REVISE SCIENCE

A COMPLETE REVISION COURSE FOR

GCSE DOUBLE *and* SINGLE AWARD

Graham Hill BA, MA, DipEd, FRSC
Deputy Head, Dr Challoner's Grammar School,
Amersham

Charles Letts and Co Ltd
London, Edinburgh & New York

First published 1990
by Charles Letts & Co Ltd
Diary House, Borough Road, London SE1 1DW

Index: Indexing Specialists, Hove
Illustrations: Tek-Art and Artistic Licence

British Library Cataloguing in Publication Data
Hill, Graham
Revise Science: a complete revision course
for GCSE. – (Letts study aids)
1. Science
I. Title

ISBN 0 85097 892 0

Printed and bound in Great Britain by
Charles Letts (Scotland) Ltd

Acknowledgements

The author and publishers are grateful to the following for permission to reproduce photographs in this book:
Aluminium Greenhouses 16.11; Arkley Manor Farm 9.3; Audience Planners (US Travel & Tourism Administration) 7.9; BAA 28.14; BASF 19.5; The British Museum, London 17.8; British Nuclear Fuels plc 22.4; British Steel Corporation 17.10; Coca-Cola Great Britain 18.1; Bruce Coleman Ltd 10.9b; Diamond Promotion Service 15.8; The Electricity Council 16.1; The Environmental Picture Library 12.3, 13.2, 19.7; Fisons plc 2.11a & b; Ford Photographic Department 23.9; Groundwork Foundation 19.1; Holt Studios Ltd/Frank Lane Picture Agency 1.2a & b, 7.3, 8.7, p. 71, 10.9a, 12.7; ICI Fertilizers 19.6; Institute of Horticultural Research 18.15; Marie Curie Cancer Care 22.1; The National Portrait Gallery, London 10.13, 15.10; Parfums Jean-Louis Scherrer 15.1; Retna Pictures Ltd 10.1: Rockwool Ltd 24.8; Science Photo Library 2.9, 3.2, 5.3, 6.3, 6.5a & b, 7.8, 10.11, 13.1, 14.3, 14.4, 14.6, 19.10, 20.6, 22.7, 22.8, 25.1, 25.21, 26.1, 28.1, 28.4; Scottish Tourist Board 17.1; Sefton Photo Library 1.1, 14.9, 15.7; Thomson Holidays 24.17; Ian Thraves 9.11; United States Travel & Tourism Administration 7.9; WHO (AHRTAG) 3.1, 12.4; Zinc Development Association 17.3.

Every effort has been made to trace all copyright holders, but if any have been inadvertently overlooked the publishers will gladly receive information enabling them to rectify any error or omission in subsequent editions.

PREFACE

This book will help you to prepare and revise for GCSE and SCE examinations in Science. It covers single and double certificated (single and dual award) syllabuses.

The book does, of course, present the important facts, but it is not simply a catalogue of facts to be learned. I have tried to identify the key areas of GCSE and SCE Science and to present them so that they are easy to understand and remember. I have also used tables, diagrams, flow charts and short sections of text to make the book concise and easy to use.

In keeping with the spirit of GCSE and SCE, emphasis is placed on the major themes of science rather than the learning of disconnected facts. Each of the twenty-eight chapters covers a major theme. Each chapter ends with a quick test of objective and/or short, structured questions similar to those in GCSE and SCE examinations. Many of these questions are taken from recent examinations. Answers are provided for all these questions so that you can check your understanding and knowledge of the topics covered in the chapter. GCSE and SCE also emphasize the social, technological, economic and environmental aspects of science and these are fully covered in the text.

The book also contains a section of longer GCSE questions taken from recent exams (pp. 317–49). Most of these are structured questions with sections requiring free response answers. Detailed specimen answers are provided for all these longer questions. Together, the questions and model answers will enable you to practise the kind of questions being set in the examination, and to check your answers. (The model answers are my own and have not been provided or approved by the Examining Boards.)

During the last four years, I have been heavily involved in setting up GCSE syllabuses through work with the School Examinations and Assessment Council (previously the Secondary Examinations Council) and the Secondary Science Curriculum Review. The development and implementation of GCSE also occupied a significant proportion of my time as an Honorary Secretary (1981–86) and then Chairman (1987–89) of the Association for Science Education.

I am grateful to the following Examining Groups for permission to reproduce questions from recent GCSE and Standard Grade examinations:

London and East Anglian Group (LEAG)
Midland Examining Group (MEG)
Northern Examining Association (NEA)
Northern Ireland Schools Examinations Council (NISEC)
Scottish Examination Board (SEB)
Southern Examining Group (SEG)
Welsh Joint Education Committee (WJEC)

In preparing this revision guide, I have valued the help and advice of Jean Mackie, Advisory Teacher of Balanced Science with Hertfordshire LEA and Graham Soar, Science Curriculum Coordinator with Essex LEA. I am also indebted to my wife, Elizabeth, for her improvements to the text and illustrations and the care with which she turned my initial manuscript into an accurate typescript. Finally, I must thank the staff of Charles Letts & Co Ltd for their support and encouragement throughout the project.

Graham Hill 1989

CONTENTS

INTRODUCTION

How to use this book

This book is specially written to help you in preparing for GCSE Science exams. It provides:

- Hints on **how to use this book during your preparation and revision** for the exam.
- Advice on what your syllabus requires in the '**Analysis of Examination Syllabuses**'. The book covers *all* GCSE and SCE Science syllabuses, both single and double certificated. So some topics in the book will not be needed for your course. Check which topics are in your syllabus using the Analysis Tables (pp. xii–xxi).
- Twenty-eight **chapters of text** covering the important ideas, facts and applications in GCSE Science courses. These chapters are concise, clear and easy to read. A lot of information is summarized in easy-to-revise tables and diagrams.
- Twenty-eight **quick tests** each covering the material in one of the twenty-eight chapters. The tests contain objective and short-answer structured questions. Many of these questions are taken from recent examinations.
- **Longer questions** from recent GCSE examinations to provide further practice in answering questions (pp. 317–38).
- **Answers** to all the quick test questions (pp. 351–59) and the longer questions (pp. 339–49).

USING THE SYLLABUS ANALYSIS TABLES

Turn to pages xii to xxi and find the Examining Group and the syllabus which relate to your science course. (If you are not sure which syllabus you are studying, check with your teacher.) The Analysis Tables show you:

- the number of examination papers you will be required to sit and their length.
- the percentage of the total mark awarded to teacher (practical) assessment.
- the types of questions used on the different examination papers.
- the syllabus content for the different grade ranges. If you are aiming for a high grade (A, B or C), you should look at the analysis in the right-hand column usually labelled 'C–A'.

The analysis of each syllabus shows the various sections of each chapter which you should revise. Two symbols are used:

● means that the section must be revised and understood.

○ means that the section is required, but with reservations–for example, 'less detail than this is required' or 'this topic illustrates important ideas and issues in the syllabus but is not specifically mentioned' or 'only an appreciation of the ideas in this section are required'.

If neither of these symbols appear for a particular section and the space is blank, it means that the topic is not in your syllabus. But remember that the tables are only a helpful guide. The most up-to-date syllabuses available have been used to compile the tables, but changes may have been made since this book was published. If you write to the Examining Group for the syllabus and for copies of past exam papers (using the addresses on page xxii), you will be able to judge the requirements of your syllabus more precisely. Your teacher will also be able to advise you, particularly on the units marked by ○.

USING THE CHAPTERS, QUICK TESTS AND LONGER QUESTIONS

In order to succeed in the examination, you need to plan and organize your revision carefully. The chapters, quick tests and longer questions in this book will help you in preparing for the exam and in carrying out your revision.

You should plan a revision timetable well before the exam. Decide how much you need to revise and how long before the exam you should start. The flow chart on the next page shows how to revise the topics in this book chapter by chapter.

1 Decide which chapter you will revise →
2 Study this chapter and any class notes which relate to it →
3 Make lists, summaries, diagrams, etc, to help your understanding (see 'Hints for Revision' below) →
4 Answer the 'Quick test' at the end of the chapter →
7 Check your answers to the 'Quick test' before going to the next chapter →
6 After covering several chapters, answer some of the longer questions →
5 Check the answers to these longer questions to improve your understanding

Hints for revision

The most important aim of GCSE Science examinations is to assess **what you know, what you understand** and **what you can do**. The key to all this is to ensure that you *understand* what you have studied. If you understand a topic, you will have little difficulty in remembering and knowing the key facts. In order to understand a topic, you must do more than just read your notes or read the sections in this book (box 2 in the flow chart).

Your learning and revision must be *active* rather than passive. Here are some activities which will help you to keep your learning active and interesting (they relate to boxes 3 to 7 in the flow chart). By revising in this way, you will practice the skills needed to show the examiner what you can do.

- **Underline or highlight important words and sentences**
- **Make lists of key words or key facts**
- **Write out important definitions**
  The very act of writing notes will help you to remember key points and fix the important facts in your memory.
- **Draw diagrams to summarize important topics**
  Label the diagrams and write notes at the side. Diagrams are a very powerful way of reinforcing your memory and your understanding of something. Most people find it easier to remember things from pictures than from words alone.
- **Summarize important ideas and explanations**
  Sometimes it is helpful to make a flow chart to summarize a sequence of events or ideas. The flow chart is simply a series of short statements connected by arrows.
- **Keep your lists, notes, diagrams and summaries** so that you can look at them again. Diagrams and summaries that you have made yourself will jog your memory and your understanding very quickly. This review of your notes should only take a few minutes. If your notes are disorganized, you will not gain much. But with concise notes, clear summaries and good diagrams similar to those in this book, you will increase your long-term knowledge and understanding significantly.
- **Try to copy your summaries and diagrams from memory**
  This won't be easy at first. You will need to look at the original to refresh your memory, but don't be discouraged. Spending time in testing yourself on work revised in previous sessions is an important part of exam preparation.
- **Answer the 'Quick tests' and the 'Longer questions'** in this book and check the answers
  Answering examination-type questions is one of the best ways to prepare for an examination. It will help you to assess your progress; it will improve your knowledge and understanding; and it will give you valuable practice in exam technique (answering an exam question in the required style).
- **Ask your teacher if you still don't understand something**
  Your teacher wants you to succeed just as much as you do. He or she will be delighted to help you with your revision, particularly if your motivation and commitment are clear.

KEEPING FIT AND WELL DURING REVISION

Keeping fit and well during revision and the exam period is just as important as keeping fit and well when training for a sports event.

- Don't overdo your revision. Set aside a realistic time for revision each day.
- Decide on a regular time for studying each day and try to stick to it.
- During revision sessions, study for 20 to 40 minutes, then take a break for 5 to 10 minutes. Continue revising for another 20 to 40 minutes, followed by another short break.
- During your breaks, try to take your mind off GCSE.
- While you are revising, avoid distractions from friends, family, radio and television.
- Finally, make sure that you have regular meals and that you get enough sleep.

Types of examination questions

This section explains and gives examples of the types of question which will be used in your examination. It also gives advice on how to answer each type of question.

OBJECTIVE (MULTIPLE CHOICE) QUESTIONS

Objective questions ask you to choose the correct answer from four or five alternatives. They are also called multiple choice questions. They usually require only a single letter for the answer.

Example:
A sparrow is
A a reptile. B a mammal. C a bird. D an amphibian.
Answer: C

At first sight, these questions appear easy because they involve simply choosing one answer from the four or five alternatives. But don't be deceived! Many objective questions are carefully designed to test difficult ideas. You should prepare just as thoroughly for a paper involving objective questions as you would for one involving longer questions.

Read the questions carefully and never leave an objective question unanswered. If necessary, make an intelligent guess. In GCSE examinations you do *not* lose marks for a wrong answer.

Sometimes, several objective questions are linked together as a set. In this case, the four or five lettered responses (labelled A, B, C, D and E) are given first followed by a series of questions.

Example:
Questions 1 to 4 concern the animals listed below
A cow
B trout
C thrush
D adder
E toad
Choose from A, B, C, D and E, the animal which is best described as
1 a bird.
2 a mammal.
3 a fish.
4 a reptile.
Answers: **1** C, **2** A, **3** B, **4** D.

SHORT ANSWER QUESTIONS

Short answer questions are very common on GCSE Science papers. Like multiple choice questions, large numbers of short answer questions can be used to cover the whole syllabus. But, unlike multiple choice questions, *you* have to come up with an answer rather than selecting one from four or five given alternatives. There are several types of short answer questions. The required answer may be a single word, several words or a sentence, or you may be asked to complete a diagram.

STRUCTURED QUESTIONS

Structured questions are probably the most common questions on GCSE papers. Usually, a structured question consists of some introductory information followed by a series of questions based on or related to that information. Sometimes, the information concerns social, environmental, industrial or economic aspects of science. It is always important to read the information carefully before starting to answer the question(s).

In structured questions, spaces are usually left for the answers on the question paper itself. Very often, the marks for each part of the question are also given. The space left and the marks given are a guide to the length of the answer required and the time you should spend. Don't feel you have to fill the space, but if your answer is much too short, think again. On the other hand, if you have average-sized writing and feel you have not been given enough space, your answer is probably more detailed than necessary.

There are examples of structured questions in almost all of the 'Quick tests'.

LONGER (FREE RESPONSE) QUESTIONS

Strictly speaking, free response questions are those in which you have to write your own answer rather than simply choosing from suggested answers. However, free response questions are usually associated with situations in which you are expected to compose at least three or four sentences. These free response sections are usually part of a longer question. A large selection of longer questions are printed at the end of this book (pp. 317–38) followed by model answers (pp. 339–49).

- **If you have a choice of longer questions**
  –read *all* the questions before making your choice.
  –answer the easiest question first. You are more likely to answer the difficult questions better, if you have already successfully completed easier ones.
- **Divide up your time sensibly**
  –if you have to answer four questions in two hours, then you should not spend more than 30 minutes on any one question.
- **Plan your answer** if you are expected to write more than two or three sentences:
  1 Read the question carefully.
  2 Jot down in rough the points to include in your answer.
  3 Decide the order in which you should present your points before starting to write the answer.
- **Don't waffle!** You will simply waste time and gain no marks.
- **Use diagrams, where appropriate**
  –make sure they are drawn clearly and labelled neatly, otherwise they are useless.
- **If a graph is required**, make sure that you
  –label the axes.
  –show the scales on the axes.
  –include the units for quantities plotted along the axes.
  –show the points clearly and neatly.
  –draw the line or curve of your graph smoothly with a well-sharpened pencil.
- **If a calculation is required**, make sure that you
  –explain your calculation. Write down the principle you are using, in words or in the form of an equation, before starting on the arithmetic.
  –follow your numerical answer by the correct units. For example, an electric current may be *2 amps*, not simply 2.

Analysis of examination syllabuses

Examination group	LEAG									
Syllabus	Science (Combined Bio., Chem. & Phys.)		Science (Syll. M)		Science (Syll. N)				Science	
Single/double certification	double (a)		double		double (d)		single (e)		single	
Type of syllabus/course	combined		modular (c)		integrated		integrated		integrated	
Range of grades	G–C	C–A	G–C	C–A	G–C	C–A	G–C	C–A	G–C	D–A (f)
Paper numbers	**1, 2, 3, 4** (b)	as for G–C **+5**	**1, 2**	**1, 2** as for G–C **+3**	**1, 3**	as for G–C **+2, 4**	**1**	as for G–C **+2**	**1, 2**	**1, 3**
(times in hours)	($1\frac{1}{4}$ + $1\frac{1}{4}$ + $1\frac{1}{4}$ + $1\frac{1}{4}$)	(2)	($2\frac{1}{2}$ + $2\frac{1}{2}$) +12 module tests during the course ($\frac{1}{2}$ hr each)	(2)	(2 + 2) +12 topic tests during the course ($\frac{1}{2}$ hr each)	(1 + 1)	(2) +6 topic tests during the course ($\frac{1}{2}$ hr each)	(1)	($1\frac{1}{4}$ + $2\frac{1}{4}$)	($1\frac{1}{4}$ + $2\frac{1}{4}$)
Teacher (practical) assessment	20%	20%	25%	25%	30%	30%	30%	30%	25%	25%
Types of questions: objective			Module tests		Topic tests		Topic tests			
short answer	all papers		Papers **1 & 2** (most questions)						Paper **1**	Paper **1**
structured	all questions	all questions	Papers **1 & 2**	Paper **3**	Papers **1&3**	Papers**2&4**	Paper **1**	Paper **2**	Paper **2**	Paper **3**
longer (free response)	all papers	all questions	Papers **1 & 2**	Paper **3**						Paper **3**

Examination group	MEG								NEA			
Syllabus	Science (Combined)		Science (Syll. B)		Science (Syll. A)		Nuffield Coordinated Science		Science (Dual Award)		Science (Modular)	
Single/double certification	double		double		single (h)		Double		double		double	
Type of syllabus/course	combined		integrated		integrated		coordinated		integrated		modular (j)	
Range of grades	G–C	C–A	G–C	C–A	G–C	C–A	G–C	C–A	G–C	E–A	G–C	C–A
Paper numbers	**1, 2, 3**	as for G–C **+4**	**1, 2, 5, 6**	as for G–C **+3, 7**	**1, 2** (h)	as for G–C **+ 3** (h)	**1, 2**	as for G–C **+3**	**1, 2, 3P**	**1, 2, 3Q** (i)	1	as for G–C **+2**
(times in hours)	(1 + 1 + 2)	(2)	($\frac{3}{4}$ + $1\frac{1}{4}$ + $\frac{3}{4}$ + $1\frac{3}{4}$) (g)	($1\frac{1}{4}$ + $1\frac{1}{4}$) (g)	($\frac{3}{4}$ + $1\frac{1}{4}$)	($1\frac{1}{4}$)	(2 + 2)	(2)	(1 + 2 + 2)	(1 + 2 + 2)	(1) 45% on module tests ($\frac{3}{4}$ hr each)	($\frac{3}{4}$)
Teacher (practical) assessment	20%	20%	32.5%	32.5%	40%	40%	30%	30%	37.5%	37.5%	30%	30%
Types of questions: objective	Paper **1** (multiple choice		Papers **1 & 5** (multiple choice		Paper **1** (multiple choice							
short answer	Paper **2**						Papers **1 & 2**		Paper **1**	Paper **1**	Module tests	
structured	Papers **2 & 3**	Paper **4**	Papers **2 & 6**	Papers **3 & 7**	Paper **2**	Paper **3**	Papers **1 & 2**	Paper **3**	Papers**2&3P**	Papers**2&3Q**	Module tests & Paper **1**	Paper **2**
longer (free response)	Paper **3**	Paper **4**	Papers **2 & 6**	Papers **3 & 7**	Paper **2**	Paper **3**		Paper **3**	Papers**2&3P**	Papers**2&3Q**	Module tests	Paper **2**

Examination group	NISEC		SEG									
Syllabus	Science		Science (Double Cert.)		Science (Single Cert.)		Integrated Science (Dual Cert.) Applications & Principles		Integrated Science (Single cert.)		Science	
Single/double certification	single		double (k)		single (m)		double		single		single	
Type of syllabus/course	coordinated		coordinated		coordinated		integrated		integrated		coordinated	
Range of grades	G–C	B–A	G–C	C–A	G–C	C–A	G–C	C–A	G–C	C–A	G–C	C–A
Paper numbers	**1, 2**	as G–C **+3**	**1, 4** (l)	as G–C **+2, 5**	**1** (m)	as G–C **+ 2**	**1, 2, 4**	as G–C **+3, 6**	**1**	as for G–C **+3**	**1, 2, 3**	as G–C **+5**
(times in hours)	(1 + 1½)	(1½)	(1½ + 1½)	(1½ + 1½) (l)	(1½)	(1½) (m)	(1½ + 1½ + 1¼) (n)	(1 + 1) (n)	(2) (o)	(1½) (o)	(½ + ¾ + 1½) (p)	(1¼) (p)
Teacher (practical) assessment	20%	20%	20%	20%	20%	20%	25%	25%	30%	30%	20%	20%
Types of questions:												
objective											Paper 2	
short answer	Paper 1		Papers 1 & 4	Papers 2 & 5	Paper 1	Paper 2	Papers 1, 2 & 4	Papers 3 & 6	Paper 1	Paper 3	Paper 1	
structured	Paper 2	Paper 3	Papers 1 & 4	Papers 2 & 5	Paper 1	Paper 2	Papers 1, 2 & 4	Papers 3 & 6	Paper 1	Paper 3	Papers 1 & 3	
longer (free response)	Paper 2	Paper 3	Papers 1 & 4	Papers 2 & 5	Paper 1	Paper 2	Papers **2** & **4**	Papers 3 & 6	Paper 1			Paper 5

Examination group	SEB		WJEC			
Syllabus	Science		Science (Single Award)		Science (Double Award)	
Single/double certification	single		single		double	
Type of syllabus/course	Coordinated (q)		Coordinated (s) (9 modules)		Coordinated (t) (18 modules)	
Range of grades	General level 3, 4 (r)	Credit level 1, 2 (r)	G–C	E–A	G–C	E–A
Paper numbers	**1**	**1**	**1** (s)	**2**	**1, 3** (t)	**2, 4**
(times in hours)	(1¼)	(1¾)	(2)	(2)	(2 + 2)	(2 + 2)
Teacher (practical) assessment	33%	33%	20%	20%	20%	20%
Types of questions						
objective	yes	yes				
short answer	yes	yes	Paper 1	Paper 2	Papers 1 & 3	Papers 2 & 4
structured	yes	yes	Paper 1	Paper 2	Papers 1 & 3	Papers 2 & 4
longer (free response)	yes	yes				

(a) It is possible to combine biology + chemistry, biology + physics, or chemistry + physics papers for a *single* certificated course. The syllabuses for these papers involve the relevant biology, chemistry and physics sections in the analysis. (b) Paper **1** Biology; Paper **2** Chemistry; Paper **3** Physics; Paper **4** Science topics; Paper **5** Extension. (c) The analysis only covers the following modules: A1, A2, A3, B1, B2(a), B3, B4, B5. These modules best equip students for further study. Your teacher will advise you on other sections to revise. (d) The syllabus is presented as section A (topics 1–13) and section B (topics 14–26). (e) This syllabus is based on section A (topics 1–13) of the double certificated Science (Syll. N). (f) Paper **3** is designed for candidates likely to achieve grades **D–A**. (Normally extension/harder papers are for those likely to achieve grades C–A.) (g) Teacher assessment is counted as Papers **4** and **8** in the overall assessment. (h) This syllabus is part of Science (Syll. B) double subject. Papers **1, 2, 3** and **4** are the same for each syllabus. (i) Papers **1** and **2** are common to each grade range. (j) The analysis covers the 4 core modules and the 7 option modules designed to provide a suitable basis for further science studies at A-level. Your teacher can advise you on other topics to revise. (k) This syllabus is displayed in two parts, Science A and Science B. (l) Papers **3** and **6** form the teacher-assessed components in the overall assessment. (m) This syllabus is the Science A portion of the Science (Double Certification) syllabus. Papers **1, 2** and **3** are the same in each syllabus. (n) Paper **5** forms the teacher-assessed component in the overall assessment. Applications and implications of science are not mentioned explicitly in the syllabus but should be included. (o) Paper **2** forms the teacher-assessed component in the overall assessment. (p) Paper **4** forms the teacher-assessed component in the overall assessment. (q) The course consists of four compulsory topics plus one or two additional topics. (r) Awards are on a seven-point scale, grade 1 being the highest: Foundation level–grades 5, 6; General level–grades 3, 4; Credit level–grades 1, 2. (s) The single award course also offers a course with alternatives to 3 of the 9 modules. If these modules are taken, the grade range is restricted to G–C and the candidate sits *Paper 1 (alternative)*. (t) The double award also offers a course with alternatives to 6 of the 18 modules. If these modules are taken, the grade range is restricted to G–C and the candidate sits *Paper 1 (alternative)* and *Paper 3 (alternative)*.

● section(s) should be revised and understood
○ section(s) required, but with reservations
(see 'How to use this book', p. viii)

	LEAG (Combined)		LEAG (Syll. M)		LEAG (Syll. N – Double)		LEAG (Syll. N – Single)		LEAG Single		MEG (Combined)		MEG (Syll. B)		MEG (Syll. A)	
	G–C	C–A	G–C	C–A	G–C	C–A	G–C	C–A	G–C	**D**–A	G–C	C–A	G–C	C–A	G–C	C–A
1 Living things																
1.1–2 Characteristics	●	●	●	●	○	○			●	●	●	●				
1.3–4 Classification	○	○	●	●	●	●			●	●			○	○	○	○
1.5–6 Cells	●	●	●	●					●	●	●	●	●	●	●	●
2 Photosynthesis																
2.1–5 Photosynthesis	●	●	●	●	○	○	○	○	●	●	●	●	●	●	●	●
2.6 Leaf structure	●	●	●	●							●	●	●	●	●	●
2.7–8 Transpiration	●	●	●	●	●	●					●	●	●	●	●	●
2.9 Essential elements	●	●	○	●							○	○	○	○	○	○
3 Food and diet																
3.1–2 Fats, proteins, carbohydrates	●	●	●	●	●	●	○	○	●	●	●	●	●	●	●	●
3.3–4 Vitamins and minerals	●	●	●	●					○	○	●	●	●	●	●	●
3.5 Diet and health	●	●	●	●	○	○	○	○			●	●	●	●	●	●
4 Digestion																
4.1–2 Digestion	●	●			○	●			●	●	●	●	●	●	●	●
4.3–5 Absorbing food into the blood	●	●							○	○	●	●	●	●	●	●
4.6–7 Teeth, tooth decay	●	●									●	●				
5 The blood system																
5.1 What is blood?	●	●	●	●					○	○	●	●				
5.2 Functions of blood	●	●	●	●					○	○	●	●				
5.3 Blood vessels	●	●	●	●					○	○	●	●	○	○	○	○
5.4–5 Circulation of blood	●	●	●	●	○	○	○	○	○	○	●	●	●	●	●	●
5.6–7 Kidneys, kidney failure	●	●			○	●	○	○			●	●	○	○	○	○
6 Respiration																
6.1–2 Breathing	●	●	○	●	●	●	○	○	●	●	●	●	●	●	●	●
6.3 The lungs	●	●	○	●	●	●	○	○	●	●	●	●	●	●	●	●
6.4 Smoking or health	●	●	●	●					○	○	●	●				
6.5–6 Cellular respiration	●	●	○	●	○	●			●	●	●	●	●	●	●	●
6.7–9 Anaerobic respiration	●	●	○	○	○	●			○	○	●	●	●	●	●	●
7 Support and movement																
7.1–2 The skeleton	●	●	●	●					○	○	●	●				
7.3 Muscles and joints	●	●	●	●							●	●	○	○	○	○
7.4–5 Broken bones, aches and pains	●	●	○	○							○	○				
7.6 Support in plants	●	●	●	●	○	○					●	●				
8 Senses and responses																
8.1 Stimuli and response	●	●	○	○	○	○					○	○	○	○	○	○
8.2 Detecting light, the eye	●	●							○	○	●	●	●	●	●	●
8.3 Detecting sound, the ear	●	●							○	○	●	●	●	●	●	●
8.4 Smell and taste																
8.5 Temp. and touch, the skin	●	●	○	●	●	●					●	●				
8.6 The nervous system	●	●	○	○							●	●	●	●	●	●
8.7 Reflex and conscious actions	●	●	○	○							●	●	●	●	●	●
8.8–9 Hormones	●	●			●	●	●	●			○	●				
9 Reproduction																
9.1 Sexual and asexual reproduction	●	●			○	○	○	○	○	○	●	●	●	●	●	●
9.2 Asexual reproduction	○	○	○	●	●	●	●	●			●	●	○	○	○	○
9.3 Sexual reproduction in plants	●	●	●	●	●	●	●	●	●	●	●	●	○	○	○	○
9.4 Reproduction in animals	○	○			●	●	●	●	●	●	●	●	○	○	○	○
9.5 Human reproduction	●	●							●	●	●	●	●	●	●	●
9.6 Puberty, menstruation	●	●							●	●	○	○	●	●	●	●
9.7 Sexual intercourse	●	●									●	●	●	●	●	●
9.8 Sexually transmitted diseases											●	●	●	●	●	●
9.9 Fertilization to birth	●	●							●	●	●	●	●	●	●	●

MEG (Nuffield Coordinated)		**NEA** (Dual award)		**NEA** (Modular)		**NISEC** (Single)		**SEG** (Double Cert.)		**SEG** (Single Cert.)		**SEG** (Integrated dual)		**SEG** (Integrated single)		**SEG** (Coordinated single)		**SEB**		**WJEC** (Single)		**WJEC** (Double)	
G–C	C–A	G–C	E–A	G–C	C–A	G–C	B–A	G–C	C–A	G–C	C–A	G–C	C–A	G–C	C–A	G–C	C–A	Gen.	Cred.	G–C	E–A	G–C	E–A
				●	●	●	●					●	●					○	○	●	●	●	●
●	●			●	●	○	○	○	○			○	○							●	●	●	●
○	○	●	●	●	●	●	●	●	●			●	●							●	●	●	●
●	●	●	●	●	●	○	●	●	●			●	●	●	●	●	●	○	●	●	●	●	●
●	●	●	●	○	○			●	●			○	○	○	○	●	●					●	●
●	●	●	●	○	○	○	●	●	●			●	●	○	○	●	●			●	●	●	●
○	○			○	○							○	○										
●	●	●	●	●	●	●	●	●	●	●	●	●	●	●	●	●	●	○	○			●	●
○	○	●	●	●	●	○	○	●	●	●	●	○	○	○	○	●	●	○	○			●	●
●	●	○	○	●	●	○	○	●	●	●	●	○	○	○	○	○	○	○	○			●	●
●	●	●	●	●	●	○	○	●	●	●	●			○	○	●	●					●	●
○	●			○	○	○	○	●	●	●	●			○	○	●	●					●	●
●	●							○	○	○	○					●	●	●	●			●	●
●	●	●	●	●	●	○	○	●	●	●	●	●	●			●	●	●	●	●	●	●	●
●	●	●	●	○	○	○	○	●	●	●	●	●	●			●	●	○	●	●	●	●	●
●	●	●	●	○	○	○	○	●	●	●	●	●	●			○	○	●	●	●	●	●	●
●	●	●	●	○	○	○	○	●	●	●	●	●	●			●	●	○	●	●	●	●	●
●	●	○	○	●	●		○	●	●	●	●	○	○			●	●			●	●	●	●
●	●	●	●	●	●	●	●	○	○	○	○	●	●	○	○	●	●	○	●			●	●
●	●	●	●	●	●	●	●	●	●	●	●	○	○	○	○	●	●	○	●	○	○	●	●
○	○	○	○	○	○			●	●	●	●	○	○	○	○	●	●	●	●	○	○	●	●
●	●	●	●	●	●	●	●	●	●	○	○	●	●	●	●	●	●	○	●			●	●
●	●	○	○	○	○		●	○	○	○	○	○	○	○	○							●	●
○	○					●	●	●	●	●	●					●	●						
●	●					●	●	●	●	●	●					●	●						
○	○																						
●	●	○	○																				
●	●	●	●	●	●	●	●	●	●	●	●	○	○			●	●	○	○	●	●	●	●
○	○					○	●	●	●	●	●	●	●			●	●			●	●	●	●
○	○					○	●	●	●	●	●					●	●			●	●	●	●
								●	●	●	●					●	●			○	○	○	○
●	●	○	○	○	○	○	○	●	●	●	●					●	●	○	○	●	●	●	●
○	○	○	○	○	○	●	●	●	●	●	●					●	●			●	●	●	●
○	○	○	○				○	●	●	●	●					●	●			○	○	○	○
●	●	●	●	○	○	●	●	●	●	●	●	○	○	○	○	●	●			○	○	○	○
●	●	●	●	●	●	●	●	●	●	●	●					●	●			●	●	●	●
○	○	○	○	○	○	○	○	●	●	○	○					●	●			○	○	○	○
●	●	○	○	●	●	○	○	●	●							●	●			●	●	●	●
●	●	○	○	●	●	●	●	○	○	○	○												
●	●			○	○	○	○	●	●	●	●					●	●			●	●	●	●
●	●							○	○	○	○					●	●			●	●	●	●
●	●	○	○	○	○			●	●	●	●					○	○			●	●	●	●
○	○	○	○					●	●	●	●									●	●	●	●
●	●	○	○	●	●			●	●	●	●					○	○			●	●	●	●

	LEAG (Combined) G–C	LEAG (Combined) C–A	LEAG (Syll. M) G–C	LEAG (Syll. M) C–A	LEAG (Syll. N – Double) G–C	LEAG (Syll. N – Double) C–A	LEAG (Syll. N – Single) G–C	LEAG (Syll. N – Single) C–A	LEAG Single G–C	LEAG Single **D**–A	MEG (Combined) G–C	MEG (Combined) C–A	MEG (Syll. B) G–C	MEG (Syll. B) C–A	MEG (Syll. A) G–C	MEG (Syll. A) C–A
10 Genetics and evolution																
10.1–3 Chromosomes and meiosis	●	●			○	●	○	●	●	●	○	●	●	●	●	●
10.4–5 Genes and genetics	○	○	○	○	○	●	○	●			○	●	●	●	●	●
10.6–7 Evolution	●	●			●	●	●	●			●	●	●	●	●	●
11 Ecosystems and ecology																
11.1 Habitats, communities, ecosystems	○	○	●	●	●	●	○	○			○	○	●	●		
11.2–3 Populations	●	●	○	○	●	●					○	○	●	●		
11.4–5 Food chains, food webs	●	●	●	●	●	●	●	●	○	○	●	●	●	●	○	○
11.6 Energy chains, C cycle	●	●	○	●	○	●	○	○	●	●	●	●	●	●	○	○
12 Our effect on the environment																
12.1 Stable/unstable ecosystems	●	●	○	○	●	●	●	●			●	●	●	●		
12.2 Agricultural practices (fertilizers, pesticides)	●	●	●	●	●	●	●	●	●	●	●	●	○	○		
12.3 Pollution	●	●	●	●	●	●	●	●	●	●	●	●	●	●		
12.4–5 Finite earth, conservation	●	●	○	○	●	●	●	●	●	●	●	●	○	○		
13 Raw materials, elements, compounds																
13.1–2 Raw materials, conservation	●	●	○	○	○	○	○	○	○	○	●	●				
13.3–4 Elements–metals/non-metals	●	●	●	●	●	●			●	●	●	●	●	●	○	○
13.5–6 Compounds and mixtures	●	●	●	●	○	○			●	●	○	○	○	○	○	○
13.7–8 Methods of separation	●	●	○	○	○	○	○	○	●	●	●	●	●	●	●	●
13.9 Testing for pure substances																
14 Air and water																
14.1 Composition of air	●	●			○	○			●	●	○	○				
14.2 Air as a source of raw materials	●	●			○	○			○	○	●	●				
14.3 Reactions of oxygen									●	●			●	●		
14.4 Burning and fuels	●	●	●	●	●	●			●	●	○	○	●	●	●	●
14.5 Air pollution	●	●	●	●	●	●	●	●	●	●	●	●	●	●	●	●
14.6–7 Water supplies/cycle	●	●	○	○	●	●			●	●	●	●	●	●	●	●
14.8 Water pollution	●	●	●	●	●	●	○	○	●	●	●	●	○	○	○	○
14.9–10 Hard water	●	●			●	●					●	●	●	●	●	●
15 Particles																
15.1–2 Evidence for particles	○	○	●	●					○	○	●	●				
15.3 Kinetic theory	●	●	●	●	●	●	○	○	●	●	●	●	●	●	●	●
15.4 Changes of state	●	●	○	●	○	○	○	○	●	●	●	●	●	●	●	●
15.5–6 Atoms, molecules	●	●	●	●	●	●	○	○	●	●	●	●	●	●	●	●
15.7 Formulas, equations	●	●			●	●	●	●			○	○	○	●	○	○
15.8 Relative atomic masses	●	●			●	●	○	●	●	●	●	●	●	●		
15.9 Moles, finding formulas, reacting amounts	○	○			○	●	○	●	○	○	○	●	○	●		
16 Electricity and electrolysis																
16.1–2 Conductors, insulators	●	●	●	●					○	○	○	○	●	●	○	○
16.3 Conduction by solids and liquids	●	●	●	●	●	●			○	○	○	○	●	●	○	○
16.4 Explaining electrolysis	●	●		●	○	●							○	○		
16.5–6 Ions and ionic compounds	●	●	○	●	●	●			○	○	●	●	●	●		
16.7 Molecular compounds	●	●									●	●	●	●		
16.8 Electrolysis in industry	●	●							●	●	●	●	●	●	○	○
16.9 Cells and batteries					○	●					○	○				
17 Metals and alloys																
17.1–2 Metallic properties/reactions	●	●							○	○			●	●		
17.3 Reactivity series									●	●						
17.4 Structure of metals	●	●			○	○							●	●		
17.5 Explaining metal properties	●	●			○	○							●	●		
17.6 Alloys	●	●									●	●	●	●		
17.7–8 Extracting metals	●	●			●	●	○	○	●	●	●	●	●	●		
17.9–10 Rusting	●	●			○	○	○	○	●	●	●	●	●	●		
17.11 Redox					○	○	○	○	●	●	●	●				

MEG (Nuffield Coordinated)		**NEA** (Dual Award)		**NEA** (Modular)		**NISEC** (Single)		**SEG** (Double Cert.)		**SEG** (Single Cert.)		**SEG** (Integrated dual)		**SEG** (Integrated single)		**SEG** (Coordinated single)		**SEB**		**WJEC** (Single)		**WJEC** (Double)	
G–C	C–A	G–C	E–A	G–C	C–A	G–C	B–A	G–C	C–A	G–C	C–A	G–C	C–A	G–C	C–A	G–C	C–A	Gen.	Cred.	G–C	E–A	G–C	E–A
○	●	●	●	●	●	○	●	●	●	●	●	●	●			○	○			●	●	●	●
○	●	●	●	●	●		●		○		○	●	●			○	○			●	●	●	●
●	●	○	○	●	●			○	○	○	○	●	●							●	●	●	●
●	●	●	●	●	●							●	●	○	○			○	○				
○	●	●	●	●	●			●	●	●	●	●	●			○	○	○	●			○	○
●	●	●	●	●	●	●	●	●	●			●	●	●	●			●	●			●	●
●	●	●	●	●	●	●	●	●	●			●	●	●	●	●	●	○	○			●	●
●	●			○	○							●	●					○	○				
●	●	○	○	○	○	○	○	●	●			○	○			●	●	○	○				
○	○	○	○	●	●	●	●	●	●			○	○			●	●	●	●				
●	●	○	○	●	●	○	○	○	○			○	○			○	○	●	●				
○	○	○	○	●	●			●	●			●	●	○	○			●	●				
●	●	○	○	●	●	●	●	●	●	○	○	●	●	●	●			●	●	○	○	○	○
○	○	○	○	●	●	●	●	●	●	●	●	●	●	○	○					○	○	○	○
●	●	○	○			●	●					○	○							○	○	○	○
						●	●	○	○			○	○	○	○								
○	○	●	●	○	○	●	●	●	●			●	●	●	●	●	●			●	●	●	●
○	○	○	○	○	○	●	●	●	●			○	○	○	○	○	○	○	○	○	○	○	○
●	●	●	●	●	●	●	●	●	●	●	●	○	○	○	○	●	●	●	●	●	●	●	●
●	●	●	●	●	●	○	○	●	●	●	●	●	●	●	●			●	●	●	●	●	●
●	●	○	○	●	●	●	●	●	●			○	○	●	●	●	●	●	●	○	○	○	○
●	●	●	●			●	●	●	●			●	●	●	●	●	●	○	○	○	○	○	○
●	●	○	○	○	○	●	●	●	●			○	○	○	○	●	●	●	●			●	●
○	●	○	○					●	●							●	●					●	●
○	○	●	●	●	●	●	●	●	●	●	●	○	○	○	○					○	○	●	●
●	●	●	●	●	●	●	●	●	●	●	●	●	●	○	○			○	○	○	○	●	●
●	●	●	●	●	●	●	●	●	●	●	●	●	●	●	●			○	○	○	○	●	●
●	●	●	●	●	●	●	●	●	●	●	●	●	●	○	○					○	○	●	●
○	○	●	●	●	●			●	●			●	●	○	○					○	○	●	●
●	●	●	●	●	●			●	●			●	●										●
	●	○	●	○	○			○	●			○	○										●
●	●	●	●	●	●	●	●	●	●	○	○	●	●	●	●			●	●			●	●
○	●	●	●	●	●	○	●	●	●			●	●	●	●			○	○			●	●
○	●	○	○	●	●	○	●	○	○			●	●	●	●							●	●
●	●	●	●	●	●	○	●	●	●	●	●	●	●	●	●							●	●
○	●	●	●	●	●		●	●	●	●	●	●	●	○	○								●
		○	○	○	○			●	●			○	○	○	○							●	●
○	○	○	○			●	●					○	○	○	○								
●	●	●	●	●	●	○	○	●	●			○	○	○	○					●	●	●	●
○	●	●	●	●	●	○	○	●	●			●	●							●	●	●	●
●	●			●	●			○	○			○	○	○	○			○	○				
○	●																	○	○				
●	●	○	○	○	○			●	●			○	○	○	○			○	●	●	●	●	●
		○	○	○	○		●	●	●			○	○	○	○					○	○	○	○
●	●	○	○	○	○	●	●	●	●			●	●	●	●			○	●	●	●	●	●
●	●					●	●	●	●									○	○	○	○	○	○

	LEAG (Combined)		LEAG (Syll. M)		LEAG (Syll. N – Double)		LEAG (Syll. N – Single)		LEAG Single		MEG (Combined)		MEG (Syll. B)		MEG (Syll. A)	
	G–C	C–A	G–C	C–A	G–C	C–A	G–C	C–A	G–C	**D**–A	G–C	C–A	G–C	C–A	G–C	C–A
18 Acids, bases and salts																
18.1 Acids in everyday life	○	○	○	○	●	●	●	●	○	○	●	●	●	●		
18.2 Indicators, pH	●	●			●	●	○	○	●	●	●	●	●	●		
18.3 Properties of acids	●	●			●	●	●	●	○	○	○	○	●	●		
18.4,6 Bases, alkalis	○	○			○	●					●	●	○	○		
18.5 Neutralization	●	●			●	●			●	●	●	●	●	●		
18.7 Preparing salts	●	●														
19 The chemical industry																
19.1 Choice of industrial site	○	○		○							●	●				
19.2–3 Sulphuric acid	●	●														
19.4–5 Ammonia	●	●							○	○	●	●	○	○	○	○
19.6 Fertilizers	●	●	○	○	○	○					●	●	○	○	○	○
19.7 Nitrogen cycle	●	●			●	●			●	●	○	○	●	●	●	●
19.8–10 Reaction rates	●	●			○	○					●	●	●	●		
19.11 Effect of conditions on reaction rates	●	●			○	●					●	●	●	●		
20 Energy and fuels																
20.1 Sources of fuels	●	●	●	●	●	●	●	●	○	○	●	●	●	●	●	●
20.2 Fuels for various purposes			●	●	●	●	●	●			●	●	●	●	●	●
20.3 Fires, fire-fighting	●	●	●	●	●	●	●	●	○	○			●	●	●	●
20.4 Energy from fuels	○	○	○	●		○			●	●			○	●	○	●
20.5 Fossil fuels	●	●	●	●	●	●	●	●			○	○	●	●	●	●
20.6 Alternative energy sources	●	●	●	●	●	●	●	●			●	●	●	●	●	●
20.7–8 Oil–alkanes	●	●	●	●					●	●	●	●	●	●	●	●
20.9–10 Alkenes–plastics	●	●		○					●	●	●	●	●	●		
20.11 Ethanol	●	●			○	○					●	●	●	●	●	●
21 Atomic structure, Periodic Table																
21.1–2 Atomic structure, atomic no., mass no.	●	●	○	●	○	○			●	●	●	●	●	●	○	○
21.3 Relative atomic mass, isotopes	●	●		○					●	●	●	●	○	○		
21.4–5 Periodic tables	●	●		●	●	●			●	●	●	●	●	●		
21.6 Electron structure	●	●			○	○			●	●	●	●	○	○		
21.7 Group II	●	●														
21.8 Group VII	●	●			●	●			○	○	●	●	●	●		
22 Radioactivity & nuclear energy																
22.1–2 Radioactivity, nuclear reactions	●	●	●	●	●	●			○	○	●	●	●	●	●	●
22.3 Nuclear equations																
22.4–5 Detecting radioactivity, half-life	●	●	●	●	●	●			○	○	●	●	○	○	○	○
22.6 Uses of radioactive materials	●	●	●	●	●	●					●	●	●	●	●	●
22.7 Dangers from radiation	●	●		○	●	●			○	○	●	●	○	○	○	○
22.8 Nuclear energy	○	○	○	●					○	○	●	●	○	○	○	○
23 Force and motion																
23.1–2 Distance, speed, velocity	●	●			●	●	●	●	●	●	●	●	●	●	●	●
23.3 Vectors and scalars									○	○	●	●				
23.4–5 Distance-time graphs, average speed	●	●			●	●	●	●	●	●	●	●	●	●	●	●
23.6–7 Acceleration–speed-time graphs	●	●			●	●	●	●	●	●	●	●	●	●	●	●
23.8 Forces	●	●	●	●	●	●	●	●	●	●	○	○	●	●	●	●
23.9 Force, weight and mass	●	●	●	●	●	●	●	●	●	●	●	●	●	●		
23.10 Stretching forces	●	●	○	○												
23.11 Frictional forces	●	●			●	●	●	●			○	○	○	○	○	○
23.12 Newton's laws of motion	●	●			○	●	○	●	○	○	○	●	●	●	○	○
23.13 Falling under gravity	○	○			○	●	○	○			●	●	●	●		
23.14 Force and pressure	●	●							●	●						
23.15 Pressure in liquids, hydraulics	●	●							●	●						
23.16 Pressure in gases									○	○	○	○	●	●	●	●
24 Energy transfers																
24.1 Work and energy	●	●	○	●	●	●	●	●	●	●	●	●	●	●	●	●

MEG (Nuffield Coordinate)		**NEA** (Dual Award)		**NEA** (Modular)		**NISEC** (Single)		**SEG** (Double Cert.)		**SEG** (Single Cert.)		**SEG** (Integrated dual)		**SEG** (Integrated single)		**SEG** (Coordinated single)		**SEB**		**WJEC** (Single)		**WJEC** (Double)	
G–C	C–A	G–C	E–A	G–C	C–A	G–C	B–A	G–C	C–A	G–C	C–A	G–C	C–A	G–C	C–A	G–C	C–A	Gen.	Cred.	G–C	E–A	G–C	E–A
●	●	○	○	○	○	●	●	●	●	○	○	○	○			○	○	○	○	○	○	○	○
○	○	●	●	●	●	●	●	●	●	●	●	●	●			●	●			○	○	●	●
○	○	●	●	●	●	●	●	●	●	●	●	○	○							○	○	●	●
○	○	●	●	●	●	○	○	○	○	○	○	●	●							○	○	●	●
●	●	●	●	●	●	○	○	●	●	●	●	●	●							○	○	●	●
		○	○																			●	●
●	●	○	○									○	○										
																						●	●
○	●	●	●					●	●			○	○									●	●
●	●	●	●	○	○			●	●			○	○	○	○	○	○					●	●
○	●	●	●	○	○			●	●			●	●	●	●	●	●			○	○	●	●
●	●	○	○	●	●			●	●			●	●	○	○					○	○	●	●
●	●	●	●	●	●			●	●			●	●	●	●					○	○	●	●
●	●	●	●	●	●	○	○	●	●	●	●	○	○	●	●	○	○	○	○	●	●	●	●
●	●	●	●	●	●			○	○	○	○	○	○	○	○			○	○	●	●	●	●
●	●	○	○									○	○					●	●	●	●	●	●
●	●			●	●	○	●					●	●	○	○							○	○
○	○	○	○	●	●	●	●	●	●	●	●	○	○	○	○	○	○	●	●	●	●	●	●
●	●	○	○	●	●	●	●	●	●			○	○	●	●	○	○	●	●	○	○	○	○
●	●	○	○	●	●	○	○	●	●	●	●	○	○	○	○	○	○	●	●	○	○	●	●
●	●	●	●	●	●			●	●	●	●			○	○	○	○	○	●			●	●
								○	○													●	●
●	●	●	●	○	○	●	●	●	●	●	●	●	●	●	●							●	●
●	●	●	●					○	●	○	●	○	○									●	●
●	●	●	●	●	●	○	●	●	●	●	●	●	●	○	○							●	●
●	●			○	○		●	●	●	●	●	○	○									○	●
○	○					○	○	●	●													●	●
○	○	○	○	○	○	○	●	●	●													●	●
●	●	●	●	●	●			●	●			●	●	●	●			○	○			●	●
	○		○																				
○	●	●	●	○	○			●	●			●	●	●	●			○	●			●	●
●	●	○	○	●	●			●	●			○	○					○	○			●	●
●	●	○	○	●	●			○	○			○	○	○	○			○	○			●	●
●	●	○	○	●	●													●	●			○	○
●	●	●	●	●	●			●	●	●	●					●	●			●	●	●	●
○	●							●	●	●	●												
●	●	○	○	●	●			●	●	●	●					●	●			●	●	●	●
●	●	●	●	●	●			●	●	●	●					●	●			●	●	●	●
●	●	●	●	●	●	●	●	●	●	●	●	●	●	○	○	●	●			●	●	●	●
●	●	●	●	○	○	●	●	●	●	●	●	●	●	●	●	●	●			●	●	●	●
●	●			●	●																		
●	●	○	○	●	●	●	●	●	●							●	●			●	●	●	●
○	●	●	●	○	○			○	○	○	○	●	●			○	○			○	○	○	○
○	●	○	○				○					●	●							○	○	○	○
		●	●	●	●																		
		○	○	●	●																		
○	○	○	○			●	●	●	●	○	○	●	●			○	○						
●	●	○	●	●	●	●	●	●	●	●	●	●	●	●	●	●	●	○	○	●	●	●	●

	LEAG (Combined)		**LEAG** (Syll. M)		**LEAG** (Syll. N – Double)		**LEAG** (Syll. N – Single)		**LEAG** Single		**MEG** (Combined)		**MEG** (Syll. B)		**MEG** (Syll. A)	
	G–C	C–A	G–C	C–A	G–C	C–A	G–C	C–A	G–C	D–A	G–C	C–A	G–C	C–A	G–C	C–A
24.2 Forms of energy	●	●	●	●	○	●	○	●	●	●	●	●	●	●	●	●
24.3–4 Efficiency and power	●	●	○	○	○	●	○	●			○	○	○	○	○	○
24.5–6 Power stations, using energy	●	●	○	○	○	○	○	○			●	●	○	○	○	○
24.7 Heat as a form of energy	●	●	●	●	○	○			●	●	●	●	●	●	●	●
24.8 Expansion and contraction	●	●	○	●	○	○			●	●			○	○	○	○
24.9 Changes of state	●	●	○	●	○	○			○	○	●	●	○	○	○	○
24.10–11 Heat transfer	●	●	○	●	●	●	●	●	●	●	●	●	●	●	●	●
25 Energy and waves																
25.1–2 Describing waves	●	●			●	●			●	●	○	●	●	●		
25.3 Transverse and longitudinal waves	●	●			○	○			●	●	●	●	○	○		
25.4 Earthquakes, seismic waves					●	●							○	○		
25.5 Electromagnetic waves	●	●			●	●			●	●	●	●	●	●		
25.6–8 Sound waves	●	●							●	●	●	●	●	●	○	○
25.9–10 Speed of sound, echoes, ultrasonics	●	●									●	●				
26 Light and colour																
26.1 Light rays					●	●	○	○	○	○	○	○	○	○	○	○
26.2 Reflecting light					●	●	○	○	●	●	●	●	●	●		
26.3 Refracting light									○	○	●	●	●	●		
26.4 Total internal reflection											●	●				
26.5–6 Converging lenses, focal length											○	●	●	●		
26.7 Ray diagrams											○	●				
26.8 Cameras											●	●				
26.9 Separating colours					●	●			○	○			●	●		
26.10 Mixing colours					○	●							●	●		
26.11 Absorbing colours					●	●			●	●			○	○		
27 Electric currents & electricity																
27.1–2 Currents and circuits	●	●	●	●	●	●	●	●	●	●	●	●	●	●	●	●
27.3–4 Current, charge, voltage	○	○	○	●	●	●	●	●	●	●	●	●	●	●	●	●
27.5 Voltage and energy	○	○	○	●	○	●	○	●	○	○	●	●	●	●	○	○
27.6–7 Resistance, resistors, Ohm's law	●	●	○	○	●	●	●	●	●	●	○	●	●	●	●	●
27.8–9 Electricity in the home	●	●	●	●	●	●	●	●	●	●	●	●	●	●	●	●
27.10–11 Power rating, electricity bills	●	●	○	●	●	●	●	●	●	●	●	●	●	●	●	●
28 Motors and generators																
28.1–3 Magnets, magnetic poles	○	○			○	○			○	○	○	○	●	●		
28.4–6 Magnetic fields	●	●			○	○			○	○	○	○	●	●		
28.7 Electromagnets	●	●	●	●	○	○			○	○	●	●	●	●	○	○
28.8 Electric motors	●	●	○	●							●	●	●	●		
28.9 Electromagnetic induction	○	○			○	○			○	○	●	●	●	●		
28.10 Alternators	●	●							○	○	●	●	●	●		
28.11 Transformers	●	●			●	●					○	●	●	●		
28.12 Transmitting electricity	●	●			●	●					●	●	●	●		

MEG (Nuffield Coordinated)		**NEA** (Dual Award)		**NEA** (Modular)		**NISEC** (Single)		**SEG** (Double Cert.)		**SEG** (Single Cert.)		**SEG** (Integrated dual)		**SEG** (Integrated single)		**SEG** (Coordinated single)		**SEB**		**WJEC** (Single)		**WJEC** (Double)	
G–C	C–A	G–C	E–A	G–C	C–A	G–C	B–A	G–C	C–A	G–C	C–A	G–C	C–A	G–C	C–A	G–C	C–A	Gen.	Cred.	G–C	E–A	G–C	E–A
●	●	●	●	●	●	●	●	●	●	●	●	●	●	●	●	●	●	○	○	○	○	○	○
●	●	●	●	●	●	●	●	●	●	●	●	●	●	●	●	●	●	○	○	○	○	○	○
●	●	○	○	●	●			●	●			○	○			●	●	○	●			○	○
●	●	○	○	●	●	○	○	●	●	○	○	●	●	○	○	●	●	○	○				
○	○	○	○			○	○	○	○	○	○	○	○	●	●	○	○	○	●				
●	●	○	○	●	●	●	●	●	●			●	●	○	○			○	○				
●	●	●	●	●	●	●	●	●	●	●	●	○	○	●	●	●	●	○	●	○	○	○	○
○	●	○	●	●	●	●	●	○	●	○	●	●	●	●	●					●	●	●	●
●	●			○	○	○	○	○	○	○	○	●	●							●	●	●	●
	●	○	○																				
●	●	●	●	●	●	●	●	○	●	○	●	●	●	○	○					●	●	●	●
●	●	○	○	○	○			●	●	●	●	○	○	○	○					●	●	●	●
	○	○	○									○	○	○	○					○	○	○	○
●	●	○	○	●	●	○	○	●	●	●	●	○	○	●	●								
●	●	○	○	●	●	●	●	●	●	●	●	●	●										
●	●	○	○	●	●	●	●	●	●	●	●	●	●										
●	●	●	●	●	●			●	●	●	●												
○	○			○	○			●	●	●	●	○	○										
●	●							●	●	●	●	●	●										
												○	○										
○	○	●	●									●	●							●	●	●	●
●	●	○	○																	●	●	●	●
●	●	○	○																	●	●	●	●
●	●	●	●	●	●	●	●	●	●	●	●	●	●	●	●	●	●	○	●	●	●	●	●
○	●	●	●	●	●	●	●	●	●	●	●	●	●	●	●	○	○	○	●	●	●	●	●
●	●	●	●	○	○	●	●	●	●	●	●	●	●	●	●	○	○	○	○	●	●	●	●
○	●	○	○	●	●	●	●	●	●	●	●	●	●	●	●	○	○	○	○	●	●	●	●
●	●	○	○	○	○	●	●	●	●	●	●	○	○	○	○	●	●	●	●	●	●	●	●
●	●	○	○	○	○	●	●	○	○	○	○	○	○	○	○	○	○	●	●	●	●	●	●
○	○	●	●	○	○	●	●	○	●	○	●	●	●	○	○	○	○			○	○	○	○
○	○	●	●	●	●	●	●	●	●	●	●	●	●	○	○	●	●					●	●
●	●	●	●	○	○			●	●	●	●	●	●	○	○	●	●					●	●
●	●	○	○	●	●	○	●	○	○			○	○	●	●							●	●
○	●	○	○	●	●	○	●	○	○			●	●	○	○							●	●
●	●	○	○	●	●	○	●					○	○	●	●							●	●
●	●	○	○			○	●	●	●			○	○	●	●							●	●
●	●	○	○					●	●			○	○	●	●							○	○

Examination Groups: Addresses

NORTHERN EXAMINING ASSOCIATION (NEA)

JMB	Joint Matriculation Board Devas Street, Manchester M15 6EU
ALSEB	Associated Lancashire Schools Examining Board 12 Harter Street, Manchester M1 6HL
NREB	Northern Regional Examinations Board Wheatfield Road, Westerhope, Newcastle upon Tyne NE5 5JZ
NWREB	North-West Regional Examinations Board Orbit House, Albert Street, Eccles, Manchester M30 0WL
YHREB	Yorkshire and Humberside Regional Examinations Board Harrogate Office–31-33 Springfield Avenue, Harrogate HG1 2HW Sheffield Office–Scarsdale House, 136 Derbyshire Lane, Sheffield S8 8SE

MIDLAND EXAMINING GROUP (MEG)

Cambridge	University of Cambridge Local Examinations Syndicate Syndicate Buildings, 1 Hills Road, Cambridge CB1 2EU
O & C	Oxford and Cambridge Schools Examination Board 10 Trumpington Street, Cambridge CB2 1QB, *and* Elsfield Way, Oxford OX2 8EP
SUJB	Southern Universities' Joint Board for School Examinations Cotham Road, Bristol BS6 6DD
WMEB	West Midlands Examinations Board Norfolk House, Smallbrook Queensway, Birmingham B5 4NJ
EMREB	East Midlands Regional Examinations Board Robins Wood House, Robins Wood Road, Aspley, Nottingham NG8 3NR

LONDON EAST ANGLIAN GROUP (LEAG)

London	University of London School Examinations Board Stewart House, 32 Russell Square, London WC1B 5DN
LREB	London Regional Examining Board Lyon House, 104 Wandsworth High Street, London SW18 4LF
EAEB	East Anglian Examinations Board The Lindens, Lexden Road, Colchester CO3 3RL

SOUTHERN EXAMINING GROUP (SEG)

AEB	The Associated Examining Board Stag Hill House, Guildford GU2 5XJ
Oxford	Oxford Delegacy of Local Examinations Ewert Place, Summertown, Oxford OX2 7BZ
SREB	Southern Regional Examinations Board Eastleigh House, Market Street, Eastleigh, Southampton SO5 4SW
SEREB	South-East Regional Examinations Board Beloe House, 2-10 Mount Ephraim Road, Tunbridge Wells TN1 1EU
SWEB	South-Western Examinations Board 23-29 Marsh Street, Bristol BS1 4BP

WALES

WJEC	Welsh Joint Education Committee 245 Western Avenue, Cardiff CF5 2YX

NORTHERN IRELAND

NISEC	Northern Ireland Schools Examinations Council Beechill House, 42 Beechill Road, Belfast BT8 4RS

SCOTLAND

SEB	Scottish Examination Board Ironmills Road, Dalkeith, Midlothian EH22 1BR

1 LIVING THINGS

1.1 The variety of living things

There are a vast number of living things in the world. The study of these living things is called **biology**. Living things are often described as **organisms**.

Living things are found everywhere in the world–on land, in the air, in the sea and underground. Different organisms live in different places. *The place where an organism lives is called its* **habitat**. The habitat of a fly might be a greenhouse, a goldfish's habitat might be its tank or bowl. The Earth provides millions of different habitats–some hot, some cold, some dry, some wet. *The conditions in a habitat make up the* **environment**.

Fig. 1.1 How many different organisms can you identify in this photograph?

In general, living things prefer a moderate environment with warm temperatures, water and a supply of food. This is why there are many different organisms in Britain, but very few organisms in hot deserts and cold Arctic regions.

Fig. 1.2 These foxes are each well adapted to their very different environments. The fennec fox (left) is a native of the Sahara Desert. It has short fur (pale gold in colour, blending in with its sandy surroundings) and its large ears radiate heat. The Arctic fox (right) is insulated so well by its long, thick fur that it can sit comfortably in snow at −40°C. Its small ears retain heat.

Most organisms are suited or **adapted** to the particular habitat in which they live. For example, they may have streamlined bodies or long legs which enable them to move very quickly or thick fur which enables them to withstand very low temperatures.

1.2 Characteristics of living things

There are thousands of different chemical reactions occurring in even the smallest living organism. These reactions are essential for life. If they stop, the organism dies. All the chemical processes in an organism are called its **metabolism**.

There are seven important characteristics common to *all* living things.

- **They grow**. Plants grow all their lives, but animals usually stop growing once they are adult. But, even when growth stops, the materials in an animal's body are being replaced by substances from its food. In an adult human being, all the chemicals in the body are replaced over a period of seven years.
- **They feed**. Organisms must feed in order to grow. Food is needed for growth, for energy and to replace worn-out parts. Animals and plants feed in different ways:

  Plants take in simple substances like carbon dioxide and water. They use these simple substances to make more complex substances which can be used as food. In order to do this, plants need energy which they get from sunlight. This process of feeding is called *photosynthesis* (see chapter 2).

  Animals eat plants or other animals. They then break down the complex chemicals in their food into simpler substances. These simpler substances are then used for growth or energy (see chapters 3 and 4).
- **They need energy**. Living things need energy to grow, to replace worn-out parts and to move. They get this energy from their food. The process of breaking down food and gaining energy is called **respiration** (see chapter 6).
- **They excrete waste products**. Organisms are like factories. Materials are constantly being taken in and used to produce other materials. Some of the products are useless, others are poisonous. The waste products of metabolism must not be allowed to collect in an organism or they will poison it. So the organism must get rid of them–this process is called **excretion** (see section 5.6).
- **They reproduce**. Organisms must produce offspring in order for the species to survive. This process is called **reproduction** (see chapter 9). Usually reproduction involves the union of a male and female of the same species. This is called *sexual* reproduction. Some organisms can reproduce on their own without needing both a male and a female. This is called *asexual* reproduction.
- **They move**. Animals can move parts of their body or even their whole body from one place to another. Plants cannot move themselves from one place to another, but they can move parts of their structure. For example, leaves may turn towards the sunlight and roots may grow towards moisture (see chapter 7).
- **They respond to stimuli**. If someone tickles you, you will probably draw back. The tickling is a **stimulus**, your drawing back is the **response** (see chapter 8). The main stimuli to which organisms respond are heat, light, sound, touch and chemicals (including taste and smell). In general, plants respond to stimuli much more slowly than animals.

The *mnemonic* **'MR GREEF'** will help you to remember the seven important characteristics of living things:

M ovement
R esponse
G rowth
R eproduction
E nergy need
E xcretion
F eeding

1.3 Classification of living things

There are more than one million different organisms. Studying them would be impossible without sorting them into groups. These groups are then divided into smaller groups, and so on. The members of a group have similar features.

Living things are first divided into **kingdoms**. These include animals and plants.

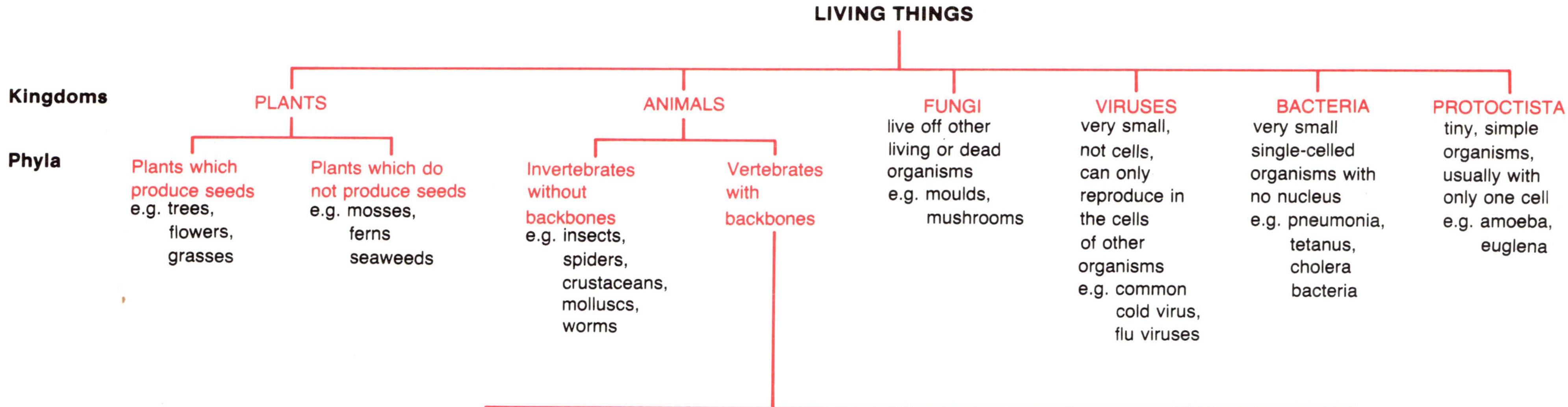

Classes	Mammals	Birds	Reptiles	Amphibians	Fish
Outer covering:	hair	feathers	dry scales	moist skin	scales
Reproduction: – fertilization:	internally on land	internally on land	internally on land	externally in water	externally in water
– eggs:	fertilized egg develops in uterus	one dozen or fewer eggs hard shell	a few dozen eggs on land soft, leathery shell	large number of eggs in water no shell	large number of eggs into water no shell
– parental care:	young cared for and fed milk from female mammary gland	care of eggs and young in nest	some care of eggs	none	none
Body temperature:	constant and warm	constant and warm	varies with surroundings	varies with surroundings	varies with surroundings
Examples:	human cat whale	hen sparrow	crocodile snake	frog newt	goldfish sardine

Fig. 1.3 The classification of living things into kingdoms, phyla and classes

Kingdoms are then divided into **phyla** (singular, *phylum*). For example, there are two phyla in the Animal kingdom–vertebrates (animals with backbones) and invertebrates (animals without backbones). Each phylum is split into **classes**. For example, there are five different classes of vertebrates. Look at Figure 1.3 and identify them. Some important characteristics of the five classes of vertebrates are shown in Figure 1.3.

In turn, classes are divided into **orders**, orders into **families**, families into **genera** (singular, *genus*) and genera into **species**. Orders, families, genera and species are not identified in Figure 1.3, but they are included in Figure 1.4 which shows how some familiar animals are classified and a full classification for human beings.

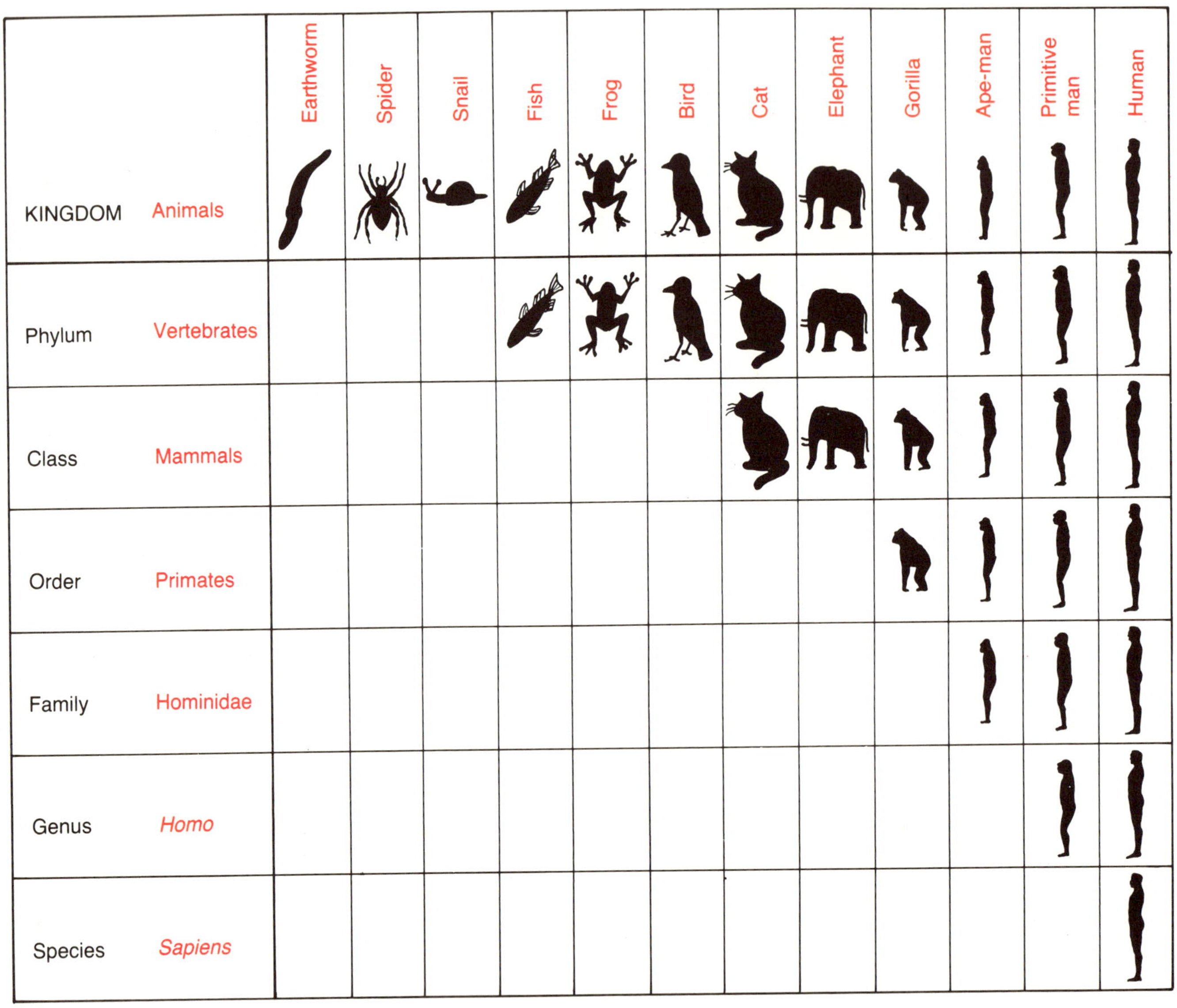

Fig 1.4

1.4 Naming living things

In 1735, Carl Linnaeus suggested a method of naming living things which we still use today. Linnaeus used *two words* to describe each organism so his method is called the **binomial system**. The words used are often derived from Latin names.

Linnaeus used the **genus** and the **species** of an organism to name it. This name is called the **proper name** of the organism because it identifies it precisely. **Common names** like cat, frog and buttercup can be confusing because the same name is sometimes used for several different organisms. Some examples of this system are given in Table 1.1.

Table 1.1 Naming organisms

Common name	Proper name	
(like a nickname)	*Genus* (like a surname, but written first)	*Species* (like a forename, but written second)
Human	*Homo*	*sapiens*
Cat (domestic)	Panthera	*catus*
Lion	*Panthera*	*leo*
Meadow buttercup	*Ranunculus*	*acris*
Creeping buttercup	*Ranunculus*	*repens*
	↑ starts with a capital letter	↑ starts with a small letter

1.5 Cells–building blocks for living things

All living things are made of cells. Cells are the building blocks for organisms in the same way that bricks are the building blocks for houses.

Looking at cells

Your body contains about one hundred million, million cells. Each cell is about one hundredth of a millimetre wide ($\frac{1}{100}$ mm). You cannot see them with your naked eye, but they can be seen under a microscope. The cells are sometimes stained with a dye so that different parts show up better (see Fig. 1.5).

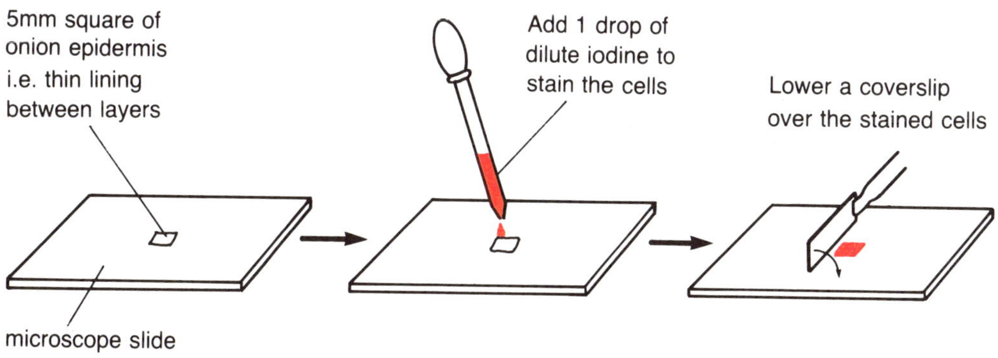

Fig. 1.5 Staining and mounting cells for examination under a microscope

Typical cells

Figure 1.6 shows a typical animal cell (e.g. a cheek cell or a liver cell) side by side with a typical plant cell (e.g. a leaf cell). The diagram emphasizes the similarities and differences between animal cells and plant cells.

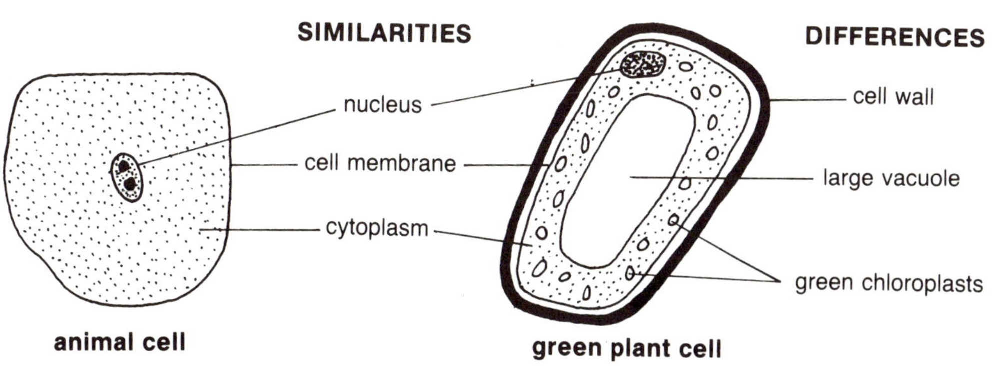

Fig. 1.6 Comparision of an animal cell and a plant cell.

All living cells contain three common features:

- **A nucleus** which contains thread-like structures called **chromosomes**. The chromosomes are composed of **DNA**. This chemical controls all the reactions inside the cell and plays an important part when the cell divides.

- **Cytoplasm** in which all the life processes take place. The cytoplasm is a jelly-like liquid containing smaller parts of the cell called **organelles**. Organelles look like little dots under the microscope. They include **mitochondria** which produce energy and small granules of stored food.
- **A cell membrane** which forms the boundary of the cell. The cell membrane is a very thin protein layer which allows food and water to pass into the cell and waste products to pass out.

In addition to these common features, **plant cells have three other features**:

- **A cell wall** outside the cell membrane. The cell wall is made of cellulose which is much tougher than the thin cell membrane. Even so, the cell wall is porous to various substances. The main function of the cell wall is to support and protect the cell.
- **A vacuole** in the centre of the cell containing a watery liquid. The vacuole occupies a large volume of the cell and is separated from the cytoplasm by a thin membrane. The vacuole has two main functions:
  (*a*) It can act as a storage space for dissolved foods and chemicals such as sugars and salts.
  (*b*) The liquid in the vacuole creates a pressure on the cell wall which helps to keep the cell wall rigid.
- **Chloroplasts**–small bodies containing the green pigment, **chlorophyll**. Chlorophyll has an essential role in **photosynthesis** (see chapter 2). Chloroplasts are only present in the green parts of a plant exposed to the light. They are not present in roots and tubers.

During the 1930s, electron microscopes were invented. They use beams of electrons instead of beams of light and are much more powerful than light (optical) microscopes. Light microscopes can magnify one thousand times, electron microscopes can magnify one million times. Electron microscopes have enabled scientists to study cells in much greater detail and to identify even smaller features than the six shown in Figure 1.6.

1.6 From atoms to ecosystems

Figure 1.7 shows how living things are built up from atoms and how these organisms themselves group to form a whole ecosystem.

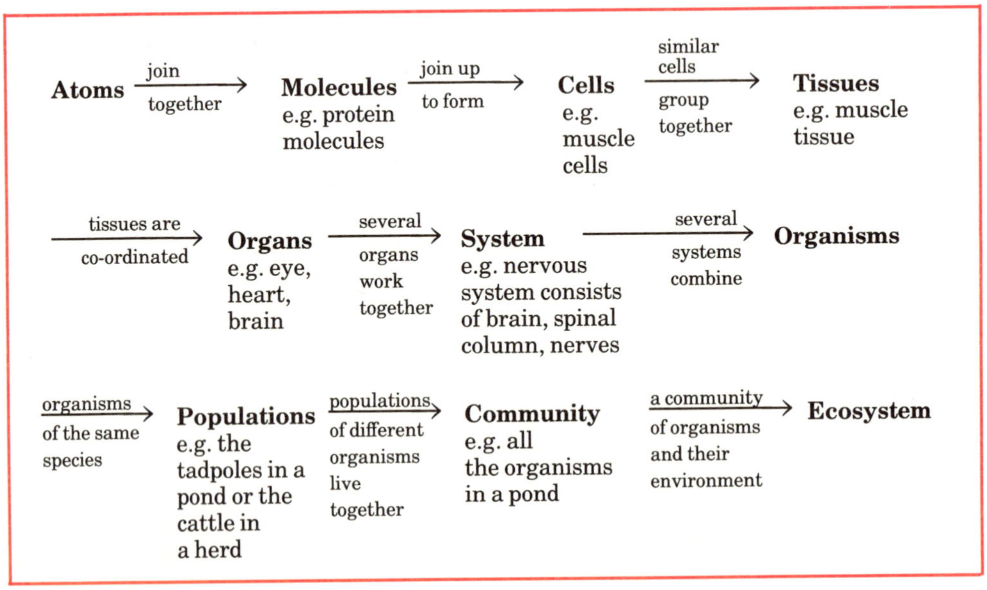

Fig. 1.7 From atoms to ecosystems

1.7 The structure of living things

In living things, cells are grouped together to form tissues such as muscle tissue, bone tissue or nerve tissue. These tissues are then built up to form organs, such as muscles or the lungs or the heart. Each organ has a particular job. The main organs in the human body are shown in Figure 1.8.

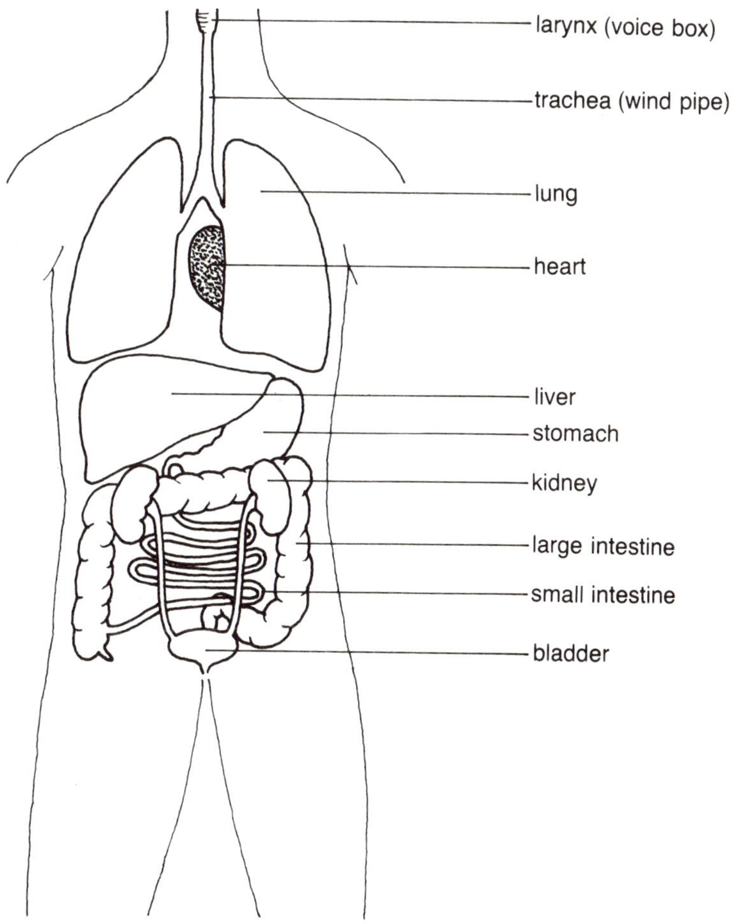

Fig. 1.8 The main organs in the human body

Quick test 1

Questions 1 to 5

Complete the following table for goldfish.

Ordinary name	Man	Goldfish
Scientific name	*Homo sapiens*	*Carassius auratus*
Name of species	*sapiens*	**1** ....
Name of genus	*Homo*	**2** ....
Name of class	Mammals	**3** ....
Name of phylum	Animals with backbones	**4** ....
Name of kingdom	Animals	**5** ....

Questions 6 and 7

Dolphins and whales are mammals that live in the sea.
A They have hairless skin.
B They have a constant body temperature.
C They give birth to their young.
D They have fins and a tail, but no legs.
E They feed their young on milk from mammary glands.

From the characteristics A, B, C, D and E above, choose
6 those which are unusual for mammals.
7 those which are possessed *only* by mammals.

Questions 8 to 13

Name the parts of the plant cell which are numbered 8 to 13 on the diagram.

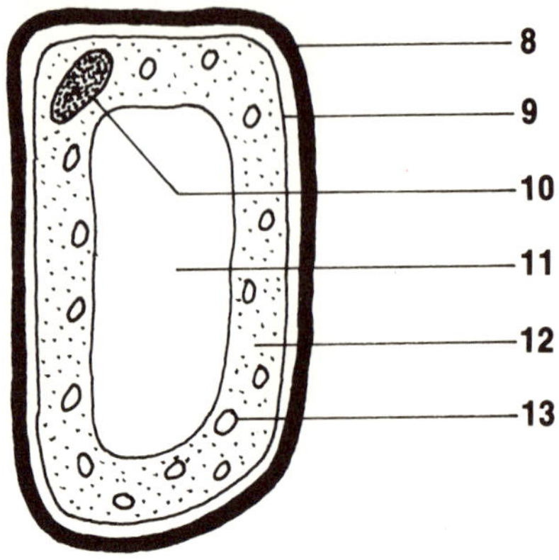

Questions 14 to 19

A cell wall
B cytoplasm
C nucleus
D chloroplast
E cell membrane

From the list A to E above, choose the part of a cell which contains

14 chromosomes.
15 cellulose.
16 chlorophyll.
17 mitochondria.
18 DNA molecules.
19 starch granules.

Questions 20 to 22

A earthworm
B trout
C frog
D ladybird
E lizard

Which of the organisms above

20 has an exoskeleton (external skeleton)?
21 is cold blooded with a dry, scaly skin?
22 has no skeleton?

Questions 23 to 25

Living things have seven important characteristics. Which characteristic is the most important to

23 someone looking through a microscope?
24 an athlete running a 100 m race?
25 a sick person taking glucose tablets?

2 PHOTOSYNTHESIS

2.1 Plants–the source of all food

One of the important differences between plants and animals is that plants make their own food. Animals cannot make their own food. Animals obtain their food by eating plants or by eating animals which have fed on plants. So humans and other animals rely on plants for their food. The process by which plants make their own food is called **photosynthesis**.

2.2 The production of starch during photosynthesis

Plants cannot grow well in the dark. Because of this, very few plants grow in caves or in the shade of a large tree. Plants need light to photosynthesize.

We can show this using two similar potted plants such as geraniums. Before the experiment, both plants must be *de-starched* by keeping the plants in the dark for several days. This uses up all the starch stored in their leaves. When the experiment starts, one plant is left in the dark and the other is placed in the light. After a few days, a leaf is taken from each plant and tested for starch using iodine (see Fig. 2.1). If starch is present, a dark blue colour forms with iodine.

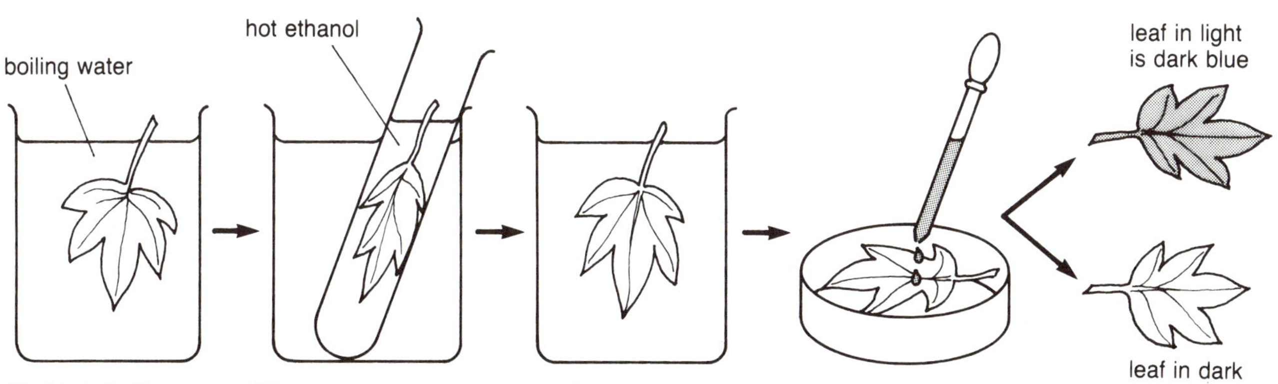

Fig. 2.1 Testing for starch using iodine

The leaf which has been in the light is stained dark blue by the iodine solution. This shows that:

starch forms during photosynthesis.

In fact, the presence of starch in the leaves of a plant is used as evidence for photosynthesis.

The leaf which is kept in the dark is stained brown by the iodine. There is no starch in this leaf. This shows that:

light is necessary for photosynthesis.

Light affects plants in their natural surroundings. On a bright sunny day, plants photosynthesize faster than on a dull day. Plants in an open meadow photosynthesize faster than those in the shade.

2.3 The role of chlorophyll in photosynthesis

Figure 2.2 (overleaf) shows the result when a variegated leaf with green and white patches is tested for starch. The green part of the leaf is coloured by a pigment called **chlorophyll**. After testing, the green part of the leaf is stained a dark blue colour

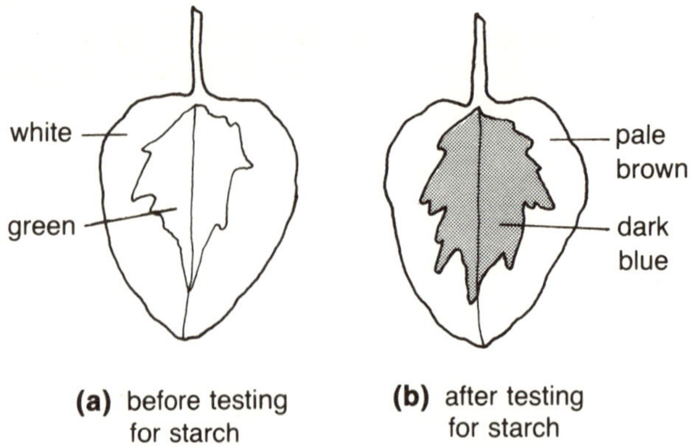

Fig. 2.2 Testing a variegated leaf for starch using iodine

showing that starch is present in this area. The white part of the leaf turns pale brown showing that it contains no starch.

This experiment shows that:

chlorophyll is needed for photosynthesis.

2.4 What chemicals do plants use to produce starch?

We have already shown that both light and chlorophyll are needed for the production of starch during photosynthesis. What chemicals are used to make the starch? Starch is a *carbohydrate*. Therefore, it contains *carbon*, *hydrogen* and *oxygen* which might come from carbon dioxide and water.

Do plants need carbon dioxide to make starch?

An experiment designed to answer this question is illustrated in Fig. 2.3. Both plants must be de-starched before the experiment. Plant A, on the left, is deprived of carbon dioxide which is absorbed by the damp soda lime. Plant B, on the right, has plenty of carbon dioxide which is provided by the slow decomposition of the sodium hydrogencarbonate.

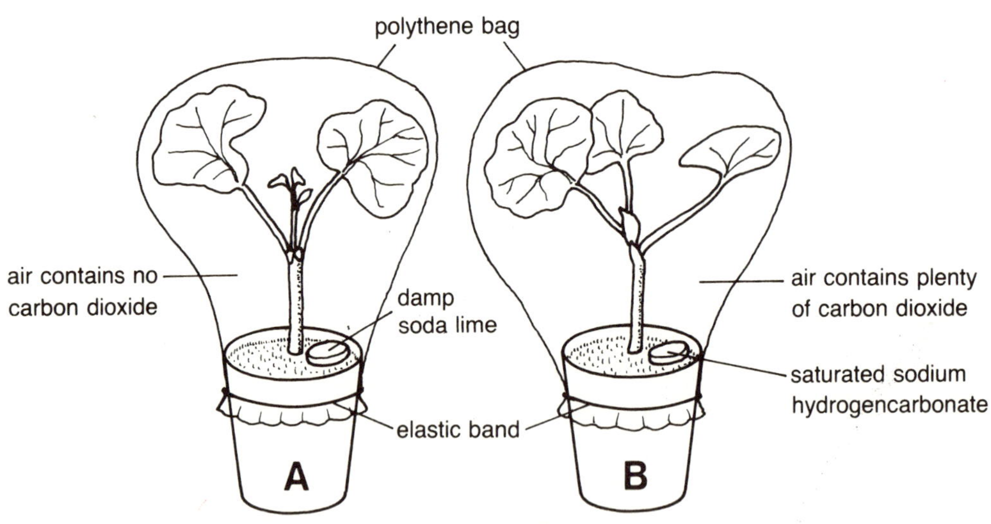

Fig. 2.3 Investigating the effect of carbon dioxide on photosynthesis

When the experiment starts, both plants are placed side by side in a well-lit room. After two or three days a leaf from each plant is tested for starch. The leaf from plant A goes brown, that from plant B goes dark blue. These results show that:

carbon dioxide is needed for photosynthesis.

Experiments show that plants photosynthesize faster if the air surrounding them contains more carbon dioxide. Carbon dioxide is sometimes pumped into greenhouses or produced from a burner to make plants grow faster.

Do plants need water to make starch?

There are no simple experiments one can carry out to answer this question. We cannot deprive the plant of all water – this would kill it. The role of water in starch production has been investigated using radioactive isotopes (see section 22.6). If plants are watered with water containing radioactive hydrogen, radioactive hydrogen is found in starch in the plants' leaves. This shows that:

water plays an important part in photosynthesis.

Plants photosynthesize more slowly if their supply of water is insufficient. However, plants need water for other processes besides photosynthesis, so the effect of water shortage on photosynthesis is not clear.

2.5 What happens in photosynthesis?

The experiments described in this chapter so far, tell us that:

plants need carbon dioxide, water, light and chlorophyll in order to make starch by photosynthesis.

If a plant is deprived of any one of these essential requirements, it cannot photosynthesize.

Experiments show that the first product of photosynthesis is *glucose*. The glucose molecules then link together to form starch. Experiments similar to the one shown in Fig. 2.4 show that *oxygen* is produced during photosynthesis as well as sugar (glucose) and starch. When the apparatus is kept in the light, the pondweed produces bubbles of gas. After a few days enough gas collects in the test tube to be able to test for oxygen. What test would you use to show that the gas is oxygen?

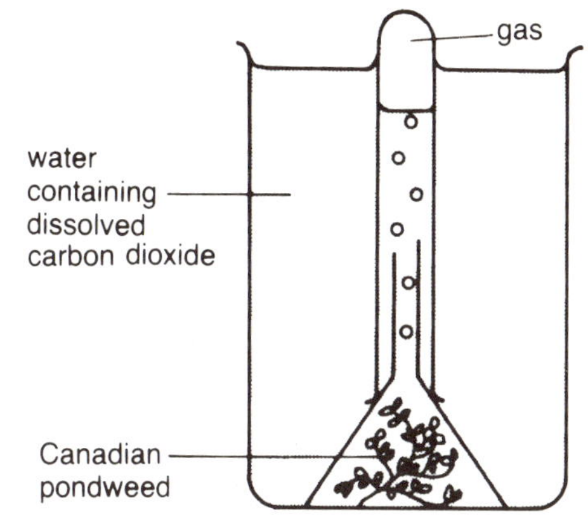

Fig. 2.4 Investigating the production of oxygen during photosynthesis

Although photosynthesis is a complicated process, we can summarize the overall reaction as:

$$\text{carbon dioxide} + \text{water} \xrightarrow[\text{and chlorophyll}]{\text{light}} \text{glucose} + \text{oxygen}$$

$$6CO_2 + 6H_2O \longrightarrow C_6H_{12}O_6 + 6O_2$$

During photosynthesis, chlorophyll absorbs light energy. This energy is used to turn carbon dioxide and water into glucose. So the overall result of photosynthesis is to turn the energy in sunlight into chemical energy in glucose.

How do plants use glucose?

The glucose which plants make by photosynthesis has three main uses. These are summarized in Figure 2.5.

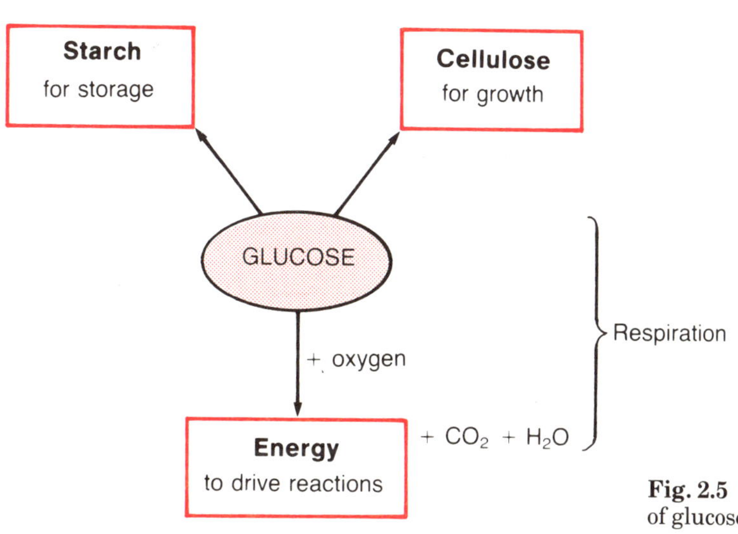

Fig. 2.5 The three main uses of glucose in plants

- Glucose is converted to **starch** and **stored** for future use. This is why the leaves of plants usually contain starch as a result of photosynthesis.
- Glucose is converted to **cellulose** which is needed to support the plant as it **grows**.
- Glucose is used to produce **energy** for the plant by **respiration** (see chapter 6). Looking at Figure 2.5, notice that the overall effect of respiration is the reverse of photosynthesis. The energy produced in respiration is used to drive the other chemical reactions which go on in plants. These reactions include the conversion of glucose to starch and cellulose.

What factors affect the rate of photosynthesis?

There are four factors that strongly influence the rate of photosynthesis:

- light intensity (section 2.2)
- concentration of carbon dioxide (section 2.4)
- water supply (section 2.4)
- temperature

Plants photosynthesize faster in warm weather. Roughly speaking, the rate of photosynthesis doubles if the temperature rises by 10 °C. This explains why plants grow so well in a greenhouse or in a sheltered garden. Although plants thrive in warm conditions, there is a limit to the temperature at which they can survive. The rate of photosynthesis increases until the temperature reaches about 40°C. Above 40°C, photosynthesis slows down and then stops. This is because some important chemicals in plants are destroyed above 40°C. These important chemicals are called **enzymes**. Enzymes are catalysts (see section 19.11). They speed up the reactions in all living things.

2.6 The structure of leaves

All plant cells which contain chlorophyll can photosynthesize (given the right conditions). These cells are mainly in the leaves. Leaves are usually flat and thin. Being flat gives them a large surface area. This helps them absorb carbon dioxide from the air and light from the sun. Being thin reduces the distance that the carbon dioxide has to travel to reach the cells once it has been absorbed.

Look closely at a leaf (Fig. 2.6). Notice the stalk or **petiole** which joins it to a stem or branch. The petiole divides into **veins**. These veins act as a kind of skeleton which supports the leaf, preventing it from drooping. The water required for photosynthesis travels up the plant from the roots and into the leaves via the veins.

The carbon dioxide needed for photosynthesis enters the leaves through tiny holes called **stomata** (singular: *stoma*). Stomata are mainly on the underside of leaves (see Fig. 2.7 opposite).

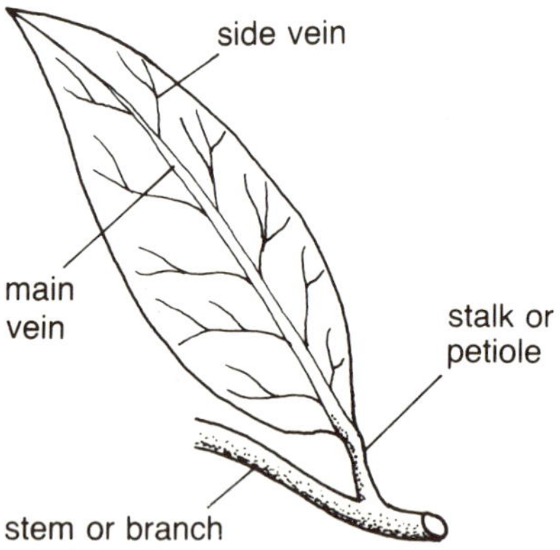

Fig. 2.6 The structure of a leaf

Very often the top side of a leaf has a smooth, shiny appearance. This is due to a thin waxy layer called the **cuticle** which reduces evaporation (water loss). Below the cuticle and on the underside of the leaf, there is a single layer of tightly fitting cells. This is called the **epidermis**. Leaves are usually a deeper green on their upper surface. This is because the cells near the upper surface contain more chlorophyll than those below. As Figure 2.7 shows, there are two distinct areas of cells between the layers of epidermis:

(*a*) long, **palisade cells** near the upper surface, containing lots of chloroplasts filled with dark green chlorophyll. These palisade cells, as their name suggests, are arranged neatly like the vertical stakes in a fence which is called a palisade.

(*b*) more rounded cells near the lower surface, containing fewer chloroplasts. These cells are arranged irregularly with air spaces between them.

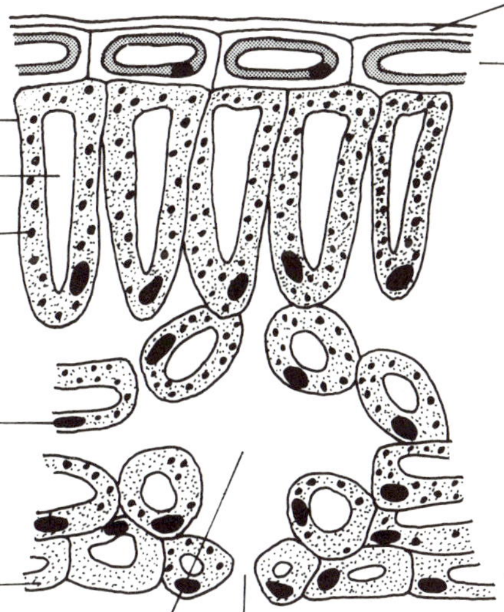

Fig. 2.7 Cells in the cross section of a leaf

2.7 Photosynthesis and transpiration

In order to live and grow, plants must transport materials from one part to another.

- Water must be transported from the roots to the leaves for photosynthesis.
- Sugars which are produced in the leaves by photosynthesis must be transported to other parts of the plant.
- Minerals (salts) such as nitrates and phosphates must be absorbed from the soil by the roots and transported to different parts of the plant.

Materials such as sugars and minerals can only be moved around a plant if they are in solution. The movement of these solutions round the plant, requires a transport system connecting the roots, stem and leaves. This is called the plant's **vascular system**. The vascular system in a plant can be compared to the blood system in animals (see chapter 5). When the stem of a plant is cut, liquid oozes out. This is **sap** escaping from the cut vascular system.

Look at Figure 2.8. This shows an experiment to investigate the uptake of water by a plant. The volume of water in the measuring cylinder was recorded over a few days. The results are shown in Table 2.1.

Table 2.1 Investigating the uptake of water by a plant

Time after start of experiment	*Volume of water/cm^3*
0	90
1 day	88
2 days	85
3 days	83
4 days	81

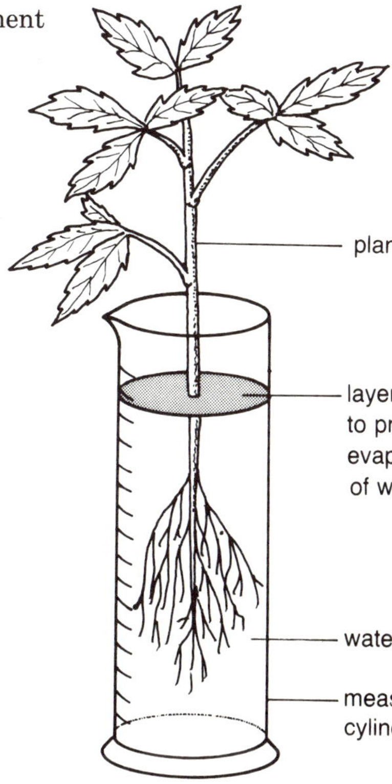

Fig. 2.8 Investigating the uptake of water by a plant

The results in Table 2.1 show that water was taken up by the plant. Some of this water is used in photosynthesis. Most of it evarporates from the leaves, escaping through the stomata. As water is lost from the leaves, it is replaced by more water from the measuring cylinder. This is drawn up from the roots to the leaves through the vascular system.

The evaporation of water from the leaves of a plant is called **transpiration**. The continuous flow of water (sap) through the plant from roots to leaves is called the **transpiration stream**. What sort of weather will increase the rate of transpiration? Why do plants wilt in this sort of weather?

2.8 The vascular system in plants

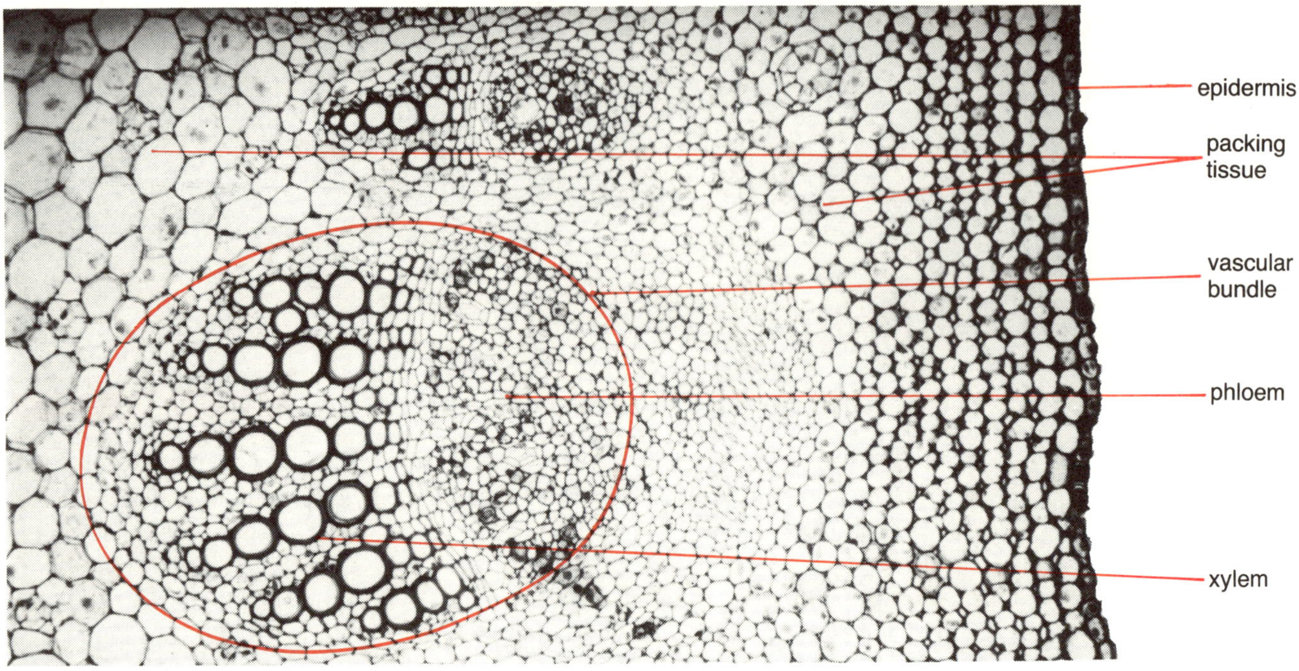

Fig. 2.9 Photomicrograph of a section through a sunflower stem (magnification 50x)

The photograph in Figure 2.9 shows the **internal structure of a plant stem**. This is composed of three main tissues:

- the **epidermis** which is the outermost layer of cells. This is a kind of skin. On the leaves and stem the epidermis is covered with waxy cuticle, pierced by stomata.
- **packing tissue** which fills most of the stem. This consists of rounded cells packed close together.
- the **vascular system** made up of **xylem** (pronounced 'zylem') and **phloem** (pronounced 'flowum'). The xylem and phloem are arranged side by side around the stem of the plant in bundles of tubes called **vascular bundles**. These are illustrated in Figure 2.10.

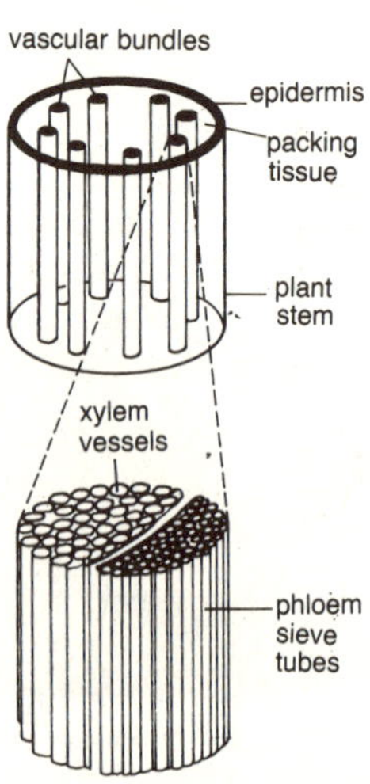

Fig. 2.10 Vascular bundles in a plant stem

In each vascular bundle, the inner tissue is xylem. This contains long, narrow, hollow vessels like capillary tubes. The walls of the vessels are composed of *dead cells*. The xylem vessels run from the roots to the leaves carrying water and dissolved salts.

Xylem carries the transpiration stream and plays an important part in the transport of water through a plant.

The outer tissue in each vascular bundle is phloem. Phloem contains very long, *living cells* joined end to end. The end walls between one cell and the next are perforated by tiny holes like a sieve. Because of this, the phloem is described as *sieve tubes*.

Phloem plays an important role in the transport of food throughout the plant.

Food (mainly carbohydrates) is made in the leaves. It is then distributed to the roots, the flowers, the fruit and the growing tip via the phloem. Notice that material in the xylem vessels travels in only one direction along a plant stem–from roots to leaves. On the other hand, material in the phloem tubes may travel up the stem to the fruits and flower or down to the roots.

In a tree trunk, the phloem is located in the soft inner part of the bark. So if a complete ring of bark is cut from a tree trunk, food cannot be transported to the roots and the tree will eventually die.

2.9 Essential elements for plants

Plants need certain elements in order to grow. These elements are therefore called **essential elements**.

Table 2.2 Essential elements for plants

Carbon	most important elements	major elements	essential elements
Hydrogen	most important elements	major elements	essential elements
Oxygen	most important elements	major elements	essential elements
Calcium		major elements	essential elements
Potassium		major elements	essential elements
Magnesium		major elements	essential elements
Iron		major elements	essential elements
Nitrogen		major elements	essential elements
Phosphorus		major elements	essential elements
Sulphur		major elements	essential elements
Aluminium	trace (minor) elements		essential elements
Chlorine	trace (minor) elements		essential elements
Copper	trace (minor) elements		essential elements
Sodium	trace (minor) elements		essential elements

Ten of the essential elements are known as **major elements** because they are needed in quite large amounts. The most important essential elements are carbon, hydrogen and oxygen. These are obtained mainly from water and from carbon dioxide in the air.

The seven other major elements are *calcium*, *potassium*, *magnesium*, *iron*, *nitrogen*, *phosphorus* and *sulphur*. These seven elements are present in the soil as soluble compounds and minerals, such as calcium phosphate and potassium nitrate. Plants absorb these through their roots (see section 19.6). Essential elements are needed by plants for important structures and functions. For example, nitrogen is used to synthesize DNA (**d**eoxyribose **n**ucleic **a**cid). Chlorophyll contains magnesium and the enzymes which make chlorophyll contain iron. So, if the plant lacks either magnesium or iron, it cannot make chlorophyll and its leaves will turn yellow. This is called **chlorosis**.

Fig. 2.11(a) The effect of nitrogen on plants. The tomato plant on the left has been deprived of nitrogen. The one on the right has had a good supply of nitrogen-rich fertilizer.

Fig. 2.11(b) The effect of potassium on plants. The tomato plant on the left has been deprived of potassium. The one on the right has had a good supply of potassium-rich fertilizer.

(Photographs courtesy of Fisons plc)

Trace elements

In addition to the ten major elements, plants also require other elements in tiny amounts. These elements are therefore called **minor elements** or **trace elements**. They include *zinc*, *copper*, *sodium*, *chlorine* and *manganese*. Trace elements are also absorbed from the soil through the roots of plants. The important point about trace elements is that they are only needed in small amounts. Too much of a trace element can be more damaging to a plant than too little.

Quick test 2

Questions 1 to 4

Choose the option, A to D, which correctly completes the sentence.

1 Photosynthesis
A is essential to all life on earth.
B uses up oxygen.
C takes place only in darkness.
D is not important to animals.

2 There is no starch in the white part of a variegated ivy leaf because that part of the leaf
A is dead.
B is too cold.
C contains no chloroplasts.
D has been in the shade.

3 Carbon dioxide enters plants through holes in the leaves called
A air spaces.
B chloroplasts.
C cuticles.
D stomata.

4 The metal present in chlorophyll is
A calcium.
B iron.
C magnesium.
D potassium.

5 The volume of oxygen produced per hour by a sample of duckweed was measured over a 12-hour period.
Which letter on the graph represents 12.00 noon?

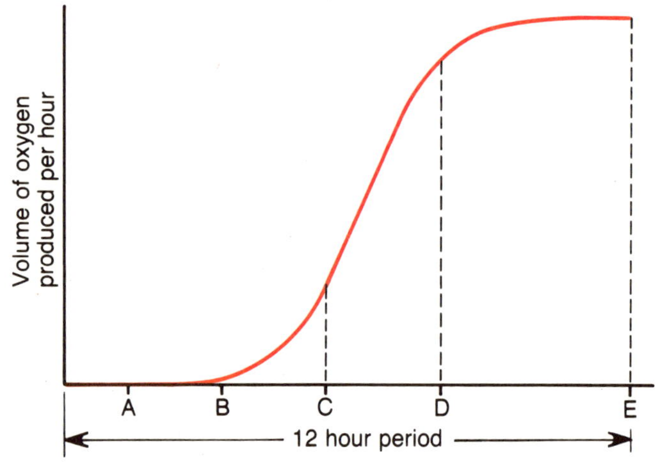

Questions 6 to 8

A carbon
B cobalt
C magnesium
D nitrogen
E phosphorus

Choose from A to E above, the essential element which
6 would improve the colour of grass.
7 would be provided by ammonium salts.
8 is required in only trace quantities.

Questions 9 to 16

The diagram (page 17) shows a cross section of a leaf.
Which of the letters A to E indicates
9 the cuticle?
10 the epidermis with stomata?
11 the layer of palisade cells?

Which of the letters V to Z indicates
12 a chloroplast?
13 a guard cell?
14 a stoma?

15 State two differences between the cells in layer C and layer D.
16 Why is layer B transparent?

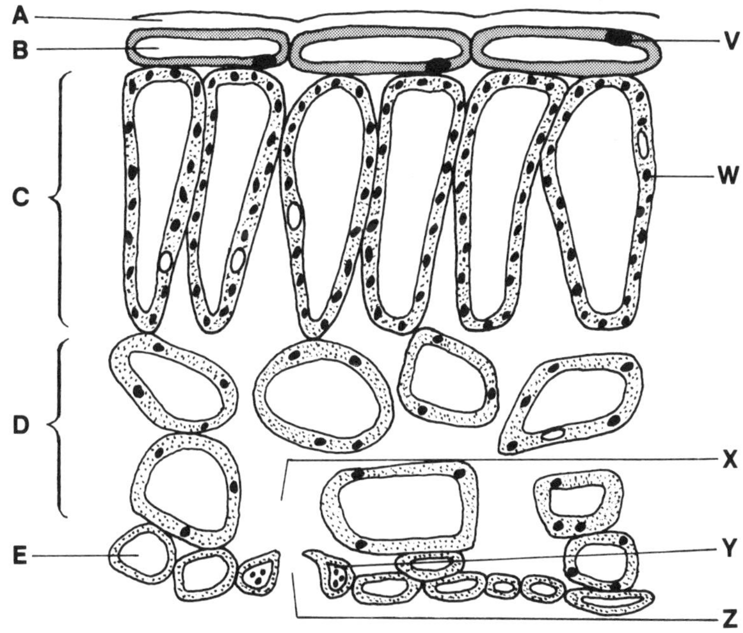

Questions 17 and 18

The diagram below shows four test tubes labelled A to D. Each tube contains the organisms shown in river water. The tubes were left in sunlight for six hours.

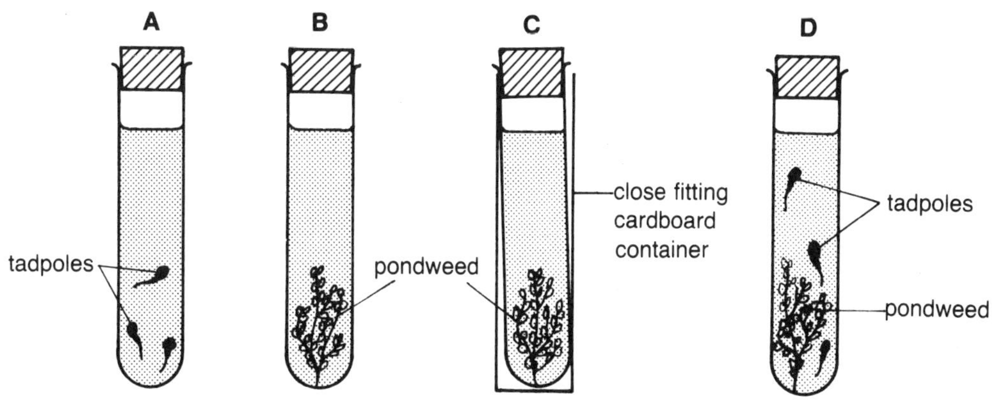

17 Which tube contains the least carbon dioxide after six hours?
18 In which tube or tubes will photosynthesis occur?

Questions 19 and 20

A market gardener found that the average mass of a lettuce grown in an ordinary greenhouse was 80 g, whereas the average mass of a lettuce grown in a greenhouse where the atmosphere contained added carbon dioxide was 115 g.

19 Why is there a difference in the average mass of the lettuces?
20 State three other ways in which the gardener could increase the mass of his/her lettuces.

Questions 21 and 22

21 Name the two products of photosynthesis.
22 What energy conversion takes place during photosynthesis?

Questions 23 and 24

There are four steps in testing a leaf for starch:

Step 1 Dip leaf in boiling water for $\frac{1}{2}$ minute.
Step 2 Dip leaf in hot ethanol for 10 minutes.
Step 3 Wash leaf in hot water.
Step 4 Add dilute iodine solution to leaf.

23 What is the purpose of step 2?
24 What happens at step 4 if starch is present?

3 FOOD AND DIET

3.1 Different kinds of food

The food that we eat and drink each day makes up our **diet**. We need different foods for different purposes. We require three types of food:

- **energy foods** which give us the energy to move and keep warm. These energy foods are sometimes called *body fuels*. The main energy foods are **carbohydrates** and **fats**. Carbohydrates include starch in bread, potatoes and rice. Fats include cream, margarine and cooking oil.
- **body-building foods** which provide the important chemicals we need to grow and to repair the worn-out parts of our bodies. The main body-building foods are **proteins**. Meat, fish, milk, cheese and eggs are rich in proteins.
- **maintenance foods** which are needed in small amounts to control our metabolism and keep our bodies running smoothly. The main maintenance foods are **vitamins** (for example, vitamin C in oranges) and **minerals** (for example, sodium in salt).

In addition to these three types of food, we also need **water**. Most people can survive several weeks without other foods, but only a few days without water. We take in most of our water by drinking, but most solid foods also contain water. For example, meat contains about 60 per cent water and cabbage is about 90 per cent water. Even so, we need to drink at least one cubic decimetre (1000 cm^3) of water every day.

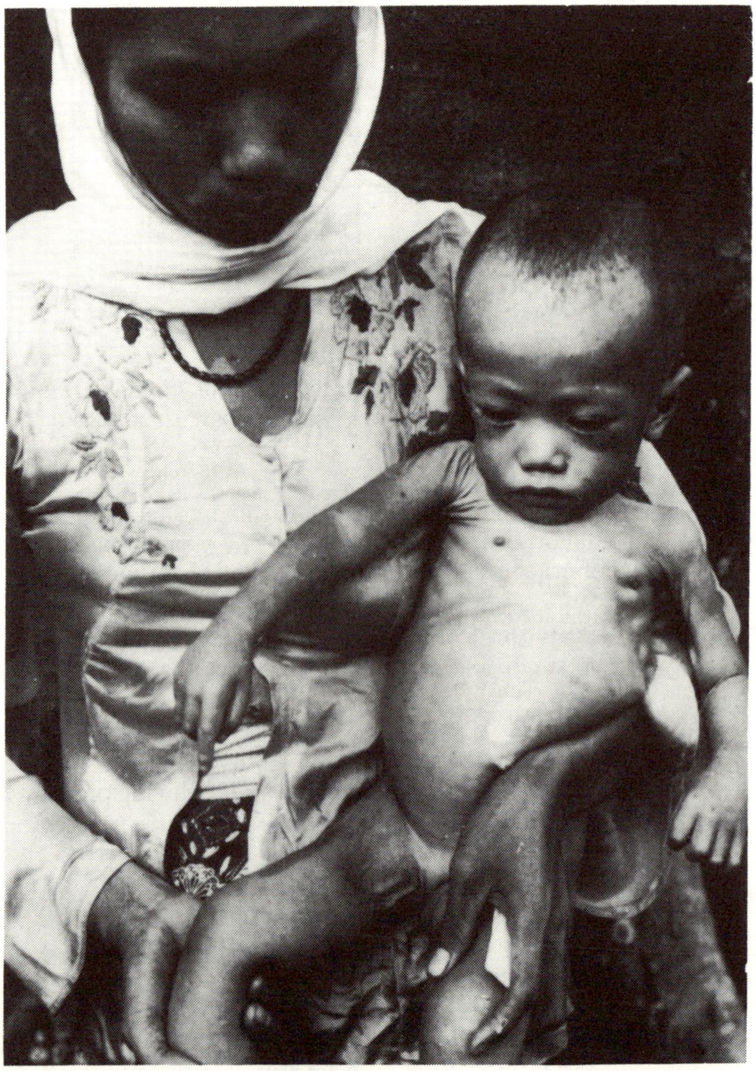

Fig. 3.1 Insufficient protein in the diet causes poor health. Children are seriously affected. They become listless and flabby with weak muscles. This condition is called kwashiorkor. This child is suffering from serious kwashiorkor.

To summarize, our diet must include the following six substances:

carbohydrates
fats
proteins
vitamins
minerals
water

} These essential requirements in our diet are called **nutrients**.

In addition to these essential nutrients, our diet should also include fibre (see section 3.5).

3.2 Carbohydrates, fats and proteins

Table 3.1 compares various characteristics and properties of carbohydrates, fats and proteins.

	Carbohydrates	**Fats**	**Proteins**
Elements present	C, H and O with H and O in the ratio 2:1	C, H and O but ratio H:O is very high (i.e. very little O)	C, H, O and N
Examples	The main forms of carbohydrate are: **glucose** ($C_6H_{12}O_6$) and fructose in fruit; **sugar** (sucrose) in sugar cane and sugar beet; **starch** in bread, potatoes, rice and cereals; **cellulose** (fibre) in the cell walls of plants in leaves, stems and wood.	Beef fat ($C_{57}H_{110}O_6$), butter, margarine, cooking oil.	Milk, eggs, meat and fish contain a high percentage of protein.
Units (monomers) and polymers	Simple **monosaccharides** (monomers), e.g. glucose (G) and fructose (F), join together to form **disaccharides**, e.g. sucrose (G)–(F), and **polysaccharides** (polymers) e.g. starch 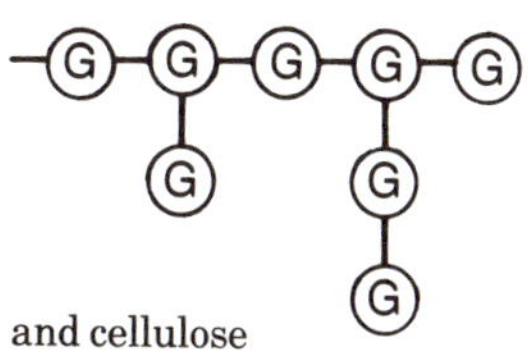 and cellulose 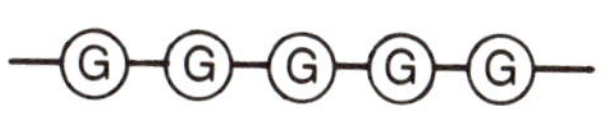	Fats are made by a reaction between **glycerol** and **fatty acids**: 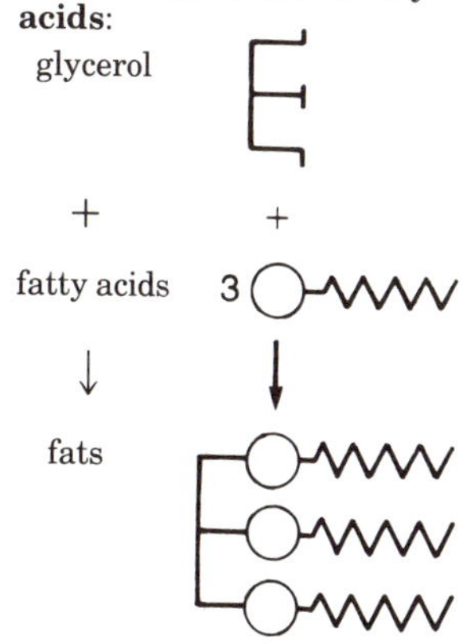	Proteins are synthesized from 23 different **amino acids**. Amino acids (monomers) join together in long chains to form proteins (polymers): 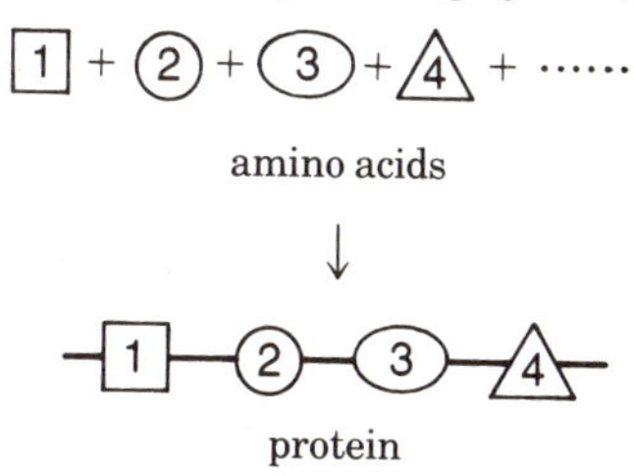 Certain amino acids can be made by our bodies so we do not need them in our diet. Others cannot be made by our bodies, so they must be in our diet–these are called **essential amino acids**.
Function	**1** Glucose and fructose are important **energy foods**. They can be oxidized to carbon dioxide and water, releasing energy. This process is called *respiration* (see section 6.5). **2** Excess carbohydrates can be stored as *starch* in plants or as *glycogen* in animals and used as energy foods at a later date. Starch and glycogen are therefore **energy stores**. **3** *Cellulose* is an important **structural substance** in the cell walls of plants. It acts as *fibre* (**roughage**) in our diet because it is not broken down in humans. Roughage keeps food moving through the gut and prevents constipation.	**1** Fats are **energy foods**. They produce about twice as much heat per gram during metabolism as carbohydrates and proteins. **2** Fats are stored under the skin (*subcutaneous fat*) in humans and other animals. This acts as **insulation**. **3** Subcutaneous fat also acts as an **energy store**.	**1** Proteins form the main structures of our body. So proteins are **body-building foods**. We need them for growth and for repairing damaged tissues. Muscles, skin, hair and nails are nearly 100 per cent protein. Bone is partly protein. **2** *Enzymes* are proteins. Enzymes catalyse the reactions in living things and help to **control the rate of metabolism**. **3** Proteins give us **energy**, but they are not as important in this role as carbohydrates and fats.
Effects and dangers of excess or lack	Excess carbohydrate of any kind can cause a person to become overweight. This can lead to heart disease. Too much sugar can cause tooth decay.	Too much fat is unhealthy. It causes a person to become overweight and may cause heart disease.	In some parts of the world, protein is very scarce. A severe lack of protein leads to a disease called **kwashiorkor** (see Fig. 3.1).

FOOD TESTS FOR FAT, SUGAR, STARCH AND PROTEIN

Test for fat

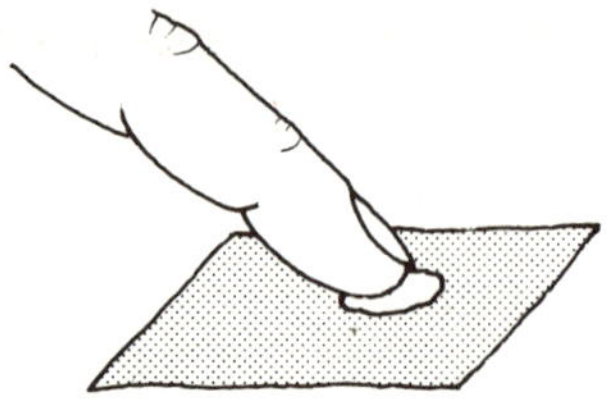

1 Rub a small sample of the food onto paper.

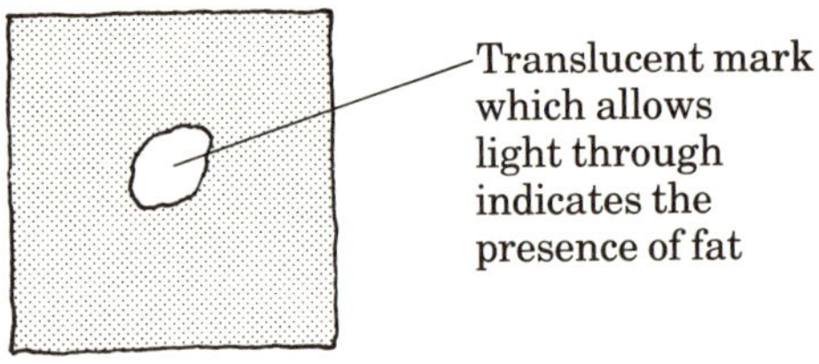

2 Allow the paper to dry, then hold it in front of a light.

Tests for starch, sugar and protein

Preparation of sample for testing

1 Mash solid foods with a pestle and mortar.

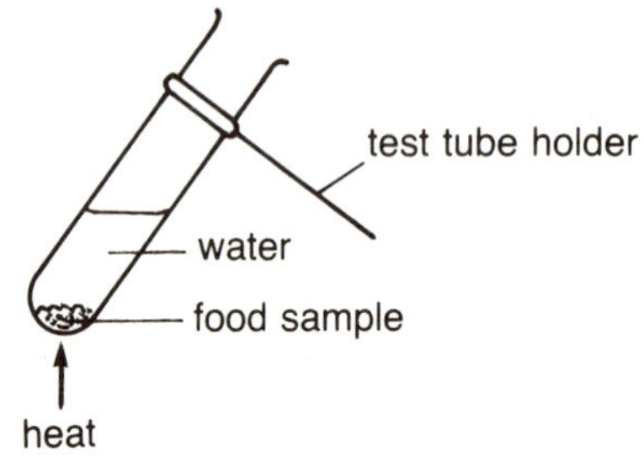

2 Put the food sample in about 5 cm^3 of water in a boiling tube. Boil gently for 1 minute. Allow to cool. Divide into 3 portions.

3 Test for starch

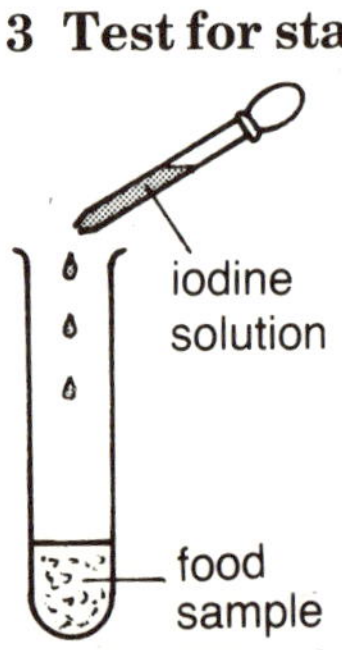

Add 5 drops of *iodine* solution.

A blue-black colour shows starch is present.

4 Test for sugar

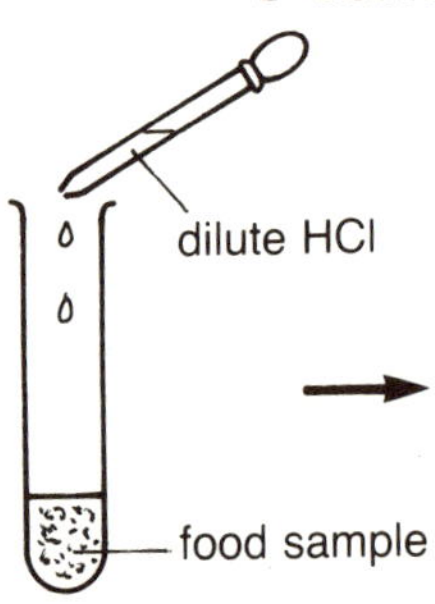

(a) Add 5 drops of *dilute hydrochloric acid* (CARE). Heat gently for 1 minute.

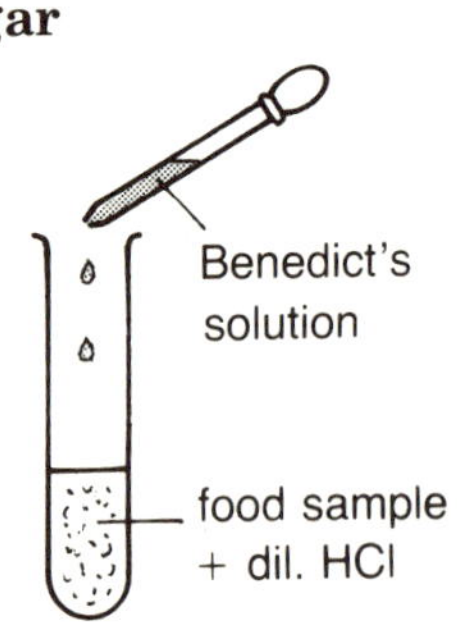

(b) Add 10 drops of *Benedict's solution*. Heat gently for 1 minute.

A green or orange-red precipitate shows glucose or sucrose is present.

5 Test for protein

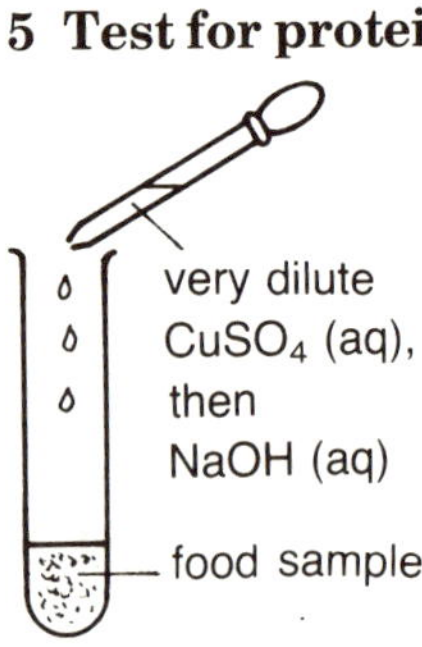

Add 1 cm^3 of very dilute *copper*(II) *sulphate* solution and 1 cm^3 of *sodium hydroxide* solution. Mix and wait for 2 minutes.

A violet colour appears if protein is present.

3.3 Vitamins

Vitamins are an essential part of our diet. They help to control the chemical reactions in our bodies. Without vitamins many of these reactions cannot take place. Most vitamins are complex chemicals. They do have chemical names, but they are usually known simply by letters of the alphabet.

We need only tiny amounts of vitamins, but without them people suffer from illnesses known as **deficiency diseases**. Table 3.2 summarizes the sources of some important vitamins, their functions and the deficiency diseases associated with them.

Table 3.2 Some important vitamins

Vitamin	*Good sources*	*Function*	*Deficiency disease*
A (retinol)	green vegetables carrots, liver	helps us to see in the dark, protects the surface of our eyes	poor vision in the dark or in dim light–*night-blindness*
B_1 (thiamine)	bread cereals (especially in the seed husks)	helps us to produce energy from foods	stomach ache, diarrhoea, vomiting, muscular weakness –*beri-beri*
B_2 (riboflavin)	green vegetables eggs fish	helps us to produce energy from foods	dry sores on the skin and around the mouth, poor growth
C (ascorbic acid)	green vegetables blackcurrants citrus fruits	helps to heal wounds and form strong skin	bleeding from the gums and the stomach–*scurvy* (see Fig. 3.2)
D (calciferol)	liver oil, eggs (also made by the skin in sunlight)	helps us to form strong, hard bones and teeth	weak bones, deformed bones –*rickets*

Fig. 3.2 The mouth of a person suffering from scurvy showing swollen and bleeding gums. Scurvy results from a diet without fresh fruit or vegetables.

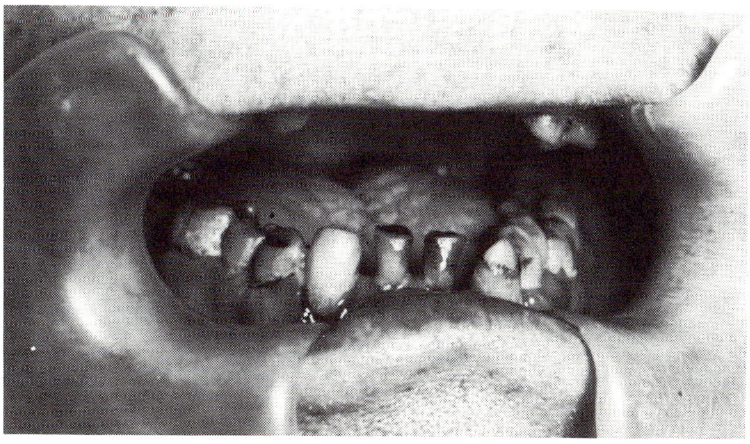

3.4 Minerals

We must have certain elements in our diet. The main elements in our bodies are carbon, hydrogen, oxygen and nitrogen. There is a good supply of these elements in the carbohydrates, fats, proteins and water in our diet.

In addition to these elements, we need many other elements in smaller quantities. These elements are usually present in the **minerals** which occur in small amounts in our food. Minerals are sometimes called **salts**. Perhaps the best example of a mineral (salt) is sodium chloride (common salt). Common salt provides us with essential small amounts of sodium. Table 3.3 shows some important minerals–their sources, their function and the effects of deficiency.

Table 3.3 Some important minerals

Mineral	*Good sources*	*Function*	*Effect of deficiency*
Sodium	common salt (table salt)	helps nerves and muscles to work smoothly	pains in muscles–*cramp*
Calcium	milk, cheese, bread	hardens bones and teeth	soft and deformed bones–*rickets*
Iron	red meat, liver, kidney, green vegetables, dried fruit	needed to form *haemoglobin* in red blood cells	tiredness, lack of energy –*anaemia*
Iodine	sea foods, table salt	needed to make the hormone *thyroxine* which controls metabolism	thyroid gland in neck swells –*goitre*

3.5 Diet and health

A balanced diet is one that maintains our health and provides the necessary amounts of carbohydrates, fats, proteins, vitamins, minerals, water and fibre. No single food contains all these nutrients, so we need to balance our diet by eating a wide variety of different foods. Table 3.4 shows the recommended amounts of energy, protein and iron needed by different people for a balanced diet.

Table 3.4 Daily amounts of energy, protein and iron recommended by the Department of Health

Person	*Energy needed*/kJ	*Protein needed*/g	*Iron needed*/mg
Baby under 1 year	3 300	20	6
Child, 5 years	7 500	45	8
Boy, 15–17 years	12 600	75	15
Girl, 15–17 years	9 600	58	15
Adult male (moderately active)	12 600	75	10
Adult female (moderately active)	9 200	55	12

The requirements of a balanced diet depend on:

- *age* (growing children need more of each type of food, relative to their weight, than adults),
- *sex* (generally, males need more food than females),
- *occupation* (people in some jobs need more energy and more water (to replace sweat) than those in other jobs),
- *climate* (in hot countries the energy required to keep warm and the water needed to replace sweat will be different from those required in cold countries).

Which two of these factors affecting a balanced diet are illustrated by the figures in table 3.4?

The dangers of over-eating

Most people enjoy food. This is healthy and natural, but it is easy to eat too much and put on weight. Some people become obese (very overweight). The reason for being overweight is not simply eating too much. It is often caused by eating too much of the wrong foods, in particular sugary and fatty foods. Being overweight can cause other health problems. People who are overweight tend to suffer more from high blood pressure, diabetes, heart disease and strokes (cerebral haemorrhages).

For health reasons, it is important to eat a balanced diet. This does not mean cutting down on all foods, but choosing a diet which is low in sugar and fat. In this way you are much less likely to suffer from weight problems. Regular exercise will also help you to maintain a healthy body.

High-fibre diets

High-fibre diets include wholemeal bread, wholegrain rice, muesli, brown pasta, vegetables and fruit. These foods are good sources of carbohydrate and fibre. By eating these foods people cut down their intake of fats and sugars which are the main causes of obesity (being overweight). Fibre acts as **roughage** in the diet. This helps **peristalsis** (the movement of food through the gut) and prevents constipation.

Vegetarianism

Some people prefer not to eat meat or fish. They are called **vegetarians**. The main constituents in their diet are vegetables, fruit, cereals, nuts, milk, eggs and cheese. The proteins in plants do not usually contain the right balance of amino acids for humans. So milk, eggs and cheese are very important in their diet (see table 3.1).

Some vegetarians prefer not to eat *any* animal products (meat, fish, eggs or dairy (milk-based) products. They are called **vegans**. By carefully combining pulses (beans, peas and lentils) and cereals, they can obtain the necessary balance of amino acids.

Quick test 3

Questions 1 to 8 refer to the information below which comes from the label on a can of baked beans.

Constituent	*Average amount per 100 g*
carbohydrate	9.3 g
fibre	7.3 g
protein	5.2 g
added sugar	2.0 g
added salt	0.8 g
fat	0.4 g

1 Which constituent of the beans provides a good source of amino acids?
2 Which constituents of the tinned beans were not present in the freshly picked beans?
3 Which constituent of the beans is good for digestion because it helps food to pass through the gut?
4 Which constituent of the beans provides an important mineral nutrient?
5 One constituent listed on the label is 'carbohydrate'. Which of the other constituents is (are) also carbohydrates?
6 In a 100 g sample, what is the total mass of the constituents shown on the label?
7 What major constituent in the baked beans is not shown on the label?
8 The label also showed that 100 g of baked beans provides 250 kJ of energy. How much energy would be provided by 200 g of baked beans?

Questions 9 to 13

Jane's meal consisted of:
a glass of water,
roast beef, boiled potatoes and carrots,
cheese,
an apple.

Assuming she eats the same mass of each food, which food will provide
9 the least energy?
10 the most protein?
11 both calcium and fat?
12 the most iron?
13 vitamin A?

Questions 14 to 16

The table below compares the average British diet with the average Eskimo diet.

Food type	*British diet*	*Eskimo diet*
carbohydrate	50%	10%
fat	40%	45%
protein	10%	45%

Use this information to complete the following sentences. Write down the food type which should go in each gap.

The diet of people in Britain contains much more ___14___ and much less ___15___ than the diet of Eskimos. The amount of ___16___ is about the same in each diet.

Questions 17 to 20

The table below shows the amount of energy a human being needs at different ages just to stay alive (breathe, keep warm, grow, etc).

	Mass/kg	*Energy (kJ) needed each day*	
		For each kg	*Total*
Infant, 1 year old	10	210	2100
Child, 7 years old	25	170	4250
Adult, 20 years old	60	100	

17 How much energy does a 7-year-old child need each day for each kilogram of body mass?

18 What is the total energy needed each day by a 20-year-old adult of mass 60 kilograms?
19 How does the total daily energy requirement of humans change as they grow from infants to adults?
20 How does the energy needed per kilogram of body mass change as humans grow from infants to adults?

Questions 21 to 24

Large food molecules such as carbohydrates, fats and proteins are broken down in our bodies to smaller molecules or monomers.

What smaller molecules or monomers do we get from
21 proteins?
22 starch?
23 sugar (sucrose)?
24 beef fat?

4 DIGESTION

4.1 What happens to food after we eat it?

A cheese sandwich contains carbohydrates, fats and proteins–carbohydrates in the bread, fats and proteins in the cheese and butter. All these foods are solids. After we eat them, they pass into the **digestive system**. The digestive system is like a long, coiled tube which runs from the mouth to the anus. It is usually called the **gut** or the **alimentary canal**.

The main purpose of digestion is to break food down into smaller particles so that these can pass through the wall of the gut into the rest of the body.

Digestion involves breaking up insoluble solid foods, like the cheese sandwich mentioned above. The solids are converted to smaller molecules which will dissolve in water. These molecules can pass through the gut wall into the bloodstream (see Fig. 4.2). Food which cannot be broken down stays in the gut. This passes out of the body, through the anus, as **faeces**.

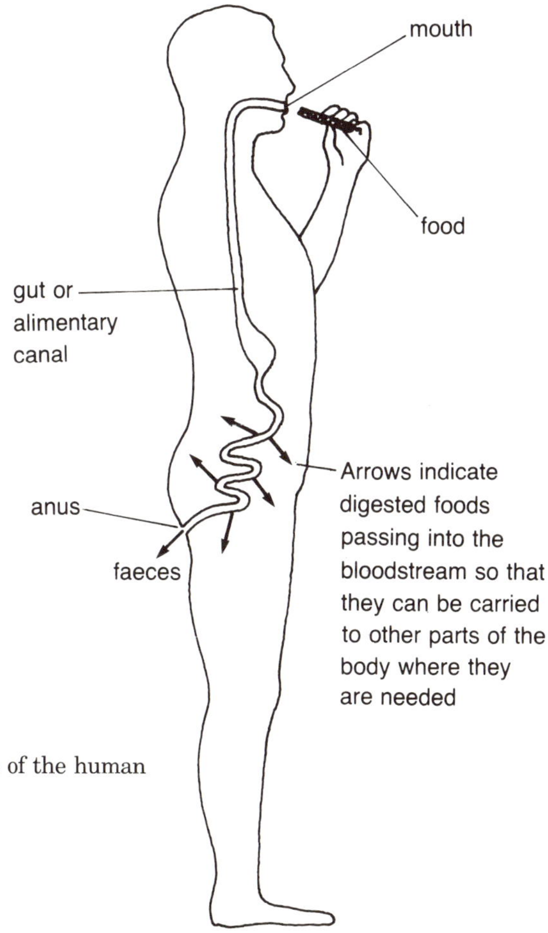

Fig. 4.1 A simple plan of the human digestive system

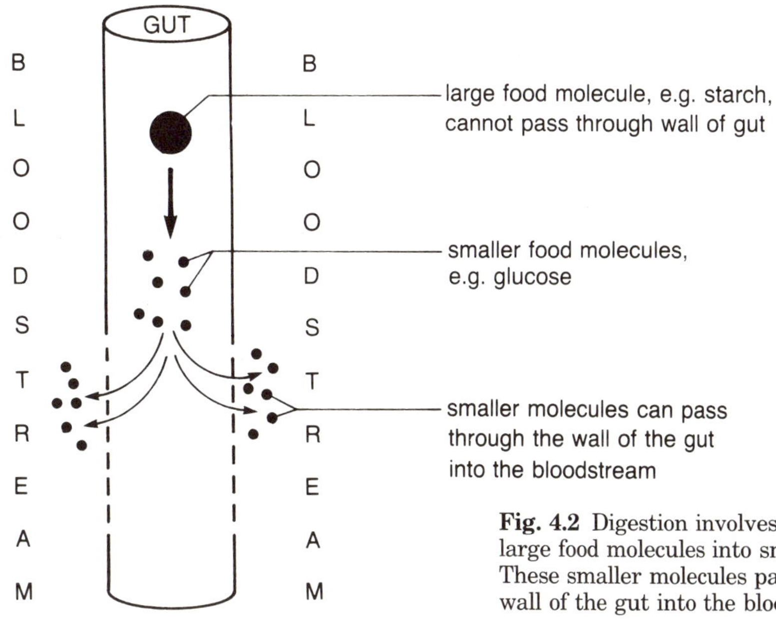

Fig. 4.2 Digestion involves breaking down large food molecules into smaller ones. These smaller molecules pass through the wall of the gut into the bloodstream.

Digestion involves two distinct sets of processes:

1 *Physical processes* which simply divide the food into smaller pieces. These include *chewing* in the mouth and *churning* in the stomach.

2 *Chemical processes* which break down chemicals in the food into smaller molecules. These chemical processes involve reactions between the food and *digestive enzymes*. Digestive enzymes are produced by glands which open into the gut.

Enzymes are biological catalysts (section 19.11). They are proteins which are affected by changes in temperature and pH (acidity level). Almost all the chemical reactions in your body are catalysed by enzymes. Every cell in your body contains dozens of different enzymes and each enzyme catalyses a different reaction.

4.2 How is food digested?

Although we said that the alimentary canal is like a long, coiled tube, it has different distinct parts. Each part has a different role in digestion. Figure 4.3 shows the main parts of the alimentary canal (gut) as they are arranged in the human body.

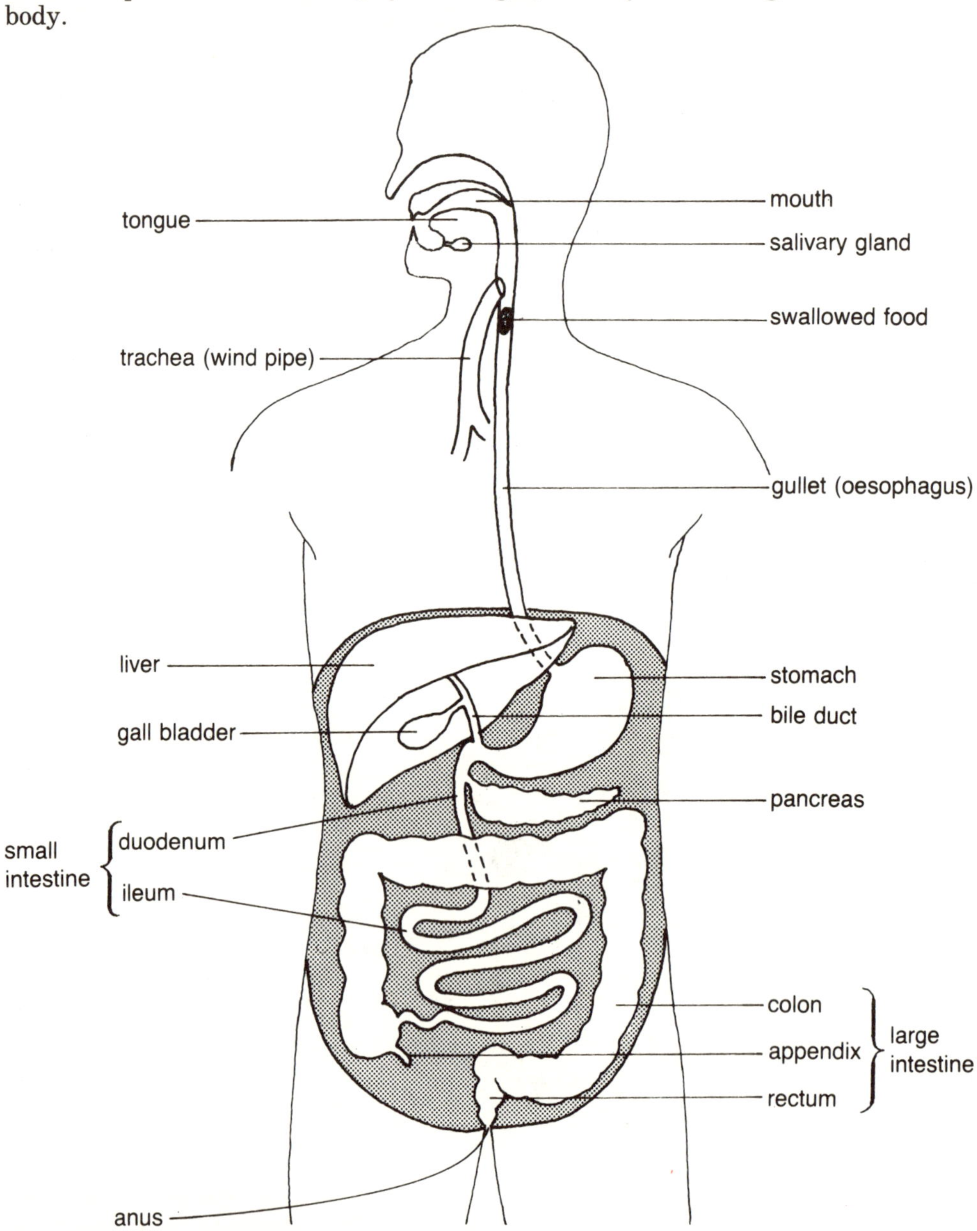

Fig. 4.3 The main parts of the human alimentary canal

Figure 4.4 shows the alimentary canal uncoiled and spread out. The role of each part of the alimentary canal is summarized at the side of the diagram.

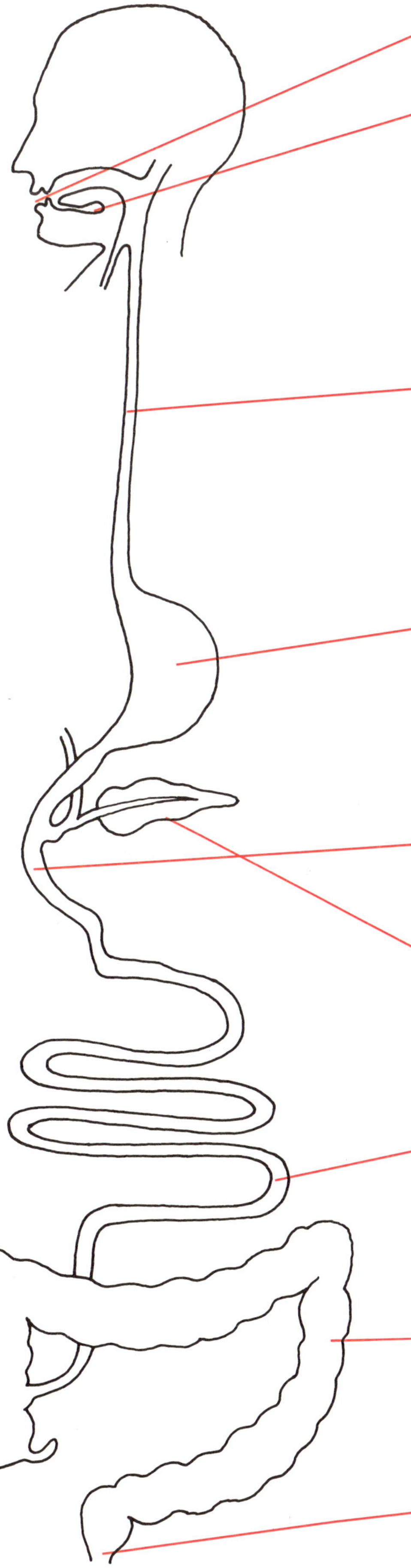

Mouth: Food chewed by teeth. This chops the food into small pieces and increases the surface area. Enzymes can then react with the food more quickly.

Salivary glands produce saliva ('spit') containing:

- *mucus* which makes food slippery and easy to swallow
- *amylase*, an enzyme which catalyses the reaction which breaks down starch to form maltose.

Gullet: The gullet has muscles in its wall. These muscles contract behind the food and push it along the gut. This process is called *peristalsis*.

Stomach: The stomach wall is thick and muscular. Muscular contractions churn up the food. Glands in the walls of the stomach (gastric glands) produce *gastric juice*. This contains *pepsin*, an enzyme which catalyses the reaction which breaks down proteins to form smaller molecules called *peptides*.

The gastric glands also produce hydrochloric *acid* which helps to break down proteins and kill germs in the stomach.

Duodenum: The **liver** produces a liquid called *bile* which is stored in the **gall bladder**. Bile enters the duodenum after a meal. It breaks up the fat in food to small droplets which can then mix with the other watery liquids. This is called *emulsification*.

The **pancreas** produces *pancreatic juice* which contains three important enzymes:

- *amylase* which catalyses the breakdown of starch to maltose
- *trypsin* which catalyses the breakdown of proteins into peptides (like pepsin in gastric juice)
- *lipase* which catalyses the breakdown of fat

Ileum: Glands in the ileum produce more enzymes:

- *maltase* which catalyses the breakdown of maltose to glucose
- *peptidases* which catalyse the breakdown of peptides to amino acids

Small molecules are absorbed through the walls of the ileum into the bloodstream (see section 4.3).

Colon: By this stage digestible foods have been broken down and absorbed into the blood. Indigestible foods, such as roughage (fibre), and water remain. In the colon, water is absorbed into the blood so the undigested material becomes more solid.

Rectum: Semi-solid matter collects in the rectum as *faeces* which pass out through the **anus**.

Fig. 4.4 The alimentary canal spread out, with a summary of the role of each part in digestion

Notice that there are digestive enzymes in saliva in the mouth, in the gastric juice of the stomach, in pancreatic juice and in the small intestine. These enzymes break down large molecules to form simpler units.

The various reactions involving enzymes are summarized below:

reactants	enzyme	products
starch + water	—amylase→	maltose
maltose + water	—maltase→	glucose
proteins + water	—pepsin and trypsin→	peptides
peptides + water	—peptidases→	amino acids
fat + water	—lipase→	fatty acids + glycerol

All these reactions involve water. They are examples of **hydrolysis**. The word 'hydrolysis' comes from two words meaning 'breaking (*lysis*) with water (*hydro*)'.

4.3 Absorbing food into the blood

Digestive enzymes in the gut break down food into small soluble molecules, e.g. glucose and amino acids. These small molecules can be absorbed into the blood through the lining of the small intestine. The inner surface of the small intestine has thousands of finger-like projections called **villi** (see Fig. 4.5). The villi give the small intestine a large surface area through which small food molecules can pass. Just below their surface, the villi are criss-crossed with a network of blood capillaries. As the soluble food molecules are absorbed through the lining of the small intestine, they pass into the capillaries and are carried away in the blood.

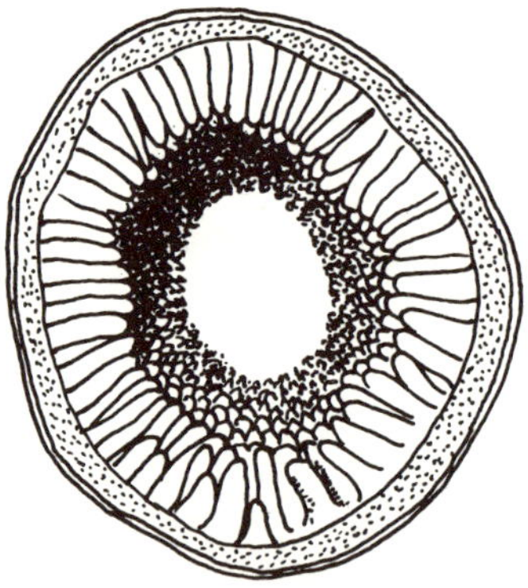

Fig. 4.5 A cross-section view looking along the small intestine. The finger-like projections are called villi.

4.4 Using the absorbed foods

Soluble food molecules are absorbed into the blood capillaries of the small intestine. From the small intestine the blood flows first to the liver. The liver acts as a food-processing factory for the absorbed foods:

- **Glucose**
  - travels in the blood to muscles to provide energy.
  - excess glucose is stored in the liver as glycogen.
- **Amino acids**
  - travel in the blood to other organs to form proteins for growth and repair.
  - some amino acids are processed in the liver to form blood proteins, e.g. fibrinogen for blood clotting.
  - excess amino acids are broken down, giving energy.
- **Vitamins** — are stored in the liver and released into the bloodstream when required.

4.5 Problems in the digestive system

Most of the time, our digestive systems work smoothly and comfortably. Problems can occur when we develop bad eating habits. The most common problems, their causes and their cures are summarized in table 4.1.

Table 4.1 Some common problems in the digestive system

Problem	*Cause*	*Cure*
Indigestion –stomach ache	Eating too quickly–gastric glands produce excess acid. If the person belches, acid comes up the gullet giving a burning sensation ('heartburn').	Indigestion tablets which contain a mild alkali to neutralize the excess acid.
Stomach ulcer	Worry and stress which cause a constant excess of acid in the stomach. The acid attacks the stomach wall making it raw and sore.	Reduce stress and worry. Indigestion tablets.
Constipation	Not going to the toilet regularly. Faeces remain in the rectum too long and more water is removed from them. This makes them hard, dry and difficult to pass out.	Regular, daily, toilet habits. Roughage in the diet helps to keep materials moving through the gut. Laxatives.
Diarrhoea –can lead to **dehydration**	Bacteria irritate the gut which produces too much mucus. Faeces move through the gut and are expelled from the anus before the colon can absorb water from them.	A short period without food allows the harmful bacteria to be expelled with the watery faeces. Drink plain water to prevent dehydration.

4.6 Teeth

Our teeth play an important part in the very first stage of digestion. They help to divide our food into smaller pieces.

Babies are born without teeth. During the next three or four years, the toddler develops a set of 20 **milk teeth**. Between the ages of six and twelve, the milk teeth fall out, one by one. They are replaced by a set of 32 **permanent teeth**.

Figure 4.6 shows the teeth on one side of an adult's jaw. From the middle outwards, in both the upper and lower jaw there are:

- two **incisors**–these are *cutting* teeth. You use them to bite food.
- one **canine**–for *gripping* and *tearing*. Animals which eat raw flesh, e.g. dogs and lions, have large canine teeth. Our own canine teeth are much less well-developed.
- two **premolars**
- three **molars**

–for *grinding* and *crushing*. They are used to grind food into small pieces. The molars at the back of the jaw are not usually present until after the age of 17. They are known as **wisdom teeth**.

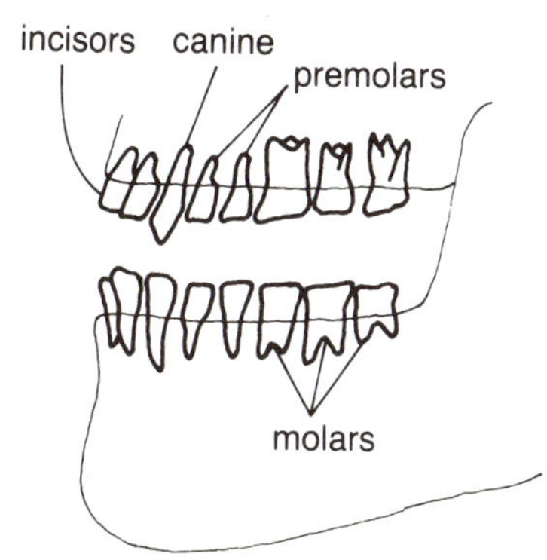

Fig. 4.6 The permanent teeth on one side of an adult's jaw

The structure of teeth

Figure 4.7 shows what complete teeth look like when they have been extracted from the jaw. They have two distinct parts:

- the **crown** which is normally above the gums
- the **root** which is normally buried in a socket in the jaw bone

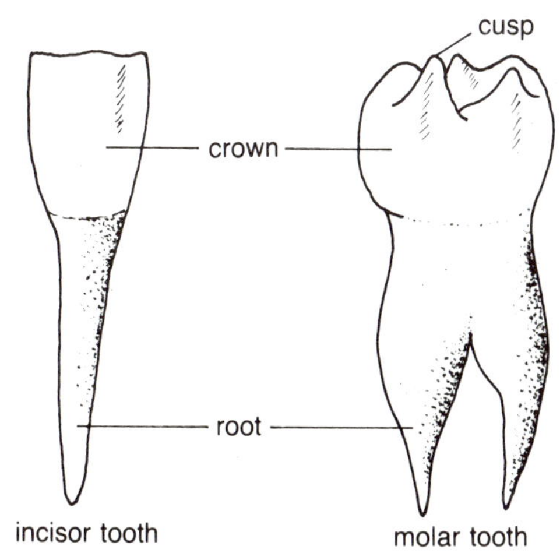

Fig. 4.7 Teeth have two parts: a crown and a root

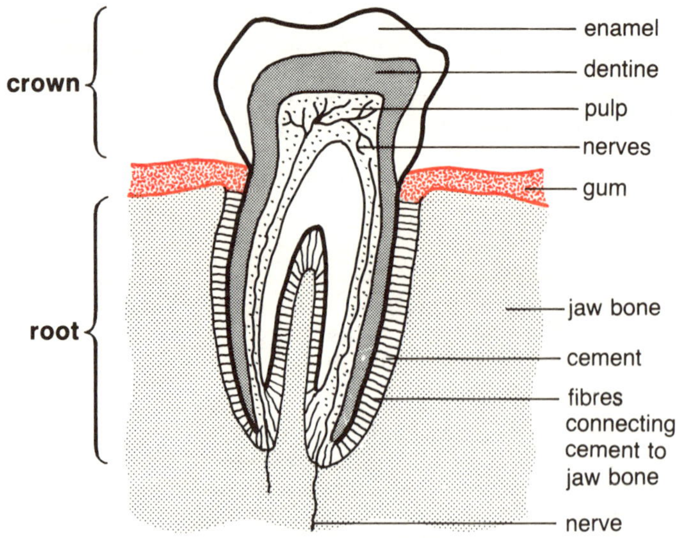

Fig. 4.8 The internal structure of a tooth

The inside of a tooth is shown in Figure 4.8. The crown has three layers:

- **enamel**–a thin outer layer giving a very hard surface for cutting and grinding.
- **dentine**–a thicker layer similar to bone.
- **pulp**–soft tissue at the centre of the tooth containing blood vessels and nerves.

The root also has three layers, but in this case the outer layer is **cement** and not enamel. Tough fibres join the cement to the jaw bone. These fibres hold the tooth in its socket. They also cushion the tooth against jolting and jarring during chewing.

TOOTH DECAY

Many people suffer from tooth decay. By middle age, some people have lost all their teeth. They have to wear 'false teeth' (dentures).

Causes of tooth decay

Saliva is slightly alkaline and does not attack teeth. During and after a meal, bacteria in the mouth break down sugary and starchy foods forming acids. These acids slowly attack the enamel and the dentine of the teeth 'tooth decay'. After a while, the saliva will neutralize these acids.

If the acid breaks through the enamel and into the dentine, bacteria can infect the pulp cavity. This causes toothache.

How can you prevent tooth decay?

Research has shown that:

- tooth decay is caused by sugary foods, such as cakes and sweets,
- the bacteria which convert sugary foods to acids form a thin layer over the surface of teeth. This layer is called **plaque**.

These findings have led dentists to make the following suggestions:

1 Clean your teeth after breakfast and before going to bed. The brushing removes plaque and toothpaste, which is alkaline, neutralizes any acids in the mouth.

2 Don't have sweets and sugary drinks between meals.

3 Visit the dentist every six months. Fillings (repairs to tooth enamel) can then be made before decay really sets in.

Dentists also believe that fluoride helps to prevent tooth decay. The fluoride helps to form stronger teeth and may also prevent plaque forming. Fluoride is present in compounds of fluorine such as sodium fluoride. It occurs naturally in the drinking water in some parts of the world. In these areas the extent of tooth decay is less than elsewhere. In many places, small amounts of fluoride are added to drinking water. This is called **fluoridation**. Some people increase their supply of fluoride by using a fluoride toothpaste or by taking fluoride tablets.

Quick test 4

1 A scientist found that 2 g of starch was changed to maltose in 1 hour when mixed with saliva at 15 °C. The experiment was repeated at a temperature of 30 °C.
How much starch was broken down in the second experiment?
A 0.5 g C 2 g
B 1 g D 4 g

Questions 2 and 3

The graph shows the rate of digestion of protein in the stomach at different temperatures.

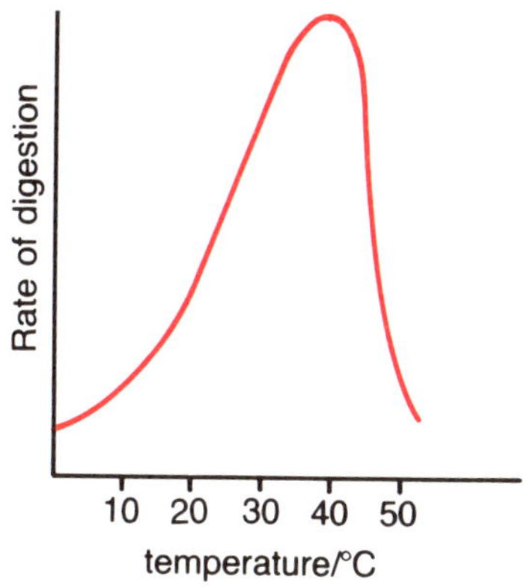

2 Digestion of protein is fastest at
A 10 °C C 30 °C
B 20 °C D 40 °C

3 If someone has a cold drink, digestion in the stomach will
A stop completely. C stay at the same rate.
B slow down. D speed up.

Questions 4 to 9
The diagram shows a section through a human canine tooth. Name the parts labelled 4 to 9.

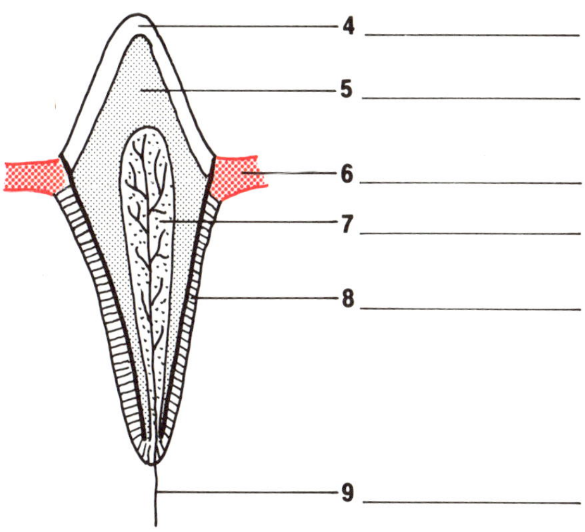

Questions 10 to 18

Look carefully at Fig. 4.4 (page 27).

10 In which parts of the alimentary canal is starch broken down?
11 In which parts of the alimentary canal are proteins broken down?
12 In which part of the alimentary canal are fats emulsified?
13 In which part of the alimentary canal are small molecules absorbed into the blood?
14 What part does hydrochloric acid play in the digestive system?
15 In which two parts of the alimentary canal does most physical digestion take place?
16 Which enzymes are involved in breaking down proteins to amino acids?
17 What is the main constituent in faeces?
18 Chewing food divides it into smaller pieces. How does this help the action of digestive enzymes?

Questions 19 to 22
Pat wants to find out how quickly amylase (an enzyme) breaks down starch at two different temperatures.
19 Which chemical (reagent) is used to test for starch?
20 What colour does the reagent change to if starch is present?
21 State *three* things which must be kept the same in the two experiments if the results are to be fairly compared?
22 In the experiment, what is produced when starch breaks down?

(*LEAG*, 1988)

Questions 23 to 33

The table below shows the pH in the mouth after eating food with a high sugar content.

Time/min	0	5	10	15	20	25	30	35	40
pH	6.9	4.6	4.4	4.8	5.2	5.6	5.9	6.4	6.9

23 What does pH measure?

24 What is the 'normal' pH of the mouth (i.e. before food is eaten)?

25 When the pH in the mouth falls below 5.5, the enamel on the teeth is likely to be attacked. About how long after eating the food could dental attack start?

26 About how long does the pH in the mouth remain at a level at which dental attack may continue?

27 Dentists advise against eating sweets between meals. Using the evidence above, suggest why it is sensible to follow this advice.

28 Name the type of organism which may cause the pH to decrease.

29 What should the pH of toothpaste be?

30 Explain your answer to question 29.

31 Dental attack may be prevented by strengthening the enamel of the tooth. This is often done using a chemical in toothpaste or in drinking water. Name one chemical that is often used in this way.

(*LEAG* (modified), 1988)

5 THE BLOOD SYSTEM

5.1 What is blood?

Blood looks like an ordinary liquid. Using a microscope, however, it is possible to see cells floating in a watery liquid called **plasma**.

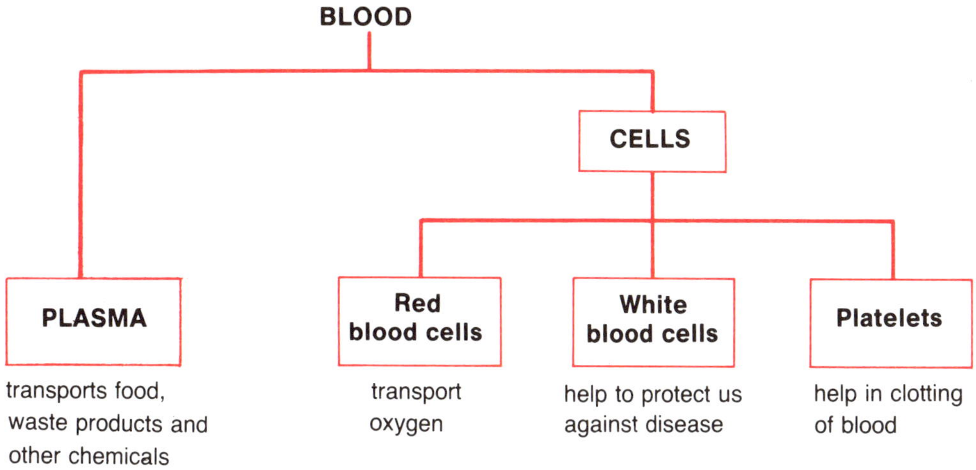

Fig. 5.1 The main constituents of blood and their functions

There are four important constituents in blood:

- **Plasma**
  Plasma is a pale yellow liquid. It is 90 per cent water and 10 per cent dissolved substances. These dissolved substances include:
  –*soluble foods* from digestion (see sections 4.2 to 4.4), e.g. glucose, amino acids and fat droplets
  –*salts (minerals)* as ions (see section 16.4), e.g. Na^+, Cl^-, Ca^{2+}
  –*hormones* (see section 8.8) in minute traces, e.g. insulin and adrenaline
  –*waste products*, e.g. carbon dioxide and urea
  –*blood proteins*, e.g. *globulin*, a protein consisting of antibodies, *albumen*, which thickens the blood, and *fibrinogen* which is needed for clotting (see Fig. 5.2).

1 Platelets form a temporary plug in any blood vessels which are cut.

2 On exposure to air, platelets produce an enzyme which converts fibrinogen (blood protein) into a mesh of fibres called **fibrin**.

3 The fibrin traps blood cells and then dries to form a **scab**. This scab allows the wound to heal and prevents harmful germs entering the body.

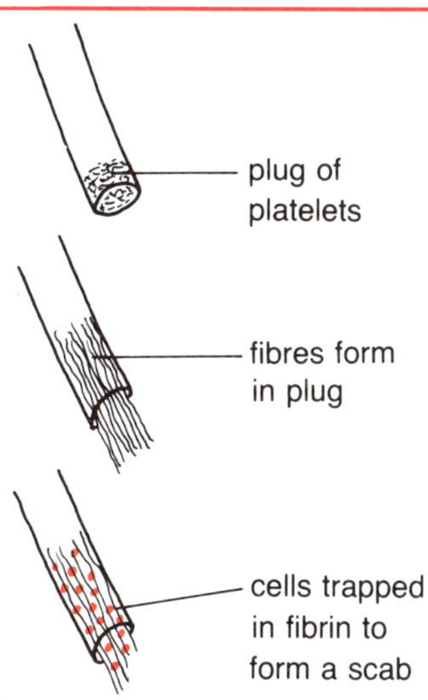

Fig. 5.2 What happens when blood clots

Fibrinogen can be removed from plasma. This is done by allowing the plasma to clot and then removing the clot. The remaining plasma without fibrinogen is called **serum**. Serum is stored in hospitals for transfusions.

- **Red blood cells**
- **White blood cells**
- **Platelets**

The structure and function of these cells are described in Table 5.1 (overleaf).

Table 5.1 The structure and function of different cells in blood

Structure	*Number of cells in 1 mm^3 of blood*	*Where are the cells produced?*	*What is the function of these cells? (What do they do?)*
Red blood cells 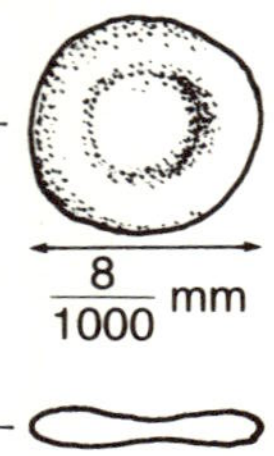 Biconcave shape (like a pressed-in disc) No nucleus Cytoplasm is mainly red haemoglobin which gives blood its colour	5 000 000	In the **red bone marrow**, the soft tissue inside certain bones such as the ribs and the back bone	Red blood cells carry oxygen around the body. **Haemoglobin** in the cells combines with oxygen in the lungs (section 6.3) to form oxyhaemoglobin. This is transported in the blood to tissues all over the body. The biconcave shape of the cells increases their surface area and enables them to absorb more oxygen. Haemoglobin contains iron. This plays an important part in enabling haemoglobin to carry oxygen. This is why we need iron in the food we eat (section 3.4).
White blood cells–there are two types: 1 **Phagocytes** 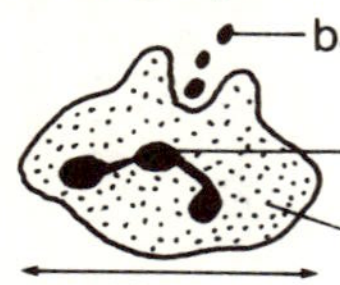	7000 phagocytes	In the **red bone marrow**	White blood cells **defend us against disease**. Their job is to kill germs which get into our body. Phagocytes kill bacteria by engulfing ('eating') them. They often die loaded with dead bacteria. This is what forms yellow 'pus'.
2 **Lymphocytes** 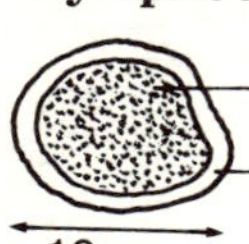	3000 lymphocytes	In **lymph tissue**	Lymphocytes produce chemicals called **antibodies**. These dissolve in the plasma, killing bacteria and reacting with poisons making them harmless.
Platelets are bits of broken up blood cells 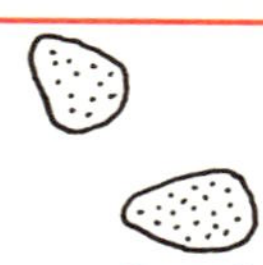	250 000	In the **red bone marrow**	Platelets **help the blood to clot** (see Fig. 5.2, page 33)

5.2 The functions of blood

The functions of the separate constituents in blood were described in section 5.1. Blood has three important functions–*transport*, *protection* and *regulation*:

1 Transport

- Blood carries *oxygen* from the lungs to other tissues. It carries *carbon dioxide* back to the lungs to be expelled (exhaled).
- Blood carries *dissolved foods* from the gut to different parts of the body.
- Blood carries *waste products* to the kidneys to be excreted in urine (see section 5.6).
- Blood carries *hormones* and *antibodies* around the body.

2 Protection

- Blood contains *platelets* and *fibrinogen* so that blood will clot preventing severe loss of blood after injury.
- Blood contains *white blood cells* which protect us against germs.

3 Regulation

- Blood helps to keep our body temperature constant by allowing us to retain or lose heat.
- Blood helps us to control the amount of water and other chemicals in different parts of the body.

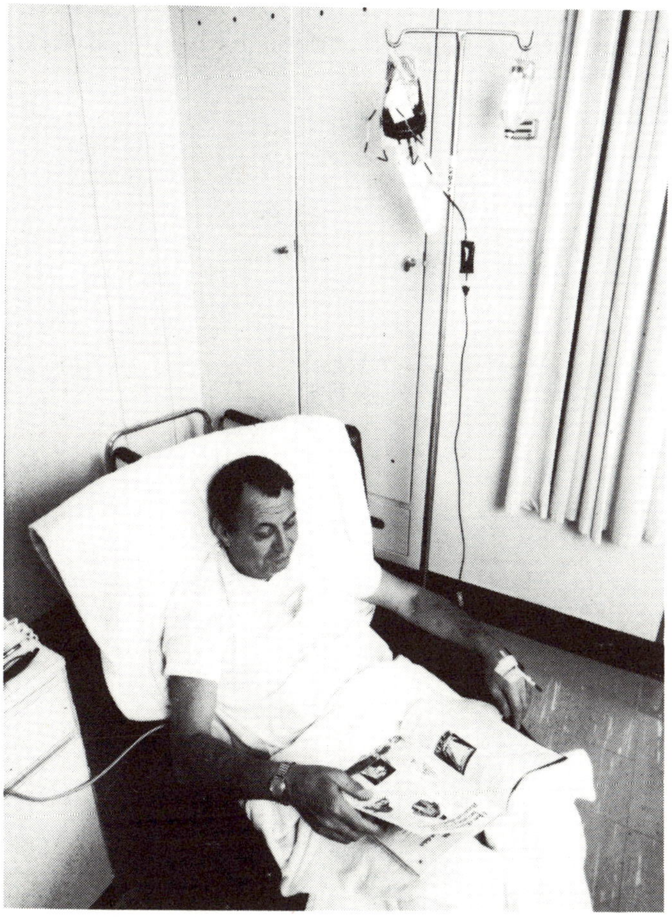

Fig. 5.3 This man is being given a blood transfusion. The blood being given must be of the same type or **blood group** as the patient's blood. To ensure this, a simple chemical test is carried out beforehand. There are four main blood groups–A, B, AB and O. The letters A and B refer to different substances in red blood cells. People in blood group A have the A substances. People in blood group B have the B substances. People in group AB have both substances and people in group O have neither. Besides the A and B substances, red blood cells may contain another substance called the **Rhesus factor** (so-called because the substance was first discovered in the Rhesus monkey). People who have this substance in their blood are described as *Rhesus positive*. People who don't are described as *Rhesus negative*.

5.3 Blood vessels

Blood flows around the body continuously. This flow is called **circulation**. The main organ involved in blood circulation is the **heart**. The heart pumps blood round the body through a system of tubes called **blood vessels**. Blood vessels are classified in three groups:

- **Arteries** carry blood away from the heart. Arteries have thick muscular walls to withstand the pumping pressure from the heart. If an artery is cut, there is a rapid loss of blood. Bleeding may be stopped by pressing on a wound or by pressure at a point where the artery comes near to the skin surface and runs close to a bone.
- **Veins** carry blood back to the heart. They tend to be closer to the surface of the body than arteries. Blood in the veins is at a lower pressure than in the arteries and there are valves to prevent the backward flow of blood. Veins have thinner, less muscular walls than arteries.
- **Capillaries** are narrow, thin-walled tubes which divide from the arteries and then rejoin to form veins. There are thousands and thousands of capillaries in every organ, and every cell in your body is close to a capillary. If your capillaries were laid end to end, they would form a very fine tube about 80 000 km long!

  As the blood flows through capillaries, water, oxygen and dissolved foods diffuse out though the thin walls to the surrounding cells. At the same time, waste materials diffuse out of the cells and into the blood capillaries. In this way, capillaries provide those materials which ce s need for good health and also remove their waste products. The capillaries in our skin play an important role in regulating our body temperature.

5.4 Circulation of blood

The main organs in our bodies through which blood circulates are shown in Fig. 5.4.

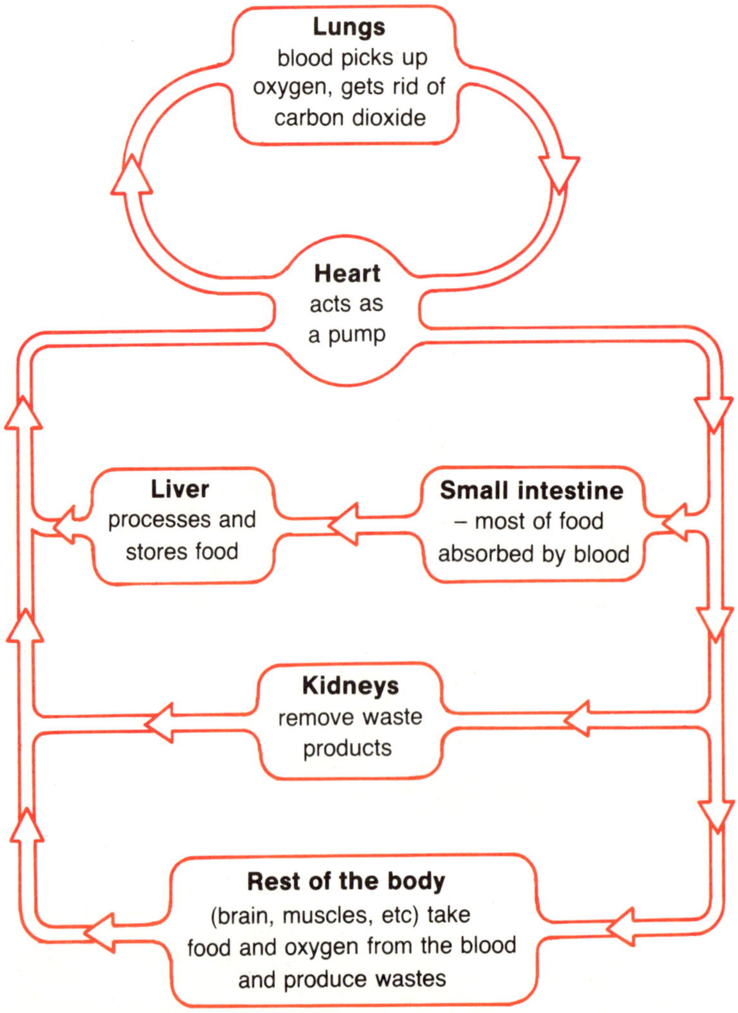

Fig. 5.4 The main organs through which blood circulates in the human body

- **The heart** pumps blood around the system. The pumping effect produces a regular beating of the heart. Every time the heart beats it produces a dull throb in the chest and a wave of pressure through the main arteries. You can feel this as a **pulse** in the artery in your wrist.
- **The lungs** allow the blood to pick up oxygen and get rid of carbon dioxide.
- **The intestines** supply digested food to the blood.
- **The liver** processes and stores some of the food carried by the blood.
- **The kidneys** remove waste products.
- **The rest of the body** uses the food and oxygen in the blood and produces waste products which are carried away by the blood. Notice in Figure 5.4 that there are two circuits from the heart. One circuit goes to the lungs and back to the heart. The other circuit goes to the rest of the body and back to the heart. To provide for these two circuits, the heart acts as two pumps side by side (see Fig. 5.5). The pumps work in unison. The pump on our right drives blood to capillaries in the lungs where oxygen is absorbed and dissolved in the blood. The pump on our left takes this oxygenated blood from the lungs and pumps it to other organs in the body. As the oxygenated blood passes through the various organs, the oxygen is used for respiration (see section 6.5) and other reactions. The deoxygenated blood then returns to the heart and the cycle is repeated. Notice that the blood passes through the heart twice during one complete cycle.

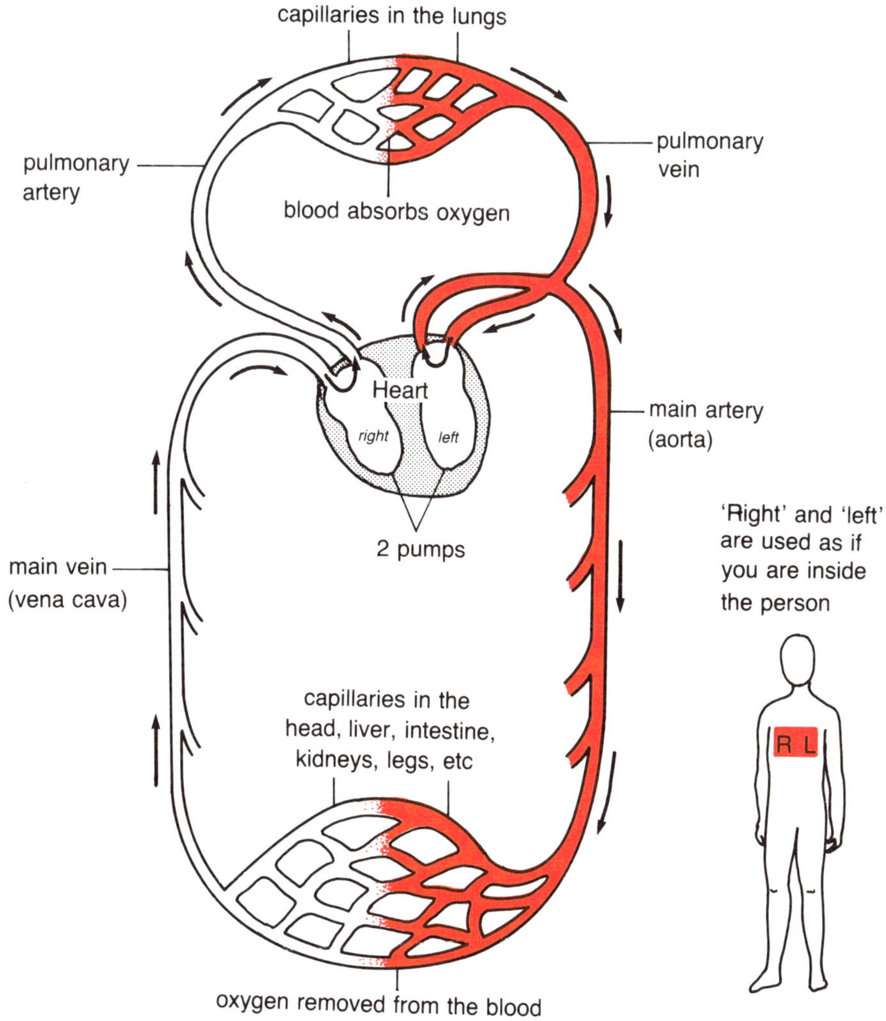

Fig. 5.5 The circulation of blood (seen from the front of a person)

THE HEART

Each pump in the heart has two chambers; an entry chamber called an **atrium** (plural: *atria*) and a pumping chamber called a **ventricle** (see Fig. 5.6). A one-way valve between each atrium and ventricle prevents blood being pumped the wrong way. There is also a one-way outlet valve from each ventricle to stop blood flowing back. The ventricles have thick muscular walls. When these contract, the pressure inside increases and blood is forced into the arteries. This causes your pulse. When the muscles relax, the ventricles expand and blood flows into them from the atria.

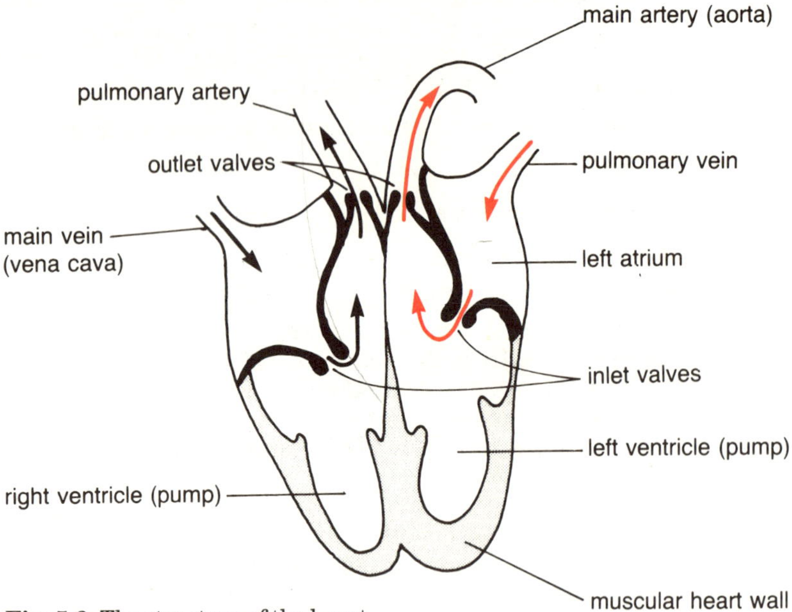

Fig. 5.6 The structure of the heart

Your heart beats about 70 times every minute, day and night. To do this, the heart muscles must have a good supply of oxygen. This is supplied through a system of arteries spread over the heart wall. These are called the **coronary vessels**.

5.5 Diseases of the circulation system

As the heart pumps blood into the arteries, there is an increase in pressure. This pressure on the walls of our arteries is called **blood pressure**. If the blood pressure is too low, blood circulates around the body too slowly. If the blood pressure is too high, there is greater strain on the heart and on the walls of the arteries. The walls of the arteries may be stretched so much that they burst. If an artery in the brain bursts, the leakage of blood will damage cells in the brain. We call this a **stroke**. This may result in paralysis (loss of use) of part of the body and speech difficulties. The causes of high blood pressure are not fully understood. However, it is more likely to occur when someone is overweight or under stress, or if they smoke heavily.

As we get older, our arteries become thicker and harder. This is due to a layer of fat forming on the inside of the vessels. The arteries get narrower and the flow of blood slows down. An artery may become blocked by a clot of blood. This is called a **thrombosis**. If a thrombosis occurs in one of the coronary vessels (a **coronary thrombosis**), the heart muscle is deprived of oxygen and may stop beating. We call this a **heart attack**. Hardening of the arteries is thought to be made worse by eating too much animal fat, by drinking too much alcohol and by smoking.

Tobacco smoke contains several poisonous substances including nicotine and carbon monoxide. Carbon monoxide affects our blood because it combines with haemoglobin in red blood cells about 300 times more readily than oxygen. This means that the blood can carry less oxygen to our body tissues. In order to improve the supply of oxygen, the heart pumps faster, putting strain on the heart and increasing the blood pressure.

5.6 Getting rid of waste

Chemical processes in our bodies produce a variety of waste products. Thelood plays an important part in helping us to get rid of waste products. This process is called **excretion**.

The main organs involved in excretion are the **lungs** and the **kidneys**:

- The lungs enable us to excrete **carbon dioxide** (section 6.3).
- The kidneys enable us to excrete **urea** and **salts**. They also control the amount of water in our bodies.

THE KIDNEYS

We take in water when we eat and drink. We lose water from our bodies as sweat and urine. When urine contains only a small amount of waste products, it is almost colourless, like water. When the waste products are more concentrated, it looks yellow. One of the important waste products in urine is urea. This is produced when proteins are metabolized (broken down into amino acids). Urea contains a high percentage of nitrogen.

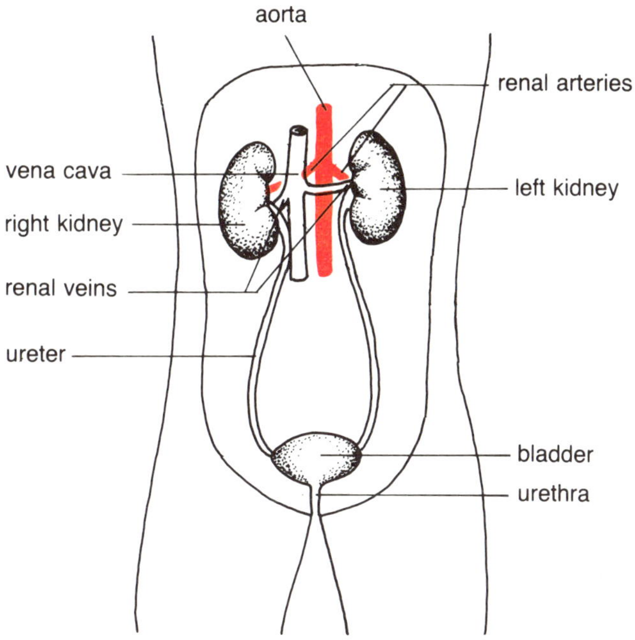

Fig. 5.7 The kidneys and the excretory system

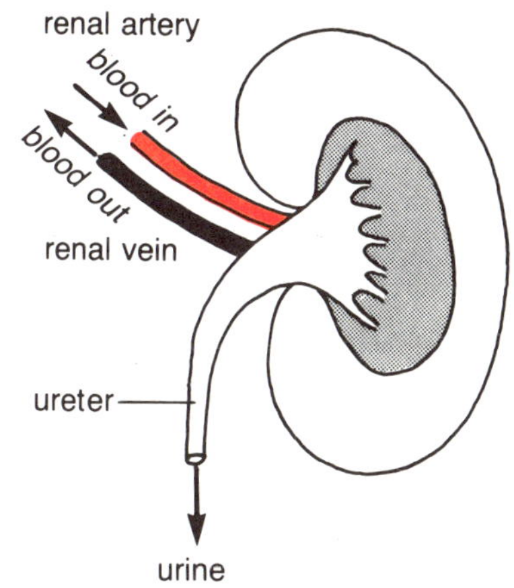

Fig. 5.8 Cross section through a kidney

Figure 5.7 shows how the kidneys are connected to the rest of the excretory system. We have two kidneys at the back of the body just above the waist.

How do the kidneys remove waste products?

As you would expect, the kidneys have an excellent supply of blood (see Fig. 5.8). The **renal artery** carries blood to the kidneys and the **renal vein** carries it back to the heart. About 1 cubic decimetre (1000 cm^3) of blood flows through the kidneys every minute.

As branches of the renal artery pass into the kidneys, they divide into a vast network of blood capillaries. These capillaries are wrapped around thousands of tiny **tubules**. As the blood flows over the tubules, excess water and waste products (**urine**) diffuse into the tubules. The tubules join up to form collecting ducts which lead into the **ureter**. At the same time, the blood capillaries join up again to form a single vein leading to the renal vein.

The ureters, one from each kidney, carry urine to the **bladder**. The bladder expands as urine collects in it. Urine is passed out of the bladder through the **urethra**. The urethra runs to an opening in front of the vagina in a female and down the middle of the penis in a male.

The ring of muscle near the top of the urethra is usually contracted. This closes the urethra and prevents urine from running out of the bladder (and out of the body). As urine collects in the bladder, pressure on the ring of the muscle increases. In time, we feel the need to urinate. When we urinate the ring of muscle relaxes.

5.7 Kidney failure

Occasionally, a person's kidneys begin to fail. This may be caused by infection or by faulty diffusion of materials from the blood into the urine.

If only one of the kidneys is affected, the person can survive. If both kidneys are affected, treatment is essential. If the person is not treated, he/she will be poisoned as urea and other waste products accumulate in the blood.

There are three kinds of treatment for kidney failure:

- A **controlled diet** with a reduced intake of water, protein and salt. This reduces the volume of urine and the amount of waste products.

- A **kidney machine** which acts as an artificial kidney. Blood from an artery in the patient's arm passes through thin tubing surrounded by special solution in the machine. Waste products diffuse out of the patient's blood into the solution. The blood then returns to the patient through a vein. This treatment is called **dialysis**. Someone with severe kidney failure must spend 15 to 20 hours each week connected to a kidney machine.
- A **kidney transplant** which replaces the failing kidney with a healthy kidney from a donor who has just died. This treatment will only work if the kidney donor has the same blood group as the patient.

Quick test 5

1 Which of the following actions is most sensible if your finger is bleeding badly?
A Submerge your finger in very cold water.
B Put your head between your knees.
C Hold your finger above your head.
D Put a tight bandage around the wound.

2 Which of the following tissues makes up the wall of the heart?
A cartilage B muscle
C plasma D tendon

3 Healthy people have about 500 red blood cells for every white blood cell. After some infections, this changes to about 100 red blood cells for every white blood cell. These changes may have occurred because
A extra white blood cells are produced to fight the infection.
B the blood has been diluted.
C white blood cells are destroyed by the infection.
D red blood cells destroy white blood cells.

Questions 4 to 8

The figure below shows a section through a human heart.

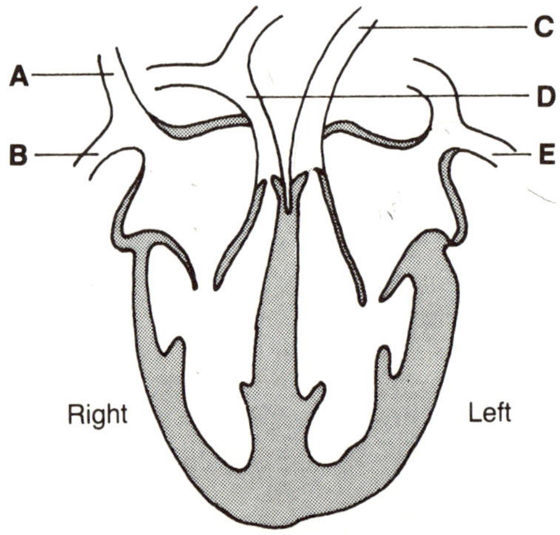

Which of the lettered blood vessels
4 carry oxygenated blood?
5 is/are attached to the right atrium?
6 is the aorta (main artery)?
7 is the pulmonary artery to the lungs?
8 carries blood from the liver and kidneys to the heart?

Questions 9 to 11

Blood is composed of several parts each of which has a particular job. Name the part of the blood whose main job is
9 transport of oxygen.
10 fighting against disease.
11 transport of dissolved foods. *SEG* (part question)

Questions 12 to 15

The chart (top of the next page) shows the death rates from heart diseases, of men and women between the ages of 35 and 74 in different countries.
12 Which country has the lowest death rate from heart diseases for men?
13 Which country has the highest death rate from heart diseases for men and women together?

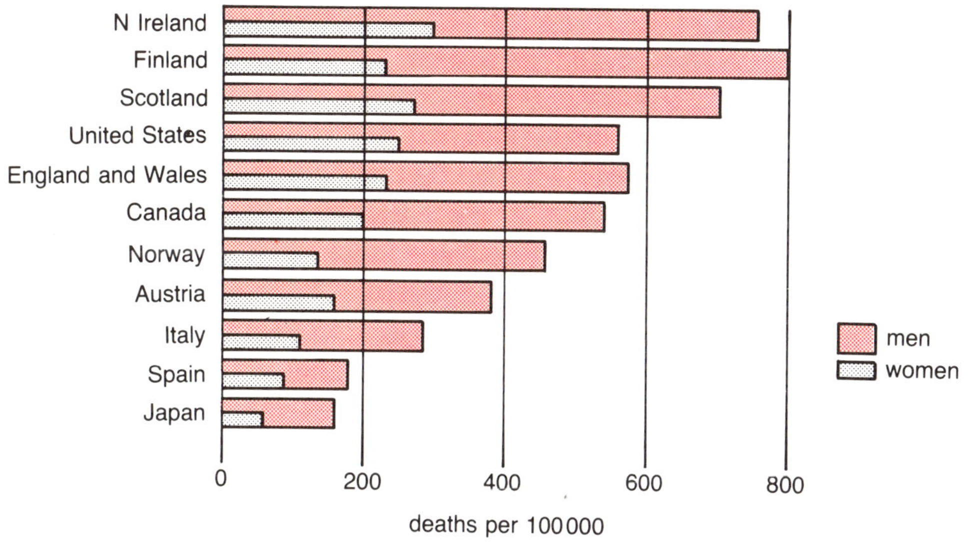

14 Which countries have the same death rate from heart diseases for women?
15 Which *one* of the following conclusions can be made from the chart?
A Smoking causes an increase in the death rate from heart diseases.
B People who suffer from heart disease should visit Japan.
C More men die of heart disease than women.
D Heart diseases are more common in colder countries.

(*LEAG*, modified)

Questions 16 to 17

Jean and Paula go jogging. They measured their heart rates before and after jogging.

	Heart rate (beats per minute)	
	Jean	*Paula*
Before jogging	75	65
Immediately afterwards	150	150
2 mins afterwards	120	100
4 mins afterwards	85	65

16 Which girl is the fitter?
17 Give two reasons for your choice in question 16.

Questions 18 to 22

18 Give four factors that can affect the pulse rate.
19 What causes a coronary thrombosis?
20 What causes anaemia?
21 Give two differences between an artery and a vein.
22 What test must be carried out before someone has a blood transfusion?
23 Humans belong to one of four blood groups: A, B, AB and O. In a recent survey, 40 per cent were type A; 10 per cent were type B; 5 per cent were type AB; 45 per cent were type O. Display this information in a pie chart.

6 RESPIRATION

6.1 Introduction

The term 'respiration' is used to summarize three processes in organisms which lead to the release of energy from foods: **breathing, gaseous exchange and cellular respiration**. These processes are outlined below.

RESPIRATION

Breathing	**Gaseous exchange**	**Cellular respiration**
Chest movements which bring air (oxygen) into the lungs.	Diffusion of oxygen into the blood and of carbon dioxide out of the blood. Diffusion occurs through the thin moist tissue in the lungs.	Chemical reactions occurring in cells which result in the release of energy from foods.

Breathing and gaseous exchange are physical processes occurring *outside cells*. They are sometimes referred to together as **external respiration**. On the other hand, cellular respiration involves chemical processes *inside cells*. It is sometimes called **internal respiration**. In this chapter, we shall look at breathing, gaseous exchange and cellular respiration in that order.

6.2 Breathing

Our bodies cannot work without a continuous supply of oxygen. When we breathe in (inhale), air enters our lungs. Oxygen from the inhaled air can then pass through the thin tissue of the lungs into the blood. At the same ti , carbon dioxide passes from the blood into the lungs. This carbon dioxide is then expelled when we breathe out (exhale). In order to help this exchange of gases, the chest and ribs act like a pump, transferring gases into and out of the lungs.

The lungs are situated inside the chest cavity or **thorax** (see Fig. 6.1). The sides of the thorax are bounded by the rib cage and there are muscles linking the ribs. At the bottom of the thorax, there is a flexible sheet of muscular tissue called the **diaphragm**.

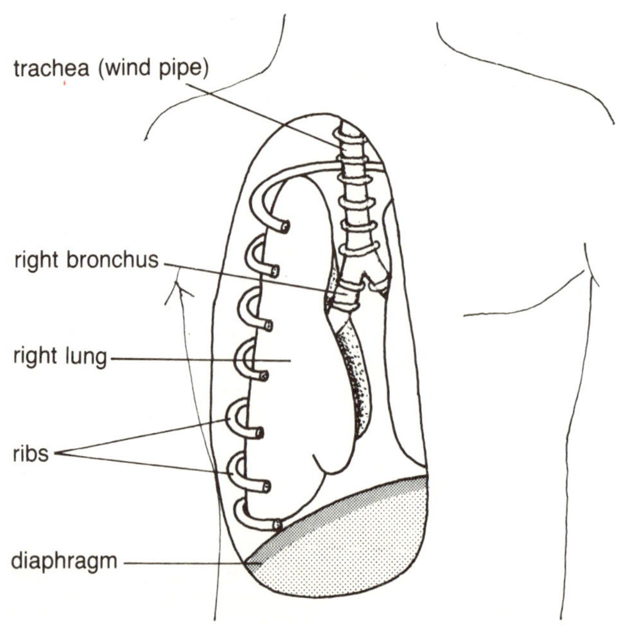

Fig. 6.1 Part of the human thorax (chest cavity)

Although the lungs have a spongy consistency, they behave like a pair of large, elastic bags. These bags stretch and inflate when the thorax increases in volume. When we breathe in, muscles pull the diaphragm downwards and the ribs upwards and outwards. The thorax increases in size and air is drawn into the lungs. When we breathe out, the diaphragm relaxes and moves upwards and the ribs move inwards. The thorax decreases in size, increasing pressure on the lungs and air is forced out.

The total volume of an adult's lungs is between 4 and 5 dm^3 (4000–5000 cm^3). Whilst resting, we inhale about 0.5 dm^3 of air each breath. After exercise, we breathe more deeply and inhale as much as 2 dm^3 with each breath. Table 6.1 shows the composition by volume of atmospheric air and exhaled air. What can you conclude from the figures given in the table?

Table 6.1 The percentage composition by volume of atmospheric and exhaled air

	Atmospheric air (inhaled air)	**Exhaled air**
Oxygen	21	17
Carbon dioxide	0.03	4
Nitrogen	78	78

6.3 Gaseous exchange in the lungs

When we breathe in, air passes through the mouth or nose. At the back of the nose there is a large space called the **nasal cavity**. This is divided up by bony partitions giving a large surface area. The surfaces are lined with fine hairs called **cilia** and they secrete slimy **mucus**. This mucus plays an important part in trapping dust and germs before they can get into the lungs. Movements of the cilia sweep the mucus towards the throat where it is swallowed, or coughed up as catarrh or phlegm (pronounced 'flem'). Mucus in the nasal passages can also be expelled by blowing your nose.

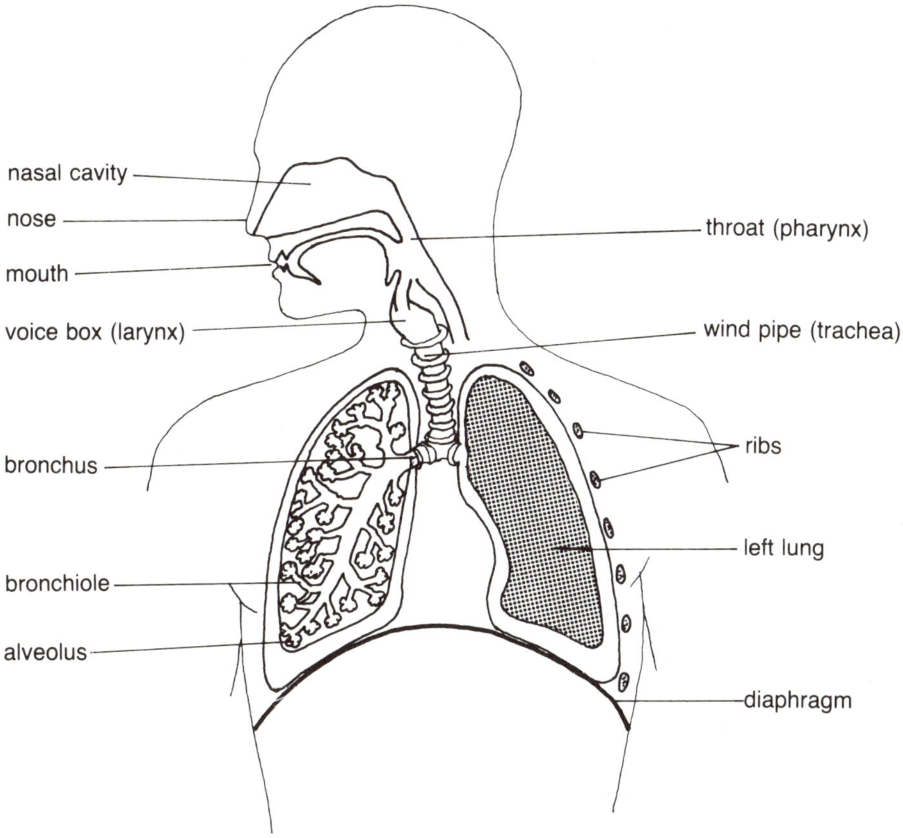

Fig. 6.2 The human respiratory system
(There are many more alveoli than the diagram shows.)

From the mouth or nose, the air passes through the **larynx** ('voice box') to the **trachea** (windpipe). The trachea branches into two **bronchi** (singular: *bronchus*) one to each lung. Rings of cartilage strengthen the trachea and bronchi to prevent them collapsing.

In the lungs, the bronchi divide into hundreds of thin tubes called **bronchioles**.

The structure of the bronchioles is like the branches and twigs on a tree. The whole network is sometimes called the **bronchial tree** (see Fig. 6.3).

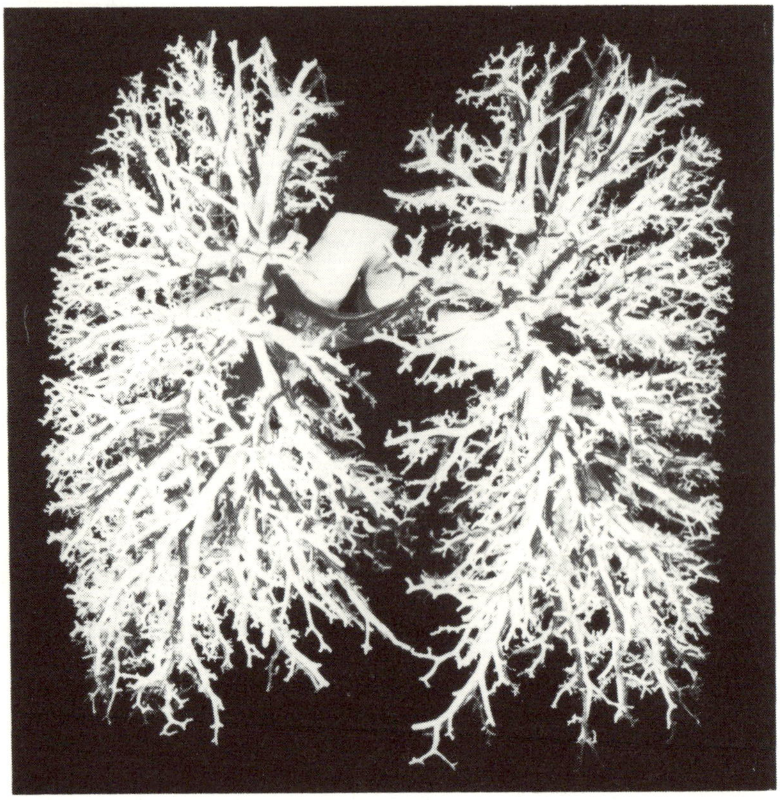

Fig. 6.3 A model of the bronchial tree

Each bronchiole ends in a bunch of tiny air sacs called **alveoli**. Each alveolus is only about 0.2 mm in diameter, but there are about 300 million alveoli in your lungs. This gives a very large surface area across which gases (oxygen and carbon dioxide) can diffuse.

The alveoli are covered with a network of capillaries like a string bag (see Fig. 6.4). The walls of the alveoli and the capillaries are extremely thin. Their surfaces are also covered in a thin layer of liquid. The thin walls and the layer of moisture make the diffusion of gases easier. Oxygen inside the alveoli dissolves in the layer of moisture and passes through the walls of the alveoli into the capillaries. It can then be carried away by red blood cells to different parts of the body.

For carbon dioxide, the process is reversed. Carbon dioxide is carried by the blood into the capillaries around the alveoli. Here, it passes out of the blood and into the alveoli. It is then expelled from the lungs when we breathe out.

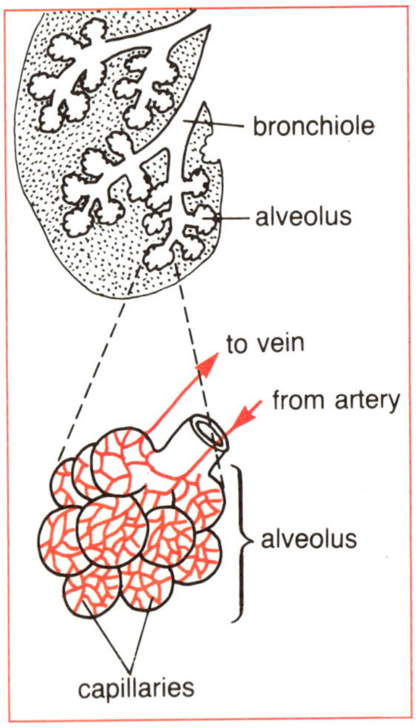

Fig. 6.4 The detailed structure of part of a lung

6.4 Smoking or health

During the last 20 years, doctors and government health departments have collected data on smokers and non-smokers. This data shows that:

- Someone who smokes 10 cigarettes a day is 8 times more likely to die from lung cancer than a non-smoker.
- A smoker who gives up smoking soon halves his/her risk of death from lung cancer.
- A smoker is twice as likely to suffer a heart attack (coronary thrombosis) as a non-smoker.

DISEASES ASSOCIATED WITH SMOKING

Lung cancer

Cigarette smoke contains fine droplets of **tar**. This tar stains the filter when a filter cigarette is smoked (but the filter does not remove all the tar). The tar contains chemicals which cause cancer. They are described as **carcinogens**. Carcinogenic chemicals make the cells of various tissues reproduce in an uncontrolled way. Affected tissue grows but cannot function in the normal way. When this happens to lung tissue, people often die of lung cancer.

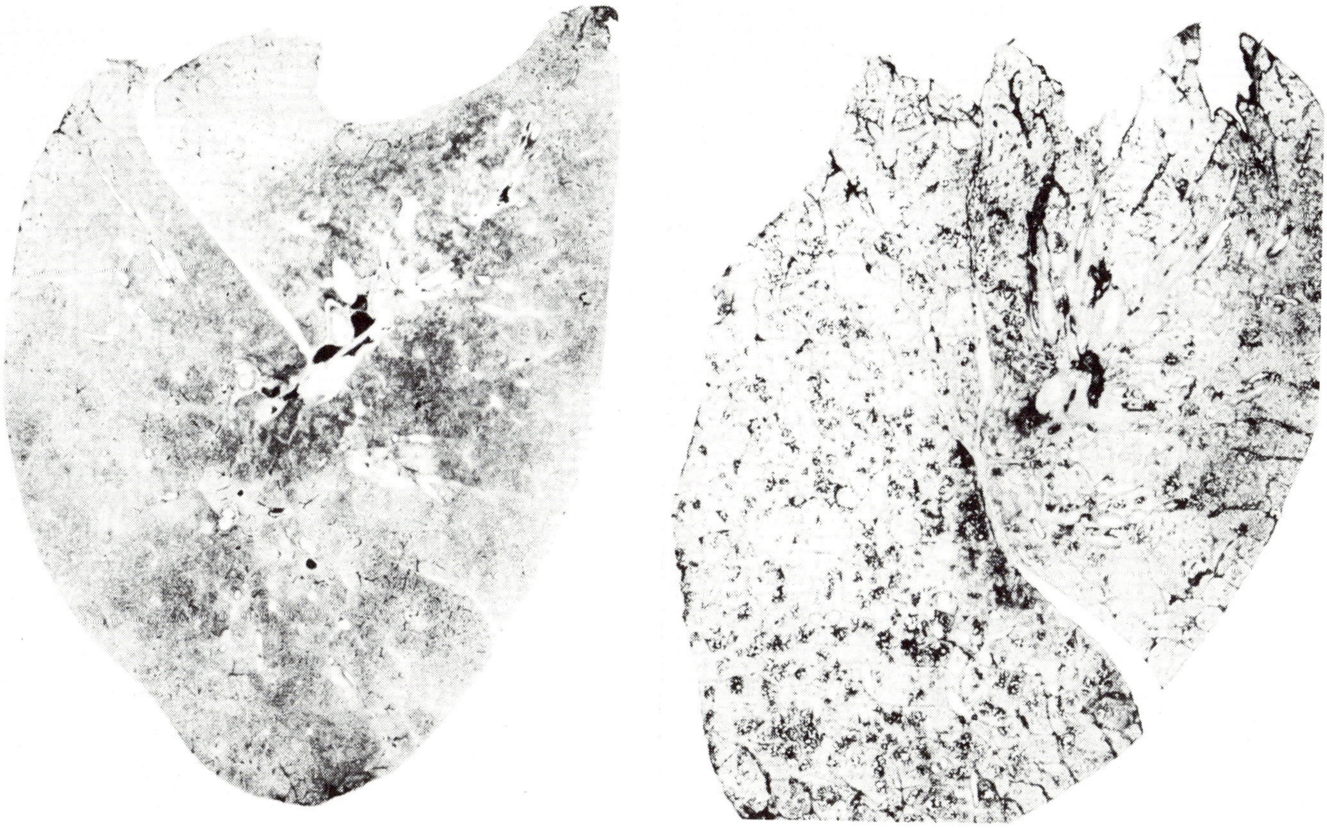

Fig. 6.5 *Left:* A section of a healthy human lung *Right:* A section of a human lung permeated with deposits of tar, caused by cigarette smoking

Bronchitis

Substances in cigarette smoke also irritate the walls of the trachea and the bronchial tubes. Extra mucus is produced which clogs up the respiratory passages. This makes breathing difficult and leads to a 'smoker's cough'. Very often, the bronchial tubes become infected and the disease lasts a long time instead of clearing up in a few days. This is called *chronic bronchitis*.

Emphysema

Cigarette smoke contains acidic and irritant substances. These substances attack the sensitive walls of the alveoli. The alveoli break down and this reduces the surface area in the lungs over which gaseous exchange can occur. The disease is called emphysema. Smokers suffering in this way become very short of breath.

Although smoking mainly affects the lungs, it has other harmful or unpleasant effects:

- It increases the risk of coronary thrombosis (heart attack) and other diseases of the blood system (see section 5.5).
- It can cause cancer of the mouth or throat.
- It reduces your senses of taste and smell.
- It makes your breath and clothes smell unpleasant.

6.5 Cellular respiration

Respiration is the overall process of breathing, gas exchange in the lungs and the breaking down of chemicals to provide energy in living things.

Cellular respiration refers to the chemical reactions which occur in cells and which result in the release of energy from foods.

During respiration we use up foods and oxygen and produce carbon dioxide, water and energy. The same thing happens during combustion when fuels burn.

The food (or fuel) reacts with oxygen, so these reactions are called *oxidation* reactions. We say that the food (or fuel) is *oxidized*.

food (or fuel) + oxygen ⟶ carbon dioxide + water + energy

Because of these similarities between foods and fuels, foods are sometimes called 'body fuels' or 'biological fuels'.

Although cellular respiration and burning are similar processes, there are important differences. When an energy food such as glucose is oxidized in our body cells, there are no flames and the reaction is very slow compared to burning. In fact, the oxidation of simple foods takes place through a large number of separate chemical reactions.

The cellular respiration of glucose can be summarized by the equation:

$$\underset{\text{glucose}}{C_6H_{12}O_6} + \underset{\text{oxygen}}{6O_2} \longrightarrow \underset{\text{carbon dioxide}}{6CO_2} + \underset{\text{water}}{6H_2O} + \underset{\text{energy}}{2900\text{ kJ}}$$

When this process occurs in our cells, about twenty separate chemical reactions are needed to convert the reactants (glucose and oxygen) into the products (carbon dioxide and water).

Notice, in the equation above, the large amount of **energy** produced. This energy from cellular respiration can be used as:

- **heat** to keep us warm,
- **mechanical energy** in our muscles to help us move around and to keep our heart and breathing muscles working.

About half of the energy from cellular respiration is released as heat. This explains why you get hot whilst running or working hard. Your body uses up more food, therefore more heat is produced. The rest of the energy from celllar respiration is used to produce a compound called **adenosine triphosphate (ATP)**. ATP reacts with muscle tissue and makes it contract. Any movement we make involves contracting (then relaxing) some muscle. In this way, about half of the energy from foods is used as mechanical energy.

6.6 Respiration in all living things

All living things respire in order to obtain the energy they need. In plants, the intake of oxygen and the release of carbon dioxide takes place through the stomata (see section 2.6).

The production of carbon dioxide during respiration

Carbon dioxide can be investigated using the apparatus shown in Fig. 6.6.

When air is drawn through the apparatus, the lime water in flask C turns cloudy after a minute or two indicating the presence of carbon dioxide. The lime water in flask A stays clear. This shows that the insects must be producing the carbon dioxide.

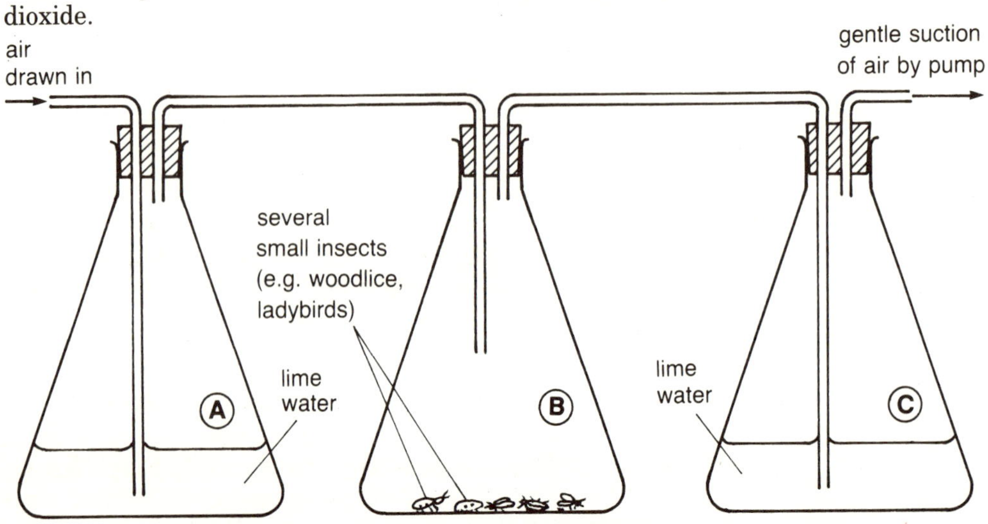

Fig. 6.6 Investigating the production of carbon dioxide when living things respire

The experiment can be carried out using different living things in flask B. If plants are used:

–flask B must be covered so that the plant will not photosynthesize using up any carbon dioxide which may be produced;

–the apparatus should be set up without the pump working and left for 24 hours. Plants respire more slowly than animals. After 24 hours, the pump is turned on gently. The lime water in flask C turns milky if it has not already done so.

The production of heat during respiration

Heat production can be investigated using the apparatus shown in Fig. 6.7. When seeds germinate and start to sprout, they respire rapidly. Food reserves (mainly carbohydrates) in the seeds are used to produce energy for the sprouting plant.

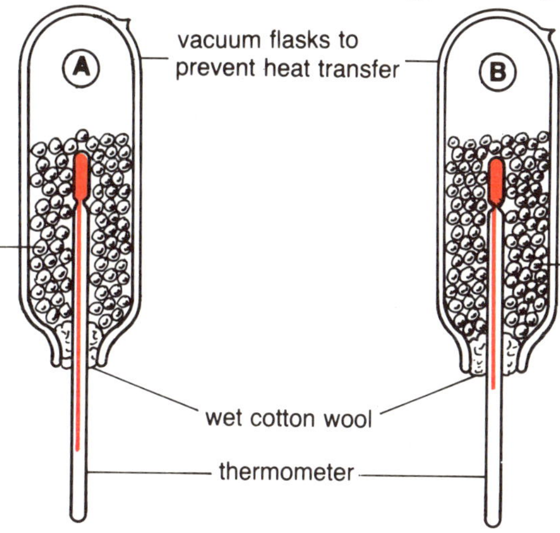

Fig. 6.7 Investigating the production of heat by germinating (respiring) peas

Flask A contains germinating peas which were soaked in water for 24 hours before the experiment. Flask B contains dead peas which cannot germinate or respire. These were killed by placing them in boiling water for 5 minutes. They were allowed to cool and soak in water for 24 hours before the experiment. The temperature rises in flask A but that in flask B stays constant. This shows that heat is being produced by the respiring seeds. If small insects are used in place of peas, the temperature in flask A rises even more quickly.

6.7 Anaerobic respiration

So far, we have only considered respiration in air (using the oxygen from the air). This kind of respiration is called **aerobic respiration**. However, respiration is also possible when there is no air and no oxygen. This is called **anaerobic respiration**. Anaerobic respiration can occur in animals and in plants.

The most important application of anaeorobic respiration is **fermentation**. Fermentation is used to make beer and wines. It involves the use of **yeast**. Yeast contains tiny single-celled organisms. Yeast can respire aerobically like animals and plants. When yeast is mixed with a solution of sugar or glucose, it quickly starts to respire. The yeast uses sugar and oxygen dissolved in the solution to produce carbon dioxide, water and energy. This, of course, is *aerobic* respiration.

$$\text{sugar (glucose)} + \text{oxygen} \longrightarrow \text{carbon dioxide} + \text{water} + \text{energy}$$

$$C_6H_{12}O_6 + 6O_2 \longrightarrow 6CO_2 + 6H_2O + 2900\ \text{kJ}$$

However, when all the available oxygen has been used, the yeast goes on respiring. Under these *anaerobic* conditions, the yeast uses up more glucose, but instead of producing carbon dioxide and water, the products are *carbon dioxide and ethanol*.

$$\text{sugar (glucose)} \longrightarrow \text{carbon dioxide} + \text{ethanol} + \text{energy}$$

$$C_6H_{12}O_6 \longrightarrow 2CO_2 + 2C_2H_5OH + 84\text{kJ}$$

Although anaerobic respiration allows the yeast to survive without oxygen, it is very inefficient. Notice, in the equations above, that one formula mass of glucose ($C_6H_{12}O_6$) produces 2900 kJ of energy in aerobic respiration, but only 84 kJ in anaerobic respiration. Under anaerobic conditions, most of the energy that the yeast could get from glucose remains 'locked up' in the ethanol.

The common name for ethanol is *alcohol*, so this example of anaerobic respiration is sometimes called **alcoholic fermentation** (see Fig. 6.8).

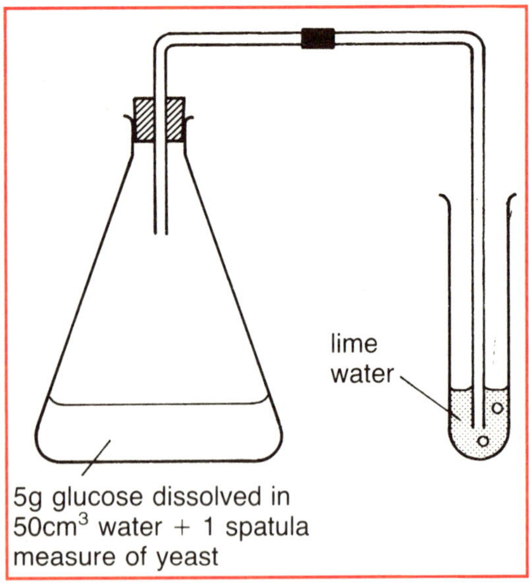

Fig. 6.8 Making alcohol by fermentation. Why does the lime water go milky?

6.8 Brewing and breadmaking

Anaerobic respiration is important in brewing and breadmaking.

BREWING AND WINE-MAKING

Alcoholic drinks are made by fermenting a sugary solution. Wine is usually made from the sugars present in grapes. The grapes are crushed to extract the juice. This contains sugar and wild yeast. The yeast ferments the sugar and gradually produces alcohol. Although the alcohol produced is always the same (ethanol), each wine has its own flavour. This depends mainly on the type of grapes used. Wines can also be made from a wide variety of flowers and fruits.

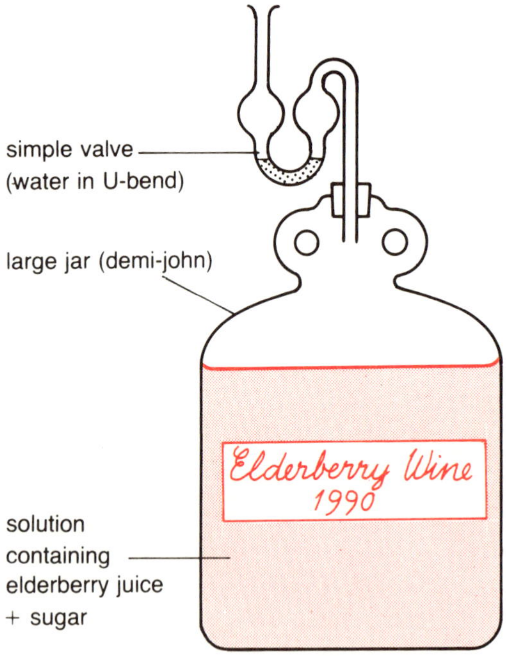

Fig. 6.9 Home-made wine can be made from various flowers and fruits. Fermentation is usually carried out in a large jar put in a warm place to speed up fermentation. The jar is fitted with a simple valve which allows carbon dioxide to escape, but prevents oxygen and bacteria entering the jar.

Yeast cannot live in solutions containing more than 14 per cent alcohol, so fermentation stops when the alcohol reaches this concentration. Stronger alcoholic drinks, 'spirits' such as whisky and gin, which contain more than 14 per cent alcohol are made by distilling wines and other weaker alcoholic solutions (see section 13.7).

Beer is made from barley. Barley grain is mashed with warm water and hops. This produces a dilute sugary liquid to which yeast is added. Fermentation converts the sugar to alcohol.

In small amounts, alcohol helps to make people relaxed and sociable, but in larger amounts it can be dangerous. It can make us aggressive and impairs our mental abilities. These effects can have disastrous results if people drink and drive. It is important to remember that alcohol is a drug which becomes addictive if taken regularly in large amounts. Addiction produces permanent damage to brain and liver cells.

BREADMAKING

Brewers are interested in the alcohol produced by fermentation, but bakers are more interested in the carbon dioxide. Bakers add yeast to their dough. The yeast respires producing bubbles of carbon dioxide which make the dough rise. When the dough is baked, heat kills the yeast and any alcohol evaporates. If dough is baked without using yeast, it is said to be *unleavened*. Unleavened bread does not rise–for example, pitta bread.

6.9 Anaerobic respiration in our muscles

Animals which live in places where there is very little oxygen, for example whales and mudworms, can respire anaerobically. In animals, anaerobic respiration produces *not* ethanol and carbon dioxide as with yeast, but **lactic acid**.

sugar (glucose) ⟶ lactic acid + energy

$$C_6H_{12}O_6 \longrightarrow 2C_3H_6O_3 + \text{energy}$$

Our own muscle cells can also respire anaerobically for short periods. This happens when our muscles have to work very hard for a short period, for example during a sprint race. Under these conditions, we cannot breathe fast enough, or pump our blood fast enough, to get sufficient oxygen to our muscles. So the muscles respire anaerobically and lactic acid is produced. Unfortunately, lactic acid is a mild poison. It causes our muscles to ache and cramp. When we rest, the blood brings oxygen to the muscles which can then respire aerobically again. This uses up the lactic acid and relieves the pain.

Quick test 6

Questions 1 to 5

The diagram shows part of the human respiratory system.

1 Name the part labelled W.
2 Name the part labelled X.
3 Name the part labelled Y.
4 Name the part labelled Z.
5 What is the important function of the rings of cartilage around part W?

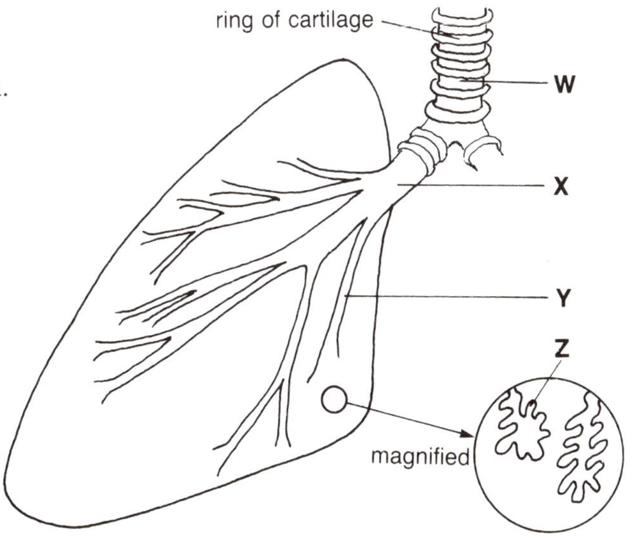

Questions 6 to 9

Billy is a runner. For a short time after he has been running, he breathes more deeply and more often.

	Normal breathing	After running
Volume of air taken in each breath/cm^3	500	1000
Number of breaths each minute	20	35
Total volume of air taken in each minute/cm^3	10 000	

6 Use the information in the table to calculate the volume of air Billy breathes during one minute after running.
7 How much *more* air does Billy take in during one minute after running compared with the volume of air taken in during one minute of normal breathing?
8 What fraction of the air is oxygen?
9 Use your answers to questions **7** and **8** to find the volume of extra *oxygen* Billy takes in during one minute after running compared with normal breathing.

(*LEAG* (part question), 1988)

Questions 10 to 12

The diagram shows how our bodies obtain the energy they need.

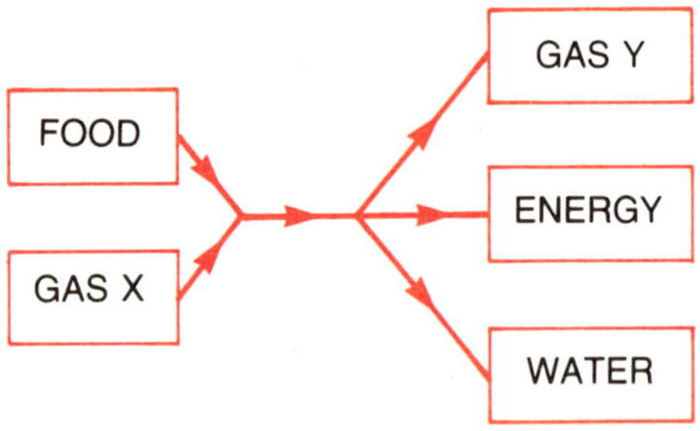

10 What is gas X?
11 What is gas Y?
12 What do we call the whole process shown in the diagram? (*NEA*, 1988)

Questions 13 to 18

In industrial brewing processes, yeast is added to a sugary solution and left at 25°C. The sugars are first converted to glucose and then this undergoes fermentation.

The equation for the reaction is

$$\underset{\text{glucose}}{C_2H_{12}O_6} \xrightarrow{\text{yeast}} \underset{\text{ethanol}}{2C_2H_5OH} + 2CO_2 + 84\text{ kJ}$$

13 What is the source of sugar for breweries?
14 What is (are) the product(s) of fermentation?
15 What will be the effect of raising the temperature to 35°C?
16 Why does boiling the yeast/sugar mixture stop the reaction?
17 How many carbon atoms are present in one molecule of ethanol?
18 How many hydrogen atoms are present in one molecule of ethanol?

Questions 19 to 24

Ian set up the apparatus shown below to find whether water is produced by a respiring plant.

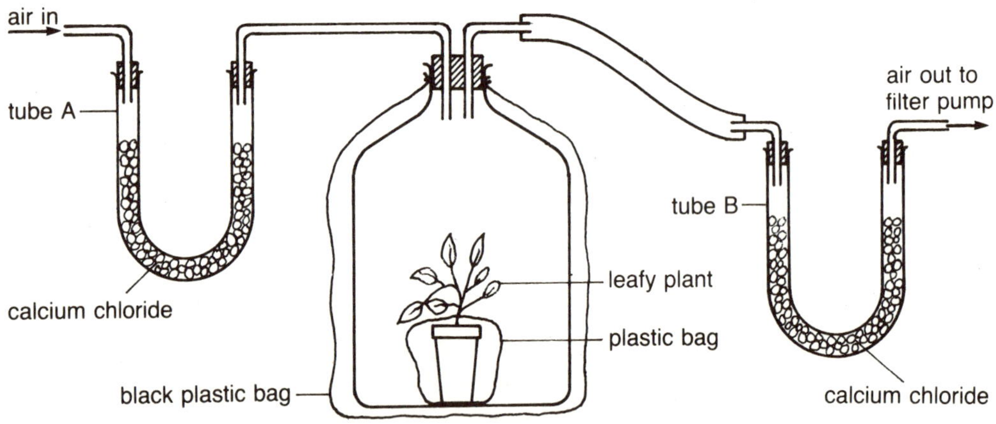

Explain why Ian took the following precautions:

19 he dried the air before it entered the bell jar, using calcium chloride;
20 he used small lumps, rather than large lumps, of calcium chloride in the–U-tubes;
21 he covered the plant pot with a plastic bag;
22 he covered the bell jar with a black plastic bag.
23 What measurements would Ian take?
24 How would Ian check that the air going to the filter pump was dry?

(*LEAG*)

Questions 25 to 30

The information in the table below was obtained by testing six brands of cigarettes.

Brand name	*Plain or filter?*	*Temperature of lighted end/ °C*	*Colour and pH of tar residue*		*Nicotine content in one cigarette/mg*
Longsmoke	plain	108	dark yellow	5	1.8
Coolburn	plain	110	brown	5	3.6
Tardust	plain	107	dark yellow	5	1.7
Coolmist	filter	127	yellow	5	0.3
Freshness	filter	135	yellow	5	1.0
Bluemist	filter	118	yellow	6	0.8

25 Are cigarette fumes acidic, alkaline or neutral?
26 Which brand has the lowest nicotine content?
27 Which two brands are almost identical?
28 What mass of nicotine (in mg) will be produced by smoking 20 Bluemist cigarettes?
29 State *two* patterns shown by the results in the table when plain cigarettes are compared with filter cigarettes.
30 Nicotine and tar in cigarette smoke cause certain lung diseases. Name *three* of these diseases.

7 SUPPORT AND MOVEMENT

7.1 The human machine

The muscles, bones and joints in your body work together like the parts of a machine. Your bones form a **skeleton** which provides a framework inside your body (see Fig. 7.1).

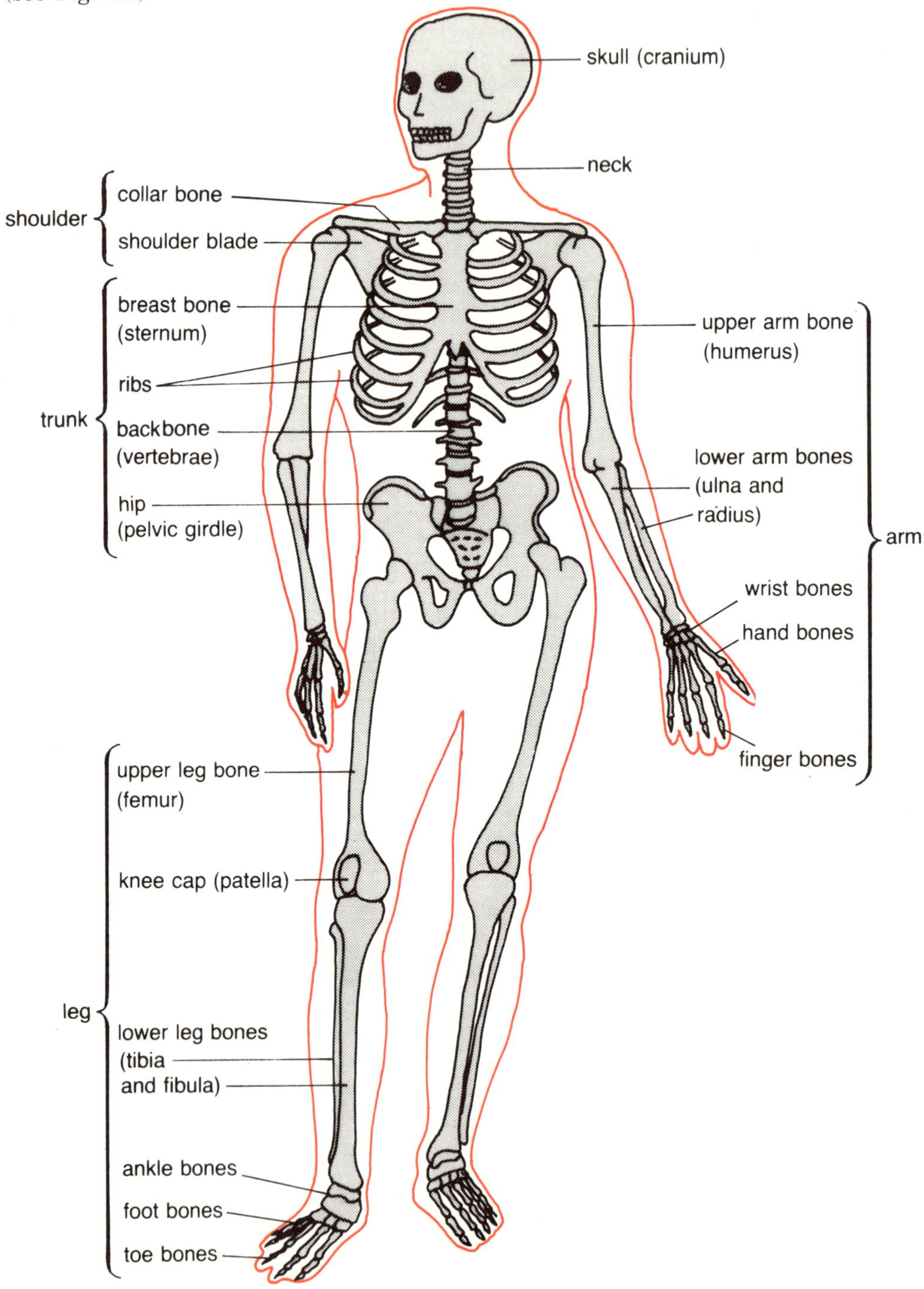

Fig. 7.1 The main bones of the human skeleton

The bones of the skeleton are connected at **joints**. The bones are actually held together by **ligaments**. These are tough, elastic strands which stretch across the joint from one bone to another. The bones and ligaments are arranged so that they can move smoothly at each joint. The bones act like rods and levers under the action of forces from our muscles.

7.2 Functions of the skeleton

The skeleton has four important jobs:

- **Support**
  The skeleton supports the body. Without a skeleton of bones we would collapse into a flabby heap.
- **Movement**
  A skeleton of bones allows us to move. Various bones in the skeleton are connected to one another at joints. Muscles attached to these bones help us to move easily.
- **Protection**
  Various parts of the skeleton protect vital organs. For example, the vertebrae in the backbone protect the spinal cord and the pelvis protects the reproductive organs. Which organs are protected by the skull and the rib cage?
- **Production of blood cells**
  Red blood cells and certain white blood cells are produced from the **marrow** found inside some bones.

What is the skeleton made of?

The skeleton is made of **bones** and **cartilage**.

Bones may look dead, but really they are very much alive. Bones contain blood vessels and nerves. They also contain special bones cells which make new bone and repair damaged bone. These living cells in bones are surrounded by a hard outer layer of calcium carbonate and calcium phosphate. This structure makes bones strong and rigid.

Cartilage (gristle) is the soft, elastic material beween bones. Cartilage acts as a shock absorber. It prevents our bones from jarring when we move about (see Fig. 7.2).

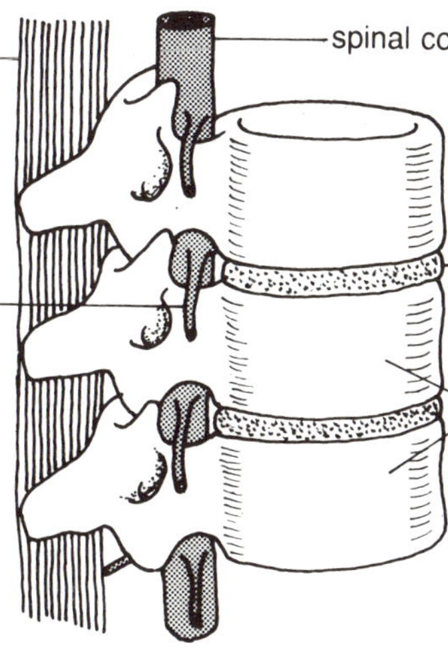

Fig. 7.2 Discs of cartilage between the vertebrae in the spinal column prevent the vertebrae from jarring and make it more flexible

All *vertebrates* have skeletons inside their bodies. You should have noticed this from eating meat, poultry or fish. Interior skeletons are called **endoskeletons**.

Some animals, such as crabs, insects and spiders, have an exterior skeleton. This is a hard outer shell enclosing soft tissue. This kind of exterior skeleton is called an **exoskeleton**. Exoskeletons have two main advantages. They protect the animal and help it to conserve water. The big disadvantage of exoskeletons is that they must be shed periodically as the animal grows.

Fig. 7.3 A blue crab–its hard outer shell is an *exoskeleton*

7.3 How do we move?

One of the important functions of your skeleton is to allow your body to move. Your skeleton contains more than 200 bones, but bones on their own are not enough. Your body will only move when forces act on the bones. These forces are provided by more than 600 **muscles**.

Almost all of the human skeleton is covered with muscles. Our arms and legs each contain several large muscles which move our limbs in different directions. The ends of each muscle are attached to different bones by **tendons** (see Fig. 7.4). For example, the Achilles tendon joins the calf muscle to the heel bone. Tendons are made of strong fibres which do not stretch much.

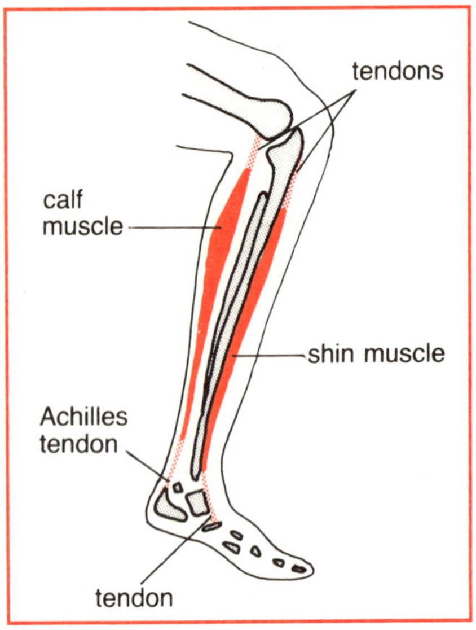

Fig. 7.4
The main muscles and tendons in the lower leg

How do muscles move bones?

The diagram in Fig. 7.5 shows the muscles which move the arm up and down. *When a muscle contracts, it gets shorter and fatter.* This causes the muscle to pull on the bones to which it is attached. After contracting, a muscle cannot lengthen itself again. It has to be pulled back to its original shape by a second muscle. Pairs of muscles which act in this way are called **antagonistic muscles**. The word 'antagonistic' is used to describe the muscles because they act in opposite ways. When one contracts, the other relaxes and vice versa. The biceps and triceps muscles which allow the arm to bend are an example of an *antagonistic pair*.

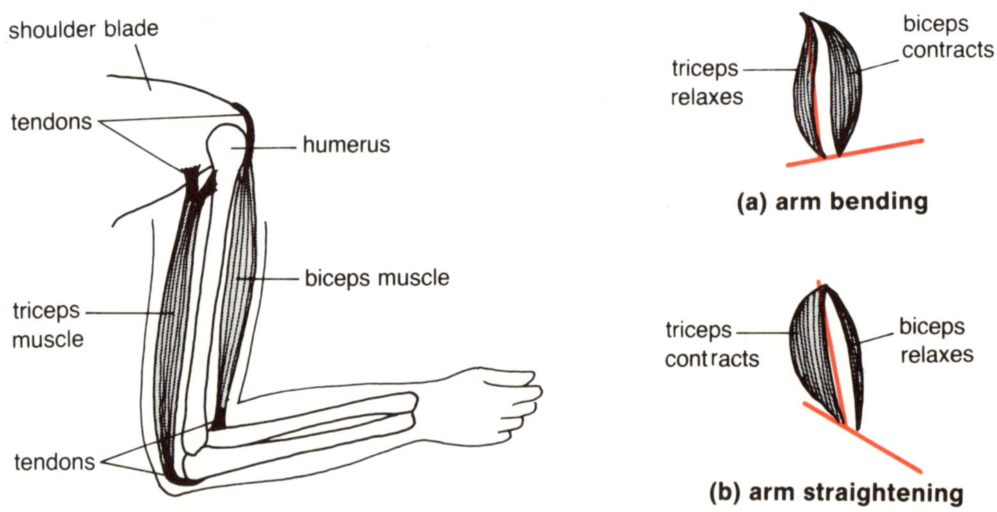

Fig. 7.5 Bones in the lower arm are moved by the biceps and triceps muscles. These muscles act as an antagonistic pair.

Although these muscles act in opposite ways, they are co-ordinated. When the biceps muscle contracts, the triceps muscle relaxes and bones in your lower arm are pulled towards your shoulder. This causes your arm to bend at the elbow (Fig. 7.5(a)). When the triceps muscle contracts, the biceps muscle relaxes and your arm straightens (Fig. 7.5(b)).

Muscles, such as the biceps, which bend limbs are called **flexors**. Muscles, such as the triceps, which straighten limbs are called **extensors**.

How do joints help bones to move?

At some joints, the bones are held together extremely tightly by ligaments. In this case, the bones cannot move. The bones which form the top of the skull are held tightly in this way.

Other joints allow a small amount of movement of neighbouring bones because they have elastic **cartilage tissue** between the bones. The joints between vertebrae in the backbone allow small movements in this way (refer back to Fig. 7.2).

Most joints can, however, move much more freely. Tough ligaments hold the ends of the bones together whilst allowing the bones to move through large angles. These joints are called **synovial joints**. Synovial joints have special features which reduce friction and allow the bones to slide over each other smoothly:

– the contact surfaces of the bones are covered with a smooth layer of elastic cartilage;
– the joint is enclosed by a tough **capsule** containing **synovial fluid**. Experiments have shown that synovial fluid is about ten times more slippery than the best man-made lubricants.

There are two main types of synovial joint:

1 Hinge joints in our knuckles, knees, wrists and elbows. Hinge joints allow our bones to move like a door on its hinges. Figure 7.6 shows the hinge joint at the knee.

2 Ball and socket joints in our shoulders and hips. At ball and socket joints, bones can move up and down or side to side. They have more freedom of movement than bones at hinge joints. Figure 7.7 shows the ball and socket joint at the hip.

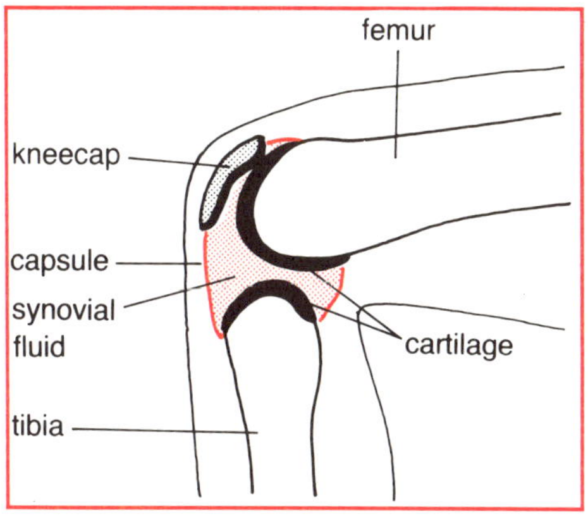

Fig. 7.6 The hinge joint at the knee

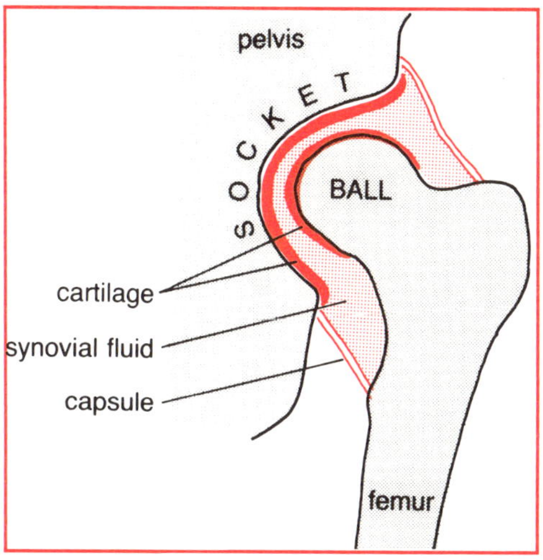

Fig. 7.7 The ball and socket joint at the hip

7.4 Broken bones

A break in a bone is called a **bone fracture**. The fracture mends in three stages:

1 A blood clot forms around the fracture. This blood may come from the broken bone or from surrounding tissue which has been damaged.

2 Bone cells multiply at the edges of the fracture and move into the blood clot. These cells make new bone tissue which eventually joins the broken pieces.

3 Unwanted fragments of broken bone around the fracture are broken down so that the final mend is almost undetectable by X-rays.

It takes a long time for bone tissue to grow and harden – some fractures can take several months to heal.

If a broken bone is to heal neatly, the two ends must be aligned correctly. This is why broken bones in our arms or legs are sometimes encased in plaster or held in position with a splint.

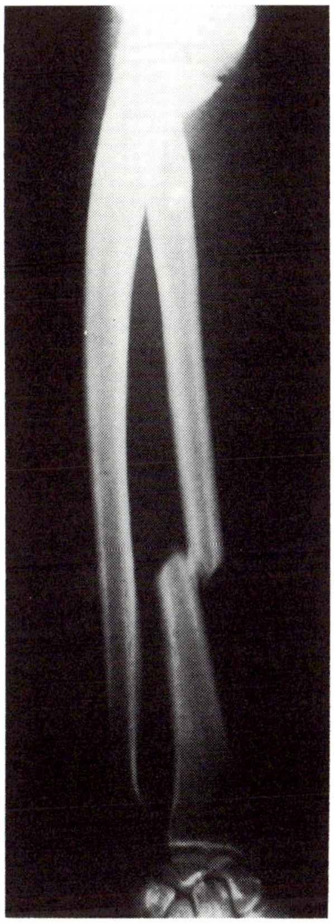

Fig. 7.8 An X-ray photograph of a right forearm showing a clean fracture of the radius. When an X-ray photograph is taken, X-rays are directed towards the fractured bone. Photographic film is placed behind the fractured bone. The X-rays pass through flesh, but not through bones. So, on the X-ray film, flesh looks dark and the bone shows up white.

7.5 Aches and pains

Table 7.1 shows some of the things that can go wrong with our bones and joints. It also indicates ways in which the problems can be relieved.

Table 7.1 Things that can go wrong with our bones and joints

Problem	*What causes the problem?*	*How is the problem relieved?*
Slipped disc	Part of a cartilage disc between two vertebrae bulges out. If this presses on a nerve, it causes much pain.	Doctors and osteopaths can sometimes manipulate the cartilage and vertebrae. An operation may be necessary to remove the protruding cartilage tissue.
Sprain	Torn ligament or tendon, particularly in a wrist or ankle joint.	Rest the joint to allow repair to take place. The joint may be supported by a bandage.
Tennis elbow, water on the knee	Swollen elbow or knee caused by the production of too much synovial fluid. This is usually caused by injury or by over-use of the joint.	The joint must be rested. Excess fluid may have to be drawn off.
Dislocated hip or shoulder	The ball of a ball and socket joint has come out of its socket. (Occasionally a baby is born with a dislocated hip.)	Doctors can manipulate the bones to replace the ball in its socket. The patient is then put in plaster or bandaged to allow the joint to become firmer.
Arthritis	Joints swell and hurt. This makes movement difficult and painful. The swelling and pain may be caused by: ● wear and tear of cartilage tissue–*osteoarthritis* ● hardening of cAtilage and other tissue around the joint–*rheumatoid arthritis*.	Drugs can be taken to relieve pain and/or to reduce swelling. Diseased joints can be replaced by artificial joints.

7.6 Support in plants

Some trees can grow to over 50 metres in height. In order to do this, they need structures to give them support. In general, plants use three structures to support themselves:
–tight packing of cells
–cellulose strands
–wood

1 Packing of cells

When cells in the leaves and stem of a plant have a good supply of water, they fill up and pack tightly. The epidermis of the leaf or the stem holds the cells in place. The cells press against one another and make the leaf or stem firm yet flexible (see Fig. 7.10). The leaf or stem is stiffened by filling the cells with water in the same way that a bicycle tyre is stiffened by filling the inner tube with air.

Plant cells can only remain swollen if they have a good supply of water. The water passes into the cells by osmosis (section 15.2). The swollen, well-filled plant cells are said to be **turgid**. **Turgor** stiffens the cells and helps to support a plant.

When plants lose their water supply, because they are cut or there is a drought, the cells are no longer turgid. The leaves, and possibly the stem, will wilt or droop.

Fig. 7.9 Giant Redwoods can grow to heights of well over 50 metres
(Photograph courtesy of the United States Travel and Tourism Administration)

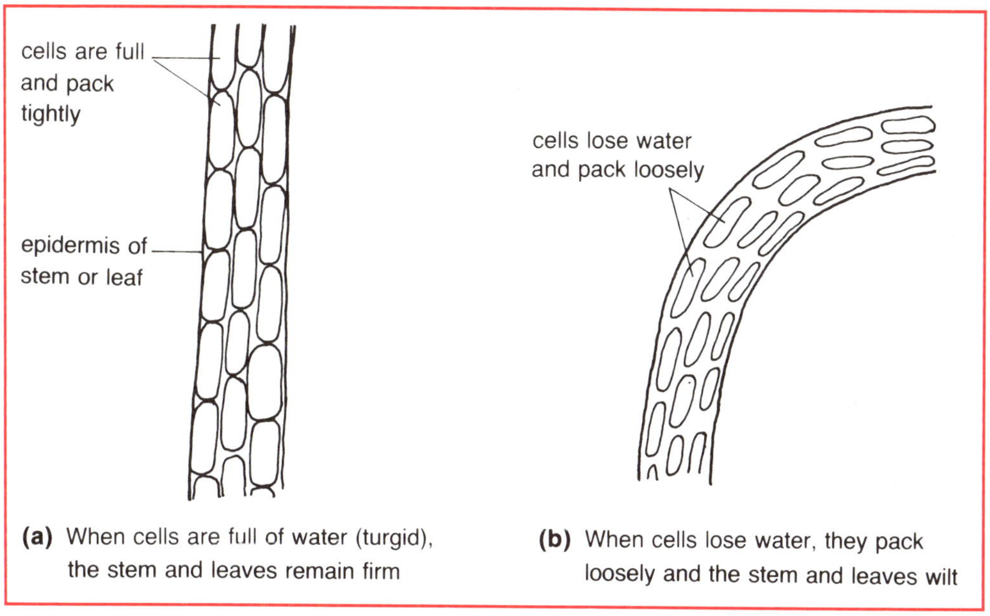

Fig. 7.10 The packing of cells can help a plant to support itself

2 Cellulose strands

Most grasses and flowering plants have strands of cellulose beneath the epidermis in their stems. These strands form part of the thick cellulose walls of the plant cells. As the plant grows, the cellulose strands increase in length with the stem. The cellulose strands make the stem strong and flexible, in the same way that carbon fibres give strength and flexibility in the handle of a tennis racket or fishing rod.

3 Wood

Plants that carry on growing from year to year (**perennials**) usually produce wood to stiffen their stems. As a plant grows, cells in the stem lengthen. As this lengthening occurs. a substance called **lignin** forms in the cell wall. Lignin does not let water pass through, so the cells die. This leaves long, thin strands of dead cells which form wood. The hard woody tissue provides good support for the plant.

In shrubs and trees, wood fills almost the whole stem. In herbacious perennials (flowering plants which appear to die off each winter and revive in spring), there is much less woody tissue.

Quick test 7

Questions 1 to 6

The diagram shows a vertical section of a synovial joint.

Choose from A to E the letter which points to

1 bone.
2 cartilage.
3 capsule tissue.
4 synovial fluid.
5 synovial membrane.

6 Which *two* of the structures labelled A to E are most important in reducing friction during movement?

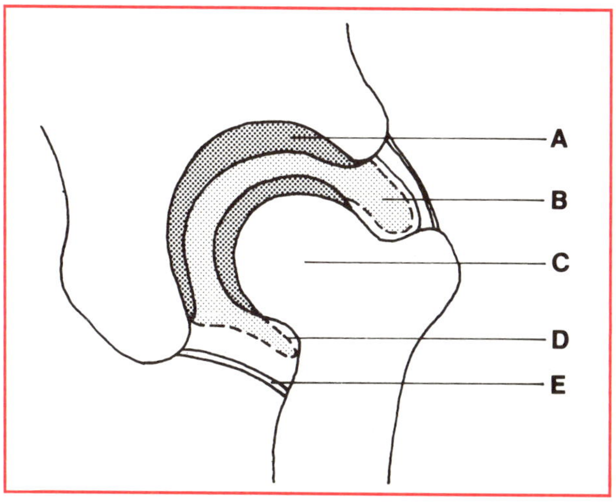

Questions 7 to 9

Choose one of the following words to fill each of the numbered gaps in the passage (overleaf):

darker	most	bone
lighter	least	air
greyer	more	paper
whiter	less	blood

When an X-ray photograph is taken, the film is ____7____ where more X-rays strike it. Therefore, the darkest areas on the photograph show where X-rays have passed through the body ____8____ easily. X-rays pass through flesh more easily than through ____9____.

Questions 10 to 17

Nagla is an athlete. She takes part in discus-throwing for her school. Nagla strengthens the muscles in her arm by lifting a dumb-bell. The diagram below shows some of the bones and muscles of her arm.

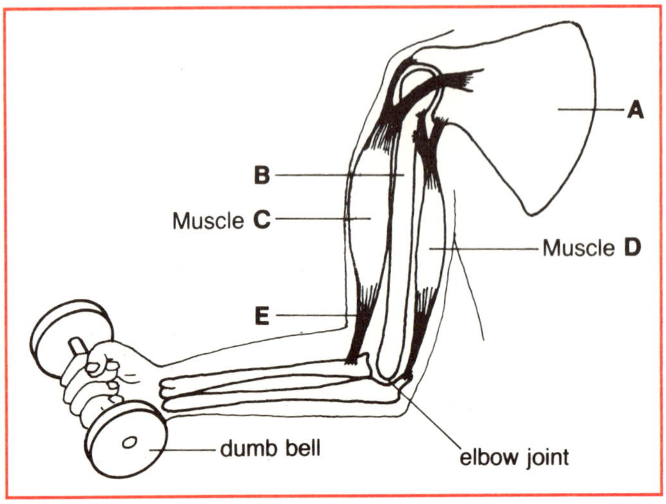

10 Name the part labelled E.
11 What does part E do?
12 Name the part labelled B.
13 What is the special name for muscle C?
14 What happens to muscle C when she lifts the dumb-bell?
15 What happens to muscle D when she lifts the dumb-bell?
16 Suppose the weight of the dumb-bell is 20 N. When the arm is held in the position shown in the diagram, the tension in E is

A much more than 20 N. C approximately 10 N.
B approximately 20 N. D approximately 3 N.

17 Pairs of muscles, like C and D, which work together to move a joint are described as

A flexors.
B extensors.
C antagonistic.
D ligaments.

(*LEAG* (modified), 1988)

Questions 18 to 20

Which parts of the human body are protected by
18 the skull?
19 the rib cage?
20 the vertebral column?

Questions 21 to 23

Five ailments that can cause aches and pains in our bones and joints are

A arthritis D sprain
B dislocated hip E tennis elbow.
C slipped disc

Which of these ailments is caused by
21 cartilage pressing on a nerve?
22 the production of too much synovial fluid?
23 a torn ligament or tendon?

24 Suggest *two* functions of bones and the skeleton besides protection.
25 Name two structures which help the stems of plants to stand upright.
26 Why do flower stems droop on cold, frosty days?

8 SENSES AND RESPONSES

8.1 Detecting changes and responding

Crossing the road can be dangerous. In order to cross safely we rely on various senses–*sight* to see the traffic;

–*hearing* to listen for the traffic;
–*touch* to move off the kerb;
–*balance* to walk steadily across the road.

Without our senses we could not survive for very long. Our senses detect changes in the environment to which we respond. They warn us about danger and help us to find food.

If someone tapped you on the shoulder, you would probably look round. The tap on your shoulder causes a change in your sense of touch. Changes like this which can be detected by our senses are called **stimuli** (singular: *stimulus*). Our reactions to stimuli are called **responses**.

Figure 8.1 summarizes our different seLes and stimuli for our sense organs. Sit very still for a moment. What stimuli are you receiving? Check your ideas against the stimuli listed in Fig. 8.1.

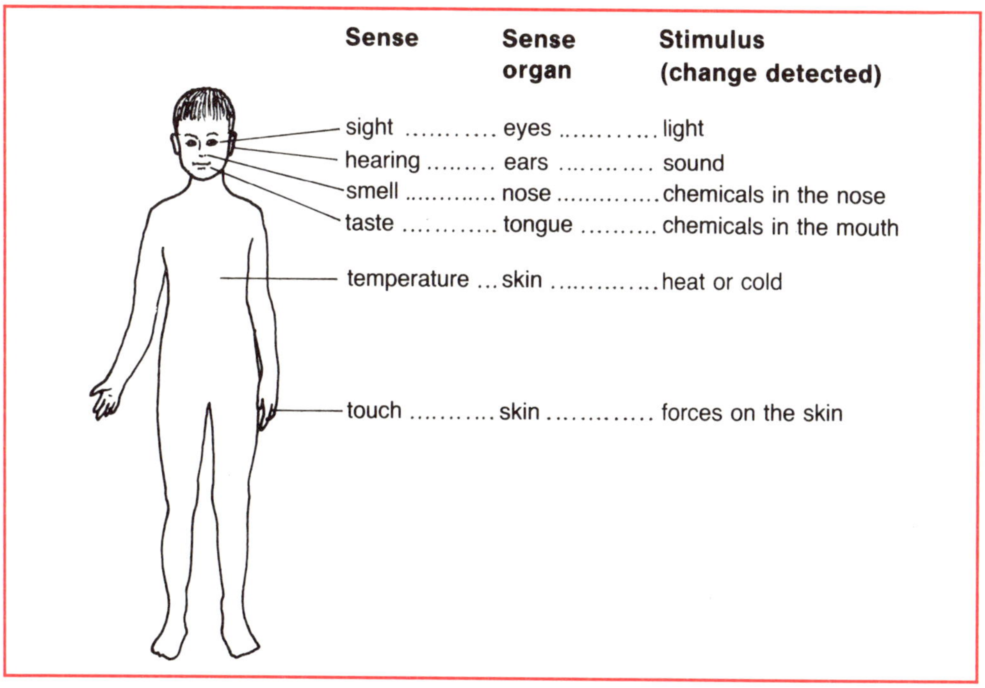

Fig. 8.1 Senses, sense organs and stimuli

When one of our sense organs has detected a stimulus, it sends impulses (messages) along nerves to the **central nervous system (CNS)**. The central nervous system consists of *the brain and the spinal cord*. When the central nervous system receives a message, it must decide whether to respond. If it responds, then impulses are sent along nerves to cause muscles to move. The flow diagram below shows what happens when you touch a hot plate.

Stimulus →	**Detection** →	**Transmission** →	**Transmission** →	**Response**
heat from hot plate	by skin (sense organ)	of messages to CNS via nerves	of messages to muscles from CNS via nerves	from muscles to move hand away from heat

We shall consider the central nervous system further in section 8.6. Our bodies have another system for responding to stimuli. This second system involves the action of chemicals, called **hormones**. Like ourselves, most animals have two methods of responding to stimuli (i.e. nerves and hormones). Plants, however, do *not* have a nervous system. They rely on hormones. We shall look at hormones in section 8.8.

8.2 Detecting light–the eye

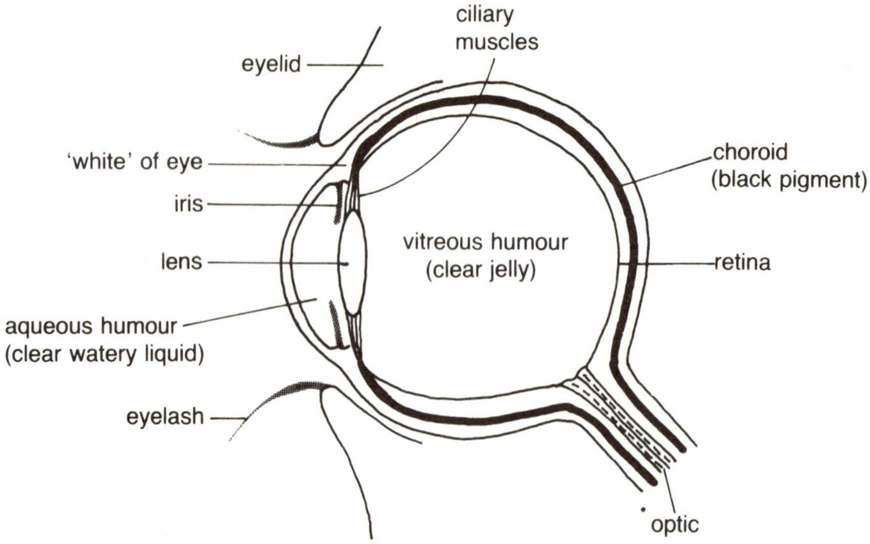

Fig. 8.2 The eye

Our eyes help us to detect light. They are very sensitive to changes in the density of light (light and dark). Although our eyes are very complex organs, they have three essential parts:

1 an **iris**, which controls the amount of light entering the eye. Your iris might be blue, brown or hazel. In bright light, the hole in the centre of your iris (the **pupil**) becomes smaller. In a dark room, the pupil becomes larger to let in more light.

2 a **lens and cornea**, which help us to form an image of the outside world on the retina. This is called *focusing*.

3 the **retina** at the back of the eye, which is sensitive to light. The retina contains more than 100 million light-sensitive cells. These cells send messages (nerve impulses) to the brain along the **optic nerve**. Our brains can use these messages to form a picture of the outside world.

HOW DO OUR EYES FOCUS?

The eye focuses on objects at different distances by changing the shape of its lens. It does this using the **ciliary muscle** which forms a ring around the lens.

Suppose you look at something *close up*, e.g. a book. The ciliary muscle *tightens* and pushes on the lens. This makes the lens fatter and more powerful (Fig. 8.3a).

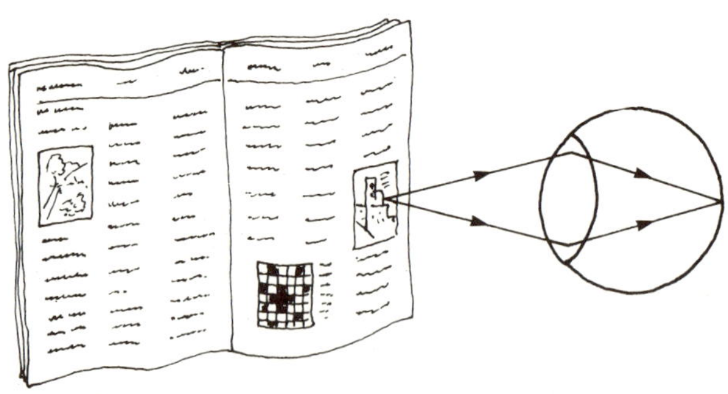

(a) Looking at something close-up.
The ciliary muscle makes the lens fatter and more powerful.

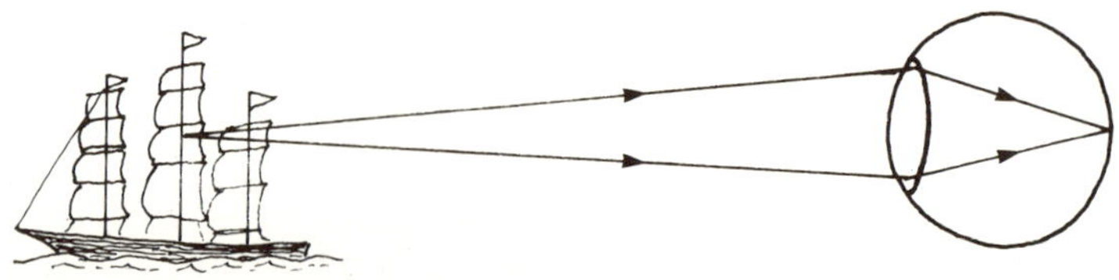

(b) Looking at something far away.
The ciliary muscle makes the lens thinner and less powerful.

Fig. 8.3 Focusing on near and distant objects

Now suppose you look at something *far away*. In this case, the ciliary muscle *relaxes* and the lens becomes thinner and less powerful (Fig. 8.3b). This change in shape of the lens to focus on near or distant objects is called **accommodation**.

If you have good eyesight, you will be able to focus on objects as near as 25 cm (the **near point**) or as far away as the stars (the **far point**).

EYE DEFECTS

Long sight

Some people cannot see close objects clearly. The lenses of their eyes cannot get fat enough to focus light on the retina. This defect can be overcome by wearing spectacles with *convex* lenses (or convex contact lenses). These help to converge the light to a focus on the retina (see Fig. 8.4).

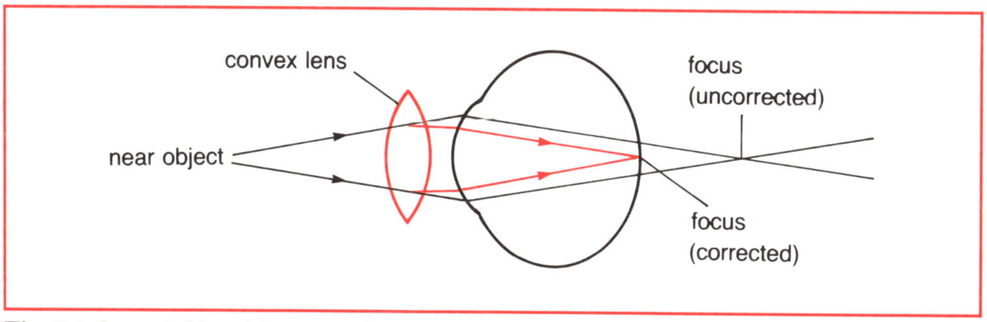

Fig. 8.4 Long sight and its correction

People who cannot focus on objects close up can usually see distant objects clearly. Because of this, we say they are *long-sighted*. People often become long-sighted in middle age as their ciliary muscles get weaker and their eye lenses are less flexible.

Short sight

People who are *short-sighted* can see close objects clearly. They cannot focus on objects in the distance. For example, someone who is short-sighted can read a book that they are holding, but not a wall poster on the other side of the street. In this case, light from distant objects is focused in front of, rather than on the retina (see Fig. 8.5).

Short-sightedness can be corrected by wearing spectacles with *concave* lenses (or concave contact lenses). These spread out (diverge) the light before it enters the eye. The light is then focused on the retina.

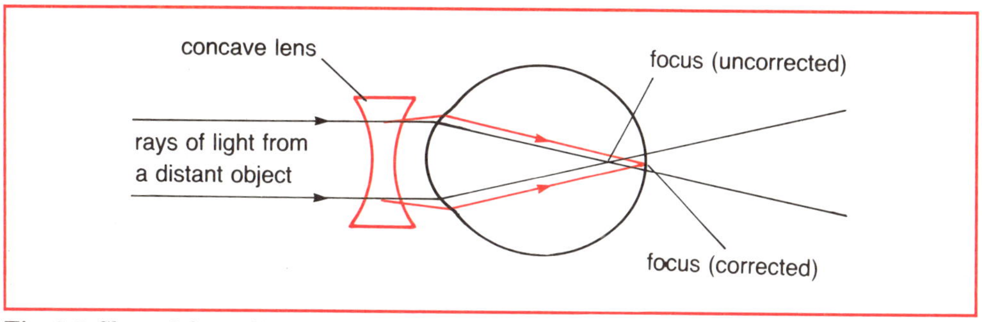

Fig. 8.5 Short sight and its correction

8.3 Detecting sound–the ear

Our ears are very sensitive to sound. They have three main sections–the outer ear, the middle ear and the inner ear (see Fig. 8.7, overleaf).

HOW DO OUR EARS HEAR?

As sound waves reach our ears, they pass down the ear canal. The waves cause the membrane of the **ear drum** to vibrate and this moves the ear bones back and forth. These vibrations pass to the membrane in the **oval window** and this causes the liquid in the **cochlea** to move. Delicate sensitive cells pick up the vibrations in the cochlea. These cells then send messages to the brain via the **auditory nerve**.

Fig. 8.6 The large ears of this North African eagle owl gather in even the faintest sounds. This helps the owl to detect its prey even in the dark.

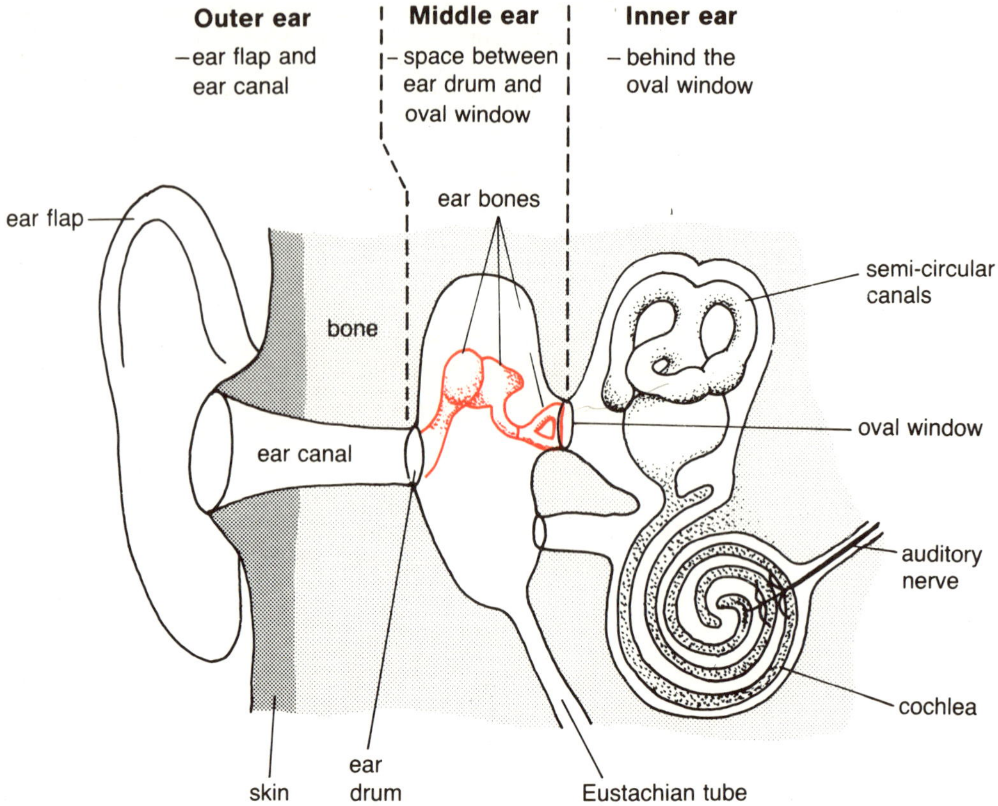

Fig. 8.7 A simplified diagram of the human ear

The inner ear also contains **three semi-circular canals** at right angles to each other. These organs are filled with liquid like the cochlea. But, unlike the cochlea which is concerned with hearing, the semi-circular canals are concerned with our sense of balance. As we move around, the liquid in the canals also moves. This stimulates nerves attached to the canals which pass messages to the brain. These messages help us to keep our balance.

8.4 Detecting smell and taste–the nose and mouth

Have you noticed how food seems to lose its flavour when your nose is blocked? This is because your sense of smell also plays an important part in detecting the taste and flavour of food.

We detect tastes with our tongues. However, our tongues are only sensitive to four different tastes – sweet, sour, bitter and salty. Other food flavours, e.g. fruity and minty, are detected by our noses.

Figure 8.8 shows the positions of cells which are responsible for our sense of taste and smell. Notice that the nasal cavity and the mouth are connected. So it is not surprising that the nose helps to detect the flavour of food.

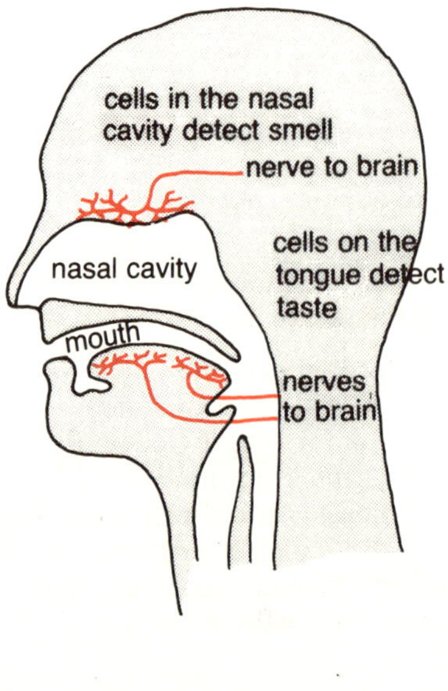

Fig. 8.8 Sense organs of smell and taste

Smell

Cells which detect smell are situated in the roof of the nasal cavity. These cells are stimulated by certain chemicals. Other chemicals have no effect on the smell cells. These chemicals have no smell–they are said to be *odourless*. Chemists think that chemicals which have similar smells have similar structures. Although our noses are sensitive to many different smells, our sense of smell is very poor compared with that of other animals.

Taste

Look at your tongue in the mirror. Notice that it is covered with dozens of short hair-like structures at the front and tiny bumps near the back. These are your **taste buds**. There are four types of taste bud. Each type is sensitive to one of the four tastes– sweet, sour, bitter and salty. The different taste buds are concentrated on different areas of the tongue (see Fig. 8.9). This is why wine tasters swill the wine around their mouths. By doing this, they are sure to detect all the flavours in the wine.

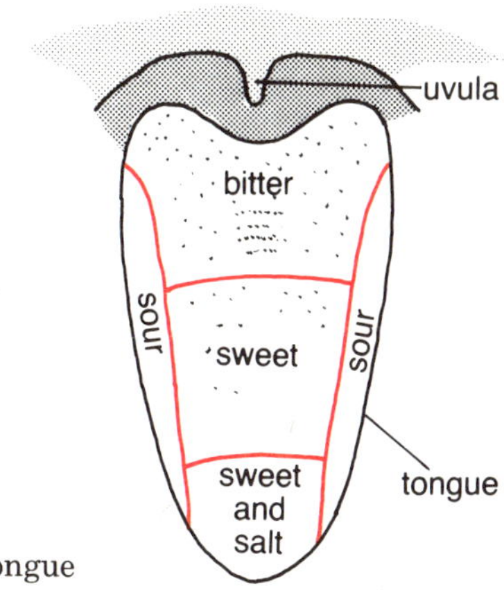

Fig. 8.9 Taste areas of the tongue

8.5 Detecting temperature and touch–the skin

Our skin forms a continuous layer over the whole of our bodies. It has two main layers: a thin outer layer, the **epidermis**, and a thicker layer, the **dermis**, underneath. The outer epidermis consists of dead cells. These flake off and are replaced from below.

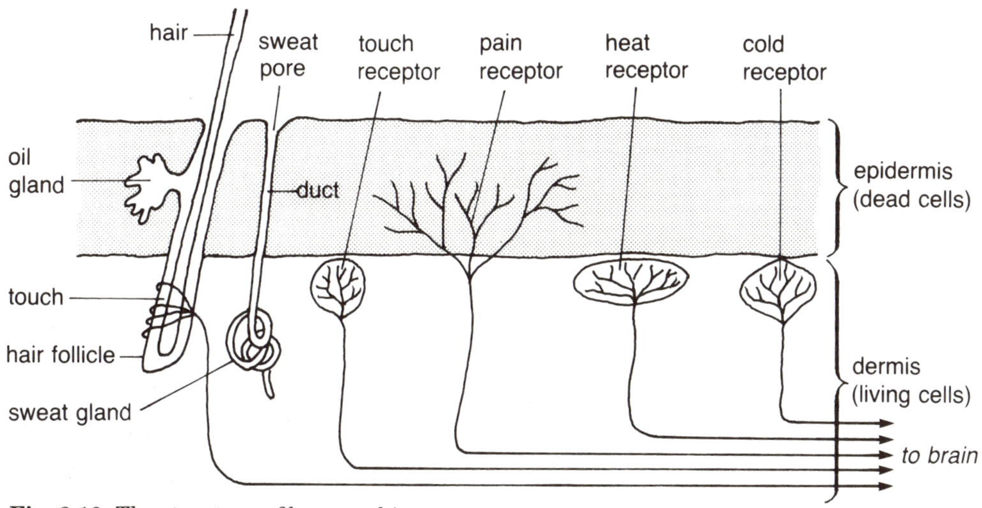

Fig. 8.10 The structure of human skin

THE FUNCTION OF SKIN

The skin has three important jobs:

1 It protects body tissues

The epidermis forms an elastic barrier which stops germs entering the body. The skin is also waterproof. Its waterproof property is increased by oil produced from **oil glands**. Oil glands open into the **follicles** from which hairs grow. The waterproof property of the skin is useful for two reasons. It stops water getting into the body, for instance when we have a bath. It also keeps essential water inside the body and stops it dehydrating (drying out).

2 It is sensitive to touch, pain and temperature

Our skin contains groups of *sensory cells* which are sensitive to different stimuli. These groups of sensory cells are called **receptors**. Some receptors are sensitive to touch, some to pain and others to heat and cold. Each receptor is connected to a nerve which carries impulses to the brain.

Gently stroke the hairs on the back of your hand. **Touch receptors** at the bottom of your hair follicles detect the stimulus and send messages to your brain. Other touch receptors are stimulated if you place the point of a needle in contact with your skin. All of our skin is sensitive to touch, but some parts, for instance our fingertips and lips, are more sensitive than others.

Touch receptors are sensitive to forces and pressure on the skin. If the pressure becomes large, then **pain receptors** start to respond by sending messages to the brain. Pain receptors in the skin consist of free nerve endings which extend into the epidermis.

Our skin also contains **temperature receptors**. Some temperature receptors detect heat, others detect cold. Temperature receptors cannot tell us the actual temperature. All they can do is to detect temperature changes and whether our skin is gaining heat or losing it.

3 It helps to control our body temperature

Warm blooded animals, like ourselves, have various ways of keeping their bodies at a more or less constant temperature:

- **Hair and feathers**
  Some animals which live in cold climates, for example polar bears and husky dogs, have thick hairy coats. The thick hair traps a layer of air close to thekin. Air is a poor conductor of heat, so heat loss is reduced. Feathers and clothing can also trap a layer of air, so they can also reduce heat loss.
- **Changes in blood vessels and capillaries**
  During cold weather, the blood vessels and capillaries near the surface of our skin contract. This means that less blood flows through them and so less heat is lost from the blood. With less blood near the skin surface, the skin can look pale, even blueish, when the weather is very cold.
  In warm weather, the reverse happens. Blood vessels and capillaries in the skin expand. More blood flows through them, so excess heat can be lost from the body. This is why we look flushed in hot weather.
- **Sweating**
  As soon as our body temperature rises above normal (37°C for humans), we begin to sweat. Sweat is mainly water. It is secreted from sweat glands just below the surface of the skin (refer back to Fig. 8.10). As the sweat evaporates, the heat needed for vaporization is taken from the skin and this causes cooling.
  If people get extremely cold, all their body processes can slow down so much that they become unconscious and may die. This condition is called *hypothermia*. Temperature control in warm-blooded animals is like the temperature control of a room using a thermostat. In a thermostat, there is a 'feed back' of information to switch the heater off if the temperature gets too high. If our skin senses that the temperature is too high it 'feeds back' a signal to the brain. The brain then passes messages to our muscles, hairs, arteries and sweat glands to put things right.
  This control of machines and living things by feedback of information, to keep conditions more or less the same at all times, is called **homeostasis**. This word comes from a Greek word *homeo*, meaning 'the same', and a Latin word *status*, meaning 'state' or 'condition'. There are many other examples of homeostasis. These include the control of traffic by police, the way you walk and balance, and the control of sugar in the blood (see section 8.8).

8.6 The nervous system

When one of our sense organs, such as our eyes or our skin has detected a stimulus, it sends impulses (messages) through the nervous system. The nervous system has two parts:

1 the central nervous system (CNS) consisting of the brain and the spinal cord;

2 a series of **nerves** which link the central nervous system with the various sense organs

Some of these nerves come out of the brain and go to sense organs in the head such as eyes and ears. Other nerves come out of the spinal cord and go directly to the arms, legs and body.

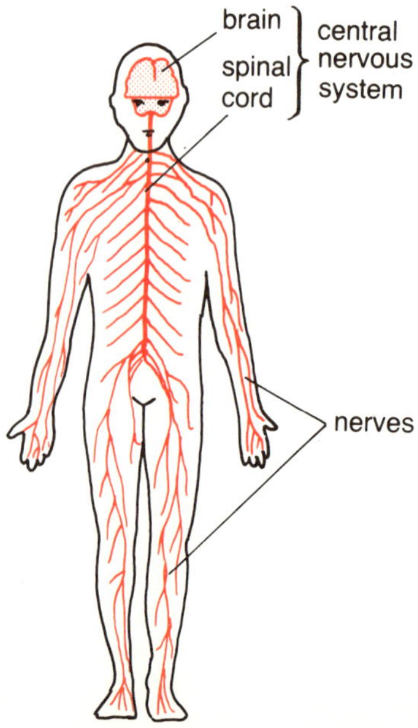

Fig. 8.11 The nervous system

The structure of a nerve cell is shown in Fig. 8.12. The main part of the cell, containing the nucleus is called the **cell body**. The cell body is located in the central nervous system. Long **nerve fibres**, called **axons**, run from the cell body to different sense organs and muscles. Usually the nerve fibres are grouped into bundles which are simply called nerves. The messages which pass along nerve fibres are tiny electric currents.

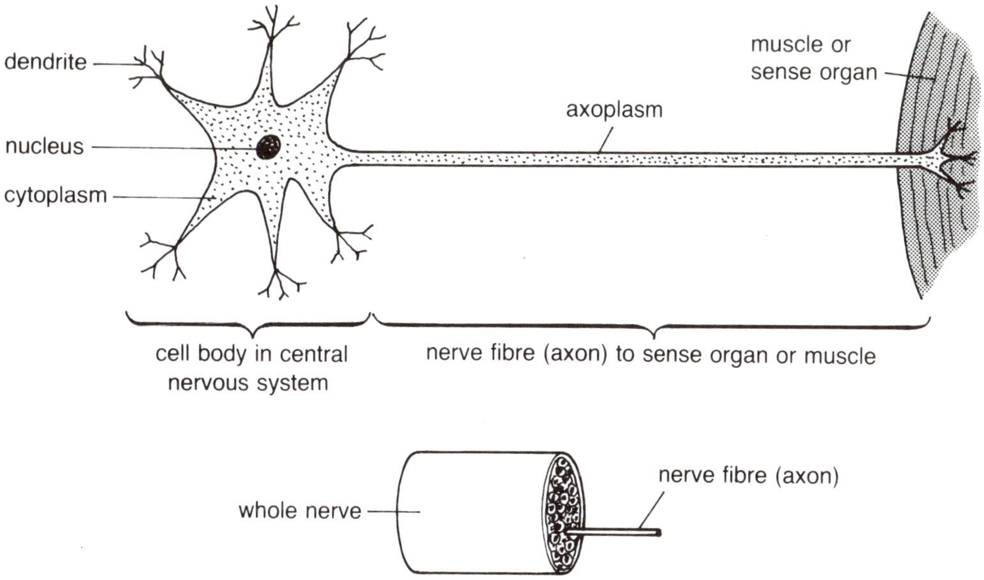

Fig. 8.12 The structure of a nerve cell and bundles of nerve fibres (axons) in a nerve

Nerve cells differ from other cells in having protruding branches called **dendrites**. These dendrites link up with other nerve cells to form a complicated network. This network enables messages to be sent in many different directions via the nervous sytem.

Experiments show that there are three distinct types of nerve cells or **neurones**:

1 **Sensory neurones** which carry messages from sense organs to the central nervous system.

2 **Motor neurones** which carry messages from the central nervous system to muscles.

3 **Connector neurones** which connect sensory neurones to motor neurones.

8.7 Reflex and conscious actions

If your throat tickles, you cough. If dust gets in your eye, you blink. If your hand touches a hot plate, you pull it away immediately. Each of these three actions happens automatically. They are spontaneous, involuntary and out of your control. You don't think about doing them. Automatic rapid responses like these are called **reflex actions**. Reflex actions are rapid because the nervous impulses travel by the shortest possible route. These shortest routes are called **reflex arcs**. The reflex arc involved in pulling your finger away from a sharp point follows the route shown in Fig. 8.13, overleaf:

1 Pain receptors in the finger produce impulses which travel via sensory neurones to the spinal cord.

2 Connector neurones in the spinal cord carry impulses to motor neurones.

3 Motor neurones carry impulses to muscles which contract pulling the finger away from the point.

The neurones are connected to each other at junctions in the spinal cord. These junctions are called **synapses**. When an impulse travels through a reflex arc, it must cross at least two synapses. These synapses allow the impulse to pass in only one direction, i.e. from sense organs to spinal cord and on to muscles.

Most of our actions are *not* involuntary, automatic reflexes, but thoughtful, **conscious actions**. Conscious actions involve the brain as well as the spinal cord. In these cases, impulses travel to the spinal cord, then up to the brain. They then travel back from the brain, down the spinal cord and out to the muscles.

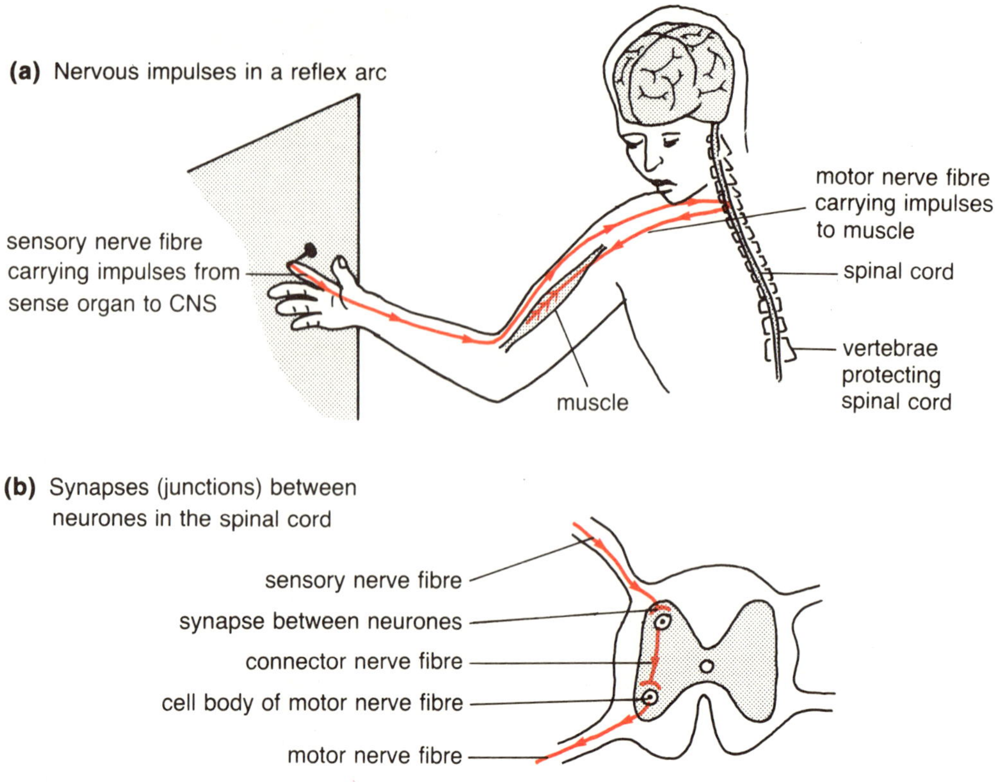

Fig. 8.13 The reflex arc involved in pulling your finger away from a sharp point

The pathways of impulses which result in conscious actions are much longer than reflex arcs. They also cross more synapses. This is why conscious actions are slower than reflex actions.

8.8 Hormones and hormonal control

The central nervous system allows messages to be sent from one part of our body to another. It can control our actions and responses second by second. The hormone system (**endocrine system**) also controls our bodies, but its effect is much slower. For example, hormones control the rate at which we grow and the development of our sexual characteristics.

The hormone system consists of a number of **glands**. These glands release chemicals called **hormones** into the bloodstream. The circulation of the blood then carries the hormones to all parts of the body. Different hormones affect different organs and different parts of the body. In effect, they carry messages from one part of the body to another. Because of this they are sometimes called **chemical messengers**.

Table 8.1 The effects of some important hormones

Hormone	*Gland*	*Effect of the hormone*
Growth hormone Tropic hormones	Pituitary Pituitary	Speeds up growth Stimulate other glands (e.g. thyroid, ovaries, testes) to produce their hormones.
Thyroxine	Thyroid	Controls the rate of chemical processes in the body
Insulin	Pancreas	Controls the amount of sugar in the blood (deficiency causes diabetes)
Adrenaline	Adrenals	Prepares body for action by –increasing heart beat and breathing rate –diverting blood from the gut to limb muscles
Female sex hormones	Ovaries	Control female sexual development and menstrual cycle (see sections 9.5 and 9.6)
Male sex hormones	Testes	Control male sexual development and sperm production (see section 9.5)

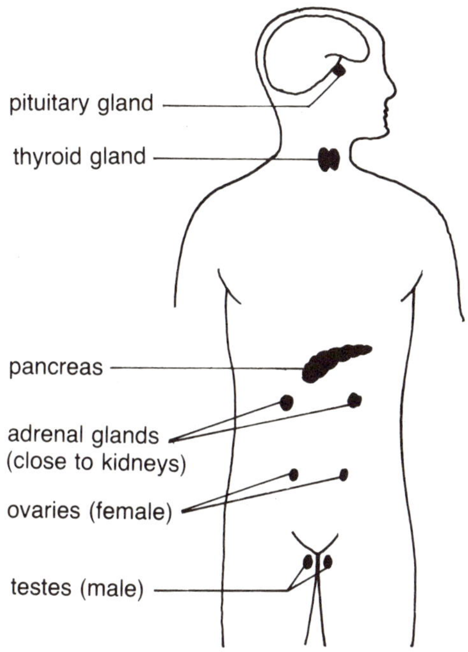

Fig. 8.14 The main hormone-producing glands in the human body

The positions of our hormonal glands are shown in Fig. 8.14. The effects of the different hormones are summarized in Table 8.1. Notice that as well as growth hormone, the pituitary gland produces other hormones which stimulate other glands. Because of this, it is sometimes called the 'master gland'.

The action of *insulin* in controlling the amount of glucose in the blood is an example of homeostasis (refer back to section 8.5). When carbohydrates are broken down, glucose is produced. If the concentration of glucose in the blood is too high, we become weak and dizzy. To prevent this happening the brain 'tells' the pancreas to release insulin into the bloodstream. Insulin triggers off the conversion of glucose to glycogen, so the concentration of glucose falls. Some people cannot produce enough insulin. Without treatment, they would go into a coma and eventually die. These people are called *diabetics* and the illness is known as **diabetes**. Diabetics can live normal lives provided they control the amount of glucose in their blood. This can be done by:

- injecting regular doses of insulin into their bodies, or taking tablets, to control the amount of glucose in their blood, and
- following a careful diet containing little carbohydrate.

8.9 Plant hormones

Plants do not have muscles or a complex central nervous system. They do, however, need to respond to stimuli and control their growth. They do this using hormones.

GROWTH HORMONES

Plants grow faster near the tip of the main shoot. This growth is controlled by a plant hormone called **auxin**. Auxin is produced in the tip of the plant and it

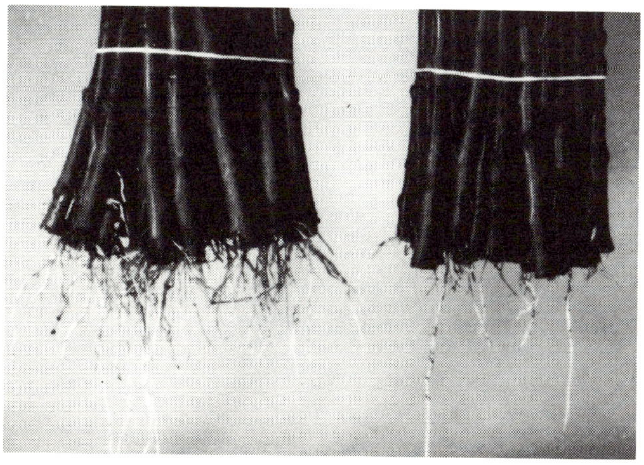

Fig. 8.15 Hardwood cuttings treated (*right*) and untreated (*left*) with IBA, a hormone rooting powder

stimulates growth. Gardeners sometimes pinch off the tips of growing plants. This stops the production of auxin and slows down growth at the tip. Side shoots begin to grow and the plant becomes more bushy. Auxin and other plant hormones are now produced commercially and used by farmers and gardeners. For example, hormone rooting powders are chemicals which stimulate plant cuttings to grow roots. Hormone weedkillers are synthetic chemicals which make weeds grow so fast that they use up all their food supply and then die.

RESPONDING TO STIMULI

Have you noticed how pot plants on a windowsill grow towards the light? The stems bend towards the window and leaves and flowers turn to the light. By responding in this way, plants can expose a larger area for photosynthesis. Responses such as this, which plants make to stimuli, are called **tropisms**. Tropisms occur much more slowly than responses in animals and they are less varied. The main tropisms involve *light* and *gravity*.

The response of plants growing towards *light* is called **phototropism**. Scientists believe that phototropism occurs because auxin collects on the side of the shoot furthest from the light. This makes the plant grow faster on the dark side, bending the shoot towards the light (see Fig. 8.16).

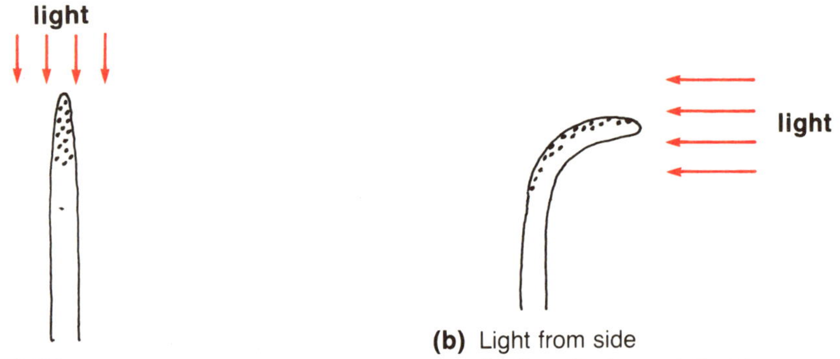

(a) Light from above
Auxin produced evenly around tip, so shoot grows equally on all sides.

(b) Light from side
Auxin collects on dark side, so shoot grows more on dark side and bends towards the light.

Fig. 8.16 Phototropism

The response of plants to *gravity* is called **geotropism**. As a result of geotropism, trees grow vertically, even on steep hillsides, and seeds produce shoots which grow upwards and roots which grow downwards (See Fig. 8.17).

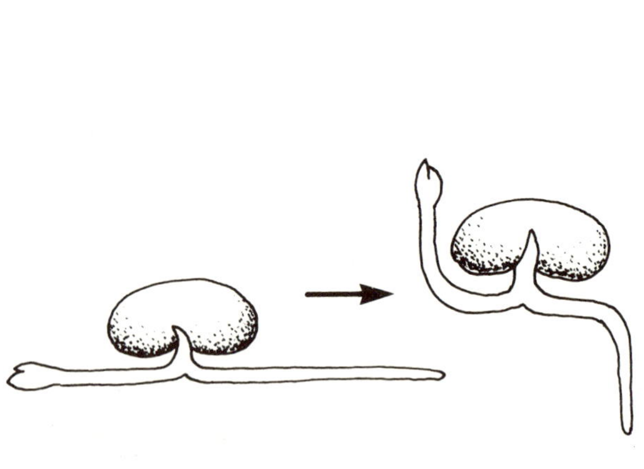

(a) Newly-germinated broad bean seedling is first placed vertically in the dark.
Shoot grows up.
Root grows down.

(b) Shoot is now turned horizontally and left in the dark.
After a while, shoot bends upwards and root bends downwards.

Fig. 8.17 An experiment to demonstrate geotropism

Quick test 8

1 Which of the following is *not* a sense organ?
A eye B hair C nose D tongue

2 A stimulus is
A a reaction to a change.
B a reflex action involving our nerves.
C something which causes a reaction.
D a nerve ending in a sense organ.

3 Plant hormones are *not* used for
A killing weeds.
B controlling fruit ripening.
C accelerating rooting in cuttings.
D increasing water movement through a plant.

Questions 4 to 8

We use many different devices to extend our senses. Consider the following senses:
A hearing B sight C smell
D taste E temperature F touch

Which of these senses are extended by
4 a barometer?
5 binoculars?
6 a thermostat?
7 a stethoscope?
8 a walking stick?

Questions 9 to 12

Name the *sense organ* in each case which makes it possible for
9 an architect to study a plan.
10 a musician to tune a piano.
11 a blind person to tell the difference between two sorts of yoghurt.
12 a cosmetic scientist to develop a new perfume. (*LEAG*, 1988)

Questions 13 to 16

Consider the following structures in the eye.
A ciliary muscles B iris C pupil
D optic nerve E retina F tear gland

Which of the structures A to F is responsible for
13 protecting the cornea?
14 detecting light?
15 carrying messages to the brain?
16 preventing too much light entering the eye?

17 Write the following in the order in which they are involved in a reflex action:
A central nervous system
B effector
C motor neurone
D receptor
E sensory neurone
F stimulus

Questions 18 to 23

The figure shows a section through the skin.

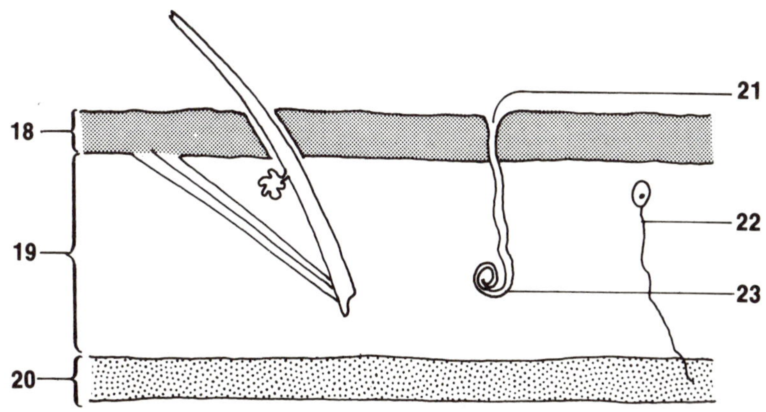

Choosing from the list below, label the structures numbered **18** to **23**.
sweat gland, dermis, pore, sensory cell, epidermis, fat

Questions 24 to 27

Javed and Debra wanted to find out if cuttings grew roots more quickly if a growth hormone was used. They set up three tests, each using a different amount of growth hormone. The figure below shows their results after 10 days.

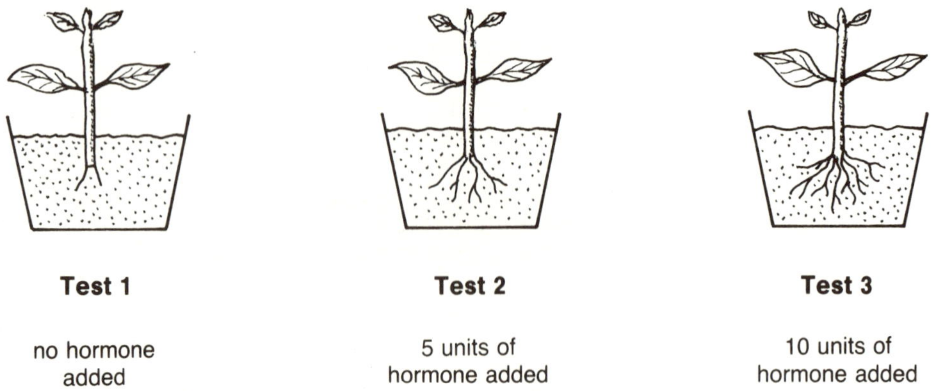

24 State which part of the plant has been cut.
25 In which test did the roots develop most quickly?
26 What was the purpose of test 1?
27 State *three* things which must be kept the same in the tests if the results are to be fairly compared. (*LEAG*, 1988)

28 Mary was trying to find how long it takes a person to press a button after seeing a bulb light up. She got one of her classmates, Julie, to be the subject of the experiment using the set-up shown below.

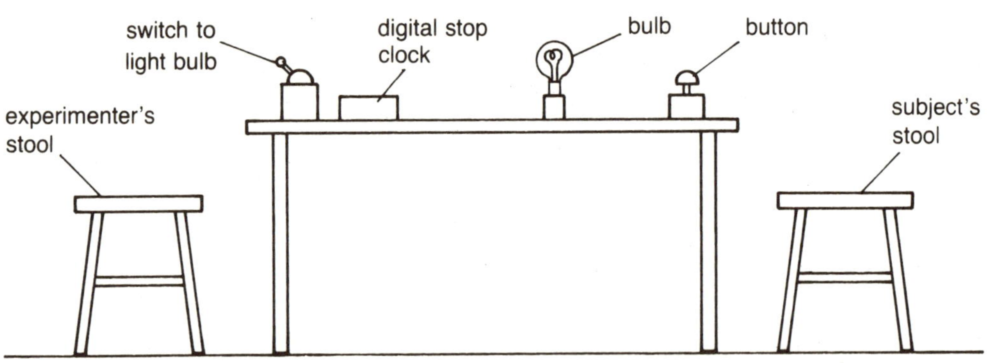

In the experiment, Mary flicked the switch to light the bulb and timed how long it took Julie to press the button.

Suggest *three* ways the experiment could have been improved to obtain a more reliable result. (*SEB*, 1988)

9 REPRODUCTION

Living things cannot live forever. They have an in-built urge to reproduce.

9.1 Sexual and asexual reproduction

Living things cannot live forever. Eventually, they die. But different animals and plants do not disappear from the Earth because they produce offspring before they die. This is called **reproduction**. Living things can reproduce in two different ways–by **sexual reproduction** and by **asexual reproduction**. Reproduction of humans is always sexual. This involves the union or mating of a male and a female. Humans, other animals and some plants reproduce sexually. But most plants and some animals can also produce offspring by asexual reproduction. Asexual reproduction does not involve the union of male and female. It takes place when part of the parent is detached and allowed to grow separately.

Sexual reproduction

Sexual reproduction is similar for all organisms. It involves special sex cells called **gametes**. Gametes are formed by a process of cell division called **meiosis** (see section 10.2). *Female gametes* are called **egg cells**. These are produced in the ovary of the female animal or plant. *Male gametes* are called **sperms** in animals and **pollen** in plants. When a male gamete meets a female gamete, the two join together. This is called **fertilization** and the fertilized cell is called a **zygote**. The zygote grows by dividing into two cells, then again into four cells and so on. Eventually, the cells form an **embryo**, which grows into an adult.

As both parents contribute part of themselves to the fertilized egg, the offspring has similarities to each. But it is not identical to the mother or the father.

Asexual reproduction

In contrast to sexual reproduction, asexual reproduction requires only *one parent*. It involves a different type of cell division called **mitosis** (see section 10.2), in which new cells are produced simply by the division of old ones. Each new cell is a copy of the original, so if reproduction is asexual, the offspring is identical to its parent.

The two methods of reproduction are summarized and compared in Fig. 9.1 (p. 72).

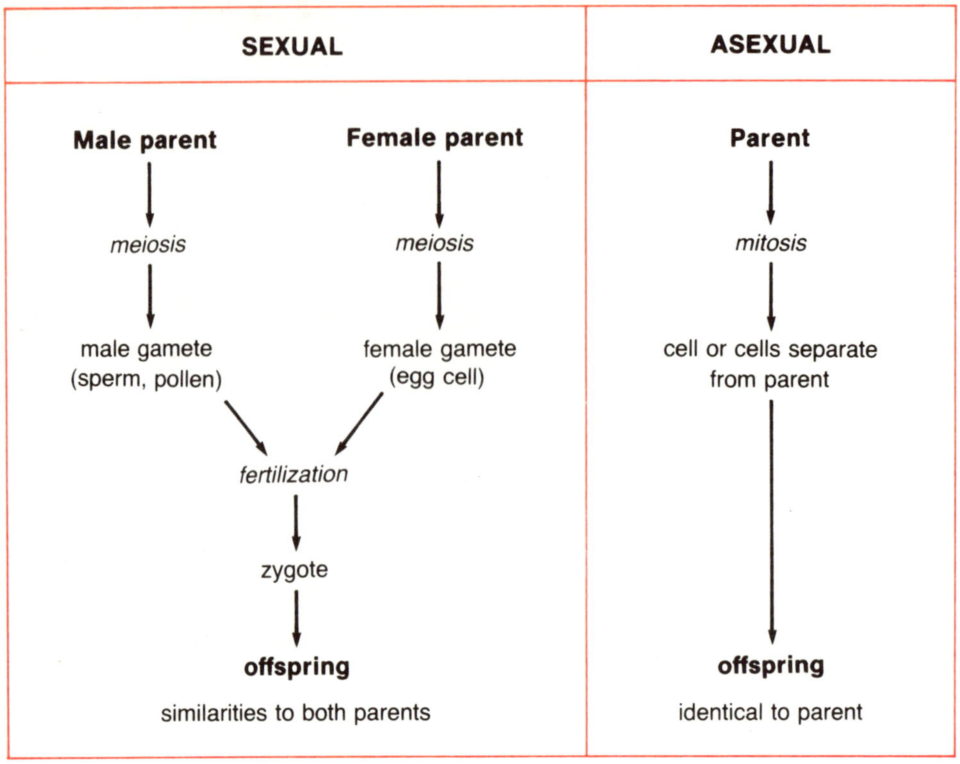

Fig. 9.1 Comparing sexual and asexual reproduction

9.2 Asexual reproduction

There are various methods of asexual reproduction. Three of these are described below.

1 Binary fission

This method is used by simple organisms such as amoeba, and by bacteria. The 'parent' cell divides to produce two identical 'daughter' cells.

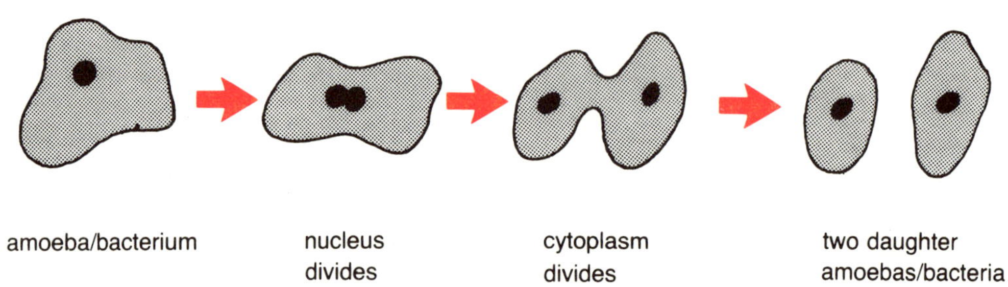

Fig. 9.2 An amoeba or bacterium reproducing by binary fission

2 Budding

In some organisms, such as yeasts, budlike growths start to form on the parent. These eventually separate from the parent and form a new organism.

3 Vegetative reproduction

Vegetative reproduction is an important form of asexual reproduction in plants. The most common methods of vegetative reproduction are:

- **Cuttings** A short stem with a few leaves is cut from the parent plant, such as a geranium. When this is put into damp soil, it produces roots and grows into a new plant.
- **Runners and stolons** Some plants, for example strawberries, send out side branches (runners) from the main stem. Roots and shoots form at intervals along the runner and these make new plants. Some plants, for example spider house-plants, form drooping branches (stolons) which develop roots and shoots for a new plant.

Fig. 9.3 This gardener is inspecting runners from his strawberry plant

- **Tubers** Potatoes are tubers. They are formed as the potato plant grows during the summer. They contain a store of carbohydrate (starch). Each tuber (potato) provides a food supply for a new young plant which grows from each potato the following year.

- **Bulbs** Bulbs are storage organs like tubers. But, unlike tubers, they enable the *same plant* to survive the winter and come back year after year. Onions, daffodils and tulips all form bulbs. During the growing season, the bulb may sprout a new bulb from its side. The following spring, a new plant grows from this. Figure 9.4 shows how a bulb reproduces vegetatively.

Fig. 9.4 Growth and vegetative reproduction in a bulb

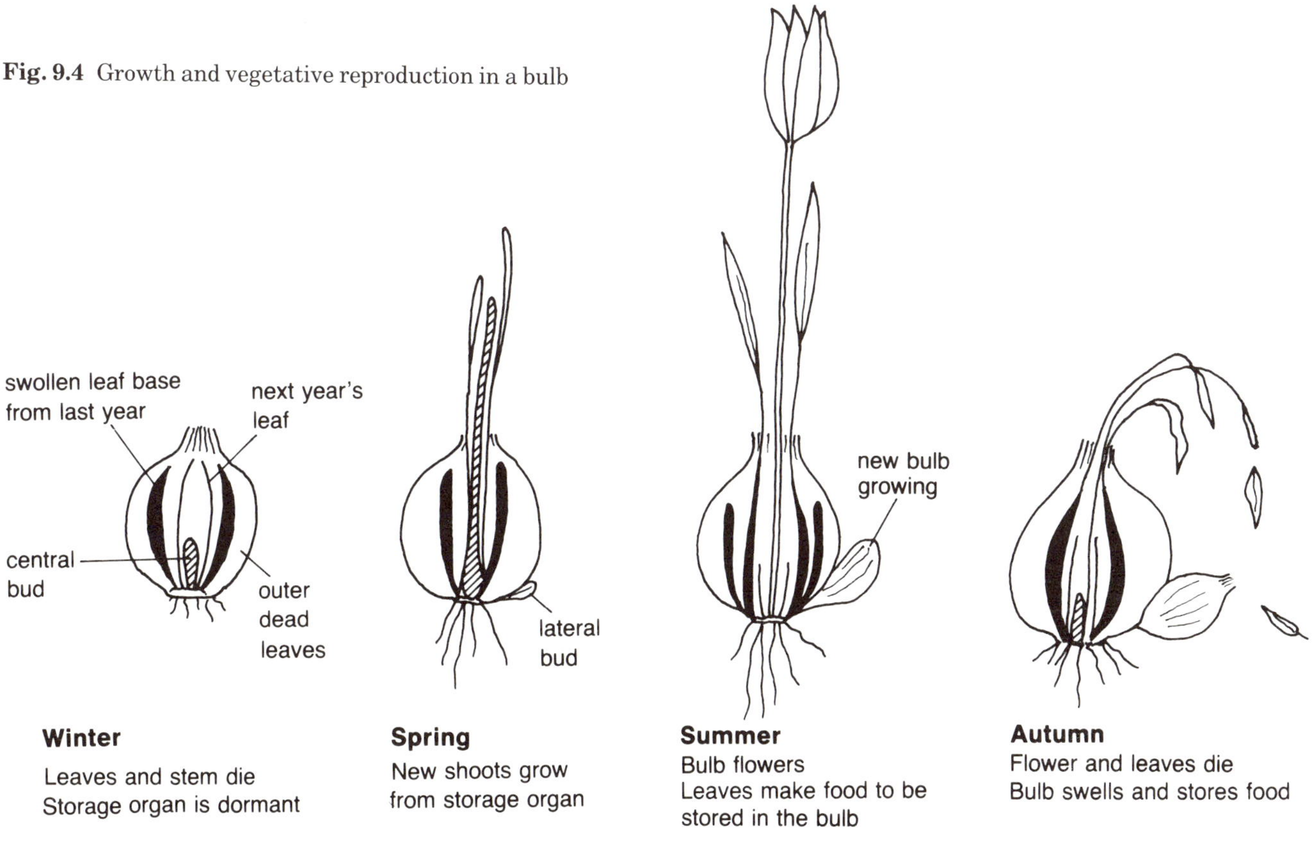

9.3 Sexual reproduction in plants

Flowers may look beautiful and smell attractive, but their colour and scent are not for our benefit. Flowers are the centre for sexual reproduction in plants. Flowers attract insects, birds and other animals. Sometimes, this enables the sex cells of different plants to meet and fertilization to take place.

THE STRUCTURE OF A FLOWER

Although there are dozens of different shapes of flowers, their basic parts are similar. Look at a flower such as a buttercup or a daffodil and try to identify the structures shown in Fig. 9.5 (overleaf).

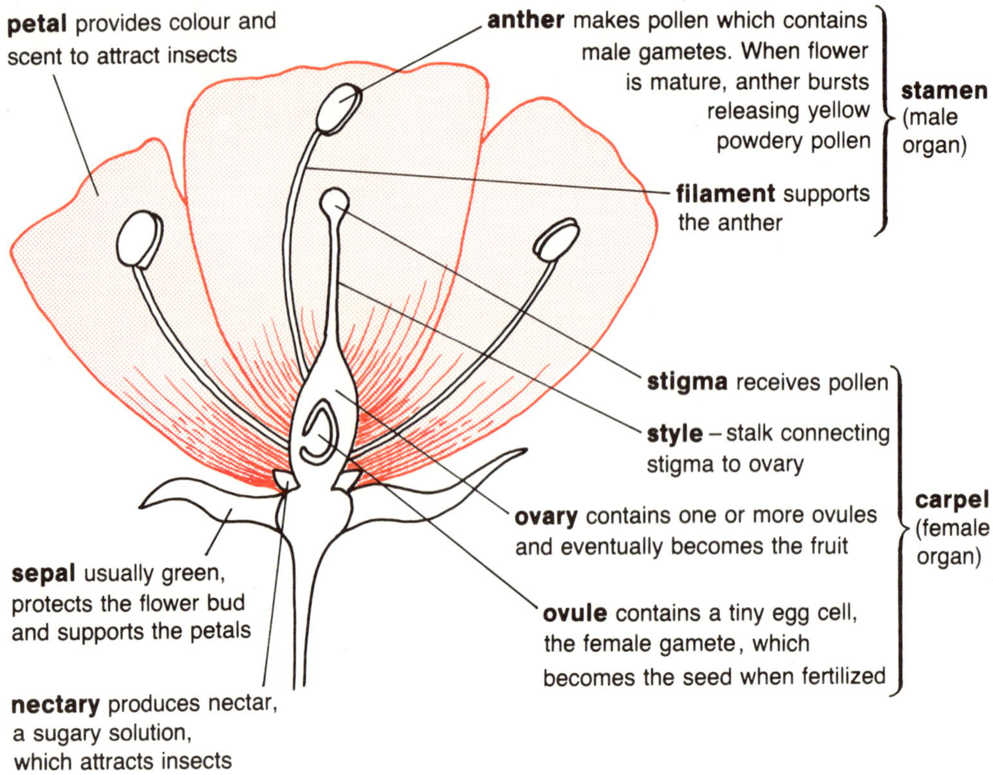

Fig. 9.5 The structure of a typical flower

POLLINATION AND FERTILIZATION

There are two stages to sexual reproduction in plants–*pollination* then *fertilization*.

Pollination is the transfer of pollen from the stamen to the stigma. Most flowering plants have both stamens and stigmas in the same flower. It is therefore possible for a single flower to pollinate itself–this is called **self-pollination**.

It is better, however, if the stigma of one flower is pollinated by the pollen from another flower of the same species. This allows the mixing of characteristics in the new plants. This is called **cross-pollination**. Very often, the anthers and stigma of one flower mature at different times. This makes cross-pollination more likely than self-pollination.

Pollen may be transferred from one plant to another by insects or by the wind. Brightly coloured and highly scented flowers often require insects to transfer pollen. The insects are attracted by the colourful flowers and by the scent of the solution (nectar) produced by the plants. When insects visit the flowers to collect nectar, pollen gets on their bodies. The pollen is then transferred to other flowers which the insects visit.

Other plants rely on the wind to blow pollen from one flower to another. In the summer, wind-blown pollen irritates the eyes and noses of people who suffer from hayfever. Trees, grasses and cereals are usually wind-pollinated.

After a pollen grain has landed on a stigma, it begins to grow a **pollen tube**. The pollen tube grows down the style and into the ovary. Inside the ovary, the nucleus from the pollen grain (male gamete) fuses with the nucleus of the egg cell (female gamete). This fusion of the male and female gametes is called **fertilization**.

SEEDS AND FRUIT

After fertilization, the fertilized egg (zygote) develops in the ovary. The zygote divides many times and becomes a **seed**. As the seed or seeds grow, the ovary, also becomes larger. Most of the other flower parts wither and die and the ovary swells to form a **fruit**. For example, on pea plants the pod is the fruit and the peas inside are the seeds. Strictly speaking, a fruit is a fertilized ovary, so nuts, sycamore spinners and dandelion 'clocks' are fruits, just as much as apples, oranges and tomatoes (see Fig. 9.6).

Plants make fruits to protect the developing seeds and help them to disperse. **Seed dispersal** ensures that the offspring do not compete with their parents for light, water and nutrients in the soil. Plants have developed many different methods for seed dispersal.

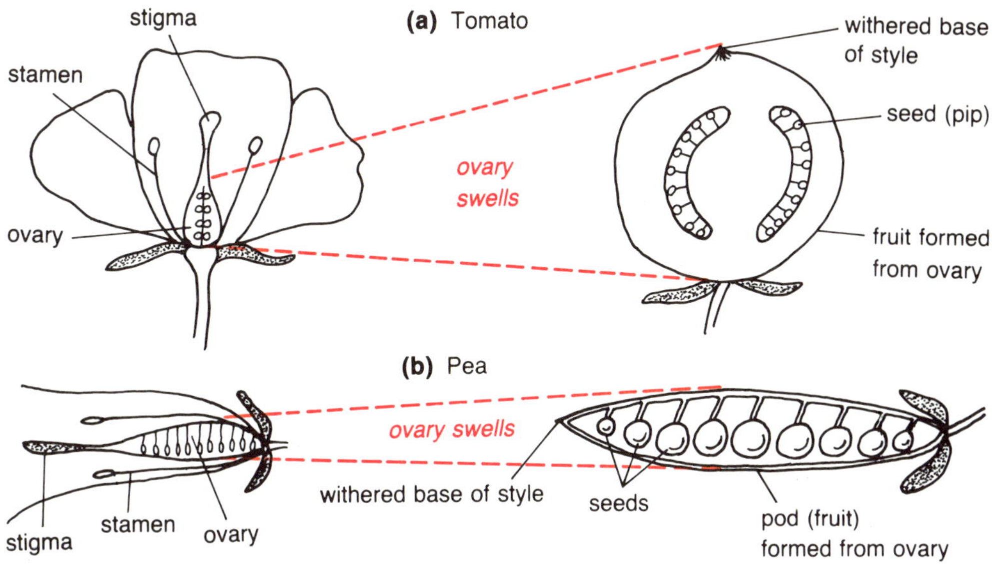

Fig. 9.6 Fruit formation in tomato and pea plants

Some examples of seed dispersal:

- *feathery 'parachutes'* (e.g. dandelions) or *'spinners'* (e.g. sycamores) which are dispersed by the wind.
- *exploding seed cases* (e.g. lupins, sweet peas) which burst open as they dry out and shrivel up.
- *small hooks* (e.g. burdocks and goosegrass) which cling to animals or clothing.
- *brightly-coloured and edible fruits* which are eaten by animals and birds. The seeds are either discarded by the animal or pass through the digestive system and are deposited in the animal's faeces.

GERMINATION

After seeds have been dispersed, they may start to grow into a new plant. This is called **germination**. Germination will only occur if the conditions are suitable:

- **Water** is essential for germination. Water causes the seeds to swell up and burst open, allowing the new plant to grow.
- **Oxygen** is also needed. This enables the seed to respire and produce the energy it needs for growth.
- **Suitable temperatures** are necessary. Seeds will not usually germinate below 5°C or above 45°C.
- The effect of **light** on seed germination varies from one plant to another. Most seeds will germinate in the light or in the dark. However, some seeds only germinate in the dark and others must have light.

9.4 Reproduction in animals

Almost all animals reproduce sexually. This involves the mating of a male and a female. For fertilization to occur, a sperm cell from the male must fuse (join) with an egg cell from the female (see Fig. 9.7 overleaf). Notice, in Fig. 9.7, that sperm cells are much smaller than egg cells. Sperm cells have a 'tail' which enables them to move around in search of egg cells. Only one sperm cell needs to enter the egg cell for fertilization to occur.

In some animals, including fish and amphibians, the female lays unfertilized eggs. The male then pours his sperm over them. This is called **external fertilization** because it takes place *outside the female's body*. External fertilization can only occur in water because sperms will die if they become dry. This is why frogs, toads and newts must return to water in order to mate.

Most land animals mate by passing sperm from the male into the female's body. Fertilization takes place *inside the female*, so this is called **internal fertilization**.

In birds and reptiles, the male passes sperm into the female. The sperms swim up the female's reproductive passage until they meet an egg. After fertilization, a shell is added to the egg before it is laid. A period of incubation is then necessary before young hatch from the fertilized eggs.

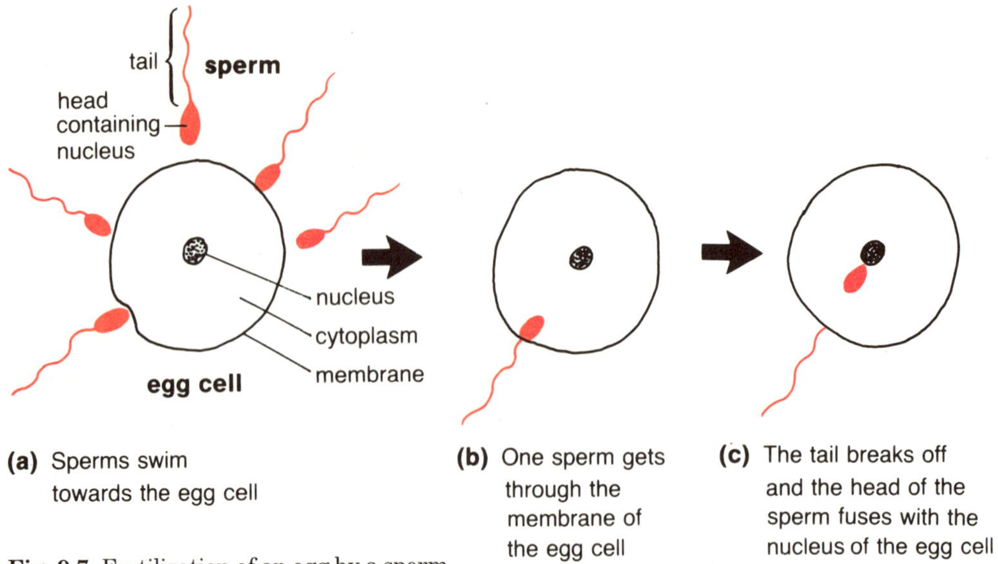

Fig. 9.7 Fertilization of an egg by a sperm

In humans and most other mammals the fertilized egg develops inside the female. The fertilized egg becomes a **foetus** (pronounced 'feetus') and grows into a young animal before it is born.

9.5 Human reproduction

THE MALE REPRODUCTIVE SYSTEM

The male reproductive system is shown in Fig. 9.8. Sperms are made in the **testes** and then stored in the **epididymis**. The sperms leave a man's body by passing along the **sperm duct**. In the sperm duct they mix with a white liquid produced by the prostate gland and the seminal vesicles. This mixture of white liquid plus sperms is called **semen** (pronounced 'seemen'). During sexual intercourse, semen passes down the urethra very quickly and is ejected from the penis by a muscular reflex action.

Notice in Fig. 9.8 that both urine and semen pass out through the urethra. However, urine and semen cannot pass through the urethra at the same time. It is impossible for a man to urinate when his penis is erect (see section 9.7) and impossible to release semen (ejaculate) when his penis is not erect.

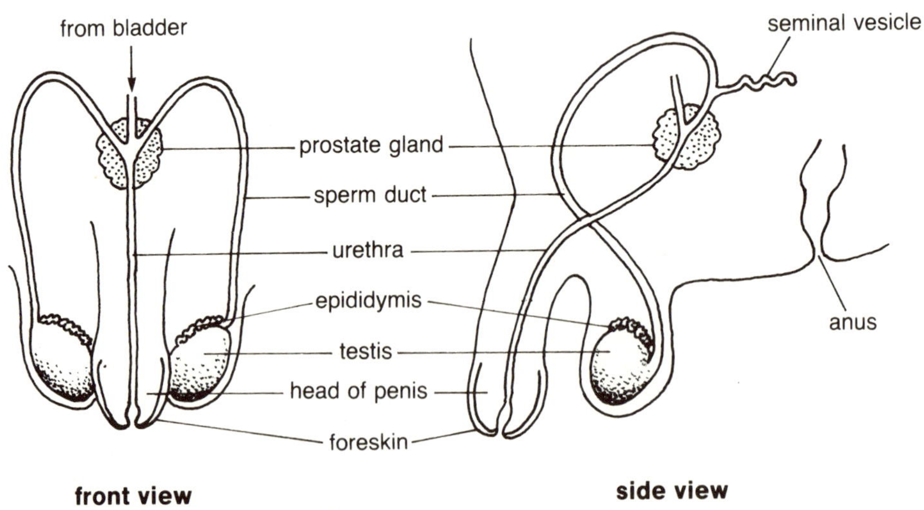

Fig. 9.8 The male reproductive system

THE FEMALE REPRODUCTIVE SYSTEM

Figure 9.9 shows the female reproductive system. Eggs are released from the **ovaries**. At roughly monthly intervals, an egg moves into the **oviduct** (egg tube) and down towards the **uterus** (womb). If the woman has sexual intercourse at this time, the egg may be fertilized by sperms which swim up the egg tube. If fertilization occurs, the fertilized egg (zygote) passes down the egg tube and into the uterus where it embeds itself in the lining. The lower end of the uterus opens into the **vagina**. Notice that a woman's urethra has a separate exit. Just in front of the urethra is a small lump called the **clitoris**. Like the man's penis, this becomes erect and sensitive when it is stimulated during sexual intercourse.

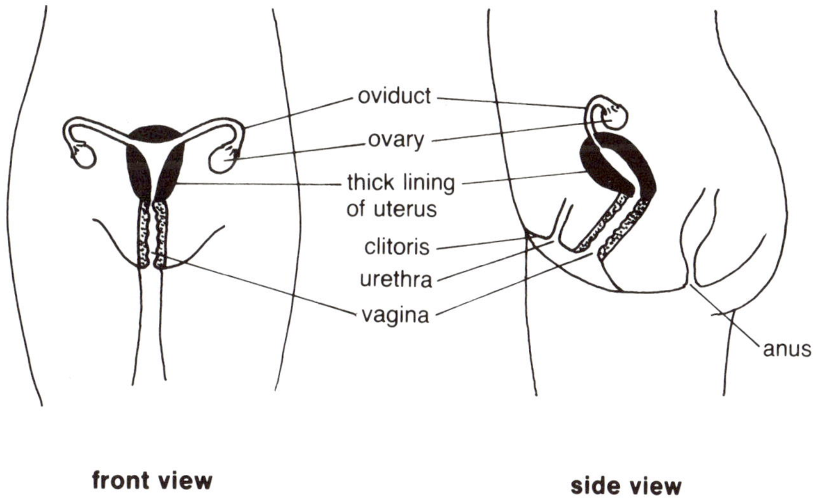

Fig. 9.9 The female reproductive system

9.6 Puberty and menstruation

Boys and girls cannot reproduce until they become sexually mature. Between the ages of 10 and 14, girls and boys start to develop sexually. This period of sexual development is called **puberty**. During puberty, boys start to produce sperms and girls produce eggs.

The changes which take place at puberty are summarized in Table 9.1. These changes are caused by hormones released from the pituitary gland and the sex organs.

Table 9.1 Changes in boys and girls at puberty

Girl	Boy
• Female sex hormones released from ovaries	• Male sex hormones released from testes
• Eggs produced by ovaries	• Sperms produced by testes • Ejaculation possible
• Menstruation starts	
• Breasts develop and nipples become larger	• Penis and testes grow
• Hair grows around sex organs in pubic area and in armpits	• Hair grows around sex organs in pubic area, in armpits and on face
• Hips get wider and buttocks fuller	• Muscular development increases
	• Voice gets deeper

At puberty, girls start to have 'periods'. The scientific word for 'period' is **menstruation**. During menstruation, blood is lost from the uterus through the vagina. At intervals of about 28 days, a ripe egg is released from one of the ovaries into its egg tube. In the week or so before this happens, hormones are released into the blood from the ovaries causing the lining of the uterus to become thicker and full of blood vessels. The uterus is preparing to receive a fertilized egg. In most cases, fertilization does not take place and the unfertilized egg dies. At the same time, the thickened lining of the uterus starts to break down and blood starts to seep from the vagina. Generally, the bleeding lasts for four to seven days. After the 'period' (menstruation), a new egg begins to ripen and the whole process, called the **menstrual cycle**, starts again.

9.7 Sexual intercourse

When a couple are sexually excited, the male penis and female clitoris become hard and stiff. This is called an **erection**. During intercourse, the erect penis is inserted into the woman's vagina. The walls of the vagina produce a lubricant which helps this process. The couple move in rhythm so that the penis moves up and down the vagina. This movement stimulates the sensitive head of the penis and the woman's clitoris. As the stimulation continues, the man and woman may have an **orgasm** (climax). During the male's orgasm, about a teaspoonful of semen is ejaculated in a few sudden bursts into the vagina. The woman may also have an orgasm, but not necessarily. Her climax may be before or after the man's ejaculation.

As soon as the sperm are ejaculated into the vagina, they 'swim' up the uterus and into the oviducts (refer to Fig. 9.9). If there is an egg in the oviduct, fertilization may occur.

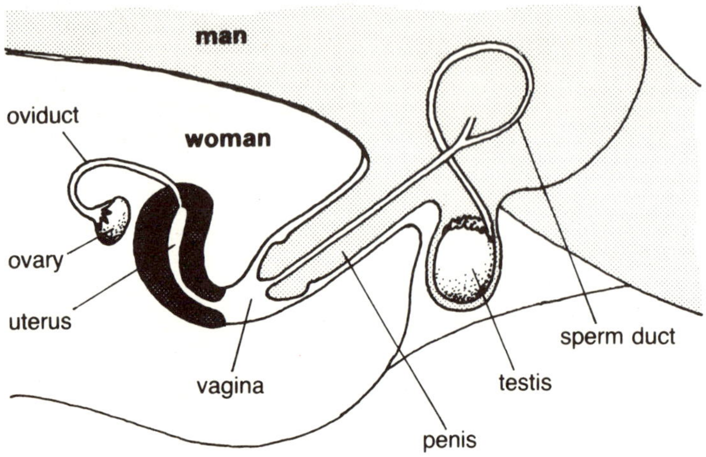

Fig. 9.10 Sexual intercourse

CONTRACEPTION

Very often, a couple may have sex regularly without the woman becoming pregnant. They can do this by using some form of **contraception**. Various methods of contraception are listed in Table 9.2 and illustrated in Fig. 9.11. Some of the methods are more reliable than others.

Table 9.2 Methods of contraception

Method used	*How does it work?*	*Comment*
Condom or **sheath** (Durex, French letter, rubber)	A thin lubricated sheath is put over the erect penis. This catches the semen and stops sperms entering the vagina.	Reliable if used properly. Putting on the condom interrupts sex. Condoms are sold at chemist shops, some supermarkets and from machines in public toilets.
The **contraceptive pill** ('the pill')	Taken by the woman. Contains hormones that prevent eggs being released from ovaries.	Very reliable provided that the pill is taken according to the instructions. There may be health risks if the pill is taken over many years. Must be prescribed by a doctor.
Diaphragm or **cap** (Dutch cap)	The cap is a dome-shaped ring of rubber which is fitted over the neck of the uterus before sex. This stops sperm entering the uterus. (Spermicidal cream is used to coat the cap.)	Reliable if the diaphragm is the right size and is correctly fitted. It may slip out of place if not put in correctly.
Spermicides	Spermicides are substances which kill sperms. They are sold as sprays or creams.	Unreliable unless used with the cap. Sold at chemists shops.
Inter-uterine devices (IUDs) (coil, loop)	IUDs are loops of metal or plastic inserted in the uterus. The IUD prevents a fertilized egg becoming implanted in the uterine lining.	Very reliable. The IUD is inserted into the uterus through the vagina by a doctor.
Sterilization	Either the sperm duct is cut in male sterilization (vasectomy), or the oviduct is cut in the female.	Totally reliable. Requires an operation by a doctor. The procedure cannot usually be reversed.
The '**safe period**' (rhythm method)	Couple only have sex during the 'safe period' when there is no egg available to be fertilized around the time of menstruation.	Very unreliable as the time and length of the 'safe period' are difficult to predict.

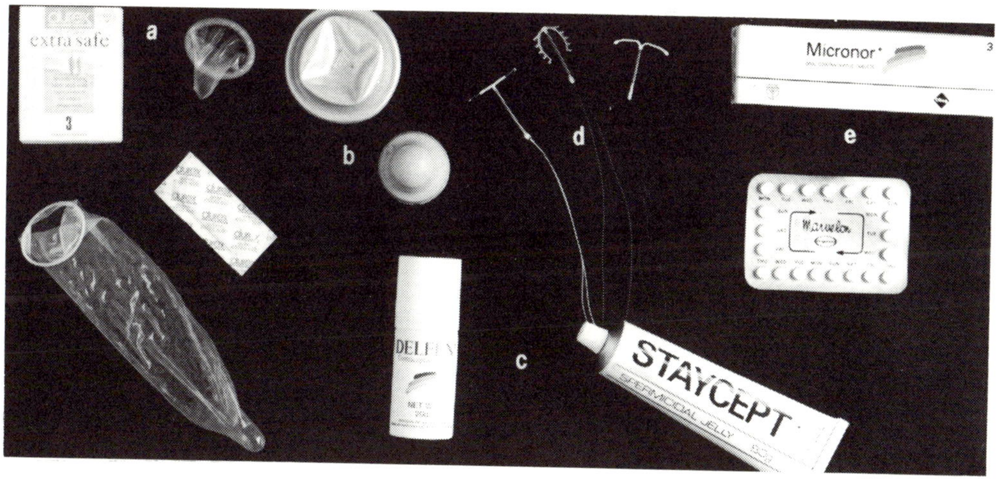

Fig. 9.11 Various contraceptives: **(a)** condoms; **(b)** two diaphragms used with **(c)** spermicides; **(d)** IUDs; **(e)** contraceptive pills

ABORTION

In spite of the various methods of contraception, fertilization sometimes occurs when it is *not* planned. To avoid giving birth to an unwanted baby, the foetus can be removed from the uterus (aborted). This is called an **abortion**.

An abortion must be carried out by a doctor and there are several ways it can be done. The operation is more difficult the older the foetus. There are continuing arguments over the time during pregnancy after which an abortion should be illegal. Some people want abortion to be easily available for as long as possible into pregnancy. Others want abortion to be illegal at any time during pregnancy.

9.8 Sexually Transmitted Diseases

A number of diseases can be passed from one person to another during sexual intercourse. These diseases are called **sexually transmitted diseases** or **venereal diseases** (VD). The micro-organisms which cause these diseases cannot survive outside the body. Sexually transmitted diseases *cannot* be picked up from cups, towels or lavatory seats.

The only sure way to avoid these diseases is never to have sex with an infected person. Very often it is impossible to tell whether someone is infected. If you have sex with several different partners, you are taking a higher risk. The contraceptive pill prevents pregnancy, but it gives no protection against venereal diseases. Although the use of a condom over the penis does not give complete protection, it helps to prevent infection and the spread of diseases such as AIDS. Four of the most common sexually transmitted diseases are described in Table 9.3.

Table 9.3 Some common sexually transmitted diseases

Disease	*Cause*	*Symptoms*	*How is it cured?*
Gonorrhoea	a bacterium	Burning sensation when urine is passed, due to an inflamed urethra. Yellow discharge from urethra. Infected person eventually becomes sterile.	Easily treated by a course of antibiotics in the early stages.
Syphilis	a bacterium	A sore at the end of the penis or just inside the vagina. After a week or two, the sore heals and the bacteria move to other parts of the body causing a mild fever. Without treatment, infected person may go blind and/or insane.	Easily treated by a course of antibiotics in the early stages. In later stages it is incurable.
Herpes	a virus	Sores on the end of the penis or just inside the vagina.	Cannot be cured.
AIDS Acquired Immune Deficiency Syndrome	a virus	The virus attacks the immune system which protects the body against infections. AIDS sufferers are therefore prone to illnesses, such as pneumonia and skin cancers, which kill them.	Cannot be cured.

9.9 From fertilized egg to baby

A fertilized egg (a zygote) is about half a millimetre in diameter. After fertilization it takes about a week to pass down the oviduct to the uterus. During this time, the zygote divides many times, first into two cells, then four cells, then eight and so on. When it reaches the uterus, the zygote has become a ball of cells called an **embryo**. The embryo implants itself in the thick lining of the uterus (see Fig. 9.12). The woman is now described as *pregnant* and *menstruation ceases*.

The embryo continues to develop and after six weeks it is about a centimetre long. Its heart and brain can be identified and it lies in a watery liquid called **amniotic fluid**. The embryo and amniotic fluid are enclosed by a membrane called the **amnion**. This protects it from bumps and jolts.

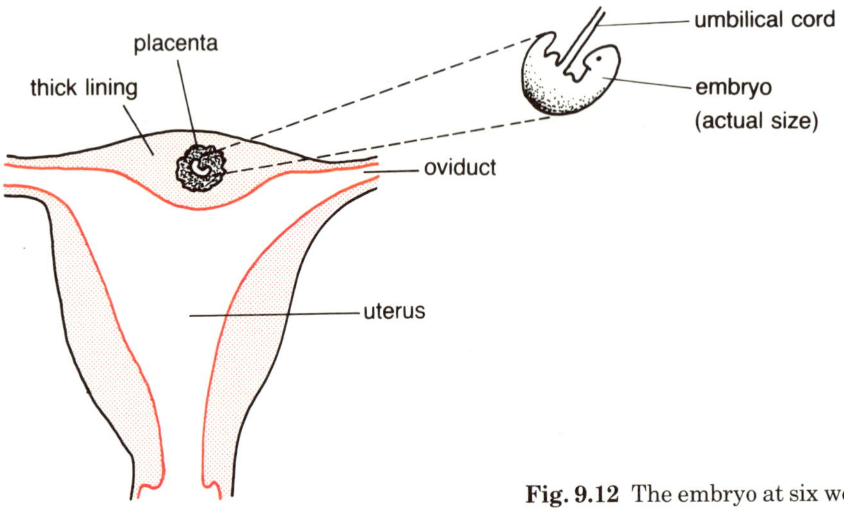

Fig. 9.12 The embryo at six weeks

At first the implanted embryo obtains food and oxygen from the uterus wall, but gradually a special organ called the **placenta** grows from tissues of the embryo and the uterus (see Fig. 9.13). The embryo is connected to the placenta by the **umbilical cord**. The embryo's blood circulates through the placenta. As it does so, it absorbs oxygen and food from the mother's blood and passes carbon dioxide and other waste products into the mother's blood. Notice, in Fig. 9.13, that the two blood systems are quite separate. The embryo's blood never mixes with the mother's blood. However, capillaries in the placenta are very close to those in the uterus wall, so substances can diffuse (move) between the two very easily.

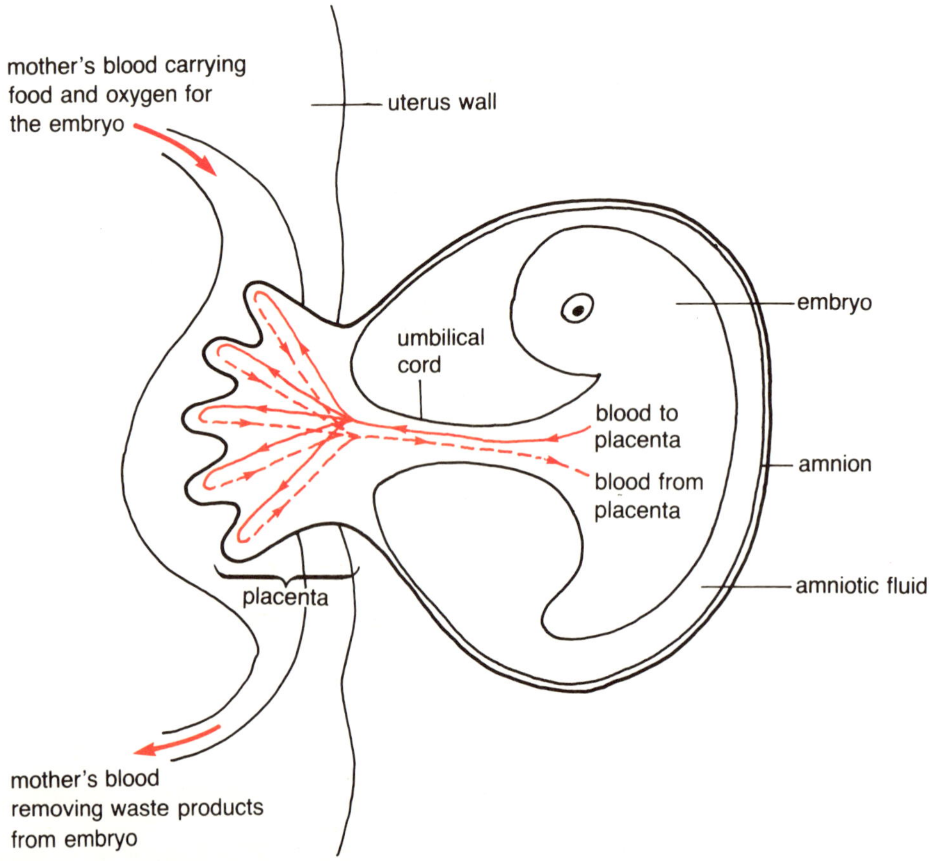

Fig. 9.13 An embryo and its placenta in the uterus

Two months after fertilization, the embryo looks like a tiny baby. It has a face, limbs, fingers and toes. It is now called a **foetus**. The foetus continues to develop inside the mother and, about nine months after fertilization, the baby is born. This period of time between fertilization and birth is called the **gestation period**. The flow diagram below summarizes the stages occurring during gestation.

FERTILIZATION ——— *gestation* ——→ BIRTH
↓ ↓
fertilized egg (zygote) ——→ embryo ——→ foetus ——→ baby

BIRTH

A few days before birth, the foetus normally positions itself with its head downwards near the opening of the uterus (Fig. 9.14).

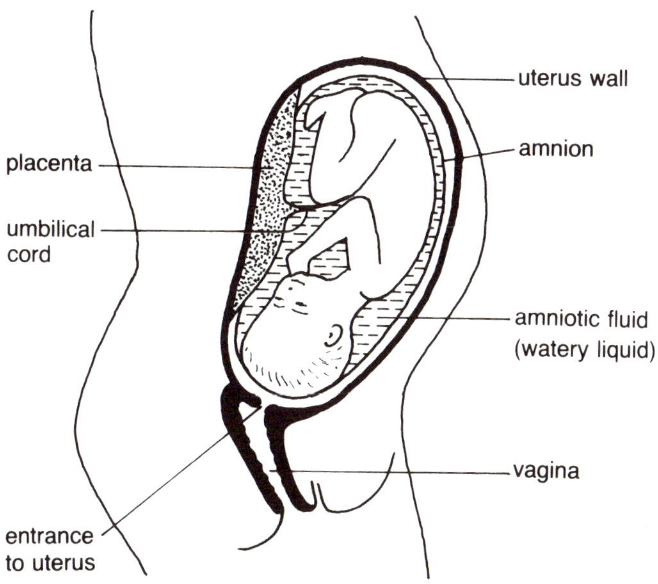

Fig. 9.14 The normal position of the foetus a few days before birth

Shortly before birth, muscles which have developed in the walls of the uterus start to make regular **contractions**. This is called **labour**. The powerful contractions push the foetus downwards and the entrance to the uterus becomes wider. The amnion bursts and the watery amniotic fluid flows out through the vagina. This is called the '*breaking of the waters*'.

As the contractions continue, the entrance to the uterus is made wide enough for the baby's head to pass through (Fig. 9.15). Once the head is out, the rest of the body slides out relatively easily.

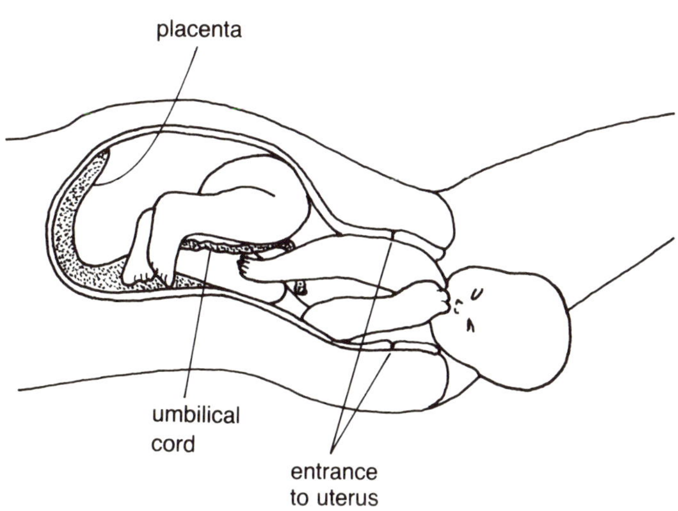

Fig. 9.15 The birth of a baby

Immediately after birth, the baby is encouraged to fill its lungs with air and cry. This ensures that the baby is breathing independently. Sometimes this requires a slap on the bottom from the midwife. The umbilical cord is then cut and tied. The remains of the cord will shrivel up, leaving the baby's **navel** (belly button). Finally, the uterus contracts again and the remains of the placenta (the **afterbirth**) are pushed out.

For animals such as fish, amphibians and reptiles, the involvement of parents ceases once the eggs are laid. But some animals, particularly birds and mammals, care for their young for quite some time after birth. Humans care for their young longer than any other animal. For most children, the period of adult care lasts until they are at least sixteen.

Quick test 9

Questions 1 to 4

Diagrams A to E show five different cells as seen through a microscope.

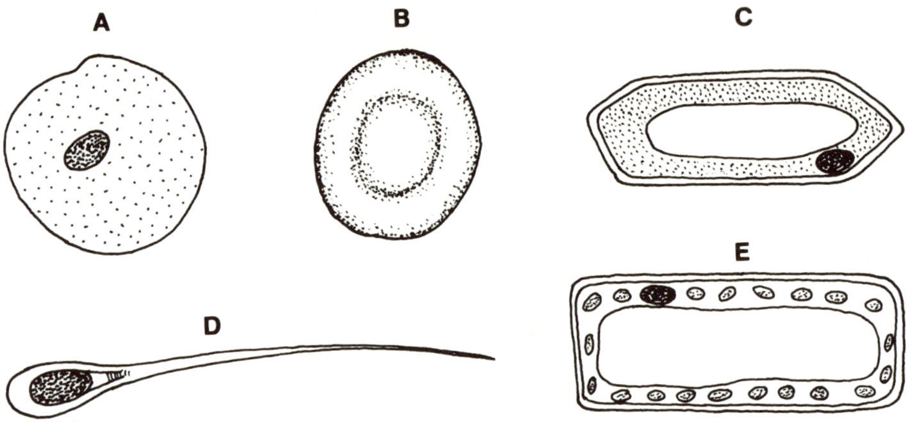

From the letters A to E, choose the one cell which
1 has no visible nucleus.
2 must be a plant cell.
3 is a sperm cell.
4 might be a female gamete.

Questions 5 to 8

The graph shows the relative growth rate of girls and boys from 6 to 18 years of age.
5 At what age are boys growing most rapidly?
6 At what age are boys growing least rapidly?
7 At what age are girls growing most rapidly?
8 At what age are girls growing least rapidly?

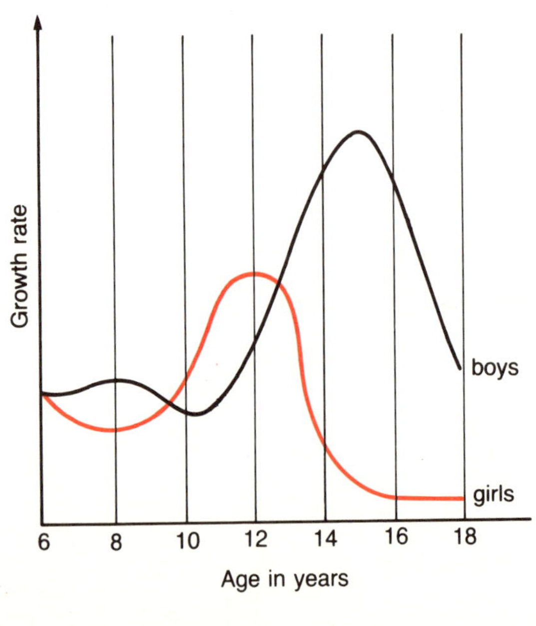

Questions 9 to 13

The diagram shows a side view of the male reproductive organs.

9 Name the part labelled A.
10 Name the part labelled B.
11 Name the part labelled C.
12 Name the part labelled D.
13 Name the part labelled E.

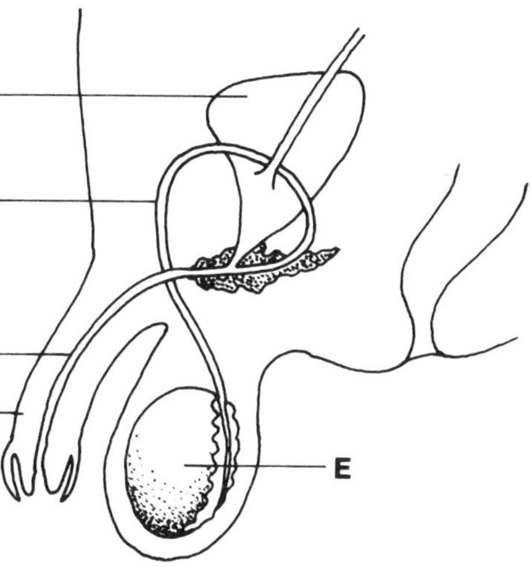

Questions 14 to 16

Look at Fig. 9.13 and then answer the following questions.

14 What is the function of the amniotic fluid?
15 What is the function of the placenta?
16 What is the function of the umbilical cord?

Questions 17 to 19

A embryo   B fruit   C gamete
D seed   E zygote

Which *one* of the words A to E above is best used to describe

17 a pollen grain?
18 a pea?
19 a peanut?

Questions 20 to 22

What are the functions of the following flower parts?

20 sepals
21 petals
22 stamens

23 The following events labelled A to E occur during sexual reproduction in a flowering plant. Arrange them in correct order.
A meiosis occurs in anther
B male nucleus fuses with ovum
C pollen tube grows down into ovary
D anther splits releasing pollen
E insect transfers pollen from anther to stigma

24 Gardeners often use methods based on asexual reproduction to produce beautiful plants. Give *two* reasons why they prefer to use these methods rather than methods based on sexual reproduction (pollination–seeds–growth).

10 GENETICS AND EVOLUTION

10.1 Introduction

Clare has dark brown hair like her mother and blue eyes like her father. Perhaps you also have some characteristics from your mother and some from your father. The way in which we inherit characteristics from our parents and grandparents is called **heredity**. The branch of science which studies the inheritance of characteristics is called **genetics**.

Fig. 10.1 Some features persist from generation to generation. Look at the similar features of father and son, Donald and Kiefer Sutherland

10.2 Chromosomes and cell division

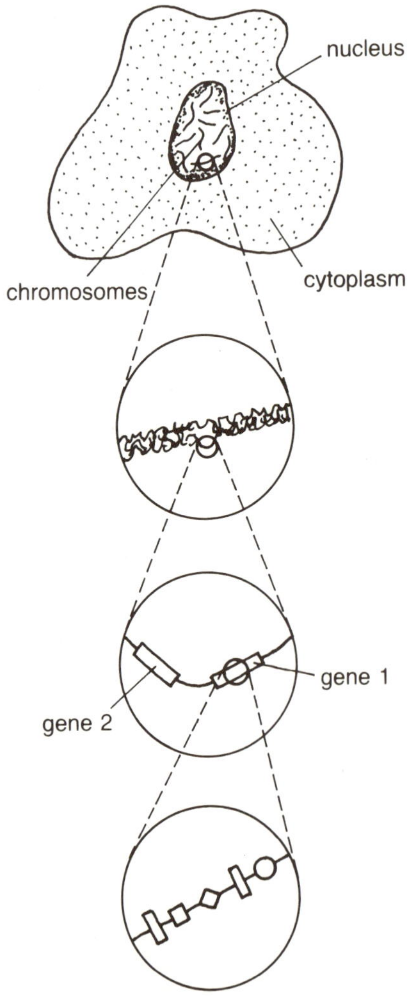

Fig. 10.2 A cell with its nucleus, chromosomes, DNA, genes and monomers

In order to understand how characteristics are passed from parents to offspring, we need to know how information is carried in cells and what happens when cells divide.

Every cell in your body contains enough information to make a complete copy of you. Normally, however, one particular cell (e.g. a nerve cell) only uses that part of the information which is needed to make a copy of itself. The information to copy is stored in long thin strands called **chromosomes** in the nucleus of the cell.

When the nucleus of a cell is stained with a dye, the chromosomes look like fine pieces of thread under the microscope. The chromosomes are made up of a complex *polymer* (see section 20.10) called **DNA** (**deoxyribonucleic acid**).

Each chromosome has thousands of shorter portions called **genes**. Each gene is responsible for making a particular protein. These proteins make up a large part of your body and the enzymes which control the chemical reactions in your body. For example, if you have brown hair, you must have a gene which makes the enzyme needed to produce brown hair pigment. Each of your genes is responsible for one of your characteristics, e.g. hair colour, eye colour, freckles, long fingers, etc.

Like all polymers, the DNA in genes is composed of small units or monomers joined together. In DNA, there are *four different monomers*. These can be joined together in millions of different ways like beads on a string. The order of the monomers in the DNA is the coded information which the cell uses to make a copy of itself.

Different organisms have different numbers of chromosomes. *Humans have 46 chromosomes in each cell*, chickens have 36, peas have 14 and fruit flies have only 8. These chromosomes can be arranged in pairs. The members of each pair look alike and carry genes which control the same characteristics. They are called **homologous pairs**. For example, the homologous pair of chromosomes which control eye colour will contain the eye colour gene at the same position. However, the two genes may not carry the same instructions. One gene might carry information for blue eyes, the other gene might carry information for brown eyes. Later, we shall see how the different information leads to only one eye colour.

In each homologous pair, one chromosome comes from the male parent and the other comes from the female parent. So, 23 of your chromosomes came from your father and the other 23 came from your mother.

CELL DIVISION

There are two different kinds of cell division–*mitosis* and *meiosis*. **Mitosis** occurs when an organism is growing or when its cells are being replaced. It occurs in the formation of all cells, *except* male sex cells (sperms, pollen) and female sex cells (eggs). **Meiosis** occurs only in the formation of male and female sex cells during reproduction.

Mitosis

Most of the time, the chromosomes in a cell are thin and difficult to see even with a microscope. But, just before cell division, the chromosomes get shorter and fatter and can often be seen with a microscope. At the same time, each chromosome makes a copy of itself. The original chromosome and its copy are joined somewhere near the middle (Fig. 10.3(b)).

The chromosomes, joined to their copies, then arrange themselves near the centre of the cell (Fig. 10.3(c)). The copies separate and the cell begins to divide (Fig. 10.3(d)). Each of the new cells has exactly the same chromosomes as the parent cell (Fig. 10.3(e)).

Notice that **mitosis produces exact copies**. This is what happens when an organism grows and when an organism reproduces **a**sexually, producing offspring which are exact copies of the parent.

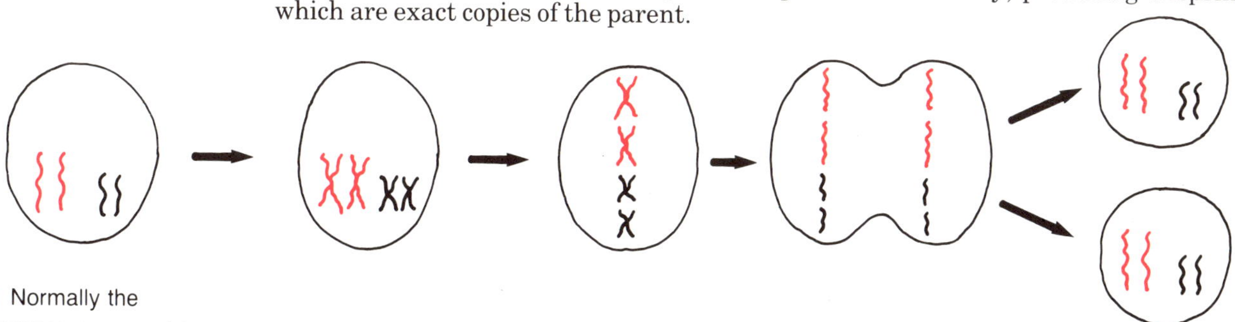

(a) Normally the chromosomes consist of single threads. The nucleus of this cell has four chromosomes – two homologous pairs

(b) Just before cell division, each chromosome makes a copy of itself

(c) Chromosomes joined to their copies move to the centre of the cell

(d) The copies separate and the cells begin to divide

(e) Each of the new cells has exactly the same chromosomes as the parent cell

Fig. 10.3 The stages in mitosis

Mitosis in human cells occurs by the process shown in Fig. 10.3, except that human cells have 46 chromosomes (i.e. *23 homologous pairs*) not four chromosomes (two homologous pairs).

During mitosis, the process of cell division is very carefully controlled. Scientists think that many cancers start when this control of cell division is lost.

Meiosis

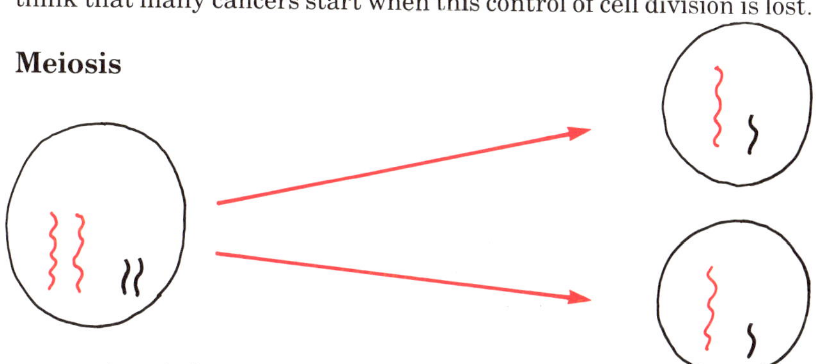

Fig. 10.4 Separation of chromosomes in meiosis

Sex cells (sperms and eggs) contain only half the normal number of chromosomes. Sex cells cannot be produced by mitosis because this would produce cells with the normal number of chromosomes.

When sex cells are produced, cell division occurs by meiosis (Fig. 10.4, p.85). In this case, one chromosome from each homologous pair is taken at random by each of the new cells.

10.3 Sexual reproduction and meiosis

Meiosis occurs during sexual reproduction. When an egg is fertilized by a sperm, the two nuclei join together. The egg and the sperm each contain only half the normal number of chromosomes. But, after fertilization, the fertilized egg will contain the normal number of chromosomes.

Figure 10.5 summarizes the process in humans. Notice that 23 chromosomes come from the mother and 23 from the father. These form 23 homologous pairs. After fertilization, the zygote starts to grow by cell division. These cell divisions involve mitosis.

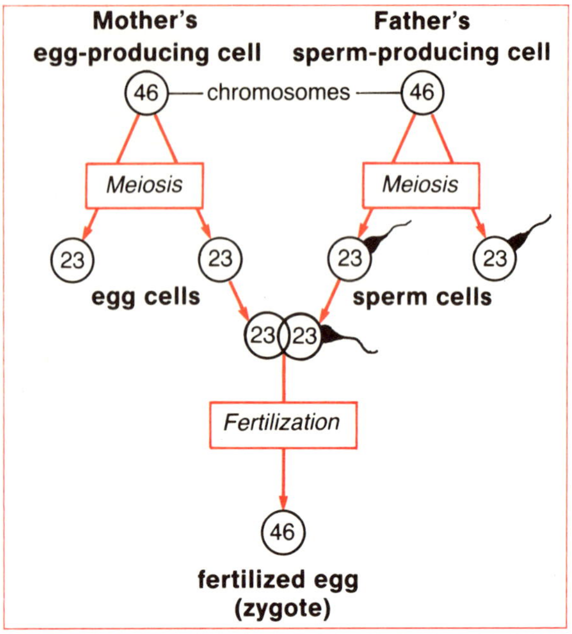

Fig. 10.5 The numbers of chromosomes involved in meiosis and sexual reproduction in humans

BOY OR GIRL?

The sex of a baby is determined by one of its 23 pairs of chromosomes. The chromosomes in this pair are called the **sex chromosomes**. There are two types of sex chromosomes. A long one called the **X chromosome** and a short one called the **Y chromosome**.

In females every cell has two X chromosomes.
In males every cell has one X and one Y chromosome.

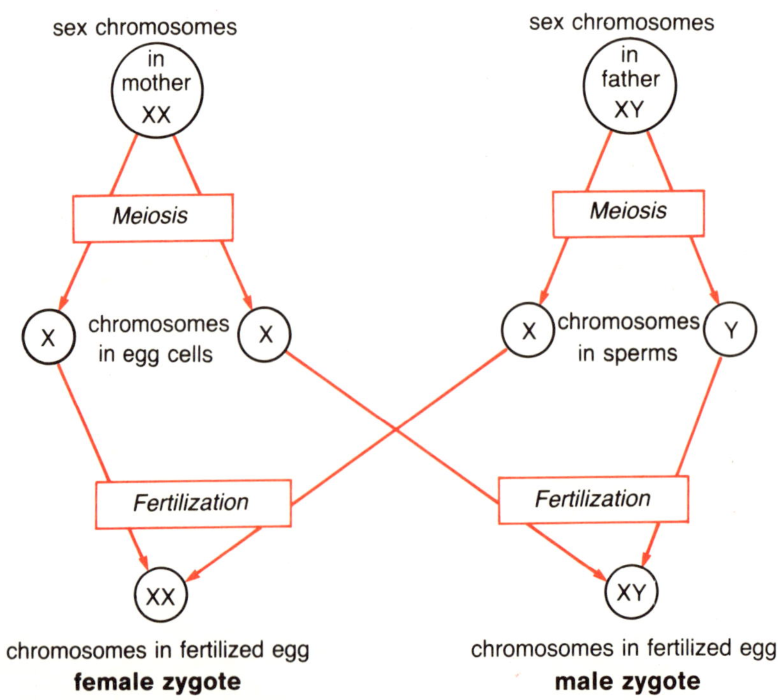

Fig. 10.6 The sex of a fertilized egg depends on the sex chromosomes

Figure 10.6 shows what happens to the sex chromosomes when:

1 eggs and sperms are produced by meiosis;
2 the eggs and sperms fuse to produce a fertilized egg.

All the eggs which the mother produces contain an X chromosome. But half the sperms from the father contain an X chromosome and the other half contain a Y chromosome. So there is an equal chance that an egg will be fertilized by an X sperm or by a Y sperm. If an X sperm fertilizes the egg, the zygote will contain two X chromosomes. This zygote will develop into a girl. If a Y sperm fertilizes the egg, the zygote will contain an X and a Y chromosome. This will develop into a boy.

10.4 Genes and genetics

During the 19th century, an Austrian monk called **Gregor Mendel** studied the way in which characteristics were passed on from one generation to the next. Mendel carried out experiments with **pea plants**. He studied the inheritance of various characteristics such as height, flower colour and seed shape. The patterns which Mendel deduced from his experiments with pea plants have been found to apply to all plants and animals, including humans.

As a result of his experiments, Mendel made some important statements. These statements are now called the **rules of genetics**:

- An organism gets its characteristics (e.g. eye colour, nose shape) from its **genes**.
- The genes for each characteristic exist in **pairs**. One gene in the pair comes from the father, the other from the mother.
- Genes may be **dominant** or **recessive**.
- If a dominant gene and a recessive gene are both present, the dominant one will decide the characteristic.

These simple rules can be used to explain how characteristics are passed on from one generation to the next. They can also be used to predict characteristics in the next generation.

EXPLAINING EYE COLOUR

Suppose a brown-eyed man and a blue-eyed woman have a baby with brown eyes. Why does the baby have brown eyes and not blue eyes?

Scientists use the word **phenotype** to *describe the characteristics of an organism.* So, in this case:

father's phenotype is brown,
mother's phenotype is blue,
baby's phenotype is brown.

Each parent has a pair of genes which control eye colour. These genes can produce brown eyes or blue eyes. We can represent the brown-eye gene with the letter **B** and the blue-eye gene with the letter **b**.

Now suppose the father has two brown-eye genes which we represent as **BB**, and the mother has two blue-eye genes which we represent as **bb**. Combinations of genes such as **BB** and **bb** are called **genotypes**. Genotypes *describe the genetic make-up of an individual.*

Figure 10.7 shows what happens to the genes for eye colour when:

1 eggs and sperm are formed;
2 fertilization takes place.

All sperms contain one **B** gene and all eggs contain one **b** gene. So, after fertilization, the baby's cells will have one **B** gene and one **b** gene. The baby's *genotype* is **Bb**.

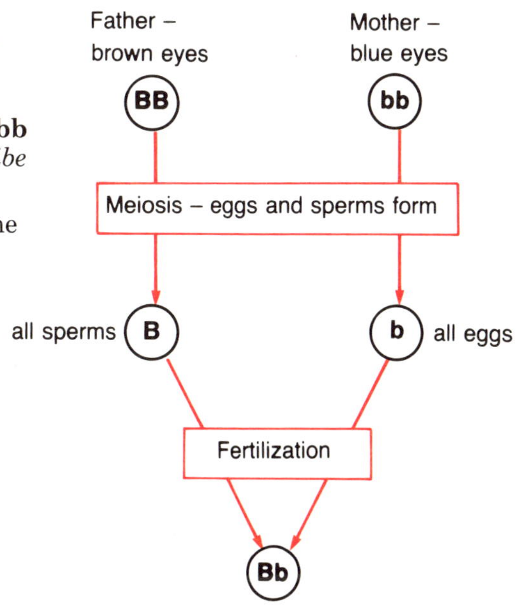

Figure 10.7 Baby – brown eyes

The baby has brown eyes, even though its cells have one blue gene, **b**. This is because the brown gene, **B**, is dominant and the blue gene, **b** is recessive. Mendel's rule stated that if a dominant gene and a recessive gene are both present, the dominant one will decide the characteristic. So the baby with a genotype of **Bb** has brown eyes. In genetics, *a dominant gene is represented by a capital letter and a recessive gene by a small (lower-case) letter.*

Notice that there are three possible genotypes for eye colour: **BB**, **Bb** and **bb**. Two of these genotypes, **BB** and **Bb**, result in brown eyes. One genotype, **bb**, gives blue eyes.

We can now use the rules of genetics to predict what happens when parents with *different eye-colour genotypes* have children. Remember that the brown-eye gene, **B**, is always dominant over the blue-eye gene, **b**. We have already seen what happens when one parent has brown eyes, **BB**, and the other has blue eyes, **bb** (Fig. 10.7). Two other possible combinations are shown in Fig. 10.8.

Draw diagrams like those in Fig. 10.8 to see what happens, on average, when:

(a) both parents have blue eyes, **bb**.
(b) both parents have brown eyes, one **BB** and the other **Bb**;

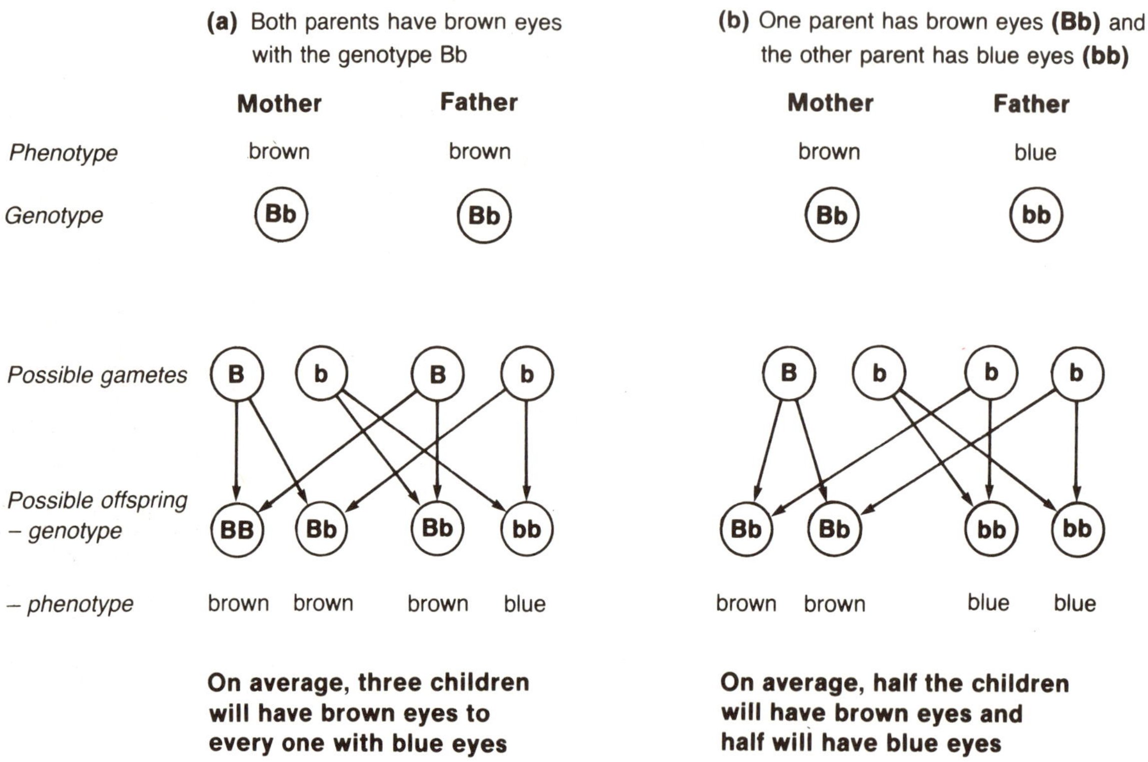

Fig. 10.8 What happens when parents with different eye-colour genotypes have children?

10.5 Why is genetics important?

UNDERSTANDING HEREDITARY DISEASES

The study of genetics has helped us to understand and treat several diseases. Most people don't mind whether they have brown eyes or blue eyes. However the genes which children inherit from their parents are sometimes faulty. In some cases, the faulty genes cause serious diseases or disabilities.

Diseases which offspring inherit from their parents are called **hereditary diseases**. The genes which cause hereditary diseases can be dominant or recessive. For example, the gene which causes **cystic fibrosis** is recessive just like the gene for blue eyes. So, if both parents carry the faulty recessive gene, their children may suffer from cystic fibrosis.

Two other diseases caused by faulty genes are **colour blindness** and **haemophilia**. These diseases are *more common in males* than females. This is because the disease is caused by a *recessive gene on the X chromosomes*. Females have two X chromosomes, but males have only one. It is unlikely that both a female's X-chromosomes will carry the recessive, disease-causing gene.

Down's syndrome is another hereditary disease. People with Down's syndrome have an abnormal extra chromosome. They have *47 chromosomes* instead of the usual 46 (23 pairs).

The diseases caused by abnormal genes can sometimes be spotted in 'family trees'. Couples with a family history of hereditary diseases often have a higher risk of passing the diseases to their children. A *genetic counsellor* can often give these couples help and advice. The counsellor may also be able to estimate the risk of the disease occurring in their children.

One of the most common methods of detecting abnormal genes is by **amniocentesis** during pregnancy. A small volume of *amniotic fluid* (refer back to section 9.9) is collected by inserting a needle through the mother's abdomen into the uterus. Laboratory tests can then be carried out on the baby's cells which are present in the fluid.

SELECTIVE BREEDING

Farmers and gardeners have been using genetics for hundreds of years. Year by year, they have taken seeds for their next crop from the most attractive, the highest yielding and the most disease-resistant plants. Farm animals and domestic animals, like cats and dogs, have also been selected and bred in the same way.

Decades of **selective breeding** have resulted in cows which yield high quantities of milk, cereal crops which are resistant to plant diseases and fruits with distinctive flavours. Nowadays, geneticists can breed varieties more systematically and advise farmers and gardeners on ways in which they can improve their animals and plants.

Fig. 10.9 Pigs (left) have been produced from wild boars (right) by centuries of selective breeding

GENETIC ENGINEERING

During the last 10 years, scientists have found ways in which they can change the genes in a chromosome. It has even become possible to remove one gene and replace it with another. These techniques are called **genetic engineering**. Genetic engineering has already been used to:

- produce antibiotics by adding a particular gene to bacteria;
- produce insulin and growth hormones by adding genes to bacteria.

At the present time, scientists are looking for ways in which they can replace the 'faulty' genes which cause hereditary diseases such as haemophilia. The possibilities for genetic engineering are endless, but some of them raise difficult moral questions. For example, suppose it was possible to make people permanently happy by genetic engineering. Do you think we should use the process for this sort of purpose?

10.6 Evolution

Have you ever wondered how living things first began. Where did all the many plants and animals come from?

Some people believe in **creation**. They believe that the Earth and all its living things were created by God. This theory of creation says that organisms are more or less the same now as when they were created.

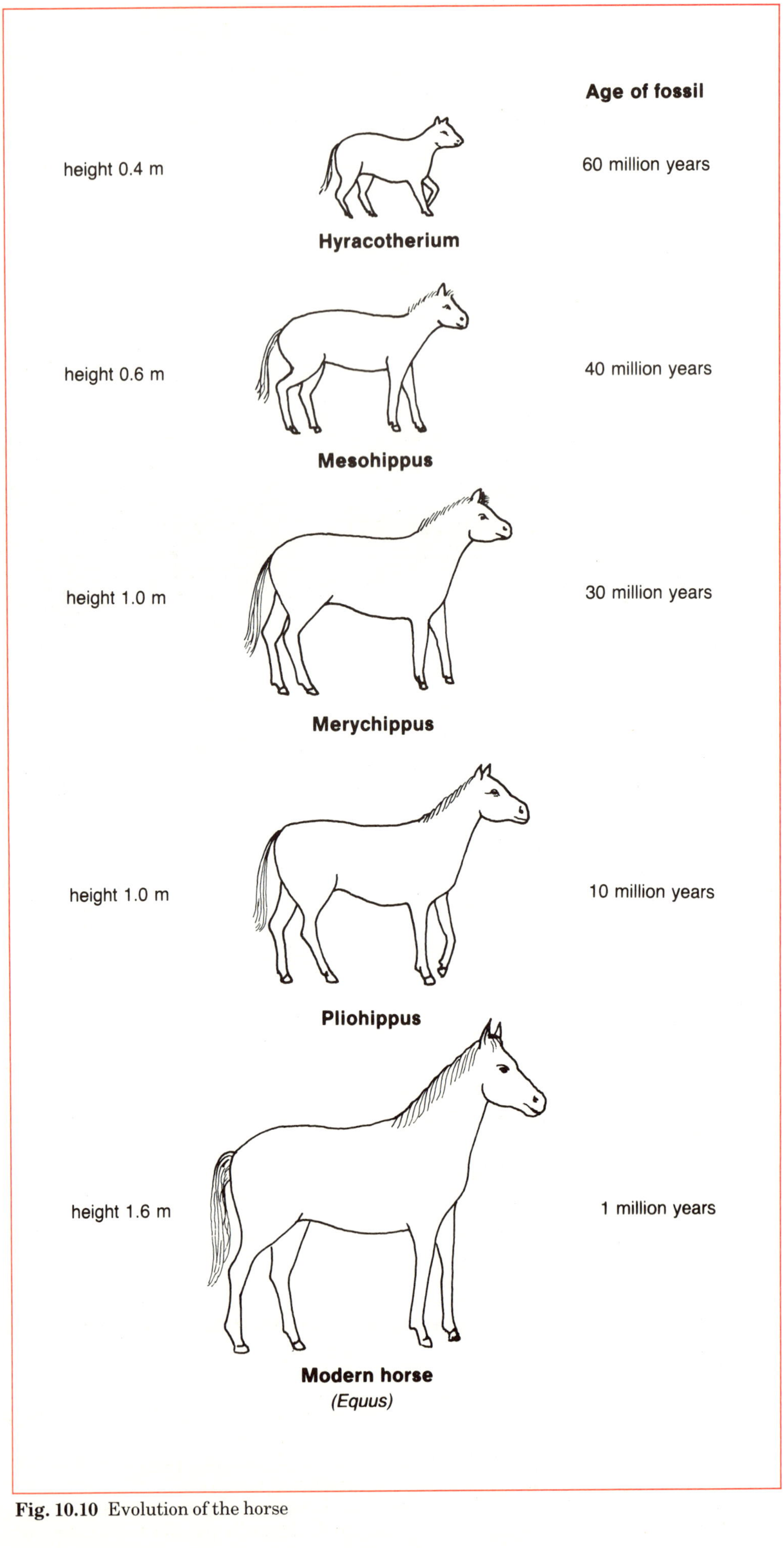

Fig. 10.10 Evolution of the horse

Other people believe in the **theory of evolution**. This is the idea that the first living things on Earth were very simple. Slowly, over millions of years, these simple creatures developed (evolved) into the thousands of organisms in the world today. The theory of evolution suggests that the very first single-celled creatures appeared on the Earth over 3000 million years ago. The theory also suggests that these simple creatures had themselves 'evolved' from chemicals which were being formed all the time in warm seas.

EVIDENCE FOR EVOLUTION

The main evidence for evolution comes from **fossils**. Fossils are the remains of animals and plants that lived long ago. When an animal or plant dies, it usually decays. Sometimes, however, the animal or plant is buried in mud which eventually becomes sedimentary rock. The animal or plant may then be preserved in the rock for millions of years.

Fig. 10.11 Fossil ammonites in a sample of rock from the lower Jurassic period (195 to 172 million years ago). The sample was found at Robin Hood's Bay, Yorkshire.

By studying these fossils, scientists can work out what the animal or plant was like when it was living. Using a technique called carbon dating (see section 22.6), they can also work out when the animal or plant lived. From the fossil record, a detailed picture can be built up of the time at which different plants and animals appeared on the Earth. The fossil record also shows that plants and animals have developed and evolved very slowly over millions of years. Figure 10.10 (opposite) shows how the modern horse has evolved over 60 million years.

The first human fossils come from rocks which are about one million years old. Figure 10.12 compares the skull of one of these fossils (*Homo erectus*) with that of modern man (*Homo sapiens*). Do you think that modern man has evolved from *Homo erectus*?

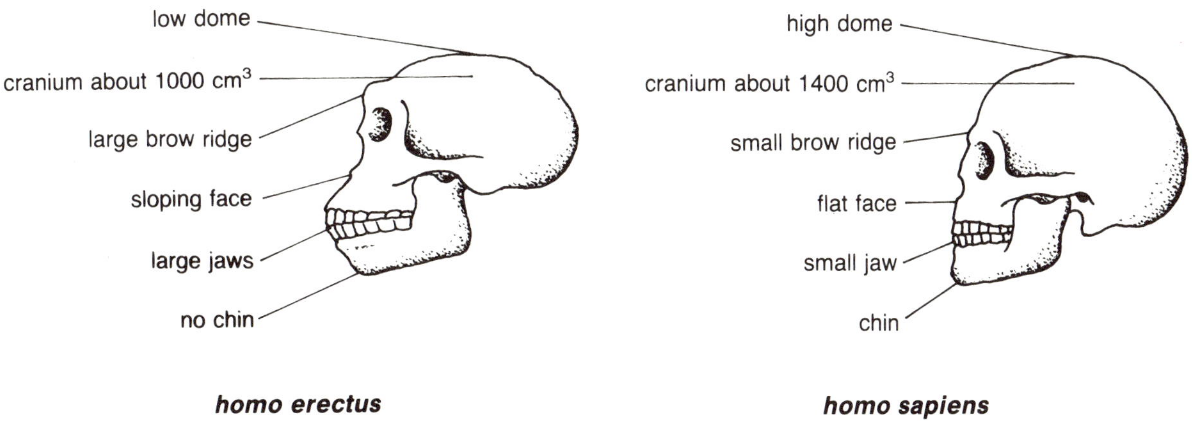

Fig. 10.12 Comparing the skulls of modern man, *Homo sapiens*, and *Homo erectus*

10.7 How has evolution occurred?

In 1831, a young scientist called **Charles Darwin** was appointed naturalist on HMS *Beagle*. During the next five years, Darwin sailed around the world in HMS *Beagle* taking part in important scientific and geographical expeditions. Darwin visited many different countries where he studied the animals and plants. He gradually became convinced that the various species which he observed had come into being by a slow process of evolution.

In 1859, Darwin published his observations and ideas in a book called *The Origin of Species*. In this book, Darwin put forward evidence to support the theory of evolution and also a theory to explain how evolution may have occurred.

Fig. 10.13 Charles Darwin (1809–82)

DARWIN'S THEORY OF NATURAL SELECTION

Darwin's theory of natural selection involved three key ideas:

- **variations within a species;**
- **survival of the fittest;**
- **adaptation of organisms.**

Variations within a species

Even within the same species, there are many differences between the individuals. Look at all the boys or all the girls in your class. Features such as height, weight, hair colour, hair texture, skin colour, speed at running and intelligence vary greatly from one person to another. These differences between individuals are called **variations**. Variations within a species can occur in four ways:

1 **Meiosis**: Meiosis 'shuffles' the chromosomes. When gametes (eggs and sperms) are formed by meiosis, the pairs of chromosomes divide in a completely random way (refer back to section 10.2).

2 **Fertilization**: Fertilization brings together new sets of chromosomes from the father and mother.

3 **Environmental influences**: For example, poor soil will result in stunted plants and a poor diet will affect a person's weight.

4 **Mutation**: A mutation is a sudden change in the genetic make-up of an organism. For example, the structure of a gene may be changed by harmful chemicals or by radioactivity. Alternatively, bits of chromosomes may be lost or extra bits may be added during abnormal meiosis or fertilization. For example, children who suffer from Down's syndrome have an extra chromosome.

Mutations are occurring all the time. Very often the mutations go unnoticed. Sometimes they are harmful, causing mental and physical handicap. Occasionally, mutations produce useful new characteristics. In this case, the animal or plant affected has advantages over other members of its species.

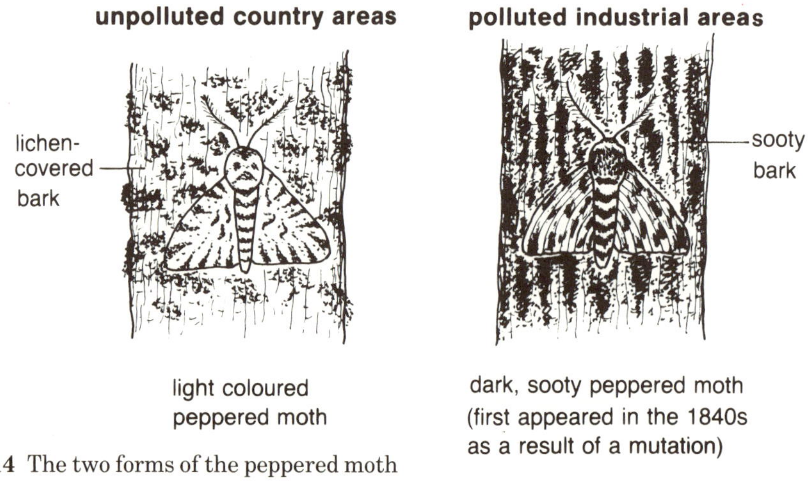

Fig. 10.14 The two forms of the peppered moth

A good example of *beneficial mutation* is provided by the peppered moth (Fig. 10.14). The peppered moth inhabits woodland areas. For most of the time, it rests on tree trunks. In unpolluted areas, the lighter form is well camouflaged by lichen-covered trunks. The darker form is easily seen and is taken by predatory birds such as thrushes. In polluted areas where the trunks of trees are blackened by soot, the darker mutant moth is better camouflaged and is more likely to survive.

Survival of the fittest

In the course of his travels, Darwin noticed the wide variations within a species. Some were taller, others were fatter or could run faster. Darwin also noticed that both animals and plants had a continual struggle to survive.

–They had to avoid **predators**.
–They had to avoid **disease**.
–They were in **competition** for food, space and shelter.
–They had to survive the **climate**.

The animals and plants that survive are usually the fittest. They are less likely to suffer from disease and are more able to find food and escape from predators. They have favourable variations in their characteristics which give them a better chance of survival. For example, tall plants will receive more light and faster deer will escape from lions. Darwin summed up these ideas using the term '**survival of the fittest**' (Fig. 10.15).

In turn, the survivors would be more likely to reproduce and pass on the favourable characteristics to their offspring. The whole process is called **natural selection**.

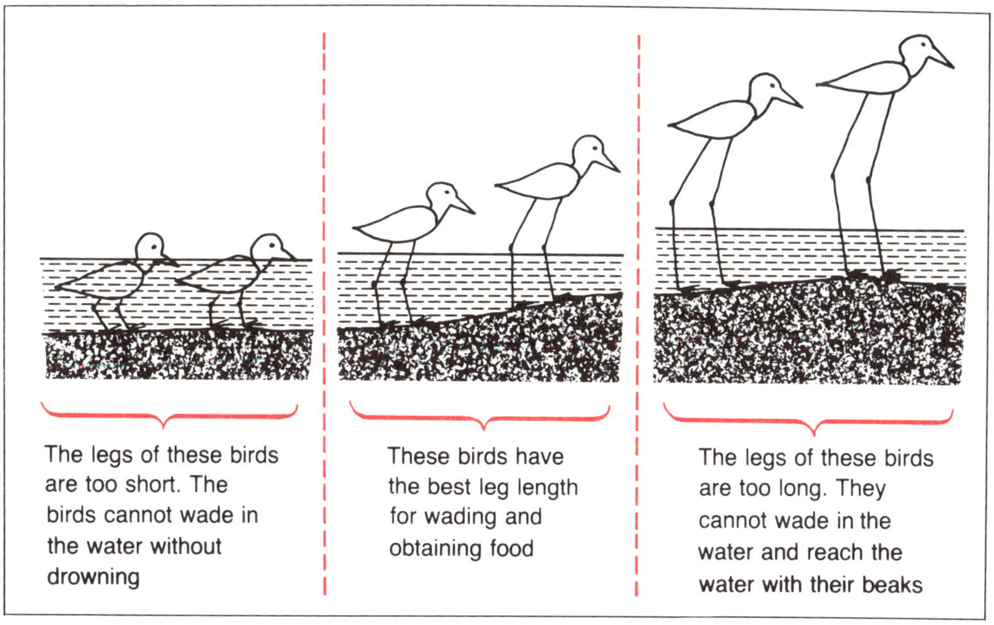

Fig. 10.15 Survival of the fittest: waders with the right leg length for the depth of water in their area are more likely to survive

Adaptation of organisms

The variations which help a species to survive are most likely to be passed on to the next generation. This is because those organisms with the most favourable characteristics are most likely to reproduce. For example, if thicker winter coats help rabbits to survive, thick-coated animals are most likely to live long enough to produce young. So later generations will tend to inherit thicker winter coats.

By this process of natural selection, a species evolves so that individual animals and plants are better suited to their environment. The *changes which take place and allow an organism to survive more easily* are called **adaptations**.

The key ideas in Darwin's theory of evolution are summarized in Fig. 10.16.

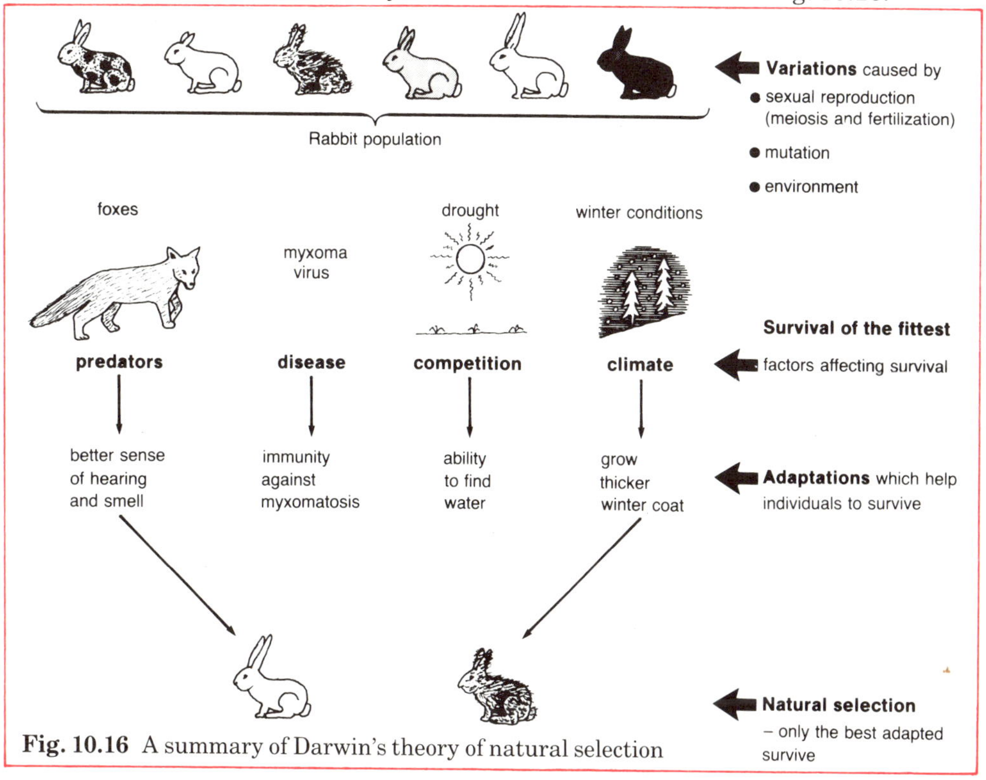

Fig. 10.16 A summary of Darwin's theory of natural selection

Quick test 10

1 Cells contain information which controls how they develop. This information is contained in
A the cell wall. C the cytoplasm.
B the chloroplasts. D the nucleus.

2 Kangaroos have 12 chromosomes in each body cell. This means that each sperm cell of the kangaroo will have
A 6 chromosomes. C 18 chromosomes.
B 12 chromosomes. D 24 chromosomes.

3 Which one of the following statements is correct?
A Chromosomes are made of DNA and contain genes.
B Genes are made of DNA and contain chromosomes.
C Genes are made of chromosomes and contain DNA.
D DNA is made of genes and contains chromosomes.

4 Which *one* of the following is *least* likely to bring about evolution?
A artificial selection
B mutation of genes
C temporary changes in the environment
D naturally occurring radiation

5 In a breed of cattle, the gene for horns, **n**, is recessive to the genes for no horns, **N**. Hornless cows (genotype **NN**) are mated with horned bulls (genotype **nn**). What proportion of the calves will be hornless?
A none B half C three quarters D all

6 The fusion of two sex cells in a plant is called
A pollination B fertilization C meiosis D germination

Questions 7 to 9

Human sex chromosomes may be represented as X and Y. The sex chromosomes of parents may be represented as (XX) or as (XY).

7 Which parent's sex chromosomes are represented as (XX)?
8 What are the possible sex chromosomes of female egg cells?
9 What are the possible sex chromosomes of male sperms?

Questions 10 to 13

The table below shows some external characteristics of two organisms which look very similar.

	Honey bee	**Hoverfly**
Body	3 segments	3 segments
Legs	3 pairs	3 pairs
Wings	2 pairs	1 pair
Colour	yellow and black stripes	yellow and black stripes
Length	1.5 cm	2 cm
Sting	present	absent

A predator of insects will not eat either of these organisms even though the hoverfly is harmless.

10 Explain the reason for the predator's behaviour. (3 marks)
11 What is the meaning of the term 'genetic mutation'? (1 mark)
12 Explain how genetic mutations in the ancestors of the hoverfly account for the similarities between it and the bee. (2 marks)
13 Mutations in disease-causing bacteria are a serious medical problem. Suggest a reason for this. (1 mark)

(*LEAG*, 1988)

Questions 14 to 17

A boy has two rabbits. The male is grey and the female is white. He has allowed them to mate so that he can make some money from selling baby rabbits. ALL the baby rabbits were grey.

Figure. A

When the grey baby rabbits had grown, he let two of them mate several times. One quarter of their babies turned out to be white.

Figure B

14 Which coat colour was dominant? (1 mark)

15 Explain why the first two rabbits (shown in Fig. A) did not have any white babies. (2 marks)

16 Explain why the grey offspring were able to have white babies (see Fig. B). (2 marks)

17 White rabbits are easier to sell, and fetch a higher price than grey rabbits. Suggest how the boy could arrange mating so that only white babies were produced. (2 marks)

(*LEAG* (part question), 1988)

Questions 18 to 20

Rabbit populations which live in different environments have evolved in different ways. The table below contains some information about four different rabbit populations.

Population	**A**	**B**	**C**	**D**
ear size	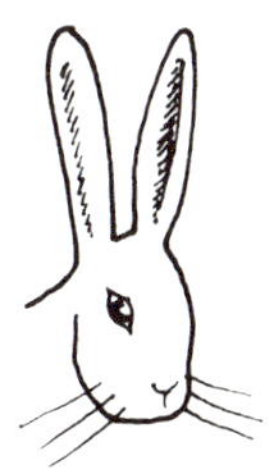			
habitat	hot desert	open grassland	evergreen forest	cold desert
main feeding time	night	early morning and late evening	day	day

18 State *two* reasons why the rabbits in population **A** have evolved with very large ears. (4 marks)

19 Rabbit populations **B** and **C** both live in a temperate climate. The temperature never gets very hot or very cold. Explain why they have evolved with different sized ears. (4 marks)

20 State *one* feature of the rabbits in population **D** not shown in the table which you would expect to see on animals which live in a cold environment. (1 mark)

(*LEAG*, 1988)

11 ECOSYSTEMS AND ECOLOGY

11.1 Ecosystems as habitats and communities

Look under a stone, or in a pond, or in a garden. Notice that organisms exist in groups rather than as single individuals. There might be several woodlice under the stone, several stickleback in the pond and several daisies in the garden. These *groups of organisms of the same species which are found in one particular area* are called **populations**. For example, we might talk about the population of humans in Liverpool, the population of woodlice under a stone or the population of rabbits in a wood.

Usually there will be populations of many different species within a given area. For example, under a stone there may be woodlice, mosses, fungi and ants. These *different populations living together in an area* are called a **community**. The *area in which the community lives* is called its **habitat**. Habitats can be very large, e.g. a forest or a city, much smaller, e.g. a garden or a pond, or tiny, e.g. a small stone or a puddle.

In any habitat there are many different interactions between the organisms in the community and the habitat itself. These interactions include finding and providing food, water and shelter. In fact, each organism depends upon the habitat and the community for its survival.

The combination of a habitat and a community living together is called an ecosystem. The study of ecosystems is called ecology.

For example, the soil, the rotting vegetation and the trees in a wood together with all the other plants and animals which live in the wood make up a woodland ecosystem.

The key words and ideas introduced in this chapter so far are summarized in Fig. 11.1 which shows a simple ecosystem in an aquarium.

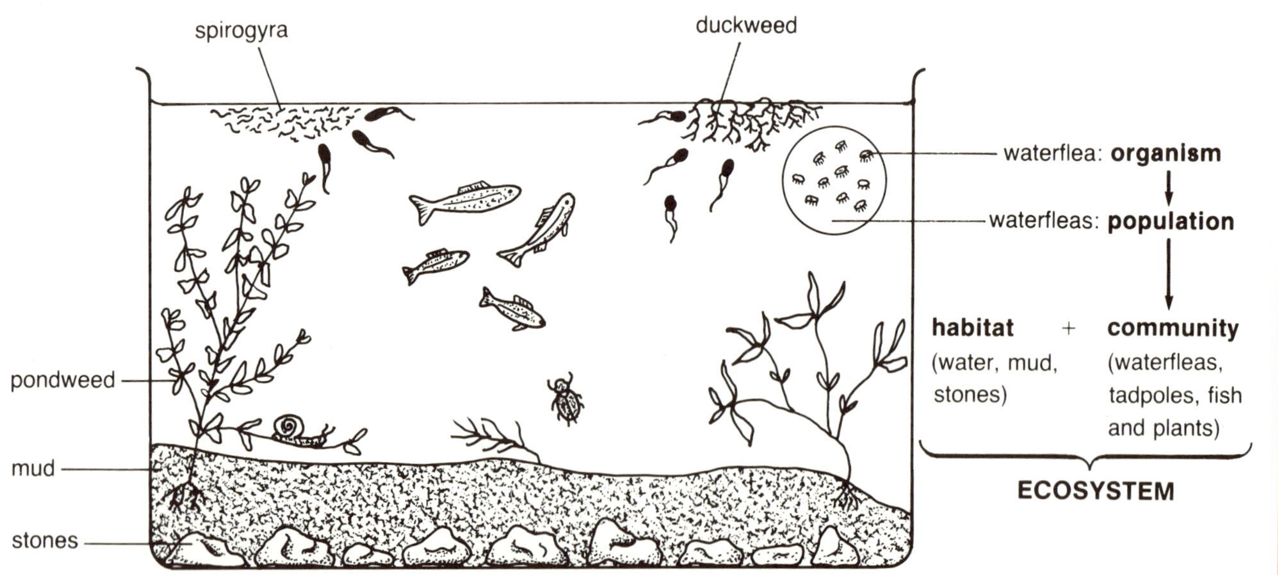

Fig. 11.1 A simple ecosystem in an aquarium

Ecosystems are not usually separate. They interact with each other. For example, flies and insects from other ecosystems may settle and feed on the surface of the aquarium in Fig. 11.1. Even ecosystems as far apart as Europe and Africa are linked by migrating birds, e.g. swallows, which feed in both areas depending on the time of the year.

11.2 The growth of populations

If a species is well adapted to its habitat, the population will start to grow. Look at Table 11.1. This shows the number of mice which inhabited a newly built barn. The results are plotted on a graph in Fig. 11.2.

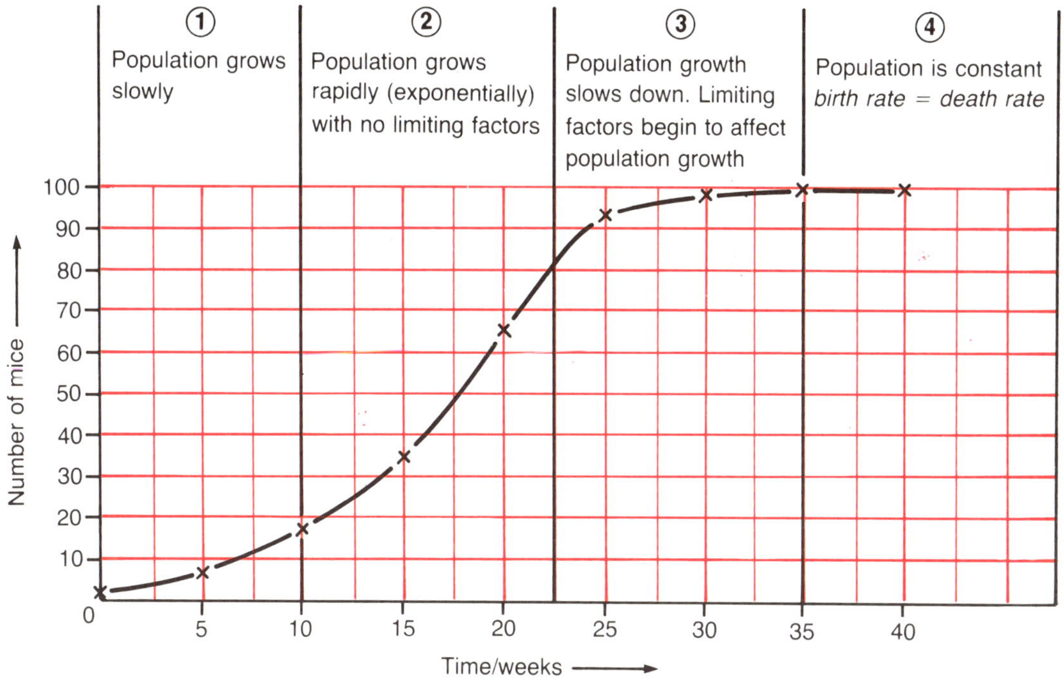

Fig. 11.2 Size of the mouse population in a newly built barn

Table 11.1 The number of mice which inhabited a newly built barn

time/weeks	0	5	10	15	20	25	30	35	40
number of mice	2	7	17	35	66	94	99	100	100

Notice (from the graph) that the number of mice increases very rapidly at first. For the first 20 weeks, the population of mice seems to double every four or five weeks. This is called **exponential growth**. Fortunately for the farmer who owns the barn, this does not go on forever. The growth rate slows down after about 23 weeks and the number in the population becomes steady after 35 weeks.

All populations grow in a similar way to the mice in the barn. Growth occurs in four distinct phases as outlined at the top of Fig. 11.2.

FACTORS AFFECTING POPULATION GROWTH

The maximum size of a population of organisms may be affected by various factors. These include:

- **food supplies**
- **water supplies**
- **space**
- **waste products** from the organisms produce poisonous substances and cause pollution
- **disease**
- **predators**
- **climate**–may become too cold or too wet
- **light**–particularly important for plants in order that they can photosynthesize, grow and reproduce

Which of these factors might have limited the growth of the mice population in the barn?

When the number of organisms in a population reaches a constant value, the rate at which new organisms are born (**the birth rate**) equals the rate at which organisms are dying (**the death rate**).

11.3 The human population

Fewer factors limit the human population than limit the populations of other organisms. Although space, food and water supplies are a problem in some parts of the world, they are not so in many places. Medicines, particularly antibiotics, have reduced the problems caused by many diseases. Predators are no real problem to humans and extremes of climate can be counteracted with appropriate shelter and clothing.

During the last century, improved hygiene, better diets and increased medical care have enabled people in most parts of the world to live longer. At the same time, the birth rate has increased because there are more healthy men and women able to reproduce. This has brought about a dramatic increase in the world population since 1850 (see Fig. 11.3).

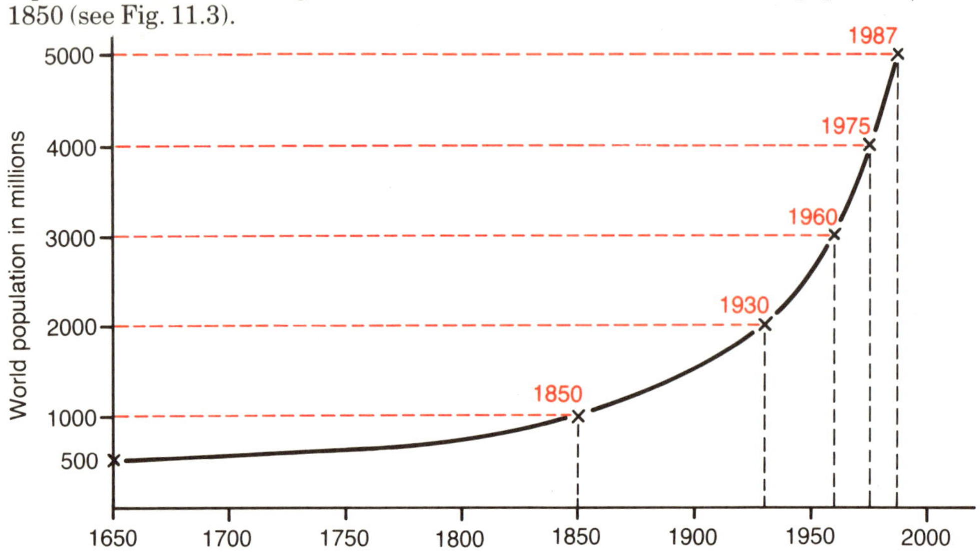

Fig. 11.3 Growth of the human population since 1650

Population growth varies from one country to another. In many developed countries, such as Britain, France and the USA, methods of birth control have almost brought the population to a steady level. But in the developing countries of Africa and Asia, the population continues to grow and grow. The world population growth is still exponential. Notice how the human population graph resembles the first two phases of the mouse population graph in Fig. 11.2.

The human population graph has not begun to level off yet, but the population explosion cannot go on forever. Eventually one of the limiting factors listed earlier will make it level off–shortage of food, overcrowding, pollution or, perhaps, disease. Many people believe that the only way to avoid these disasters is to introduce reliable methods of birth control throughout the world.

11.4 Interactions in ecosystems–food chains

Some of the most important interactions in any ecosystem involve feeding patterns. Plants are the only living things which can photosynthesize and *produce* their own food–they are called **producers**. All other living things depend on plants for their food. They *consume* the food which plants have produced or animals which have eaten plants–they are called **consumers**. Figure 11.4 shows an example of the relationship between producers and consumers.

Table 11.2 Producers and consumers

Producer	*First consumer*	*Second consumer*	*Third consumer*
grass	cow	human	–
algae	waterflea	stickleback	pike
grass seeds	mouse	owl	–
seaweed	crab	seagull	–

Table 11.2 shows three more examples of producer/consumer combinations. Notice that producers are always plants. Very often, the first consumers are **herbivores**, animals that eat *only plants*. The second and third consumers are either **carnivores**, animals that eat *only animals* (meat), or **omnivores**, animals that eat *both plants and animals*.

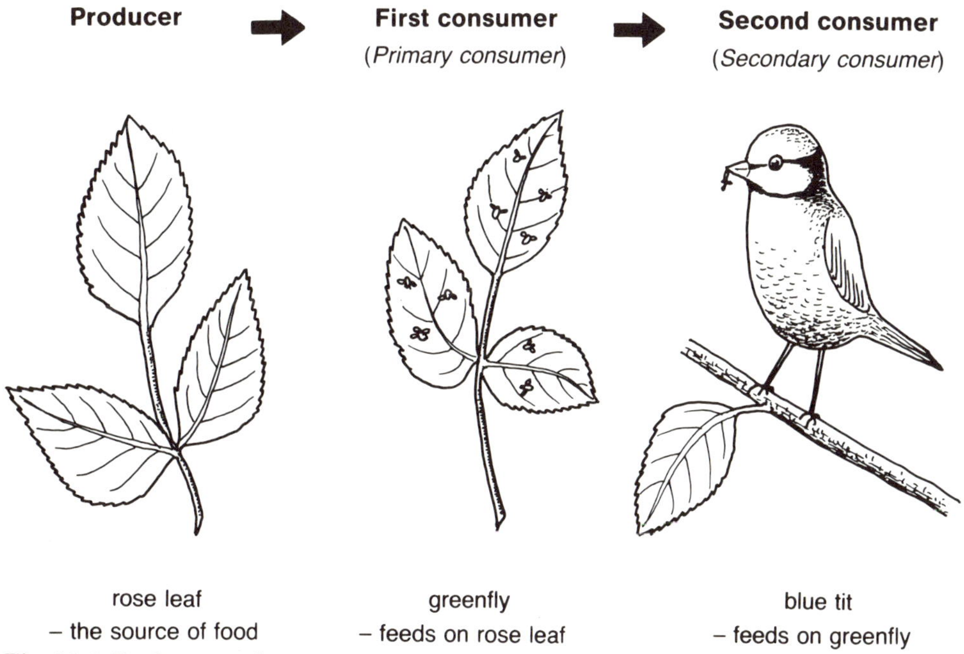

Fig. 11.4 Producers and consumers

Sequences of producers to consumers, such as

grass seeds ⟶ mice ⟶ owls

are examples of **food chains**. A food chain has a minimum of three organisms. It always begins with a producer (a green plant) and the following links in the chain are all consumers. Animals, such as owls, which hunt and eat other animals besides being carnivores are also called **predators**. The animals, which they eat, such as mice, are the predators' **prey**. The food chain always ends with an animal, such as an owl, which has no predator. These ideas are illustrated in Fig. 11.5.

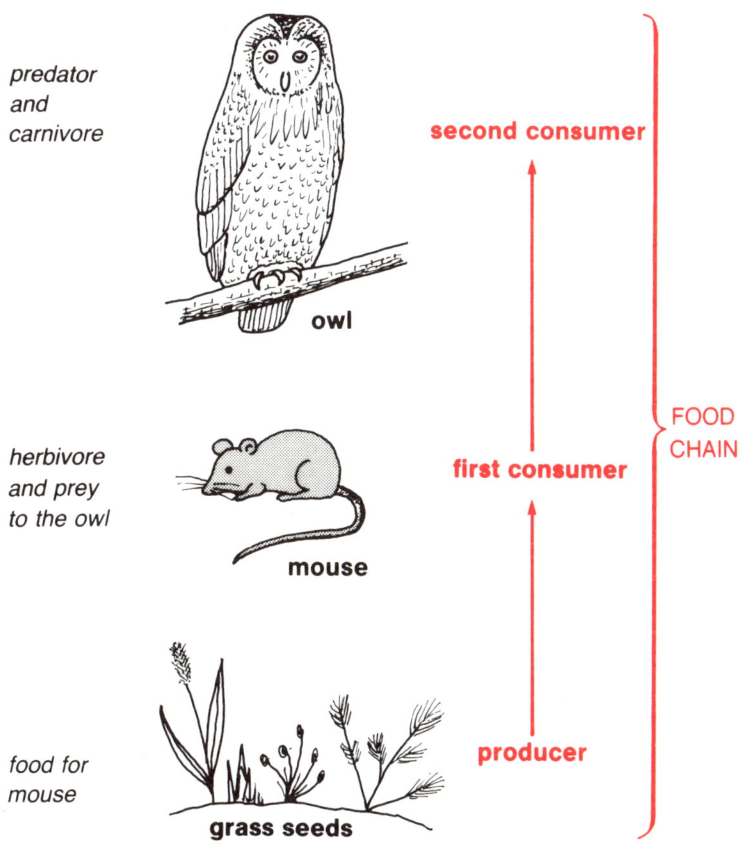

Fig. 11.5 Producers, consumers, predators and prey in a food chain

11.5 Food chains and food webs

In an ecosystem, feeding patterns are not usually as simple as those shown in Table 11.2 and Figures 11.4 and 11.5. For example, mice will eat food other than grass seed, such as fruit and small insects. The owl will also eat other prey. In any community of animals and plants, complex feeding patterns will emerge. Many food chains will exist and some of these will be interlinked. These interlinked food chains are described as a **food web**.

Figure 11.6 shows a food web for a simple pond community.

Which organisms are producers?

Which organisms are consumers?

Which animals are prey only?

Which animals are predators only?

Which animals are both predators and prey?

Which animals are herbivores?

Which animals are carnivores?

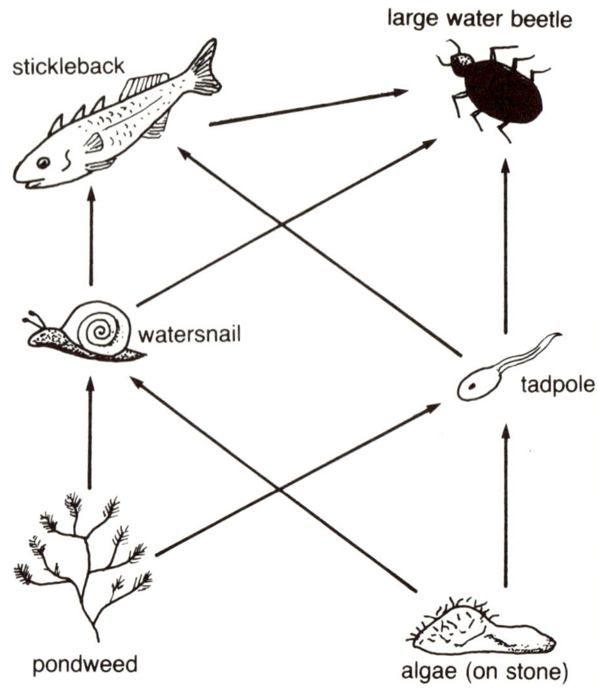

Fig. 11.6 A food web for a simple pond community

PYRAMIDS OF NUMBERS

As you pass along a food chain, the number of each type of organism usually gets less. An illustration of this is given in Fig. 11.7. Along a stretch of river there may be only one pair of herons. These herons feed on hundreds of small fish in the river which in turn are supported by thousands of tadpoles. The tadpoles feed on millions of algae growing on the stones of the river bed. Diagrams like that in Fig. 11.7 are called **pyramids of numbers**.

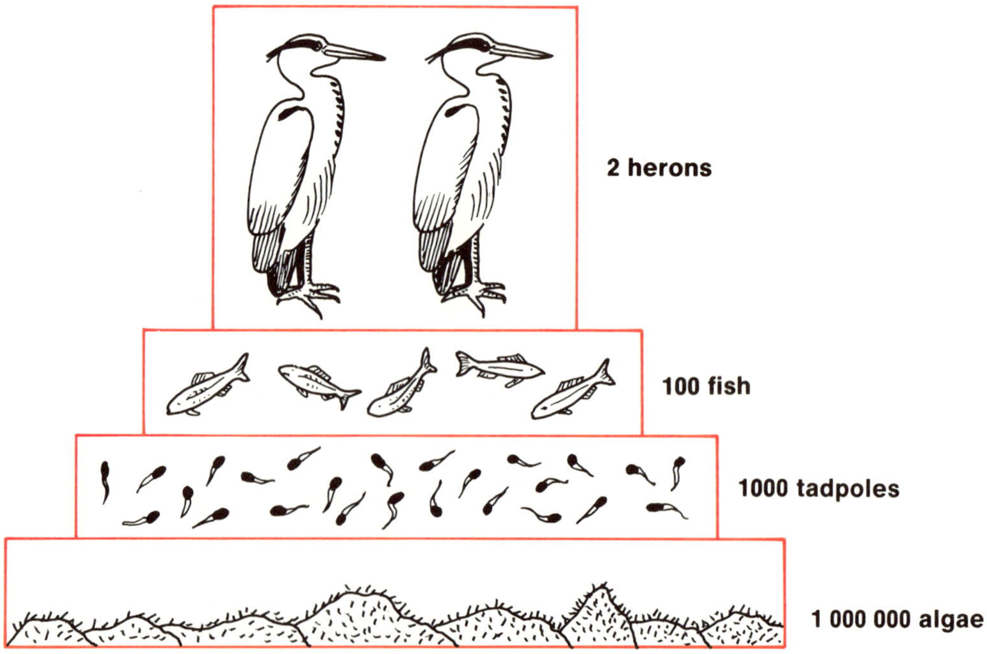

Fig. 11.7 A pyramid of numbers for a food chain in a river

Sometimes, the numbers in a pyramid are converted to masses. This shows the reduction in *the mass of living material* (**biomass**) at each stage along the food chain. The result is a **pyramid of biomass** like that in Fig. 11.8.

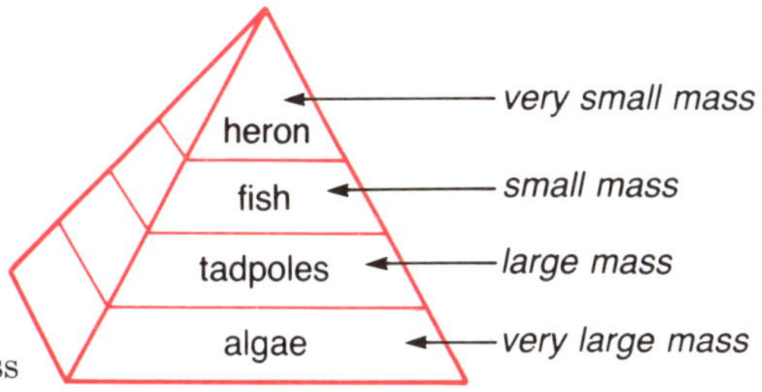

Fig. 11.8 A pyramid of biomass

Pyramids like these can be drawn for all food chains. They help to explain why:

- top carnivores like herons, eagles and foxes are rare;
- the biomass of each species is ultimately limited by the ability of green plants at the bottom of the pyramid to produce food;
- there is a great waste of energy along a food chain. For example, only a small percentage of the energy in the algae eventually helps the herons to grow. Most of the energy in the algae is lost along the food chain as heat, in urine and in faeces. Less energy is wasted if the food chain is shorter. This explains why humans can get more energy from cereals by eating them directly, than by feeding the cereals to cattle and then eating meat (see Fig. 11.9).

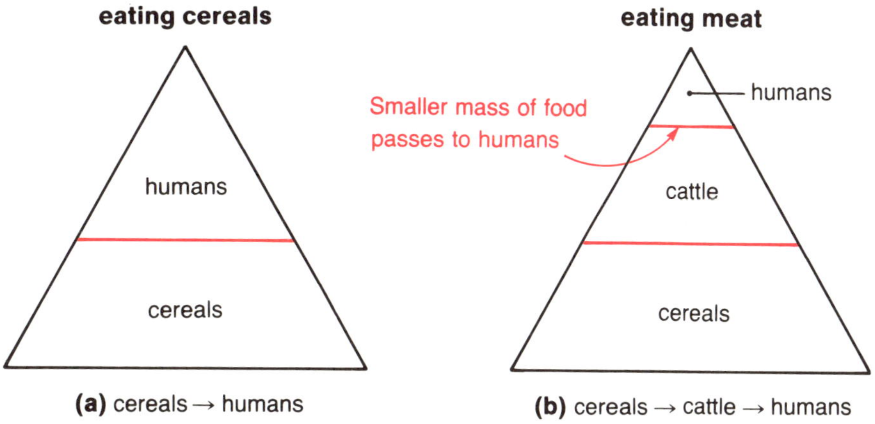

Fig. 11.9 Pyramids of mass for two comparable food chains

11.6 Energy chains and important cycles

The source of energy for every food chain is, of course, the sun. Energy from sunlight allows green plants (producers) to photosynthesize at the start of the food chain. The sun's energy is converted into chemical energy in carbohydrates, fats and proteins in the plants. The energy in these foods is then passed along the food chain to animals (consumers). Eventually, all the energy is lost from the chain as the animals and plants die and decay (Fig. 11.10, overleaf).

Superimposed on this energy chain, there is a continual cycling of the elements and compounds in plants and animals, including carbon, nitrogen, water and minerals.

THE CARBON CYCLE

The cycle of carbon compounds through the air, plants, animals and decaying remains is usually called the **carbon cycle**. This is shown in more detail in Fig. 11.11 (overleaf). Notice the following points:

- Photosynthesis (chapter 2) and respiration (chapter 6) play an important part in the carbon cycle. Plants gain carbon through photosynthesis and lose it through respiration. Animals gain carbon by eating plants and lose it through respiration.
- Carbon dioxide is removed from the atmosphere by photosynthesis and returned to the atmosphere by respiration, combustion and the decomposition of dead plants and animals. This decomposition is speeded up by bacteria and fungi which feed on the decaying remains. For this reason, fungi and bacteria are sometimes called **decomposers**. They play an important part in recycling carbon, nitrogen, minerals and water by releasing carbon dioxide and nitrogen into the air and nitrogen compounds, water and minerals into the soil.

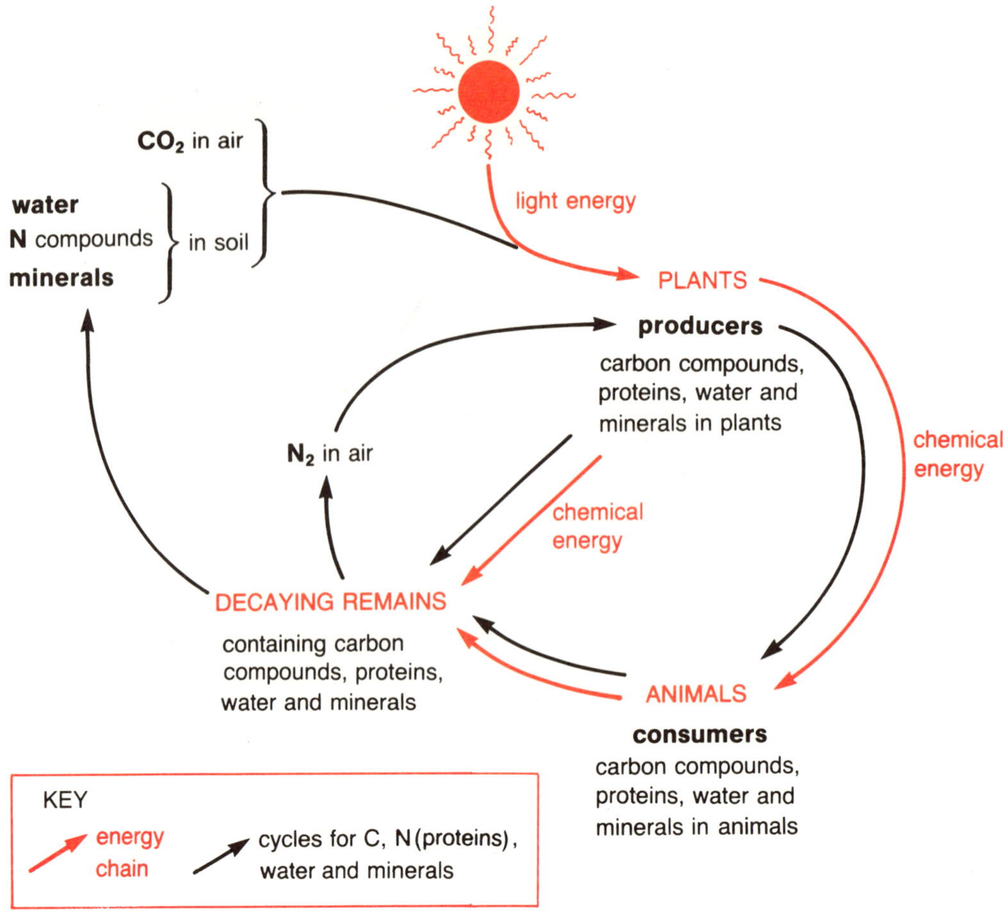

Fig. 11.10 The energy chain and cycles for carbon, nitrogen, water and minerals

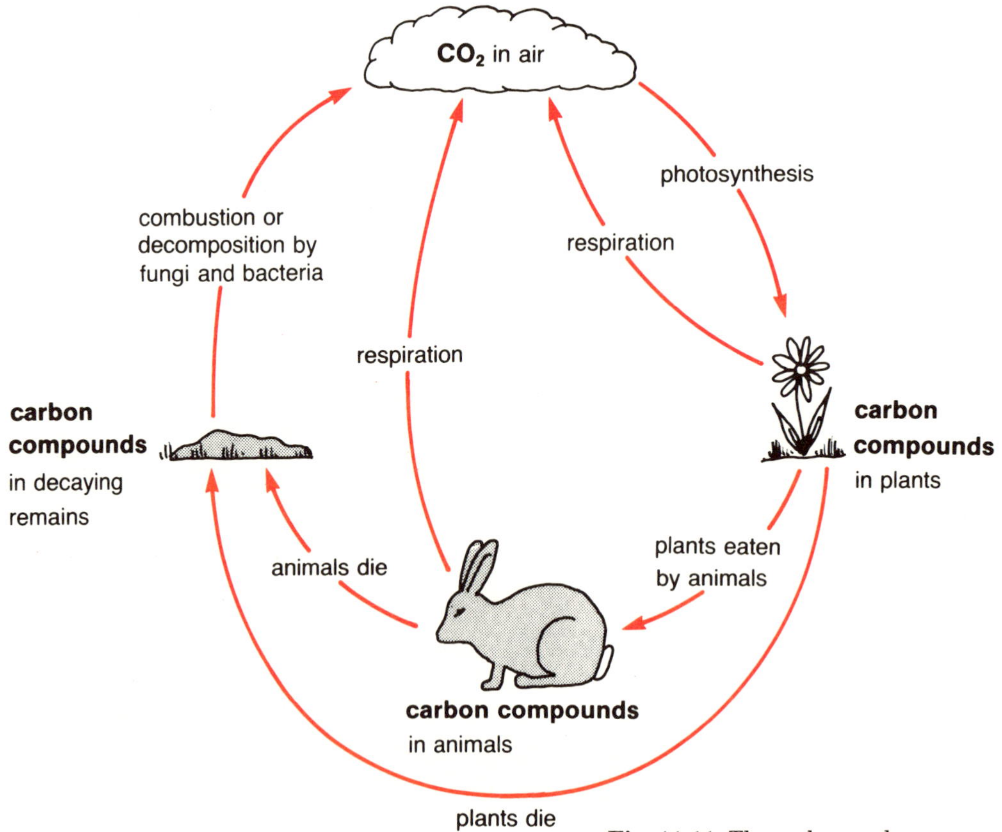

Fig. 11.11 The carbon cycle

Under natural circumstances, the amount of carbon dioxide in the atmosphere would stay about the same. Unfortunately, the carbon dioxide balance is being disturbed by the activities of human beings. This is leading to problems such as the 'greenhouse effect' (see section 14.5). The cycling of nitrogen compounds through plants and animals is discussed more fully in section 19.7 and the essential features of the water cycle are considered in section 14.7.

Quick test 11

Questions 1 to 3

The graph below shows the number of yeast cells in a vat of beer during fermentation.

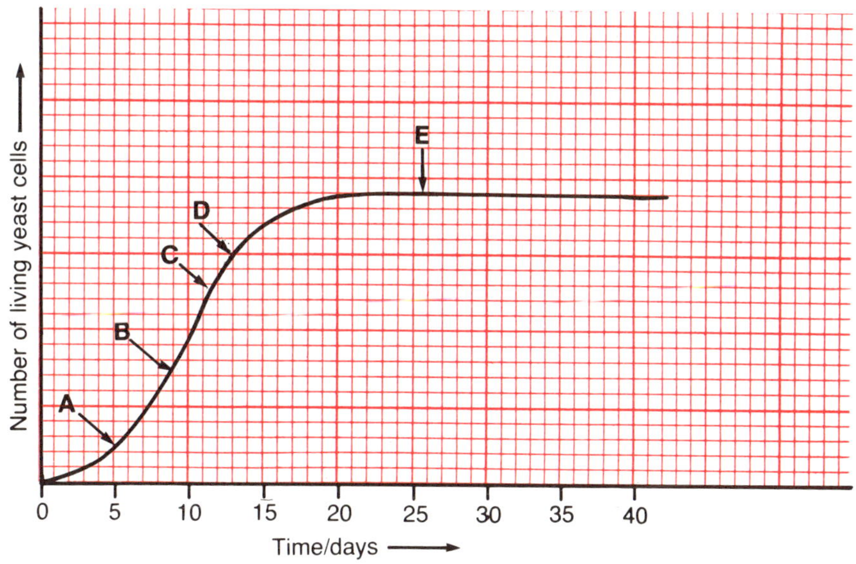

Which letter, A–E, identifies the time when

1 the yeast cells are dying at the same rate as they are being produced?
2 the yeast cells are multiplying at the fastest rate?
3 there are half as many cells as there are after 13 days?

Questions 4 to 7

Here is a simple food chain:

4 Which of the organisms in the chain is a producer?
5 The hare gets its energy by eating grass. From where does the grass get its energy?
6 What name do we give to animals that eat only meat?
7 What happens to the numbers of organisms as you go further up this food chain?

Questions 8 to 13

The diagram below shows how different living things depend on others.

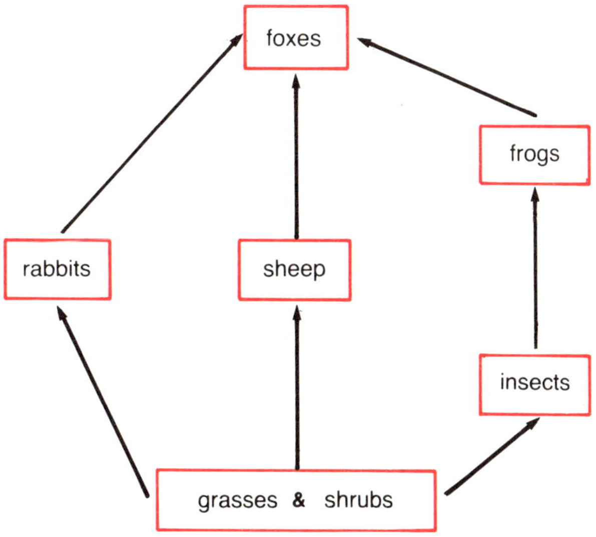

8 What is the name or term given to this type of diagram? (1 mark)

9 Which group would contain the smallest number of individual living things? (1 mark)
10 Which group would contain the greatest total weight of living things? (1 mark)
11 Which box contains the primary producers? (1 mark)
12 Where do these primary producers get their energy from? (1 mark)
13 If the rabbit population was killed off by disease, what two effects could this have on sheep farming in the area? (2 mark)
(*WJEC*, 1988)

Questions 14 to 16

The diagram shows a wheat field with a hedge.
Land up to one metre away from the hedge has received just as much seed and fertilizer as the rest of the field and has been just as well cultivated.

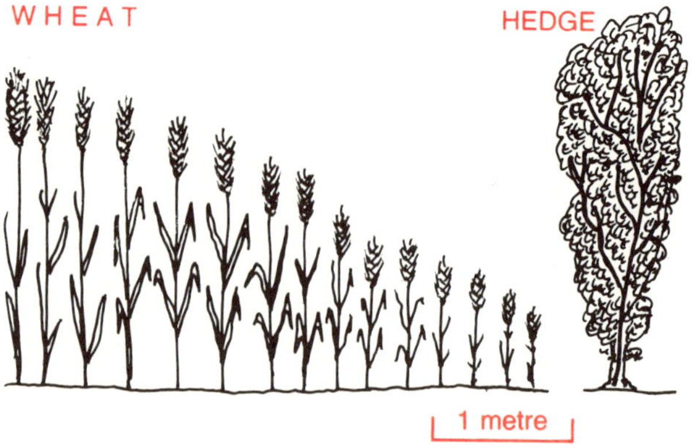

14 Suggest *three* reasons why the wheat does not grow so well between 1 and 3 metres from the hedge. (3 marks)
15 Why does a good variety of wild plants grow close to the hedge but nowhere else in the field? (2 marks)
16 Lots of hedgerows have been torn up so that more crops can be grown. How does tearing up hedgerows damage the environment? (1 mark)
(*NEA*, 1988)

Questions 17 to 23

The diagram shows part of the constant recycling of materials which occurs in nature.

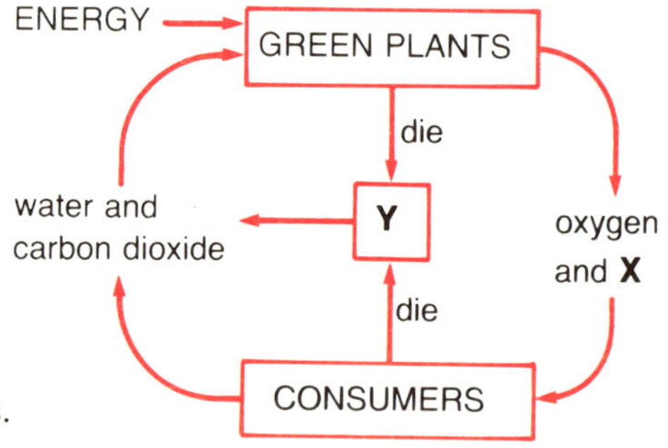

17 What is the energy source which keeps the whole system going?
18 **X** represents an important group of energy-storing foods. What is this group called?
19 Name one member of this group.
20 The producers of food are all green plants. What makes them green?
21 What do we call the process in which green plants use energy to make food?
22 What do we call the living organisms labelled **Y**?
23 How does the amount of energy leaving the cycle compare with the amount of energy entering it? (*NEA*, 1988)

Questions 24 to 28

The diagram represents the flow of energy through a food chain.
24 Where does the energy in the system come from?
25 Explain why grass is called the primary producer.
26 How much energy is passed on to
(a) the grasshopper?
(b) the chicken?
(c) the human?
27 At each step, energy is lost. Give *two* examples of how it is lost.
28 Use the diagram to explain why meat (animal food) is more expensive to produce than vegetables (plant food).
(*LEAG*, 1988)

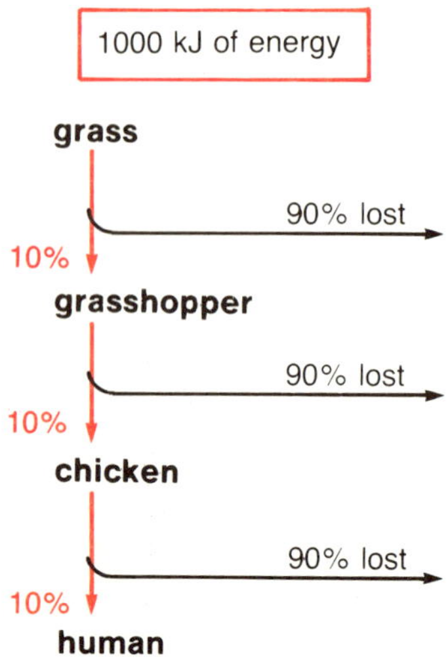

12 OUR EFFECT ON THE ENVIRONMENT

12.1 Stable and unstable ecosystems

In a well-established ecosystem, such as a large park, an open moorland or a beechwood, the number of organisms will rise and fall according to the time of year (see Fig. 12.1).

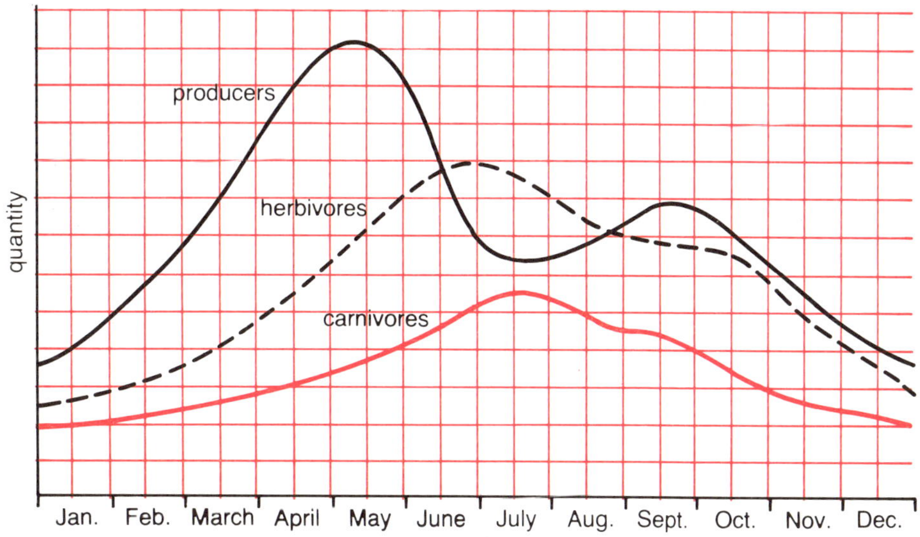

Fig. 12.1 The rise and fall of producer, herbivore and carnivore populations in a stable pond ecosystem during one year

Points to notice in Fig. 12.1:

1 The number of producers increase until April when herbivores begin to check their increase.

2 The number of herbivores increase until May/June when carnivores begin to check their increase.

3 As the amount of light and the temperature begin to fall in October, the numbers of all organisms begin to fall to winter levels. Lower light and temperature levels mean reduced rates of photosynthesis in plants. This results in fewer producers which means less food for herbivores, so fewer herbivores survive. In turn, fewer herbivores results in fewer carnivores.

Although the populations within an established (stable) ecosystem fluctuate in this way, they are in fact very similar at one particular time of year from one year to the next. Habitats with a well-balanced community like this are **stable ecosystems**.

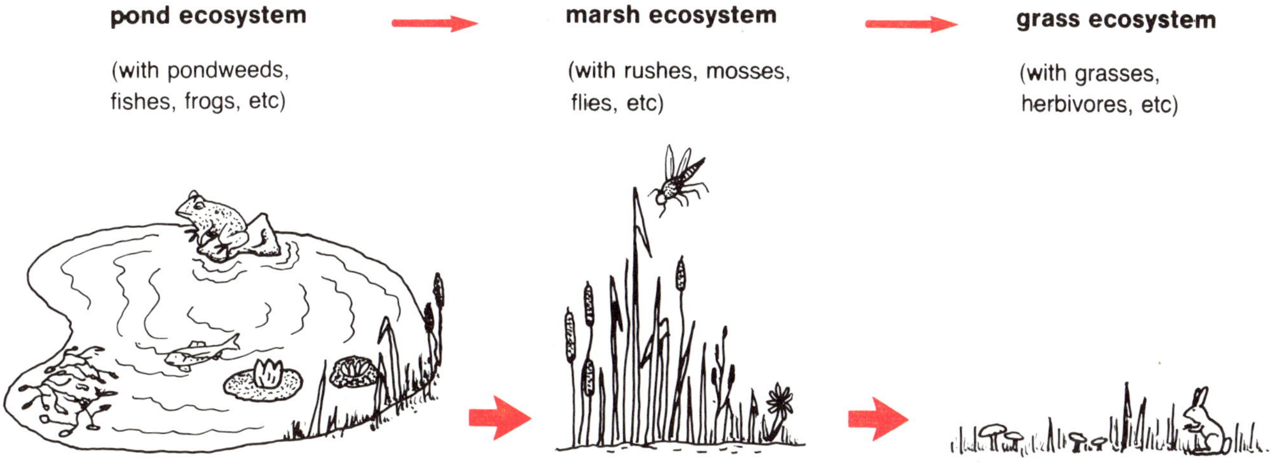

Fig. 12.2 Change in an *unstable* pond ecosystem

Sometimes, however, the whole balance within a community in an ecosystem can change. This may happen naturally when one dominant population 'out-competes' another or because of a change in the environment, for example when a pond is silting up (see Fig. 12.2, previous page).

When there are large changes in the environment, as are shown in Fig. 12.2, the ecosystem is **unstable**.

Although ecosystems and environments can change naturally, the main causes of instability are activities of human beings. Many of our disruptive effects on the environment fall into two areas:

1 **Agricultural practices**: Throughout the world, vast areas of woodland, marshland and heathland have been cleared in order to grow crops. This has destroyed entire ecosystems. In addition to this, deforestation (clearing of forests) has sometimes resulted in soil erosion and pesticides have been used to kill unwanted plants and animals. Modern mechanized farming has resulted in artificial unnatural ecosystems (see section 12.2).

2 **Pollution**: Various forms of pollution have damaged communities, habitats and food webs. Smoke from factories has killed lichens and, in the worst-affected areas, whole forests have been affected by acid rain. Industrial chemicals have been discharged indiscriminately into the air and into rivers and this has damaged animals, plants and habitats (see section 12.3).

Our effects on ecosystems and on the environment have been appreciated more fully during the last few years. Fortunately, steps are now being taken to conserve ecosystems and protect the environment.

12.2 Agricultural practices

Modern agricultural methods have allowed humans to produce increasing amounts of food. This has involved:

- ploughing which aerates the soil, improves the drainage and turns organic matter, such as stubble, into the soil to decay;
- breeding better plant and animal species (section 10.5);
- using fertilizers to increase soil fertility (section 19.6);
- using pesticides to remove the pests which attack cattle and crops.

Fertilizers and pesticides have been responsible for significant changes in ecosystems. We must now consider these in more detail.

FERTILIZERS

When plants are grown year by year on the same land, the soil becomes depleted of vital elements. This results in weak and stunted plants. Most farmers get round the problem of soil depletion by using fertilizers. Fertilizers add to the soil those elements removed by crops. Three of the most important elements which are needed to keep the soil fertile are **nitrogen**, **potassium** and **phosphorus**.

Fig. 12.3 'Organically grown' produce is widely available today. Such produce comes from farms which use only organic fertilizers.

There are two types of fertilizer–organic and inorganic.

Organic fertilizers

Organic fertilizers are obtained from plants and animals. They include bone meal, manure and compost. Leguminous crops, such as clover and peas, are sometimes ploughed into the soil as organic fertilizers because they are rich in nitrogen. Farming methods which use only organic fertilizers are described as **organic farming**.

Inorganic fertilizers

Inorganic fertilizers are obtained from non-living (inorganic) materials such as rocks, minerals and nitrogen in the air. Millions of tonnes of inorganic fertilizers are used every year. They include compounds such as ammonium nitrate, ammonium sulphate and potassium nitrate.

Table 12.1 A comparison of organic and inorganic fertilizers

	Organic fertilizers	**Inorganic fertilizers**
Examples	manure, compost	ammonium sulphate, potassium nitrate
Cost	cheap	expensive
Ease of use	awkward–bulky and sticky	easy to use as powder or granules
Speed of action	slow	rapid
Effect on ecosystem	provide food for decomposers such as earthworms, fungi, ants and bacteria	can harm decomposers and other small insects

Table 12.1 compares organic and inorganic fertilizers. Notice that inorganic fertilizers can disrupt an ecosystem by harming small insects and decomposers in the soil. The excessive use of fertilizers has also resulted in problems in our rivers and lakes. The fertilizers dissolve in rain water and get washed into streams and rivers. This enrichment of waterways with minerals such as fertilizers is called **eutrophication**. Once in the waterways, the fertilizers encourage the growth of bacteria, algae and water plants. These organisms increase exponentially (refer back to section 11.2) and deplete oxygen dissolved in the water. Eventually, all the oxygen is used up. Without oxygen, the bacteria, algae and plants die and decay and the river becomes a stinking sewer.

Despite these problems, we could not manage at present without inorganic fertilizers. Without them, we could not grow enough food to feed the ever-increasing world population. The manufacture of fertilizers and the world's food supply problem are considered further in sections 19.5 and 19.6.

PESTICIDES

Pests are organisms which compete with humans for food or spread disease. They include weeds, rats, mice and, worst of all, insects like locusts, mosquitos, aphids and caterpillars.

There are three main methods of controlling pests:

- **Chemical control**
  This involves using a chemical which poisons and kills the pest. The chemical poison is called a **pesticide**.
- **Biological control**
  This involves using a natural enemy (a predator) to control the pest.
- **Mechanical control**
  This involves using machines and labour to remove the pest or to prevent the population of the pest increasing.

These three methods of pest control are summarized and compared in Table 12.2. Notice that both chemical control using pesticides and biological control using natural predators can disrupt food chains and damage ecosystems.

Fig. 12.4 Pesticide being sprayed on to a crop from a low flying aeroplane (Photograph courtesy of WHO)

Table 12.2 Comparing the methods of pest control

Method of pest control	**Chemical**	**Biological**	**Mechanical**
How does it work?	**Pesticide** (chemical) kills the pests	Natural enemy (**predator**) controls the pest numbers	Machines or labour control the pest numbers
Examples	• **Weedkillers** (herbicides) are used to control weeds. Some are **selective** (e.g. broad-leaved weedkillers destroy dandelions and daises, but not the grass, in a lawn.) • **Insecticides**, such as DDT, have been used to control locusts and mosquitos. • **Poison** is used to kill rats and mice.	• Cats are used to control populations of rats and mice. • Ladybirds are welcomed by gardeners because they eat aphids.	• Weeds are controlled by hoeing or ploughing. • In the home, scraps of food are not left around to attract mice and insects and rooms are regularly cleaned. • Traps can be used to kill mice and control insects.
Advantages	Quick acting	1 Natural method of control 2 Safer than chemical control, because it does not introduce toxic chemicals into the environment	1 Natural method of control 2 Least likely to interfere with food webs and ecosystems (provided it is not on a large scale)
Disadvantages	1 Expensive 2 Kill harmless and helpful organisms as well as pests, e.g. pets, ladybirds, insects which pollinate flowers 3 Pesticides (e.g. DDT) get into food chains where they can accumulate and damage organisms further along the chain.	1 Once the predator has killed all the pests, it will look for other prey (e.g. cats will hunt small birds). 2 Interferes with feeding patterns in the food web. This can have unexpected effects.	1 Time consuming 2 Machinery/labour may be expensive.

12.3 Pollution

Some of the worst damage to our environment is caused by pollution. Pollution is caused by waste materials or waste energy from the activities of humans. The word pollution normally brings to mind waste materials such as sewage, pesticides and CFC's (chlorofluorocarbons), but pollution also includes excessive noise (e.g. aircraft noise) and waste heat (e.g. from power stations).

The effects of pollution can be divided into three categories:

- **Air pollution**
  This leads to problems such as acid rain and the 'greenhouse effect'. See section 14.5.
- **Water pollution**
  The worst sources of water pollution are sewage, oil, fertilizers and detergents. See section 14.8.
- **Land pollution**
  The main causes of land pollution are summarized in Table 12.3. This also shows the effects of the different pollutants and the different methods of control. The most common land pollutants are plastics. Unfortunately, plastics are *not* **biodegradeable** like wood and paper. This means that they are not broken down by bacteria and other decomposers.

Table 12.3
Major land pollutants

Land pollutant	*Source*	*Effect*	*Methods of control*
Pesticides 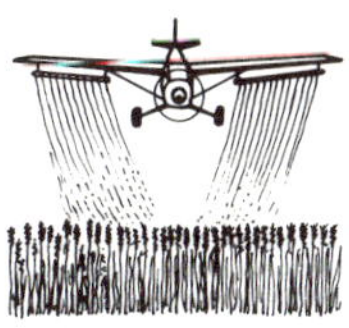 (see section 12.2)	Spraying of crops with chemicals to kill certain plants and insects	Plants are contaminated. Poisonous substances get into the bodies of animals, and sometimes humans, that eat these plants. Harmless and helpful organisms are killed as well as pests.	Limited use. Ban undesirable insecticides, such as DDT, wherever possible.
Radioactive waste  (see chapter 22)	Used material from nuclear power stations.	Waste is still very radioactive. The radioactivity can cause: –cancers –mutations	Improved methods of disposal, e.g. –underground stores (silos) for nuclear waste –solidify waste in glass or concrete and dump it in the deepest oceans
Plastics 	Plastic wrappings and food containers. Unlike paper and wood, plastics are not attacked and broken down by bacteria. They are **non-biodegradable**.	Plastic waste contaminates the countryside and city streets.	Stricter litter laws. Development of biodegradable plastics.

12.4 Finite Earth–depleting the Earth's resources

Human beings have always wanted more possessions and easier living. In order to create our present lifestyles, we have spoilt large areas of the Earth with mines, quarries, motorways and pylons. Large buildings have turned our cities into concrete jungles and a lot of countryside has been destroyed, some of it forever. At the same time, we are using up scarce resources such as copper, oil and natural gas. During the last 200 years, society has benefited greatly from improvements in living standards. These improvements have resulted from the use of raw materials in the Earth. But the Earth's resources will not last forever. Some raw materials, like coal, will last for centuries yet, but others like oil and natural gas will only last a few more decades unless we use them more sparingly (see Fig. 12.5).

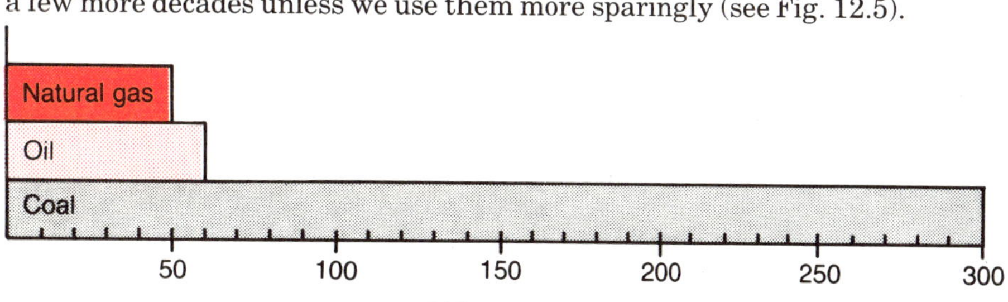

Fig. 12.5 Estimates of how long the Earth's reserves of fossil fuels will last if we continue to use them at present rates. How long will coal last? How long will natural gas last?

Our supplies of metal ores and other minerals are also being depleted. Figure 12.6 shows the predicted lifetimes of reserves of some metal ores. The estimates refer to the lifetimes of **known reserves**. These are the reserves of ores known to be present in the Earth. As these reserves are used up, it is likely that new reserves will be discovered. But, this cannot go on forever. *The reserves of the Earth are finite, not limitless.*

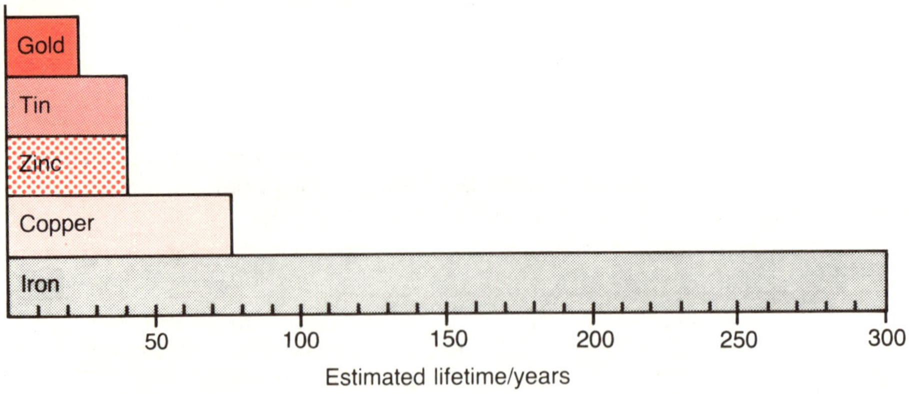

Fig. 12.6 The estimated lifetimes of reserves of some metal ores. Which metal will last longest? Which metal will run out first?

The following steps are already being taken to overcome the problems caused by depletion of resources:

- **Materials are being conserved and used more sparingly**. For example, cars are being designed to use fuel more efficiently.
- **Chemists are developing new materials** to replace those made from scarce resources. For example, plastic pipes are replacing those made from lead and copper.
- **Materials are being recycled** for example, scrap iron, aluminium, glass, paper and plastics.
- **New (renewable) sources of energy are being developed**. These include solar power, wind power, tidal power and hydroelectric power (see section 20.6).

12.5 Conservation of wildlife and the countryside

In some parts of the world, our effect on the environment has been disastrous. Agricultural practices, industrial pollution and the hunting of animals for 'sport' or fashionable items, like skins and ivory, have destroyed natural habitats and caused the extinction of whole species. The dodo is probably the best known example of an extinct species, but there are thousands of others, for example, the Cape lion, the great auk and the passenger pigeon. In addition to these species which have disappeared forever, there are thousands of other **endangered species**. These animals and plants are in real danger of extinction. They include pandas, whales and even the African elephant.

In some cases, it is already too late to prevent the extinction of certain species and the destruction of large habitats. In other areas, however, important and successful conservation projects and regulations are in operation. They include:

- **Regulations to reduce pollution**
  –The Clean Air Acts to reduce soot in the atmosphere
  –laws to reduce the amount of lead in petrol from 0.4 to 0.15 g/dm^3
- **Restoration of areas damaged by mining and quarrying**
  –In the Thames valley, gravel pits have been reclaimed and converted into water sports areas
  –In parts of South Yorkshire, mining tips have been landscaped and turned into parks and gardens.
- **Increasing management of habitats and strict guardianship of nature reserves and National Parks**.
  In some countries, such as Britain and the USA, National Parks are well managed. There is little danger to the animals and plants within their boundaries. However, this is not always the case. Rare animals in the game parks of central Africa are still in danger from hunters.
- **Restriction on the number of animals slaughtered for food**.
  This applies particularly to fish and whales in areas which have been over-fished in the past.

Fig. 12.7 In many parts of central Africa the elephant has been hunted almost to extinction. The hunters kill the animals to obtain their tusks which are made of ivory.

Quick test 12

1 Detergents should be biodegradable in order to
A reduce the pollution of rivers.
B increase their cleaning power.
C cause less damage to clothes.
D remove fat and oil more quickly.

2 The additives in petrol have changed since 1980. As a result of these changes, our environment will contain less
A acid rain. C lead.
B carbon monoxide. D radioactivity.

3 Which of the following would be a method of biological control of ants?
A Destroy the ants' nests C Introduce birds which eat ants
B Spray the area with insectide D Keep all food away from the ants

4 A habitat is
A a collection of plants and animals.
B a place with a given environment.
C a study of a particular environment.
D a web of animals which depend on each other.

5 Which of the following is a pollutant from fertilizers?
A mercury C lead
B DDT D nitrate compounds

Questions 6 to 10

Consider the following agricultural practices:
A crop rotation
B spreading manure
C spreading lime
D scattering artificial fertilizers
E using pesticides

Which practice
6 quickly increases the nutrient level in the soil?
7 provides food for decomposers?
8 raises the pH level in the soil?
9 acts as a mechanical control of infectious plant diseases?
10 causes the greatest disruption to food webs?

Questions 11 to 15

The graph shows how the numbers of carnivorous birds and of field mice, and the mass of wheat grown, varies throughout the year in a particular field.

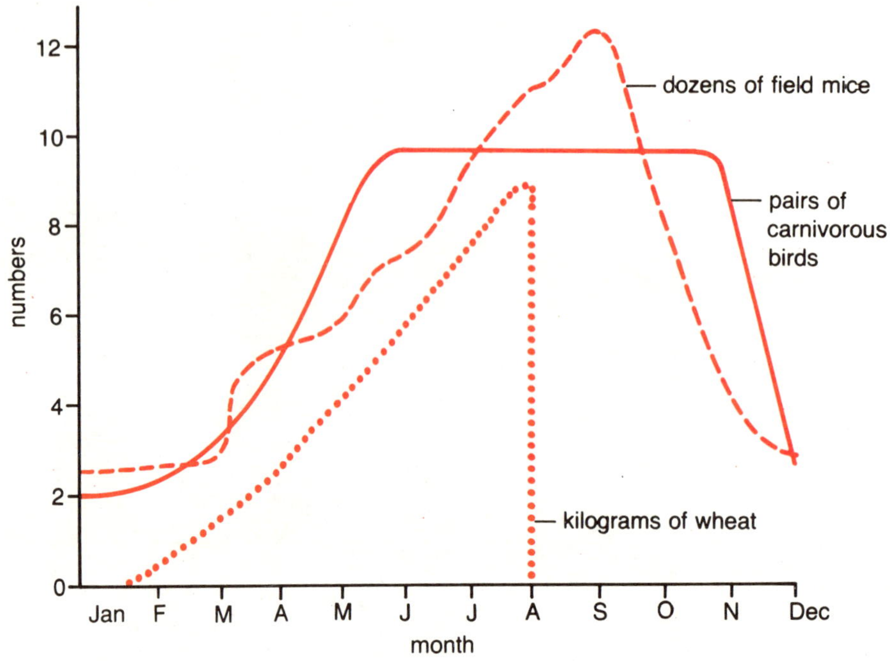

11 Describe how the mass of wheat varies throughout the year.
12 Carefully explain *why* these changes take place.
13 Give *two* possible reasons for the increase in the number of birds from January to May.
14 Explain carefully why the graph line for the number of field mice follows the shape of the wheat line.
15 Suggest a reason why the line for field mice numbers does not rise as smoothly as the line for wheat? (*LEAG*)

Questions 16 to 19

The graph shows the general trend of how the bee population in Britain has declined since 1968.

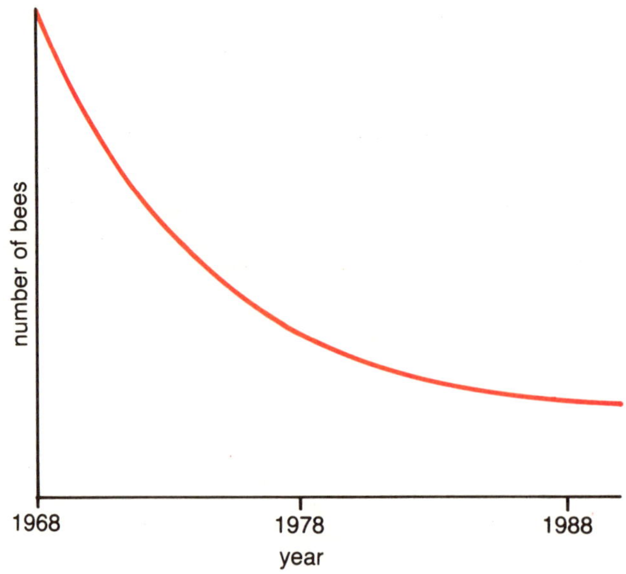

16 Suggest one reason for the decline.
17 Why do you think the decline is less since 1978?
18 Why do you think people are concerned about the decline?
19 How could the decline be stopped?

(*WJEC* (modified))

Questions 20 to 22

Scrap aluminium can often be used again (recycled). The bar chart shows how much of the aluminium in each 100 tonnes of scrap could be recycled and how much is actually recycled.

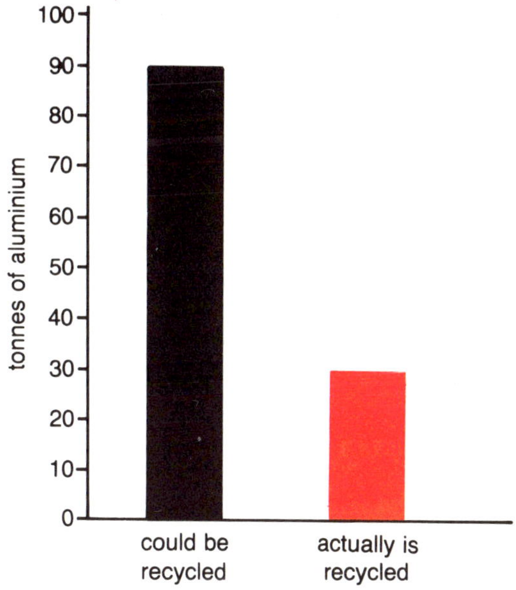

20 How much scrap aluminium is actually recycled?

21 How does the amount of scrap aluminium that *is* recycled compare with the amount that *could be* recycled?

22 Recycled aluminium costs the same as aluminium made from ore. Why then should people bother to recycle thc aluminium? (*NEA*, 1988)

13 RAW MATERIALS, ELEMENTS AND COMPOUNDS

13.1 Raw materials from the Earth

Look around you. Everywhere you will see a large number of different materials. These include air, sand, glass, water, wood, rocks and steel.

These different materials are called **substances**. Some substances, such as air, sand, water, rocks and wood, occur naturally in the world around us. These *naturally-occurring substances* are the **raw materials** from which we can make other substances, for example, glass and steel. The chemical and mining industries produce valuable substances such as metals, fuels, plastics and fertilizers from raw materials in the Earth.

Table 13.1 The most important raw materials and the substances we obtain from them

Raw material	*Substances obtained from the raw material*
Plants	foods (e.g. sugar, flour, cooking oil), timber, dyes, rubber, cotton
The air	oxygen, nitrogen, argon
Coal	coke, plastics, detergents, paints, explosives, perfumes
Crude oil	petrol, diesel oil, waxes, polishes, lubricants, road tar, plastics
The sea	salt (sodium chloride), magnesium, bromine
Rocks	sand, bricks, lime, glass, metals (e.g. iron, aluminium, copper)

Fig. 13.1 What materials are used to build houses? What are the sources of these materials?

13.2 Conserving and recycling

The Earth, the sea and the atmosphere provide a vast source of raw materials for the chemical industry. Table 13.2 lists some important raw materials in Britain.

Limestone
Salt
Sand
Iron ore
Clay
Coal
Oil
Natural gas

Table 13.2 Some important raw materials in Britain. What are these raw materials used for?

Our industries have only been using natural resources on a large scale for about one hundred years. Even so, scientists believe that many important raw materials will become scarce in the near future. For example, natural gas may be used up in fifty years' time if we continue to use it at present rates.

This depletion of resources has had three important results:

- We are now more cautious about the use of scarce resources. **Conservation** is essential.
- Materials, such as scrap steel, aluminium, copper, glass and plastics, are being recovered and **recycled**.
- Chemists and engineers are producing cheaper **alternative materials** to those already in use.

Fig. 13.2 Most local authorities provide collection points for materials to be recycled

13.3 Elements as building blocks

Although there are millions of different substances, they can be sorted into just three groups–*elements*, *mixtures* and *compounds*.

ELEMENTS

An element is a substance which cannot be broken down into simpler substances by chemical reactions.

Elements are the building blocks for other substances. So far we know of 106 elements. These include iron, aluminium, copper, gold, oxygen, nitrogen and carbon. Every substance in the universe can be split up into one or more of these 106 elements. For example, glass is made of calcium, silicon and oxygen; wood is made of carbon, hydrogen and oxygen.

13.4 Classifying elements as metals and non-metals

Elements can be sorted into groups with similar properties. The simplest way of sorting elements is into two groups–metals and non-metals. The main differences between metals and non-metals are summarized in Table 13.3.

Table 13.3 Comparison of the properties of metals and non-metals

Property	**Metals** *e.g. aluminium, iron, copper, gold*	**Non-metals** *e.g. oxygen, nitrogen, chlorine, sulphur*
State	usually solids at room temperature	mostly gases at room temperature
Melting point and boiling point	usually high	usually low
Density	usually high	usually low
Effect of hammering	malleable–can be hammered into shapes	solids are brittle or soft
Conduction of heat and electricity	good	poor (except graphite which conducts well)

The best way to check whether an element is a metal or a non-metal is to test its electrical conductivity. This can be done using the apparatus in Fig. 13.3.

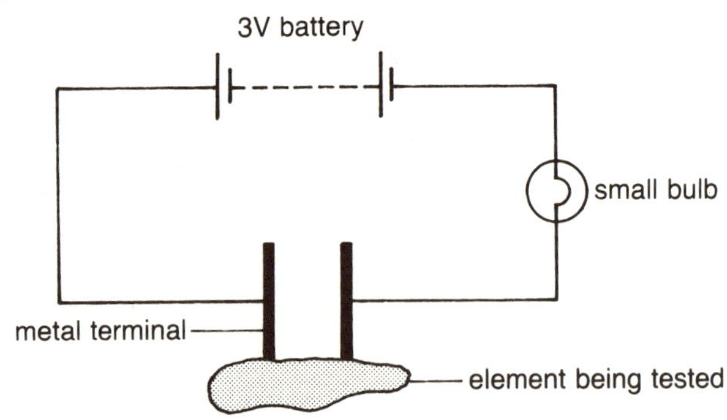

Fig. 13.3 How does this apparatus tell you whether the element being tested is a metal or a non-metal?

(If the element is a metal, the bulb will light up –a metal will conduct electricity completing the circuit.)

13.5 Elements and compounds

When aluminium window frames are new they are shiny. Gradually, the frames go dull as a layer of white aluminium oxide forms on the surface. The aluminium has **reacted** or **combined** with oxygen in the air to form aluminium oxide. The aluminium oxide is a completely new substance. Changes such as this, which result in new substances, are called **chemical reactions**. The new substance is called the **product** of the reaction.

We can summarize the reaction which takes place when aluminium goes dull by writing a **word equation**:

aluminium + oxygen ⟶ aluminium oxide

Aluminium and oxygen are elements. They have combined together to form a **compound** called aluminium oxide.

A compound is a substance which contains two or more elements combined together.

The product of the reaction, the compound aluminium oxide, has very different properties from the starting elements. See Table 13.4.

Table 13.4 Comparison of the properties of aluminium and oxygen, and aluminium oxide, the compound they form when they combine.

Elements				Compound
aluminium	+	**oxygen**	⟶	**aluminium oxide**
shiny		colourless		white
metal		gas		solid
fairly reactive		very reactive		very unreactive

When two elements react together to form a compound, the name of the compound ends in **–ide**. For example,

aluminium + oxygen ⟶ aluminium ox**ide**

sodium + chlorine ⟶ sodium chlor**ide**

hydrogen + sulphur ⟶ hydrogen sulph**ide**

When a metal reacts with a non-metal, the non-metal forms the –ide part of the name of the compound. When two non-metals react, the more reactive non-metal forms the –ide part of the name.

When elements combine to form compounds the reaction is an example of **synthesis**. Photosynthesis is another example of synthesis.

Unlike elements, compounds can be split up into simpler substances. For example, aluminium oxide can be split into aluminium and oxygen. This occurs when electricity is passed through molten aluminium oxide. When compounds are split into simpler substances, the reaction is an example of **decomposition**.

> **Synthesis** is the *building up* of more complex substances by joining together simpler substances.
> **Decomposition** is the *breaking down* of more complex substances into simpler substances.

Notice that decomposition is the opposite of synthesis.

$$\text{aluminium + oxygen} \underset{\textit{decomposition}}{\overset{\textit{synthesis}}{\rightleftarrows}} \text{aluminium oxide}$$

13.6 Mixtures

Most substances which occur naturally are mixtures. They may be *mixtures of elements*, for example air which is mainly oxygen and nitrogen, or *mixtures of compounds*, for example sea water which contains water (a compound of hydrogen and oxygen) and salt (sodium chloride).

The important point about mixtures is that the different substances in them are *not* combined together. This is different from compounds in which the elements are combined together. The differences between compounds and mixtures are summarized in Table 13.5.

Table 13.5 The differences between compounds and mixtures

Compounds	Mixtures
1 A new substance is produced when the compound forms.	**1** No new substance is produced when the mixture forms.
2 Contain one substance.	**2** Contain two or more substances.
3 Properties are different from the elements in them.	**3** Properties are similar to the substances in them.
4 The elements in them can only be separated by a chemical reaction.	**4** The substances can often be separated easily.
5 The percentages of elements in the compound are constant.	**5** The percentages of substance in the mixture can vary.

13.7 Separating mixtures

Very often mixtures have to be separated before we can use them. Just think what might happen if we used gritting salt for cooking or crude oil in place of petrol in a car. Figure 13.4 (overleaf) shows what happens when solids are mixed with liquids. It also includes some important words relating to **solutions**.

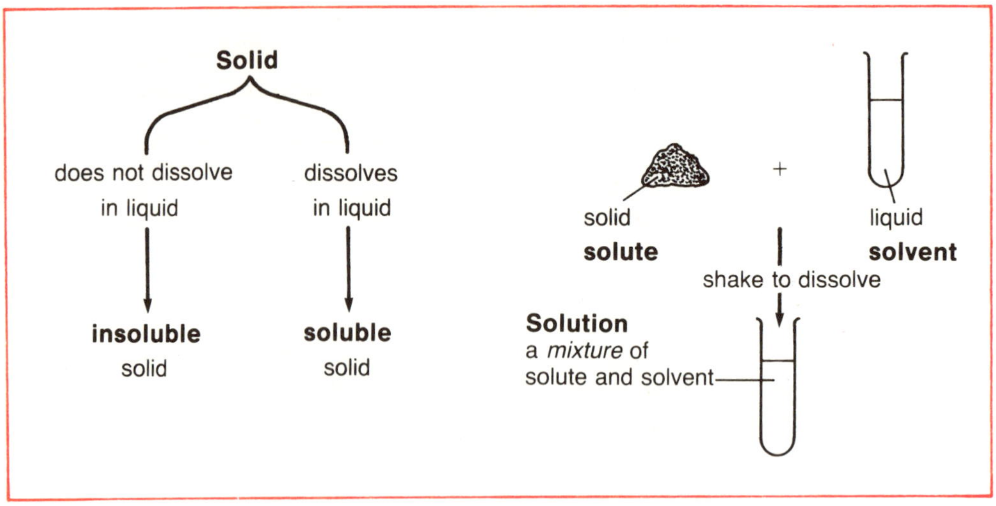

Fig. 13.4 Mixing solids and liquids

SEPARATING INSOLUBLE SOLIDS FROM LIQUIDS

It is usually easy to separate an insoluble solid from a liquid. There are three possible methods:

Decanting (pouring off)

This method is often used when the solid is in large pieces–for example, separating peas, potatoes or other vegetables from the water in which they have been cooked.

Filtering

This method is used when the particles of solid are small. It is used in making filter coffee (Fig. 13.5) and in separating fine particles from drinking water.

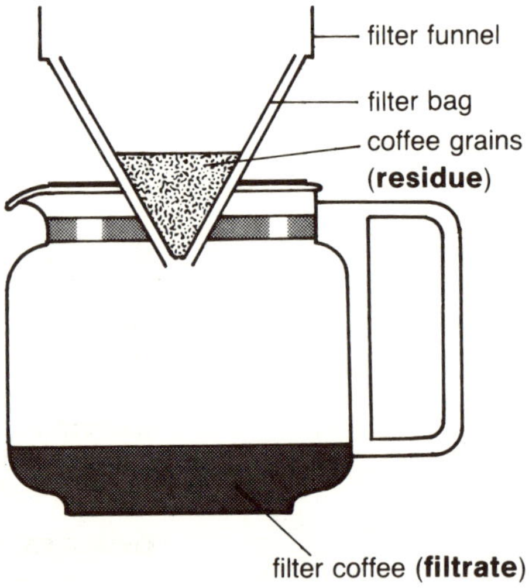

Fig. 13.5 How does the filter bag let the filter coffee through?

Centrifuging

This method is used when the particles are so small that they float in the liquid and form a cloudy **suspension**. The suspension is spun around very quickly in a machine called a centrifuge. This forces the denser, solid particles to the bottom of the container. The liquid can then be poured off (decanted) easily. Centrifuging is used to separate cream from milk. Do you think the milk or the cream is forced to the bottom of the centrifuge?

SEPARATING SOLUTIONS

Tap water is clean but it is *not* pure. It contains dissolved gases such as oxygen and probably dissolved solids which make the water 'hard' (see section 14.9). Tap water is, of course, a solution. Clear sea-water is another example of a solution. It contains salt (sodium chloride) dissolved in water. You cannot see the salt in sea-water, but it is there–you can taste it. The salt has been broken up into tiny particles. The particles are too small to be seen, even with a microscope. They can pass through the holes in filter paper very easily during filtration.

Evaporation

When sea-water is left to dry in the sun, the water turns into a vapour (*evaporates*). Salt is left behind as a white solid.

The *change of a liquid into a gas* or a vapour is called **evaporation**. Evaporation can be used to separate a dissolved solid from its solvent. If the solvent evaporates slowly, the dissolved solid is often left behind as evenly-shaped *crystals*. This process of forming crystals by evaporation of the solvent from a solution is called **crystallization** (see Fig. 13.6).

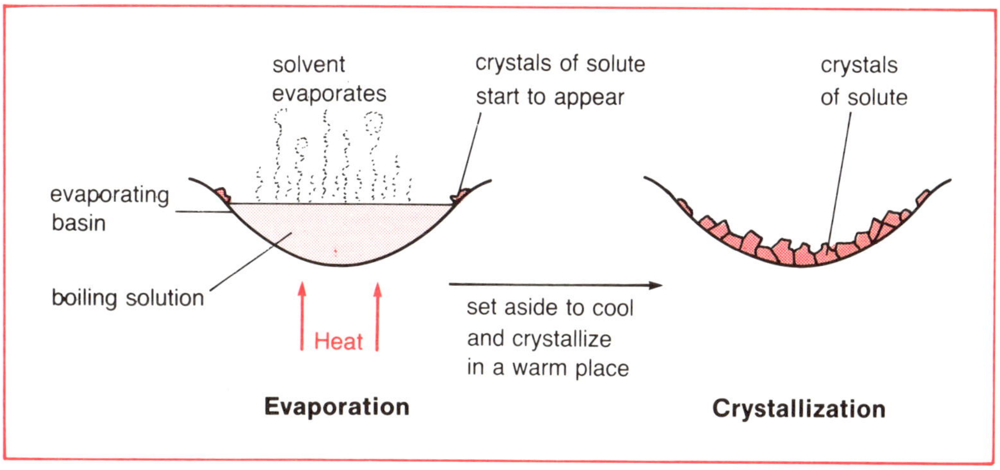

Fig. 13.6 Evaporation and crystallization

Evaporation is an essential process in

- obtaining salt from sea-water in hot countries;
- drying wet clothes;
- producing concentrated evaporated milk;
- obtaining sugar from sugar cane and sugar beets (see Fig. 13.7).

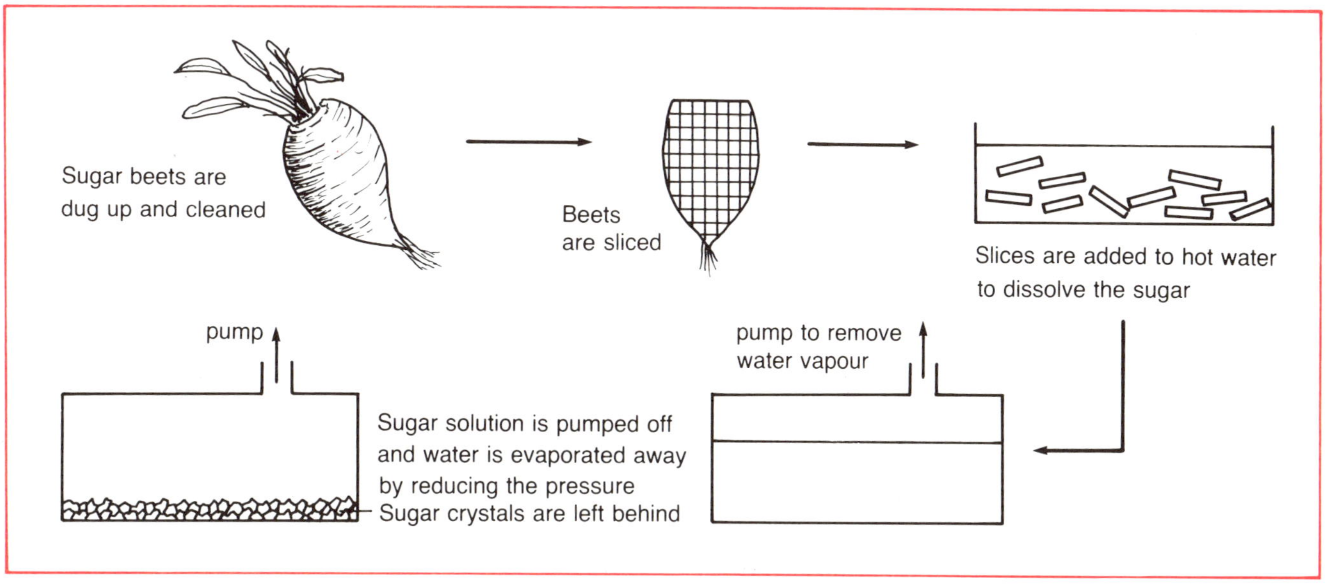

Fig. 13.7 Obtaining sugar from sugar beets

Distillation

When sea-water is heated, water vapour escapes into the air. If the water vapour is passed into a second container and cooled, it will turn back to water. This process in which a *vapour changes to a liquid* is called **condensation**. Figure 13.8 shows how pure water can be obtained from sea-water by evaporating the water and then condensing the water vapour. This process of *evaporating a liquid and condensing the vapour* is called **distillation**.

distillation = evaporation + condensation

When sea-water is heated in apparatus like that shown in Fig. 13.8, water vapour passes into the inner tube of the condenser. This is cooled by cold water in the outer jacket. The water vapour condenses and drips from the lower end of the condenser into the conical flask. The liquid which collects after distillation is called a **distillate**.

Distillation is an essential process in

- making 'spirits', such as whisky, gin and vodka, from weaker alcoholic liquids;
- obtaining pure water from sea-water in parts of the Middle East where fuel is cheap.

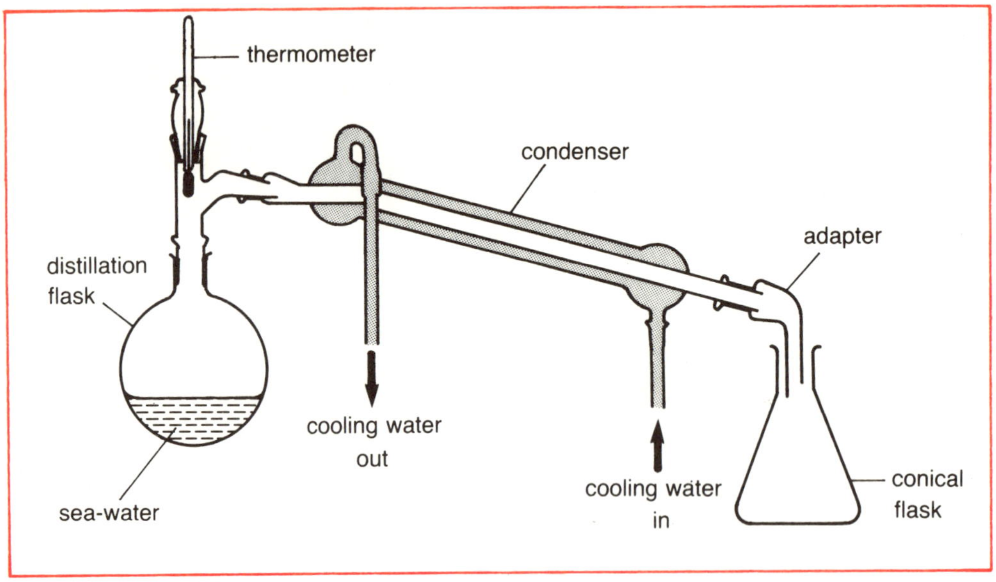

Fig. 13.8 Obtaining pure water from sea-water by distillation

SEPARATING LIQUIDS

If oil is added to water, the two liquids do not mix. Liquids, such as oil and water, which do not mix are described as **immiscible**. These liquids can be separated by decantation or by using a separating funnel (Fig. 13.9).

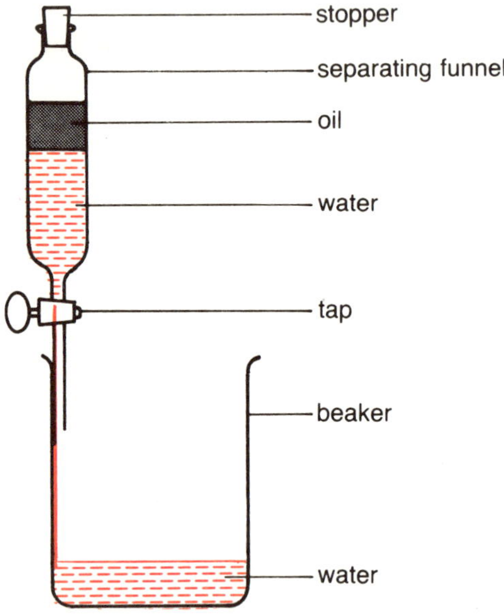

Fig. 13.9 Separating oil and water using a separating funnel

If oil is added to petrol, the two liquids *do* mix. These liquids are described as **miscible**. Miscible liquids can be separated by a special kind of distillation called **fractional distillation**. Different liquids in the mixture boil at different temperatures. When the mixture is heated vapours of the different liquids boil off at different temperatures as each reaches its boiling point. As the different liquids boil off they can be condensed separately.

Fractional distillation is an essential process in:

- separating the different constituents in crude oil (see section 20.7);
- separating oxygen and nitrogen from liquid air.

13.8 Chromatography

Chromatography is another important technique which can be used to separate mixtures. It is used to separate substances which are very similar, for example dyes in ink, natural colours in foods and drugs in blood and urine.

Figure 13.10 shows how the dyes in inks can be separated by chromatography. As the solvent soaks up the paper, the dyes separate. Some dyes stick to the paper, other dyes tend to dissolve in the solvent. The dyes which dissolve in the solvent travel further up the paper. This method was first used to separate coloured substances. The process was therefore called **chromatography** from the Greek word *khroma* meaning colour. The paper with the substances separated out is called a **chromatogram**. Nowadays, chromatography is also used with colourless substances. When chromatography is used to separate colourless substances, the paper is sprayed with a locating agent after chromatography. The locating agent reacts with the colourless substances to form coloured substances.

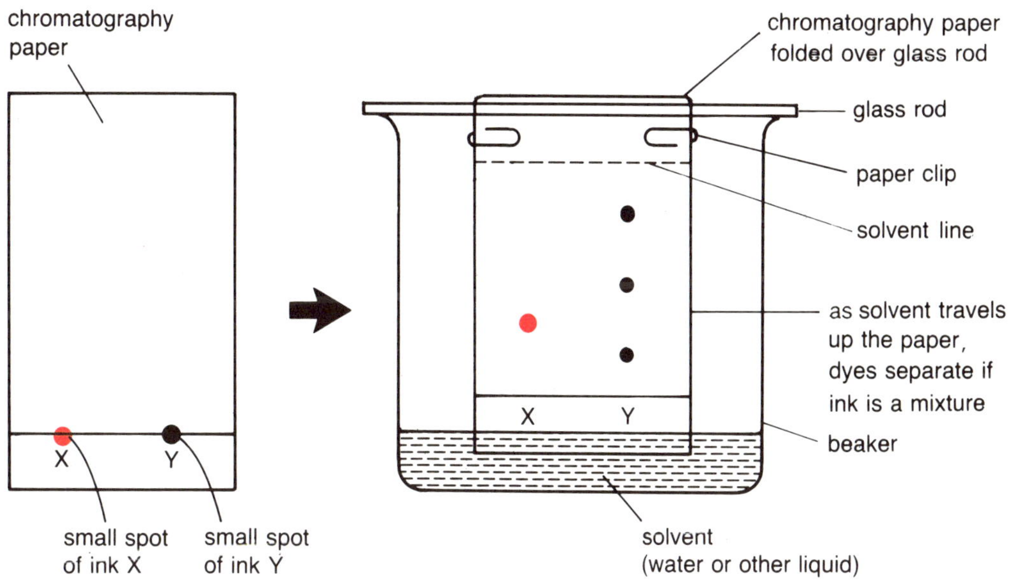

Fig. 13.10 Separating the dyes in inks by chromatography. How many dyes are there in each of inks X and Y?

13.9 Testing for pure substances

Supermarkets often sell cartons of 'Pure Orange Juice'. This means that the carton contains only the juice of oranges. No colouring or flavouring has been added. However, a scientist would *not* describe the orange juice as pure. To a scientist, **somethings is pure if it contains only one substance**. Orange juice contains water, sugar, citric acid and often colouring and other additives. So, it is a mixture.

If a substance is pure, it is all the same. So all of it will behave in the same way. When a pure solid is heated, it all melts at the same temperature. When a pure liquid is heated, it all boils at the same temperature. The melting points and boiling points of most pure substances have been measured accurately. If a substance contains impurity, its melting point and boiling point will be different from that of the pure substance.

The most useful methods of testing whether a substance is pure are
1 checking the melting point;
2 checking the boiling point.

Quick test 13

Questions 1 to 4

The dyes in two food flavourings, X and Y, were analysed using chromatography. five pure dyes (labelled A to E) were tested at the same time. The final chromatogram is shown below.

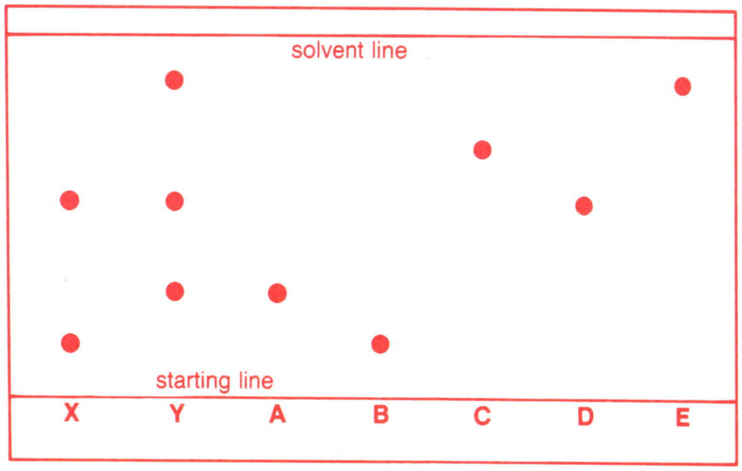

1 Which pure dye is present in both X and Y?
2 How many different dyes are present in X?
3 Which pure dye is not present in X or Y?
4 Which dyes could be mixed to make X?

Questions 5 to 9

A a pure element
B a pure compound
C a mixture of elements
D a mixture of compounds
E a mixture of elements and compounds

Choose from A to E above, the best description for

5 water.
6 steel.
7 copper.
8 air.
9 petrol.

Questions 10 to 14

A chromatography
B condensation
C crystallization
D distillation
E filtration

Choose from A to E above, the process that occurs when

10 solid sugar is obtained from its solution.
11 tea leaves are separated from tea.
12 sugar is detected in urine.
13 whisky is produced from wort.
14 water vapour turns to water.

Questions 15 to 17

The table shows the melting points and boiling points of substances A, B, C and D.

Substance	*Melting point/°C*	*Boiling point/°C*
A	650	1500
B	−8	60
C	−150	−30
D	40	100

15 Which substance is a liquid at room temperature?
16 Which substance is a gas at room temperature?
17 Which substance may be a metal?

18 Crude oil can be separated by fractional distillation. This shows that crude oil is
A a compound of carbon.
B a mixture of substances.
C a mixture of carbon compounds.
D a fossil fuel mixture.

Questions 19 to 20

A word equation for respiration is

$$\text{food} + \text{oxygen} \rightarrow \text{carbon dioxide} + \text{water} + \text{energy}$$

19 What is (are) the reactant(s) in this process?
20 What is (are) the product(s) in this process?

14 THE ENVIRONMENT – AIR AND WATER

14.1 Composition of air

We cannot live without air. The oxygen present in air is essential for all living things. Figure 14.1 shows an experiment to find the percentage of oxygen in the air.

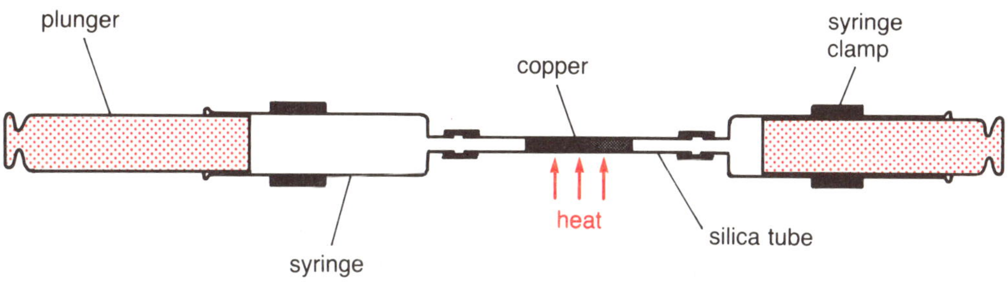

Fig. 14.1 Apparatus used to find the percentage of oxygen in air

One of the syringes is first filled with 100 cm^3 of air. This air is then passed slowly backwards and forwards over the heated copper. The copper reacts with oxygen in the air forming solid copper oxide. This removes oxygen from the air, so there is a decrease in the volume of air in the syringe. The final volume of the air is measured when the apparatus has cooled. The percentage of oxygen can be calculated from the decrease in volume. Some results are shown below:

Initial volume of air in syringe	= 100 cm^3
Final volume of gas in syringe	= 79 cm^3
Decrease in volume	= 21 cm^3
$\therefore$ Volume of oxygen combining with copper	= 21 cm^3
Percentage volume of oxygen in air	= **21**

The main constituents of air are **nitrogen** and **oxygen** (see Table 14.1). There are also **noble gases** (see section 21.5), **carbon dioxide** and **water vapour**. The amount of water vapour varies with the weather.

Table 14.1 Gases present in dry air

Nitrogen	78.07%
Oxygen	20.97%
Argon	0.93%
Carbon dioxide	0.03%
Noble gases (helium, neon, krypton and xenon)	traces

14.2 Air as a source of raw materials

Air is an important source of oxygen, nitrogen and noble gases. These gases are separated by liquefying air, then fractionally distilling the liquid air. As the liquid air warms, the different constituents boil off at different temperatures.

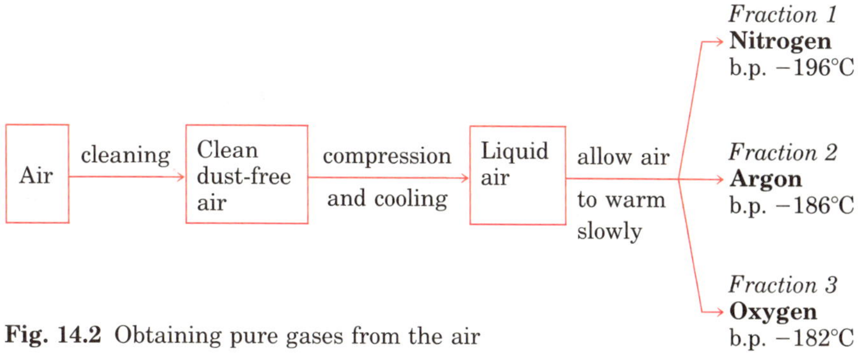

Fig. 14.2 Obtaining pure gases from the air

The main products from air are nitrogen, argon and oxygen. The important uses of these gases are summarized in Table 14.2.

Table 14.2 The important uses of nitrogen, argon and oxygen

Nitrogen	● Manufacture of ammonia, nitric acid and fertilizers (see sections 19.5 and 19.6) ● Used as a cheap unreactive gas 'blanket' to stop materials reacting with oxygen (e.g. in petrol storage tanks)
Oxygen	● Manufacture of steel (see sections 17.7 and 17.8) ● Welding and cutting–oxyacetylene flames are hot enough to melt metals ● Breathing apparatus, e.g. for fire fighting, deep sea diving, mountaineering and in hospitals
Argon	● Used as an unreactive gas to stop materials reacting with air, e.g. in electric light bulbs where the very hot filaments would react with the nitrogen in air

Fig. 14.3 Pure oxygen is used in oxyacetylene welding and cutting. When acetylene burns in oxygen, the temperature may reach 3000°C. This is hot enough to melt metals which can then be cut or welded together. The operator must wear goggles and heavy gloves for protection against the shower of sparks.

14.3 Reactions with oxygen

Oxygen is the most reactive gas in the air. When substances burn in air they react with oxygen forming **oxides**, e.g.

magnesium + oxygen → magnesium oxide

When something combines with oxygen, it is **oxidized**. The process is described as **oxidation**. Burning, breathing (refer back to sections 6.2 and 6.5) and rusting (see section 17.9) are important oxidation processes.

The test for oxygen relies on the fact that oxygen is so reactive. When a glowing splint is inserted into oxygen, it bursts into flame.

Most elements will combine with oxygen. Some elements will even react slowly with oxygen at room temperature. For example, things made of iron are slowly covered with rust (*iron oxide*) when exposed to moist air. Similarly, shiny aluminium articles become covered with a layer of white *aluminium oxide* as the aluminium reacts with oxygen in air. Table 14.3 shows the type of oxides produced when metals and non-metals react with oxygen.

Table 14.3 The types of oxides produced when metals and non-metals react with oxygen

Type of element	*Type of oxide produced*	*Properties of oxides*
Non-metals e.g. sulphur carbon	**Acidic oxides** e.g. sulphur dioxide carbon dioxide	**Gases** React with water to produce acidic solutions (pH < 7), e.g. sulphur dioxide + water → sulphurous acid carbon dioxide + water → carbonic acid (Water is an exceptional non-metal oxide (hydrogen oxide) being neutral and liquid.)
Metals e.g. sodium aluminium iron	**Basic oxides** e.g. sodium oxide aluminium oxide iron oxide	**Solids** Oxides of less reactive metals are insoluble in water but they will neutralize acid. Oxides of the reactive metals (K, Na, Ca, Mg) react with water to form alkaline solutions (pH > 7), e.g. calcium oxide + water → calcium hydroxide These oxides are called **alkaline oxides**.

14.4 Burning and fuels

Burning is probably the most important chemical process. We use burning to keep warm, to cook food, to drive vehicles and to generate electricity. Burning is sometimes called **combustion**.

Burning involves the oxidation of fuels to produce heat.

The most important fuels are **coal, oil** and **natural gas**. These are all **fossil fuels** which come from the decay of dead animals and plants. Fossil fuels are mostly **hydrocarbons**–*compounds of hydrogen and carbon*. During burning, the hydrogen and carbon in fossil fuels react with oxygen in the air to produce water, carbon dioxide and heat:

fuel (compound of carbon and hydrogen) + oxygen in air —*burning*→ carbon dioxide + water (hydrogen oxide) + heat

Reactions like burning which give out heat are called **exothermic reactions**. When fuels burn, a lot of heat is produced. This causes the reactants to burst into flame. This happens in a gas cooker or in a Bunsen burner when natural gas reacts with oxygen in the air to produce a flame. Natural gas is mainly **methane**. The equation for the burning of methane is:

methane + oxygen → carbon dioxide + water

$$CH_4(g) + 2O_2(g) \rightarrow CO_2(g) + 2H_2O(g)$$

(Symbols and equations for chemical reactions are dealt with fully in chapter 15.)

Other fossil fuels are more complex substances than natural gas. They contain mixtures of many hydrocarbons. However when they are burnt they all produce the same products–carbon dioxide and water. If fuels burn in a limited supply of air, they produce *carbon monoxide* instead of carbon dioxide. This is why carbon

Fig. 14.4 The launch of the Space Shuttle Discovery with its two solid rocket boosters and enormous external fuel tank (Kennedy Space Centre, Florida, 29 September 1988)

monoxide is present in car exhaust fumes. Carbon monoxide is very poisonous so you should avoid inhaling exhaust gases.

FIRE FIGHTING

All fires need fuel, oxygen and heat in order to burn. This is often summarized in the *fire triangle* (Fig. 14.5). A fire can be put out by removing any one of these three factors. For example, *water* extinguishes a fire by removing heat and, possibly, oxygen. A *fire blanket* cuts off the supply of oxygen. A *fire break* in a forest cuts off the supply of fuel if there is a forest fire. Firefighting is discussed in section 20.3.

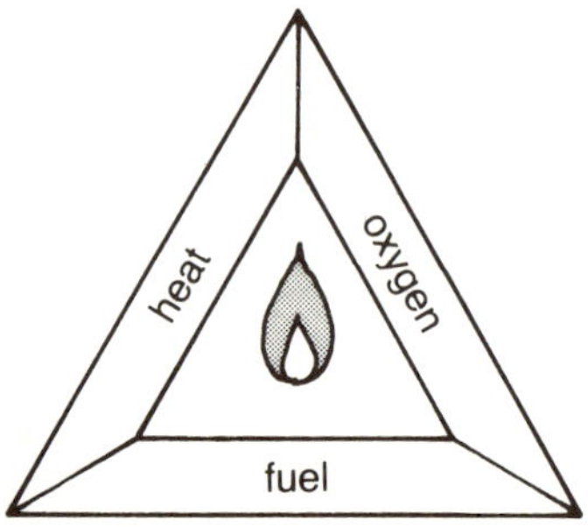

Fig. 14.5 The fire triangle

14.5 Air pollution

Air pollution is caused by the release of poisonous or damaging gases into the air. These gases may harm living things and non-living things (e.g. stonework).

Most air pollution is caused by burning fuels, so the problems are worse in industrial areas. However, pollutant gases may be carried by prevailing winds to affect areas miles from the source of pollution. For example, scientists in Scandinavia believe that sulphur dioxide emitted from industrial areas in Britain is responsible for the acid rain in Sweden.

In the last few years, many scientists and politicians have become increasingly concerned about the use of CFCs (chlorofluorocarbons) as refrigerants and aerosol propellants. One of the most widely used CFCs is dichlorodifluoromethane, CCl_2F_2. CFCs increase the dangers from ultraviolet radiation and also increase 'the greenhouse effect' on our climate.

Table 14.4 summarizes the substances which cause most air pollution. It also shows the effects of these pollutants and some methods of control.

Table 14.4 Major air pollutants

<table>
<tr><th>Air pollutant</th><th>Source</th><th>Effects</th><th>Method of control</th></tr>
<tr><td>Soot and smoke</td><td>Burning fuels</td><td>Deposit of soot on buildings
Make clothes and fabrics dirty</td><td>Use of smokeless fuel
Improve supply of air to burning fuels</td></tr>
<tr><td>Carbon dioxide</td><td>Burning fuels</td><td>Increased percentage of carbon dioxide in the air causes more heat to be retained by the Earth– this affects our climate (the 'greenhouse effect').</td><td>Burn less fossil fuels</td></tr>
<tr><td>Carbon monoxide</td><td>Burning fuels particularly car exhausts</td><td>Poisonous to humans and all other animals because it prevents haemoglobin in the blood from carrying oxygen (refer back to section 5.5)</td><td>Make sure vehicle engines are burning fuel efficiently</td></tr>
<tr><td>Sulphur dioxide</td><td>Burning fuels particulary coal: small amounts of sulphur in coal and oil burn to form sulphur dioxide. This reacts with rain water to form sulphurous acid ('acid rain')</td><td rowspan="2">Acid rain
–harms plants
–gets into rivers and lakes and kills fish
–attacks the stonework of buildings</td><td>Burn less coal and oil
Remove sulphur dioxide from waste gases</td></tr>
<tr><td>Nitrogen oxides</td><td>Vehicle exhaust gases– these react with rain water to form nitrous and nitric acids which cause acid rain</td><td>Adjust vehicle engine so that nitrogen oxides do not form during sparking
Fit catalytic converters to exhaust systems</td></tr>
<tr><td>Lead compounds</td><td>Vehicle exhaust gases</td><td>Poisonous to humans and all other animals</td><td>Reduce the lead additives in petrol
Use unleaded petrol</td></tr>
<tr><td>CFCs chlorofluoro-carbons</td><td>Solvents in aerosols and in refrigerator liquids</td><td>React with and remove ozone in the upper atmosphere. This allows more ultraviolet radiation in sunlight (normally absorbed by ozone) to penetrate to the Earth. The extra ultraviolet radiation causes
–damage to plants
–increased risk of skin cancers
CFCs also retain heat more than normal atmospheric gases, increasing the 'greenhouse effect'</td><td>Limit the use of CFCs
Develop alternative, less harmful, chemicals to do the same jobs</td></tr>
</table>

Fig. 14.6 A church wall in Chelsea, London, soot-stained from decades of air pollution, showing sections before and after cleaning

14.6 Water supplies

All living things need water. Every day your body needs about two litres ($3\frac{1}{2}$ pints) of water to replace the water lost in urine, in sweat and when you breathe. In some ways, water is more important to us than food. We can survive about fifty or sixty days without food, but only five to ten days without water.

In addition to the water we must drink, we also need water for personal washing, clothes washing, dish washing, toilet flushing, etc. Every time you flush the toilet, about ten litres of water are used.

Industry uses even larger amounts of water. Most of this water is used for cooling. For example, a large power station uses about five million litres of water for cooling every day. This water need not be pure, so it can be taken straight from rivers or from the sea.

The public water supply which comes to our homes is, of course, treated (cleaned) by the water authorities. The main stages in the treatment of this water are shown in Fig. 14.7.

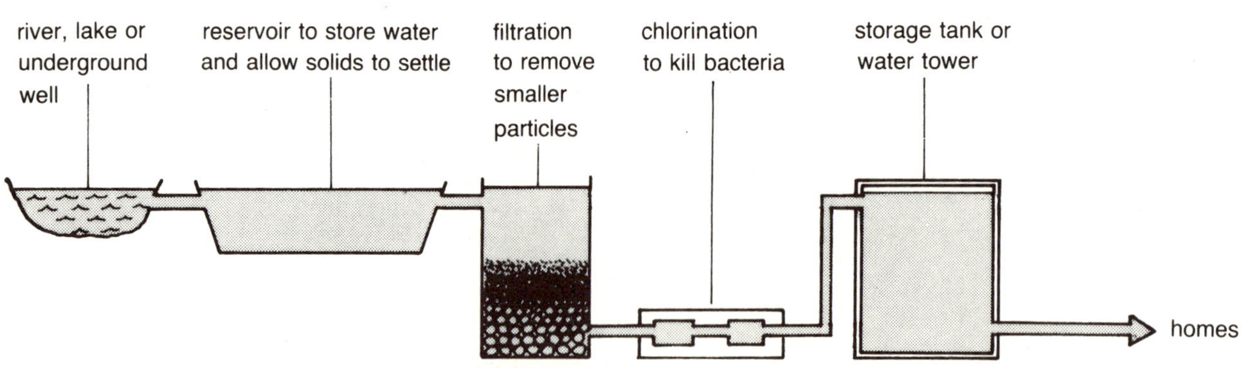

Fig. 14.7 The main stages in the treatment of water for public supply

14.7 The water cycle

The source of water for the public supply is usually a river, a lake or an underground well. We can, however, trace our water supply further back than this. Water on the Earth's surface and underground comes from rain. Rain comes from clouds and clouds come from water which has evaporated from rivers, lakes and seas. This cycle of water from the Earth's surface into the clouds and then back to Earth as rain, is called the **water cycle** (see Fig. 14.8).

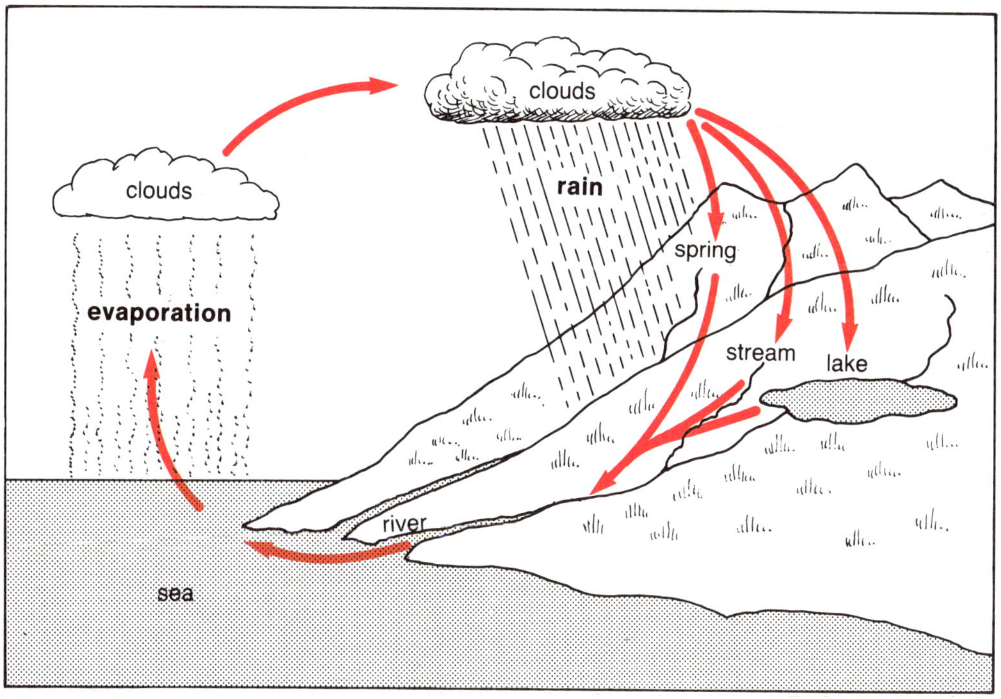

Fig. 14.8 The water cycle

14.8 Water pollution

The main pollutants of our rivers, lakes and oceans are listed in Table 14.5. The table also shows the sources and effects of these pollutants.

Table 14.5 Major water pollutants

Water pollutant	*Source*	*Effect*
Sewage	Homes, schools, factories	Bacteria grow on nutrients in sewage. This uses up the dissolved oxygen in the water. Lack of oxygen causes the bacteria and other water organisms to die. The decaying matter makes the water smelly.
Oil	Refineries and spillages from tankers	Covers sea birds with oil, pollutes beaches
Fertilizers	Rain water washes fertilizers into rivers, lakes	Bacteria and water plants grow rapidly, use up all the oxygen and then die. The decaying matter makes the water smelly (eutrophication – refer back to section 12.2).
Detergents	Homes, schools, factories	Water produces a foam. The detergents themselves are often poisonous to organisms in the water

The main cause of water pollution is **sewage**. At one time, sewage was simply piped into rivers or into the sea. This led to widespread disease and sometimes poisoned the living things in the water. In order to overcome these problems, sewage plants treat the waste before it is returned to rivers and the sea. Sewage is first pumped into large tanks. Here it is aerated (mixed with air) and decomposed by bacteria to harmless products.

14.9 Hard water

Although water from the public supply is treated, it is *not* pure. Water from the tap may look pure, but it is really a solution. It contains dissolved gases, such as oxygen and carbon dioxide, and also dissolved solids picked up by the water as it travels over rocks in rivers and streams. Some of these dissolved solids cause 'hard' water.

Hard water forms a scum with soap and does not easily produce a lather.

Hard water is common in chalk and limestone areas. The main cause of hard water is a high concentration of calcium ions, Ca^{2+} (see section 16.4). When hard water is mixed with soap, the Ca^{2+} ions in the water react with complex anions (see section 16.5) in the soap to form an insoluble solid. This insoluble solid is the scum. If you live in a hard water area, notice that detergents, for example washing-up liquid, do not produce scum. This is because detergents do not contain the anions which react with Ca^{2+} ions to form an insoluble solid.

The formation of hard water

As rain falls, it reacts with carbon dioxide in the air to form **carbonic acid**:

rain water + carbon dioxide ⟶ carbonic acid

$$H_2O(l) + CO_2(g) \longrightarrow H_2CO_3(aq)$$

When this dilute solution of carbonic acid comes in contact with limestone or chalk, it reacts with **calcium carbonate** in the rocks. The product is **calcium hydrogencarbonate**.

carbonic acid + limestone/chalk ⟶ calcium hydrogencarbonate

$$H_2CO_3(aq) + CaCO_3(s) \longrightarrow Ca(HCO_3)_2(aq)$$

Unlike calcium carbonate, calcium hydrogencarbonate is soluble in water. Its calcium ions (Ca^{2+}) make the water hard.

Fig. 14.9 Stalactites on the roof of a cave. Stalactites are made of calcium carbonate. They form when hard water containing calcium hydrogen carbonate slowly decomposes in the cave leaving insoluble calcium carbonate

SOFTENING HARD WATER

In some areas, the water is so hard that the calcium ions must be removed. This is called **water softening**. There are various ways of softening hard water.

- **Distilling the water**
  The water is evaporated and then condensed (refer back to section 13.7). Ca^{2+} ions are left behind. Energy is needed to vaporize the water so this process is expensive.

- **Adding washing soda**
  Washing soda and bath salts contain sodium carbonate (Na_2CO_3). When this is added to hard water, it removes the Ca^{2+} ions by forming insoluble calcium carbonate ($CaCO_3$):

$$\underset{\text{in hard water}}{Ca^{2+}} + \underset{\text{in washing soda}}{CO_3{}^{2-}(aq)} \longrightarrow \underset{\text{precipitate}}{CaCO^3(s)}$$

- **Using excess soap**
  Soap will react with Ca^{2+} ions in hard water until they are all precipitated as scum. Further soap will then lather. This, of course, wastes soap and forms a lot of scum.

- **Using ion-exchange resins**

In this method, the hard water runs through a tube packed with an insoluble material called a resin. The resin has a complicated structure, but like the washing soda it contains sodium ions (Na^+). As the hard water runs over the resin, Ca^{2+} ions in the water exchange places with Na^+ ions in the resin. Calcium ions in the water are replaced by sodium ions which do not form insoluble scum with soap, so the water is softened.

After a while, all the Na^+ ions on the resin are replaced by Ca^{2+} ions, so it will no longer soften water. The resin can be restored by pouring a strong solution of salt (sodium chloride) through it. This puts Na^+ ions back on the resin and washes out Ca^{2+} ions.

Once the equipment (the resin tube) has been installed, this is the cheapest method of softening water.

Quick test 14

Questions 1 to 5

Four methods of softening water are

A distillation
C using washing soda
B using excess soap
D using ion-exchange resins

Choose from A to E the method that

1 produces pure water.
2 precipitates scum.
3 is the most expensive.
4 precipitates calcium carbonate.
5 uses an insoluble complex sodium compound.

Questions 6 to 9

Four important fuels are

A coal B oil C natural gas D uranium

Choose from A to D the fuel that

6 cannot cause acid rain.
7 causes most pollution from sulphur dioxide.
8 contains more than 90 per cent of one compound
9 is used to produce petrol.

Questions 10 to 12

Five water pollutants are

A sewage
D pesticides
B oil
E detergents
C fertilizers

Choose from A to E the pollutant which

10 causes water to foam.
11 is most likely to contaminate our food.
12 gets into rivers near arable farmland.

Questions 13 to 17

A calcium B copper C sulphur D iron E hydrogen

Choose from the elements labelled A to E, the element or elements that

13 produce acidic oxides.
14 produce alkaline oxides.
15 produce neutral oxides.
16 form solid oxides at room temperature.
17 form oxides which are insoluble in water.

Questions 18 to 21

The following are five important chemical processes

A chlorination
B neutralization
C condensation
D oxidation
E distillation

Choose the process which occurs when

18 water vapour forms droplets of rain.
19 water is treated for use in our homes.
20 river water is used to make pure water.
21 water is produced from a burning fuel.

Questions 22 to 25

The table shows the percentage of four gases present in air.

Gas	*Percentage in air*
A	1
B	78
C	0.03
D	less than 0.01

Which of the gases, A to D, is

22 neon.

23 carbon dioxide.

24 argon.

25 nitrogen.

26 A candle burns in a jam jar of fresh air for 8 seconds and in an identical jam jar containing exhaled air for 2 seconds. This shows that exhaled air contains

A less nitrogen than fresh air

B more carbon dioxide than fresh air.

C more water vapour than fresh air.

D less oxygen than fresh air.

27 Water is stored in reservoirs before it passes into the public water supply so that

A bacteria are killed.

B dissolved solids will crystallize.

C solid particles can settle.

D water plants can clean the water.

15 PARTICLES

15.1 Introduction

Try to answer the following questions:

- How does the coffee get through the filter paper when filter coffee is made? Why do the coffee grains stay in the filter paper?
- Why does it only require a tiny amount of curry to flavour a large meal?
- Why can a small amount of dye colour a large piece of fabric?

In order to answer these questons effectively you need to use the idea that:

all substances are made up of particles.

There is plenty of everyday evidence that matter is composed of particles. Can you think of two more examples? In the next section we will look at the evidence that these particles are *moving*.

Fig. 15.1 Why is it possible to smell the perfume someone is wearing from several metres away?

(Photograph courtesy of Parfums Jean-Louis Scherrer)

15.2 Evidence for moving particles

The best evidence that particles of matter are constantly moving comes from studies of **diffusion** and **Brownian motion**.

DIFFUSION

Most people like the smell of fish and chips. You can smell them a long way away. How does the smell get from the fish and chips to your nose?

Particles of gas are released from the fish and chips. The particles mix with air particles and move away from the fish and chips. *This movement and mixing of particles* is called **diffusion**.

Gases diffuse to fill all the space available to them–even heavy gases like bromine will behave in this way (see Fig. 15.2, overleaf).

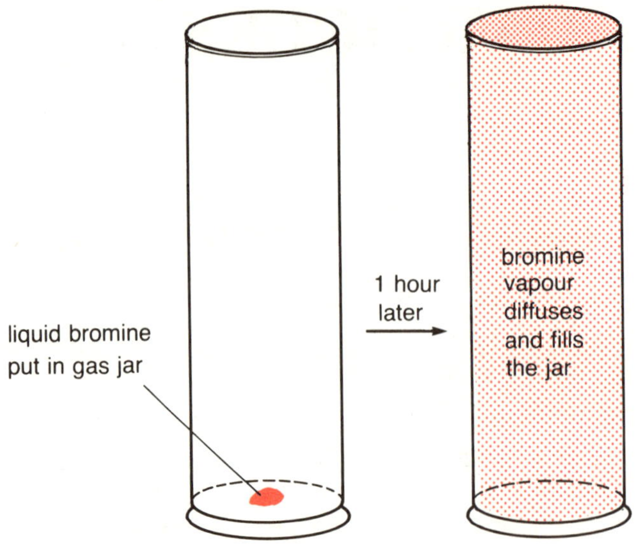

Fig. 15.2 Diffusion of bromine vapour in air

How does the bromine vapour get to the top of the gas jar? Gases consist of tiny particles, moving around haphazardly. These particles collide with each other and with the walls of their container. The gas particles don't care where they go. Sooner or later they will spread into all the space available.

Diffusion also occurs in liquids, although it takes place more slowly than in gases (see Fig. 15.3). This indicates that liquid particles move around more slowly than gas particles.

Solids do *not* diffuse through other solids, but gases and liquids can diffuse through some solids. For example, dyes can diffuse into fabrics and nutrients (in solution) can diffuse through membranes in living organisms.

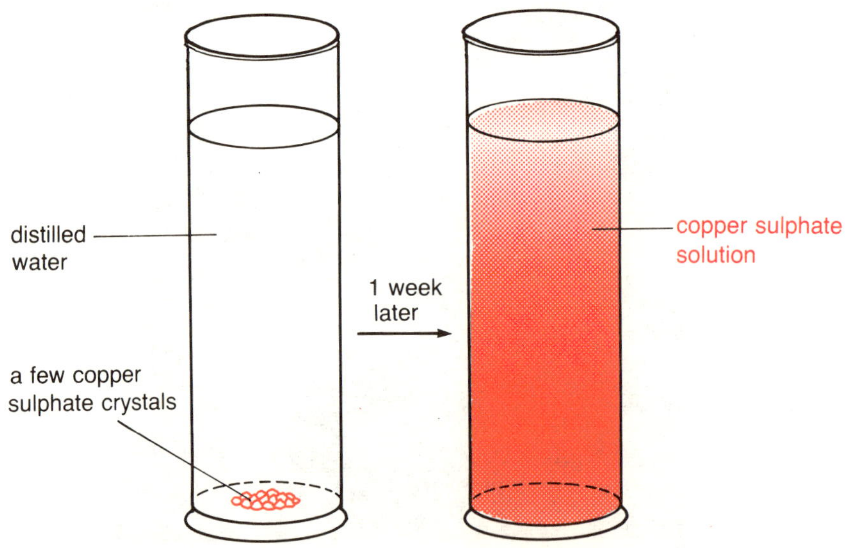

Fig. 15.3 The copper sulphate dissolves in the water then begins to diffuse through the water. Notice that the solution contains more copper sulphate and is darker near the bottom of the gas jar. Eventually all the solution will have the same blue colour. Why is this?

Diffusion is very important in living things. It explains how the food you eat gets to different parts of your body. After a meal, food passes into your stomach, then into your intestines. Large food particles are broken down into smaller ones. These smaller particles can diffuse through the walls of your intestines into your bloodstream (refer back to section 4.1).

BROWNIAN MOTION

In 1827 a biologist called Robert Brown was using a microscope to look at pollen grains in water. To his annoyance, the pollen grains kept moving about randomly. Similar random movements can be seen when you look at smoke particles through a microscope (Fig. 15.4). *This movement of tiny particles in a gas or liquid is called* **Brownian motion**.

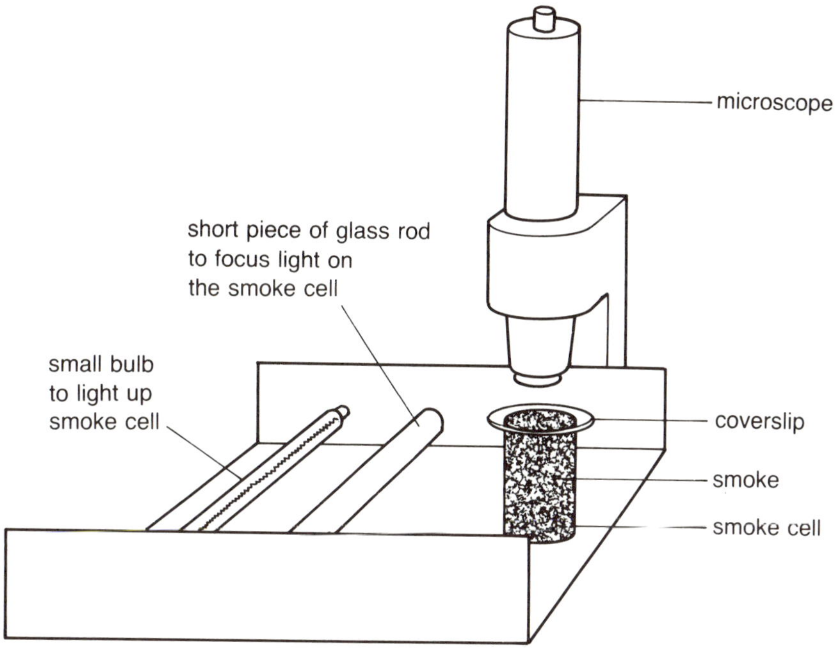

Fig. 15.4 Observing the movement of smoke particles

Smoke from smouldering string is injected into the smoke cell using a teat pipette. Under the microscope, the smoke particles look like tiny pinpoints of light which jitter about.

The movement of the smoke particles is caused by the random motion of particles in the air around them. The particles of smoke are small, but they are much larger than air particles. We can see individual smoke particles through the microscope. The air particles are much too small to be seen. The air particles move very rapidly and hit the smoke particles at random. The smoke particles are therefore knocked first this way, then that way, so they appear to jitter about (Fig. 15.5).

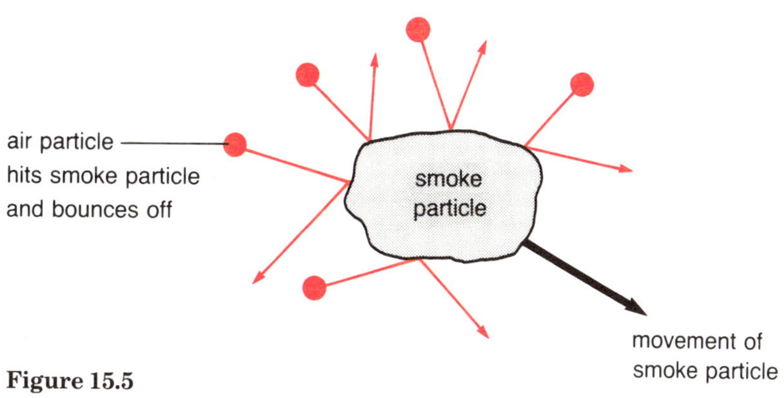

Figure 15.5

15.3 Particles in motion–the kinetic theory

The idea that everything is made of moving particles is called the **kinetic theory of matter**. The word *kinetic* comes from a Greek word which means 'moving'.

The main points of the kinetic theory are:

1. All matter is made of particles. There are particles in everything you can see–glass, wood, paper, water, concrete, petrol, grass, air, etc.
2. The individual particles are very, very small. We cannot see them.
3. The particles of different subtances have different sizes. Particles of elements, such as aluminium, iron and oxygen, are small. Particles of compounds, for example sugar, are larger. Particles of some complex compounds, such as rubber and proteins, are thousands of times larger.
4. The particles in all substances are continually moving. Small particles move faster than heavier particles at the same temperature.

continued

5 As the temperature rises, the particles get hotter. They have more energy and move around faster.

6 In a solid, the particles are very close with strong forces between them. Solid particles can only vibrate about fixed positions (Fig. 15.6**a**).

7 In a liquid, the particles are a little further apart. The forces between the particles are not as strong. Liquid particles can move around each other (Fig. 15.6**b**).

8 In a gas, the particles are much further apart. There are no forces to hold the particles together. The particles rush around in all directions in all the space they can find (Fig. 15.6**c**).

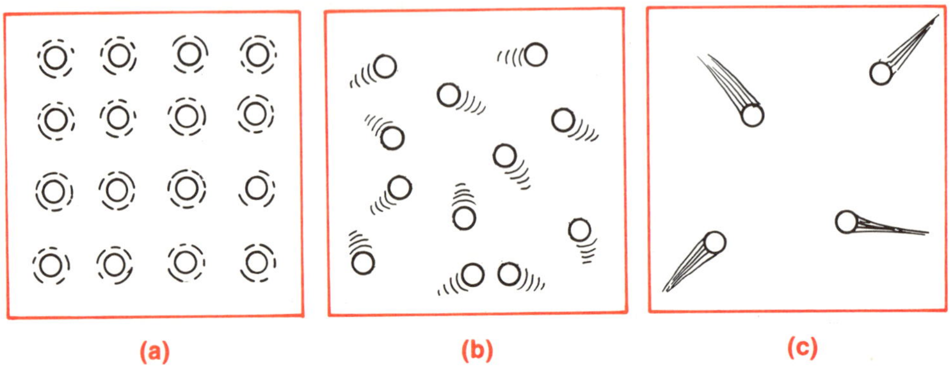

Fig. 15.6 The movement of particles in (**a**) a solid, (**b**) a liquid and (**c**) a gas

Fig. 15.7 The forces between metal particles in steel are so strong that thin steel cables can be used to lift heavy loads

Fig. 15.8 Diamond is the hardest natural substance. Diamond-tipped cutters are used to cut glass and engrave glass objects. What does this suggest about the forces between particles in diamond?
(Photographs courtesy of the Diamond Information Service)

15.4 Changes of state

All materials can be classified as either **solid** or **liquid** or **gas**–concrete and ice are solids, petrol and water are liquids, air and steam are gases. *Solid*, *liquid* and *gas* are called the **states of matter**.

The kinetic theory can be used to explain what happens when a substance changes from one state to another. For example, when ice (solid) melts to become water (liquid). A summary of the different changes of state is shown in Fig. 15.9. These changes are usually caused by heating or cooling. Notice that when a solid changes directly to a gas it is **subliming**. Ice sublimes when it disappears into the air without forming water first.

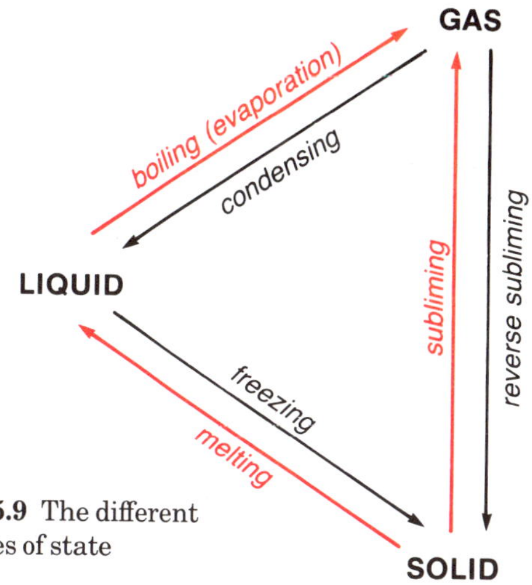

Fig. 15.9 The different changes of state

MELTING AND FREEZING

When a solid is heated, the particles vibrate more and more quickly. Eventually they break free from their fixed positions and begin to move around each other–the solid melts to form a liquid. *The temperature at which the solid melts* is called the **melting point**.

The melting point of a solid tells us how strongly its particles are held together. Substances with high melting points have strong forces between their particles. Substances with low melting points have weak forces between their particles. Metals and alloys, such as iron and steel, have very high melting points. This suggests that there are strong forces between their particles. This is why metals can be used for girders, supports and cables.

When a liquid is cooled, the particles move around each other more and more slowly. Eventually, the particles are moving so slowly that they only vibrate about a point. When this happens the liquid has **frozen** to form a solid.

EVAPORATING, BOILING AND CONDENSING

When a liquid is heated, the particles move around each other more and more quickly. Some particles near the surface of the liquid have enough energy to escape from the liquid into the air. When this happens, the liquid **evaporates** to form a gas.

As the temperature rises, more and more particles escape from the liquid and evaporate. Eventually, particles are moving so rapidly that bubbles of gas start to form inside the liquid. The temperature at which this *evaporation occurs in the middle of the liquid* is the **boiling point**. Liquids which evaporate and boil at low temperatures are described as **volatile**.

Boiling points tell us how strongly the particles are held together in liquids. Liquids with high boiling points have stronger forces between their particles than liquids with low boiling points.

When a gas is cooled, the particles move around more slowly. As the temperature falls the particles move more and more slowly. Eventually the particles do not have enough energy to bounce off each other when they collide. The particles cling together as a liquid. **Condensation** has occurred.

(Energy considerations involved in changes of state are discussed in section 24.9.)

15.5 Atoms and molecules

So far we know that all matter and materials can be classified in two ways:
- **as solids, liquids and gases**, or
- **as elements, compounds and mixtures.**

Remember:
- **Elements** are substances that cannot be broken down any further.
- **Compounds** are formed from elements and can be broken down into elements.
- **Mixtures** contain two or more different substances.

Fig. 15.10 John Dalton (1766–1844)

In section 15.3, we saw that the particle picture of matter could explain the differences between solids, liquids and gases. But how does the particle model explain the difference between elements, compounds and mixtures? The answer to this question was first suggested by **John Dalton** in 1807.

Dalton's theory of atoms and molecules

In 1807, Dalton put forward his *Atomic Theory of Matter*. In this theory, Dalton was the first scientist to use the word *atom* for the smallest particle of an element.

The main points in Dalton's theory are:

1. All matter is made up of tiny particles called *atoms*.
2. Atoms cannot be made or broken apart.
3. All the atoms of one element are exactly alike. An element is a substance made of only one kind of atom.
4. Atoms of one element are different from those of another element. They have different masses, different colours, etc.
5. Atoms of one element can combine with atoms of other elements to form compounds. We now call these larger particles *molecules*.
6. A mixture contains two or more kinds of atoms or molecules, but the different particles are not combined together in a single compound.

Figure 15.11 shows how Dalton pictured the elements iron and sulphur, the compound iron sulphide and a mixture of iron and sulphur. Although Dalton put forward his ideas nearly two hundred years ago, they are still very useful.

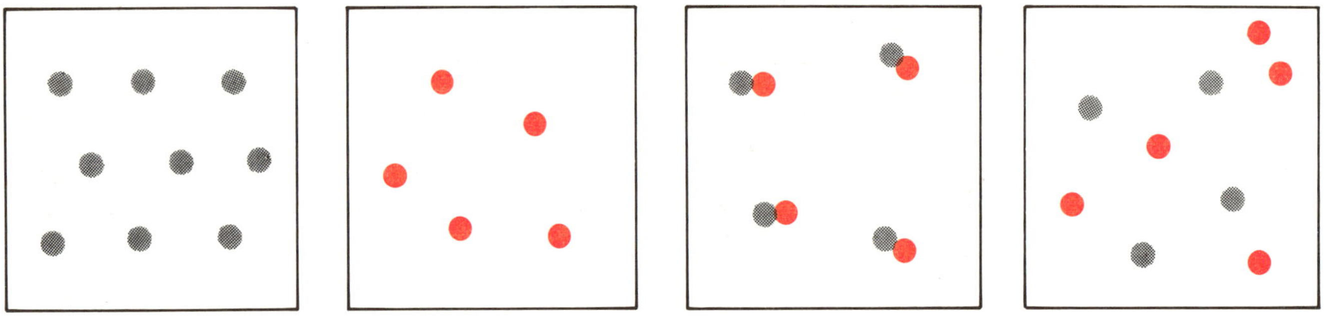

Atoms in the *element* iron

Atoms in the *element* sulphur

Molecules in the *compound* iron sulphide

Atoms in a *mixture* of iron and sulphur

Figure 15.11

15.6 Symbols and formulas

Dalton also invented symbols to represent the atoms of different elements. The symbols which we use today are based on Dalton's suggestions. Table 15.1 gives a list of the symbols for some of the common elements. Notice that most elements have two letters in their symbol. The first is a capital letter and the second is always small (lower case). These symbols come from either the English name (e.g. O for **o**xygen, Al for **al**uminium) or from the Latin name (Au for gold from the Latin name ***au**rum*; Cu for copper from the Latin name ***cu**prum*).

Table 15.1 The symbols for some elements

Element	*Symbol*	*Element*	*Symbol*	*Element*	*Symbol*
Aluminium	Al	Helium	He	Oxygen	O
Argon	Ar	Hydrogen	H	Phosphorus	P
Bromine	Br	Iodine	I	Potassium	K
Calcium	Ca	Iron	Fe	Silicon	Si
Carbon	C	Lead	Pb	Silver	Ag
Chlorine	Cl	Magnesium	Mg	Sodium	Na
Chromium	Cr	Mercury	Hg	Sulphur	S
Cobalt	Co	Neon	Ne	Tin	Sn
Copper	Cu	Nickel	Ni	Uranium	U
Gold	Au	Nitrogen	N	Zinc	Zn

We can use these symbols to represent compounds as well as elements. For example, water is represented as H_2O. The smallest particle of water is a molecule. This contains two hydrogen atoms (H_2) and one oxygen atom (O). Carbon dioxide is written as CO_2–one carbon atom and two oxygen atoms. 'H_2O' and 'CO_2' are called **formulas**. Formulas show the relative numbers of atoms of the different elements in a compound.

Scientists use symbols as a form of shorthand. It is much easier and much quicker to represent substances and chemical changes using symbols than writing their names out in full.

15.7 Formulas and equations

In the last section, we revised the use of symbols and formulas to represent the particles in a substance. For example, we can represent aluminium using the symbol Al. This shows that aluminium is composed of single atoms. In the same way, water is represented by the formula H_2O, showing that water is composed of molecules each containing two hydrogen atoms and one oxygen atom (Fig. 15.12).

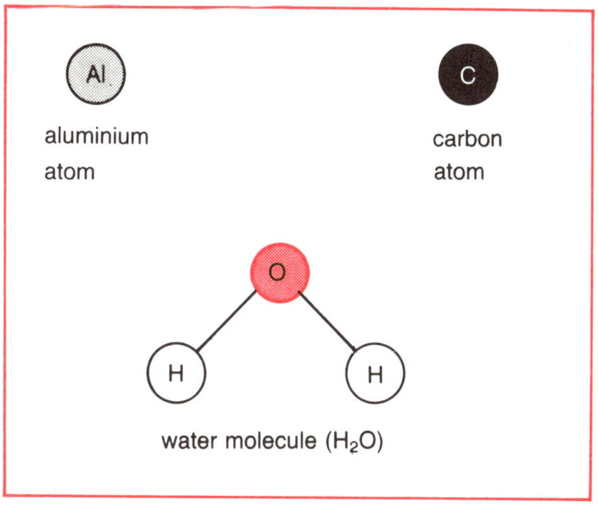

Fig. 15.12 Using symbols and formulas to represent the particles in substances

Like aluminium, most elements can be represented by their symbols because they contain single atoms. But this is not the case for oxygen, hydrogen, nitrogen, chlorine, bromine and iodine. Experiments show that these elements contain *particles with two atoms joined together* (see Fig. 15.13). So the best way to represent oxygen gas is by $\mathbf{O_2}$, not O, and the best way to represent hydrogen gas is $\mathbf{H_2}$, not H. These molecules containing two atoms are described as **diatomic molecules**.

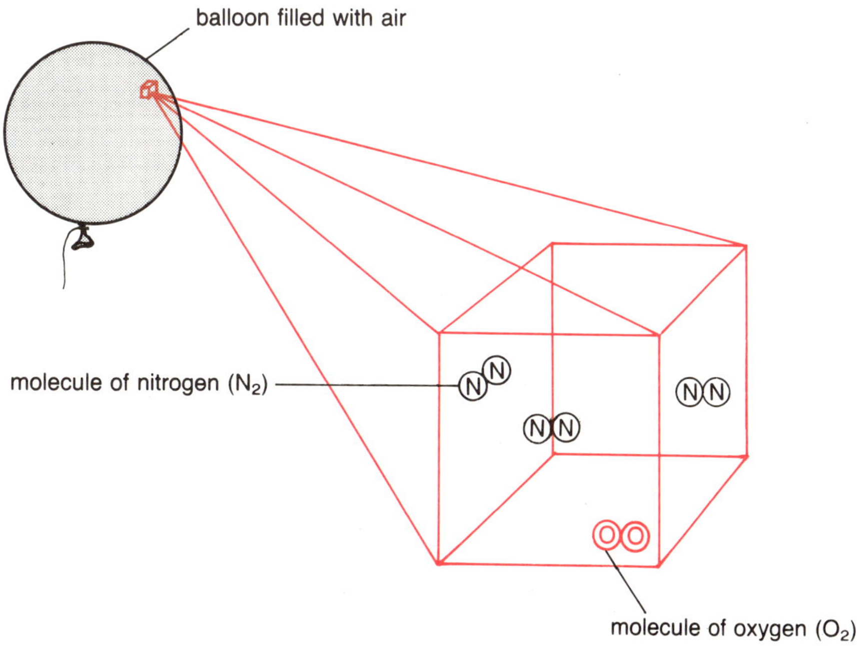

Fig. 15.13 Molecules of oxygen and nitrogen in air

CHEMICAL EQUATIONS

A chemical equation is a summary of the starting substances and the products in a chemical reaction.

So far we have used **word equations** to summarize what happens when substances react. Word equations show the names of the reactants and the products. When zinc and oxygen react, the product is zinc oxide. The word equation for this simple reaction is:

zinc + oxygen ⟶ zinc oxide

Balanced equations go further than word equations. They show

- *the formulas* of the reactants and products, and
- *the relative numbers of particles* of the reactants and products.

For example, in the word equation above we could write zinc as Zn, oxygen as O_2 and zinc oxide as ZnO:

$Zn + O_2 \longrightarrow ZnO$

But notice that this does not *balance*. There are two oxygen atoms in the O_2 molecule on the left and only one oxygen atom in the product, ZnO, on the right. So ZnO on the right must be doubled:

$Zn + O_2 \longrightarrow \mathbf{2}ZnO$

Unfortunately the equation still does not balance. There are now two Zn atoms on the right in 2ZnO, but only one on the left. This can easily be corrected by writing 2Zn on the left, i.e.:

$\mathbf{2}Zn + O_2 \longrightarrow 2ZnO$

This equation is now **balanced**.

Writing balanced equations

The last example used the three steps for writing a balanced equation:

Step 1 Write a word equation

e.g. hydrogen + oxygen ⟶ water

Step 2 Write formulas for reactants and products

e.g. $H_2 + O_2 \longrightarrow H_2O$

Remember that oxygen, nitrogen, hydrogen and the halogens are written as O_2, N_2, H_2, Cl_2, Br_2 and I_2. All other elements are shown as single atoms, e.g. Mg for magnesium, S for sulphur, etc.

Step 3 Balance the equation by making the number of atoms of each element the same on both sides.

e.g. $2H_2 + O_2 \longrightarrow 2H_2O$

N.B. *Never change a formula* to make an equation balance. For example, the formula of zinc oxide is always ZnO. Zn_2O and ZnO_2 do not exist. To balance an equation *put a number in front of the whole formula*, e.g. 2ZnO, 2MgO or 3MgO.

15.8 Measuring atoms

HOW LARGE ARE ATOMS?

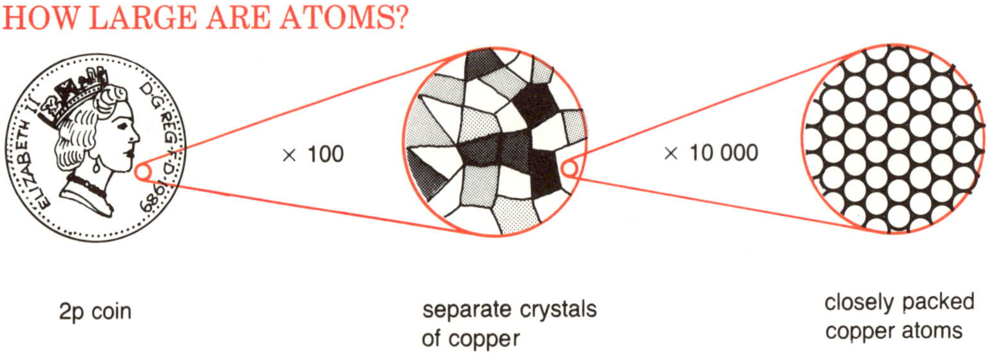

Fig. 15.14 You would have to magnify a copper coin to about 10 000 times its actual size to be able to see individual copper atoms

Atoms are about one hundred millionth ($\frac{1}{100\,000\,000}$) of a centimetre across. This means that if you put 100 million of them side by side, together they would measure about one centimetre. It is very difficult to imagine anything as small as this, but Fig. 15.14 might help you.

If the surface of a two pence coin is magnified one hundred times using an ordinary microscope, it is possible to see crystals of copper. If these crystals were then magnified ten thousand times, it would be possible to see copper atoms. The coin would have been magnified first 100 times, then 10 000 times, i.e. one million times in total (100 × 10 000). By doing this, it is possible to see the individual copper atoms in the coin.

HOW HEAVY ARE ATOMS?–RELATIVE ATOMIC MASSES

A single atom is far too small to be weighed on a balance. However the mass of one atom can be compared with that of another atom using a **mass spectrometer** (see Fig. 15.15).

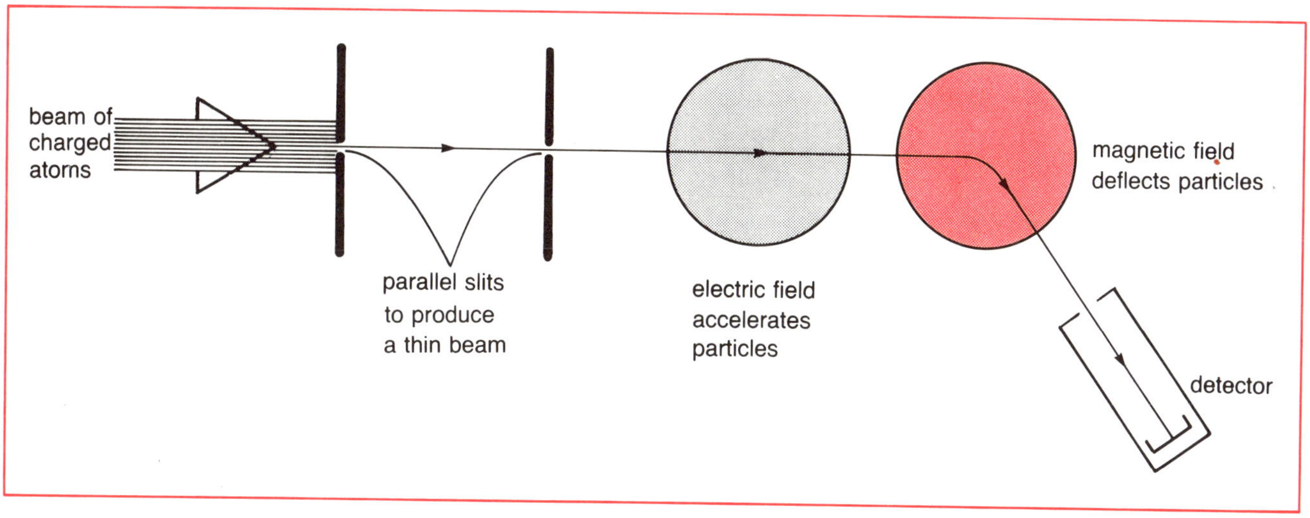

Fig. 15.15 A simplified diagram of a mass spectrometer

In a mass spectrometer a beam of charged atoms is passed along a tube and focused into a thin beam. This beam of particles passes first through an electric field which speeds them up, then through a magnetic field which deflects them. The extent to which an atom is deflected depends on its mass. The greater the mass, the smaller the deflection. By comparing the deflections, it is possible to compare the masses of different atoms and make a list of the **relative masses**. The relative masses which scientists use for different atoms are called **relative atomic masses** (RAM).

The element **carbon** has been chosen as the *standard* for relative atomic masses. Carbon atoms are given a *relative mass of 12* and the relative masses of other atoms are obtained by comparison with the mass of a carbon atom. A few relative atomic masses are listed in Table 15.2. From the table you will see that carbon atoms are twelve times as heavy as hydrogen atoms. Oxygen atoms are sixteen times as heavy as hydrogen atoms.

The symbol A_r is sometimes used for relative atomic mass. We write $A_r(C) = 12.0$ and $A_r(Cu) = 63.5$.

Table 15.2 The relative atomic masses of a few common elements

Element	*Symbol*	*Relative atomic mass*
Carbon	C	12.0
Hydrogen	H	1.0
Oxygen	O	16.0
Copper	Cu	63.5
Iron	Fe	55.8

15.9 How much?

Scientists often ask the question 'How much?'. They want to know *how much* of one substance is used up or formed in a chemical reaction. We can answer these questions using the idea of relative atomic masses. Relative atomic masses show that one atom of carbon is twelve times as heavy as one atom of hydrogen. Therefore 12 g of carbon contains the same number of atoms as 1 g of hydrogen. An atom of oxygen is sixteen times as heavy as an atom of hydrogen. So 16 g of oxygen also contains the same number of atoms as 1 g of hydrogen or 12 g of carbon. In fact,

the relative atomic mass of any element will contain the same number of atoms as 12 g of carbon

Experiments show that the relative atomic mass of an element in grams always contains 6×10^{23} atoms. The number $\mathbf{6 \times 10^{23}}$ is called the **Avogadro constant** in honour of the Italian scientist Amedeo Avogadro (1776–1856).

The amount of a substance which contains 6×10^{23} particles is often called a **mole**. Chemists use the mole as their unit for counting atoms. In the same way as we might use dozens to count eggs or hundreds to count people (Table 15.3).

Table 15.3 Some counting units

1 pair	= 2
1 dozen	= 12
1 gross	= 20
1 hundred	= 100
1 million	= 10^6
1 mole	= 6×10^{23}

So 12 g of carbon is one mole of carbon because it contains 6×10^{23} atoms. 1 g of hydrogen is also 1 mole. 24 g of carbon is 2 moles and 240 g of carbon is 10 moles. Notice that:

$$\text{number of moles} = \frac{\text{mass in grams}}{\text{RAM}}$$

RELATIVE FORMULA MASS

So far we have considered *elements*, *atoms* and *relative atomic masses*. We must now consider **compounds**, **molecules** and **relative formula masses** (also called relative molecular masses). Relative formula masses are compared in the same way as relative atomic masses. For example:

- the relative atomic mass of hydrogen (H) = 1, and
- the relative atomic mass of oxygen (O) = 16.

From these relative atomic masses we can calculate:

- the relative formula mass of hydrogen gas (H_2) = 1 + 1 = 2,
- the relative formula mass of oxygen (O_2) = 16 + 16 = 32, and
- the relative formula mass of water (H_2O) = 1 + 1 + 16 = 18.

Notice that *the relative formula mass of a compound is obtained by simply adding up the relative atomic masses of all the atoms in the formula.*

FINDING FORMULAS

We have used some formulas already. But how are they obtained? How do we know, for example, that the formula of water is H_2O?

Formulas are obtained by carrying out experiments. First we must find the masses of each of the elements in a sample of the compound. These masses can then be used to work out the number of moles of each element present and hence the formula of the compound.

Example

Some iron pyrites was purified. 12 g of the purified ore contained 5.6 g of iron and 6.4 g of sulphur. What is its formula?

$A_r(\text{Fe}) = 56$; $A_r(\text{S}) = 32$.

Ratio of masses of iron and sulphur in the ore $= 5.6 : 6.4$

Ratio of moles of iron and sulphur in the ore $= \frac{5.6}{56} : \frac{6.4}{32}$

$= 0.1 : 0.2$

So the iron pyrites sample contained 0.1 moles of iron and 0.2 moles of sulphur. The iron and sulphur were present in a ratio of 1:2.

The formula of a compound shows the number of moles of each element in the compound as well as the number of atoms. So the formula of iron pyrites is $\mathbf{FeS_2}$.

The calculations we have just made are summarized in Table 15.4.

Table 15.4 Calculating the formula of iron pyrites

	Fe	S
Masses present	5.6 g	6.4 g
Mass of 1 mole	56 g	32 g
∴ moles present	0.1	0.2
Ratio of moles	1	2
∴ formula for the compound is $\mathbf{FeS_2}$.		

REACTING AMOUNTS

In industry it is often important to know the amounts of reactants and products in a chemical process. Industrial chemists need to calculate how much product they can get from a given amount of starting material. In order to do this they use formulas, equations and relative atomic masses.

For example, suppose we want to know how much aluminium we can get from 1 kg of pure bauxite (aluminium oxide, Al_2O_3). The necessary calculations are as follows:

aluminium oxide	$\longrightarrow$	aluminium	*(word equation)*
Al_2O_3	$\longrightarrow$	$2Al$	*(balanced equation)*
$\therefore$ 1 mole Al_2O_3	$\longrightarrow$	2 moles Al	*(moles reactants & products)*
$(27+27+16+16+16)$g Al_2O_3	$\longrightarrow$	$(27+27)$g Al	*(RAMs: $A_r(Al)=27; A_r(O)=16$)*
i.e. 102 g Al_2O_3	$\longrightarrow$	54 g Al	
$\therefore$ 1 g Al_2O_3	$\longrightarrow$	$\frac{54}{102}$ g Al=0.53 g Al	*(Divide both sides by 102)*

So 1 kg of bauxite will produce 0.53 kg of aluminium.

Quick test 15

1 If you look at smoke particles through a microscope, you will see them moving about randomly. This movement is due to
- A air currents blowing on the smoke particles.
- B air molecules bumping into smoke particles.
- C forces of attraction between the smoke particles.
- D smoke particles reacting with oxygen in the air.

2 Gases diffuse faster than liquids because gas molecules are
- A freer to move than liquid molecules.
- B more compressible than liquid molecules.
- C lighter than liquid molecules.
- D more elastic than liquid molecules.

3 Solids do *not* diffuse like liquids because the particles of a solid
- A are stationary.
- B are too close to move.
- C are too heavy to move.
- D cannot move around each other.

4 As a liquid freezes, its particles
- A slow down, but continue to move around each other.
- B stop moving and form a regular arrangement.
- C slow down, until they only move around fixed points.
- D stop moving as they get closer to each other.

5 Which *one* of the following will change the temperature at which a liquid boils?
- A The amount of liquid.
- B Solid dissolved in the liquid.
- C The air temperature.
- D The temperature of the Bunsen flame.

6 An element is described as *diatomic* if it has two
- A symbols in its formula.
- B formulas in its symbols.
- C atoms in each molecule.
- D molecules in each atom.

7 Which one of the following is the correctly balanced equation for the reaction between iron and chlorine to form iron(III) chloride, $FeCl_3$?
- A $Fe + 3Cl \longrightarrow FeCl_3$
- B $Fe + Cl_2 \longrightarrow FeCl_3$
- C $Fe + 3Cl_2 \longrightarrow FeCl_3$
- D $2Fe + 3Cl_2 \longrightarrow 2FeCl_3$

Questions 8 to 12

In the boxes below, ● and ● represent different atoms.

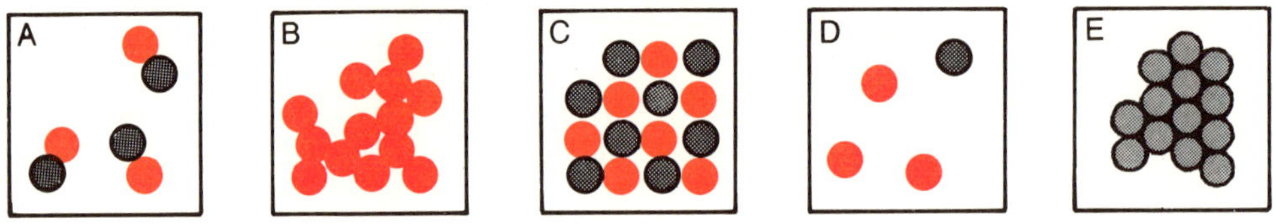

Which box contains

8 a close packed metal?

9 a solid compound?

10 a liquid?

11 a mixture?

12 diatomic molecules?

Questions 13 to 14

How many atoms are there in one molecule of

13 methane, CH_4?

14 sulphuric acid, H_2SO_4?

Questions 15 to 18

Write balanced equations for the reactions of

15 charcoal (carbon) burning in oxygen to give carbon dioxide.

16 natural gas (methane, CH_4) burning in oxygen to give carbon dioxide and water.

17 copper oxide with sulphuric acid (H_2SO_4) to give copper sulphate ($CuSO_4$) and water.

18 nitrogen with hydrogen to give ammonia (NH_3).

Questions 19 to 20

What is the mass of

19 6 moles of bromine ($A_r(\text{Br}) = 80$)?

20 $\frac{1}{5}$ mole of calcium ($A_r(\text{Ca}) = 40$)?

Questions 21 to 22

Calculate the formula of

21 the compound which is 75 per cent carbon and 25 per cent hydrogen (by weight) ($A_r(\text{C}) = 12$, $A_r(\text{H}) = 1$),

22 the compound which contains 0.26 g of chromium combined with 0.07 g of nitrogen ($A_r(\text{Cr}) = 52$, $A_r(\text{N}) = 14$).

16 ELECTRICITY AND ELECTROLYSIS

16.1 Introduction

Electricity plays an important part in our lives. We use it for lighting, for heating and for cooking. Most of the electricity we use is *mains electricity*. We use this to operate electric lights, electric cookers, electric kettles, hair dryers and other electrical gadgets. In addition to the dozens of everyday appliances which use mains electricity, there are many others which use electricity from *cells and batteries*. These include radios, watches, torches and calculators.

Fig. 16.1 City lighting – the sky line of Croydon, Surrey, at night (Photograph courtesy of the Electricity Council)

This chapter will cover:

- ideas about electric currents;
- the properties of different substances as conductors or non-conductors;
- the important uses of electrolysis in industry;
- the generation of electricity from cells and batteries.

16.2 Electric currents

All atoms are composed of just three particles–**protons**, **neutrons and electrons**. Different atoms have different numbers of these particles. For example, every hydrogen atom has one proton and one electron; helium atoms, the next simplest, each have two protons, two neutrons and two electrons (see Fig. 16.2, overleaf).

Protons and neutrons occupy the centre of the atom, the **nucleus**. Protons are positively charged, but neutrons have no charge. Electrons occupy the outer areas of the atom and move around the nucleus. Electrons have a negative charge.
During chemical reactions and other processes, the electrons in the outer parts of atoms can be transferred from one substance to another.

Metals are the only common solids whose atoms give up their electrons easily. Metals allow electrons to pass through them–because of this they are called **conductors** and are used for fuses, wires and cables in electrical machinery.

Most other solids, particularly plastics like polythene and PVC, hold on to their

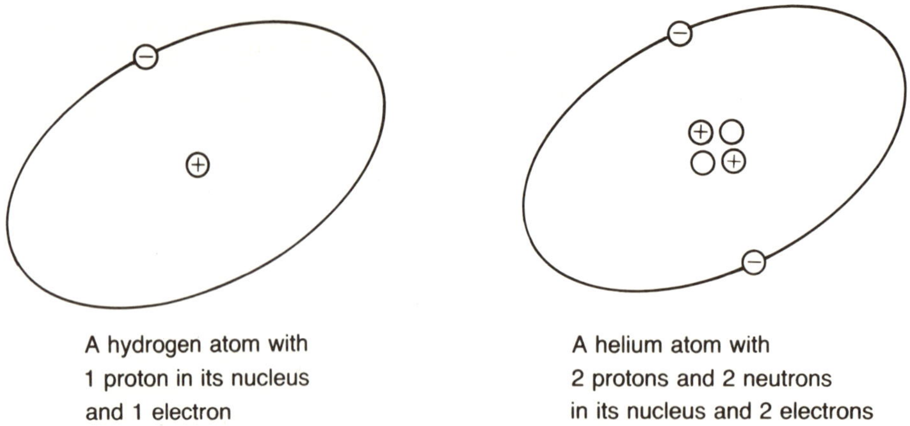

Fig. 16.2 Protons, neutrons and electrons in **(a)** a hydrogen atom and **(b)** a helium atom (⊕= proton, ⊖ = electron, ○ = neutron)

electrons very strongly. They do *not* allow electrons to pass through them, so they are used as **insulators** for electrical wires and cables.

When an electric current flows through a metal wire, the outermost electrons in the metal atoms are attracted to the positive terminal of the battery. At the same time, more electrons are repelled from the negative terminal into the metal wire (see Fig. 16.3). In a metal, **an electric current is simply a flow of electrons**. Electrons flow through the metal, like traffic flowing along a road or water flowing through a pipe.

Electric currents, voltages and circuit diagrams are discussed in detail in sections 27.2 to 27.4.

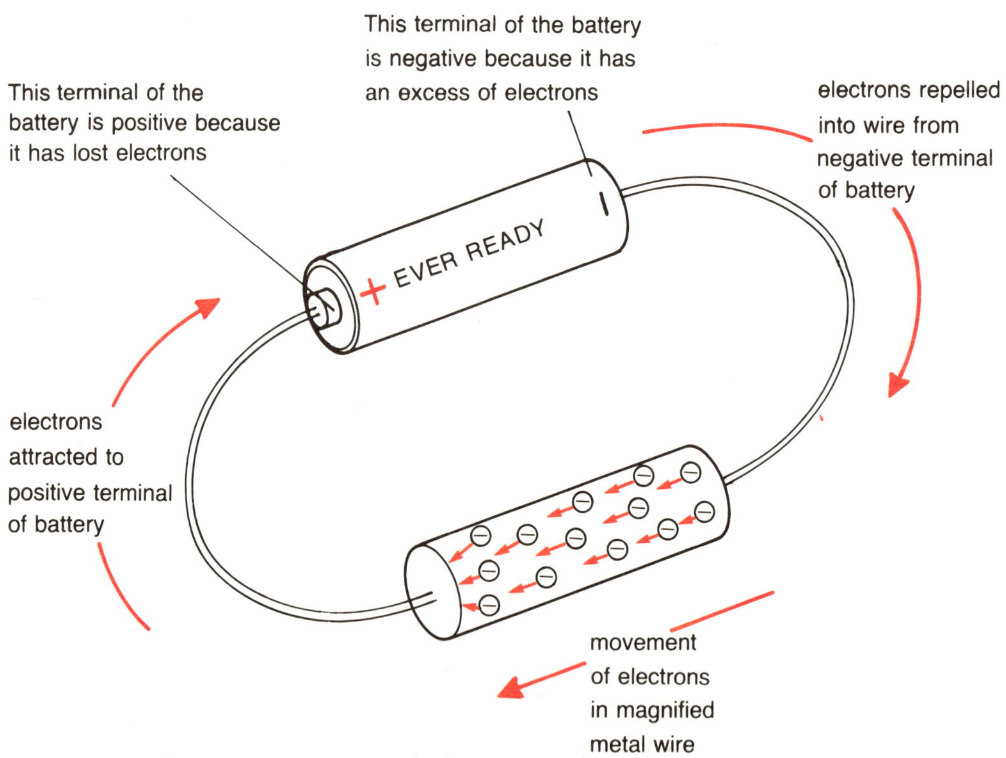

Fig. 16.3 An electric current in a metal wire

16.3 Conduction of electricity by solids and liquids

CONDUCTION

Which solids conduct electricity?

The apparatus shown in Fig. 13.3 (page 116) can be used to check whether a solid conducts electricity. Experiments show that

> **the only common solids which conduct electricity at low voltages are metals and graphite.**

When metals and graphite conduct electricity

- electrons flow through the material.
- there is no chemical reaction.
- no new substances are produced.

Which liquids conduct electricity?

Figure 16.4 shows the apparatus which we can use to test the conductivity of liquids. The terminals through which the electric current enters and leaves the liquids are called **electrodes**. The electrode connected to the positive terminal of the battery is positive itself. It is called the **anode**. The electrode connected to the negative terminal of the battery is negative itself. It is called the **cathode**.

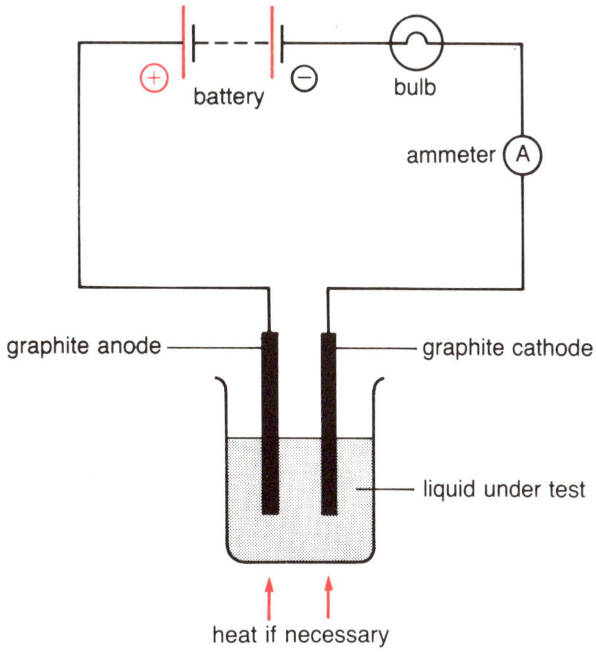

Fig. 16.4 Investigating the conductivity of liquids

Experiments show that **the following liquids will conduct electricity**:

- liquid metals (e.g. molten iron, mercury)
- liquid metal/nonmetal compounds (e.g. *molten* sodium chloride).
- aqueous solutions of metal/nonmetal compounds (e.g. sodium chloride *solution*).
- aqueous solutions of acids (e.g. sulphuric acid).

ELECTROLYSIS

Liquid metals conduct electricity by allowing a flow of electrons in the same way as solid metals.

Unlike metals, liquid and aqueous compounds which conduct electricity are *decomposed* during the process. For example, when liquid (molten) sodium chloride conducts electricity, it is decomposed into sodium and chlorine. This can be summarized by the following word equation:

$$\text{sodium chloride} \xrightarrow{\text{electricity}} \text{sodium} + \text{chlorine}$$

This *decomposition of compounds by electricity* is called **electrolysis**. The *compound which is decomposed* is called an **electrolyte**.

The products of electrolysis

When compounds are electrolysed, new substances are produced at the electrodes. For example, when electricity is passed through potassium iodide solution using the apparatus in Fig. 16.5 (overleaf), brown streaks of iodine appear near the anode and

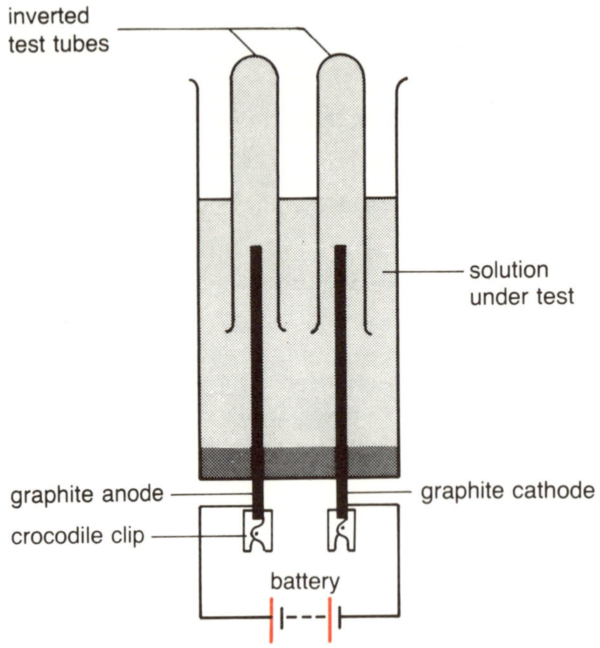

Fig. 16.5 Investigating the products at the electrodes when liquids are electrolysed

bubbles of a colourless gas stream off the cathode. When tested with a lighted splint, the gas gives a 'pop'. This shows that the gas is hydrogen.

Table 16.1 shows the products formed at the anode and cathode when various liquid and aqueous compounds are electrolysed. Remember that water is present in the aqueous compounds and this may give rise to one or both of the products at the electrodes.

Table 16.1 Products at the anode and cathode when various liquid and aqueous compounds are electrolysed

Compound electrolysed	*Product at cathode*	*Product at anode*
molten sodium chloride	sodium	chlorine
molten lead bromine	lead	bromine
aqueous potassium iodide	hydrogen	iodine
aqueous sodium chloride	hydrogen	chlorine
aqueous copper sulphate	copper	oxygen
hydrochloric acid	hydrogen	chlorine

In Table 16.1, all the compounds are decomposed by electrical energy. An element is produced at each electrode. For example,

$$\text{lead bromide} \xrightarrow[\text{energy}]{\text{electrical}} \text{lead} + \text{bromine}$$

Look at the results in Table 16.1 and notice the following pattern amongst the products:

When metal/nonmetal compounds and acids are electrolysed

- a metal or hydrogen forms at the cathode.
- a nonmetal (except hydrogen) forms at the anode.

16.4 Explaining electrolysis

When liquid sodium chloride is electrolysed, sodium is produced at the cathode and chlorine at the anode. Sodium particles in the electrolyte have been attracted to the negative cathode, so they are probably positively charged. Scientists write these positively charged sodium particles in sodium chloride as Na^+. At the same time, chlorine is produced at the positive anode, so the chlorine particles in the electrolyte must be negatively charged. These negatively charged chlorine particles in sodium chloride can be written as Cl^-.

Charged particles, such as Na^+ and Cl^-, which move to the electrodes during electrolysis, are called **ions**.

During electrolysis, Na^+ ions near the cathode combine with negative electrons on the cathode forming neutral sodium atoms:

$$Na^+ + e^- \longrightarrow Na$$

At the anode, Cl^- ions lose an electron to the positive anode and form neutral chlorine atoms:

$$Cl^- \longrightarrow e^- + Cl$$

The chlorine atoms then join up in pairs to form diatomic molecules of chlorine gas, Cl_2.

$$\underbrace{Cl + Cl}_{\text{2 chlorine atoms}} \longrightarrow \underset{\text{chlorine molecule}}{Cl_2}$$

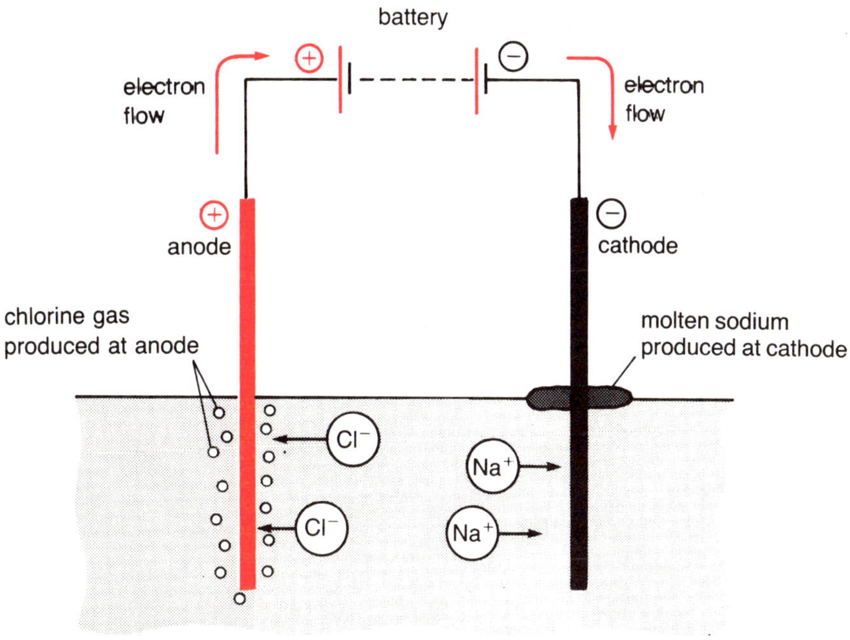

Fig. 16.6 Electrolysis of molten sodium chloride

The movement of ions in the electrolyte and the movement of electrons in the circuit is shown in Fig. 16.6. Notice that the electric current is being carried through the molten sodium chloride by ions. Na^+ ions remove electrons from the cathode and Cl^- ions give up electrons at the anode. The electron flow in Fig. 16.6 has been shown *by drawing an arrow at the side of the circuit*. This is the usual way in which electron flow should be shown in a circuit.

The electrolysis of other molten and aqueous electrolytes can also be explained in terms of ions.

16.5 Charges on ions

As we saw in section 16.3 (Table 16.1), when electrolysis occurs

- metals and hydrogen are produced at the cathode, and
- non-metals (except hydrogen) are produced at the anode.

The negative cathode will attract only positive charges and the positive anode will attract only negative charges. From these results and ideas we can deduce that:

- **Metals and hydrogen have positive ions.**
  Positive ions are called **cations** because they are *attracted to the cathode.*
- **Non-metals (except hydrogen) have negative ions.**
  Negative ions are called **anions** because they are *attracted to the anode.*

Electrolysis experiments show that it requires twice as much electricity (twice as many electrons) to produce a magnesium atom as to produce a sodium atom. Earlier in this section, we wrote the formation of sodium during electrolysis as follows:

$$\underset{\text{sodium ion}}{Na^+} + \underset{\text{electron}}{e^-} \longrightarrow \underset{\text{sodium atom}}{Na}$$

Using the information about the relative amounts of electricity needed, we can therefore write the formation of magnesium as follows:

Mg^{2+}	+	$2e^-$	$\longrightarrow$	Mg
magnesium ion		2 electrons		magnesium atom

In this way we can build up a table of ions showing their charges, e.g. Table 16.2.

Table 16.2 Common ions and their charges

Cations						Anions			
+1		+2		+3		−1		−2	
Hydrogen	H^+	Copper	Cu^{2+}	Aluminium	Al^{3+}	Chloride	Cl^-	Oxide	O^{2-}
Sodium	Na^+	Magnesium	Mg^{2+}	Chromium	Cr^{3+}	Bromide	Br^-	Carbonate	CO_3^{2-}
Potassium	K^+	Calcium	Ca^{2+}	Iron(III)	Fe^{3+}	Iodide	I^-	Sulphide	S^{2-}
Silver	Ag^+	Zinc	Zn^{2+}			Hydroxide	OH^-	Sulphite	SO_3^{2-}
		Iron(II)	Fe^{2+}			Nitrate	NO_3^-	Sulphate	SO_4^{2-}
		Lead	Pb^{2+}						

Most metal ions have a charge of +2.
–the only common metal ions with a charge of +1 are Ag^+, Na^+ and K^+.
(To remember this, say *AgNaK*.)
–the only common metal ions with a charge of +3 are Cr^{3+}, Al^{3+} and Fe^{3+}
(To remember this, say *CrAlFe*.)
–Notice that **iron can form two different ions**, Fe^{2+} and Fe^{3+}. We show this in the names of compounds by writing iron(II) for Fe^{2+} and iron(III) for Fe^{3+}. Thus iron forms two oxides, two chlorides, etc. For example, its two oxides are iron(II) oxide, which is black, and iron(III) oxide, which is red-brown.

16.6 Ionic compounds

All metal/nonmetal compounds are composed of ions. They are therefore called **ionic compounds**. Ionic compounds include salt (sodium chloride), rust (iron(III) oxide) and limestone (calcium carbonate).

FORMULAS OF IONIC COMPOUNDS

To obtain the formulas of ionic compounds we must *balance the charges* on the positive ions with those on the negative ions. For example:

- The formula of sodium chloride is Na^+Cl^-, or simply NaCl. The one positive charge on Na^+ is balanced by one negative charge on Cl^-.

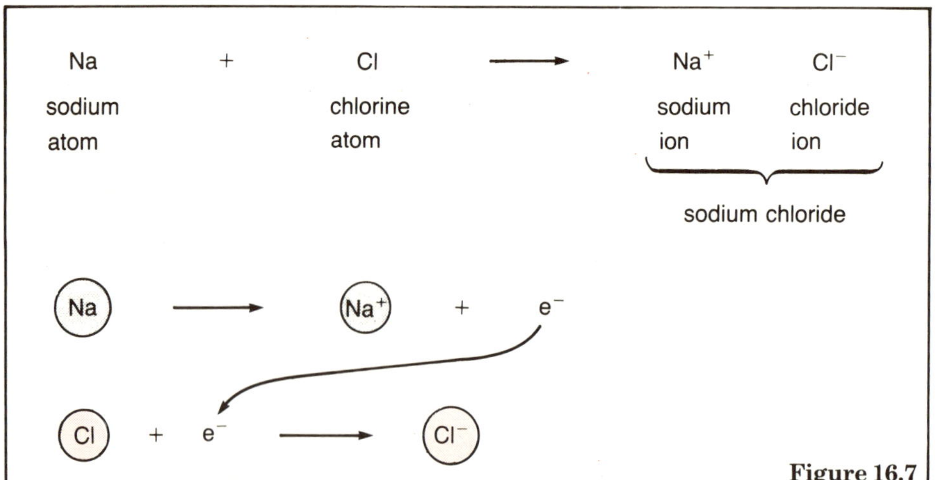

Figure 16.7

- The formula of magnesium chloride is $Mg^{2+}(Cl^-)_2$ or $MgCl_2$. Here the charges on two Cl^- ions are balanced by one Mg^{2+} ion.
- What is the formula for slaked lime (calcium hydroxide)? Like magnesium ions, calcium ions have a +2 charge. Two hydroxide ions (OH^-), each −1, will be needed to balance the charges. The formula is therefore $Ca^{2+}(OH^-)_2$ or $Ca(OH)_2$.

Notice that brackets are required around the OH in $Ca(OH)_2$. The brackets show that OH is a single unit containing one oxygen atom and one hydrogen atom. The 2 means that there are two of these units. (It would be quite wrong to write $CaOH_2$ for the formula of calcium hydroxide. This would mean that there is only one oxygen atom for every two hydrogen atoms in calcium hydroxide.)

Other ions, for example NO_3^-, SO_4^{2-} and CO_3^{2-}, must also be regarded as single units and put in brackets when there are two or three of them in a formula. For example, the formula for iron(III) nitrate is $Fe(NO_3)_3$.

FORMATION OF IONIC COMPOUNDS

Ionic compounds form when metals react with nonmetals. During these reactions, *metal atoms lose electrons and form positive ions*. At the same time, *nonmetal atoms gain electrons and form negative ions*. Figure 16.7 represented what happens when sodium reacts with chlorine to form sodium chloride. In this case, one electron is transferred from each Na atom to each Cl atom.

PROPERTIES OF IONIC COMPOUNDS

In solid ionic compounds, the ions are held together by the attraction between positive ions and negative ions. Figure 16.8 shows the arrangement of ions in a layer of sodium chloride. Notice that Na^+ ions are surrounded by Cl^- ions and vice versa. Structures like sodium chloride in which large numbers of atoms or ions are packed together in a regular pattern are called **giant structures**.

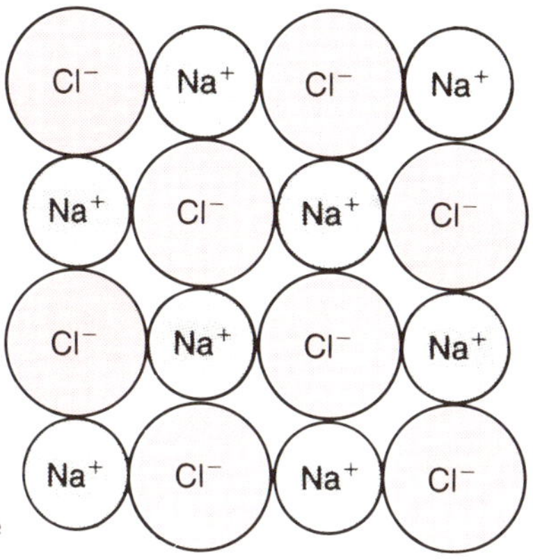

Fig. 16.8 The arrangment of ions in solid sodium chloride

In solid sodium chloride, there are strong forces of attraction between the oppositely charged ions. These forces are called **ionic bonds** or **electrovalent bonds**. The strong ionic bonds hold the ions together very firmly, giving ionic compounds the following properties:

Ionic compounds

- are solids at room temperature.
- have high melting points and high boiling points.
- are hard substances.
- cannot conduct electricity when solid because the ions cannot move to the electrodes.
- conduct electricity when molten or in aqueous solution because the ions are free to move to the electrodes.

16.7 Molecular compounds

When metals react with non-metals, ionic compounds are formed. Non-metals can also react with each other to form compounds, e.g. water (H_2O), carbon dioxide (CO_2) and ammonia (NH_3). These nonmetal compounds are composed of *small neutral molecules*. They *do not contain ions*. They are called **simple molecular compounds**.

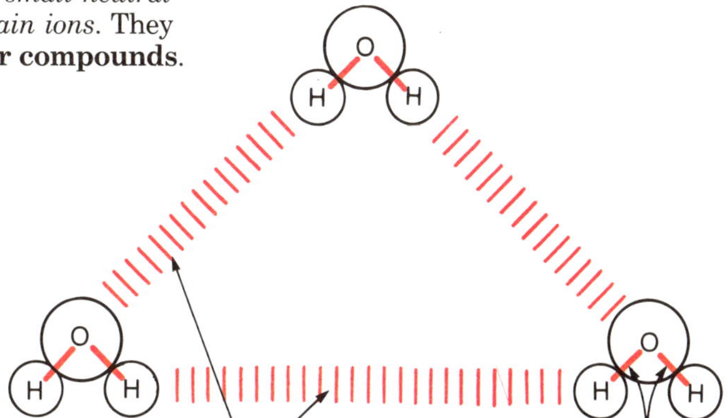

Fig. 16.9 Bonds in simple molecular compounds

In simple molecular compounds, such as water, there are strong bonds which hold the atoms together *within each molecule*. These are called **covalent bonds**. There are also weak bonds *between the separate molecules*. These are known as **intermolecular bonds** (see Fig. 16.9).

Intermolecular bonds hold the separate molecules together in liquids such as water and in solids such as sugar and dry ice (solid carbon dioxide). Even so, the intermolecular bonds are very weak, so simple molecular compounds have the following properties:

Simple molecular compounds

- are liquids or gases at room temperature.
- have low melting points and boiling points.
- are soft when solid.
- cannot conduct electricity as solids or liquids because they have neither ions (like ionic compounds) nor mobile electrons (like metals).

16.8 Electrolysis in industry

Electrolysis is very important in industry. Three of its important applications are:

1 the manufacture of aluminium;

2 electroplating; and

3 the manufacture of hydrogen, chlorine and sodium hydroxide from salt.

We will look at each of these applications in some detail.

THE MANUFACTURE OF ALUMINIUM

Reactive metals such as sodium and aluminium cannot be obtained by reduction of their oxides with coke (carbon) (see section 17.7). These metals have to be manufactured by electrolysis of their molten (liquid) compounds. We cannot use electrolysis of their aqueous solutions because hydrogen from the water would be produced at the cathode, *not* the metal. For example, when aqueous sodium chloride is electrolysed, hydrogen is produced at the cathode, *not* sodium.

Aluminium is manufactured by the *electrolysis of molten aluminium oxide*. The aluminium oxide is obtained from *bauxite*.

The melting point of pure aluminium oxide is 2045°C. It would be very expensive to carry out electrolysis at this high temperature. The aluminium oxide is therefore dissolved in molten *cryolite* ($Na_3Al_3F_6$) which melts at less than 1000°C.

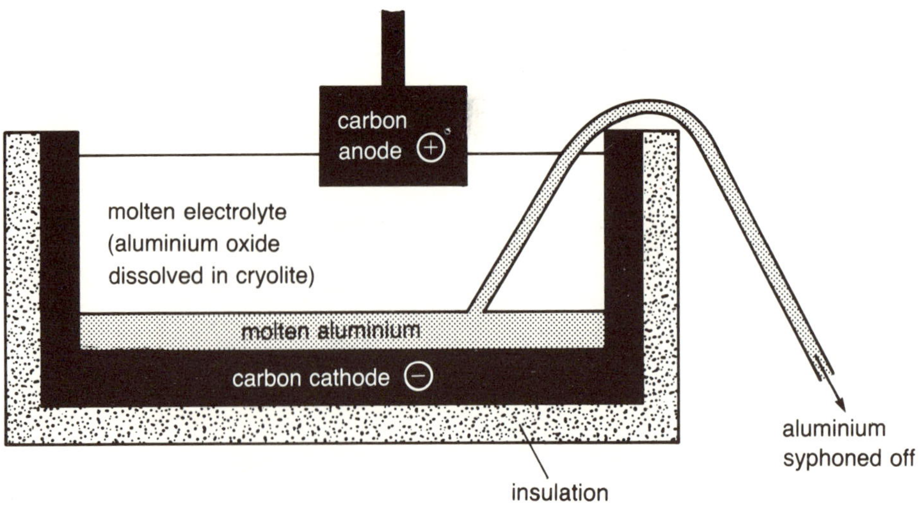

Fig. 16.10 The electrolytic cell for the manufacture of aluminium

Figure 16.10 shows a diagram of the electrolytic cell used. Aluminium ions (Al^{3+}) in the electrolyte are attracted to the carbon cathode lining the cell. Here they accept electrons and form aluminium.

Cathode (−) $Al^{3+} + 3e^- \longrightarrow Al$

Molten aluminium collects at the bottom of the cell and is syphoned off at intervals.

Oxide ions (O^{2-}) are attracted to the carbon anode. Here they give up electrons and produce oxygen (O_2).

Anode (+) $2O^{2-} \longrightarrow 4e^- + O_2$

It takes about 16 kilowatt hours of electricity to produce 1 kg of aluminium. Because of this, plants manufacturing aluminium are usually sited near sources of cheap electricity.

Fig. 16.11 Aluminium is a very useful metal. This photograph shows a greenhouse with an aluminium frame. Aluminium is strong, it has a low density and it does not rust. Because of these properties the aluminium supports the glass firmly, it is relatively light and it never needs painting (Photograph courtesy of Aluminium Greenhouses)

ELECTROPLATING

Electroplating is used to protect metals from corrosion and make articles more attractive. Bicycle frames and the steel bodywork of cars are protected from corrosion by copper plating. Car bumpers and kettles are protected in a similar way by chromium plating. Unfortunately, chromium will not stick to iron (steel) or copper during electroplating. Steel articles which are to be chromium plated are first plated with nickel. Nickel forms a firm deposit on the steel which can then be plated with chromium.

Copper, nickel, chromium and *silver* are the metals most commonly used for electroplating. The metal coating is deposited on the cathode, so the object to be plated must be used as the cathode during electrolysis. The electrolyte must also contain a compound of the metal which forms the coating.

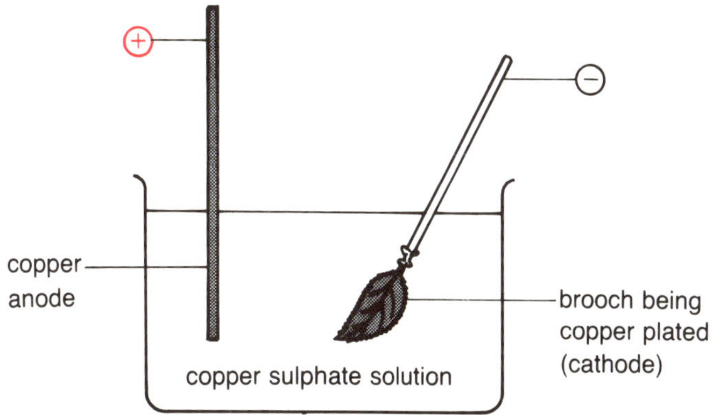

Figure 16.12

Figure 16.12 shows a steel brooch being electroplated with copper. During electrolysis, copper ions (Cu^{2+}) in the electrolyte are attracted to the cathode (the brooch). Here they gain electrons and form a deposit of copper.

Cathode (−) $Cu^{2+} + 2e^- \longrightarrow Cu$

The anode is a piece of pure copper. Sulphate ions (SO_4^{2-}) in the electrolyte are attracted to the anode, but they do not react in any way. Instead, copper atoms in the anode give up electrons to the anode and go into solution as Cu^{2+} ions.

Anode (+) $Cu \longrightarrow Cu^{2+} + 2e^-$

Notice that this process at the anode replaces the copper ions which are removed from the electrolyte at the cathode.

THE MANUFACTURE OF HYDROGEN, CHLORINE AND SODIUM HYDROXIDE FROM SALT

Salt (sodium chloride) is one of the cheapest and most widely available raw materials. It is found in vast quantities underground and in sea water. The electrolysis of **sodium chloride solution (brine)** is used to manufacture hydrogen, chlorine and sodium hydroxide. Figure 16.13 shows how the process is carried out in a **diaphragm cell**.

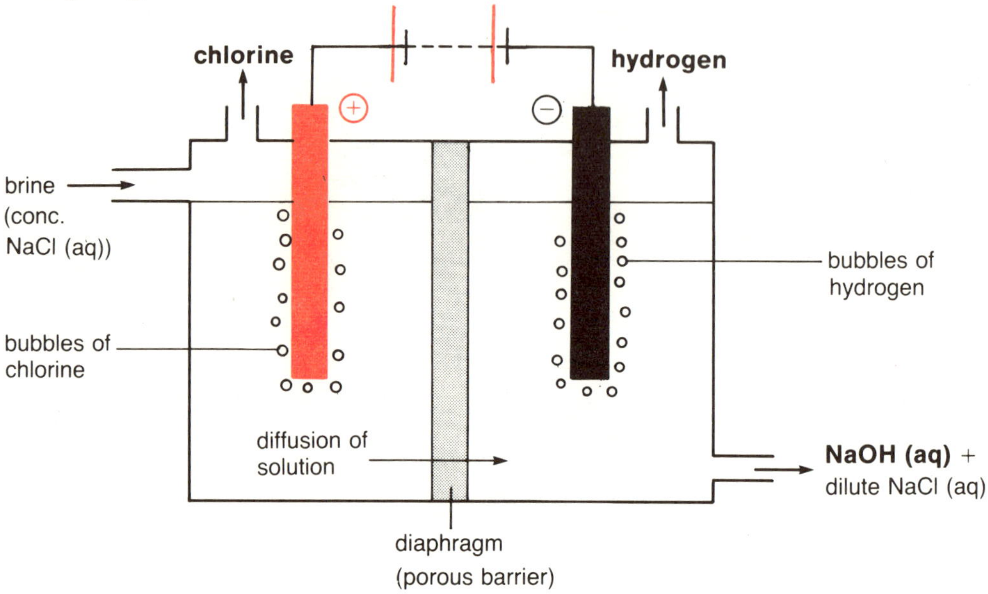

At the anode ⊕

Chlorine is produced

$2Cl^- \rightarrow 2e^- + Cl_2$

At the cathode ⊖

Hydrogen is produced

$2H^+ + 2e^- \rightarrow H_2$

The removal of Cl^- ions from NaCl (aq) and H^+ ions from water, leaves behind Na^+ and OH^- ions. These form a solution of sodium hydroxide.

Fig. 16.13 The manufacture of hydrogen, chlorine and sodium hydroxide

16.9 Making electricity

When electrolysis occurs, electricity (electrical energy) is used to decompose substances and produce new chemicals. Electrical energy is coverted into chemical energy in the products at the electrodes.

In cells and batteries, this process takes place in reverse. Chemical energy in the materials of cells is converted into electricity.

$$\text{Electrical energy} \underset{\text{cells/batteries}}{\overset{\text{electrolysis}}{\rightleftarrows}} \text{Chemical energy}$$

Cells and batteries are very convenient sources of electricity. They are used in torches, radios, watches, calculators and vehicles.

THE DRY CELL

The dry cell is one of the most widely used type of cell. Dry cells are used in torches, bicycle lamps and door bells. They are called *dry* cells because the electrolyte is a paste of ammonium chloride. This avoids the danger of liquid spilling out.

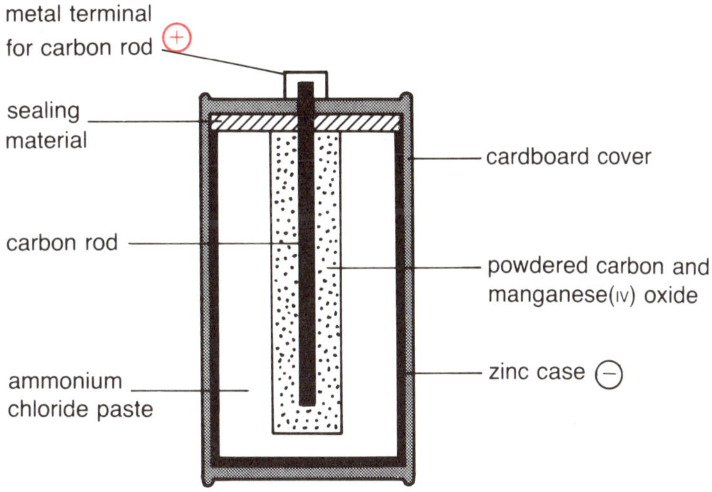

Fig. 16.14 A dry cell

When the cell is being used, the zinc case acts as the negative terminal. Zinc atoms give up electrons which form the electric current from the cell.

$$Zn \longrightarrow Zn^{2+} + 2e^-$$

The electrons flow through the torch or radio, etc, to the carbon rod which is the positive terminal. Here, ammonium ions (NH_4^+) in the ammonium chloride paste accept electrons and form ammonia and hydrogen.

$$2NH_4^+ + 2e^- \longrightarrow 2NH_3 + H_2$$

Arrangements like the dry cell which generate electric currents are called **cells**. When *two or more cells are joined together* they form a **battery**. One dry cell produces about 1.5 volts. Batteries of dry cells can be used to give up to 100 volts. When dry cells are used, the zinc case forms Zn^{2+} ions which dissolve in the paste. Eventually the zinc case is worn away and the paste leaks out. The paste is corrosive and acidic, so old batteries should be replaced as soon as they have run out.

RECHARGEABLE CELLS

When dry cells produce electricity, their chemicals are used up. Dry cells cannot be *recharged* and used again. Cells like this are called **primary cells** or simple cells. In contrast, **secondary cells** or **rechargeable cells** can be recharged and used again.

The most common rechargeable cells are **lead-acid cells** which are used in car batteries. One lead-acid cell produces about 2 volts. In a lead-acid cell:

- The negative terminal is a lead plate;
- the positive terminal is a lead plate covered in lead(IV) oxide (PbO_2);
- the electrolyte is sulphuric acid (H_2SO_4).

When a lead-acid cell produces electricity (discharges), lead atoms on the negative terminal give up electrons to form lead ions.

$$Pb(s) \longrightarrow Pb^{2+}(aq) + 2e^-$$

These electrons form the electric current which operates the starter motor and the electrical gadgets (e.g. the dashboard lights and the radio) in a car.

The electrons flow to the positive terminal of the cell. Here lead(IV) oxide takes the electrons and H^+ ions from the electrolyte to form lead ions and water.

$$PbO_2(s) + 4H^+(aq) + 2e^- \longrightarrow Pb^{2+}(aq) + 2H_2O(l)$$

As the battery discharges, H^+ ions are used up and water forms. This lowers the concentration of the acid and also the density of the electrolyte. The state of charge of a lead-acid cell can therefore be checked by measuring the density of the electrolyte. Lead-acid cells must be recharged before they get 'flat' (fully discharged). The cell is recharged automatically during long journeys. As the car moves, a small dynamo generates electricity. This passes through the cell in the opposite direction to the working current, reversing the reactions at the terminals.

Quick test 16

Questions 1 to 5

Chlorine is made by passing an electric current through a solution of sodium chloride. The chlorine collects at the positive electrode.

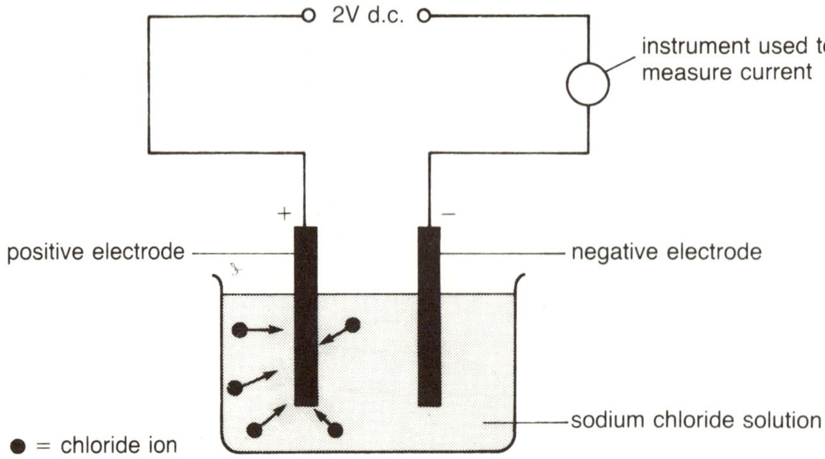

1 What is the type of charge on the chloride ions?
2 Explain why the chloride ions move towards the positive electrode.
3 Name the instrument used to measure current.
4 Name the unit of current.
5 What quantity is measured in volts? (*NEA*, 1988)

(Information for questions **3** to **5** and **7** to **9** can be found in sections 27.2 to 27.4.)

Questions 6 to 10

The apparatus shown below was set up to silver plate a metal spoon.

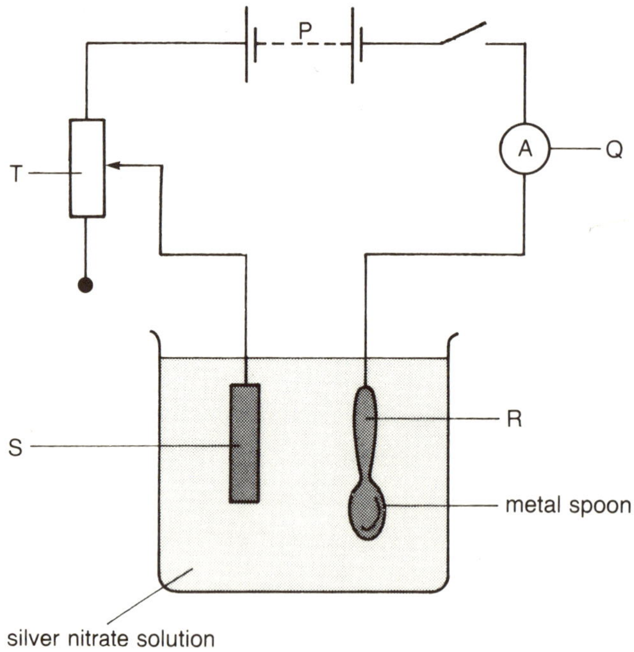

6 Which piece of apparatus (P, Q, R, S or T) is the cathode?
7 What is T used for?
8 What should S be made of?
9 Which *one* of the following would be the safest and most effective conditions for the experiment?

	current	*voltage*	*time*
A	20 A	200 V	30 minutes
B	1 A	240 V	30 minutes
C	0.5 A	6 V	30 minutes
D	0.5 A	6 V	1 minute

10 Which *one* of the following equations represents the process which coats the spoon?

A $Ag^+ + e^- \longrightarrow Ag$

B $Ag \longrightarrow Ag^+ + e^-$

C $Ag^{2+} + 2e^- \longrightarrow Ag$

D $Ag \longrightarrow Ag^{2+} + 2e^-$

Questions 11 to 14

Read these two passages and then answer the questions.

'When food stuck to the frying pan, my grandmother would heat the pan until it was very hot, pour salt into it and rub the salt crystals round the pan with a thick cloth.'

'Sugar melts when gently heated. But if the temperature goes above 160°C, the liquid goes brown and then black and smells burnt.'

11 Sugar is a carbohydrate. What is the black substance likely to be?

12 What type of bonds hold the particles together in
(a) a molecule of sugar?
(b) a crystal of sodium chloride (common salt)?

13 Explain why the salt did not melt even in a very hot pan.

14 What are the particles in solid sodium chloride called? (*MEG*, 1988)

Questions 15 and 16

The diagram shows two electrodes dipping in a beaker of liquid. The electrodes are connected to a voltmeter.

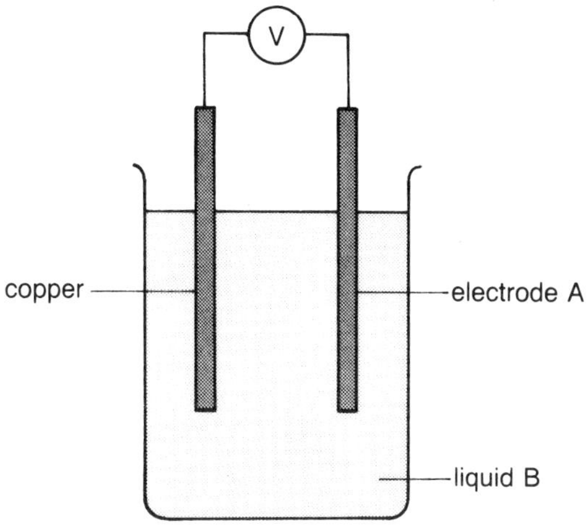

15 When A is sulphur and B is alcohol, the voltmeter shows no voltage. Give a reason for this.

16 When A is zinc and B is dilute acid, a voltage is recorded. Give *two* reasons why this arrangement would *not* be suitable for a torch battery.

Questions 17 to 19

17 Describe briefly how aluminium is manufactured.

18 Write an equation for the formation of aluminium in the process.

19 Aluminium manufacture often takes place near hydroelectric power stations because
A water is needed to clean the ore.
B aluminium ore is dissolved in water before it is electrolysed.
C the process uses large quantities of electricity.
D aluminium cable and alloys are used in the power station.

Questions 20 to 24

A one B two C three D four E five

Choose from A to E above

20 the number of charges on a tin(IV) ion.

21 the number of magnesium ions which combine with one sulphide ion.

22 the number of atoms joined together in one sulphate ion.

23 the number of silver ions which combine with one oxide ion.

24 the number of sodium ions which combine with one nitride ion (N^{3-}).

17 METALS AND ALLOYS

Fig. 17.1 The Forth Rail Bridge, Edinburgh, is made of thousands of tonnes of steel.
What properties of steel make it useful for building bridges such as this?

17.1 Metallic properties

Metals and alloys are some of the most useful and important materials. Nowadays, the whole of society is dependent upon the use of metals and alloys. We use them in large quantities to build homes, bridges and vehicles. Most of our work and leisure activities also require the use of metals, whether we use a keyboard, a typewriter, a tractor, a saucepan or a pen.

Most metallic materials used today are alloys, mixtures of metals, not pure metals. For example, practically all the metal parts in a car are alloys. If the bodywork was pure iron, it would rust far more rapidly than steel (an alloy of iron and carbon). If pure metals were used for other car components, they would be very malleable and would buckle under strain.

We have already considered the physical properties of pure metals and compared metals with nonmetals (Table 13.3). Then, in chapter 14, we looked at the reactions of elements with oxygen (air) and compared metal oxides with nonmetal oxides (Table 14.3).

The important differences in the physical and chemical properties of metals and nonmetals are summarized in Table 17.1.

Table 17.1 Comparing the physical and chemical properties of metals and nonmetals

Property	**Metals** e.g. aluminium, copper, iron	**Nonmetals** e.g. oxygen, sulphur, chlorine
Melting and boiling points	usually high	usually low
Conduction of heat and electricity	good	poor (except graphite)
Reaction with air (oxygen)	form metal oxides which are –solids –basic	form nonmetal oxides which are –gases –acidic
Ions	form positive ions e.g. Al^{3+}, Cu^{2+}	form negative ions e.g. O^{2-}, Cl^{-}
Compounds	react only with nonmetals to form ionic compounds e.g. $Na^{+}Cl^{-}$	react with metals to form ionic compounds react with other nonmetals to form molecular compounds

17.2 Reactions of metals with air, water and acids

REACTIONS WITH AIR (OXYGEN)

As soon as the surface of sodium is exposed to the air, it begins to dull. This is because the sodium starts to react with oxygen in the air to form sodium oxide.

$$\text{sodium} + \text{oxygen} \longrightarrow \text{sodium oxide}$$
$$4Na + O_2 \longrightarrow 2Na_2O$$

Other metals, such as aluminium, react much more slowly. A clean, shiny aluminium surface can take several days to dull through the formation of aluminum oxide.

$$\text{aluminium} + \text{oxygen} \longrightarrow \text{aluminium oxide}$$
$$4Al + 3O_2 \longrightarrow 2Al_2O_3$$

Perhaps you have noticed how shiny new aluminium articles, e.g. window frames, lose their shine after a period of time.

Unreactive metals, such as copper, take months or even years before we notice any formation of oxide.

$$\text{copper} + \text{oxygen} \longrightarrow \text{copper oxide}$$
$$2Cu + O_2 \longrightarrow 2CuO$$

REACTIONS WITH WATER

The reactions of some metals with water are summarized in Table 17.2.

Table 17.2 The reactions of some metals with water

Metal	*Reaction with water*
Sodium	Reacts violently with water, forming hydrogen and an alkaline solution sodium + water ⟶ sodium hydroxide + hydrogen $2Na + 2H_2O \longrightarrow 2NaOH + H_2$
Aluminium	Clean aluminium reacts slowly with water forming hydrogen and aluminium hydroxide aluminium + water ⟶ aluminium hydroxide + hydrogen $2Al + 6H_2O \longrightarrow 2Al(OH)_3 + 3H_2$
Copper	Does not react with water

REACTIONS WITH ACIDS

Figure 17.2 shows what happened when six common metals were added to dilute hydrochloric acid at room temperature (21°C).

Which metal reacts most vigorously? Which metal reacts least vigorously?

Write the metals in order of decreasing reactivity with dilute hydrochloric acid.

Check your answers by looking at Table 17.3 (p.160).

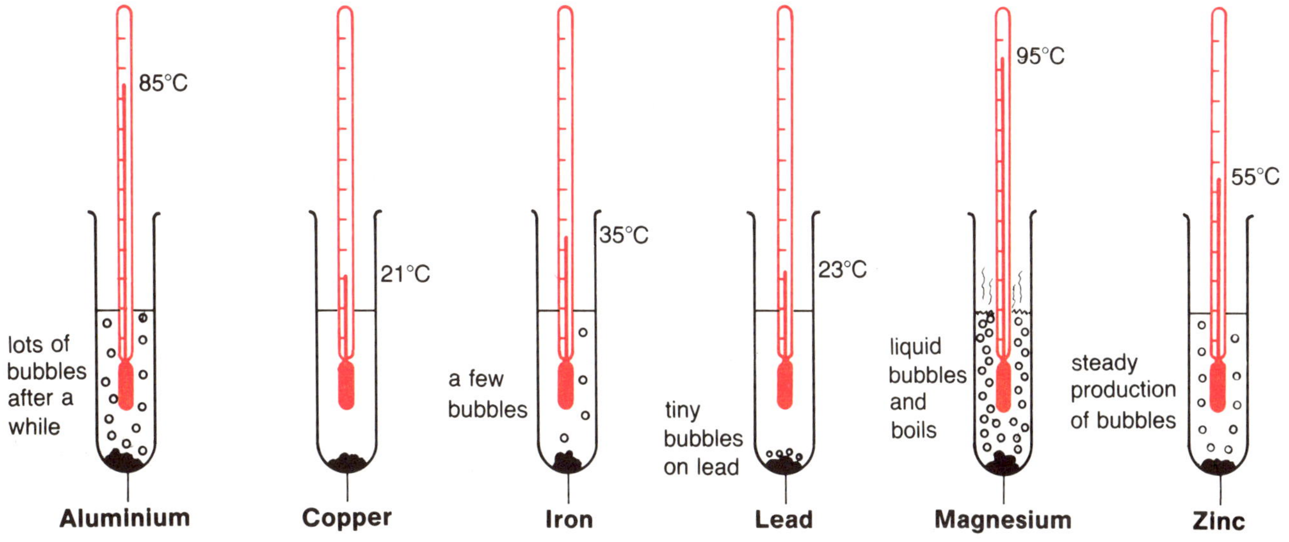

Fig. 17.2 The reactions of six common metals with dilute hydrochloric acid

All the metals shown in Fig. 17.2, except copper, react with dilute hydrochloric acid. The bubbles which form are hydrogen. The other product of the reaction is the chloride of the metal, i.e.

metal + hydrochloric acid ⟶ metal chloride + hydrogen

e.g. zinc + hydrochloric acid ⟶ zinc chloride + hydrogen

$$Zn + 2HCl \longrightarrow ZnCl_2 + H_2$$

A similar reaction occurs between metals and dilute sulphuric acid. This time the products are hydrogen and a metal sulphate. In general, metals above copper in the reactivity series (see section 17.3) react with acids to give the metal compound and hydrogen.

Metal (above Cu in reactivity series) + Acid ⟶ Metal Compound + Hydrogen

17.3 The reactivity series

The reactions of metals can be summarized using a reactivity series. Metals at the top of the series, such as sodium and calcium, react most vigorously. Metals at the bottom of the series, such as copper and silver, are the least reactive.

Table 17.3 shows the reactivity series and summarizes the reactions of metals with oxygen, water and acids. Notice that the order of reactivity is the same in all four columns. This is not surprising because metal atoms react to form metal ions in each case, i.e.

$$M \longrightarrow M^{2+} + 2e^-$$

Table 17.3 The reactions of metals with air, water and dilute acids

Reactivity series	*Reaction with air or oxygen*	*Reaction with water*	*Reaction with dilute acids*
K potassium **Na** sodium	React immediately to give a layer of oxide Burn very vigorously	react with decreasing vigour to produce hydrogen	react with dilute HCl and dilute H_2SO_4 with decreasing vigour to produce hydrogen
Ca calcium **Mg** magnesium **Al** aluminium	React with decreasing vigour to form a layer of oxide Burn with decreasing vigour Pb and Cu only form a layer of oxide		
Zn zinc **Fe** iron **Pb** lead		**Do not react** with cold water	
Cu copper			**Do not react** with dilute acids
Ag silver **Au** gold	**Do not react** with air or oxygen		
General equation	$2M + O_2 \rightarrow 2M^{2+}O^{2-}$ oxide	$M + H_2O \rightarrow M^{2+}O^{2-} + H_2$	$M + 2HCl \rightarrow M^{2+}(Cl^-)_2 + H_2$ $M + H_2SO_4 \rightarrow M^{2+}SO_4^{2-} + H_2$

Notice that iron does not react with pure water. It does, of course, rust in water *if air (oxygen) is also present.* Rusting is looked at in more detail in sections 17.9 and 17.10.

The results in Table 17.3 help to explain some important uses of metals:

- **Copper** is the least reactive metal which can be produced at a reasonable cost. Because of this it is used for hot water tanks, water pipes and cooking utensils. However, copper is much more expensive than iron (steel) which is used for cold water tanks and saucepans.
- **Aluminium** is more widely used for everyday articles such as window frames, ladders and foil, than you might expect from Table 17.3. This is because when aluminium is exposed to the air it forms a thin layer of aluminium oxide. This layer of oxide is tough and non-porous. It protects the aluminium underneath from reaction with air or water.

17.4 The structure of metals

Look closely at the surface of some galvanized iron on a bucket or a dustbin. You will see irregularly shaped areas separated by clear boundaries (Fig. 17.3). The

Fig. 17.3 Grain boundaries on the surface of galvanized iron. The distinct areas are crystals of zinc. Galvanized iron is iron coated with zinc.
(Photograph courtesy of the Zinc Development Association)

irregular areas are called **grains** and the boundaries between grains are **grain boundaries**.

The grains of zinc on the galvanized iron are usually easy to see. The grains in most other metals are too small to see without the help of a microscope. The oxide coating on many metals can also obscure the grains. But if a metal surface is clean and smooth, the grains can be seen under a microscope.

X-ray analysis shows that the atoms in metal grains are packed in a regular pattern, but the grains are irregularly shaped crystals which have grown into each other.

In most metals, the atoms are packed as close as possible. This arrangement is called **close-packing**. Figure 17.4 shows a few close-packed atoms in one layer of a metal crystal. Notice that each atom in the middle of the crystal touches six other atoms in the same layer.

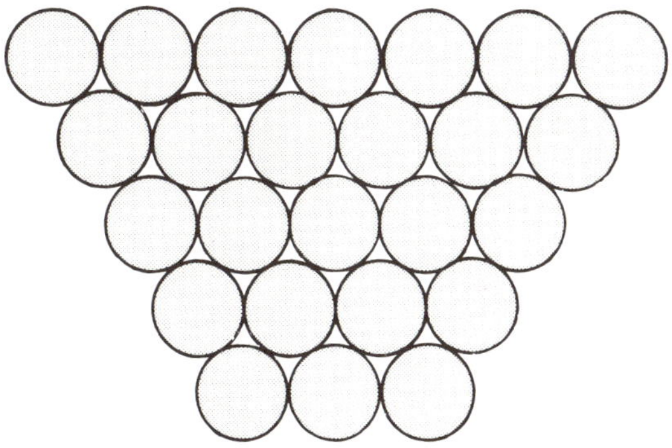

Fig. 17.4 A bird's eye view of close-packed atoms in one layer of a metal crystal

When another layer is placed on top of the first layer, atoms in the second layer sink into the dips between atoms in the first layer (Fig. 17.5).

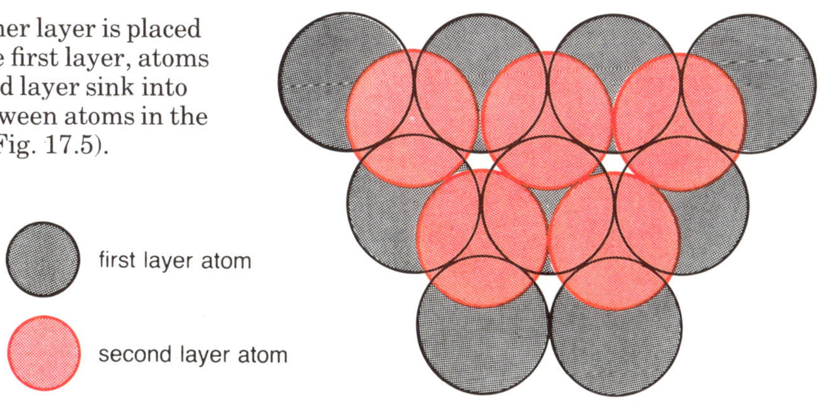

Fig. 17.5 The arrangement of atoms in two consecutive layers in a metal structure

17.5 Explaining the properties of metals

Most metals:

- have high densities;
- have high melting points and boiling points;
- are good conductors of heat and electricity;
- are malleable (can be hammered into different shapes);
- are ductile (can be pulled into wires).

These properties of metals can be explained in terms of the close-packed structure of metals:

High density

The close packing of metal atoms gives a *high mass per unit volume*. This results in a high density.

High melting points and boiling points

Scientists think that the outermost electrons in metal atoms can move around fairly freely. So metals consist of positive ions surrounded by a 'sea' of moving or mobile electrons (see Fig. 17.6). The negative electrons attract all the positive ions and 'cement' all the atoms together. Overall, there are strong forces of attraction between the moving electrons and the positive ions. This results in high melting points and high boiling points.

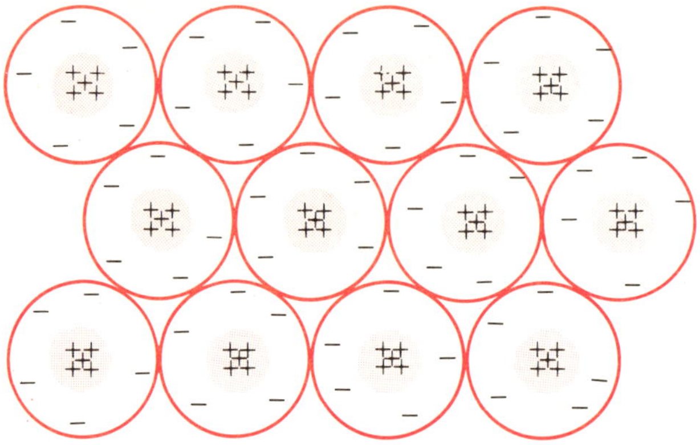

Fig. 17.6 Close-packed atoms with mobile electrons in a metal structure

Good conductivity

When a metal is connected in a circuit, freely moving electrons in the metal move towards the positive terminal. At the same time, electrons can be fed into the other end of the metal from the negative terminal (refer back to Fig. 16.3). This flow of electrons through the metal forms the electric current.

Malleable and ductile

The bonds between atoms in a metal are strong, but they are not rigid. When a force is applied to a metal crystal, the layers of atoms can 'slide' over each other. This is called '**slip**'. After slipping, the atoms settle into position again and the close-packed structure is restored. Figure 17.7 shows the position of atoms before and after slip. This is what happens when a metal is hammered into different shapes or drawn in a wire.

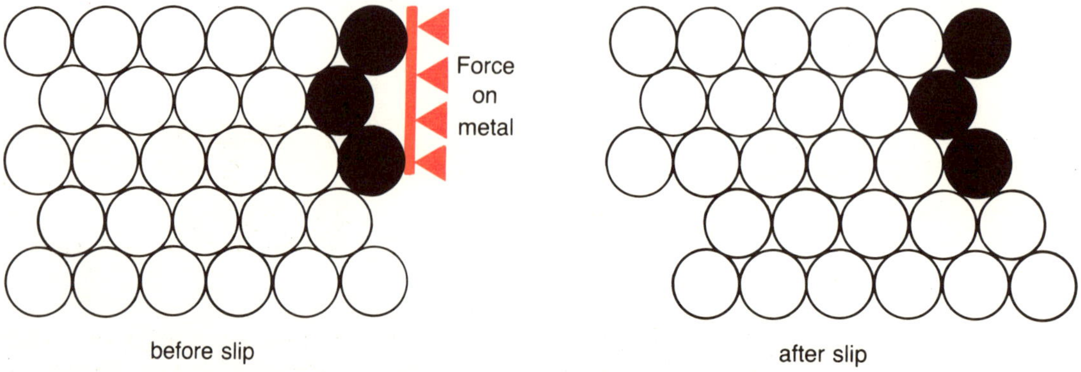

Fig. 17.7 The positions of atoms in a metal crystal before and after 'slip'

17.6 Alloys and their uses

As soon as our ancestors had built furnaces which could melt metals, they began to make **alloys**.

Most alloys are mixtures of metals. However, **steel** (probably the most important alloy) is a mixture of iron and carbon.

The first alloy to be used was probably **bronze**. This is a mixture of *copper and tin*. Bronze swords, ornaments and coins were being made as early as 1500 BC.

Fig. 17.8 This Bronze Age shield from Rhyd-y-Gorse, Dyfed in Wales dates from about 1500 BC. (Reproduced by Courtesy of the Trustees of the British Museum)

Alloys are more useful than pure metals because they can be made with specific properties to suit particular uses. Some alloys are made for hardness, some for resistance to corrosion. Other alloys have unusually low melting points and densities. Yet others have special magnetic or electrical properties.

MAKING ALLOYS

Alloys are made by mixing together the appropriate amounts of the constituent metals as liquids. For example, solder is made by adding a small amount of molten tin to molten lead (see Fig. 17.9).

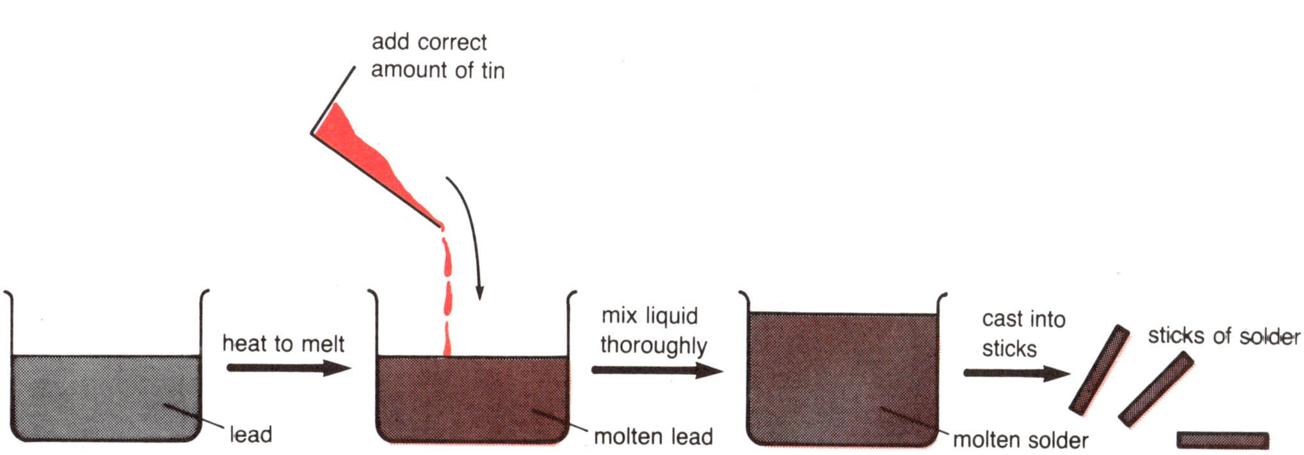

Fig. 17.9 Making solder

The most important alloys are those based on steel. Other important alloys are those based on copper and aluminium. The constituents, properties and uses of some of the most useful and common alloys are shown in Table 17.4 (overleaf).

Table 17.4 The constituents, properties and uses of some common alloys

Alloy	*Constituent elements*	*Properties*	*Uses*
Solder	lead and tin	very low melting point	joining electrical components
Mild steel	iron with 0.12 to 0.25% carbon	cheap, easily manufactured, hard and strong can be pressed into sheets and cast into different shapes	used as girders in buildings, bridges and towers sheets used as bodywork for vehicles
Stainless steel	iron with about 15% chromium and 0.12 to 0.25% carbon	similar to mild steel and also resists corrosion	cutlery, surgical instruments
Aluminium alloys including duralumin	aluminium with about 4% copper	low density, high strength, resists corrosion	aircraft bodywork, window frames, lightweight tubing
Brass	copper with up to 20% zinc	easily worked, hard, does not corrode, golden appearance	ornaments, picture frames

17.7 Extracting metals

The extraction of metals involves **three stages**:

1 **Mining and concentrating the ore**
Very often the ore must be separated from soil and other impurities before it can be processed.

2 **Converting the ore to the metal**
Table 17.5 shows the ores from which some important metals are obtained.

Table 17.5 The ores from which some important metals are obtained

Metal	*Common ore of metal*	*Chemical name of ore*	*Formula of ore*
Sodium	rock salt	sodium chloride	$NaCl$
Aluminium	bauxite	aluminium oxide	Al_2O_3
Zinc	galena	zinc sulphide	ZnS
Iron	iron ore (haematite)	iron(III) oxide	Fe_2O_3
Copper	copper pyrites (chalcopyrites)	copper(II) sulphide and iron(II) sulphide	$CuS + FeS$ ($CuFeS_2$)

3 **Purifying the metal**
The iron produced from iron ore contains 8 per cent of impurities. It is called *pig iron*, which is very hard and brittle compared to pure iron or steel. These impurities must be removed if iron or steel are required.

METHODS

We must now turn our attention to stage 2 in the extraction process and the methods used to convert ores to metals. The method used for a particular metal depends on two key factors:

- the position of the metal in the reactivity series;
- the cost of the process.

Heating the ore

This is the *cheapest method* of extraction. But, it only works with compounds of *metals at the bottom of the reactivity series*. These compounds decompose to the metal on heating. For example, mercury is extracted from cinnabar (HgS) by heating in air:

mercury sulphide (cinnabar) + oxygen ⟶ mercury + sulphur dioxide

$$HgS + O_2 \longrightarrow Hg + SO_2$$

Reducing the ore with carbon

This method is commonly used for *metals in the middle of the reactivity series* such as zinc, iron, lead and copper. The metals are usually obtained by heating their *oxides* with *carbon (coke)*. The carbon reduces the metal oxide to metal. This is discussed further in section 17.11.

e.g. zinc oxide + carbon ⟶ zinc + carbon monoxide

$$ZnO + C \longrightarrow Zn + CO$$

In some cases, air is bloL into the furnace so that the coke will react with oxygen to form carbon monoxide.

coke + oxygen ⟶ carbon monoxide

$$2C + O_2 \longrightarrow 2CO$$

Carbon monoxide will also remove oxygen from the metal oxides to produce metals and carbon dioxide, e.g.

iron(III) oxide + carbon monoxide ⟶ iron + carbon dioxide

$$Fe_2O_3 + 3CO \longrightarrow 2Fe + 3CO_2$$

Sometimes the metal ores are *sulphides*, not oxides. These ores *must be converted to oxides* before reaction with carbon or carbon monoxide. This is done by heating the sulphide in air, e.g.

zinc sulphide + oxygen ⟶ zinc oxide + sulphur dioxide

$$2ZnS + 3O_2 \longrightarrow 2ZnO + 2SO_2$$

The extraction of iron from iron ore is described fully in section 17.8.

Electrolysis of molten compounds

Metals at the top of the reactivity series, for example sodium and aluminium, *cannot* be obtained from their ores by heating with coke (carbon) or carbon monoxide. Also, these metals *cannot* be obtained by electrolysis of their aqueous solutions, because hydrogen from the water is produced at the cathode instead of the metal.

The only way to extract these reactive metals is by *electrolysis of their liquid (molten) compounds*. For example, sodium is obtained by electrolysis of molten sodium chloride (section 16.4) and aluminium is obtained by electrolysis of aluminium oxide dissolved in molten cryolite (Na_3AlF_6) (section 16.8).

17.8 Extracting iron

Iron is the most important metal. The world production of iron is about 700 million tonnes per year. Most of it is made into steel. This is used for large machines, vehicles and girders in buildings.

The main ore used to obtain iron is iron ore (*haematite*). This contains iron(III) oxide. Iron ore is converted to iron in special tall furnaces called **blast furnaces**. Figure 17.11 (overleaf) shows a diagram of a blast furnace and includes a summary of the reactions to produce iron.

Fig. 17.10 The blast furnace at British Steel's Teesside Works, Cleveland (Photograph courtesy of the British Steel Corporation)

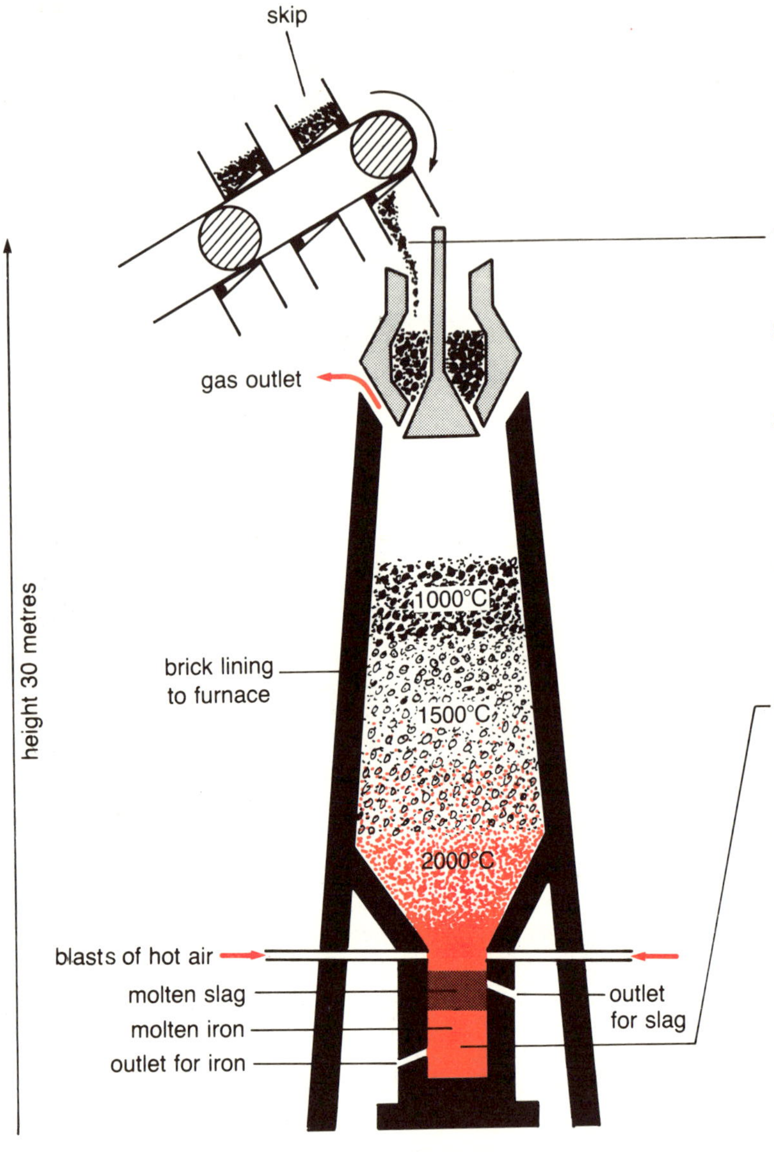

1 A mixture of iron ore, coke and limestone is added to the furnace

2 Blasts of hot air are blown through small holes near the bottom of the furnace

3 The coke burns in oxygen in the hot air producing carbon monoxide and great heat

$$\underset{\text{(coke)}}{2C} + O_2 \rightarrow 2CO$$

4 The carbon monoxide reacts with iron ore (iron (III) oxide) to form iron

$$Fe_2O_3 + 3CO \rightarrow 2Fe + 3CO_2$$

5 Molten iron runs to the bottom of the furnace where it is tapped off from time to time. Most of it is used to make steel

6 Limestone is added to the furnace to remove impurities like sand (SiO_2) in the ore.
The limestone first decomposes to calcium oxide

$$CaCO_3 \rightarrow \underset{\text{(calcium oxide)}}{CaO} + CO_2$$

The calcium oxide then reacts with impurities to form slag

$$CaO + SiO_2 \rightarrow \underset{\text{(calcium silicate in slag)}}{CaSiO_3}$$

7 Molten slag collects on top of the molten iron and is tapped off from time to time

Fig. 17.11 Extracting iron from iron ore in a blast furnace.

17.9 Rusting

Although iron (steel) is the most widely used metal, it rusts more easily than most other metals. You may have carried out an experiment similar to that shown in Fig. 17.12 to decide whether oxygen and/or water are involved in rusting. The test tubes are set up as shown and left for about a week.
The results of the experiment are given in Fig. 17.12. They show that iron does *not* rust when

- there is no water (tube 2),
- there is no air (tube 3).

Iron will only rust when both air (oxygen) and water are present.

During rusting, iron reacts with oxygen to form iron(III) oxide.

$$\text{iron} + \text{oxygen} \longrightarrow \text{iron(III) oxide}$$

$$4Fe + 3O_2 \longrightarrow 2Fe_2O_3$$

At the same time, the iron combines with water to form hydrated iron(III) oxide, which is rust.

$$\text{iron(III) oxide} + \text{water} \longrightarrow \text{hydrated iron(III) oxide (rust)}$$

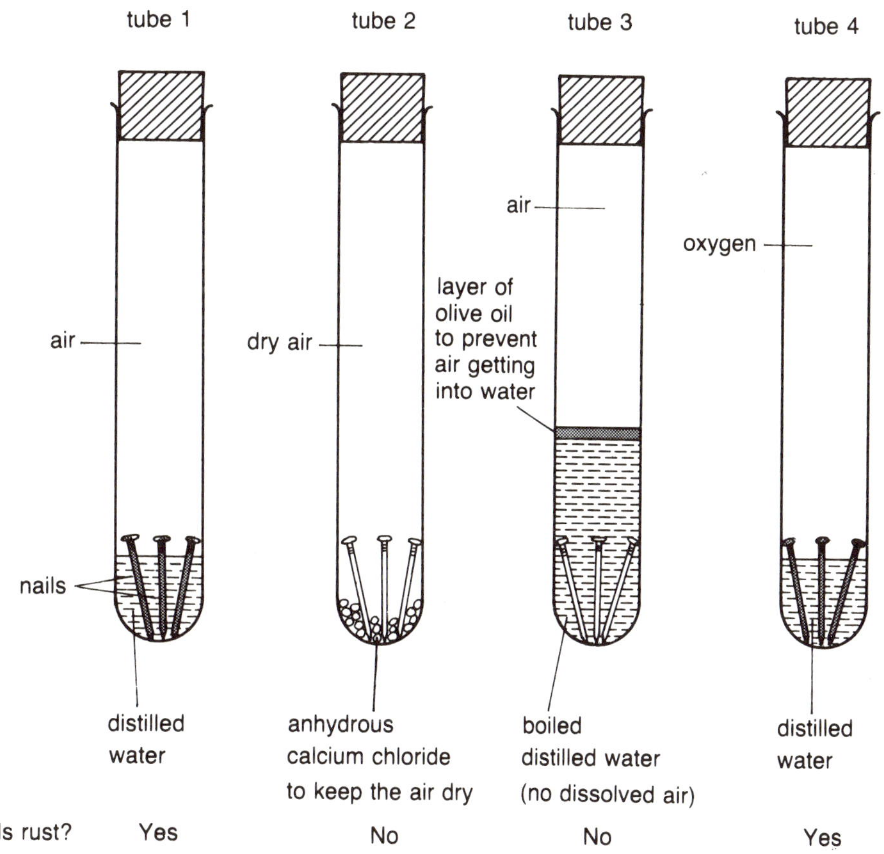

Fig. 17.12 Investigating rusting

17.10 Preventing rust

Rusting costs millions of pounds every year because of the need to protect iron and steel and the replacement of rusted articles.

We can protect iron and steel from rusting by:

- **painting**
- **oiling**
- **plastic coating**
- **tin plating**
- **chromium plating**

These methods keep air and water away from the iron or steel

- **alloying**–This method changes the properties of the metal. Stainless steel contains chromium, nickel and/or manganese, as well as iron and carbon.
- **galvanizing** (zinc plating)–This method allows a coating of a more reactive metal (zinc) to react rather than the iron or steel.

17.11 Redox

Many common reactions, including burning, rusting and metal extractions, are examples of *oxidation* (refer back to section 14.3). For example, during rusting iron reacts with oxygen and water to form hydrated iron(III) oxide.

iron + **oxygen** + water ⟶ hydrated iron(III) **oxide**

Reactions in which substances combine with oxygen are called **oxidations**. But if one substance gains oxygen, another substance (possibly oxygen itself) must *lose* oxygen. We say that *substances which lose oxygen* in chemical reactions are **reduced**. The process is called **reduction**. Figure 17.13 (overleaf) shows the reduction and oxidation processes when iron rusts and iron is extracted from iron ore.

Reduction and oxidation always occur together. If one substance loses oxygen and is reduced, another substance must gain oxygen and be oxidized. The combined process of **RED**uction and **OX**idation is called **REDOX**.

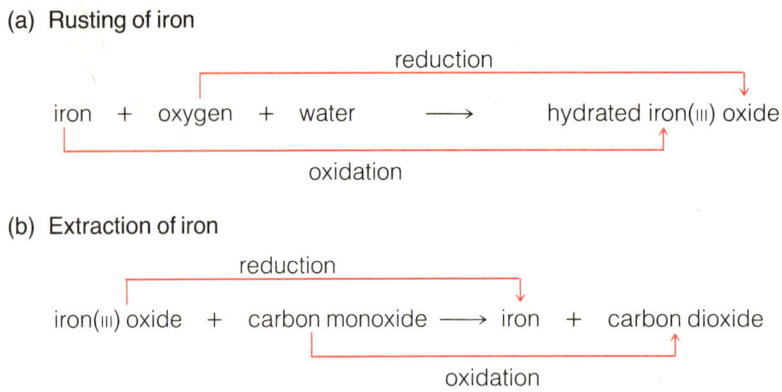

Fig. 17.13 Reduction and oxidation processes when **(a)** iron rusts, **(b)** iron is extracted from iron ore

Quick test 17

Questions 1 to 5

Consider the following five alloys labelled A, B, C, D and E.

Alloy	*Elements in the alloy*	*Properties*
A	lead and tin	melts at 203°C
B	bismuth, cadmium, lead and tin	melts at 70°C
C	carbon, iron and tungsten	unaffected at very high temperatures
D	copper and zinc	golden colour does not tarnish
E	aluminium and lithium	low density high strength

Which alloy would you use for

1 joining electrical wires?
2 making jewellery?
3 'plugging' an automatic fire sprinkler?
4 making aircraft bodywork?
5 making a drill for bricks and stone?

Questions 6 to 8

The equation below summarizes the chemical reaction between sodium and water. The equation is incomplete.

$2Na(s) + 2H_2O(l) \longrightarrow x\,NaOH(aq) + y\,H_2(g)$

6 What is the value of x?
7 What is the value of y?
8 What happens to the pH of the solution during the reaction?

Questions 9 to 11

The table below shows how certain metals react with cold water.

Metal	*Reaction with cold water*
Calcium	a steady reaction
Iron	little reaction
Magnesium	slightly more reactive than iron
Copper	no reaction

9 Place the metals in order of their reactivity, the most reactive first.
10 Give *one* commercial use of copper which depends upon the fact that it does not react with water.

11 Why do you think that the metals sodium and potassium should be removed as a matter of urgency from a laboratory store that had been flooded?
(*WJEC*, 1988)

Questions 12 to 17

12 Explain why some metals corrode when they are left in the open air.
13 A student left the following items in the garden for three months to see whether they would corrode. Say whether you would expect each item to corrode *a lot*, *a little* or *not at all*.
(a) a stainless steel fork
(b) a new penny
(c) a copper bracelet
(d) an iron nail.
14 What *two* treatments could be used to prevent corrosion of iron?
15 Iron is extracted from its ore in the *blast furnace*. Name *one* ore from which iron may be extracted.
16 What are the *raw materials* needed to make iron in a blast furnace (other than iron ore)?
17 Which chemical reduces (takes the oxygen away from) iron ore in the top of the blast furnace? (*LEAG*, part question)

Questions 18 to 22

Mineral ores containing metals do not usually conduct electricity.
18 What is done to some ores to make them conduct electricity?
19 Why is it useful to be able to pass electricity through some ores?
20 Iron can be extracted by heating the ore with carbon (coke). Explain why this method will not work with the ores of all metals.
21 Name a metal that does not have to be extracted from an ore?
22 Explain why the metal you have named is not found combined with something else, for example as an ore containing the metal oxide. (*MEG*, 1988)

Questions 23 to 27

When iron rusts it combines with oxygen in the air to form hydrated iron(III) oxide.

The rusting of six identical nails was investigated by treating each nail as shown in the table below. All six nails were left exposed to the air for a few months.

Treatment given	*Cost of treatment*	*Mass of nail + coating before exposure to air*	*Mass of nail + coating after exposure to air*
A waxed	cheap	5.0 g	5.3 g
B oiled	cheap	5.0 g	5.2 g
C painted	cheap	5.0 g	5.4 g
D galvanized	expensive	5.0 g	5.1 g
E dipped in salt	cheap	5.0 g	6.7 g
F untreated	nil	4.9 g	6.1 g

23 Which treatment gives the best protection?
24 Which treatment would be the most practical to use to protect iron railings from rusting?
25 Which treatment is worse than no treatment at all?
26 Give the name of the other substance which, with oxygen, causes iron to rust.
27 Give the name of the process that takes place when a metal reacts with oxygen to form an oxide. (*WJEC* (modified))

18 ACIDS, BASES AND SALTS

18.1 Acids in everyday life

Acids are important in everyday life and in the chemical industry (see chapter 19). They are used to make our clothes, our food and the medicines that protect us from disease.

ACIDS IN OUR FOOD

Acids are present in many of our foods. For example:

Citric acid is present in all citrus fruits (oranges, lemons, grapefruit, etc).

Acetic acid is present in vinegar and in most spicy sauces such as mint sauce, tomato sauce and brown sauce.

Ascorbic acid is vitamin C which is present in fruits and vegetables (see section 3.3).

Carbonic acid is present in all fizzy drinks. It is made by dissolving carbon dioxide in the drink under pressure. The carbon dioxide reacts with water in the drink to form carbonic acid.

$$\text{carbon dioxide} + \text{water} \longrightarrow \text{carbonic acid}$$

$$CO_2 + H_2O \longrightarrow H_2CO_3$$

Soda water is simply water containing dissolved carbon dioxide and carbonic acid. Coke, Pepsi, lemonade and champagne also contain carbonic acid. Why do you think these drinks fizz as soon as they are opened?

Fig. 18.1 Drinks like Coke, lemonade and champagne do not fizz while their container is closed. Gas builds up in the space above the liquid and the pressure of this gas stops more gas escaping. Once the bottle or can is opened, pressure above the liquid suddenly falls. This enables the dissolved gas to escape from the liquid.
(Photograph courtesy of Coca-Cola Great Britain)

ACIDS IN THE SOIL

The pH of different soils varies from about 6 to 8, but most soils have a pH between 6.5 and 7.5.
– In chalk and limestone areas the soil is usually alkaline with a pH between 7.0 and 7.5.
– In forests, moorland areas and sandstone regions, the soil is usually acidic (pH 6.5 to 7.0). Peat and clay areas also have acidic soils.

For gardening and arable farming, the best crops are usually obtained with neutral or slightly acid soil (pH 6.5 to 7.0). Below pH 6.5 the soil is too acidic for most plants, particularly vegetables. However, some heathers and rhododendrons grow best in more acidic soil (i.e. pH less than 6.5).

In areas where the soil is too acidic, it can be improved by treatment with powdered slaked lime (calcium hydroxide). The slaked lime reacts with acids in the soil and raises the pH to the desired level. Substances like this which neutralize acids are called **bases** (see section 18.4 and 18.5).

ACID RAIN

Large areas of Scandinavia are covered with lakes and pine forests. During the last ten years, scientists have noticed more and more damage the trees and to the organisms in the lakes of Scandinavia. Most of the scientists think that the damage is being caused by **acid rain**.

Fig. 18.2 Because prevailing winds blow from Britain to Scandinavia, many people blame British power stations and factories for the damage Scandinavian lakes and forests suffer from acid rain.

When fuels burn, sulphur in the fuel forms *sulphur dioxide*. Because of this, city air may contain ten times as much sulphur dioxide as clean air. Sulphur dioxide reacts with water vapour and rain in the air to form *sulphurous acid*.

$$\text{sulphur dioxide} + \text{water} \longrightarrow \text{sulphurous acid}$$

$$SO_2 + H_2O \longrightarrow H_2SO_3$$

Sulphurous acid makes the rain much more acidic than normal and this has led to the term **acid rain**. (Without pollution rainwater is only slightly acidic. This is because it contains carbonic acid.)

Acid rain causes damage to:
- trees and other plants;
- fish and other organisms in rivers and lakes;
- stonework and metal on buildings and other structures.

18.2 Measuring acidity

We can use substances called **indicators** to find out whether a solution is acidic or alkaline. Indicators change colour depending on how acidic or how alkaline a solution is.

The most commonly used indicators are **litmus** and **Universal Indicator**.

- Acidic substances dissolve in water to produce solutions which turn litmus red and give an *orange or red* colour with Universal Indicator.
- Alkaline solutions turn litmus blue and give a green, blue or purple colour with Universal Indicator.

It would be very clumsy if we had to use the colour of an indicator to describe how acidic something was. So chemists use a scale of numbers known as the **pH scale**. On this scale:

- acidic substances have a pH below 7 ($pH < 7$);
- alkaline substances have a pH above 7 ($pH > 7$);
- neutral substances have a pH of 7 ($pH = 7$).

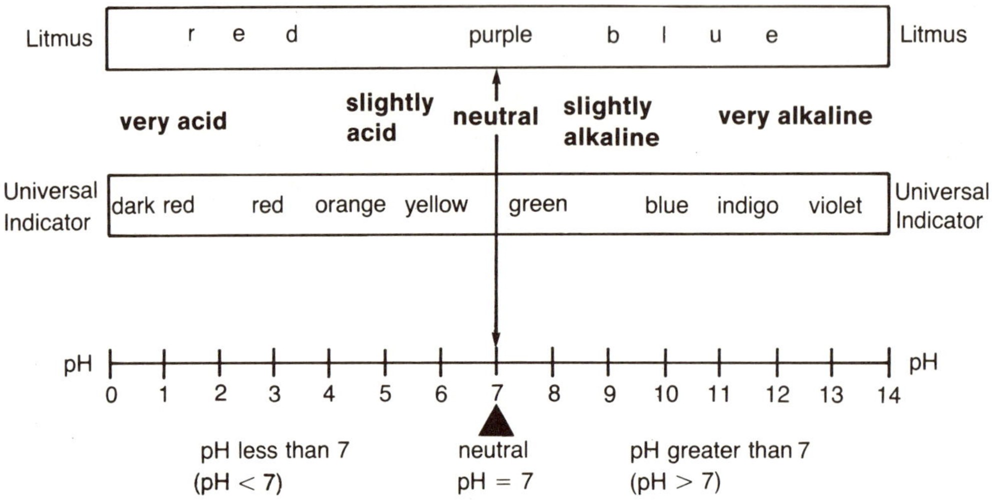

Fig. 18.3 The colours of litmus and Universal Indicator at different pHs

Notice in Fig. 18.3 that Universal Indicator shows a different colour at each pH value. Because of this, it can be used to measure the pH of a solution. It can tell us *how* acid or *how* alkaline a solution is. It is therefore more useful than litmus which can only tell us whether a solution is acid, alkaline or neutral. Figure 18.4 shows the pH of some common substances.

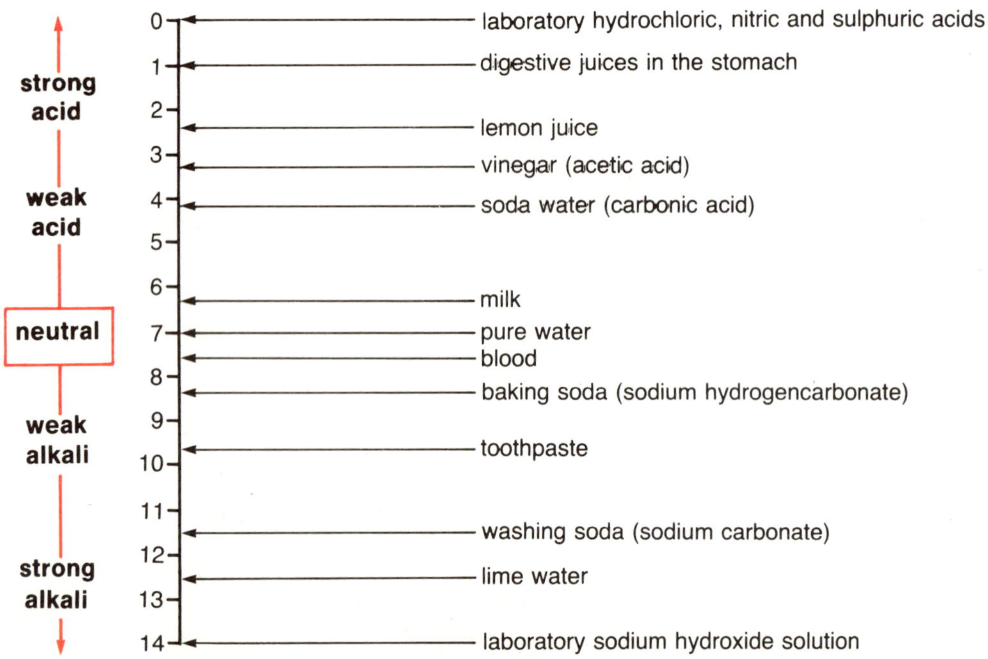

Fig. 18.4 The pH of some common substances

18.3 The properties of acids

The main properties of acids are summarized in Table 18.1.

ACIDS

- are soluble in water
- have a pH less than 7
- turn litmus red
- turn Universal Indicator orange or red
- conduct electricity
- react with metals above Cu in the reactivity series to produce hydrogen
- react with bases to form salts and water
- react with carbonates to produce carbon dioxide

Table 18.1 The main properties of acids

Notice that acids conduct electricity. When this happens, the acids are decomposed by the electric current. This shows that solutions of acids contain ions (refer back to section 16.4). All acids produce hydrogen at the cathode during electrolysis. This indicates that all acids contain **H^+ ions** (Table 18.2).

Table 18.2 The ions in some common acids

Acid	*Formula*	*Ions in the acid*
Hydrochloric acid	HCl	$H^+ + Cl^-$
Nitric acid	HNO_3	$H^+ + NO_3^-$
Sulphuric acid	H_2SO_4	$2H^+ + SO_4^{2-}$
Carbonic acid	H_2CO_3	$2H^+ + CO_3^{2-}$
Sulphurous acid	H_2SO_3	$2H^+ + SO_3^{2-}$
Acetic acid	CH_3COOH	$H^+ + CH_3COO^-$

The H^+ ions in acids are responsible for their chemical reactions with indicators, metals, bases and carbonates. Because of this:

Acids are defined as substances which donate H^+ ions.

REACTION WITH METALS

Acids react with metals above copper in the reactivity series to form a **salt** and **hydrogen** (refer back to sections 17.2 and 17.3).

metal + acid ⟶ salt + hydrogen

e.g. iron in steel + sulphurous acid ⟶ iron sulphite + hydrogen
in acid rain

Salts are *ionic compounds*. Nearly all salts contain a metal cation (e.g. Fe^{2+}, Na^+, Al^{3+}) and an anion (e.g. Cl^-, SO_3^{2-}, SO_4^{2-}). Three important salts are sodium chloride (NaCl) usually known as common or table salt, iron(II) sulphate ($FeSO_4$), the main form of iron present in iron tablets, and ammonium nitrate (NH_4NO_3) the main ingredient in 'Nitram' fertilizer.

REACTION WITH CARBONATES

Acids react with carbonates to give a **salt**, **carbon dioxide** and **water**.

carbonate + acid ⟶ salt + carbon dioxide + water

This is the reaction which occurs when sulphurous acid in acid rain reacts with calcium carbonate in buildings made from limestone.

calcium carbonate	+	sulphurous acid	⟶	calcium sulphite	+	carbon dioxide	+	water
$CaCO_3$	+	H_2SO_3	⟶	$CaSO_3$	+	CO_2	+	H_2O

REACTION WITH BASES

Acids react with bases to form a **salt** and **water**.

base + acid ⟶ salt + water

These reactions are described as **neutralizations**. They are discussed more fully in section 18.5.

18.4 Bases and alkalis

Certain substances can **neutralize acids**. Farmers and gardeners use slaked lime (calcium hydroxide) to neutralize acids in acidic soil. We all use toothpaste to neutralize the acids which are produced from food and which cause tooth decay. You may also have taken indigestion tablets (antacid tablets e.g. Rennies) to neutralize excess acid produced in your stomach.

These substances which neutralize acids are called **bases**.

Bases are the chemical opposites of acids.
- **Acids give up H^+ ions**
- **Bases take H^+ ions**

Table 18.3 lists some important bases and their uses. Notice that these bases include the **oxides, hydroxides and carbonates of metals**.

Table 18.3 Some important bases and their uses

Base	*Formula*	*Use*
Sodium hydroxide	$NaOH$	oven cleaner, grease remover
Iron(III) oxide	Fe_2O_3	manufacture of iron and steel
Magnesium oxide	MgO	antacid medicine (Milk of Magnesia)
Ammonia	NH_3	manufacture of fertilizers, toilet cleaner
Sodium hydrogencarbonate	$NaHCO_3$	baking powder, antacid tablets
Calcium carbonate	$CaCO_3$	building, manufacture of iron, lime and cement
Calcium hydroxide	$Ca(OH)_2$	neutralizing soil acidity
Aluminium oxide	Al_2O_3	manufacture of alumunium

ALKALIS

Most bases are insoluble in water, but a few are soluble. These *soluble bases* are called **alkalis**. The Venn diagram in Fig. 18.5 illustrates the relationship between bases and alkalis.

The commonest alkalis are *sodium hydroxide* ($NaOH$), *calcium hydroxide* ($Ca(OH)_2$) and *ammonia* (NH_3). Calcium hydroxide is much less soluble in water than sodium hydroxide and ammonia. A solution of calcium hydroxide in water is usually called *lime water*.

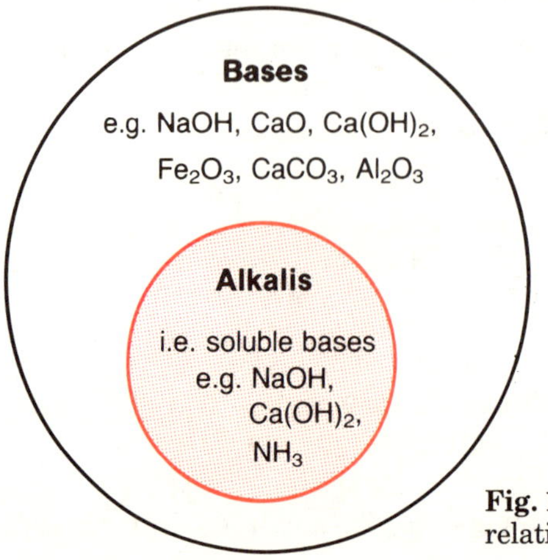

Fig. 18.5 A Venn diagram showing the relationship between bases and alkalis

Table 18.4 shows the important properties of alkalis.

Table 18.4

ALKALIS

- are soluble in water
- are bases
- are electrolytes
- neutralize acids
- have a pH greater than 7
- give a blue colour with litmus
- give a green, blue or violet colour with Universal Indicator

Sodium oxide and **calcium oxide** react with water to form their hydroxides. So the reactions of these metal oxides with water form alkalis.

$$\text{sodium oxide} + \text{water} \longrightarrow \text{sodium hydroxide}$$
$$Na_2O + H_2O \longrightarrow 2NaOH$$

$$\text{calcium oxide} + \text{water} \longrightarrow \text{calcium hydroxide}$$
$$CaO + H_2O \longrightarrow Ca(OH)_2$$

Most other metal oxides and hydroxides are insoluble in water. They are bases, *but not* alkalis.

18.5 Neutralization

We have already seen some important examples of neutralization reactions in section 18.4: curing indigestion, making soil less acidic and preventing tooth decay. Neutralization is also used to treat splashes of acid or alkali on skin and clothing and to remove carbon dioxide from the air in air-conditioned buildings. Carbon dioxide is an acidic oxide (when dissolved in water it forms carbonic acid). It is removed from the stale air using either sodium hydroxide (soda) or calcium hydroxide (slaked lime) or a mixture of the two (soda lime).

The most important industrial application of neutralization is in the manufacture of fertilizers. For example, ammonium nitrate fertilizer is manufactured by neutralizing nitric acid with ammonia:

$$\text{ammonia} + \text{nitric acid} \longrightarrow \text{ammonium nitrate}$$
$$NH_3 + HNO_3 \longrightarrow NH_4NO_3$$

Ammonium sulphate fertilizer is manufactured by neutralizing sulphuric acid with ammonia:

$$\text{ammonia} + \text{sulphuric acid} \longrightarrow \text{ammonium sulphate}$$
$$2NH_3 + H_2SO_4 \longrightarrow (NH_4)_2SO_4$$

The largest group of bases are metal oxides and metal hydroxides such as sodium oxide, aluminium oxide, sodium hydroxide and aluminium hydroxide. These bases neutralize acids to form a salt and water.

Neutralization is the reaction
acid + base ⟶ salt + water

e.g.
$$\text{sodium oxide} + \text{hydrochloric acid} \longrightarrow \text{sodium chloride} + \text{water}$$
$$Na_2O + 2HCl \longrightarrow 2NaCl + H_2O$$

$$\text{sodium hydroxide} + \text{hydrochloric acid} \longrightarrow \text{sodium chloride} + \text{water}$$
$$NaOH + HCl \longrightarrow NaCl + H_2O$$

During neutralization, H^+ ions in the acid react with either oxide ions (O^{2-}) or hydroxide ions (OH^-) in the base to form water.

$$2H^+ + \underset{\text{(oxide)}}{O^{2-}} \longrightarrow H_2O \qquad H^+ + \underset{\text{(hydroxide)}}{OH^-} \longrightarrow H_2O$$

18.6 Alkalis in industry

The most important industrial alkalis are *sodium hydroxide* (**caustic soda**), *calcium hydroxide* (**slaked lime**), *calcium oxide* (**lime**) and *ammonia* (see section 19.4). Figure 18.6 summarizes the manufacture of lime and slaked lime from limestone.

Limestone (calcium carbonate) $CaCO_3$ —heat→ **Lime** (calcium oxide) CaO + carbon dioxide CO_2

Lime CaO —add water (H_2O)→ **Slaked lime** (calcium hydroxide) $Ca(OH)_2$

Fig. 18.6 The manufacture of lime and slaked lime from limestone

Lime and slaked lime are used as cheap alkalis in agriculture to neutralize acid soils. They are also used in the manufacture of cement.

Large amounts of sodium hydroxide are used to manufacture soap, paper, rayon and cellulose acetate (Tricel). These processes are illustrated in Fig. 18.7 and 18.8.

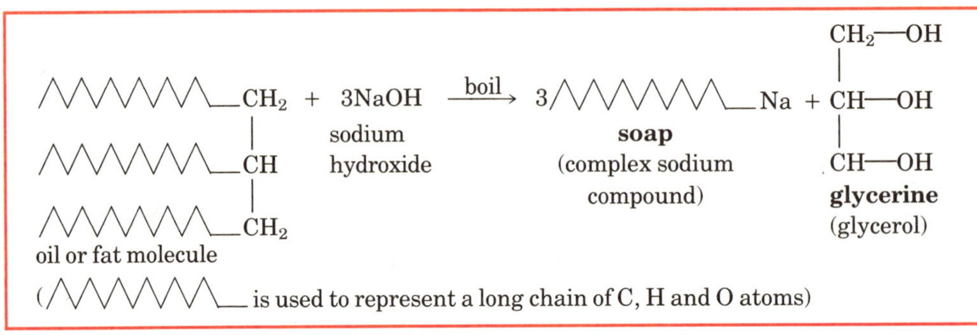

Fig. 18.7 The use of sodium hydroxide in the manufacture of soap

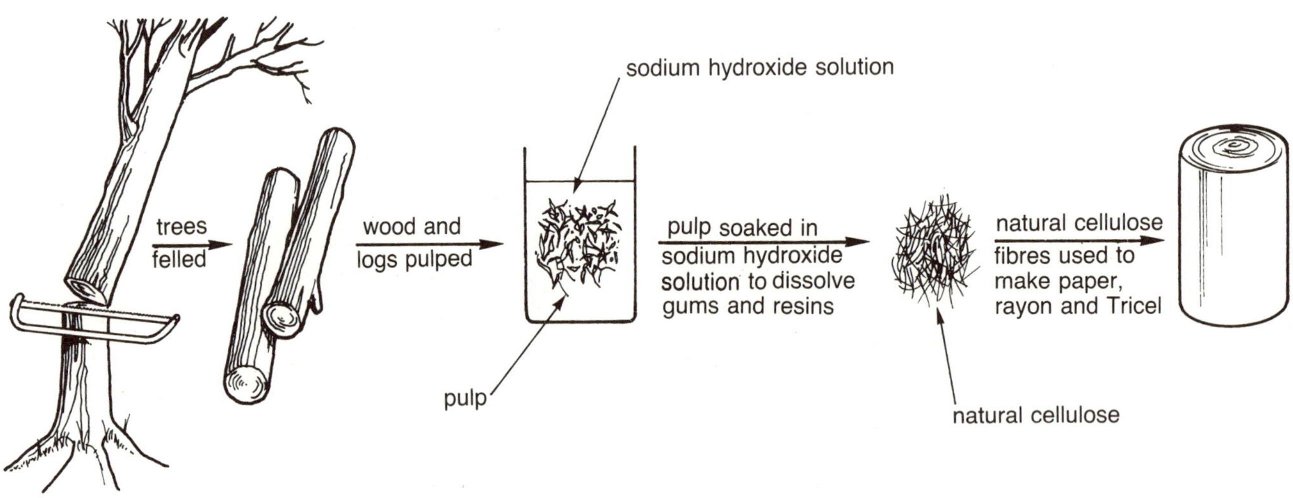

Fig. 18.8 The use of sodium hydroxide in the manufacture of paper, rayon and Tricel

18.7 Preparing salts

In preparing a salt, it is important to know whether the salt is soluble or insoluble.

- If the salt is soluble, it is usually prepared by reacting an acid with either a metal or a base.
- If the salt is insoluble, it is usually prepared by precipitation.

The flow diagram in Fig. 18.9 can be used to decide how to prepare a particular salt.

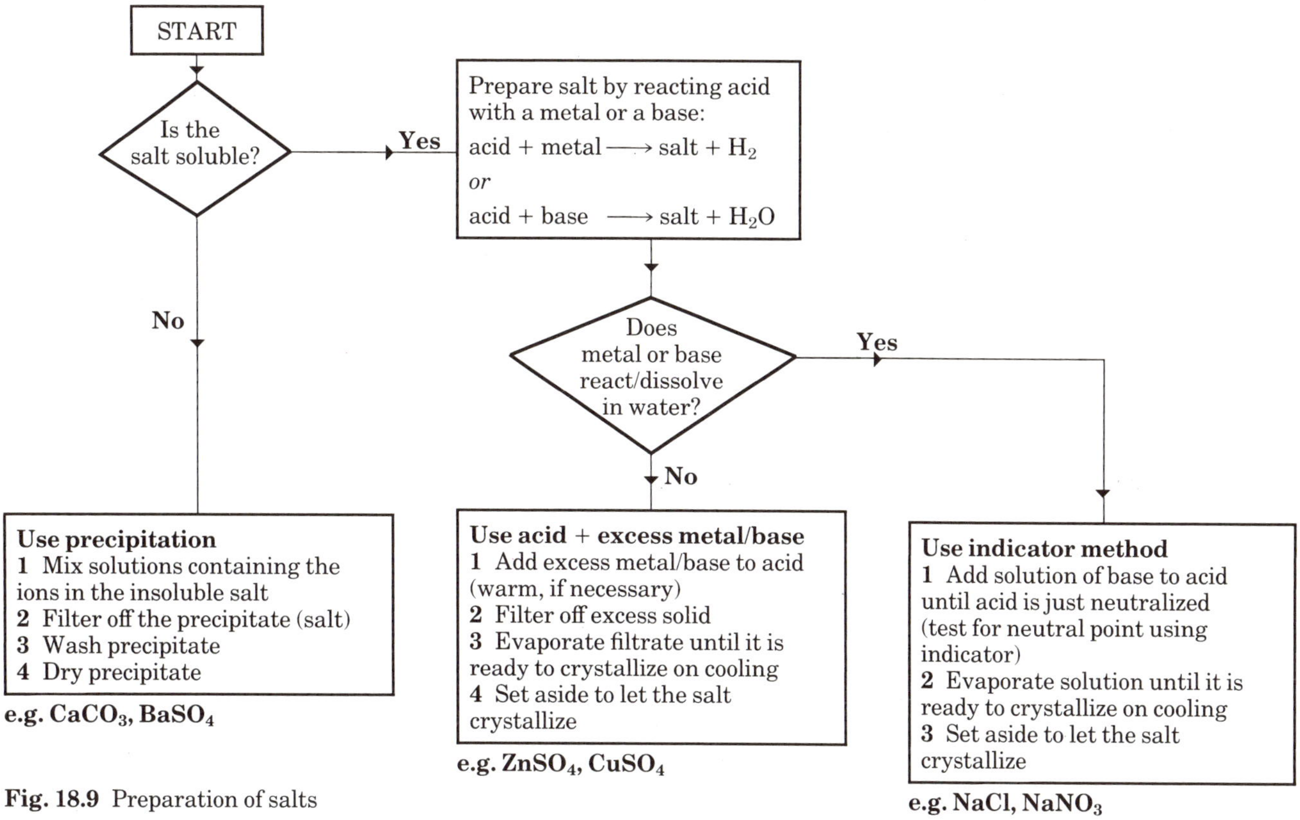

Fig. 18.9 Preparation of salts

Quick test 18

Questions 1 to 4

Questions 1 to 4 concern the following five types of chemical reaction labelled A to E.

A condensation
B decomposition
C neutralization
D oxidation
E precipitation

Choose from A to E the type of reaction which occurs when

1 acid soils are treated with lime.
2 sulphur in coal burns to form sulphur dioxide.
3 lime is manufactured from limestone.
4 scum is formed when soluble sodium salts in soap are mixed with hard water.

Questions 5 to 9

Five liquids, A to E, were found to have the following pHs:

A pH=1 B pH=4 C pH=6 D pH=8 E pH=12

Choose from A to E the liquid which

5 is most acidic.
6 would be most suitable for use in preserving food by pickling.
7 would be most suitable for treating indigestion.
8 would be most suitable as an oven grease remover.
9 might be lemonade.

10 Read through these lists of chemicals, then answer the questions which follow.

acids	*metals*	*compounds*
hydrochloric	copper	copper(II) oxide
nitric	sodium	sodium hydroxide
sulphuric	zinc	copper(II) sulphate
ethanoic		sodium carbonate

(a) State the *two* chemicals you would need from the above lists to make the following:

(i) zinc sulphate **(ii)** sodium chloride **(iii)** copper carbonate (3 marks)

(b) Using labelled diagrams and short notes, describe how you would make a solid sample of *either* zinc sulphate *or* sodium chloride *or* copper carbonate, using the chemicals you have chosen from the lists and normal laboratory equipment. (4 marks)

(*WJEC*, 1988)

Questions 11 to 14

Some power stations are thought to cause acid rain. In January 1985 children from all over Britain took part in a survey to measure the acidity of the acid rain that fell.

11 The children collected rain water and tested it for acidity. Complete the table using the following:

teat pipette, 1 m^2 polythene sheet, test tube, clean beaker.

Job to be done	*Apparatus used*
(a) Collect water over a large area	
(b) Store water	
(c) Take a small sample of water for testing	
(d) Put 3 drops of indicator solution into the small sample of water	

(4 marks)

12 Why is it important that the beaker is clean?

13 Many lakes in Scotland are very acidic and have to be neutralized by adding limestone which is a carbonate.

(a) What gas will be given off when the carbonate is added to the acid in the lake?

(b) What effect does this have on the pH value of the water? (2 marks)

14 Sulphuric acid (H_2SO_4) and nitric acid (HNO_3) are the two main acids in acid rain. What ion is removed when acidic lakes are neutralized? (1 mark)

(*NEA*, 1988)

15 The four subtances listed in the table below are all used in the home. The table shows the results expected for each substance in each of three simple tests.

Substance	*Add water then indicator*	*Action of gentle heat on sample*	*Action of acid on substance*
sodium carbonate	alkaline	no reaction	odourless gas
sodium hydrogen -carbonate	alkaline	gas evolved	odourless gas
tartaric acid	acidic	no reaction	no reaction
calcium hypochlorite	alkaline	no reaction	gas with a strong smell

(a) Devise an identification key will show how this information could be used to identify an unknown solid as one of these substances. (5 marks)

(b) One type of fire extinguisher produces carbon dioxide by reacting a metal carbonate with an acid. The balanced equation for the reaction between sodium carbonate and hydrochloric acid is

$$Na_2CO_3 + 2HCl \longrightarrow 2NaCl + H_2O + CO_2$$

Given the relative atomic masses Na = 23, C = 12, and O = 16,

(i) what is the relative mass of CO_2? (1 mark)

(ii) what is the relative mass of Na_2CO_3? (1 mark)

(c) What mass of CO_2 would be formed by reacting 212 grams of sodium carbonate with excess acid?

(3 marks)

(*MEG*, 1988)

19 THE CHEMICAL INDUSTRY

19.1 Choosing an industrial site

The chemical industry provides vital materials for our society. Everyday we depend on industrial chemicals for materials such as fertilizers, fibres, foodstuffs, alloys, plastics and paints. Many factors are involved in choosing the site for an industrial plant such as a nuclear power station, an oil refinery, an electrolytic plant or a waste tip. Most of the factors are concerned with:

1 Social issues

- Will it provide employment?
- Is there a readily available and skilled workforce?
- Will it cause a strain on existing social, medical, and other community services?
- Will it disrupt or benefit the present community?

2 Environmental issues

- Will it disfigure the countryside with roads, pylons, large buildings, etc?
- Will it produce large amounts of waste or pollution?
- Will it cause high levels of noise?

3 Financial issues

- Is there enough cheap land available?
- What is the cost of raw materials?
- Will it provide sufficient profits for investors?
- Will the profits benefit the local community?

4 Location issues

- Are the raw materials available and accessible nearby?
- Are the existing transport facilities (road, rail and/or sea links) suitable for bringing in raw materials and distributing products?

Suppose there are plans to develop a large waste tip near your home and a public meeting is planned to discuss the development. Some people will be in favour and others will be against the proposal. Think of one important point that each of the following people could make at the public meeting. Give a different point for each person.

– The secretary of the local house owners' association
– The manager of a local haulage firm
– A representative of the local Trade Unions
– The local MP

Fig. 19.1 The site of the Moss Nook Trout Fishery was once a clay excavation pit in an industrial part of St. Helens, Merseyside. It was reclaimed and landscaped by the Groundwork Trust, St. Helens, Knowsley and Sefton, and is now used for recreation. In the background of the photograph you can see the chimneys of a local power station.

19.2 Sulphuric acid–an important industrial acid

The chemical industry is one of the largest manufacturing industries. But, unlike many other industries, its products are used to make other things rather than being used themselves. Sulphuric acid is a very good example of this.

Sulphuric acid is vital to the chemical industry. About 2½ million tonnes are manufactured in the UK each year. Most of this is then used to make a wide variety of other materials (see Fig. 19.2).

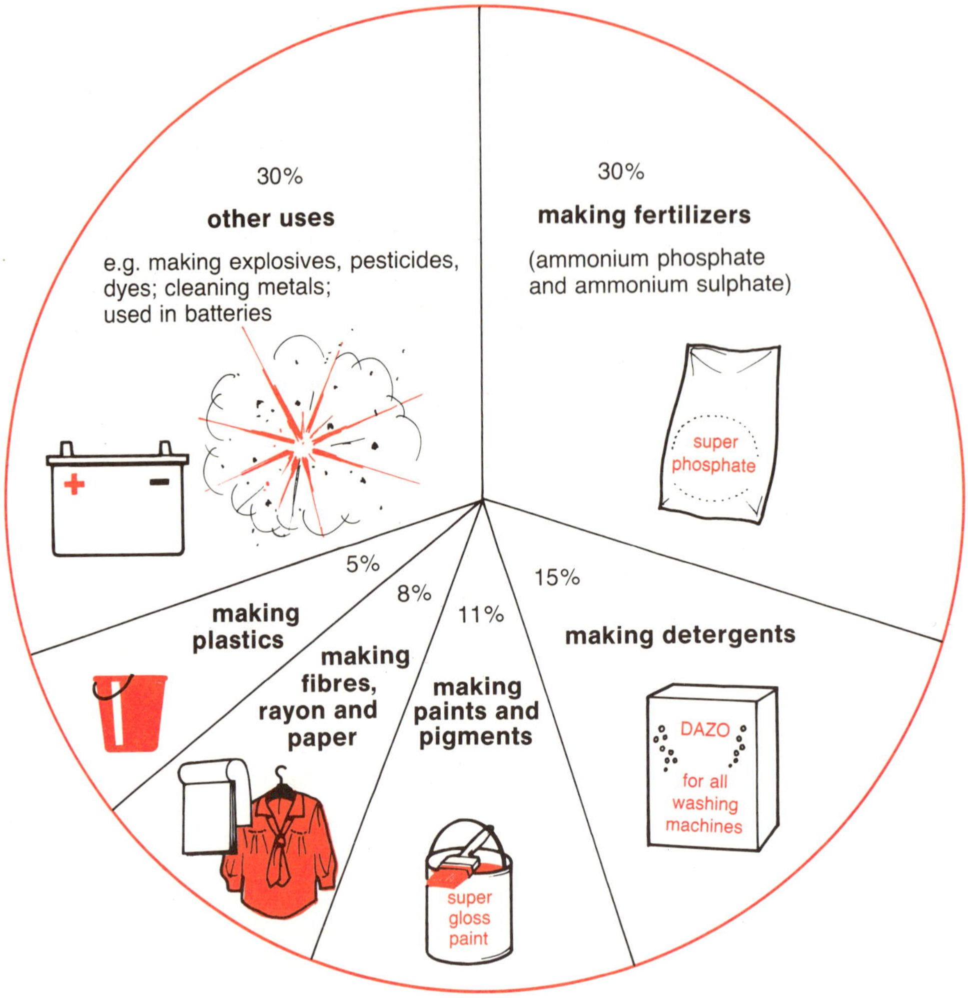

Fig. 19.2 The uses of sulphuric acid

Sulphuric acid is used by the chemical industry in two forms–either **dilute** or **concentrated**. These two forms are compared in Table 19.1.

Table 19.1 Comparing dilute and concentrated sulphuric acid

	Sulphuric acid	
	Dilute	*Concentrated*
Composition	10% H_2SO_4, 90% water	98% H_2SO_4, 2% water
Constituents	H^+ and SO_4^{2-} ions in water	H_2SO_4 molecules (very few H^+ and SO_4^{2-} ions)
Reactions	Typical reactions of a dilute acid with –indicators –metals –bases –carbonates (see section 18.3)	Does *not* show the same properties as dilute acids which require H^+ ions. Strong dehydrating agent (removes water from other materials such as hydrates and carbohydrates) e.g. removes water rapidly from living tissues such as skin. This causes burns. **Use with caution!**

19.3 Manufacturing sulphuric acid

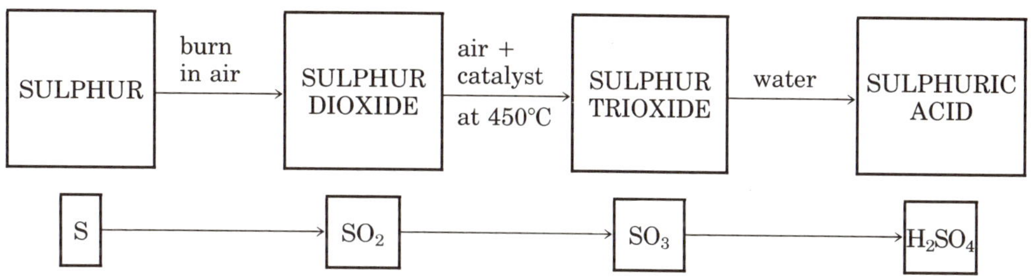

Fig. 19.3 A flow diagram for the manufacture of sulphuric acid

RAW MATERIALS

Notice in Fig. 19.3 that the raw materials for the process are **sulphur**, **air** and **water**. Air costs nothing, water is very cheap and sulphur is relatively inexpensive. This helps to keep down the cost of manufacture. This is important when so much sulphuric acid is needed by industry.

Most of the sulphur used in Britain is imported. It comes from two sources;

- underground deposits of sulphur in the USA, Mexico and Poland;
- 'recovered' sulphur–sulphur which has been removed from crude oil and natural gas.

CHEMICAL PROCESSING

Stage 1

Sulphur is burnt in air to produce sulphur dioxide:

$$\text{sulphur} + \text{oxygen} \longrightarrow \text{sulphur dioxide}$$
$$S + O_2 \longrightarrow SO_2$$

Stage 2

The sulphur dioxide is converted to sulphur trioxide by reacting it with oxygen in air. This is called the **Contact Process**. At room temperature, sulphur dioxide and oxygen react very slowly. The reaction is speeded up by using a **catalyst** of vanadium(V) oxide (V_2O_5) and by raising the temperature to 450°C.

$$\text{sulphur dioxide} + \text{oxygen} \xrightarrow[V_2O_5 \text{ catalyst}]{450°C} \text{sulphur trioxide}$$
$$2SO_2 + O_2 \longrightarrow 2SO_3$$

(Catalysts are discussed in section 19.11.)

Stage 3

The sulphur trioxide is then converted to sulphuric acid.

$$\text{sulphur trioxide} + \text{water} \longrightarrow \text{sulphuric acid}$$
$$SO_3 + H_2O \longrightarrow H_2SO_4$$

19.4 Ammonia–an important industrial alkali

Ammonia is an important industrial alkali. It is made from nitrogen and hydrogen. About two million tonnes are manufactured in the UK each year. About three quarters of this ammonia is used to make fertilizers. The other quarter is used to make a variety of products from nylon, plastics and fibres to dyes and explosives.

The properties of ammonia are summarized in Table 19.2. Unlike most bases, ammonia is a **gas**. It has a very pungent smell which you may have met in laboratory experiments. You might also have smelled ammonia in toilet cleaners which contain ammonia dissolved in water.

AMMONIA
NH_3

- gas at room temperature
- colourless
- pungent smell
- less dense than air
- very soluble in water

Table 19.2 Properties of ammonia

AMMONIA AS A BASE

Ammonia acts as a base in most reactions. It has typical alkaline reactions with
–indicators,
–acids, forming **ammonium salts**.

Most fertilizers are made by reacting ammonia with acids. For example, 'Nitram' (ammonium nitrate) is made by reacting with nitric acid:

ammonia + nitric acid ⟶ ammonium nitrate

$$NH_3 + HNO_3 \longrightarrow NH_4NO_3$$

19.5 Manufacturing ammonia

RAW MATERIALS

The chemical industry uses so much ammonia that its cost must be kept to a minimum. This means that a cheap source of raw materials is essential. Look back at the formula of ammonia given in Table 19.2. Ammonia contains **nitrogen** and **hydrogen**. These starting materials are obtained from **air**, **water** and **natural gas**.

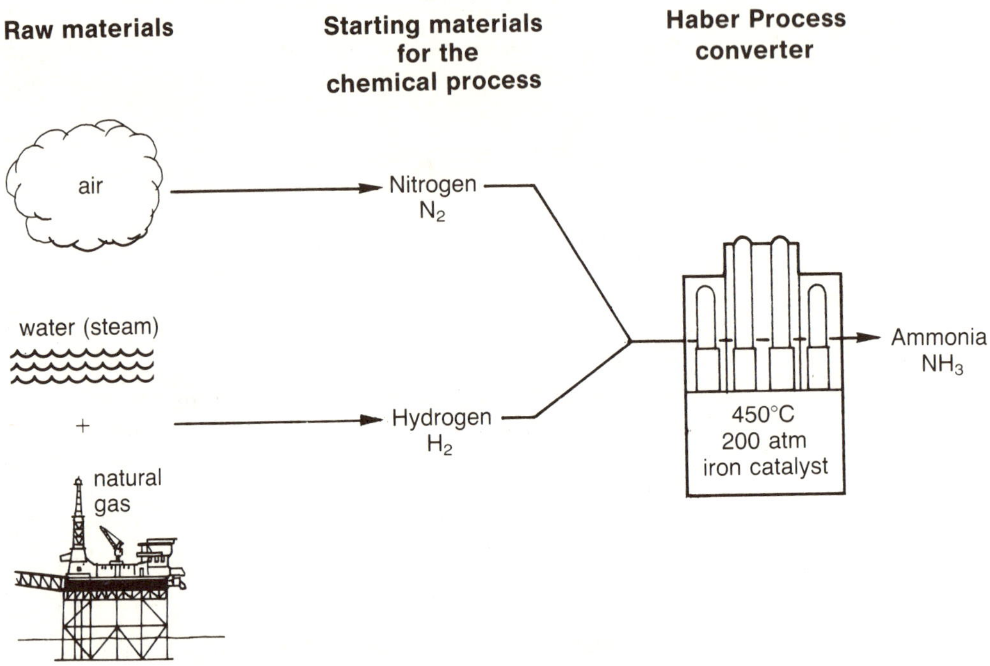

Fig. 19.4 Raw materials and starting materials for the manufacture of ammonia

CHEMICAL PROCESSING–THE HABER PROCESS

During the last century, the population of Europe rose very rapidly. More crops and other foods were needed to feed more people. To increase production, farmers began to use nitrogen compounds as fertilizers. At first, the main source of fertilizers was sodium nitrate from Chile.

By 1900, the deposits of sodium nitrate in Chile were almost used up. Another source of nitrogen had to be found. The obvious source of nitrogen was the air, but nitrogen is very unreactive. No-one had yet found a way of converting nitrogen gas into ammonium salts and nitrates for fertilizers.

The problem was solved by the German chemist, **Fritz Haber** (1868–1934). Haber found the conditions needed to make ammonia from hydrogen and nitrogen from the air. In time, the **Haber Process** became the most important method of manufacturing ammonia.

The Haber Process uses high temperature (450°C), high pressure (200 atmospheres) and a catalyst of iron to make nitrogen and hydrogen combine. Even so, only about 15 per cent of the mixture is converted to ammonia.

$$\text{nitrogen} + \text{hydrogen} \xrightarrow[\text{iron catalyst}]{450^\circ\text{C, 200 atm}} \text{ammonia}$$

$$N_2 + 3H_2 \longrightarrow 2NH_3$$

The hot gases from the converter are cooled to liquefy and separate the ammonia. The unreacted nitrogen and hydrogen are recycled.

Fig. 19.5 The ammonia plant at the BASF Aktiengesellschaft works in Ludwigshafen, West Germany. The first commercial ammonia manufacturing plant was built at Ludwigshafen in 1913

(Photograph courtesy of BASF)

19.6 Fertilizers from ammonia

Plants need certain essential elements in order to grow well (refer back to section 2.9). Some of these essential elements are obtained from the air or from water in the soil. Others are obtained from soluble compounds in the soil. Three essential elements which plants obtain from soluble compounds in the soil are nitrogen, phosphorous and potassium. Plants need more of these three elements than other elements (except carbon, hydrogen and oxygen). So if plants are to grow successfully year after year, nitrogen, phosphorus and potassium must be rcplaced in the soil by adding fertilizers.

Table 19.3 The role of nitrogen, phosphorus and potassium in plants

Essential element	*Role in plant growth*	*Effect of shortage*
Nitrogen	Needed for synthesis of proteins and chlorophyll	Plants are short and stunted
Phosphorus	Needed for synthesis of nucleic acids	Plants grow slowly Seeds and fruit are small
Potassium	Takes part in the synthesis of carbohydrates and proteins	Leaves become yellow and curl inwards

Fertilizers can be used as single compounds such as ammonium nitrate ('Nitram') or a mixture of compounds containing nitrogen, phosphorus and potassium ('NPK' fertilizers). The proportions of nitrogen, phosphorous and potassium in NPK fertilizers are usually given as percentage nitrogen (N), percentage phosphorous(v) oxide (P_2O_5) and percentage potassium oxide (K_2O) (see Fig. 19.6).

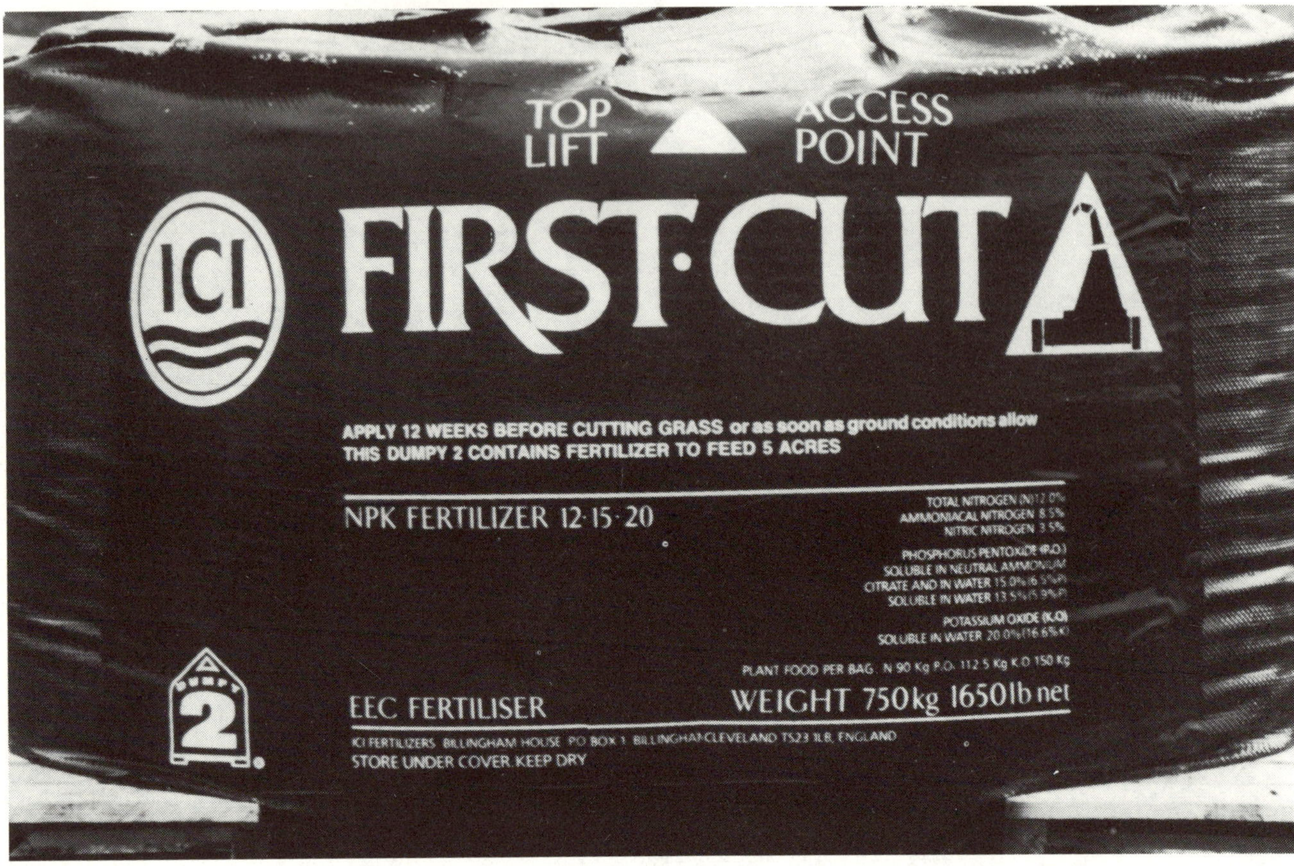

Fig. 19.6 The numbers 12·15·20 on this bag tell us that this NPK fertilizer contains 12 per cent N, 15 per cent P_2O_5 and 20 per cent K_2O

(Photograph courtesy of ICI Fertilizers)

NITROGEN FERTILIZERS

Nitrogen fertilizers are usually ammonium salts or nitrates. All of these are made from ammonia. **Ammonium nitrate** ('Nitram') is the most widely used fertilizer because

–it is soluble,
–it can be stored and transported as a solid,
–it contains a high percentage of nitrogen (see Table 19.4).

The higher the percentage of nitrogen the better, because a smaller amount of useless material is stored and transported. Use the method in Table 19.4 to calculate the percentage of nitrogen in ammonia (NH_3). Why do you think pure ammonia is not usually used as a fertilizer?

Table 19.4 Calculating the percentage of nitrogen in ammonium nitrate

Fertilizer	Ammonium nitrate
Formula	NH_4NO_3
Relative formula mass	Assuming the relative atomic masses $H = 1, N = 14$ and $O = 16$; $NH_4NO_3 = 14 + (4 \times 1) + 14 + (3 \times 16)$ $= 80$
Mass of nitrogen in relative formula mass	$14 + 14 = 28$
Percentage nitrogen	$\frac{\text{Mass of nitrogen}}{\text{Relative formula mass}} \times 100 = \frac{28}{80} \times 100 = 35$

OVER-USING FERTILIZERS

Fertilizers are important in that they provide plants with essential elements, but their over-use can cause problems:

- They may change the soil pH.
- They may harm plants and animals in the soil (refer back to section 12.2).
- They allow elements not required by plants to accumulate in the soil.
- They may be washed out of the soil and into waterways. This causes eutrophication and eventually leads to the pollution of rivers (refer back to section 12.2).

Fig. 19.7 Dead and decaying material in a polluted waterway as a result of eutrophication

19.7 The nitrogen cycle

In the last section we looked at man-made inorganic fertilizers like ammonium nitrate. Large quantities of **organic fertilizers** are also used by farmers and gardeners (refer back to section 12.2, particularly Table 12.1).

The most widely used organic fertilizers are **animal manure** and **compost** formed from the decaying remains of plants. The nitrogen compounds in manure and compost are decomposed by bacteria in the soil to produce nitrates and ammonium salts. The nitrates and ammonium salts are then absorbed through the roots of plants and used for growth. Animals have to eat plants or other animals in order to get the nitrogen and the proteins which they need. Eventually the animals and plants die and their decaying remains act as organic fertilizers again.

This cycle involving nitrogen in the air and nitrogen compounds in plants, in animals and in decaying remains, is called the **nitrogen cycle** (Fig. 19.8).

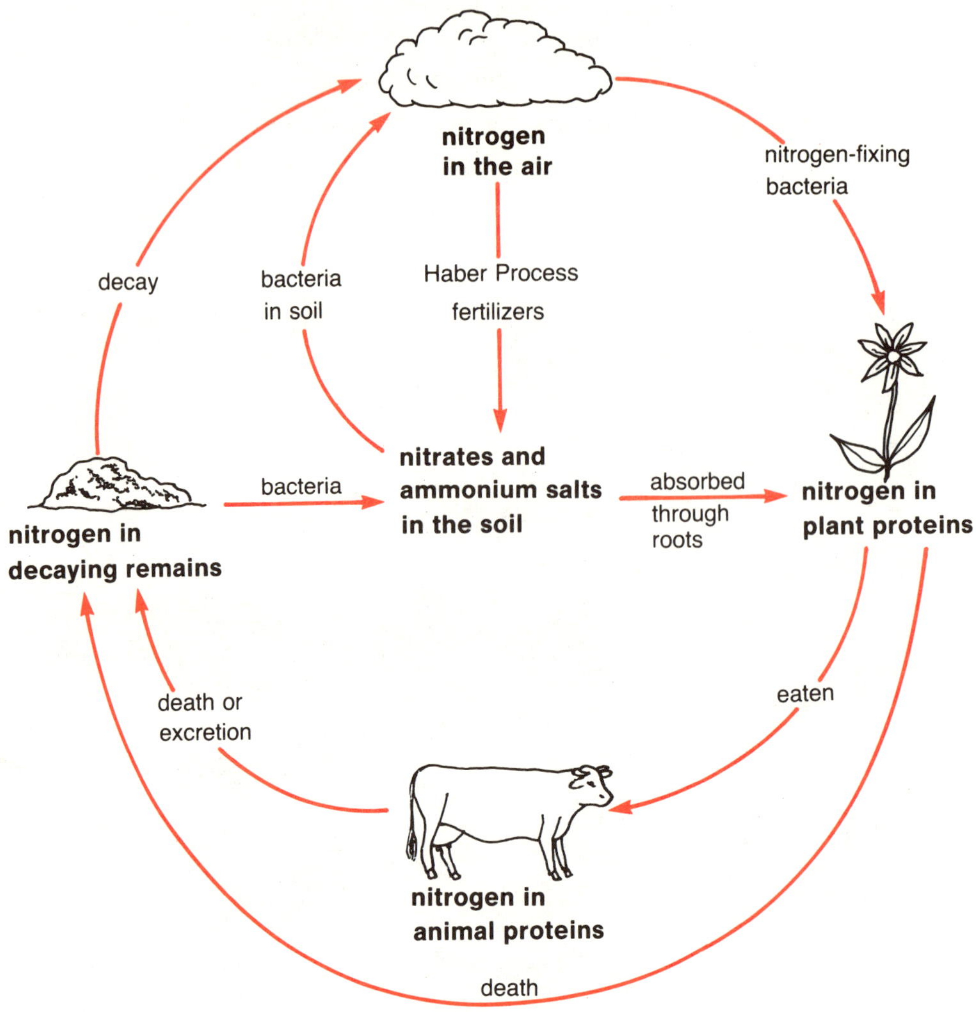

Fig. 19.8 The nitrogen cycle

Notice that some of the nitrogen that crops need is provided by **nitrogen-fixing bacteria**. These bacteria live in nodules on the roots of **leguminous plants** such as peas, beans and clover. The nitrogen-fixing bacteria can convert nitrogen from the air into nitrogen compounds for use by the plants. This conversion of atmospheric nitrogen to nitrogen compounds in plants is sometimes called *natural* nitrogen fixation. The conversion of atmospheric nitrogen to ammonia in the Haber process is called *industrial* nitrogen fixation.

19.8 Reaction rates and industrial processes

The chemists who work in industry try to produce materials as cheaply as possible. In order to do this they choose conditions which
–increase reaction rates,
–use the cheapest methods and raw materials.

Reaction rates can be speeded up by:

- **increasing the concentration of the reacting solutions** (or increasing the pressure of reacting gases);
- **increasing the surface area** of contact betwen reacting materials;
- **increasing the temperature** of reactants;
- **using a suitable catalyst**.

Look back at the descriptions of the Contact Process (section 19.3) and the Haber Process (section 19.5). What conditions are used to increase the reaction rates in these processes? By speeding up the reaction rates, sulphuric acid and ammonia can be made more quickly and cheaply. This is important because sulphuric acid and ammonia are major industrial chemicals.

19.9 How fast?

Every day we are concerned about how fast certain reactions occur. We want to know how long it takes to bake a cake, how long it takes to digest a meal and how quickly steel articles rust if they are left outdoors.

Different chemical reactions happen at different rates. Some reactions are so fast that they are almost instantaneous.

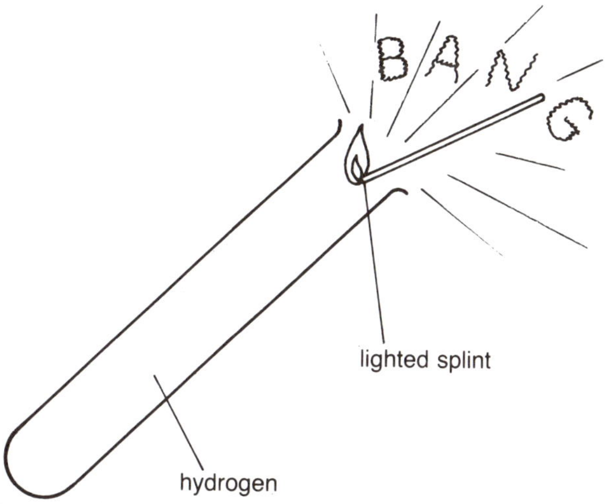

Fig. 19.9 The 'pop' test for hydrogen produces an almost instantaneous result

Other reactions, like the weathering of limestone on buildings, happen so slowly that it may be centuries before we notice the effect.

Fig. 19.10 This limestone statue has reacted with rain water so slowly that it has taken four or five centuries to begin to crumble away

Most reactions take place at steady speeds, somewhere between the extremes of explosions and weathering. The reactions involved in cooking food, in digesting a meal and in burning fuels, usually take place at steady rates.

19.10 Measuring reaction rates

During a reaction, reactants are being used up and products are forming. So the amounts of the reactants fall and the amounts of the products rise. The reaction rate tells us *how fast the reaction is taking place*. We can calculate the reaction rate by measuring *how much reactant is used up* or *how much product forms in a given time*.

$$\text{Reaction rate} = \frac{\text{change in amount of a substance}}{\text{time taken}}$$

The rate of the reaction between limestone and acid can be studied using the apparatus shown in Fig. 19.11 (overleaf).

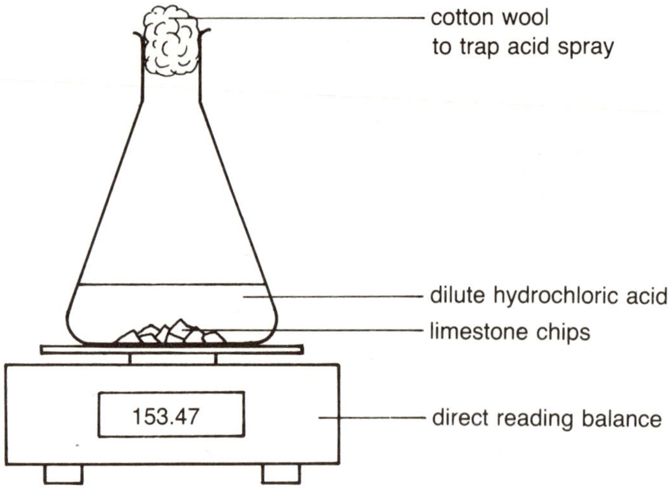

Fig. 19.11 Studying the reaction between limestone and acid

As the reaction occurs, carbon dioxide is produced.

$$CaCO_3(s) + 2HCl(aq) \longrightarrow CaCl_2(aq) + H_2O(l) + CO_2(g)$$

The carbon dioxide escapes from the flask as a gas and the mass of the flask and its contents decrease. The loss in mass is the mass of carbon dioxide produced. The results of one experiment have been plotted on a graph in Fig. 19.12.

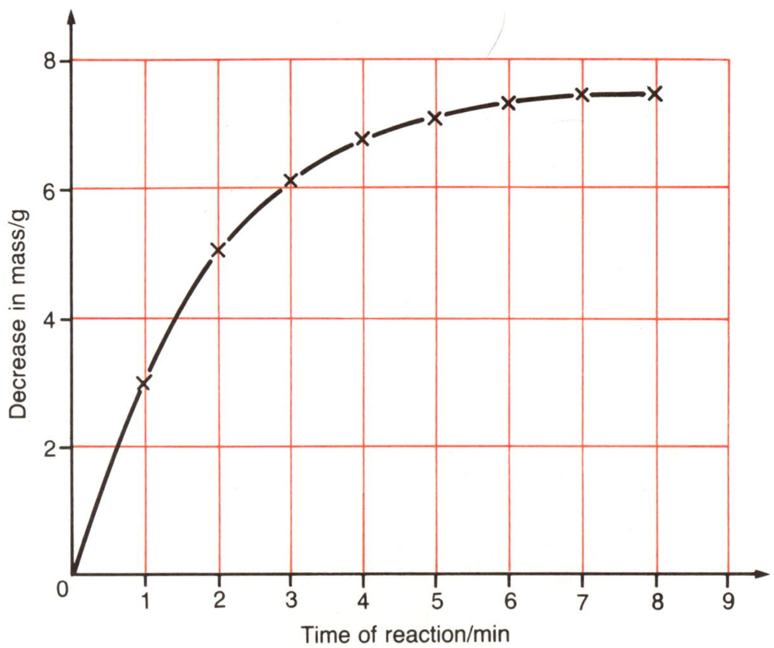

Fig. 19.12 A graph of the loss in mass against time, when limestone reacts with dilute hydrochloric acid

Notice from the graph that there is a decrease in mass of 3 grams in the first minute. We can calculate the reaction rate as follows:

$$\text{Reaction rate in first minute} = \frac{\text{change in mass of carbon dioxide}}{\text{time taken}}$$

$$= \frac{3\text{ g}}{1\text{ min}} = \mathbf{3\ g/min}$$

During the second minute (from time = 1 min to time = 2 min), 2 grams of carbon dioxide are lost. Therefore,

$$\text{Reaction rate in second minute} = \frac{2\text{ g}}{1\text{ min}} = \mathbf{2\ g/min}$$

These calculations and the graph show that the reaction rate is fastest at the start of the reaction. The faster the reaction, the steeper the graph. During the reaction, the rate decreases and the slope of the graph levels off. Eventually, the reaction stops (reaction rate = 0 g/min) and the graph becomes flat (gradient or slope = 0).

19.11 Speeding up reactions

- Why do large potatoes take longer to boil than small potatoes?
- Why does milk go sour more quickly on a hot summer's day?
- Why does concentrated detergent clean dishes faster than detergent?
- Why are stains removed by soaking a tablecloth in biological detergent?

These questions illustrate four important factors which affect the rates of chemical reactions:

- surface area
- temperature
- concentration
- catalysts

SURFACE AREA

The surface area of a solid is the *area of solid which is exposed*. If the solid is cut up into smaller pieces, more surface is exposed and this means it can react faster. This explains why smaller potatoes can be cooked faster than larger potatoes–with more surface exposed, the smaller potatoes cook more quickly.

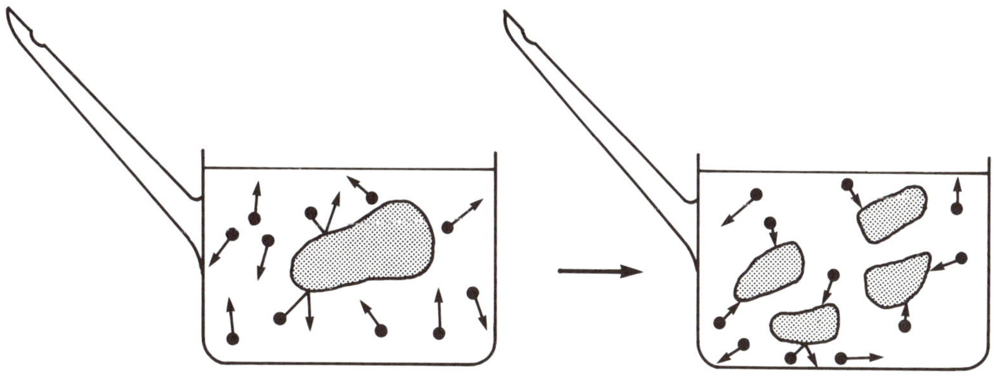

Fig. 19.13 When a potato is cut into smaller pieces, there are more collisions per minute with hot water particles, so the potatoes cook more quickly

TEMPERATURE

Milk sours in a few hours if left out on a bench on a hot, sunny day, but it will keep for days in a refrigerator. The chemical reactions which take place when milk goes sour occur more quickly at higher temperatures.

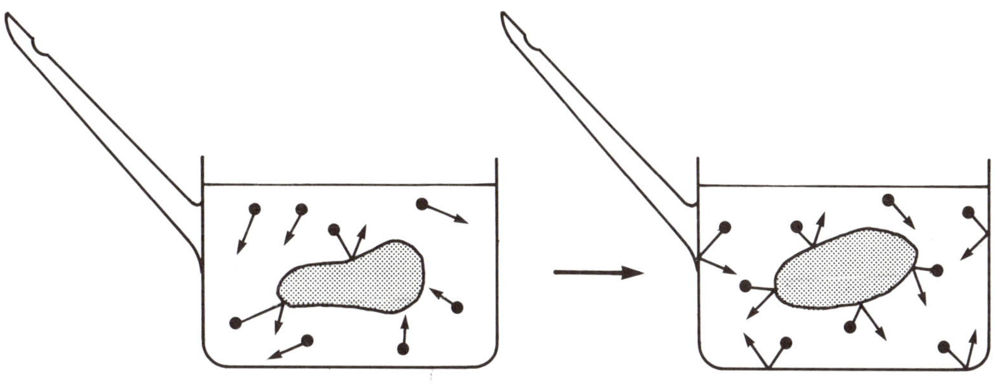

Fig. 19.14 At higher temperatures, particles collide more frequently and with more energy, so reactions proceed more quickly

CONCENTRATION

Concentrated solutions react more quickly than dilute ones. This is why concentrated detergent removes grease from dishes more quickly than dilute detergent. (See Fig. 19.15 overleaf.)

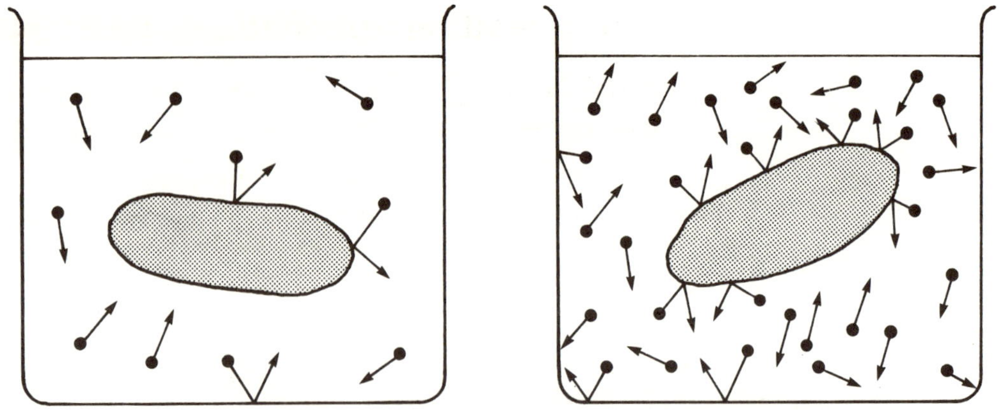

Fig. 19.15 In the more concentrated solution there are more collisions per second between the reacting particles, simply because there are more particles present, so the reaction proceeds more quickly.

CATALYSTS

Catalysts enable substances to react more easily. They do this by helping bonds within and between molecules to break more easily. The particles need less energy to react, so the reactions proceed more quickly.

For example, at room temperature hydrogen peroxide decomposes very slowly into water and oxygen.

$$\text{hydrogen peroxide} \longrightarrow \text{water} + \text{oxygen}$$
$$2H_2O_2 \longrightarrow 2H_2O + O_2$$

When powdered manganese(IV) oxide (MnO_2) is added, the hydrogen peroxide decomposes very rapidly. However *none of the manganese(IV) oxide is used up during the reaction*. The mass of manganese(IV) oxide is the same after the reaction as before. The manganese(IV) oxide has acted as a **catalyst**.

> **A catalyst is a substance which alters the rate of a reaction without being used up.**

Most catalysts speed up their reactions. However, a few catalysts are used to *slow down* reactions. These are called **negative catalysts** or **inhibitors**.

Catalysts play an important part in industry. Sulphuric acid (section 19.3), ammonia (section 19.5) and petrol (section 20.10) are all produced by processes involving catalysts. These catalysts allow their respective reactions to take place at lower temperatures. Less energy (heat) is therefore needed for the processes and they are more economical.

Catalysts are also vitally important to all living things. Catalysts in biological processes are called **enzymes**. Enzymes are proteins. At this moment, thousands of different chemical reactions are going on in your body. Every one of these reactions is catalysed by a specific enzyme. Without enzymes the reactions in your body would stop and you would die. Reactions in plants, e.g. photosynthesis, are also catalysed by enzymes (refer back to the end of section 12.5).

Enzymes are used in biological detergents and washing powders. They break down foods, blood and other biological substances. These biological detergents are more effective than ordinary detergents because they contain enzymes as well as soaps and detergents.

More and more industrial processes are being developed which use enzymes. These processes include the manufacture of fruit juices, yoghurt, vitamins, cheese and pharmaceuticals. The enzymes for these processes are often extracted from living material such as animal tissues, plants, yeast and fungi.

Quick test 19

Questions 1 to 4

The diagram below shows the supplies of water (labelled A, B, C, D and E) to a large lake.

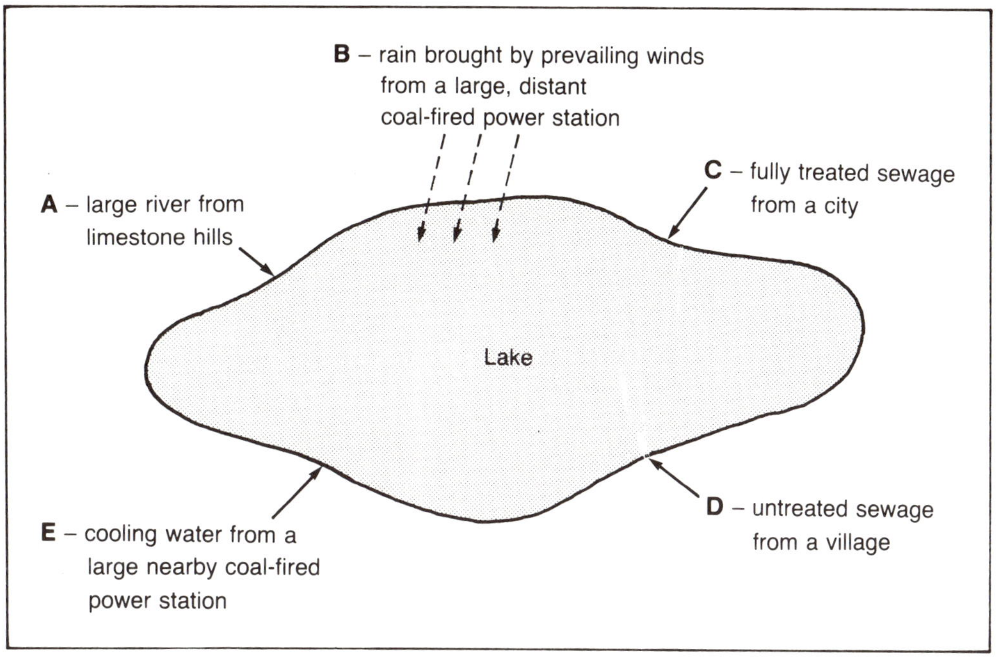

Which supply is most likely to
1 make the water in the lake more acidic?
2 raise the temperature of water in the lake?
3 lead to eutrophication in the lake?
4 neutralize any acidic substances in the lake?

Questions 5 to 7

Consider the following changes which might be made to the reaction between dilute hydrochloric acid and marble chips (calcium carbonate):

A decreasing the temperature
B diluting the acid further with water
C using a larger reaction vessel
D using larger marble chips
E using smaller marble chips

Which change or changes would
5 increase the rate of the reaction?
6 not affect the rate of the reaction?
7 decrease the rate of the reaction?

Questions 8 to 14

Plants need compounds containing nitrogen in order to grow healthily. These compounds are absorbed through the plant roots from soil water. They enter the soil both by natural processes and with the help of people. This century it has become possible to manufacture ammonia on a large scale by the Haber process. The ammonia produced is used to make compounds which are used as fertilizers.

8 Why can nitrogen gas in the air in soil *not* be used by most plants?
9 Name one natural process which produces nitrogen compounds that can enter the soil in a form that can be used by plants?
10 Explain why natural sources of nitrogen compounds are not sufficient for repeated crop growing on the same land.
11 What raw materials are used as a source of hydrogen and nitrogen in the production of ammonia in the Haber process?
12 In the Haber process, the nitrogen and hydrogen are reacted at 450°C. Why do you think the reaction is carried out at high temperature instead of ordinary temperature?
13 Ammonia is usually converted into a solid chemical such as ammonium nitrate for use as a fertilizer. Write the word equation for the reaction which is used to make ammonium nitrate from ammonia.

14 The formula of ammonium nitrate is NH_4NO_3. The relative atomic masses of the elements present are

N = 14 H = 1 O = 16

Calculate the percentage by mass of nitrogen in ammonium nitrate.

(*MEG*, 1988)

Questions 15 and 16

Ammonia is used to make fertilizers. It is made from nitrogen and hydrogen. The graph shows the percentage of ammonia that can be made from the same mixture of nitrogen and hydrogen at different temperatures and pressures.

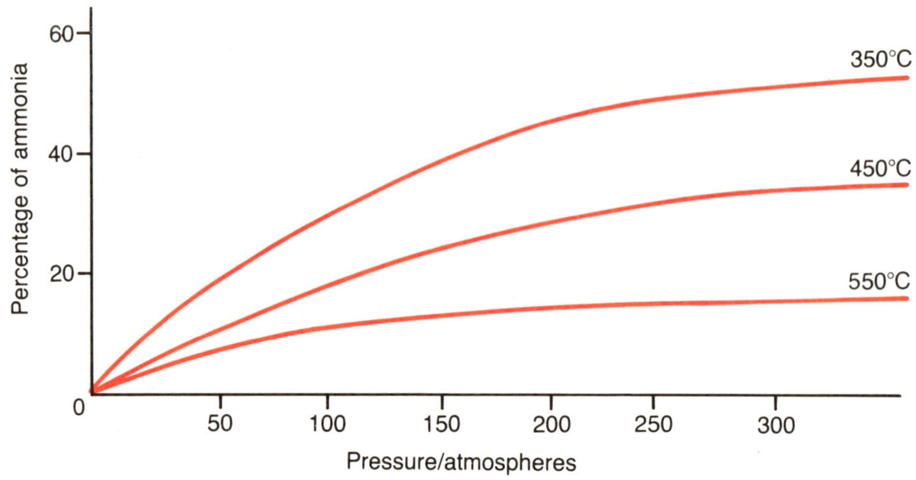

15 What *two* general conclusions can you draw from the information in the graph?

16 Under what conditions of temperature and pressure might you expect that part of a factory producing ammonia to operate? (*SCE*)

Questions 17 to 20

The diagram of the nitrogen cycle in Fig. 19.8 may help you to answer some of these questions.

17 What do the letters NPK on a bag of fertilizer stand for?

18 What part do the bacteria in the roots of pea plants take in the nitrogen cycle?

19 Suggest *two* reasons why most of the nitrates in the soil are not used by plants.

20 Some bacteria in the soil decompose nitrates to nitrogen. These bacteria work best in soil containing little or no air. Suggest conditions in which these bacteria will be most active.

20 ENERGY AND FUELS

20.1 Sources of energy and fuels

We cannot live without energy and fuels. We need them to keep warm, to cook our food, to drive our cars and to manufacture different products. Our main sources of energy are:

- **the sun** which provides the energy for plants to photosynthesize;
- **fuels**, such as coal and natural gas;
- **electricity** which is generated from fuels;
- **food** which is sometimes described as 'fuel for our bodies' (chapter 3).

A fuel is a substance which burns in air to produce heat.

The most important fuels are:

- **coal**
- **oil**
- **natural gas**

These three are described as **fossil fuels** because they have formed through the decay of dead animals and plants.

In addition to fossil fuels, *uranium* and *plutonium* are sometimes called **nuclear fuels**. They produce heat as a result of nuclear fission (see section 22.8).

Exothermic and endothermic reactions

Fossil fuels are composed mainly of hydrocarbons, compounds containing carbon and hydrogen. During burning, these compounds react with oxygen in the air forming carbon dioxide and water and producing heat:

	fuel	+ oxygen ⟶	carbon dioxide	+ water	+ heat
e.g.	$CH_4(g)$	$+ 2O_2(g) \longrightarrow$	$CO_2(g)$	$+ 2H_2O(l)$	+ heat
	methane in natural gas				

Reactions like this, which *give out heat*, are called **exothermic reactions**.

Some reactions are the opposite of this. They take in (require) heat. Reactions which *take in heat* are called **endothermic reactions**. One important endothermic reaction is the decomposition of limestone. This reaction is used to manufacture lime (refer back to Fig. 18.6).

$CaCO_3(s)$	+ heat ⟶	$CaO(s)$	$+ CO_2(g)$
limestone (calcium carbonate)		lime (calcium oxide)	

In *exo*thermic reactions heat is a product; in *endo*thermic reactions heat can be thought of as an input.

20.2 Fuels for various processes

Each year in the UK, we need energy equivalent to that which could be provided by about 300 million tonnes of coal. Figure 20.1 (overleaf) shows the percentages of this energy which we obtain from coal, oil, natural gas, nuclear power and hydroelectric power. Which of these sources provide most of our energy needs?

Some fuels, for example coal and coke, are difficult to set alight. Other fuels, e.g. natural gas, burn so rapidly and produce so much heat that they quickly burst into flames. A few fuels, for example hydrogen and petrol vapour, react so rapidly that they can cause explosions.

Because of the dangers of fire and explosion, all fuels must be used and handled with great care.

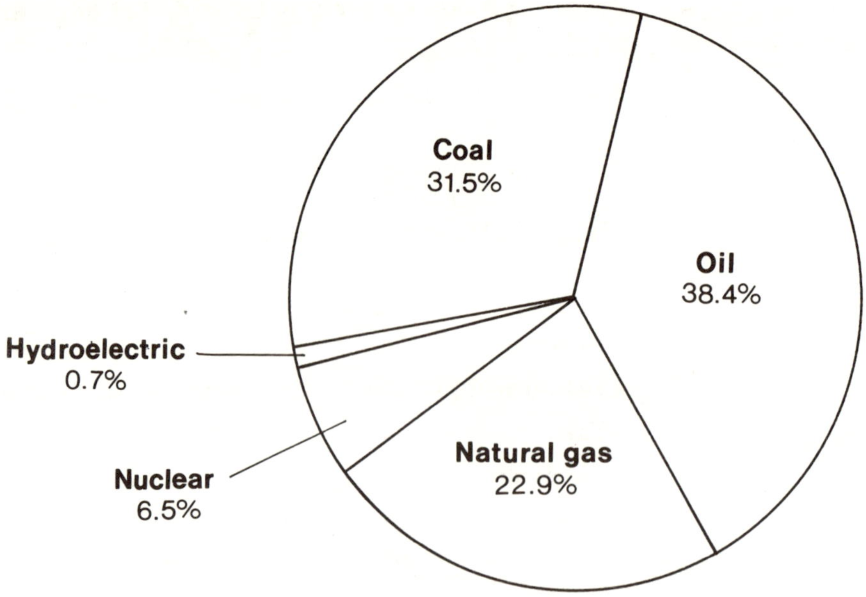

Fig. 20.1 The percentages of our energy needs from different sources (1988)
(Source: *BP Statistical Review of World Energy*, July 1989)

CHOOSING A FUEL

The properties of different fuels are very different. Because of this, different fuels are suitable for different purposes. What is more, industrial chemists have found ways of producing new fuels for specific purposes. These special man-made fuels include firelighters, coke, petrol, GAZ and lighter fuel.

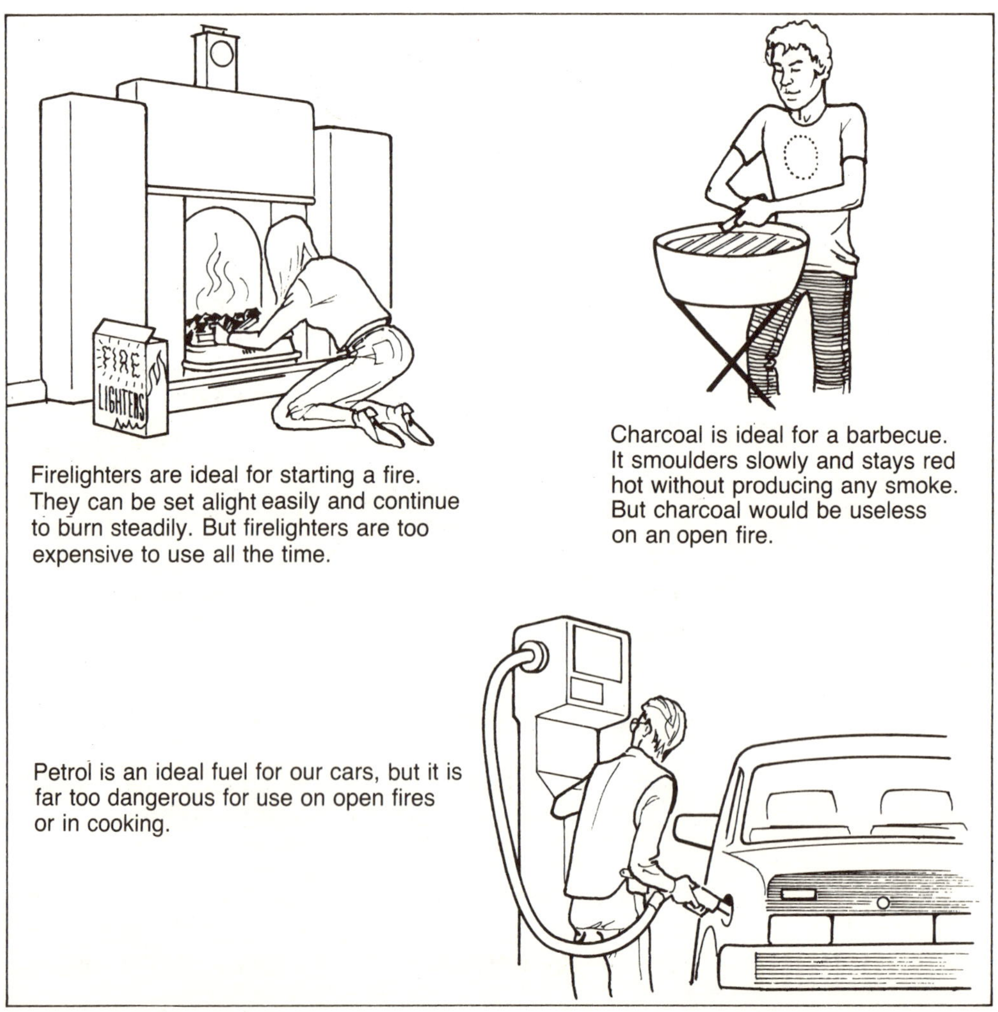

Fig. 20.2 Different fuels are needed for different purposes. Think carefully before choosing a fuel for a particular purpose

The important criteria to consider in choosing a fuel

- **Cost** Is it important to have a cheap supply of fuel?
- **Availability** Are large amounts of fuel required? If so, how easily can it be obtained?
- **Storage** How easily can the fuel be stored? Will special facilities be needed to store the fuel safely?
- **Transport** How easily can the fuel be transported? Solid fuels are easier to store and transport than liquid fuels. Liquid fuels are easier to store and transport than gaseous fuels.
- **Pollution** Does the fuel produce a lot of ash? Does the fuel produce much smoke?
- **Combustibility** How easily can the fuel be set alight? Does the fuel burn steadily?
- **Safety** Does the fuel pose any risk of fire or explosion?

Look at the criteria above and try to decide why more people prefer to use gas rather than coal or oil for cooking and heating in their homes.

20.3 Fires and fire-fighting

Figure 20.3 shows the **fire triangle** which was mentioned in chapter 14. Fuel, oxygen and heat are shown along its sides because all these are needed to start a fire and to keep a fire burning.

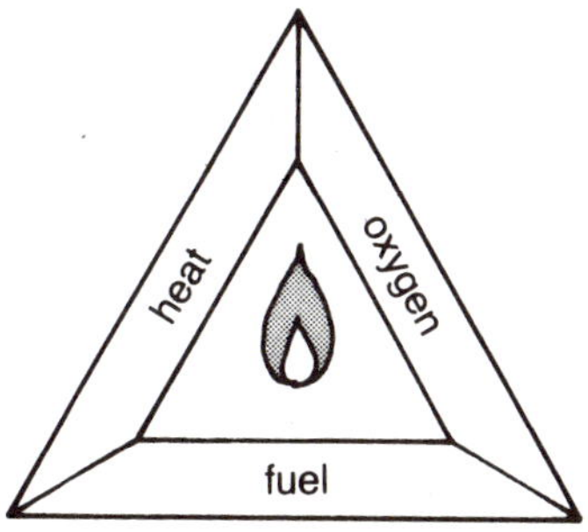

Fig. 20.3 The fire triangle

Very often fires are easy to start but difficult to put out. To put out a fire you need to remove one or more of the components in the fire triangle. Some of the methods of fire-fighting are summarized in Table 20.1.

Table 20.1 Methods of fire-fighting

Fire-fighting method	*How it works*
Fire blanket (damp cloth)	A blanket of cloth which will not burn is used to cover the fire. This removes the supply of air (oxygen).
Sand	Sand is thrown over the fire. This cuts off the supply of air (oxygen).
Water	Cold water is poured on the fire. This reduces the temperature and removes heat from the fire. Water should *not* be used with fires from petrol or oil (which will float on the water) or with electrical fires (because of the danger of electrocution).
Carbon dioxide	A jet of carbon dioxide is directed at the fire. This dense gas covers the fire and cuts off the supply of air (oxygen).
Fire breaks in forests	A fire break is a 'corridor' through a forest which is cleared of trees. If a forest fire reaches a fire break it dies down because the supply of fuel is cut off.

20.4 Measuring the energy from fuels

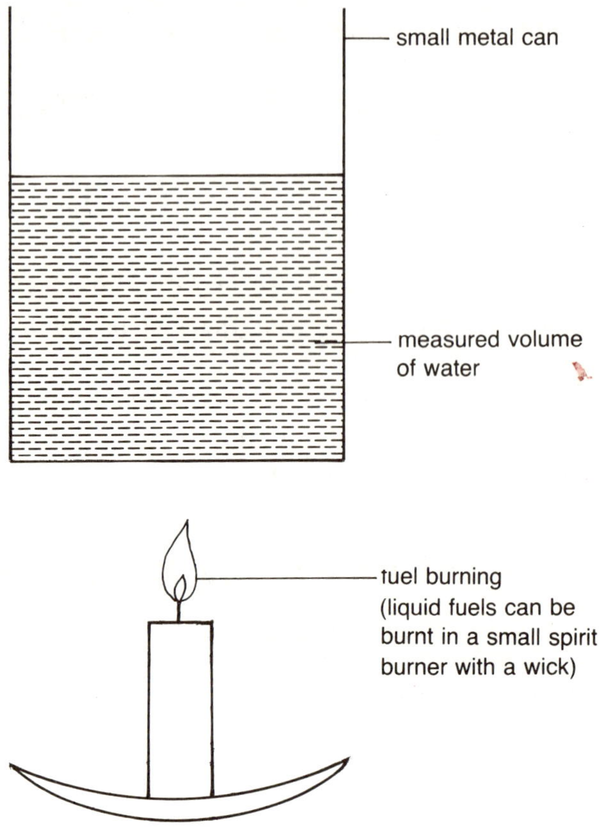

Fig. 20.4 Measuring the energy from a fuel

It is useful to know how much energy is produced when a fuel burns. Figure 20.4 shows the apparatus which can be used to find this. The heat from the burning fuel is used to heat the water in the metal can. By measuring

–the volume of water in the can,
–the temperature rise of the water and
–the mass of fuel burnt,

we can calculate the energy (heat) produced when one gram of the fuel burns. The results of one experiment using methylated spirits (meths) are shown in Table 20.2.

Table 20.2 Results of an experiment to measure the energy produced when meths is burnt

Volume of water in metal can	300 cm^3
∴ *mass of water in can*	300 g
Rise in temperature of water	8°C
Mass of meths burnt	0.5 g

In the experiment, the temperature of 300 g of water was raised 8°C.

4.2 joules* of energy (heat) will warm up 1 g of water by 1°C

therefore 300×4.2 joules will warm up 300 g of water by 1°C
and $300 \times 4.2 \times 8$ joules will warm up 300 g of water by 8°C.

This amount of heat (energy) was produced by 0.5 g of meths

$\Rightarrow$ 0.5 g meths produced $300 \times 4.2 \times 8 = 10080$ joules (J)
$= 10.08$ kilojoules (kJ) of energy.

therefore, when it is burnt, 1 g of meths produces 20.16 kJ of energy.

*The measurement of energy in joules is discussed in section 24.1.

20.5 Fossil fuels–coal, oil and natural gas

300 million years ago, the earth was covered in forests and the sea was teeming with tiny organisms. As these plants and animals died, large amounts of decaying

material began to pile up. Where the decaying material was in contact with air, it rotted away completely. During this process, complex compounds in the rotting material, containing carbon, hydrogen, oxygen and nitrogen, reacted with oxygen in the air. The products were carbon dioxide, water and nitrogen.

In some areas, however, the decaying material was covered by the sea, by sediment from rivers or by rocks from earth movements. In these places, the material decayed in the absence of oxygen. It was still attacked by bacteria, but instead of rotting away completely it was compressed by the water and rocks above. Over millions of years this led to the slow formation of coal from plants and to the formation of oil and natural gas from sea creatures.

The formation of these fossil fuels involved energy changes over millions of years. Energy from the sun was originally trapped by photosynthesis in plants. This energy was eventually converted to chemical energy in coal, oil and natural gas.

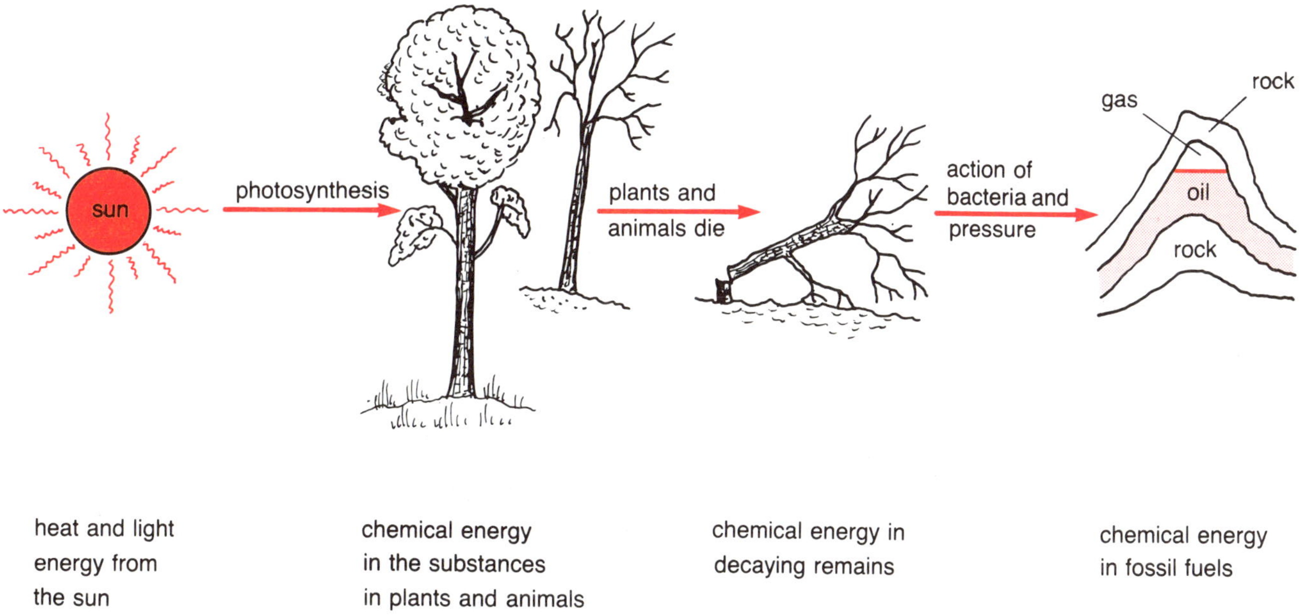

Fig. 20.5 Energy changes in the formation of fossil fuels

Conserving fossil fuels

For the last 150 years, industrialized nations have relied on fossil fuels, particularly oil, as sources of energy and for important chemicals. We depend on oil for transport and as the source of chemicals to manufacture important materials like plastics, nylon, polythene, Terylene, paint and antifreeze liquid. Unfortunately, supplies of fossil fuels will not last forever. Coal is still plentiful, but oil and natural gas are likely to run out in fifty to sixty years' time. We need to conserve fossil fuels and prevent waste of energy. This has led to:

- the search for and use of alternative energy sources (see section 20.6);
- improved methods of insulation (see section 24.13);
- more efficient use of fuels.

20.6 Alternative energy sources

In time, our supplies of fossil fuels are bound to run out. This means that we must look for alternative energy sources. It is particularly important to find other sources of energy for transport and for generating electricity, both of which rely on oil.

At present, the most viable alternative source of large amounts of electrical energy is nuclear power. This and other alternatives to fossil fuels are summarized in Table 20.3 (overleaf).

Fossil fuels and uranium are sometimes described as **non-renewable energy sources**. Once used, they are gone forever. They cannot be replaced. On the other hand, tidal power, wind power, hydroelectric power, solar power and biomass are **renewable energy sources**. They keep on being replaced – however much they are used the tide continues to rise and fall, the wind continues to blow, . . .

Table 20.3 Alternative energy sources

Energy source	*How is the energy source used?*
nuclear power	Nuclear fission of uranium-235 produces heat (see section 22.8). This heat is used to produce steam which drives turbines generating electricity.
tidal power	As the tides come in and flow out, the water is made to drive turbines which generate electricity.
wind power	The wind is used to drive giant windmills (wind turbines) which generate electricity.
hydroelectric power	Falling water is used to drive turbines which generate electricity. Sometimes the electricity is used to pump water into a high reservoir. In this way, energy can be stored in the water for later use.
solar power	Energy from the sun is used to heat water in solar panels or to generate electricity using photo cells.
biomass	Material from plants and animals is used to provide fuel for heat, e.g. wood, charcoal, vegetable oils. Sometimes the animal and plant materials (such as manure and compost) are allowed to decompose in the absence of air. This produces **biogas** which is about 60 per cent methane and 40 per cent carbon dioxide.

Fig. 20.6 An experimental wind turbine being tested at Exeter University

20.7 Crude oil

Crude oil (petroleum) is our main source of fuel and organic (carbon-based) chemicals. The crude oil comes to refineries in the UK from oil wells in the North Sea and the Middle East.

Crude oil is a thick, smelly, dark brown liquid. It contains hundreds of different compounds. These vary from simple substances like methane (CH_4) to complex substances with dozens of atoms per molecule. Most of the compounds in crude oil are **hydrocarbons**, i.e. they contain only hydrogen and carbon.

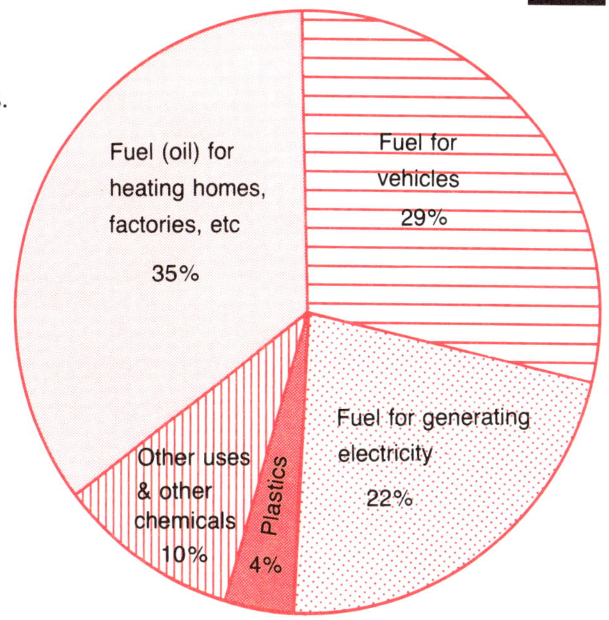

Fig. 20.7 The uses of crude oil

FRACTIONAL DISTILLATION OF CRUDE OIL

Crude oil itself is useless. It must be separated into different parts or **fractions** before it is used. Each fraction contains a mixture of hydrocarbons with similar properties. Some of the fractions contain *volatile* hydrocarbons – these are easily vaporized. These fractions can be used as petrol. Other fractions are much less volatile. They can be used as fuel for ships or power stations.

The separation of crude oil into fractions is carried out by **fractional distillation**. (This process was described at the end of section 13.7.) Figure 20.8 shows how this is carried out at an oil refinery. It also shows the temperatures and products at different heights in the fractionating column.

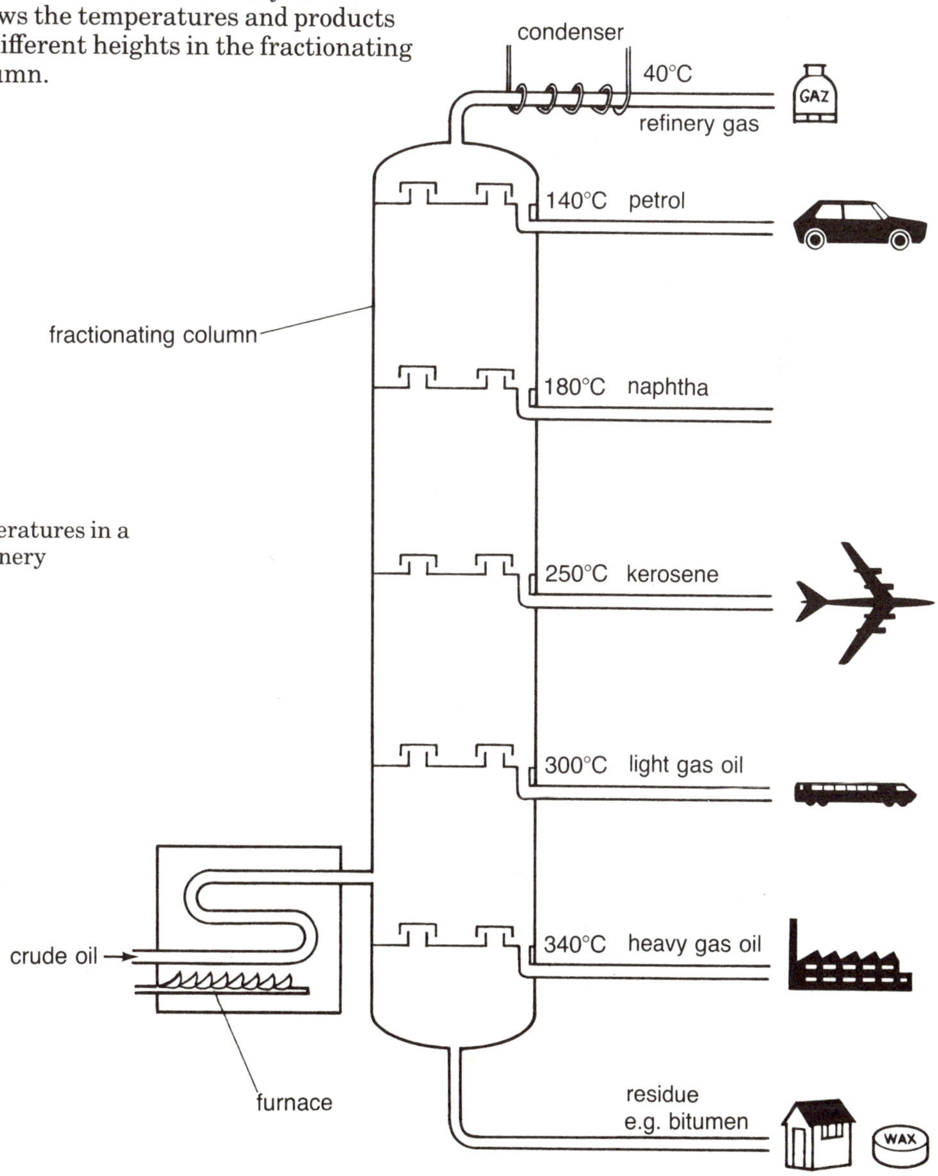

Fig. 20.8 The products and temperatures in a fractionating column at an oil refinery

The crude oil is heated by a furnace and the vapours pass into the lower part of the fractionating column. As the vapours rise up the column through holes in the trays, the temperature falls. Vapours of different compounds condense at different heights in the column as the temperature falls below the boiling point of the compounds. Liquids such as petrol (gasoline), which boil at low temperatures, condense high up the column. Liquids such as diesel oil, which boil at higher temperatures, condense lower down.

Each of the fractions from crude oil contains a mixture of similar compounds which have about the same number of carbon atoms. Table 20.4 summarizes the properties and uses of the different fractions collected at an oil refinery. The uses of the various fractions depend on their properties. For example, refinery gases burn easily at a jet without producing any smoke, so they are ideal for cooking. The residue contains viscous materials which can be used as lubricants or sealants (e.g. bitumen).

Table 20.4 The properties and uses of the different fractions produced by fractional distillation of crude oil at a refinery

Fraction	*Boiling range/°C*	*Number of carbon atoms in molecules*	*Uses*
refinery gas	up to 40	1–4	fuel for gas cookers, LPG, GAZ, plastics
petrol (gasoline)	40–140	5–10	fuel for vehicles, chemicals
naphtha	140–180	8–12	raw material for chemicals and plastics
kerosine (paraffin)	180–250	10–16	aircraft fuel, heating and raw material for chemicals
light gas oil (diesel oil)	250–300	14–20	fuel for trains and lorries, raw materials for chemicals, plastics
heavy gas oil	300–340	20–30	fuel for ships, factories, central heating
residue	above 340	more than 25	lubricants, waxes, bitumen for roads and roofing

20.8 Chemicals in crude oil – alkanes

Most of the chemicals in crude oil are hydrocarbons. The simplest series of hydrocarbons is the **alkanes**.

Table 20.5 The first four members of the alkanes

Alkane	*Molecular formula*	*Structural formula*
Methane	CH_4	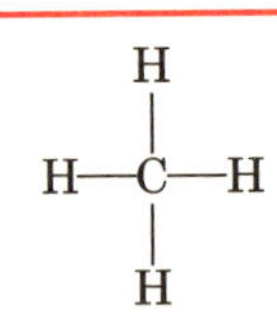
Ethane	C_2H_6	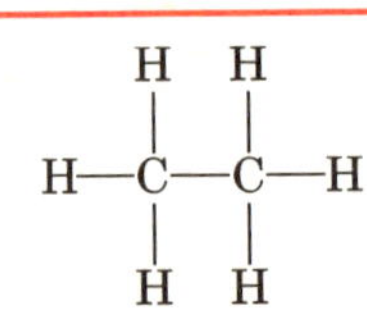
Propane	C_3H_8	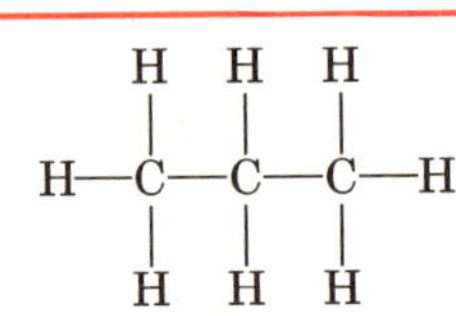
Butane	C_4H_{10}	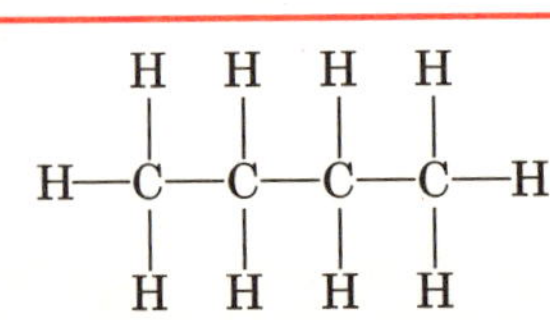

Table 20.5 describes the first four members of the alkanes. Crude oil and natural gas are the main sources of alkanes. Natural gas is mostly methane (CH_4), with small amounts of ethane (C_2H_6). Propane (C_3H_8) and butane (C_4H_8) are the main constituents of 'Calor gas' and GAZ used as fuel when camping and caravanning.

Alkanes with between 5 and 17 carbon atoms are liquids at room temperature. For example, octane (C_8H_{18}) is one of the main constituents of petrol. Alkanes with 18 or more carbon atoms are solids at room temperature.

Notice how the alkanes become less volatile and change from gases through liquids to solids as their molecular size increases.

Alkanes are typical **molecular compounds** (refer back to section 16.7). They are:

- **volatile** compared to ionic compounds;
- **insoluble in water**;
- **fairly unreactive** – petrol, for example, will not react with sodium or with concentrated sulphuric acid.

The most important reaction of alkanes is **combustion**. They burn in oxygen producing carbon dioxide and water.

$$\underset{\text{butane}}{C_4H_{10}} + 6\tfrac{1}{2}O_2 \longrightarrow 4CO_2 + 5H_2O$$

The combustion reactions of alkanes are very exothermic, so alkanes in natural gas and crude oil are important as fuels.

20.9 Alkenes

After alkanes, the next most important series of hydrocarbons are the **alkenes**. Alkenes can be obtained from crude oil. They are very important in the manufacture of plastics and other polymers (see section 20.10).

In alkanes, all the bonds between carbon atoms are single bonds (C—C). Alkenes differ from alkanes because they contain a **double bond** between two of their carbon atoms (C═C).

The simplest alkene is ethene (C_2H_4). The next alkene in the series is propene (C_3H_6) (see Fig. 20.9).

Ethene **Propene**

C_2H_4 C_3H_6

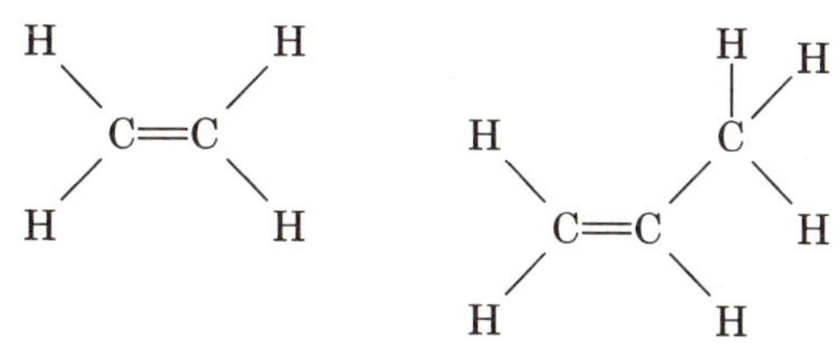

Fig. 20.9 The first two alkenes

STRUCTURE AND REACTIONS OF ALKENES

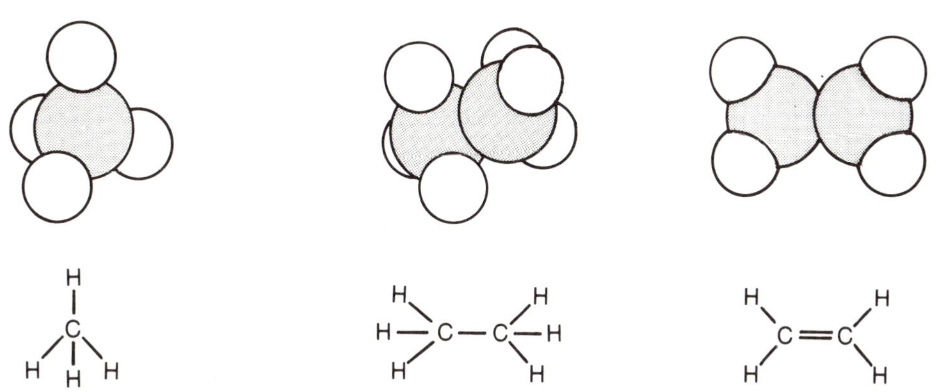

methane **ethane** **ethene**

Fig. 20.10 Models showing the tetrahedral arrangement of atoms bonded to carbon atoms in alkanes (methane and ethane), and the triangular arrangement in an alkene (ethene)

The most stable arrangement for the four bonds to a carbon atom is a tetrahedral one. Alkenes, such as ethene, have a triangular arrangement of bonds to those carbon atoms joined by a double bond. This makes alkenes much more reactive than alkanes. Other atoms can *add* across the double bond to make two single bonds. So alkenes readily undergo **addition reactions**. Table 20.6 summarizes three important addition reactions of ethene.

Table 20.6 Three important addition reactions of ethene

Reaction of ethene	*Conditions needed*	*Equation and product*
with bromine or bromine water	reacts easily at room temperature	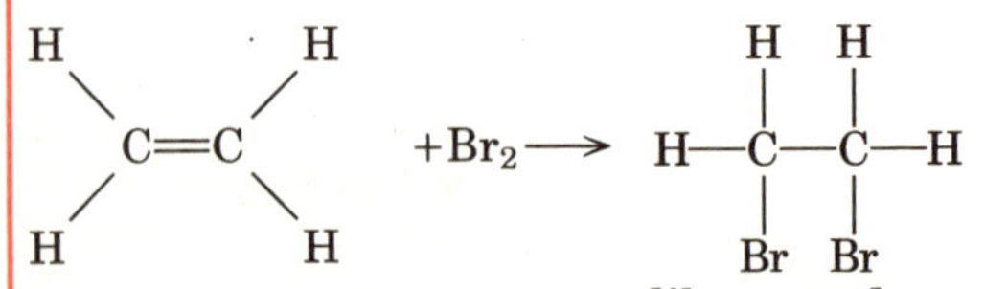 **dibromoethane**
with steam	300°C, very high pressure	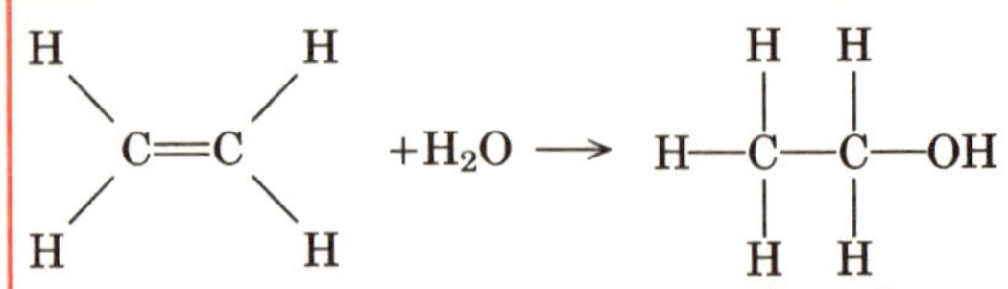 **ethanol**
with itself	high temperatures, high pressures, a suitable calalyst	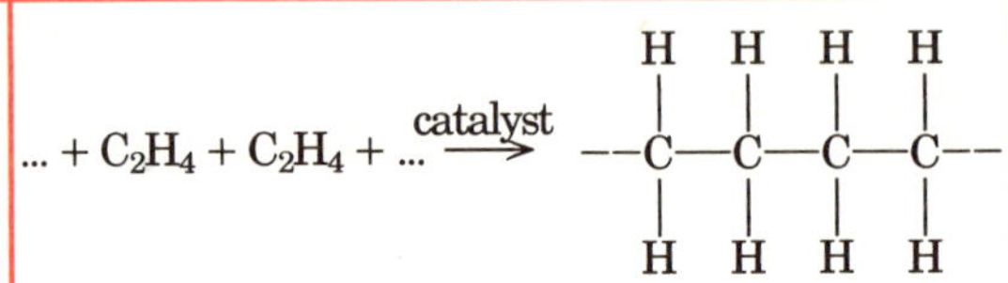 **polythene**

Bromine water is a yellow-orange liquid. During the reaction with ethene it becomes colourless. (The product, dibromoethane is colourless). Other alkenes react with bromine water in a similar way so this reaction is used as a **test for alkenes**.

The reaction of ethene with steam is important in the manufacture of alcohol and methylated spirits (see section 20.12).

The reaction of ethene with itself produces polythene. This is discussed further in the following section.

20.10 Plastics

POLYMERIZATION

Plastics (e.g. polythene, nylon and PVC) are **polymers**. The plastics are made by **polymerization**. This involves joining together small molecules called **monomers**.

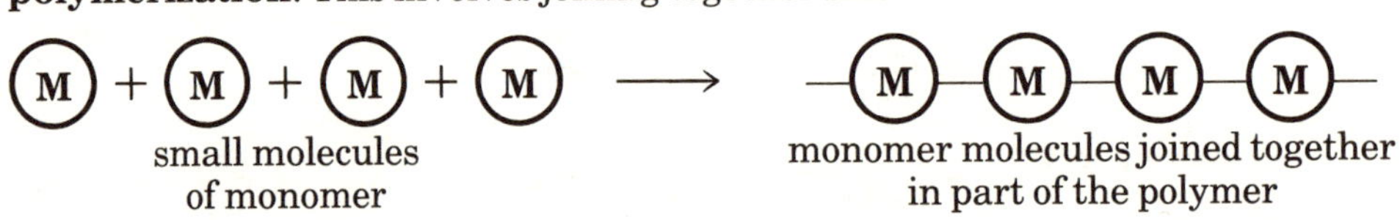

Fig. 20.11 Polymerization

The most important plastic is **polythene**. This is made by polymerization of ethene. This is an addition reaction in which ethene reacts with itself. The process requires high temperature, high pressure and a catalyst.

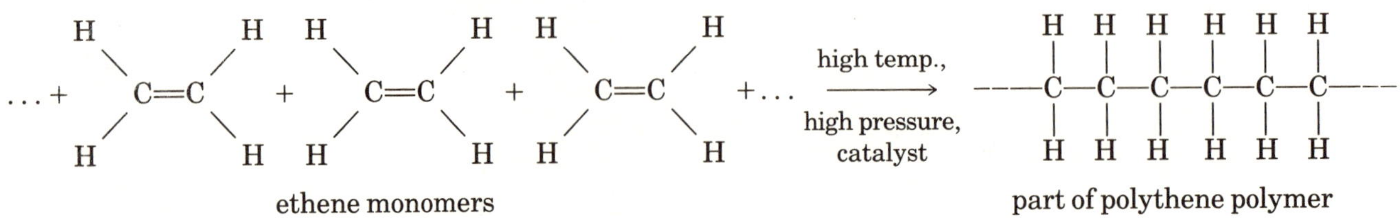

Fig. 20.12 Polymerization of ethene to form polythene

POLYMERS FROM CRUDE OIL

Chemists have found ways of obtaining ethene from the heavier fractions of crude oil, such as naphtha and gas oil. These methods involve a process called **cracking**.

During cracking, larger molecules are broken apart forming two smaller molecules. Alkanes, such as decane ($C_{10}H_{22}$), are broken down into smaller alkanes like octane (C_8H_{18}) and alkenes such as ethene (C_2H_4):

$$\text{decane} \longrightarrow \text{octane} + \text{ethene}$$
$$C_{10}H_{22} \longrightarrow C_8H_{18} + C_2H_4$$

Unlike distillation, cracking is a chemical reaction. It involves breaking a bond between carbon atoms to form two new substances. Because of this, it requires high temperatures of about 800°C.

Ethene and the other alkenes produced during cracking are used to make plastics. The other products of cracking, e.g. octane, provide additional supplies of petrol. Larger fragments than octane (molecules with more than eight carbon atoms) can be cracked further.

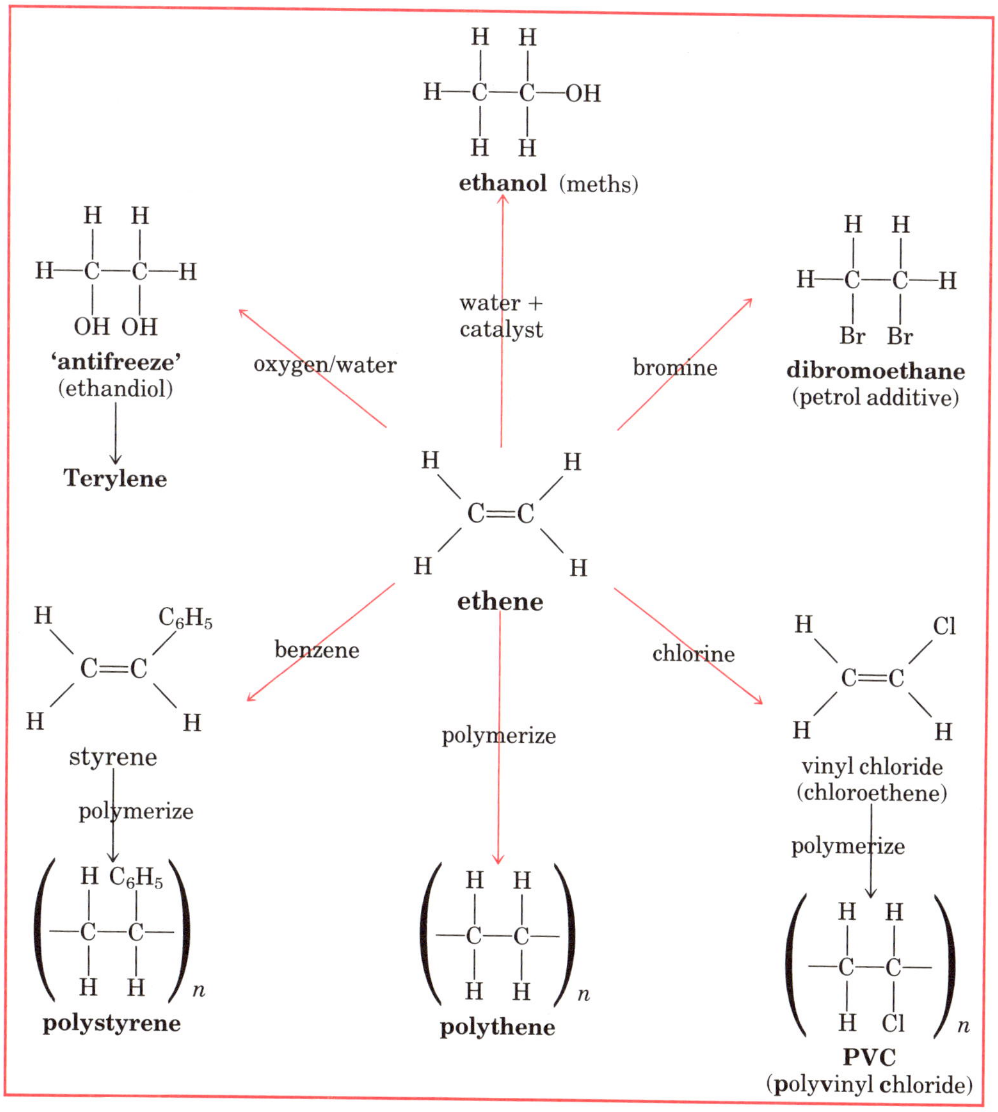

Fig. 20.13 Important plastics and other products from ethene

Some of the important plastics and other products from ethene are shown in Fig. 20.13. Notice that polythene, polystyrene and PVC are all made from monomers containing a C=C double bond. This is also the case with Perspex, polypropene and Teflon (polytetrafluoroethene, PTFE).

USING PLASTICS

Different plastics have very different properties and therefore very different uses. In fact, one of the important advantages of plastics is that by mixing different monomers, or by melting and mixing the final polymers, it is possible to make a plastic with specific properties. Plastics are chosen for their different uses because they have a suitable combination of properties. The examples in Table 20.7 (overleaf) show why different plastics are chosen for different uses.

Table 20.7 The choice of plastics for different uses

Plastic	**Polythene**	**PVC** (polyvinyl chloride)	**Perspex**
Important properties	cheap, flexible, light, can be dyed	cheap, strong, easily moulded	strong, clear, easily moulded, resistant to chemicals
Uses	bags, wrappers, cling film 	artificial leather for furniture, luggage cases and clothes 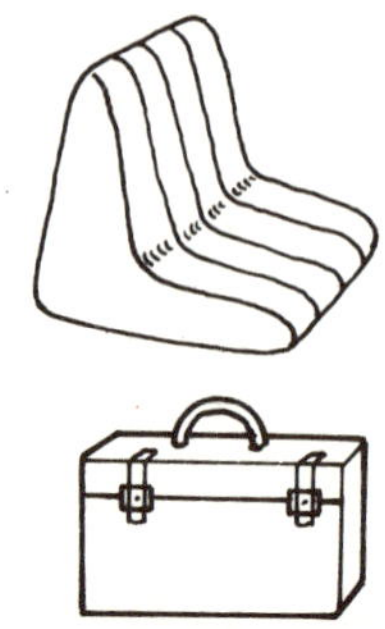	safety glasses 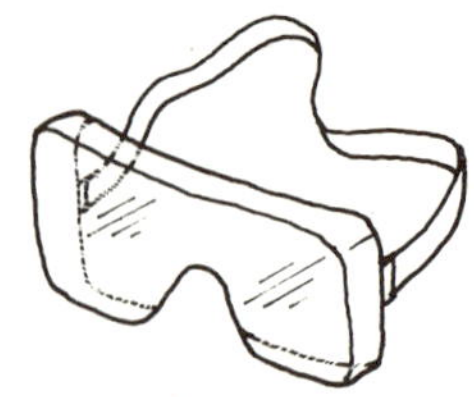

20.11 Ethanol

Ethanol is another important product from ethene (refer back to Fig. 20.13). The structure of ethanol is shown in Fig. 20.14.

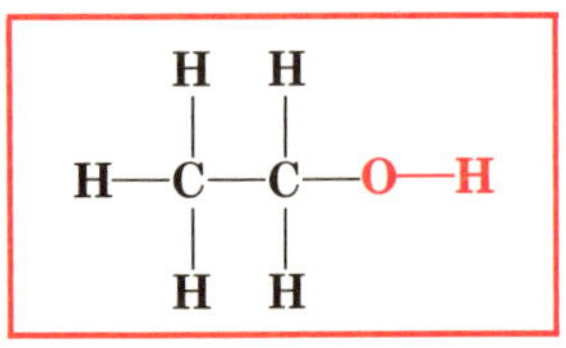

Figure 20.14

Ethanol is a member of a group of compounds called **alcohols**. All alcohols have an oxygen and a hydrogen atom in their molecule. These two atoms are bonded together as an —O—H group (highlighted in Fig. 20.14.). Ethanol is the most important member of the alcohols. Because of this, it is often just called *alcohol*.

USES OF ETHANOL

Ethanol has three important uses:

1 As a solvent

Ethanol is a very good solvent. It will dissolve many different substances. It is also very volatile, so it is used as a solvent in paints, varnishes and perfumes which need to dry quickly when used.

2 As a fuel

Ethanol burns easily without smoking. This makes it suitable for use in spirit burners for cooking, lighting and heating. The ethanol for this purpose is usually sold as *methylated spirits*, commonly called meths. Meths is approximately 95 per cent ethanol. The other 5 per cent includes colourings and poisonous substances to stop people drinking it.

In some countries, for instance Brazil, ethanol is used as a fuel for vehicles in place of petrol.

3 In alcholic drinks

Alcoholic drinks such as beer, wine and whisky contain ethanol in varying amounts. The ethanol in these drinks is produced by fermentation of sugars from different sources. The percentage of ethanol and the source of sugar for some different drinks are shown in Table 20.8. There is more about alcoholic drinks and fermenation in sections 6.7 and 6.8.

Table 20.8 The percentage of ethanol and the source of sugar in different drinks

Drink	*Approximate percentage of ethanol*	*Source of sugar (and flavour)*
Beer	4	Barley
Wine	10	Grapes
Sherry	20	Grapes
Whisky	40	Barley
Gin	40	Wheat

ETHANOL PRODUCTION

Ethanol is produced by two methods:

1 By fermentation

This method is used in the production of alcoholic drinks (refer back to sections 6.7 and 6.8).

2 From ethene

The addition reaction which produces ethanol from ethene and steam was mentioned in section 20.9 and Table 20.6. Most of the ethanol which is used as a solvent or as fuel is manufactured from ethene.

Quick test 20

Questions 1 and 2

The table below gives information about three different fuels.

Fuel	*State* (at 20°C)	*Uses*	*Products of burning*
coal	solid	open fire	CO_2, water, ash, SO_2
methane	gas	cooking stove	CO_2, water
petrol	liquid	car engine	CO_2, water, CO

1 Which fuel does least harm to living things in the environment? (1 mark)
2 Give *two* reasons for your answer to question **1**. (2 marks)
(*NEA*, 1988)

Questions 3 and 4

The movement of sea water can be used to generate electricity.
3 State *two* different movements of the sea which could be used to generate electricity. (2 marks)
4 Consider the following statements:
- Your uncle says that some power stations use 'sea' power.
- He says that they are more expensive to build than nuclear or coal-fired power stations.
- That is why he thinks there is no point in building any 'sea' power stations.

Give *three* reasons why you might disagree with your uncle. (3 marks)
(*NEA*, 1988)

Questions 5 and 6

Crude oil contains many useful chemicals which have to be separated before they can be used.
5 **(a)** How is crude oil separated into the different chemicals? (1 mark)
(b) Put the missing words into the following sentence.
This method of separation can be used because chemicals made of ____________ molecules have ____________ boiling points whereas chemicals made of ____________ molecules have ____________ boiling points. (2 marks)
6 Long- and short-chain molecules are obtained when the chemicals in crude oil are separated out, but the short-chain ones are in greater demand and so are easier to sell. Oil companies break some of the spare long-chain molecules into short ones.

(a) What name is given to the 'breaking' of long-chain molecules from oil into short ones? (1 mark)
(b) Briefly describe *one* of the ways in which this is done. (1 mark)
(*NEA*, 1988)

Questions 7 to 12

Oil and natural gas are produced by the action of bacteria on organic matter. Scientists have found that this process is going on at this moment in the Gulf of Mexico.

Oil and gas contain mostly hydrocarbons. But organic matter contains a lot of carbohydrates.

7 What element must be removed from carbohydrates to change them into hydrocarbons? (1 mark)
8 How do living micro-organisms convert carbohydrates to hydrocarbons? (1 mark)
9 Name one other element which must be removed from organic material to produce hydrocarbons. (1 mark)
10 In removing this element the micro-organisms produce a waste gas. What is it? (1 mark)
11 Methane (CH_4) and ethane (C_2H_6) are the main substances in natural gas.
(a) Complete the table below to show the structural formulas of methane and ethane. (2 marks)

Name	*Formula*	*Structural formula*
methane	CH_4	
ethane	C_2H_6	
propane	C_3H_8	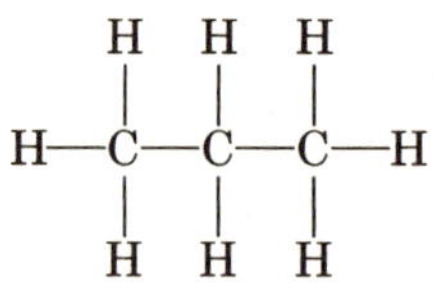

(b) Draw a diagram to show the tetrahedral arrangement of bonds in methane. (2 marks)
12 Methane, ethane and propane are part of an *homologous series* in which the formulas differ by CH_2.
How can an homologous series of compounds be compared with a group of elements in the periodic table? (2 marks)
(*LEAG*, 1988)

Questions 13 to 17

A pupil wanted to calculate the cost of energy from a portable butane burner. She used the burner to heat water in a metal can. The table below shows the readings she made during the experiment.

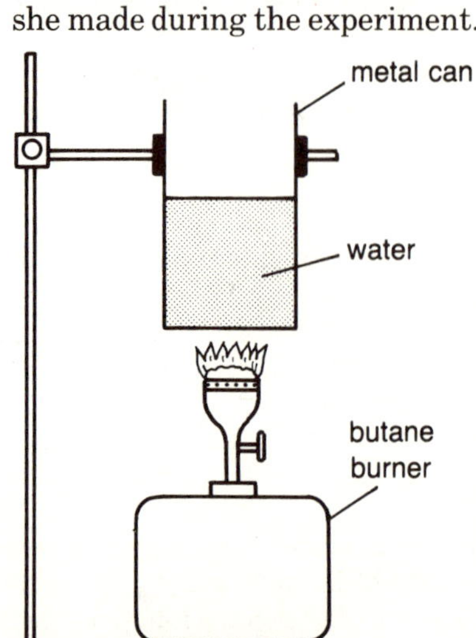

mass of empty can	106.3 g
mass of can + water	306.3 g
mass of butane burner at start	467.8 g
mass of butane burner at end	467.2 g
temperature of water at start	21° C
temperature of water at end	57° C

In answering the following questions you should show the stages in your working.

13 Calculate the heat energy given out when the butane burns.
(The specific heat capacity of water is 4200 J/kg/°C. 4200 J will heat 1 kg of water by 1°C.) (2 marks)

14 Calculate the heat energy given out when 1 kg of butane burns. (2 marks)

15 If butane costs 50p per kg, calculate the cost of producing 100 000 kJ of heat energy. (2 marks)

16 Name the products formed when butane is burnt. (2 marks)

17 Suggest *two* ways of improving the accuracy of this experiment. (2 marks)

(*LEAG*, 1988)

21 ATOMIC STRUCTURE AND THE PERIODIC TABLE

21.1 Atomic structure

One hundred years ago, scientists believed that atoms were hard, solid particles like tiny snooker balls. Since then, experiments have shown a different structure for atoms. From current evidence, we can make the following statements about atomic structure:

- All atoms are composed of just three particles: **protons**, **neutrons** and **electrons**.
- The centre of an atom is called the **nucleus**.
- The nucleus contains protons and neutrons.
- Protons and neutrons have virtually the same mass. Their mass is almost the same as that of a hydrogen atom. So the proton and neutron are given a relative mass of one like the hydrogen atom.

- Protons are **p**ositively charged, but **n**eutrons are **n**eutral.
- The nucleus takes up a minute part of the volume of the whole atom.
- More than 99.9 per cent of the atom is empty space occupied by moving **electrons**.
- Electrons have a mass about 2000 times less than that of protons and neutrons.
- Electrons are negatively charged. The negative charge on one electron just balances the positive charge on one proton.
- The electrons move around the nucleus very rapidly. They tend to remain in layers or **shells** at different distances from the nucleus.

Most of these key points about atomic structure are summarized in Table 21.1.

Table 21.1 The position, relative mass and charge of protons, neutrons and electrons

Particle	*Position within the atom*	*Mass relative to a hydrogen atom*	*Charge*
Proton	nucleus	1	+1
Neutron	nucleus	1	0
Electron	'shells'	0.0005	−1

Protons, neutrons and electrons are the building blocks for atoms. Different atoms have different numbers of protons, neutrons and electrons. Hydrogen atoms are the simplest of all atoms. Each hydrogen atom has only one proton and one electron (Fig. 21.1). The next simplest atoms are those of helium. Each helium atom has two protons, two electrons and two neutrons. After helium comes lithium (three protons, three electrons and four neutrons), then beryllium (four protons, four electrons and five neutrons; Fig. 21.2).

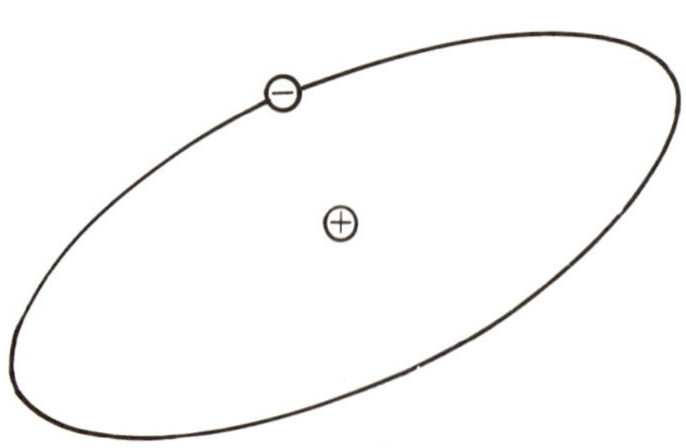

Fig. 21.1 A hydrogen atom has one proton (⊕) in its nucleus and one orbiting electron (⊖)

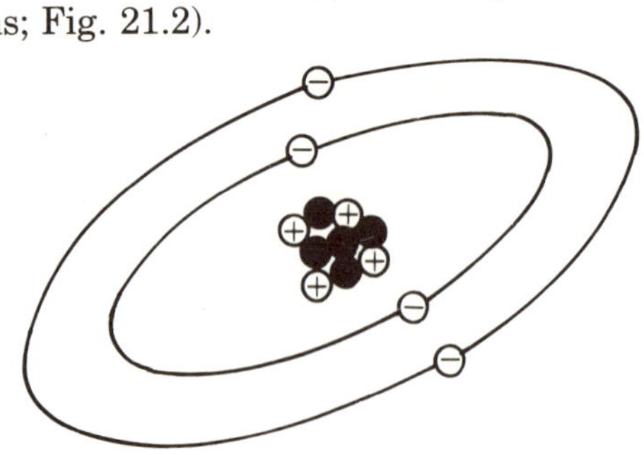

Fig. 21.2 A beryllium atom has four protons and five neutrons (●) in its nucleus, and four orbiting electrons. Two electrons are in a 'shell' close to the nucleus and the other two electrons are in a second 'shell' further away

Some of the heaviest atoms have 100 or more protons, neutrons and electrons. For example, each atom of lead has 82 protons, 82 electrons and 125 neutrons. Notice that in all the examples given each atom has the **same number of protons and**

electrons. This allows the positive charges on the protons to balance the negative charges on the electrons, so each atom is **neutral** overall.

21.2 Atomic number and mass number

The only atoms with one proton are those of hydrogen;
The only atoms with two protons are those of helium;
The only atoms with three protons are those of lithium; and so on.

Can you see that the number of protons in an atom tells you which element it is? Because of this, scientists use a special name for *the number of protons in an atom*. They call it the **atomic number**. Thus, hydrogen's atomic number is one, helium's atomic number is two, lithium's atomic number is three, and so on.

The mass of the electrons in an atom is negligible compared to the mass of protons and neutrons (refer back to Table 21.1). In fact, the mass of an atom depends on the number of protons and neutrons in its nucleus. Because of this, scientists use the term **mass number** for *the number of protons plus neutrons* in an atom.

atomic number = number of protons
mass number = number of protons + number of neutrons

So carbon atoms, with six protons and six neutrons, have an atomic number of six and a mass number of twelve. Sodium atoms, with 11 protons and 12 neutrons, have an atomic number of 11 and a mass number of 23.

Sometimes the symbol A is used for mass number and the symbol Z is used for atomic number. So for sodium; $A = 23$ and $Z = 11$.

Figure 21.3 shows how the mass number and the atomic number can be shown with the symbol for an element. How many protons, neutrons and electrons are there in an aluminium atom?

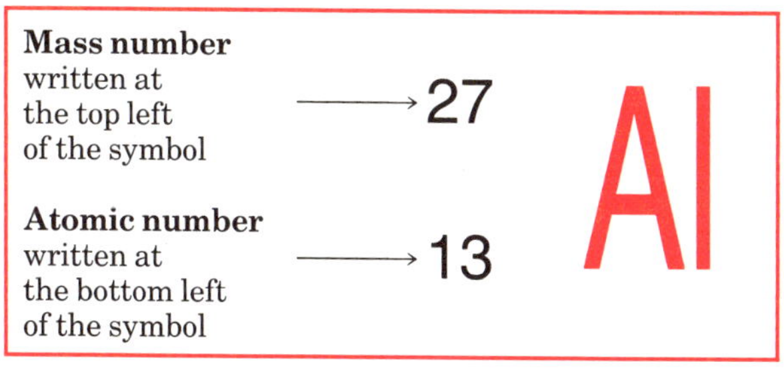

Fig. 21.3 Writing the mass number and the atomic number with the symbol for aluminium

21.3 Relative atomic mass and isotopes

Several elements have relative atomic masses which are whole numbers. For example, the relative atomic mass of oxygen is 16.0 and that of aluminium is 27.0, the same as their mass numbers. This is what we might have expected because the mass of an atom depends on its protons and neutrons both of which have a relative mass of 1.0. For example, we can find the relative atomic mass of $^{27}_{13}Al$ as follows:

$^{27}_{13}Al$ atoms have:

13 protons – relative mass	= 13.0
13 electrons – relative mass	= 0.0
14 neutrons – relative mass	= 14.0
therefore, relative atomic mass of $^{27}_{13}Al$	= 27.0

ISOTOPES

Unlike oxygen and aluminium, some elements have relative atomic masses that are *not* whole numbers. For example, the relative atomic mass of neon is 20.2 and that of magnesium is 24.3. These unexpected results were explained in 1919 when F. W. Aston discovered that one element could have atoms with different masses.

Atoms of the same element with different masses are called **isotopes**. Each isotope has a relative mass which is a whole number, but the average atomic mass for the mixture of isotopes is not always a whole number.

We will look at chlorine as an example. Naturally-occurring chlorine has two isotopes, $^{35}_{17}Cl$ and $^{37}_{17}Cl$. Each of these isotopes has 17 protons and 17 electrons and therefore both have an atomic number of 17. However, one istope ($^{35}_{17}Cl$) has 18 neutrons and the other isotope ($^{37}_{17}Cl$) has 20 neutrons. Their mass numbers are therefore 35 and 37, respectively. They are referred to as **chlorine-35** and **chlorine-37**.

Isotopes are atoms with the same atomic number, but different mass numbers.

Table 21.2 The isotopes of hydrogen

	Hydrogen-1	**Hydrogen-2** (also called **deuterium** or heavy hydrogen)	**Hydrogen-3** (also called **tritium**)
Symbol	${}^{1}_{1}H$	${}^{2}_{1}H$	${}^{3}_{1}H$
Number of protons	1	1	1
Number of neutrons	0	1	2
Number of electrons	1	1	1
Atomic number	1	1	1
Mass number	1	2	3

Table 21.2 illustrates these points by looking at the isotopes of hydrogen. The three isotopes of hydrogen have *identical chemical properties* because they have the same number of electrons. However, they have *different physical properties* because they have different numbers of neutrons and therefore different masses. Samples of hydrogen-1, hydrogen-2 and hydrogen-3 have different densities, different melting points and different boiling points. The similarities and differences between isotopes of the same element are summarized in Table 21.3.

Table 21.3 The similarities and differences between isotopes of the same element

Isotopes have the same	**Isotopes have different**
• number of protons • number of electrons • atomic number • chemical properties	• numbers of neutrons • mass numbers • physical properties

The relative atomic mass of an element is the **average mass** of one atom. This can be calculated from the relative masses and the relative proportions of the different isotopes. Table 21.4 shows how the relative atomic mass of chlorine can be calculated.

Table 21.4 Calculating the relative atomic mass of chlorine

Naturally-occurring chlorine contains three chlorine-35 atoms for every chlorine-37 atom:

${}^{35}_{17}Cl$ relative atomic mass $= 35$

${}^{37}_{17}Cl$ relative atomic mass $= 37$

Relative atomic mass of chlorine $= \dfrac{(3 \times 35) + 37}{4}$

$= \dfrac{105 + 37}{4} = \dfrac{142}{4}$

$= 35.5$

21.4 The Periodic Table

During the nineteenth century, several scientists tried to arrange the known elements in a systematic way. The most successful attempt to find a pattern for the elements was made by the Russian chemist, **Dmitri Mendeléev** in 1869.

Mendeléev arranged all the known elements in order of their relative atomic masses.

He arranged the elements in horizontal rows so that elements with similar properties appeared in the same vertical column.

The vertical columns of similar elements are called **groups**.

The horizontal rows are called **periods**.

Because of the *periodic* repetition of elements with similar properties, Mendeléev called his arrangement a **periodic table**. Figure 21.4 shows part of Mendeléev's periodic table. Notice that elements with similar properties – for example, sodium and potassium – fall in the same vertical column. Look for other pairs or trios of similar elements which appear in the same column of Mendeléev's table.

	Group							
	I	II	III	IV	V	VI	VII	VIII
Period 1	H							
Period 2	Li	Be	B	C	N	O	F	
Period 3	Na	Mg	Al	Si	P	S	Cl	
Period 4	K Cu	Ca Zn	* *	Ti *	V As	Cr Se	Mu Br	Fe Co Ni

Fig. 21.4 Mendeléev's periodic table

Mendeléev left gaps in his periodic table so that similar elements were in the same vertical column. Three of these gaps are shown by asterisks in Fig. 21.4.

Mendeléev predicted the properties of the missing elements. He did this by studying the properties of the elements above and below them in his table. Within 15 years of Mendeléev making his predictions, the missing elements had been discovered. The three missing elements were called scandium, gallium and germanium. Their properties were very similar to Mendeléev's predictions.

The success of Mendeléev's predictions showed that his ideas were probably correct. His periodic table was quickly accepted by scientists as an important summary of the properties of elements.

21.5 Modern periodic tables

Modern periodic tables like the one overleaf are based on Mendeléev's table.

Notice that the elements are numbered along each period, starting with period 1, then period 2, and so on. These numbers are the same as the atomic numbers of the elements.

The atomic number of an element can be defined as:
the number of protons in one atom of the element,
or **the order of the element in the periodic table.**

There are some important points to appreciate about modern periodic tables:

1. Moving from left to right across each period, the elements change from metals to non-metals.
2. In each group, the elements have similar properties, but there is a gradual change in properties from one element to the next.
3. Some groups have special names. These names are shown below the group numbers in Fig. 21.5.
4. In modern periodic tables, metals are clearly separated from non-metals. There are about 20 non-metals. These are all found in the top right-hand corner of the table, above the thick steps in Fig. 21.5. Some elements close to the steps are **metalloids**. Metalloids have some properties like metals and some properties like non-metals.
5. Modern periodic tables show **transition elements** in a different way to Mendeléev. Transition elements are ten or more elements in the middle of each period. In modern periodic tables, these are taken out of the simple groups. Period 4 is the first period to contain transition elements. These include chromium, iron, copper and zinc.
6. If we exclude the noble gases, elements get more reactive towards the right and left edges of the periodic table.

- The most reactive metals are those in Group I (alkali metals) along the left-hand edge. These include potassium and sodium.
- The next most reactive metals are those in Group II (alkaline-earth metals).
- Transition metals are less reactive again. These are nearer the centre of the table.
- The most reactive non-metals are the halogens in Group VII, near the right-hand edge of the table.

KEY: H (symbol) / Hydrogen (name) / 1 (atomic number)

Group ► / Period ▼	I Alkali metals	II Alkaline-earth metals	Transition elements										III	IV	V	VI	VII Halogens	0 Noble gases
1									H Hydrogen 1									He Helium 2
2	Li Lithium 3	Be Beryllium 4											B Boron 5	C Carbon 6	N Nitrogen 7	O Oxygen 8	F Fluorine 9	Ne Neon 10
3	Na Sodium 11	Mg Magnesium 12											Al Aluminium 13	Si Silicon 14	P Phosphorus 15	S Sulphur 16	Cl Chlorine 17	Ar Argon 18
4	K Potassium 19	Ca Calcium 20	Sc 21	Ti 22	V 23	Cr Chromium 24	Mn Manganese 25	Fe Iron 26	Co 27	Ni 28	Cu Copper 29	Zn Zinc 30	Ga 31	Ge 32	As 33	Se 34	Br Bromine 35	Kr Krypton 36
5	Rb 37	Sr 38	Y 39	Zr 40	Nb 41	Mo 42	Tc 43	Ru 44	Rh 45	Pd 46	Ag Silver 47	Cd 48	In 49	Sn Tin 50	Sb 51	Te 52	I Iodine 53	Xe 54
6	Cs 55	Ba 56	57–71 See below	Hf 72	Ta 73	W 74	Re 75	Os 76	Ir 77	Pt Platinum 78	Au Gold 79	Hg Mercury 80	Tl 81	Pb Lead 82	Bi 83	Po 84	At 85	Rn 86
7	Fr 87	Ra 88	89–103 See below	Ku 104	Ha 105													

Lanthanides	La Lanthanum 57	Ce 58	Pr 59	Nd 60	Pm 61	Sm 62	Eu 63	Gd 64	Tb 65	Dy 66	Ho 67	Er 68	Tm 69	Yb 70	Lu 71
Actinides	Ac Actinium 89	Th 90	Pa 91	U Uranium 92	Np 93	Pu 94	Am 95	Cm 96	Bk 97	Cf 98	Es 99	Fm 100	Md 101	No 102	Lr 103

Fig. 21.5 A modern periodic table

21.6 Electron structures and the Periodic Table

During chemical reactions, changes occur in the number of electrons belonging to atoms. Some atoms gain electrons, some lose electrons and others share electrons. Once these changes in electron structure have taken place, the atoms or ions are usually more stable, i.e. less reactive.

Some atoms, for instance those of helium and neon, never react. This indicates that atoms of helium, neon (and the other noble gases) must have very stable electron structures. Scientists have therefore concluded that atoms and ions will have very stable electron structures if they have 2 electrons (like helium), 10 electrons (like neon), 18 electrons (like argon) and so on.

These stable electron structures are closely related to the way in which electrons are arranged in layers or shells. We now know that:

- the first shell is stable when it contains **2** electrons;
- the second shell is stable when it contains **8** electrons;
- the third shell is stable when it contains **8** or **18** electrons.

Neon atoms, with 10 electrons, have 2 electrons in their first shell and 8 electrons in their second shell. The electron structure of neon is therefore written as 2,8.

Argon, the next noble gas, is stable because its atoms have 18 electrons: 2 in the first shell, 8 in the second shell and 8 in the third shell. The electron structure of argon is written as 2,8,8.

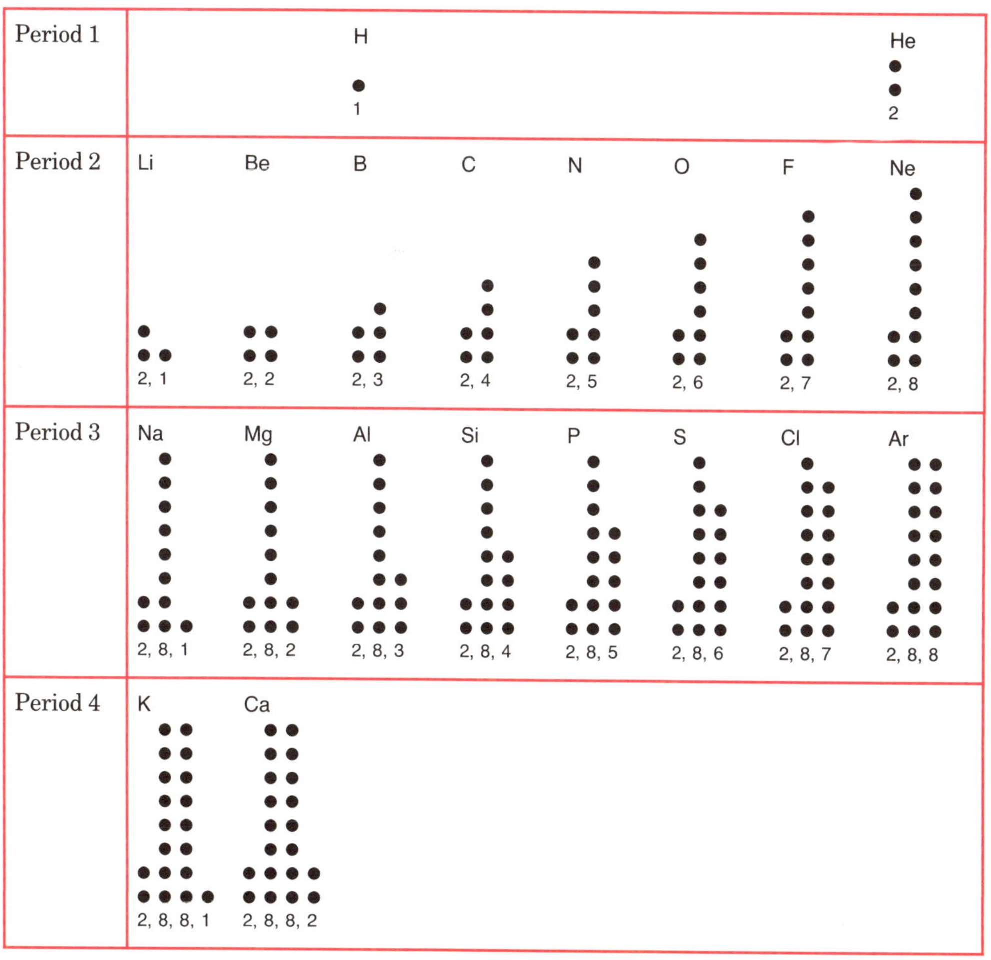

Fig. 21.6 Electron structures of the first 20 elements in the periodic table

Figure 21.6 shows the electronic structures of the first 20 elements in the periodic table. When the first shell is full (in helium), electrons go into the second shell. So the electron structure of lithium is 2,1, beryllium is 2,2, boron is 2,3 and so on. Once the second shell is full (at neon), electrons go into the third shell. So the electron structure of sodium is 2,8,1, etc.

Using these electron structures, we can explain why elements in the same vertical column of the periodic table have similar properties (see the following sections, 21.7 and 21.8).

21.7 Group II–the alkaline-earth metals

Group II

Be
Mg
Ca
Sr
Ba
Ra

Alkaline-earth metals

The elements in group II include magnesium and calcium. They are called **alkaline-earth metals** because:

- their oxides and hydroxides are *alkaline*;
- their compounds are important rocks in the *earth's* crust. These rocks include:
    - chalk, limestone and marble–calcium carbonate ($CaCO_3$)
    - gypsum and anhydrite–calcium sulphate ($CaSO_4$)
    - granite and sandstone which contain calcium silicate ($CaSiO_3$)
    - magnesium silicate ($MgSiO_3$)

REACTIONS OF THE GROUP II METALS

Table 21.5 The chemical properties of magnesium, calcium and barium

Element	*Reaction with dry air*	*Reaction with cold water*	*Formula of oxide*	*Symbol of ion*
Magnesium	reacts very slowly to form a layer of oxide	reacts very slowly to give tiny bubbles of hydrogen on its surface	MgO	Mg^{2+}
Calcium	reacts slowly to form a layer of oxide	reacts steadily forming bubbles of hydrogen and an alkaline solution of calcium hydroxide	CaO	Ca^{2+}
Barium	reacts rapidly to form a layer of oxide	reacts rapidly forming bubbles of hydrogen and an alkaline solution of barium hydroxide	BaO	Ba^{2+}

Table 21.5 summarizes the chemical properties of magnesium, calcium and barium. Notice how the elements react more vigorously with air and with water as we go down the group magnesium to barium. This illustrates an important feature of the Periodic Table (point 2, section 21.5).

> **Although elements in a group are similar, there is a steady change in property from one element to the next.**

We can use this to predict the properties of the different elements in a group.

Each alkaline-earth metal appears two places after a noble gas in the periodic table. So alkaline-earth metals have two electrons in their outer shell (see Table 21.6). By losing these two electrons, their atoms form **positive ions** (e.g. Be^{2+}, Mg^{2+}, Ca^{2+}) with stable electron structures like a noble gas. For example, Mg^{2+} ions have the same electron structure as neon (2,8) and Ca^{2+} ions have the same electron structure as argon (2,8,8).

Table 21.6 The electron structures of the atoms and ions of the first three alkaline-earth metals

Alkaline-earth metal	*Atom*	*Ion*
Beryllium	Be 2,2	Be^{2+} 2
Magnesium	Mg 2,8,2	Mg^{2+} 2,8
Calcium	Ca 2,8,8,2	Ca^{2+} 2,8,8

All group II metals:

- form ions with a charge of 2+,
- are fairly reactive because they are keen to lose the two electrons in their outer shell.

21.8 Group VII – the halogens

Group VII

F
Cl
Br
I
At

Halogens

The elements in group VII are called the **halogens**. The common elements in the group are chlorine (Cl), bromine (Br) and iodine (I).

The halogens are so reactive that they never occur naturally as uncombined elements. They always occur with metals in **salts**, e.g. sodium chloride (NaCl), magnesium bromide ($MgBr_2$) and calcium fluoride (CaF_2). This is the reason for their name, 'halogens', which means 'salt formers'.

In these salts, the halogens occur as **negative ions**, the **halides** – e.g. chloride (Cl^-), bromide (Br^-) and iodide (I^-). The commonest chlorine compound is sodium chloride (NaCl). This occurs in rock salt and in sea water. Every kilogram of sea-water contains about 30 grams of sodium chloride. Sea-water is also the commonest source of bromine. The bromine is present in sea-water as bromide ions. Sea-water also contains traces of iodides, but the main source of iodine is sodium iodate ($NaIO_3$), which is mined in Chile.

Some of the important uses of fluorine, chlorine and their compounds are summarized in Table 21.7.

Table 21.7 Important uses of fluorine, chlorine and their compounds

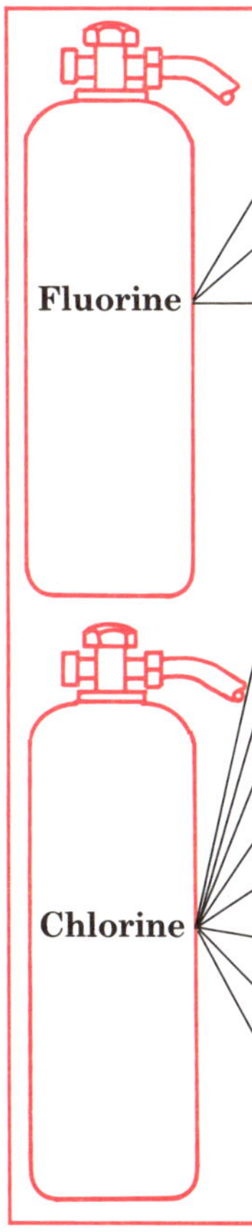

Fluorine:
- fluoride (e.g. NaF) is added to toothpaste and drinking water to reduce decay
- PTFE (polytetra*fluoro*ethene) is used as the non-stick coating on frying pans and skis
- CFCs (***chlorofluoro***carbons) are used as aerosol propellants (this is being discouraged since it was found that CFCs damage the ozone layer)

Chlorine:
- CFCs (***chlorofluoro***carbons) are used as aerosol propellants (this is being discouraged since it was found that CFCs damage the ozone layer)
- PVC (**poly**v**inyl** ***chloride***) is used as artificial leather for suitcases, furniture, etc.
- various solvents contain chlorine, e.g.
  – dry cleaning liquid (tetra*chloro*ethene, $CCl_2=CCl_2$)
  – degreasing solvent (di*chloro*methane, CH_2Cl_2)
- some bleaches contain chlorine and chlorine compounds, e.g. Harpic
- chlorine is used to kill bacteria and viruses in drinking water and in swimming pools
- various pesticides contain chlorine, e.g. DDT (**d**i*chloro***d**iphenyl**t**ri*chloro*ethane)
- common salt (sodium chloride) is used in cooking – it provides the sodium which is essential in our diet
- rock salt is used to grit icy roads

PROPERTIES OF THE HALOGENS

Table 21.8 Some properties of chlorine, bromine and iodine, the first three halogens

Halogen	*Relative atomic mass*	*Structure*	*Colour and state at room temperature*	*Melting point/°C*	*Boiling point/°C*
Chlorine	35.5	Cl_2 molecules	pale green gas	−101	−35
Bromine	79.9	Br_2 molecules	orange-red liquid	−7	58
Iodine	126.9	I_2 molecules	dark purple solid	114	183

Table 21.8 shows that the halogens are a typical group of elements in the periodic table – they show similarities to one another, but there is a gradual change in properties down the group.

Look at Table 21.8. How do the following properties of the halogens change as their relative atomic mass increases?

- state at room temperature (*gas* ⟶ *liquid* ⟶ *solid*)
- melting point (*increases*)
- boiling point (*increases*)
- colour (*darkens*)

All the halogens have **simple molecular structures** (refer back to section 16.7) with **diatomic molecules**, e.g. Cl_2, Br_2, I_2. Strong bonds hold the two atoms together as a molecule, but the bonds between separate molecules are weak. This means that their molecules are easily separated, so their boiling points are relatively low.

Moving down the group, the halogen molecules get larger and heavier. Therefore, from chlorine to iodine, they are gradually more difficult to melt and to vaporize. This is reflected by the increasing melting and boiling points from chlorine to iodine.

REACTIONS OF THE HALOGENS

Like the physical properties, the chemical reactions of the halogens are similar within the group, with gradual changes from one element to the next. Fluorine is the most reactive of all non-metals. Chlorine is also very reactive, but iodine is only moderately reactive. Table 21.9 summarizes the reactions of chlorine, bromine and iodine with cold water and hot iron. Notice how the elements get less reactive as we go down the group from chlorine to iodine.

Table 21.9 Some reactions of chlorine, bromine and iodine

Halogen	*Reactions with cold water*	*Reaction with hot iron*
Chlorine	forms a mixture of hydrochloric acid and hypochlorous acid the solution is very acidic and a strong bleach (the bleaching of damp indicator paper is used as a test for chlorine)	reacts rapidly and vigorously forming iron(III) chloride ($FeCl_3$)
Bromine	forms a mixture of hydrobromic acid and hypobromous acid the solution is acidic and a bleach	reacts slowly forming iron(III) bromide ($FeBr_3$)
Iodine	reacts slightly with water the solution is slightly acidic and a very mild bleach	reacts very slowly forming iron(II) iodide (FeI_2)

Electron structures

In the Periodic Table, each halogen comes just before a noble gas. This means that they have seven electrons in their outer shell (see Table 21.10). By gaining one electron, halogens form **negative ions** with stable electron structures like a noble gas. Therefore, all the halogens form stable ions with one negative charge (e.g. F^-, Cl^-, Br^-).

Table 21.10 The electron structures of the atoms and ions of the first three halogens

Halogen	*Atom*	*Ion*
Fluorine	F 2,7	F^- 2,8
Chlorine	Cl 2,8,7	Cl^- 2,8,8
Bromine	Br 2,8,18,7	Br^- 2,8,18,8

Quick test 21

Questions 1 to 4

Questions 1 to 4 concern the following five sets of elements labelled A, B, C, D and E.

A Group I D Group 0
B Group II E Transition metals
C Group VII

1 Which set of elements are also known as the noble gases?
2 Which set of elements contains the most reactive metal?
3 Which set contains elements used in jewellery?
4 Which set contains an element which is used as a germicide?

Questions 5 to 7

The table below shows how well different treatments kill bacteria and protozoa in drinking water.

Treatment	*Effect on bacteria*	*Effect on protozoa*
chlorine added	all killed	some killed
iodine added	some killed	all killed
fluoride added	none killed	none killed

5 Which treatment does *not* involve the use of an uncombined element?
6 Which treatment would be the best in countries where there could be bacteria in the drinking water but no protozoa?
7 What treatment would you suggest in countries where the drinking water could contain both bacteria and protozoa?

Questions 8 to 11

The table below gives information about some elements.

Atom	Number of protons	Number of neutrons
W	6	6
X	6	8
Y	7	8
Z	8	9

8 What is the mass number of element X?
9 What is the atomic number of element Y?
10 How many electrons will one atom of element Z contain?
11 How many different elements are shown in the table?

Questions 12 to 15

Questions 12 to 15 concern the halogens in group VII of the Periodic Table. In the table below, the halogens are arranged in the same order as they appear in the Periodic Table.

Element	*Symbol*	*Relative size of atom*	*Melting point/°C*	*Colour*	*Formula of compound with hydrogen*
Fluorine	F	○	−220	very pale yellow	HF
Chlorine	Cl	○	−101	pale green	HCl
Bromine	Br	○	−7	reddish	HBr
Iodine	I	○	114	nearly black	HI
Astatine	At				

12 As you go down group VII from fluorine to iodine, what happens to
(a) the size of their atoms?
(b) their boiling points?
(c) their colour?
13 What pattern can you see in the formula of their compounds with hydrogen?
14 Astatine lies below iodine in group VII. Complete the last row of the table by making a prediction of its properties.

15 A sample of iodine contains 80 per cent $^{127}_{53}I$ and 20 per cent $^{131}_{53}I$.

(a) What is the mass number of $^{127}_{53}I$?

(b) What is the mass number of $^{131}_{53}I$?

(c) What is the relative atomic mass of iodine in the sample?

Questions 16 to 18

Chemical elements can be grouped in families. Elements belonging to the same family are similar to each other in many ways. Differences between elements in the same family are related to how heavy the atoms of the elements are (their relative atomic mass).

16 The table contains information about the first three elements in the alkali metal family.

Element	*Relative atomic mass*	*Melting point/°C*	*Boiling point/°C*	*Reacting with water*
Lithium	7	181	1331	not very fast
Sodium	23	98	890	fairly fast
Potassium	39	64	766	fast
Rubidium	85			

Even before the next element in the family, rubidium, was discovered, scientists knew what they were looking for.

Complete the table to show what you would expect rubidium to be like.

(5 marks)

17 The following table contains information about another family of elements – the halogens.

Element	*Relative atomic mass*	*Melting point/°C*	*Boiling point/°C*	*State at 20°C*	*Reaction with hot iron*
Fluorine	19	−220	−188	gas	very fast
Chlorine	35.5	−101	−34	gas	fast
Bromine	80	−7			
Iodine	127	114	183	solid	not very fast

Complete the table for the element bromine. (4 marks)

18 The increase in relative atomic mass affects the halogen family in different ways than it affects the alkali metal family. Describe these differences.

(3 marks)

(*NEA*, 1988)

22 RADIOACTIVITY AND NUCLEAR ENERGY

22.1 Radioactivity

In 1896, **Henri Becquerel** was investigating the reactions of uranium compounds. After one set of experiments, Becquerel left one of his uranium compounds in a drawer near a photographic plate wrapped in black paper. When Becquerel developed the photographic plate, he was surprised to find that it had been darkened in the part nearest the uranium compounds.

This prompted Becquerel to carry out further tests. He found that the uranium compound was emitting **radiation** which could pass through the black paper and affect the photographic plate. Becquerel called the phenomenon **radioactivity** and he described the uranium compound as **radioactive**.

Marie Curie, one of Becquerel's assistants, decided to examine the radioactivity of uranium compounds in more detail. Marie Curie made the following discoveries:

- All uranium compounds are radioactive.
- The radiation from radioactive substances carries a charge.
- **Pitchblende** (impure uranium sulphide) contained two other elements which were more radioactive than uranium. Marie named these elements **radium** and **polonium**. Radium was about two million times more radioactive than uranium.

Fig. 22.1 Marie Curie (1867 – 1934) spent nearly four years in isolating the radioactive elements polonium and radium from pitchblende. In 1903, she shared the Nobel Prize for Physics with her husband, Pierre, and Henri Becquerel. Then in 1911, she was awarded the Nobel Prize for Chemistry. She was the first person to win two Nobel Prizes.
(Photograph courtesy of Marie Curie Cancer Care)

22.2 Nuclear reactions

Radioactivity (radioactive decay) is the spontaneous break up (decay) of atoms.

When radioactive atoms break up they release energy and lose three different kinds of radiation. These radiations are called **alpha-rays**, **beta-rays** and **gamma-rays**. The Greek letters α (alpha), β (beta) and γ (gamma) are often written instead of the words.

α-rays (alpha rays) and β-rays (beta-rays) are made up of *particles*, so they are often described as α-particles or β-particles. Gamma rays are *electromagnetic waves* with the greatest penetrating power (section 25.5 and figure 25.12). The nature and properties of the three kinds of radiation are summarized in Table 22.1 and Fig. 22.2.

Table 22.1 The nature and properties of α-rays, β-rays and γ-rays

Radiation	*Nature*	*Distance travelled in air*	*Effect of electric and magnetic fields*
α-rays	α-particles = helium nuclei	a few centimetres	very small deflection
β-rays	β-particles = electrons	a few metres	large deflection
γ-rays	electromagnetic waves	several kilometres	no deflection

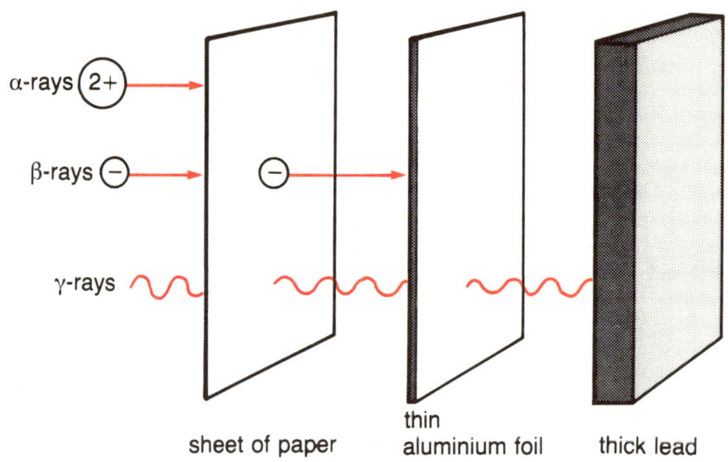

Fig. 22.2 The relative penetrating powers of α, β and γ-rays

Notice (in Table 22.1 and Fig. 22.2) that γ-rays travel much further in air and have much greater penetrating power than α-rays and β-rays. γ-rays can penetrate paper and aluminium foil very easily. In fact, γ-rays will penetrate bricks and metal sheets. They carry enough energy to damage cells and kill organisms. Because of this, radioactive materials which emit γ-rays are often stored in thick lead containers. As radioactive materials give off γ-rays, they lose energy and become stable.

The other important point to notice from table 21.1 is the effect of electric and magnetic fields. Gamma rays have no charge. Therefore, they are unaffected by electric and magnetic fields. Alpha- and beta-particles are charged so they are affected. β-rays are much smaller and lighter than α-rays so they are affected the most.

22.3 Nuclear equations

Experiments show that:

- radioactive atoms with an *atomic number greater than 83* usually undergo α-**decay**;
- radioactive atoms with an *atomic number less than 83* usually undergo β-**decay**;

The changes in mass number and atomic number during α-decay and β-decay are summarized in Table 22.2. The symbol for an electron can be written as ${}_{-1}^{0}e$ because its relative mass is effectively zero and its charge is -1.

Table 22.2 Changes in mass number and atomic number during α-decay and β-decay

Type of radioactivity	*Particle lost*	*Change in mass number*	*Change in atomic number*
α-decay	helium nucleus $^{4}_{2}He^{2+}$	−4	−2
β-decay	electron $^{0}_{-1}e$	0	+1

Uranium-238, an example of α-decay

We can illustrate α-decay with uranium-238. When an atom of $^{238}_{92}U$ loses an α-particle, the part left behind will have a mass number which is four less than $^{238}_{92}U$ and an atomic number which is two less than $^{238}_{92}U$. That is, the atom left behind will have a *mass number of 234* and an *atomic number of 90*. Atoms with an atomic number of 90 are those of *thorium, Th*. Thus, the products of the decay of $^{238}_{92}U$ are $^{234}_{90}Th$ and $^{4}_{2}He$.

This can be summarized in a nuclear equation as follows:

$$^{238}_{92}U \longrightarrow {}^{234}_{90}Th + {}^{4}_{2}He + \text{Energy}$$

Carbon-14, an example of β-decay

We can illustrate β-decay with $^{14}_{6}C$. This time, the products are $^{0}_{-1}e$ and $^{14}_{7}N$. The nuclear equation is:

$$^{14}_{6}C \longrightarrow {}^{14}_{7}N + {}^{0}_{-1}e + \text{Energy}$$

Notice in both these nuclear equations that the *total* mass in the superscripts and the *total* charge in the subscripts are the same before and after decay.

During β-decay, a neutron in the radioactive atom splits up into a proton and an electron.

$$\underset{\text{neutron}}{^{1}_{0}n} \longrightarrow \underset{\text{proton}}{^{1}_{1}p} + \underset{\text{electron}}{^{0}_{-1}e}$$

The electron is emitted in the β-rays, but the proton stays in the nucleus. In this way the mass number of the remaining fragment (number of protons plus neutrons) is the same as the original radioactive atom, but its atomic number (number of protons) goes up by one.

22.4 Detecting radioactivity

Various rocks in the Earth, including granite, contain radioactive uranium, thorium and potassium compounds. In addition to this, we are also exposed to radiation from the sun. These two *natural sources* of radiation are usually called **background radiation**. Normal background radiation is very low. It causes no risk to our health.

Background radiation and other radioactivity can be detected using a **Geiger-Muller (GM) tube**. Figure 22.3 shows a diagram of a GM tube.

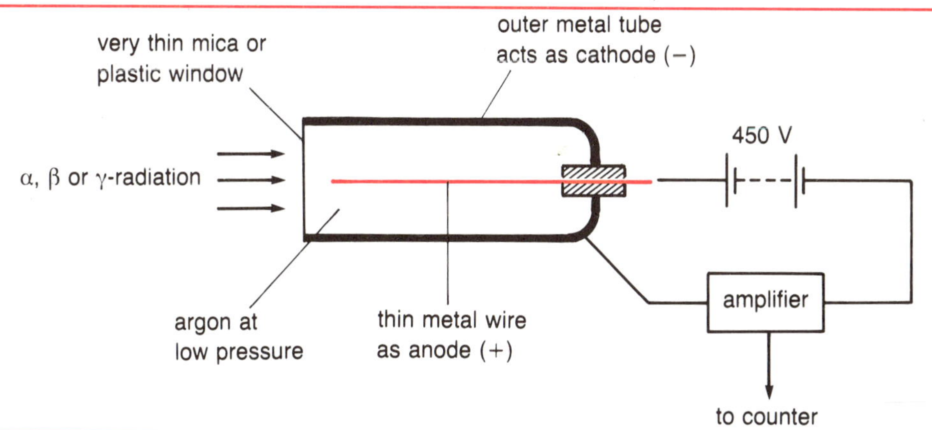

Fig. 22.3 A Geiger-Muller tube

When α, β or γ-rays enter the tube, they ionize the argon atoms inside.

$$Ar \longrightarrow Ar^{+} + e^{-}$$

The Ar^+ ions and the electrons are attracted to the electrodes in the tube and a tiny current flows in the circuit. This current is then amplified and a counter can be used to measure the amount of radiation entering the tube.

Fig. 22.4 A scientist using a Geiger-Muller counter to check the levels of radiation at Saltmarsh near the Sellafield site of British Nuclear Fuels plc in Cumbria
(Photograph courtesy of BNF plc)

22.5 Half-life

Table 22.3 The half-lives of some radioactive isotopes

Isotope	*Half-life*	*Stability*
Carbon-14	5500 years	decreasing stability ↓
Uranium-238	4500 years	
Cobalt-60	5·3 years	
Iodine-131	8 days	
Technetium-99	6 hours	
Polonium-234	0.15 milliseconds	

The *rate of decay* of a radioactive isotope is shown by its **half-life**. This is the time it takes for half of any given amount of the isotope to decay.

Half-lives can vary from less than a second to millions of years. The half-life tells you how stable an isotope is. The longer the half-life, the slower the decay process, therefore the more stable the isotope (see Table 22.3).

Figure 22.5 shows how a sample of iodine-131 will decay. If you start with one gram of iodine-131, only half a gram is left after eight days (one half-life). After another eight days, the half gram will have decayed to a quarter of a gram. Eight days later (i.e. 24 days from the start), only one eighth of a gram will remain.

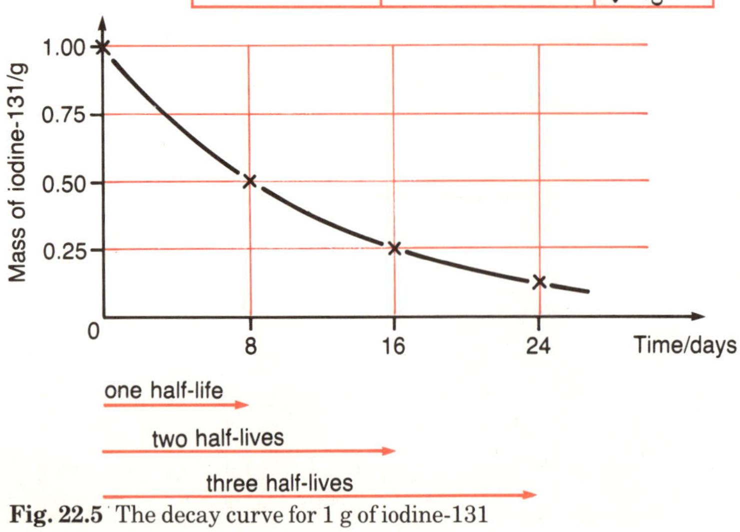

Fig. 22.5 The decay curve for 1 g of iodine-131

Radioactive iodine-131 is used by doctors to measure the activity of the thyroid gland. The thyroid gland plays an important part in our metabolism of iodine. First of all, the patient drinks some liquid containing a tiny amount of iodine-131. Then by measuring the amount of radioactivity in the thyroid gland using a scanner, doctors can tell how fast iodine is being taken up by the gland.

22.6 Uses of radioactive materials

Radioactive materials have a large number of uses in industry, in medicine, in agriculture and in archaeology.

Industrial uses

Two important industrial uses of radioactive materials are illustrated in Fig. 22.6.

Detection of leaks in pipes without digging

Thickness gauges
e.g. during production of polythene or paper

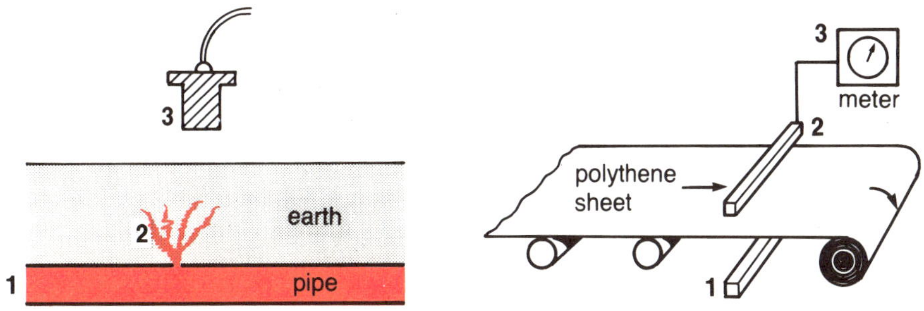

1 Radioactive tracer fed into pipe, then discontinued

2 Radioactive tracer leaks into soil

3 Geiger-Muller tube used to detect radiation and therefore the position of the leak

1 Long radioactive source emits radiation

2 Long Geiger-Muller tube used to detect radiation

3 Meter measures radiation level – the thicker the polythene or paper, the lower the reading

Fig. 22.6 Two important industrial uses of radioactive materials – detection of leaks in underground pipes without digging being necessary, and in systems to monitor thickness in production processes

Medical uses

Treatment of cancer

Penetrating γ-rays from cobalt-60 are used to kill cancer cells and treat growths inside the body. Skin cancer can be treated with less penetrating β-rays. This is done by strapping a sheet containing phosphorus-32 or strontium-90 on the affected area.

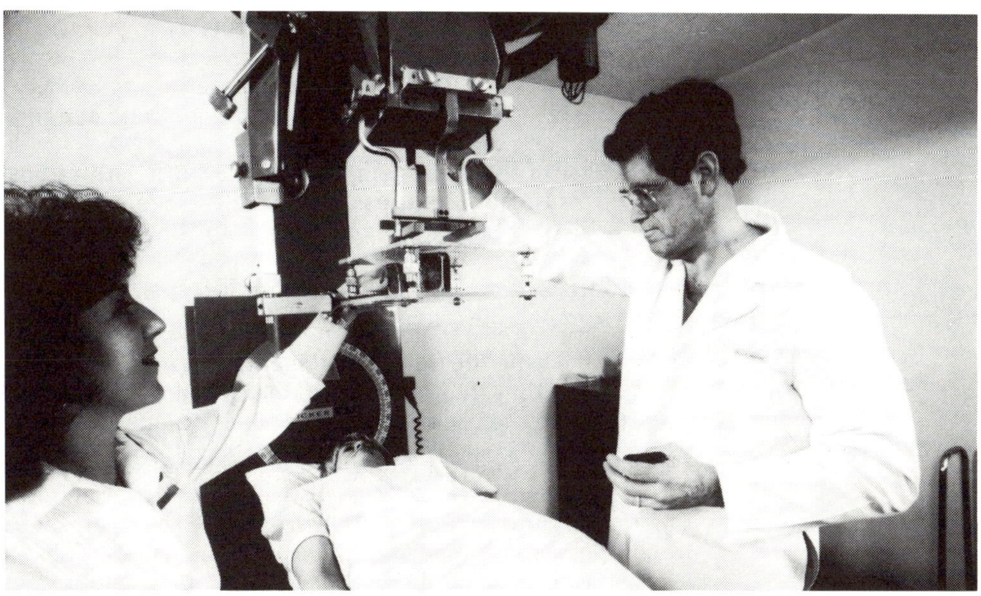

Fig. 22.7 Treatment for cancer by radiotherapy can be very unpleasant, but it is becoming more and more successful in slowing down and curing the disease

Sterilization of medical items

Medical items such as dressings and syringes are sealed in plastic bags and sterilized by intense γ-rays from cobalt-60. The γ-rays kill any micro-organisms on the articles.

Archaeological uses

The common isotope of carbon is carbon-12. Therefore, carbon in living things and in carbon dioxide is mainly carbon-12 with a small fraction of radioactive **carbon-14**. The fraction of carbon as carbon-14 in living things always stays at the same level. Although the carbon in the organism is continually decaying, it is also being replaced from food or by photosynthesis. When an animal or plant dies, its level of carbon-14 starts to fall.

Carbon-14 has a half-life of 5500 years. So after 5500 years, the fraction of carbon-14 in the dead remains will be half that in living specimens. By measuring the fraction of carbon-14 in ancient remains of animals and plants, scientists can calculate the age of the specimens. Carbon dating was used to show that the Turin Shroud was made in the 13th century. Previously, it was thought to be the burial shroud of Jesus.

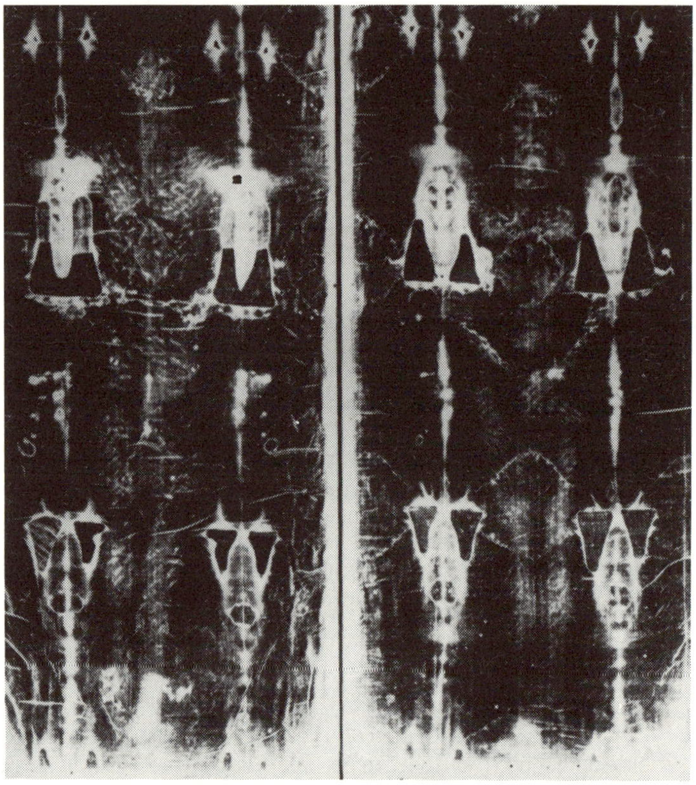

Fig. 22.8 The Turin Shroud. Carbon dating was used to show that the shroud could not have been used to cover the body of Jesus

22.7 Dangers from radiation

People who work with radioactive materials must be aware of the dangers from radiation. With very penetrating radiation, these dangers include skin burns, loss of hair, sickness, cancers and sterility.

Because of these dangers, people who work with radioactive materials must wear special **radiation badges**. These badges contain film sensitive to radiation. The film is developed at regular intervals to show how much radiation the wearer has been exposed to.

Scientists and technicians whose work involves dangerous isotopes emitting **γ-rays**, must take **extra safety precautions**. These include:

- manipulating the isotopes by remote control from a safe distance;
- ensuring that they are exposed to any radiation for only the minimum time;
- protecting themselves by lead or concrete shielding.

Special precautions must also be taken in the **disposal of radioactive waste**. Some isotopes in radioactive waste have half-lives of hundreds of years. These waste materials must be sealed in concrete or steel containers, then buried deep underground or dropped to the bottom of the sea. The disposal of radioactive waste has become an issue of great concern.

22.8 Nuclear energy

NUCLEAR FISSION

Large heavy atoms, like those of uranium and radium, can become more stable by losing an α-particle or a β-particle (refer back to Section 22.3). Some of these heavy atoms such as uranium-235 can also become stable by **nuclear fission**. Figure 22.9 shows how nuclear fission works.

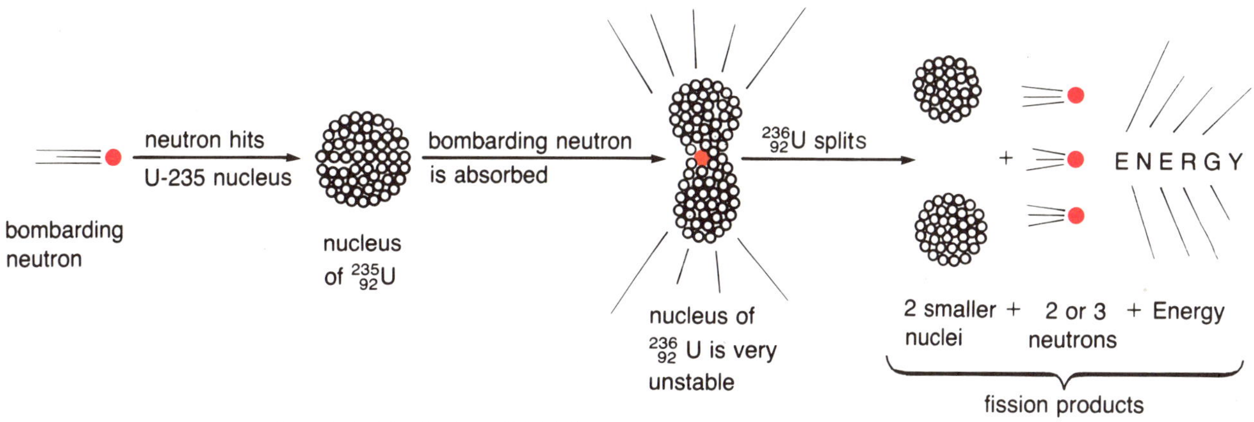

Fig. 22.9 The fission of U-235

Unlike radioactive decay which is quite random, nuclear fission is caused by bombardment of a nucleus with a neutron. The final products of fission are two smaller nuclei, two or three separate neutrons and enormous amounts of **energy**. The fission of a nucleus provides about 40 times more energy than the loss of an alpha particle.

Controlling fission

Natural uranium consists of 0.7 per cent uranium-235 and 99.3 per cent uranium-238, but only the uranium-235 atoms will undergo nuclear fission. However, scientists realized that if a uranium sample contained a larger percentage of U-235, the neutrons released during fission would split other U-235 nuclei. This could cause a **chain reaction**.

Figure 22.10 shows an exploding chain reaction with uranium-235. One reaction releases 3 neutrons. These 3 neutrons release 9 more neutrons, then 27, 81 and so on. Each time, more and more energy is produced.

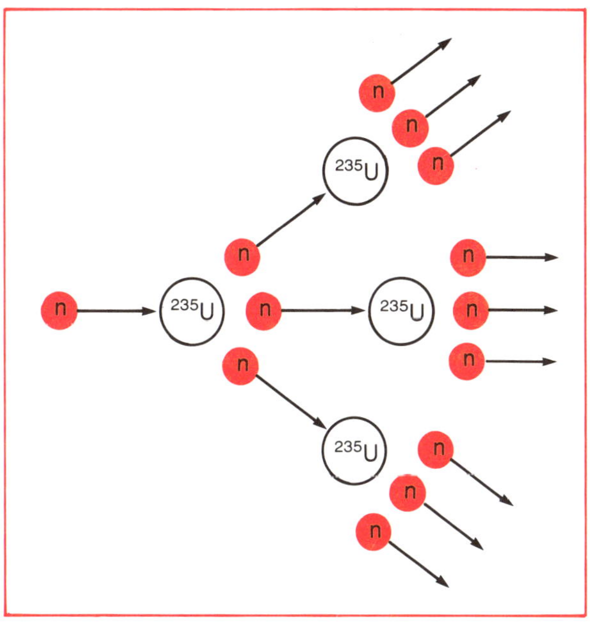

Fig. 22.10 An exploding chain reaction with U-235

If we can control this chain reaction, we can use it in different ways. For example:

- **In an atomic bomb**, the fission of *pure* uranium-235 happens in an *uncontrolled* exploding chain reaction. All the neutrons released by fission cause further fissions. Enormous amounts of energy and radiation are released.
- **In an atomic (nuclear) reactor**, a *mixture* of 3 per cent uranium-235 and 97 per cent uranium-238 is used. This gives a *controlled* chain reaction. In this case, an average of only one neutron from each fission causes further fission. The heat produced is then used to generate electricity.

Nuclear reactors

Figure 22.11 is a simplified diagram of a **gas-cooled nuclear reactor**. The function of each part of the reactor is shown in the diagram.

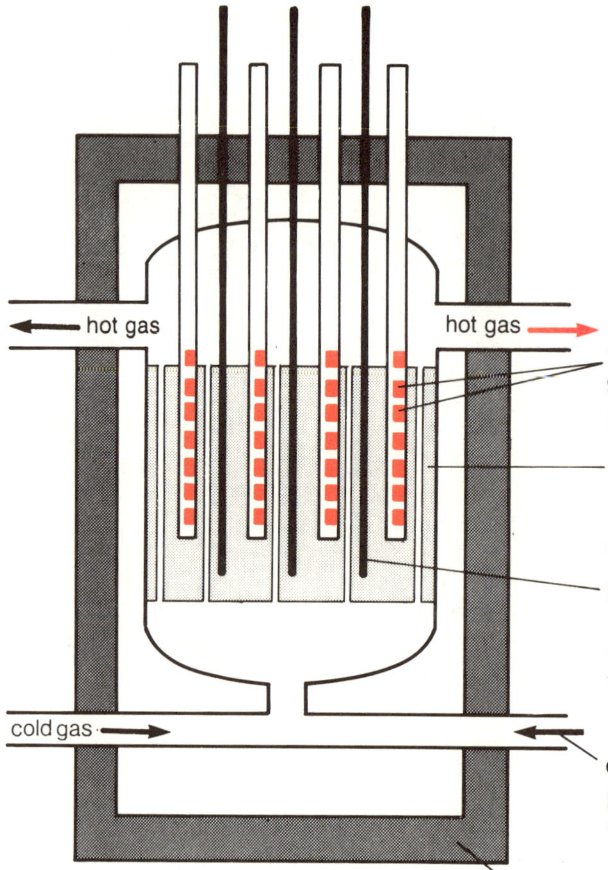

Fig. 22.11 A gas-cooled nuclear reactor

THE FUTURE

At present about 18 per cent of our electricity is generated from nuclear energy. In 1987, the government announced plans to build more nuclear power stations. By the year 2000, as much as 50 per cent of our electricity may come from nuclear power.

The reason for this increased use of nuclear fuel is that fossil fuels are running out. However, there is also concern about the supplies of uranium-235. In order to reduce our reliance on uranium-235, scientists are trying to develop a new type of fission reactor called a **breeder reactor**. The first prototype breeder reactor was built at Dounreay in Scotland. This started working in 1976. The reactor uses **plutonium-239** as the fuel, not uranium-235. The plutonium-239 can be produced ('bred') from the stable uranium-238 which makes up 99.7 per cent of natural uranium. By using U-238 to 'breed' plutonium, our stocks of nuclear fuel will last for a few hundred years.

Fusion

In the distant future, scientists hope to harness energy from **fusion** rather than fission. Fusion involves joining two nuclei together. The energy produced by the sun comes from the fusion of heavy hydrogen (deuterium) nuclei (see Fig. 22.12).

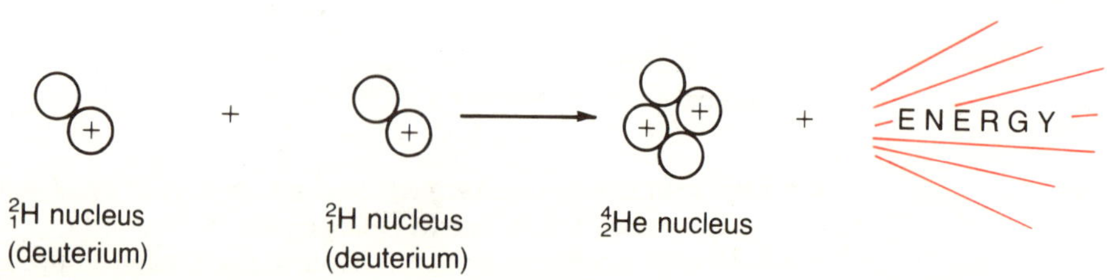

Fig. 22.12 The fusion of two deuterium nuclei

For many years, scientists have tried to fuse deuterium nuclei by producing very high temperatures, similar to those on the sun. Recently, however, scientists have claimed to produce fusion at room temperature (cold fusion) and this has caused great excitement. The energy liberated by the fusion of two nuclei is much greater than that liberated by fission. If we can harness the energy from fusion, we will have solved our energy problems forever.

Quick test 22

Questions 1 to 4

Questions 1 to 4 concern the five isotopes labelled A, B, C, D and E below.

	Mass number	*Atomic number*
A	1	1
B	3	2
C	4	2
D	4	3
E	7	4

1 Which is an isotope of hydrogen?
2 Which two are isotopes of the same element?
3 Which isotopes contain only one neutron?
4 Which isotope contains the most electrons?

Questions 5 to 10

A neutron
B hydrogen atom
C alpha particle
D beta particle
E hydrogen ion

Which type(s) of particle labelled A to E above
5 would be attracted by a positive plate?
6 is the heaviest?
7 could be used in a thickness guage for polythene or paper?
8 causes fission of uranium-235?
9 is a proton?
10 contains the same number of protons and electrons?

Questions 11 to 13

The table below gives information about alpha, beta and gamma radiation.

Type of radiation	*What it consists of*	*How far radiation penetrates*
Alpha	positively charged particles – each particle contains two protons and two neutrons	stopped by paper
Beta	negatively charged electrons	stopped by a thin sheet of aluminium
Gamma	electromagnetic waves	stopped by thick blocks of lead or concrete

11 The diagram shows alpha and beta particles passing between two charged plates.

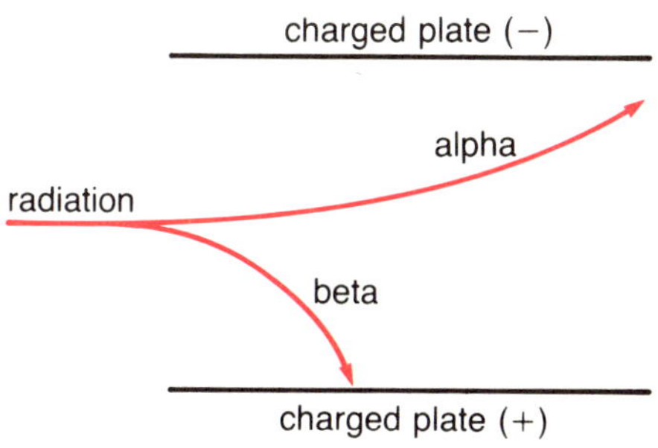

(a) Explain why alpha particles are deflected upwards in the electric field, but beta particles are deflected downwards. (2 marks)
(b) Explain why a radioactive source which gives out only alpha and beta particles can be safely stored in an aluminium container. (2 marks)

12 Radioactivity is used in hospitals to investigate the inside of a person's body without having to cut them open. Technetium-99 (^{99}Tc) gives out gamma rays and has a half-life of six hours.

(a) Why is lead used to shield hospital workers while they are using ^{99}Tc? (1 mark)

(b) Explain why a radioactive substance having a short half-life is used. (2 marks)

(c) Medical equipment such as disposable syringes can be sterilized using gamma rays. Gamma rays kill bacteria and other micro-organisms. Before being sterilized by the gamma rays the plastic syringes are sealed in aluminium foil packets.

Discuss why this is a better method of sterilizing the syringes than heating them at high temperatures using steam and then packing them. (2 marks)

13 **(a)** Radiation is always present in the environment. What is the general name given to this radiation? (1 mark)

(b) Give *two* causes of this radiation. (2 marks)

(c) Name the instrument used to measure the radiation level. (1 mark)

(*NEA* 1988)

Questions 14 to 20

The diagram shows a gamma ray unit used in a hospital. A is a container of radioactive material. The unit is made 'safe' by moving the container to position B. Lead absorbs gamma rays.

The radioactive material is either cobalt-60 (^{60}Co) or caesium-137 (^{137}Cs). Cobalt-60 decays after a few years and must be replaced, but a container of caesium-137 usually lasts for the working life of the unit, which is about 20 years. The table below shows some information about these isotopes.

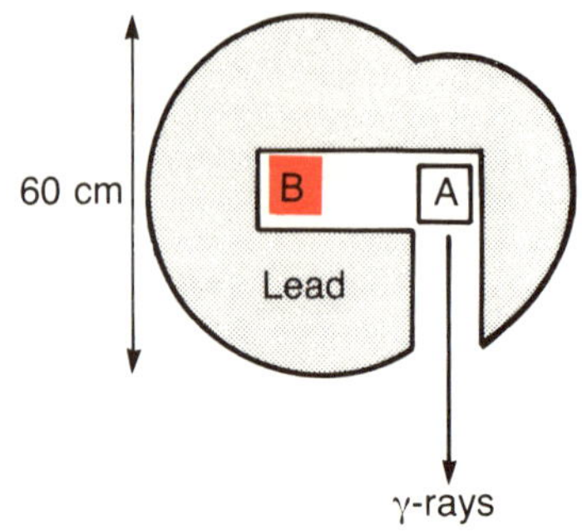

Isotope	*Proton number (atomic number)*	*Nucleon number (mass number)*	*Half-life*
Cobalt-60	27	60	5.3 years
Caesium-137	55	137	35 years

In 1987, an old gamma ray unit was broken open by people who did not know how dangerous it could be. Some of them were killed by radiation after they touched caesium-137 from the unit.

14 Name the *two* types of particle in the nucleus of the isotope cobalt-60. (2 marks)

15 What is the proton number of the isotope cobalt-59? (1 mark)

16 What is the number of electrons in a neutral atom of caesium-137? (1 mark)

17 Explain the meanings of *decay* and *half-life*? (2 marks)

18 Why does a container of caesium-137 last longer than a container of cobalt-60? (1 mark)

19 Explain why the gamma ray unit is 'safe' when the container is in position B. (2 marks)

20 Suggest *three* safety precautions which a person should take when removing a container of cobalt-60. (3 marks)

(*LEAG*)

23 FORCE AND MOTION

23.1 Distance and displacement

Figure 23.1 shows a map of John's route to school each day. Altogether, John walks a total distance of 600 metres (200 m + 300 m + 100 m).

But John has not walked 600 metres in a straight line. He has gone east, then north, then east again.

John has ony been *displaced* 480 metres from his starting point in a north-east direction. We can say that John's *total path is 600 metres*, but his **displacement** is only *480 metres north-east*.

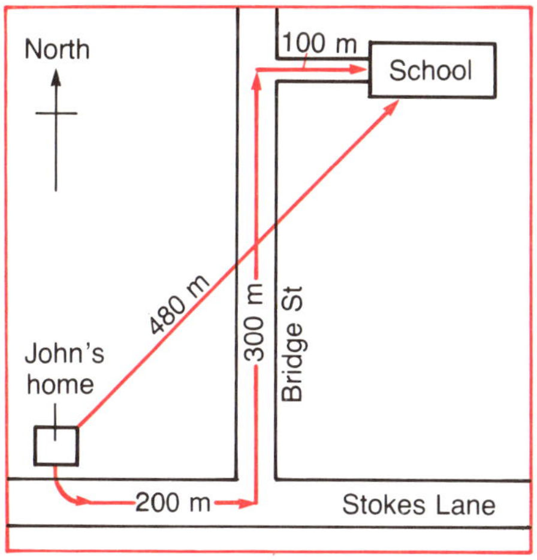

Fig. 23.1 John's walk to school

Distance moved = total path taken whatever the direction
Displacement = distance moved in a particular direction

23.2 Speed and velocity

As well as measuring how far John has moved, we may want to know how fast he has moved. We can calculate John's speed if we know the time he takes to walk to school.

$$\textbf{speed} = \frac{\textbf{distance moved}}{\textbf{time taken}}$$

Suppose John walks to school in ten minutes, what is his speed in *metres per second* (m/s)? This can be calculated as follows:

$$\text{John's speed} = \frac{\text{distance moved}}{\text{time taken}} = \frac{600 \text{ metres}}{10 \times 60 \text{ seconds}}$$

$$= \frac{600 \text{ metres}}{600 \text{ seconds}}$$

$$= 1{\cdot}0 \text{ m/s}$$

Notice that 'metres per second' is written as m/s. The slanting line stands for 'per'. When we are describing motion, **per means 'in one'**. So a speed of '2 m/s' means 'two metres per second' or 'two metres in one second'.

The **SI units** of distance and time are the metre and the second, respectively. So, speed is measured in metres/second or m/s in SI (the International System of Units). However, many other units are in everyday use such as miles per hour (mph) and kilometres per hour (km/h).

Although John walks 600 metres to school in 10 minutes, he is moving in different directions during those 10 minutes. His speed is 1·0 m/s, but it has no particular direction. If we calculate John's *speed in a particular direction*, this is called his **velocity**.

$$\textbf{velocity} = \frac{\textbf{displacement}}{\textbf{time taken}}$$

$$\textbf{In our example, John's velocity} = \frac{\textbf{480 metres north-east}}{\textbf{10} \times \textbf{60 seconds}}$$

$$= \textbf{0.8 m/s north-east}$$

Notice that whenever a velocity is given, its direction must always be stated, as well as its size.

23.3 Vectors and scalars

Quantities that have both size and direction such as displacement and velocity, are called **vectors**. *Quantities that have size but no direction* such as distance and speed, are called **scalars**.

Another example of a vector is **weight**. The weight of an object *always acts in a downward direction.*

- Which of the following quantities are vectors and which are scalars?
  temperature, volume, force, time, mass

23.4 Distance – time graphs

Katie sets off from home on her bicycle to the newsagents 330 metres away. The first part of her journey is along a narrow, bumpy lane. The second part is along a road. Table 23.1 shows the distance Katie has travelled after every 10 seconds.

Table 23.1

Time taken/s	0	10	20	30	40	50	60	70	80	90	100
Distance/m	0	20	40	60	80	130	180	230	280	330	330

Figure 23.2 shows a **distance-time graph** of Katie's journey.

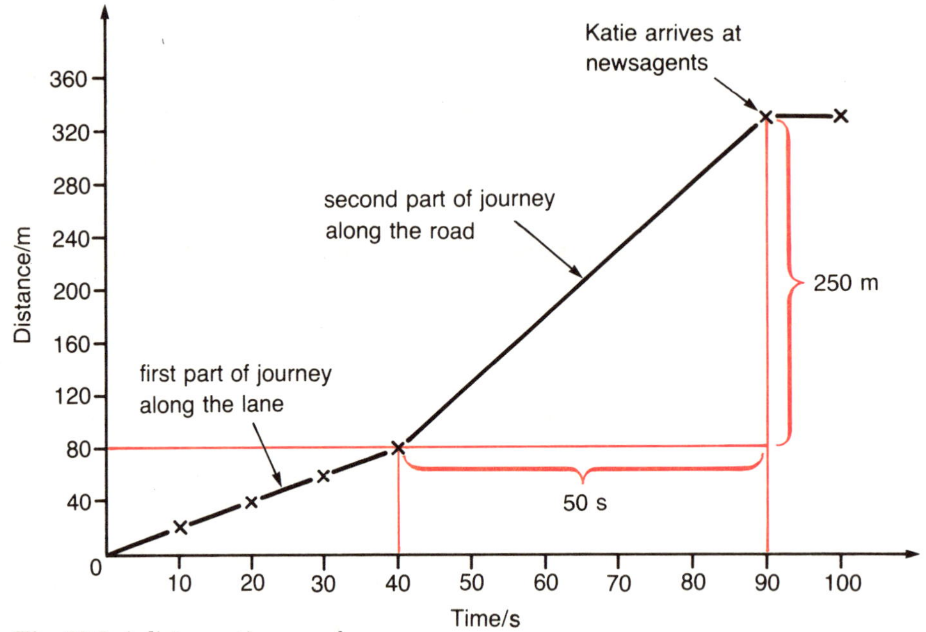

Fig. 23.2 A distance-time graph

The first part of the journey is 80 metres along the bumpy lane. This takes 40 seconds. On the graph it is shown as a straight line. We can find the gradient (slope) of the line as follows:

$$\text{Gradient (slope) of line} = \frac{\text{Distance moved}}{\text{time taken}} = \frac{80 \text{ metres}}{40 \text{ seconds}}$$

$$= 2 \text{ m/s}$$

You should recognize the units of the gradient as the SI unit of speed.

Gradient of distance-time graph = speed

During the second part of the journey, Katie's speed increases. Here she travels 250 metres in 50 seconds.

- What is Katie's speed in the second part of her journey?
- Compare the slope of the distance-time graph for the second part of her journey with that for the first part.
- What happens to the gradient of the distance-time graph between 90 and 100 seconds? Why is this?

23.5 Average and relative speed

The first part of the graph in Fig. 23.2 shows a constant speed of 2 m/s. The second part shows a constant speed of 5 m/s. Finally, the speed between 90 and 100 seconds is zero. Notice how the speed changes during the journey. If you want the speed at any moment, the best way is to find the gradient of the graph at that time. Of course, if you were travelling in a car, you could find its speed at any moment by looking at the speedometer. This works by measuring the rate at which the wheels are rotating.

Average speed is obtained from the *total distance moved* and the *total time taken*:

$$\text{average speed} = \frac{\text{total distance moved}}{\text{total time taken}}$$

For the journey described in Fig. 23.2, the average speed is calculated as follows:

$$\text{Average speed} = \frac{\text{total distance moved}}{\text{total time taken}} = \frac{330 \text{ metres}}{100 \text{ seconds}}$$
$$= 3.3 \text{ m/s}$$

Relative speed

Suppose you are travelling in the slow lane of a motorway at 80 km/h and a car in the fast lane passes at 120 km/h (Fig. 23.3). If you watch the faster car, it will seem to move past you at 40 km/h (120 – 80).

Relative to your car, the second car is moving at 40 km/h. *Relative to the ground* it is moving at 120 km/h.

The relative speed of a moving object is its speed *relative to* something else.

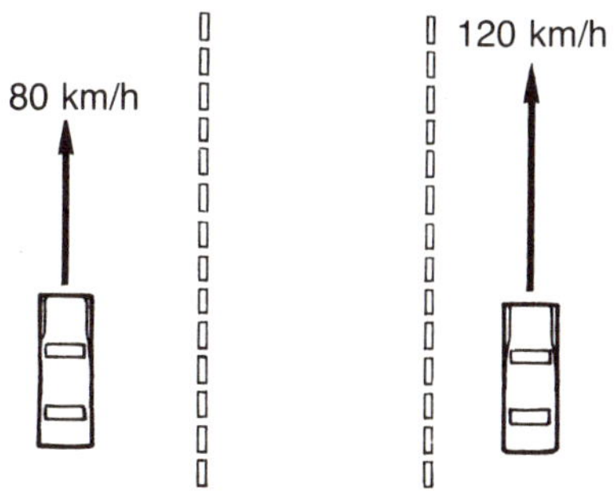

Fig. 23.3 Relative speeds

23.6 Changing speed – acceleration

The makers of a sports car claim that it will increase its speed from 0 to 40 m/s in 10 seconds. When a moving object increases its speed, we say it accelerates. The *rate at which the object increases its speed* is called **acceleration**.

$$\text{acceleration} = \frac{\text{change in speed}}{\text{time taken}}$$

e.g. the sports car's acceleration $= \dfrac{(40 - 0)\text{m/s}}{10 \text{ s}} = \dfrac{4 \text{ m/s}}{\text{s}}$

So the car accelerates by 4 metres per second every second. This means that it increases its speed by 4 metres per second every second (i.e. **4 m/s^2**).

Suppose the car is travelling at 40 m/s. The driver suddenly applies the brakes and the car stops in 2 seconds. What is the acceleration this time?

$$\text{acceleration} = \frac{\text{change in speed}}{\text{time taken}}$$
$$= \frac{\text{final speed} - \text{initial speed}}{\text{time taken}}$$
$$= \frac{0 - 40 \text{ m/s}}{2 \text{ s}} = -20 \text{ m/s}^2$$

In this case, the car is *slowing down*, not speeding up. **Negative acceleration** of this kind is called **deceleration**.

23.7 Speed – time graphs

Look at the results in Table 23.2. They show the distance moved by a rocket in each of the first five seconds after take-off.

Table 23.2

	Distance moved/m	*Average speed/m/s*
1st second	4	4
2nd second	12	12
3rd second	20	20
4th second	28	28
5th second	36	36

The **average** speed of the rocket during the first second is 4 m/s. At the beginning of the first second (i.e. zero time) the speed of the rocket will be zero. At the end of the first second (i.e. after one second), the speed of the rocket will be 8 m/s. Half way through the first second (i.e. after half a second), the speed of the rocket is 4 m/s. So, using the other results in Table 23.2,

speed of rocket after $1\frac{1}{2}$ secs = 12 m/s
speed of rocket after $2\frac{1}{2}$ secs = 20 m/s
speed of rocket after $3\frac{1}{2}$ secs = 28 m/s
speed of rocket after $4\frac{1}{2}$ secs = 36 m/s

what is the acceleration of the rocket?

(Hint: How much does the speed increase in one second?)

These results for the rocket have been plotted in a speed-time graph in Fig. 23.4.

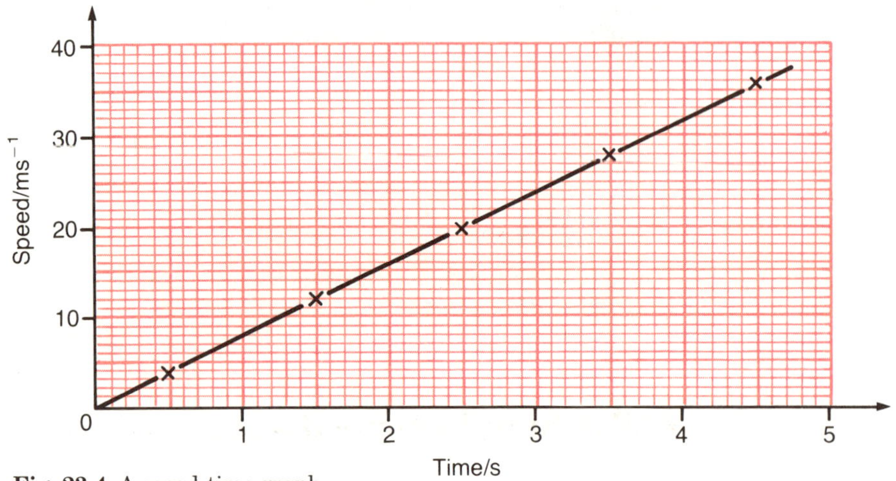

Fig. 23.4 A speed-time graph

The straight line of the graph shows that the speed is increasing at an even rate, i.e. that acceleration is constant. Acceleration is found by calculating the gradient (slope) of the graph:

$$\text{Gradient of the speed-time graph} = \frac{\text{change in speed}}{\text{time taken}} = \text{acceleration}$$

If we were asked how far the rocket travels in the first four seconds, we must first calculate its average speed in this time:

speed at time 0 seconds = 0 m/s

From the graph, Fig. 23.4:

speed after 4 seconds = 32 m/s

$$\text{therefore average speed in first 4 seconds} = \frac{0 + 32}{2} = 16\text{m/s}$$

therefore distance travelled in 4 seconds = 16 × 4 = 64 metres

Notice that:

distance moved = average speed × time taken

23.8 Forces

A force is a push or a pull. If you wanted to exert a force on something you could push it, pull it, twist it, squeeze it, etc.

The following are examples of some important forces:

- **Gravitational forces** are caused by the pull of the Earth on objects. This is sometimes called *the force of gravity*. It is the force of gravity that pulls the ski jumper back down to Earth.

- **Frictional forces** try to stop things moving. They cause the *friction* or *drag* which stops objects slipping over each other or sliding past each other. Friction eventually stops a billiard ball rolling on a billiard table and frictional forces prevent the child in the picture from moving down the slide too fast.

- **Contact forces** are produced when two objects are pushed together. The contact force from the starting block pushes the sprinter away at the start of a race.

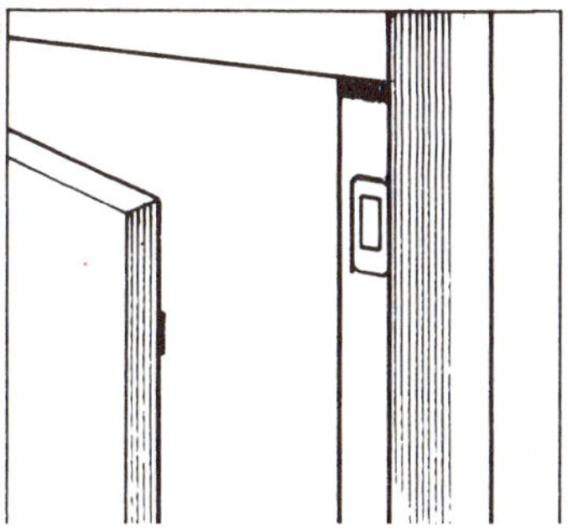

- **Magnetic forces** act on magnetic materials. The magnetic strips in magnetic door catches pull the door to the frame and keep the door closed.

- **Electric forces** act between electric charges. Electric forces (*static*) sometimes make your hair cling to a plastic comb.

Forces can:
- change the shape of objects;
- change the motion of objects;
- cause objects to move.

Think of one example for each of these effects of forces. The following sections discuss various forces and their effects in more detail.

23.9 Force, weight and mass

Forces vary enormously in size – from tiny forces to remove a cataract from someone's eye, to huge forces to cut through rock. Therefore it is important that we can measure the size of a force. **Forces are measured in newtons (N)**. This name was chosen in honour of Sir Isaac Newton, the famous physicist (1642–1727). It requires a force of about one newton (1 N) to lift an average-sized apple or orange with a mass of 100 grams.

Everyone experiences one important force all their lives. This is the **force of gravity** which is caused by the pull of the Earth on our bodies.

Experiments show that every object in the universe attracts all other objects. These attractions are called **gravitational forces**. The gravitational forces between relatively small objects like tables, chairs and people are too small to have any effect. But if one object is as large as the Earth, the gravitational force is very strong.

The gravitational force between the Earth and an object is usually called the **weight** of the object.

It is important to understand the difference between weight and **mass**:

Weight is the *force of gravity* on an object, measured in newtons (N). Mass is the *amount of matter* (or stuff) in an object, measured in kilograms (kg).

On Earth, an apple with a mass of 0.1 kg (100 g) has a weight of 1 N; a bag of potatoes with a mass of 1 kg (2.2 pounds) has a weight of 10 N; someone with a mass of 50 kg has a weight of 500 N.

If we could get the apple, the bag of potatoes and this person to the moon, their mass would stay the same because they still contain the same amount of matter. However, their weights would be only one-sixth of their weights on Earth. This is because the moon is smaller than the Earth and its gravitational pull is only one-sixth of the Earth's (see Fig. 23.5).

When an astronaut is far out in space, there is no gravitational pull from the Earth, the moon or any stars or planets. He or she just floats around in a *weightless* state.

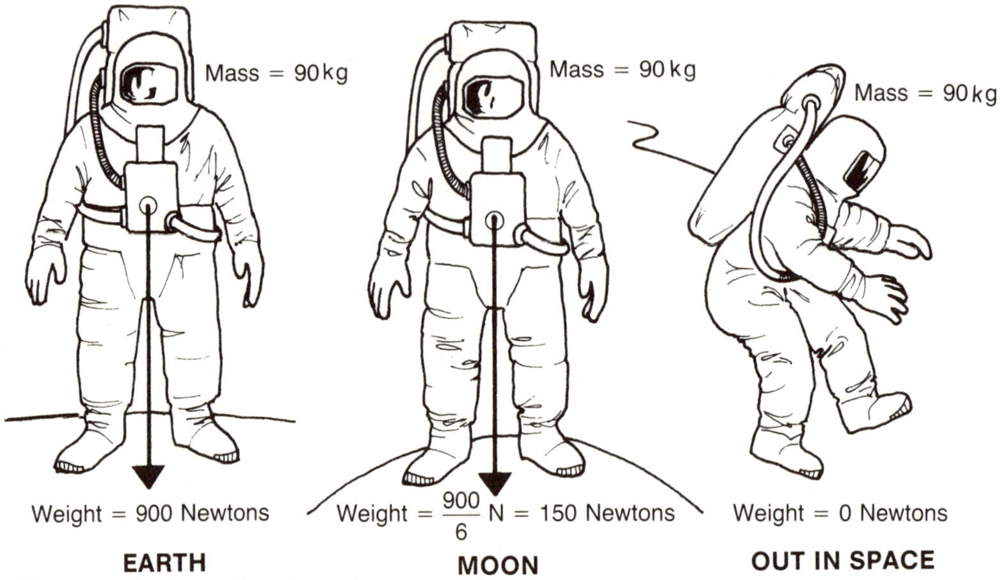

Fig. 23.5 Gravity on Earth, on the moon and in outer space

The SI unit for mass is the **kilogram** (kg). However, many people continue to measure masses in ounces (oz), pounds (lb) and stones.

1000 g = 1 kg = 2.2 pounds

1000 kg = 1 tonne

23.10 Stretching forces

When we hang weights from a spring, the spring extends (stretches). The force of gravity pulling on the weight pulls on the spring and this causes it to extend. The spring can support the weights due to the forces of attraction between particles in the spring. The pull in the spring which supports the weights is called a **tension**.

INVESTIGATING HOOKE'S LAW

Figure 23.6 shows the apparatus we can use to investigate the stretching forces acting on a spring.

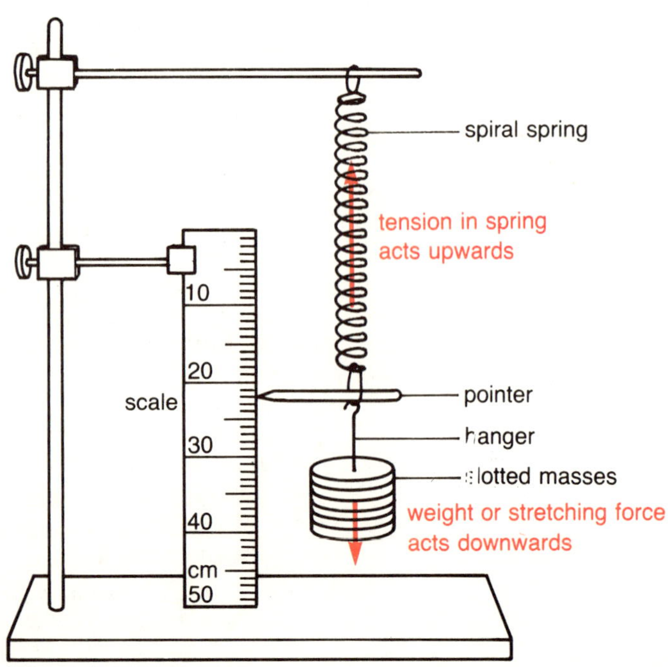

Fig. 23.6 Stretching a spring

Table 23.3 The results of an experiment using the apparatus in Fig. 23.6.

Weight added, stretching force on spring /N	*Position of pointer on scale* /cm	*Extension of spring* /cm
0	10.0	0
2	13.9	3.9
4	18.1	8.1
6	22.0	12.0
8	25.9	15.9
10	30.0	20.0

The results in Table 23.3 are plotted on a graph in Fig. 23.7.

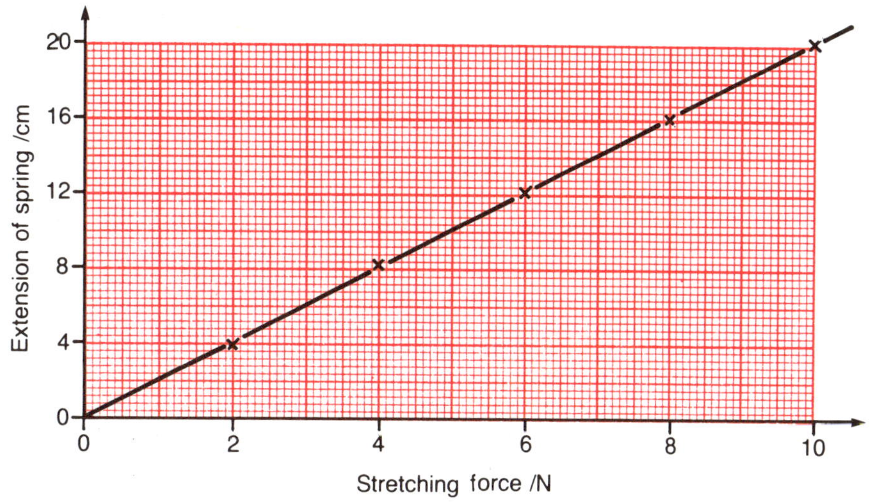

Fig. 23.7 Extension of a spring against stretching force (load)

The graph of extension against the stretching force is a straight line. When the stretching force is doubled, the extension doubles, and so on. The extension is said to be **proportional** to the stretching force. Using the symbol $\propto$, which means 'proportional to', this can be summarized as:

extension $\propto$ stretching force

This result is usually known as **Hooke's Law** after the scientist Robert Hooke who first investigated springs during the 17th century.

Provided the stretching forces are not too great, the same kind of results are obtained when:

- other materials, such as wires, wood and even concrete, are stretched;
- materials are compressed by forces.

ELASTICITY

Some materials *return to their original length when the force is removed.* These materials are said to be **elastic**. As the stretching force increases, a point is reached when a material remains deformed even when the force is removed. This *extent of elasticity* varies greatly from one material to another.

The elastic properties of springs are put to use in kitchen and bathroom scales and springs in mattresses, chairs and other furniture. Although the elasticity of wood and concrete is much less than that of most metals, it allows buildings to move slightly as a result of minor Earth movements (rather than fall down).

23.11 Frictional forces

If you have waded knee-deep in water or thick snow, you will know how difficult it is to make progress. Your movement through the water or snow is slowed down by **friction**. Frictional forces (friction) are the *forces which prevent motion*. These forces prevent an object moving over a surface or through a fluid.

What causes friction?

Friction occurs when the molecules of one object get very close to the molecules of another surface or the molecules in a fluid. The forces of attraction between the molecules must be overcome in order to move one surface over another or through another.

The effects of friction

Friction has three major effects:

1. it prevents objects moving or slows them down;
2. it produces heat when two objects rub against each other (you will notice this if you rub your hands vigorously or if you slide down a rope);
3. it wears things out as surfaces rub against each other (e.g. tyres lose their tread because of the friction between the tyres and the road).

Reducing friction

Friction can be reduced by the use of

- **bearings**,
- **lubrication**,
- **streamlining**.

Two of these methods are illustrated in Fig. 23.8. Bearings and lubrication are used to reduce friction between a wheel and its axle. The ball bearings reduce the area of contact between the moving surfaces. The oil between the bearings, wheel and axle acts as a lubricant by separating the moving surfaces with a thin layer of liquid.

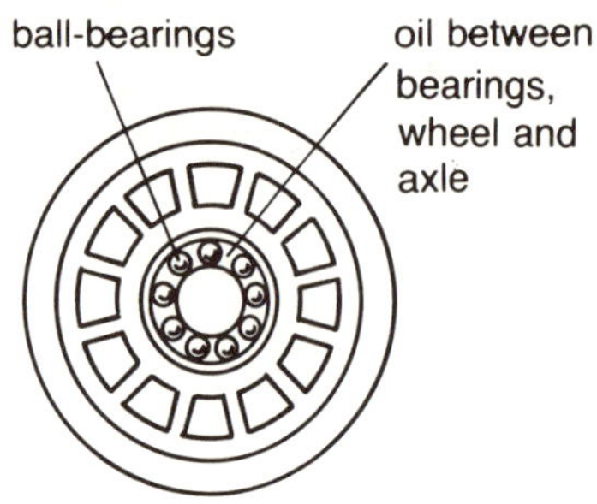

Fig. 23.8 Reducing friction between a wheel and its axle

One of the latest attempts to reduce friction is *air lubrication*. This is very useful in machine tools, in hover mowers, hovercraft and aerotrains. Air is forced between the surfaces in contact at high pressure. This forces the surfaces apart and keeps the friction to a minimum.

Lubrication is also important in our bodies. Synovial fluid is the lubricant which allows bones to slide over one another (see section 7.3).

When objects move through fluids, like air and water, there are frictional forces which resist their motion. These frictional forces are usually called **drag**. Streamlining of cars, trains, aircraft and rockets reduces drag to a minimum. The vehicles can then get to higher speeds with less fuel.

Fig. 23.9 How has this racing car been designed and built to reduce drag? (Photograph courtesy of Ford Photographic Department)

Using friction

Friction is often a nuisance, but sometimes it is essential. If you have tried to walk on ice, you will know that movement is very difficult when friction is reduced to a minimum. We depend on the friction between the soles of our shoes and the ground to be able to stop and start and to walk around easily. The tyres and brakes on vehicles also depend on friction for starting, moving and stopping.

If there was no friction, pens and pencils would not be able to leave marks on paper, anything on a slope would move downhill and screws would come loose.

23.12 Newton's Laws of Motion

NEWTON'S FIRST LAW OF MOTION

If you roll a stone or a ball over a flat, icy surface it seems to move on and on and on because there is so little friction. If we could reduce friction and air resistance (drag) to zero, the stone would go on rolling forever.

These simple ideas were first summarized by Sir Isaac Newton in his **First Law of Motion**:

> If an object is stationary it will remain so, and if it is moving it will continue to move with constant speed in a straight line, unless external forces act upon it.

In practice, most moving objects slow down because external frictional forces act on them.

NEWTON'S SECOND LAW OF MOTION

Newton's first law is concerned with objects at rest or those moving at constant speed. His second law is concerned with the motion of objects which are forced to move.

If you have tried to push a vehicle along a flat road, you will know that it accelerates away faster if two people push instead of one. When accurate investigations are made, the results show that the *acceleration doubles when the force doubles* and acceleration trebles when the force trebles, etc. This means that the **acceleration is proportional to the force applied**, i.e.

$$\text{acceleration} \propto \text{force}$$

In symbols this is written

$$a \propto F \qquad \textit{(Equation 1)}$$

Experience may also have taught you that a smaller car is easier to push and accelerate than a large van. Accurate experiments show that if you push *double the mass*, with the same force, *the acceleration is only half*. This result can be summed up as:

$$\text{acceleration} \propto \frac{1}{\text{mass}}$$

$$a \propto \frac{1}{m} \qquad \textit{(Equation 2)}$$

Equations 1 and 2 can be combined to give

$$a \propto \frac{F}{m}$$

$$\textit{or} \quad F \propto m \times a \qquad \textit{(Equation 3)}$$

Equation 3 is the mathematical form of Newton's **Second Law of Motion**, which says:

> The acceleration of an object is inversely proportional to its mass and directly proportional to the force acting on it.

The equation for Newton's second law can also be written as

$$F = k \times m \times a$$

where k is a constant. However, the unit of force (one newton) was chosen so that k equals one, so we can write

$$\textit{Force} = \textit{mass} \times \textit{acceleration}$$

$$F = m \times a \qquad \textit{(Equation 4)}$$

Using equation 4,

one newton is the force which gives a mass of 1 kg an acceleration of 1 m/s^2.

When using equation 4, remember

- F must be in newtons
- m must be in kilograms
- a must be in metres per second per second.

Example

A car of mass 1.5 tonnes accelerates from rest to 20 m/s in 4 seconds.
What is

(a) the average acceleration?
(b) the force causing acceleration?
(c) the distance travelled in the 4 seconds?

First, put all measurements in the correct units:

Mass of car = 1.5 tonnes = 1500 kg
Initial speed of car = 0 m/s
Final speed of car = 20 m/s
Time of acceleration = 4 s

(a) Average acceleration $= \dfrac{\text{change in speed}}{\text{time taken}}$

$$= \frac{20 \text{ m/s}}{4 \text{ s}} = 5 \text{ m/s}^2$$

(b) Force causing acceleration, $F = m \times a$

$$= 1500 \times 5$$
$$= 7500 \text{ N}$$

(c) Distance travelled in 4 secs = average speed × time

$$= \frac{20 \text{ m/s}}{2} \times 4 \text{ s}$$
$$= 40 \text{ m}$$

23.13 Falling under gravity

When an object is dropped, it falls to the ground and accelerates due to the force of gravity. In air, a penny falls faster than a bit of paper. But in a vacuum, when the air is removed, both the penny and the paper fall at the same rate (Fig. 23.10).

The difference in air is due to air resistance (drag). This affects the fall of less dense objects like paper more than dense objects like the penny.

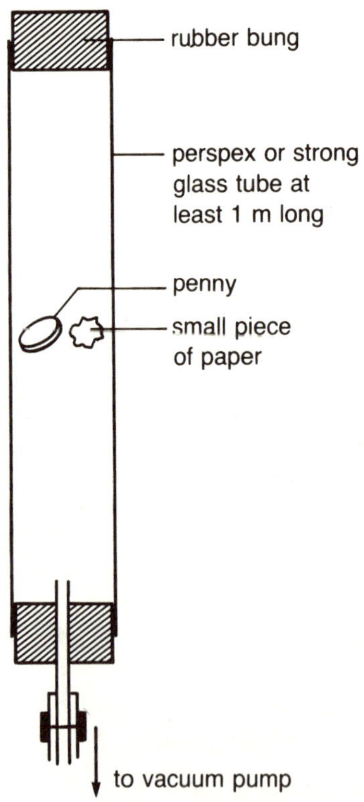

Fig. 23.10 Comparing the way in which a penny and a bit of paper fall in air, then in a vacuum

Careful experiments show that when air resistance is negligible, all objects accelerate to the ground at the same rate. The apparatus which can be used to measure acceleration due to gravity is shown in Fig. 23.11. It consists of an electromagnet, connected to a battery via a two-way switch. The current in the electromagnet holds a small ball-bearing about one metre above a hinged trap-door. When the switch is moved to position 2, the current in the electromagnet stops and the ball starts to fall. At the same time the circuit to the timer is completed and it starts counting. After falling through about one metre, the ball hits the hinged trap-door. This breaks the contact at C and stops the clock.

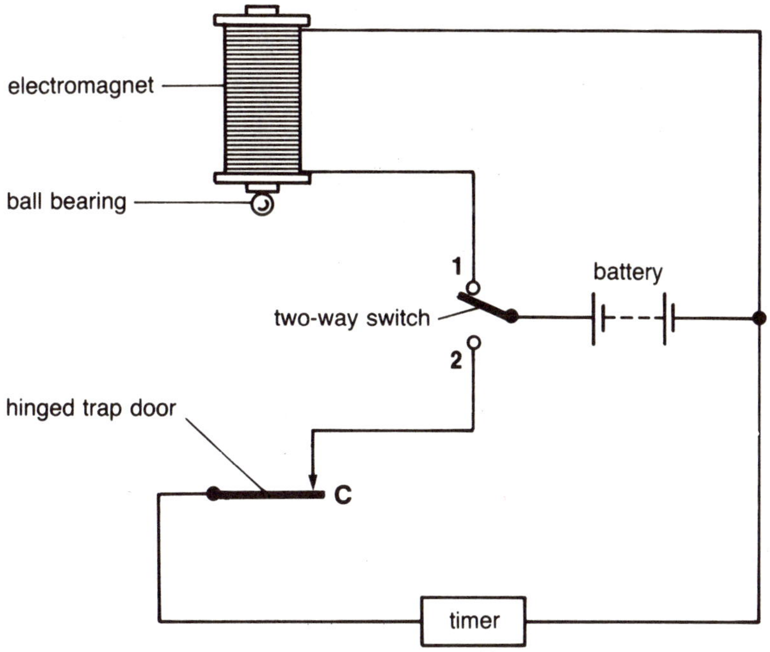

Fig. 23.11 Measuring the acceleration due to gravity

Results
Height through which ball falls = 1.25 m

Time of fall = 0.50 s

Calculations

$$\text{Average speed during fall} = \frac{\text{distance fallen}}{\text{time taken}} = \frac{1.25\text{ m}}{0.5\text{ s}}$$

$$= 2.5\text{ m/s}$$

Initial speed = 0 m/s

Final speed = 2 × average speed = 5 m/s

$$\text{Therefore, acceleration during fall} = \frac{\text{increase in speed}}{\text{time taken}}$$

$$= \frac{5\text{ m/s}}{0.5\text{ s}} = 10\text{ m/s}^2$$

Accurate experiments show that **acceleration due to gravity is 9.8 m/s²**, but its value is usually approximated to 10 m/s². It is usually given the symbol *g*.

This result means that the speed of a falling object increases by 10 m/s every second. Acceleration due to gravity also means that if an object is thrown upwards, its velocity will *decrease* by 10 m/s every second until it reaches its highest point. After that, its velocity will increase downwards at the rate of 10 m/s every second.

Example
A stone is dropped from the top of a cliff and takes three seconds to reach the beach below.
Calculate
(a) the speed of the stone as it hits the beach;
(b) the height of the cliff.

(a) Initial speed of stone = 0 m/s
Acceleration of stone = 10 m/s² (acceleration due to gravity)
Therefore, speed after 3 s (as stone hits beach) = 3 × 10 = <u>30 m/s</u>

(b) $\text{Average speed of stone} = \frac{0 + 30}{2} = 15\text{ m/s}$

Therefore, height of cliff = distance fallen by stone
= average speed × time
= 15 m/s × 3 s
= <u>45 m</u>

WEIGHT AND GRAVITY

Weight is a force exerted by a mass as a result of acceleration due to gravity.

Remember, force = mass × acceleration

so **weight = mass × acceleration due to gravity**

e.g. the weight of a 9 kg mass is given as,

weight = mass × acceleration due to gravity

= 9 kg × 10 m/s^2 = 90 N

TERMINAL VELOCITY

When objects fall, air resistance (drag) increases as they move faster. Eventually the air resistance acting upwards equals the weight of the object acting downwards. The overall force on the object is then zero and it continues to *fall with a constant velocity*. This speed is called the **terminal velocity**. It depends on the size, the shape and the weight of the falling object.

23.14 Force and pressure

Why is it possible to push a drawing pin into a piece of wood, but impossible to push your finger into a piece of wood? The answer is that the force on the drawing pin is concentrated on a small area (the point of the pin). When you press your finger on the wood, the force is spread out over a much larger area (the area of skin touching the wood).

Scientists use the word '**pressure**' to describe how concentrated a force is. If the force is concentrated on a small area, pressure is high. If the force acts on a large area, pressure is low (see Fig. 23.12).

Pressure is defined as the force per unit area and can be calculated using the formula

$$\textbf{Pressure} = \frac{\textbf{force}}{\textbf{area}}$$

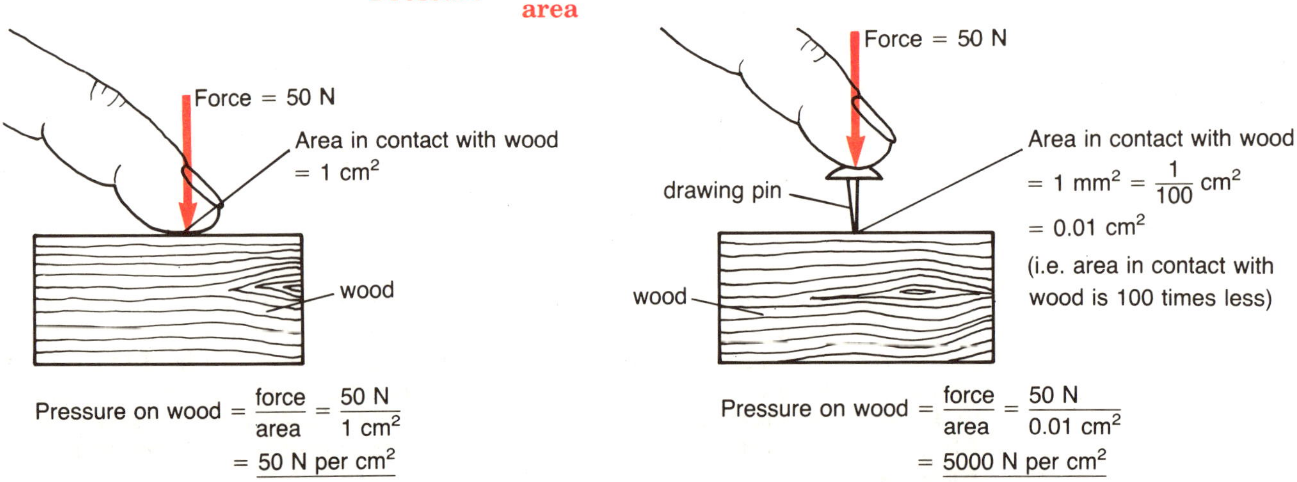

Fig. 23.12 The pressure on the wood below the point of the drawing pin is 100 times greater than the pressure from the finger

The idea of pressure as '*force divided by area*' also explains why:

- tractors working on boggy ground need wide tyres,
- it is easier to walk over snow wearing snow shoes,
- camels are more suitable than horses for riding over sandy desert (they have larger hooves),
- woodpeckers need strong pointed beaks.

23.15 Pressure in liquids

The force of gravity pulls a liquid down in its container. This exerts pressure on the container and on objects in the liquid.

Pressure increases with depth

As the liquid gets deeper, the mass of liquid pushing down increases. The force from the liquid is therefore greater and so is the pressure. Because of this, dams are built with thicker walls at their base (Fig. 23.13).

Pressure acts in all directions

A liquid pushes on every surface in contact with it, whichever way the surface is facing. This helps to explain why there is an upward force (**upthrust**) on an object in a liquid. If this upthrust is large enough, it can balance the weight (force) of the object downwards. Under these conditions, the object will float (Fig. 23.13).

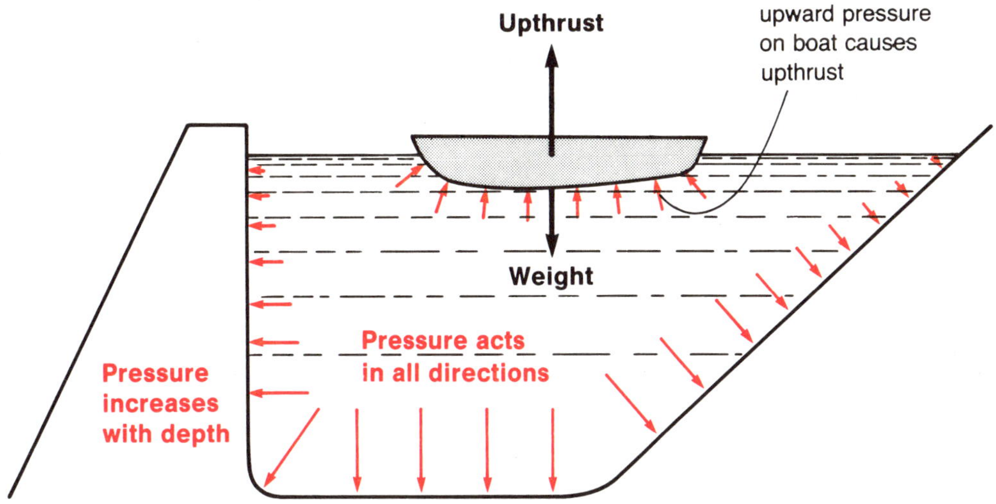

Fig. 23.13 Pressure in liquids

HYDRAULIC MACHINES

Hydraulic machines use liquids under pressure to transmit forces. Liquids have two important properties which make hydraulic machines possible.

- Unlike gases, **liquids cannot be compressed**.
  –*In a gas*, the particles are widely spaced so they are easily pushed closer together (compressed);
  –*In liquids*, the particles are close together, so they cannot be pushed together (compressed) any more.
- **Pressure on trapped liquid can be transmitted through the whole liquid**.

Hydraulic machines are important in hydraulic jacks, car brakes, fork-lift trucks and chair-lifts for the physically disabled.

The principle on which these machines work is shown in Fig. 23.14. Check the calculations at the side of Fig. 23.14. These show that when a force of 100 newtons is applied on a piston A, the pressure transmitted through the liquid is 100 000 newtons per square metre (Nm^{-2}). This creates a force on piston B of 10 000 N. This could lift a car of mass 1 tonne (1000 kg).

Hydraulic jacks, car brakes, fork-lift trucks and chair-lifts, all rely on arrangements similar to that shown in Fig. 23.14. By using pistons with different cross-sectional areas, they can magnify forces.

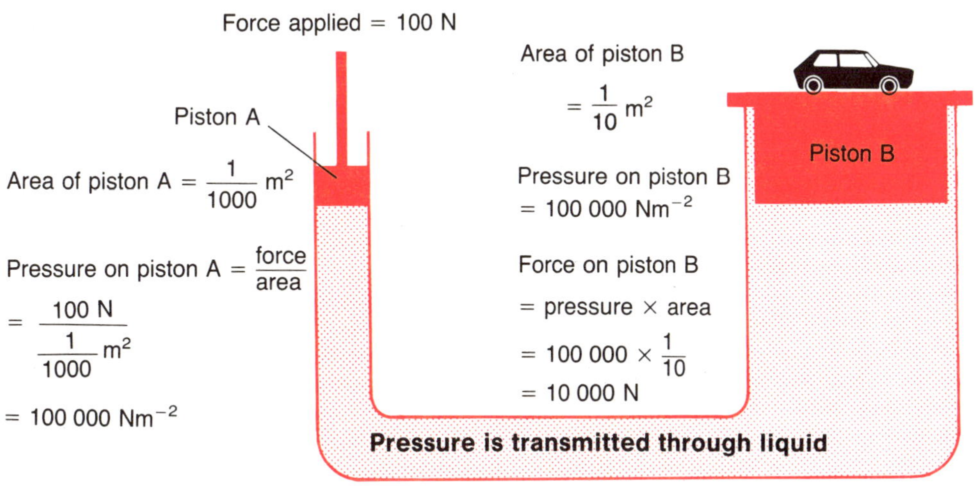

Fig. 23.14 Hydraulic machines can magnify forces. A force of 100 N on piston A, transmits a pressure through the liquid to produce a force on piston B of 10 000 N

23.16 Pressure in gases

The pressure of a gas is caused by particles bombarding the sides of their container. In Fig. 23.15(a), particles of gas are bombarding the inside and the outside of the can. The pressure is equal on both sides, so the can keeps its shape. Figure 23.15(b) shows what happens when the gas inside the can is removed. Now there are no particles bombarding the inside surface. The vacuum inside the can has zero pressure. However, air particles continue to bombard the outside of the can. This pressure from gases in the atmosphere causes the can to collapse.

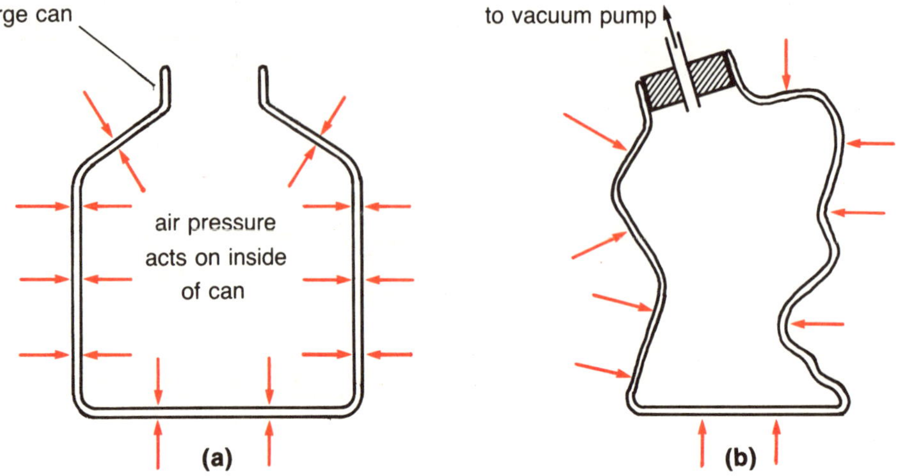

Fig. 23.15 The pressure of gases in the atmosphere can cause a metal can to collapse

ATMOSPHERIC PRESSURE

The atmosphere is like a deep ocean of air. The air is attracted to the Earth by gravity and presses down on everything below. Just as pressure increases as you go deeper underwater (refer back to section 23.15), **atmospheric pressure decreases as you rise further and further above sea level**.

Atmospheric pressure is usually about 100 000 newtons per square metre. This is approximately equal to the weight of an elephant pressing on every square metre. We don't usually feel the effects of this pressure because we have air pressure inside our lungs and the liquid pressure of our blood and other body fluids.

Measuring atmospheric pressure

Atmospheric pressure is measured by instruments called **barometers**.

The mercury barometer

A simple barometer can be made by *completely* filling a long, thick glass tube, which has been sealed at one end, with mercury. The tube is then corked and turned upside down into a dish of mercury. When the cork is removed, the mercury in the tube starts to fall. The mercury stops falling when the pressure from the mercury left in the tube is balanced by atmospheric pressure acting on mercury in the dish. Atmospheric pressure is then found by measuring the height of the mercury column above the level in the dish. This gives the atmospheric pressure in *millimetres of mercury* (mmHg). The higher the atmospheric pressure, the higher the mercury column.

At sea level, atmospheric pressure varies between 740 and 770 mmHg. At the top of Mount Everest (10 000 m above sea level), atmospheric pressure is only about 250 mmHg.

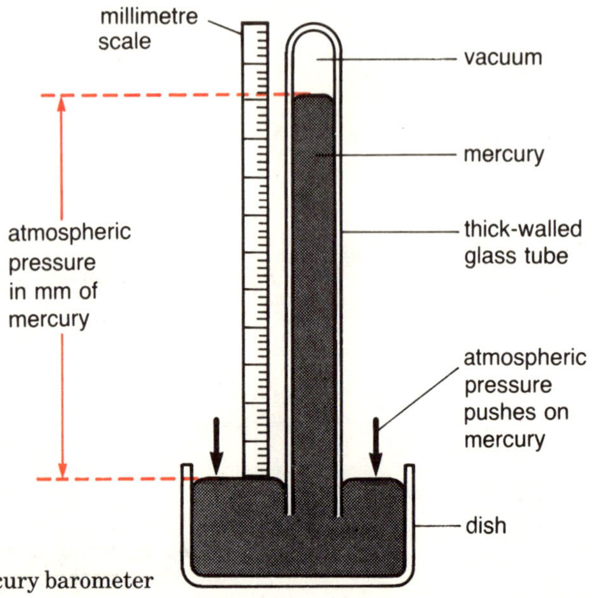

Fig. 23.16 A simple mercury barometer

Do not attempt to make a mercury barometer. Mercury is on the Hazardous Chemicals list. It gives off a poisonous vapour which can be absorbed through the skin, so do not play with spilt mercury (e.g. from a broken thermometer).

Mercury barometers are not very convenient because they use a liquid inside glassware. Also because that liquid, mercury, is poisonous. Scientists therefore looked for more convenient ways of measuring atmospheric pressure.

The aneroid barometer

Aneroid barometers are more convenient than mercury barometers. They do not use mercury. Instead, the main part of the instrument is a small corrugated metal box containing air at low pressure. As the atmospheric pressure outside the box increases, the top and bottom of the box move in. As the atmospheric pressure falls, the top and bottom of the box move out. This movement of the box is magnified by levers which are linked to a pointer. The pointer shows the atmospheric pressure on a circular scale.

Aneroid barometers are used as **pressure gauges** and as **altimeters** in aircraft. As explained earlier in this section, atmospheric pressure decreases with height above sea level. In an altimeter, the scale on an aneroid barometer is calibrated to show the altitude of the aircraft.

Quick test 23

Questions 1 to 5

What is the correct SI unit for

1 force?
2 distance?
3 mass?
4 acceleration?
5 work done (which equals force × distance)?

Questions 6 to 7

Tony and Zubair decide to walk from a youth hostel to a mountain lodge. On their map the distance is 12 km north-east. The path which they follow is 16 km and they take 4 hours.

6 What is their average speed for the walk?
7 What is their average velocity for the walk?

Questions 8 to 10

A car travels at 40 km/h for 15 minutes and then at 30 km/h for 30 minutes.

8 How far does it travel in the first 15 minutes?
9 How far does it travel in the next 30 minutes?
10 What is the average speed of the car?

Questions 11 to 14

Questions 11 to 14 relate to the graph below which shows the speed of a car at different times.

Choose the letter(s) from A to L which show where

11 the car is stationary.
12 the car is accelerating.
13 the car is decelerating.
14 the car is travelling at constant speed.

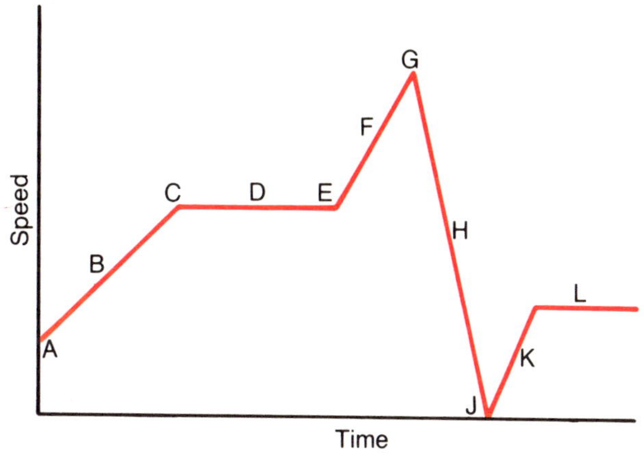

Questions 15 to 19

A cyclist and a runner had a race. The graph shows their movement during the race.

15 What distance did they race?

16 How long did the cyclist take for the race?

17 When is the runner running fastest?

18 What is the average speed of the runner during the race?

19 Who accelerates more quickly at the start of the race?

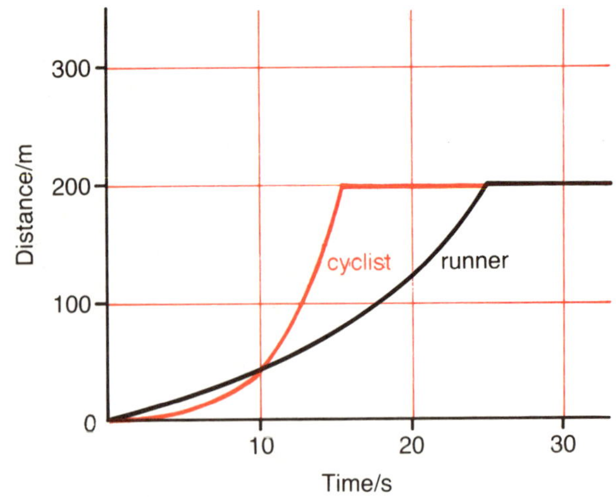

Questions 20 to 21

An astronaut has a mass on Earth of 90 kg and a weight of 900 N. He then travels to the moon where the gravitational field strength is only 1.5 N/kg.

20 What is his mass on the moon?

21 What is his weight on the moon?

Questions 22 to 25

A stone dropped from a helicoptor takes 10 seconds to hit the sea below.

22 What is the acceleration of the stone in m/s^2?

23 What is the final speed of the stone as it hits the sea?

24 What is the average speed of the stone during the fall?

25 What is the height of the helicoptor above the sea?

26 Which of the following are vector quantities?
force, mass, length, temperature, speed, velocity

27 What is a speed of 144 km/h in m/s?

28 A stone of mass 1 kg falls 180 metres in 6 seconds from a hot air balloon. How far will a 2 kg stone fall in 6 seconds? (Ignore air resistance.)

29 Which *one* of the following would help a car to stop more quickly in an emergency?
A extra luggage
B slower speed
C smooth road surface
D well-worn tyres
E wet road surface

30 The density of air is about 1 kg/m^3. What is the approximate mass of air in a telephone kiosk?
A 20 kg B 2 kg C 0.2 kg D 0.002 kg

31 A cube of steel with sides 2 m is resting on flat concrete. The cube has a mass of 6.4×10^4 kg. What is the pressure on the concrete?
A 1.6×10^4 N/m^2
B 8×10^4 N/m^2
C 16×10^4 N/m^2
D 256 N/m^2

32 Which distance should be measured in the diagram in order to obtain atmospheric pressure?
A W – Y
B W – Z
C X – Y
D X – Z

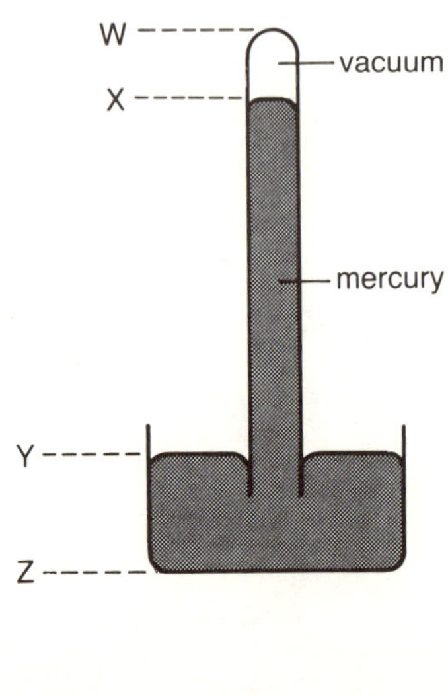

33 A gas exerts a pressure because the gas particles
A pass energy to the container.
B want to get out of the container.
C try to push each other out of the container.
D exert a force when they hit the walls.

34 A large metal container leaning against a wall is filled with water. The container has holes at A, B, C and D.
From which hole does the water squirt fastest?

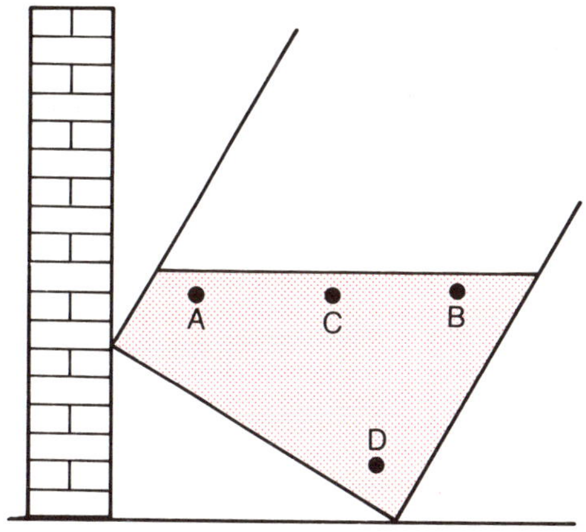

35 Mercury is the most convenient *liquid* for use in a barometer because
A it has a high density
B it is a metal.
C it has a silvery colour.
D it expands on heating.

36 If the pressure is reduced in all the tyres of a car
A the pressure exerted by the tyres on the ground is larger.
B the force exerted by the tyres on the ground is larger.
C the area of contact between the tyres and the ground is larger.
D the weight of the tyres and car on the ground is larger.

24 ENERGY TRANSFERS

24.1 Doing work and using energy

Clare is a fitness freak. She uses weight training to tone up her muscles and keep fit. Everytime Clare lifts the weights, she is doing **work**. The amount of work that Clare does depends on:

- how far she lifts the weights,
- how heavy the weights are.

Remember that weight is a force (related to mass and gravity – refer back to section 23.9).

Work is defined by the following formula:

Work = Force × Distance

In fact, **work is done whenever a force causes something to move**. We do work when we throw a stone, push a trolley or lift a bag. Vehicles do work when they climb hills, overcoming the force of gravity. When a vehicle travels along a flat road, it does work overcoming the force of friction.

Work is measured in **joules** (J). One joule of work is done when a force of one newton moves something through a distance of one metre.

Work in joules	=	Force in newtons	×	Distance in metres
1 J	=	**1 N**	×	**1 m**

Example

How much work does Clare do if she lifts two masses of 0.5 kg through 50 cm (Fig. 24.1)?

mass lifted = 2 × 0.5 kg = 1 kg

therefore weight lifted = 10 N (refer back to section 23.9)

distance lifted = 50 cm = 0.5 m

work done = force × distance
= 10 N × 0.5 m
= 5 J

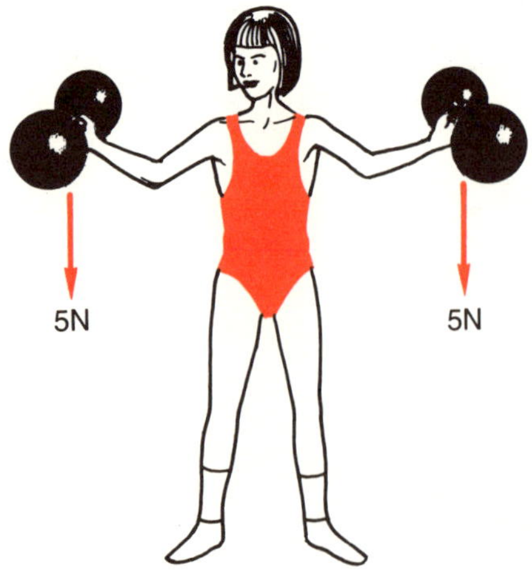

Fig. 24.1 When Clare lifts the weights she is doing work. If she holds them still, her arms get tired because her muscles use energy to hold weights up – but she is *not* doing any work because the weights are not moving.

Energetic people like Clare can usually do lots of work. We might say that Clare has 'plenty of energy'. Scientists use the word *energy* in the same way. When we do work, we use energy. When a machine does work, it uses energy.

Energy helps us to get jobs done
– it enables us, and the machines we use, to do work.

Energy can be measured in terms of the amount of work done. Therefore, the units of energy, like those of work, are **joules**.

24.2 Forms of energy

There are several forms of energy. Some of these are summarized in Table 24.1.

Table 24.1 Different forms of energy

Form of energy	*What form does the energy take?*	*Examples*
potential energy	Anything placed in a higher position has potential energy – its extra height gives it the *potential* to do work when it falls. Pot. energy = weight × height lifted (J) (N) (m)	Weight lifted above the floor; someone who has climbed some stairs; water stored in a high-level reservoir.
strain energy	Material that has been stretched and is under *strain* is storing energy, which can be released if the strain is relieved.	A stretched bow ready to shoot an arrow; a tuned (tightened) violin string; a wound-up watch spring; a stretched rubber band.
kinetic energy	*Moving* objects can do work if they hit something. The energy which they possess is called kinetic energy. Kin. energy = $\frac{1}{2}$ × mass × (velocity)^2 (J) (kg) (m/s)	Any moving object e.g. a falling stone, falling water, a moving car, you running.
heat (thermal energy)	Molecules in any material move faster when heated. The hot, fast moving molecules possess kinetic energy which can be used to do work.	Hot materials e.g. (hot water, steam, red hot charcoal)
electrical energy (electricity)	An electric current is a flow of electrons. The moving electrons can do work.	Electric currents.
chemical energy	Chemical energy is locked in the bonds between atoms. When the fuels and foods react with oxygen, this stored energy can be converted into heat or into kinetic energy.	The chemicals in fuels and in foods.
nuclear energy	Energy is stored in the nuclei of all atoms. This energy is released, mainly as heat and light, when a nuclear reaction occurs, e.g. in a power station or in a nuclear explosion.	All atoms contain nuclear energy. The nuclear energy in radioactive atoms is so great that they break up.
wave energy (see chapter 25)	Waves carry energy. This can be made to do work, e.g. wave energy from the sun causes photosynthesis.	Light waves, radio waves and sound waves

When we do work, or when a machine does work, energy is used. However, the energy is *not used up*; it is *not lost*. Instead, the energy is converted from one form to another. Some important examples of **energy conversion** are shown in Fig. 24.2.

(a) Generating hydroelectricity

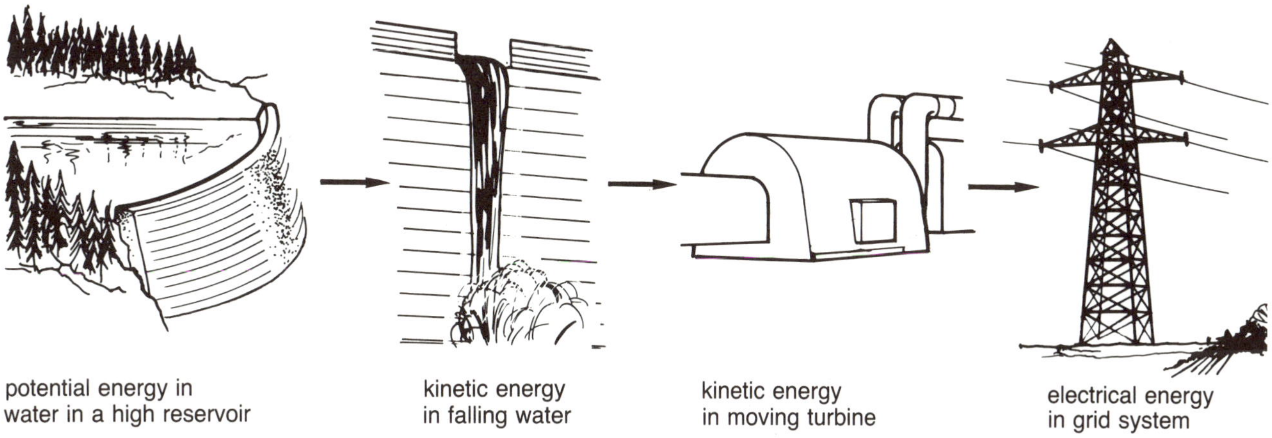

Figure 24.2a

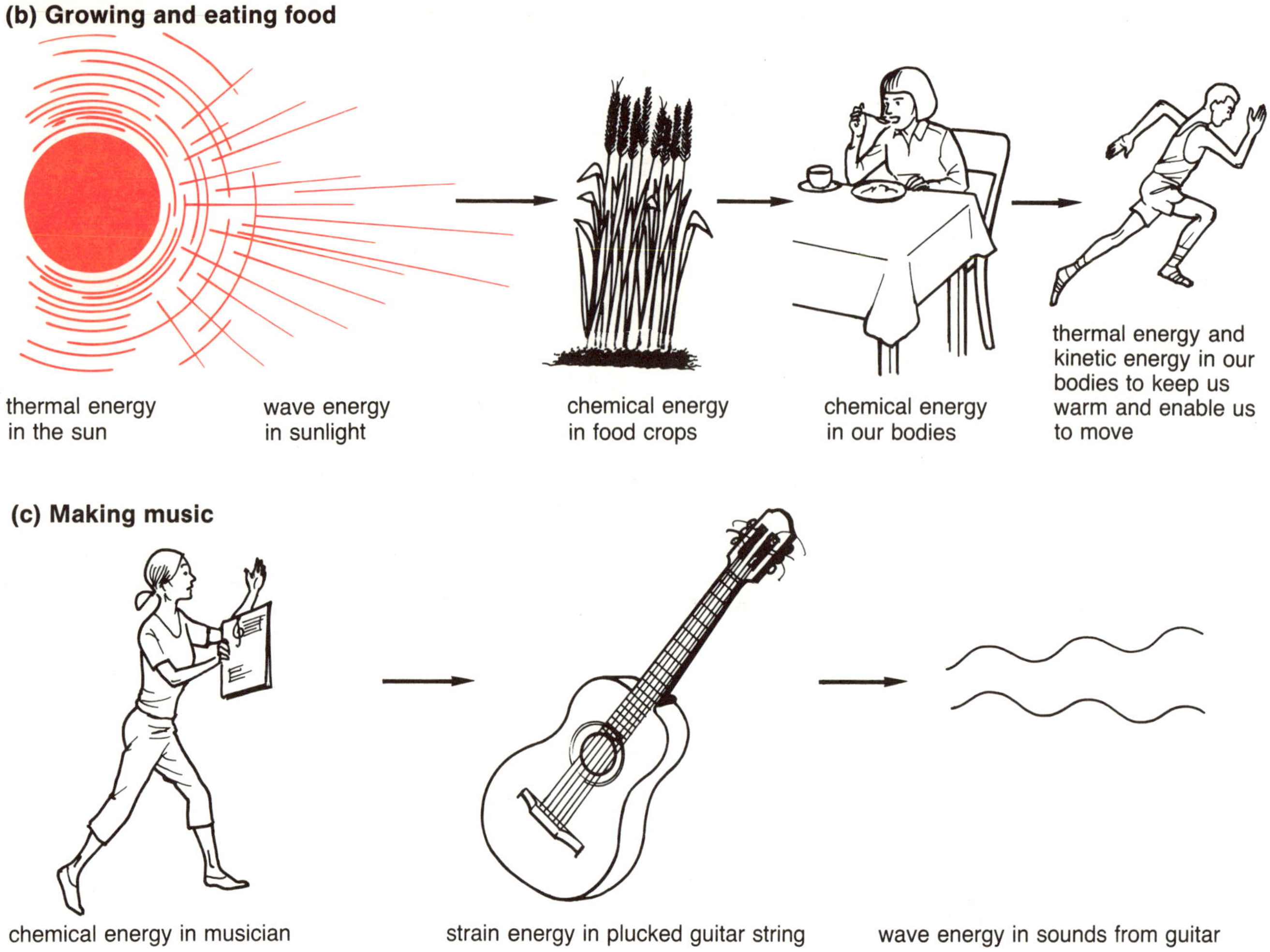

Fig. 24.2 Some important energy conversions

Notice that energy is being converted from one form to another in all the events shown in Fig. 24.2. For example, the chemical energy of food in the musician is converted into strain energy in the stretched guitar string. This strain energy is then converted into wave energy in sounds when the guitar string is released.

Notice also that energy is *not* lost when these energy conversions occur. It is simply converted from one form of energy into another form. This important point is summarized in **the law of conservation of energy**. This states:

**Energy cannot be made or lost,
it can only be changed from one form into another.**

24.3 Efficiency of energy conversions

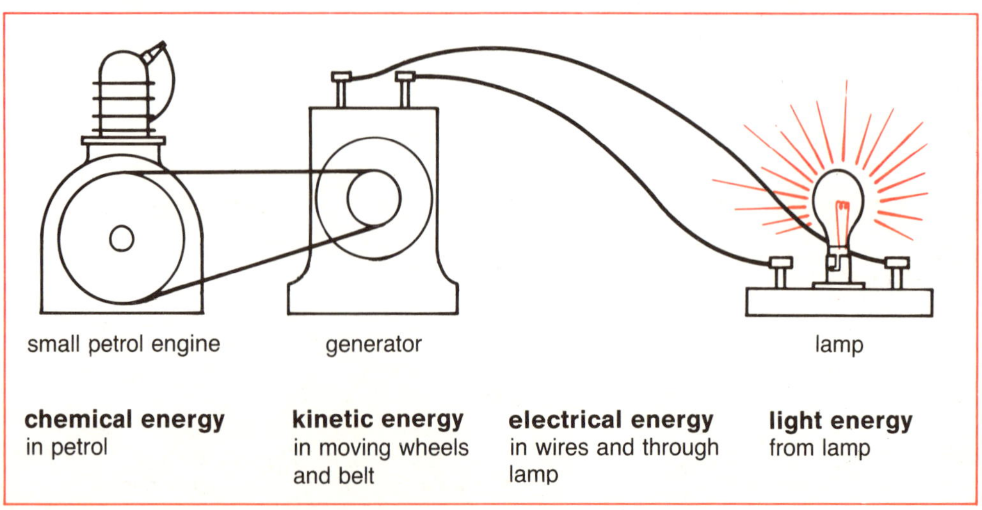

Fig. 24.3 A small petrol engine generating electricity to light a lamp

When a musician plucks a guitar, only about 25 per cent of the musician's chemical energy is being converted into strain energy in the guitar strings. The rest of the energy is converted into heat to keep the musician warm and into heat from friction between his fingers and the guitar strings. None of the chemical energy in the musician is lost, but only 25 per cent is converted into strain energy in the strings (which will go on to produce music). This means that the **efficiency** of converting the musician's chemical energy into strain energy in the strings is only 25 per cent.

Look at Fig. 24.3. This shows the energy conversions which occur when a small petrol engine is used to drive a generator which produces electricity to light a lamp. At each stage in Fig. 24.3, some energy is wasted as heat. The petrol engine, the generator and the lamp all get warm. We can show these energy changes in a flow diagram such as Fig. 24.4. Notice that energy is never completely used. Some energy is transferred usefully from one stage to the next. The rest of the energy is wasted, often as heat. Both the useful and the wasted energy should be shown at each stage in the energy flow chart.

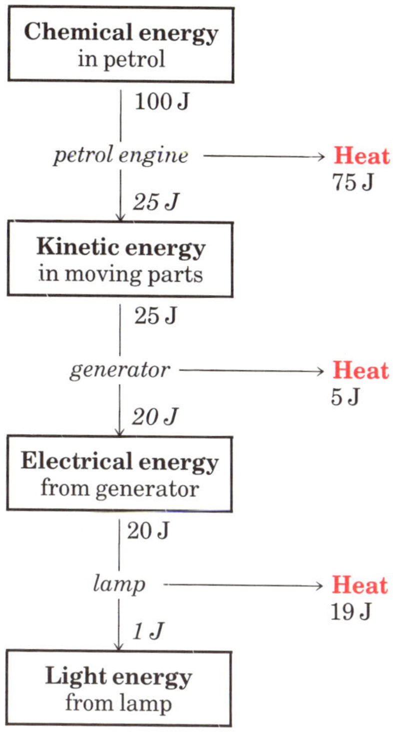

Fig. 24.4 A flow diagram showing the energy changes which occur when a petrol engine and generator are used to light a lamp

From the energy changes shown in Fig. 24.4, we can calculate the efficiency of each machine:

$$\textbf{Efficiency} = \frac{\textbf{useful energy (or work) out of machine}}{\textbf{energy (or work) put into machine}} \times \textbf{100 per cent}$$

Example

What is the efficiency of the generator in Fig. 24.4?

useful energy out of generator = 20 J

energy put into generator = 25 J

therefore efficiency $= \frac{\text{useful energy output}}{\text{energy input}} = \frac{20}{25} \times 100 = 80\%$

Use the data in Fig. 24.4 to calculate the efficiency of the lamp.

Human efficiency

Figure 24.1 showed Clare lifting weights. While she does this her body uses 20 000 J every minute. In one minute, Clare raises two 10 N weights through 0.5 metres sixty times. What is Clare's efficiency?

Energy output in lifting
two 10 N weights through 0.5 m = force × distance
$= 2 \times 10\text{ N} \times 0.5\text{ m}$
$= 10\text{ J}$

energy output in 1 minute $= 10\text{ J} \times 60$
$= 600\text{ J}$

so Clare's efficiency $= \frac{\text{useful energy output}}{\text{energy input}} \times 100$

$= \frac{600}{20\,000} \times 100$

$= 3\%$

24.4 Power

Engineers and athletes often talk about power. Engineers are concerned about the power of machines. Athletes are interested in the power they can develop in running, jumping and throwing.

We can understand the power of a machine by considering a crane lifting cargo onto a ship. Suppose the crane is lifting a weight of 50 000 N through a height of 10 m onto a ship (as in Fig. 24.5).

Figure 24.5

We can easily calculate the work done by the crane in lifting the cargo:

Work done by crane = force × distance
$= 50\,000 \text{ N} \times 10 \text{ m}$
$= 500\,000 \text{ J} = 5 \times 10^5 \text{ J}$

It is all very well to know this, but the crane would be useless if it took several hours to lift the load onto the ship. In order to appreciate the usefulness of the crane, we need to know how quickly it can do the work of lifting the cargo. Suppose the crane lifts the cargo in five seconds:

$$\text{Work done by crane per second} = \frac{5 \times 10^5 \text{ J}}{5 \text{ s}} = 10^5 \text{ J/s}$$

The *work done* by the crane *per second* is known as its **power**. Power is the *rate* of working. It can be calculated using the following formula:

$$\textbf{power} = \frac{\textbf{work done}}{\textbf{time taken}} = \frac{\textbf{energy output}}{\textbf{time taken}}$$

Power can be expressed in *joules per second* (as in the crane example above), but we usually use the word **watt** (W) in place of joules per second. The name 'watt' is used to honour the Scottish scientist, James Watt (1736–1819). Watt was the first person to investigate the power of machines. One watt is a rate of working of one joule per second.

Human power

Linford measured his power output by running up a flight of stairs. The flight of stairs was 12 m high and he ran up in 4.2 seconds. Linford's mass is 56 kg; therefore his weight is 560 N.

work done = force × distance
$= 560 \text{ N} \times 12 \text{ m} = 6720 \text{ J}$

$$\text{power} = \frac{\text{work done}}{\text{time taken}}$$

$$= \frac{6720 \text{ J}}{4.2 \text{ s}} = 1600 \text{ W}$$

We can say that Linford's working rate is 1600 watts. In other words, he can convert chemical energy into potential energy at the rate of 1600 watts.

24.5 Energy transfers in a power station

Figure 24.6 shows the important energy transfers which take place during the production of electricity in a power station. Most of our power stations use coal as their source of energy. Other stations use oil or uranium.

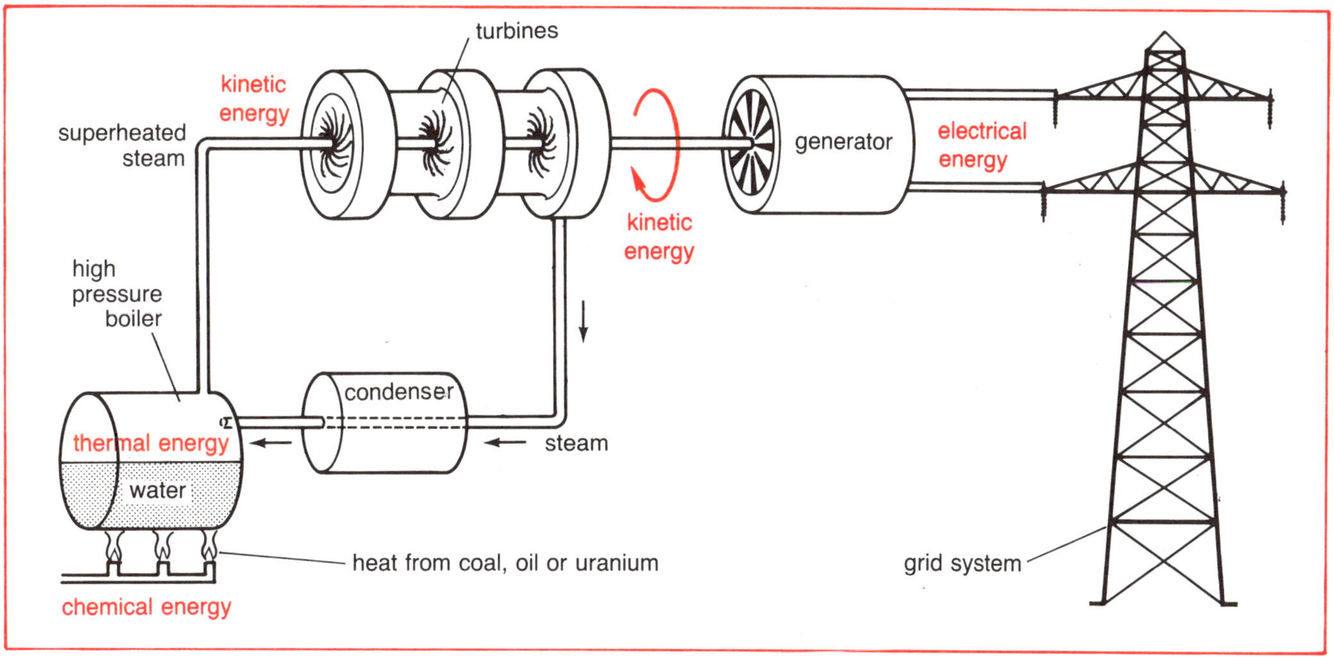

Fig. 24.6 The production of electrical energy in a power station

The main transfers of useful energy in the power station are:

- chemical energy in coal or oil or nuclear energy in uranium → thermal energy in water/steam and kinetic energy in steam
- kinetic energy in superheated steam → kinetic energy in rotating turbines
- kinetic energy in rotating turbines → kinetic energy of rotating coils in generator
- kinetic energy of rotating coils in generator → electrical energy in grid system

24.6 How do we use our sources of energy?

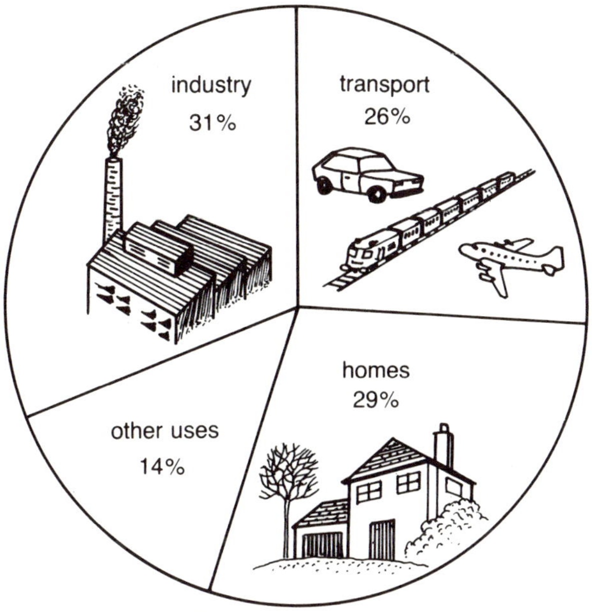

Fig. 24.7 How we use our sources of energy

Figure 24.7 shows how Britain uses its energy supplies. Notice the following points:

- The main users of energy are industry, transport and homes.
- Industry uses most of the country's energy production. This energy is used to convert raw materials like coal and crude oil into useful commodities like plastics and electricity.
- Within industry, the main user of energy is the energy industry itself. Refining oil, mining coal and generating electricity need large amounts of energy.
- Most of the fuel consumed in Britain is used to generate electricity. Unfortunately, power stations are only about 30 per cent efficient. The other 70 per cent of the energy in the fuel is wasted as heat when the fuel burns, as heat in the cooling towers and turbines or as heat due to friction in the generators.

CONSERVING OUR SOURCES OF ENERGY

In sections 20.5 and 20.6, we considered the importance of conserving fossil fuels and the search for alternative energy sources. The information in Fig. 24.7 can lead to further suggestions for conserving energy:

- **Saving energy in industry** by improving the efficiency of industrial processes. For example, it should be possible to improve the efficiency of power stations by reducing the energy wasted as heat and by using the thermal energy which would otherwise be wasted to heat homes, offices and factories.
- **Saving energy in the home** by reducing our energy demands. This could be achieved in almost every home by better insulation (see section 24.13).

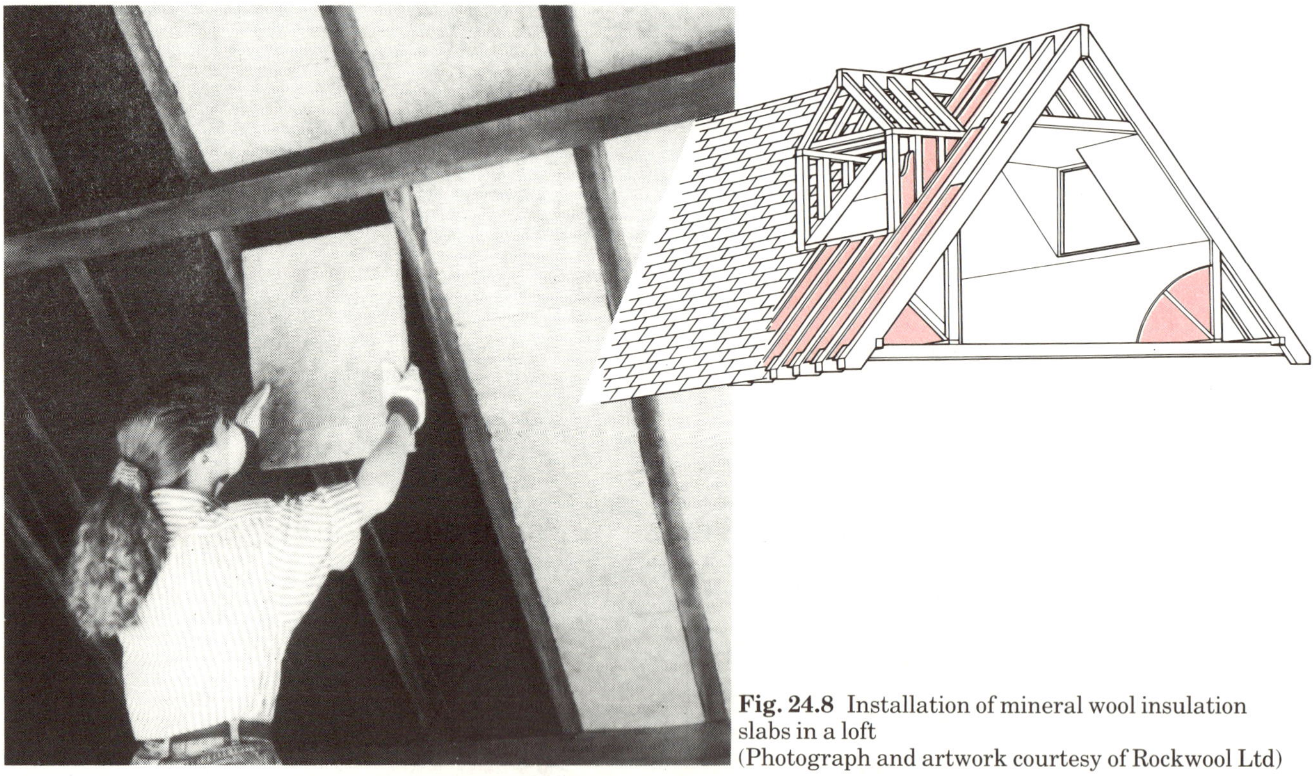

Fig. 24.8 Installation of mineral wool insulation slabs in a loft
(Photograph and artwork courtesy of Rockwool Ltd)

- **Saving energy in transport** by using fuel as economically as possible. This might involve using different methods of transport, e.g. travelling by train or coach rather than as the only passenger in a car or sharing car journeys. We should also drive cars at a steady speed so that fuel is used most economically. Car manufacturers are also designing cars with lower petrol consumption.

24.7 Heat as a form of energy

Heat is a form of energy. When materials are heated, they gain energy and their particles move faster (refer back to section 15.3). Thus heat (thermal energy) shows itself in the movement of particles.

It is important not to confuse 'heat' and 'temperature'.

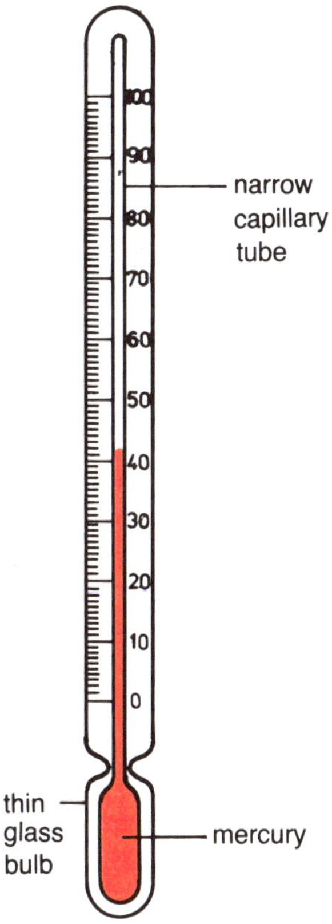

Fig. 24.9 A mercury thermometer for measuring temperatures between 0 and 100°C. What temperature does the thermometer show?

- **'Heat' tells us how much thermal energy a material has.** Heat is measured in **joules (J)**.
- **'Temperature' tells us how hot something is.** Temperature is measured in **degrees Celsius (°C)** or **Kelvins (K)**.

THERMOMETERS

Temperature is measured using a **thermometer**. The most common type is the mercury thermometer (Fig. 24.9). When the temperature rises, mercury in the bulb expands and moves further up the narrow capillary tube.

Most thermometers have a scale marked in degrees Celsius (°C). This is known as the **Celsius scale** after the Swedish scientist who suggested it. The temperature in degrees Celsius is sometimes referred to as *degrees centigrade* because the Celsius scale has one hundred divisions between 0°C (the temperature at which water freezes) and 100°C (the temperature at which water boils).

24.8 Expansion and contraction

When a substance is heated, its particles move more quickly and collide with more force. The particles push each other further apart and the substance expands.

When a substance cools, its particles move more slowly. They also collide less frequently and with less force. So the particles move closer together and the material contracts.

In theory, contraction can continue until the molecules stop moving. Scientists believe that the particles of all substances stop moving at the same temperature. They call this temperature **absolute zero**. On the Celsius scale, absolute zero is −273°C. On the Kelvin scale, absolute zero is 0 K.

Figure 24.10 compares the Celsius and Kelvin temperature scales. Notice how easy it is to convert from degrees Celsius to Kelvin. You simply add on 273. For example:

°C	**+ 273 =**	**K**
−273	+ 273 =	0
0	+ 273 =	273
37	+ 273 =	310

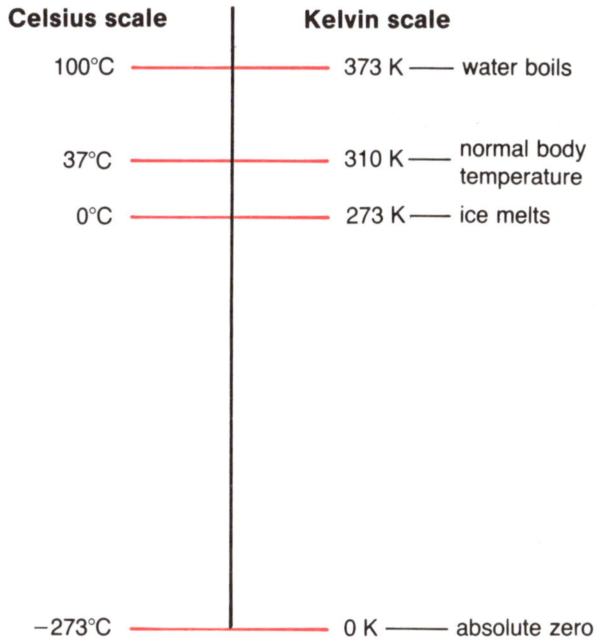

Fig. 24.10 Comparing temperatures in °C and K

USING EXPANSION AND CONTRACTION

Expansion and contraction are put to good use in thermometers.

They are also important in the workings of fire alarms and thermostats. If two thin strips of different metals such as steel and brass are riveted together, they form a **bimetallic strip** (see Fig. 24.11). When the strip is heated, both metals expand. However, brass expands more than steel, so the strip will bend with the brass on the outside.

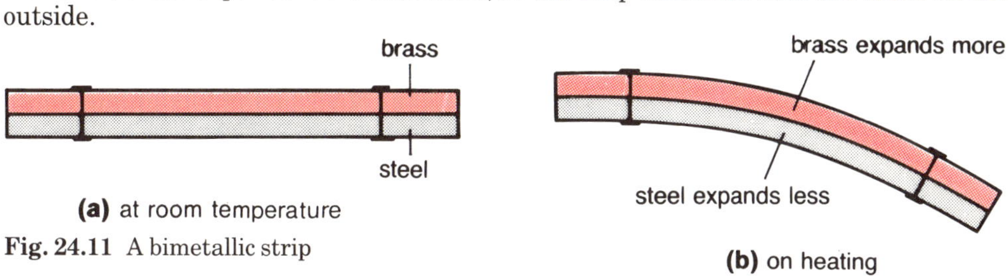

Fig. 24.11 A bimetallic strip

Bimetallic strips are used in fire alarms (see Fig. 24.12). On heating, the brass expands more than the steel, so the strip bends upwards. At a certain temperature the strip bends so much that the circuit is completed and the alarm bell rings.

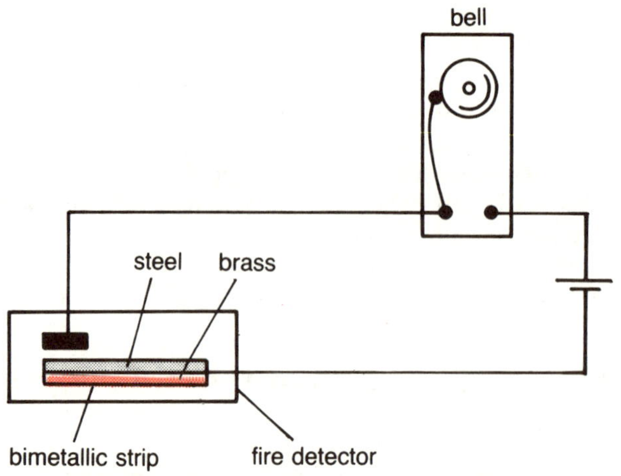

Fig. 24.12 A bimetallic strip used in a fire alarm

Bimetallic strips can also be used to control the temperature of irons, ovens and immersion heaters. The bimetallic strip forms part of a **thermostat** (Fig. 24.13). When the appliance is cold, the contacts are together and the current flows to the heating element. As the appliance gets hot, the bimetallic strip bends down and breaks the contacts. If the control knob is screwed further down, the strip must bend further before the contacts separate. So, by screwing the knob further down, the appliance will work at a higher temperature.

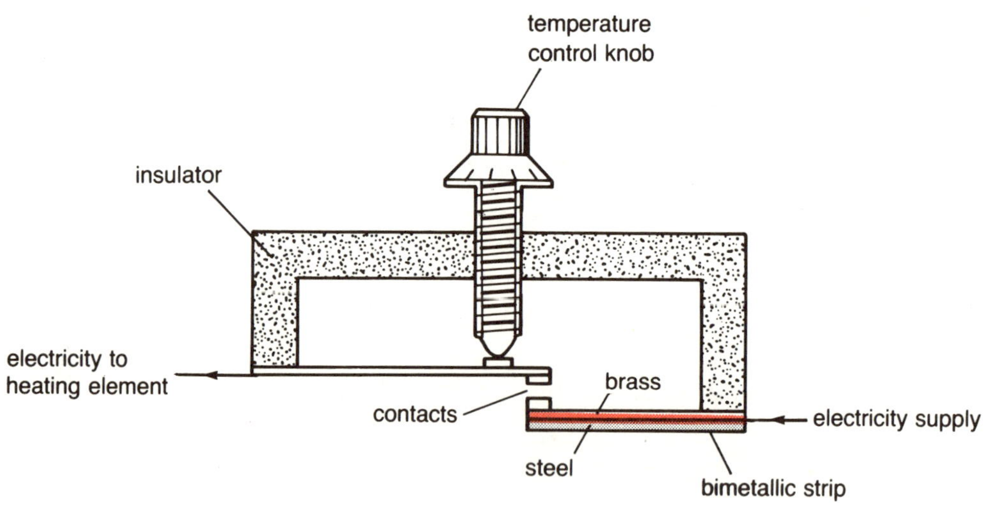

Fig. 24.13 A simple thermostat for an iron, an oven or an immersion heater

PROBLEMS OF EXPANSION AND CONTRACTION

At one time, railway lines were laid with a small gap between each rail. This allowed for expansion in hot weather, so that the rails would not buckle. Nowadays, most rails are welded together to give continuous lengths of track of a kilometre or more. The advantage of this is that the passengers have a smoother journey and the wheels and track suffer less wear. However, to avoid problems with expansion, the rails must be fastened to heavy concrete sleepers or joined on an angle with gaps over about a metre.

In order to compare the expansion of different materials, scientists calculate their **linear expansivity**. This gives the *increase in length (in metres) when one metre of the material is heated by one degree Celsius*. The linear expansivity values of some common materials are given in Table 24.2.

Notice that steel and concrete have the same linear expansivity. This makes steel ideal for reinforcing concrete because the two materials expand and contract by the same amount when the temperature changes.

Table 24.2 The linear expansivity of some materials

Material	**Linear expansivity** (increase in length of 1 m in m/°C)
brass	0.000019
copper	0.000017
iron	0.000012
steel	0.000011
concrete	0.000011
glass (ordinary)	0.000009
glass (Pyrex)	0.000003

However, concrete road surfaces cannot be laid in long stretches because they would soon crack if the temperature changed by several degrees. To avoid this, the concrete is laid in short sections separated by strips of bitumen (tar). On hot days the bitumen softens easily and is squeezed out by the expansion of the concrete. Steel bridges must also be designed so that there is room for expansion and contraction as the temperature changes.

Also notice in Table 24.2 that the linear expansivity of pyrex glass is only one third that of ordinary glass. This makes it much better than ordinary glass for kitchen and laboratory use. Unlike ordinary glass, Pyrex glass does not crack in very hot water and can withstand oven temperatures.

24.9 Changes of state

Changes of state, such as melting and evaporating, were discussed in section 15.4. We will now look at these further.

Figure 24.14 shows the temperature changes and the changes in state which occur when ice is heated from −10°C.

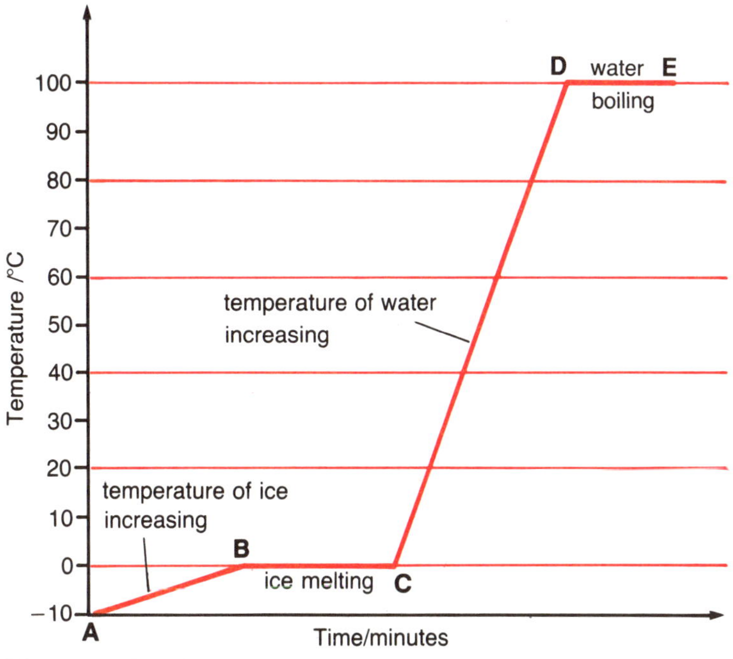

Fig. 24.14 The changes in temperature and the changes of state which occur when ice is heated

Look carefully at the captions to the different sections of the graph (Fig. 24.14). Notice that along the section BC, the ice is melting. The temperature stays at 0°C even though the ice is still being heated. This shows that *heat is needed to melt (fuse) a solid and form a liquid*. This heat is called the **latent heat of fusion**. 'Latent' means hidden. This word is used because the heat required for fusion is hidden – it cannot be detected as a temperature change.

When all the ice has melted to water, the temperature rises again along CD. When the water reaches 100°C, it starts to boil and the temperature stays constant again (DE). This shows that *heat is needed to change a liquid to a gas or vapour*. This heat is called the **latent heat of vaporization**.

SALT AND ANTIFREEZE

When an impurity is added to a liquid, particles in the liquid cannot pack in a regular fashion and crystallize easily. Particles of impurity get in the way of liquid particles and hinder the liquid crystallizing as a solid.

This is why roads are treated with rock salt in icy weather and why antifreeze is added to car radiators. The salt and antifreeze act as impurities and hinder the formation of ice. Because of this, ice does not form until the temperature falls well below 0°C, the normal freezing point.

PRESSURE COOKERS

When a liquid boils, the particles must be given enough energy to overcome the forces holding them together (i.e. they must be given enough energy to escape as a gas). The energy to overcome these forces is provided by the latent heat of vaporization. If the pressure above a liquid is increased, the particles cannot escape from the liquid as easily – the boiling point rises.

Fig. 24.15 A pressure cooker

Pressure cookers are large, heavy saucepans with a tightly-fitting lid and a weight that can increase the pressure in the pan (Fig. 24.15). During cooking, water evaporates into the space above the food and the pressure inside the pan increases. As the pressure in the pan increases, the water is prevented from boiling. The closely-fitting weight allows the pressure to rise to as much as two atmospheres (i.e. twice the surrounding air pressure) before any vapour can escape. At this pressure, the boiling point of water is raised to about 120°C, so the food is cooked much more quickly.

24.10 Heat transfer

There are three ways in which heat is transferred from one place to another – **conduction**, **convection** and **radiation**.

If you walk around in bare feet, you will notice that your feet feel much colder walking on tiles than on carpet. Your feet feel cold because they are losing heat. The transfer of heat from your feet to the tiles is an example of **conduction**.

> **Conduction is the transfer of heat through a material from places of higher temperature to places of lower temperature without the material moving as a whole.**

A second way in which heat can travel from one place to another is illustrated by electric heaters and radiators (see Fig. 24.16). Air near the heater is warm. This causes it to expand, become less dense and rise. As the air rises, cooler air falls and moves in to replace it. This flow of air is an example of **convection**.

> **Convection is the transfer of heat by movement of a liquid or gas due to differences in density.**

Sunbathing and photosynthesis rely on probably the most important method of heat transfer. Sunbathing and photosynthesis both require energy from the sun. This energy has travelled millions of miles from the sun to the Earth as electromagnetic waves (see section 25.5). This is an example of **radiation**.

> **Radiation is the transfer of energy (heat) from one place to another by means of electromagnetic waves.**

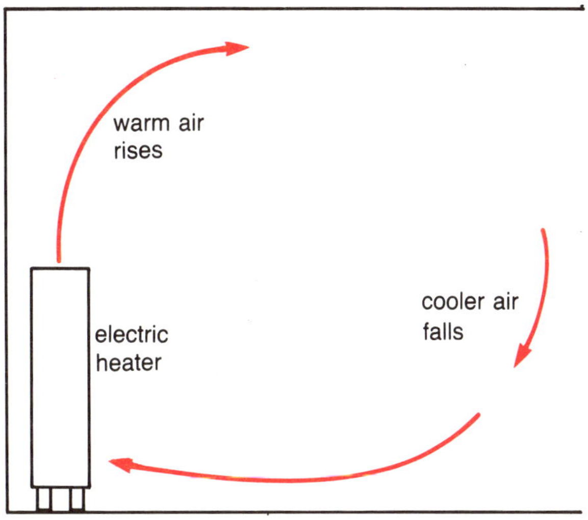

Fig. 24.16 Convection currents of air caused by an electric heater

Fig. 24.17 Sunbathers enjoy heat from the sun's rays which have travelled millions of miles as electromagnetic waves. This is an example of radiation.
(Photograph courtesy of Thomson Holidays)

24.11 Preventing heat transfer

The **conductivity** of a material is a measure of how well it transfers energy by conduction (the first of the three methods of heat transfer in section 24.10). Look closely at Table 24.3 which shows the relative **conductivities** of some different materials.

Table 24.3 The relative conductivities of some common materials

Material	*Relative conductivity*	
copper	16 000	good conductors
aluminium	8 800	↓
steel	3 100	
concrete	175	
glass	35	
water	25	
brick	23	
breeze block	9	
wood	6	
felt	1.7	
fat	1.5	
wool	1.2	poor
air	1.0	conductors

Notice the following points from Table 24.3:

- Metals are much better **conductors** than any other materials. Because of this they are used for kettles, saucepans and radiators.
- Poor conductors, such as air, wool, felt and wood, are used to *prevent heat transfer*. These materials are called **insulators**.
- Air is the worst conductor of the materials in Table 24.3. It is an excellent insulator. Materials which trap air, e.g. hair, feathers, fibreglass and wool, are also used as insulators. They are used in winter clothing, cavity wall insulation, roof insulation and in lagging for refrigerators, ovens and pipes.

KEEPING OURSELVES WARM

Fat, wool and air are the best insulators in Table 24.3. They play an important part in keeping warm-blooded animals, including ourselves, alive during the cold winter months. For example:

- Seals have a thick layer of fat (blubber) surrounding all their body. We have only a thin layer of fat. Seals can live all winter in icy Artic waters where we would not survive for more than a few minutes.

- Birds have feathers; other animals have thick fur. Fur and feathers are poor conductors. They reduce heat transfer by trapping a layer of air. In cold weather birds fluff out their feathers to trap more air. (It is also why the fine hairs on your arms 'stand up' when you are cold.)

- On cold days, we wear layers of clothing made from fabrics such as wool. These fabrics trap air which acts as an insulator to keep us warm.

KEEPING OUR HOMES WARM

If we did not wear clothes, we would lose lots of heat by convection (see Fig. 24.18). By wearing clothes, we trap a layer of air around our bodies. This prevents convection currents and the trapped air also acts as an insulator.

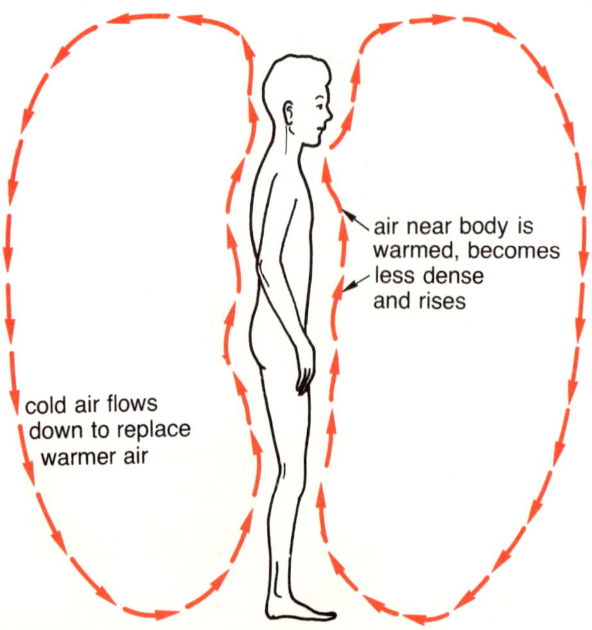

Fig. 24.18 Convection currents around a naked person

The same idea is used in several methods which we use to keep our houses warm (see Fig. 24.19). For example:

- **draught excluders** stuck around doors and windows prevent convection currents and loss of warm air to the outside.
- **cavity wall insulation** – mineral wool or polystyrene in the cavity gap traps air and prevents circulation of convection currents. The air acts as an insulator.
- **double glazing** – the layer of air between the glass sheets acts as an insulator. The layer must be thin to prevent convection currents.
- **loft insulation** – mineral wool or vermiculite traps air which acts as an insulator.

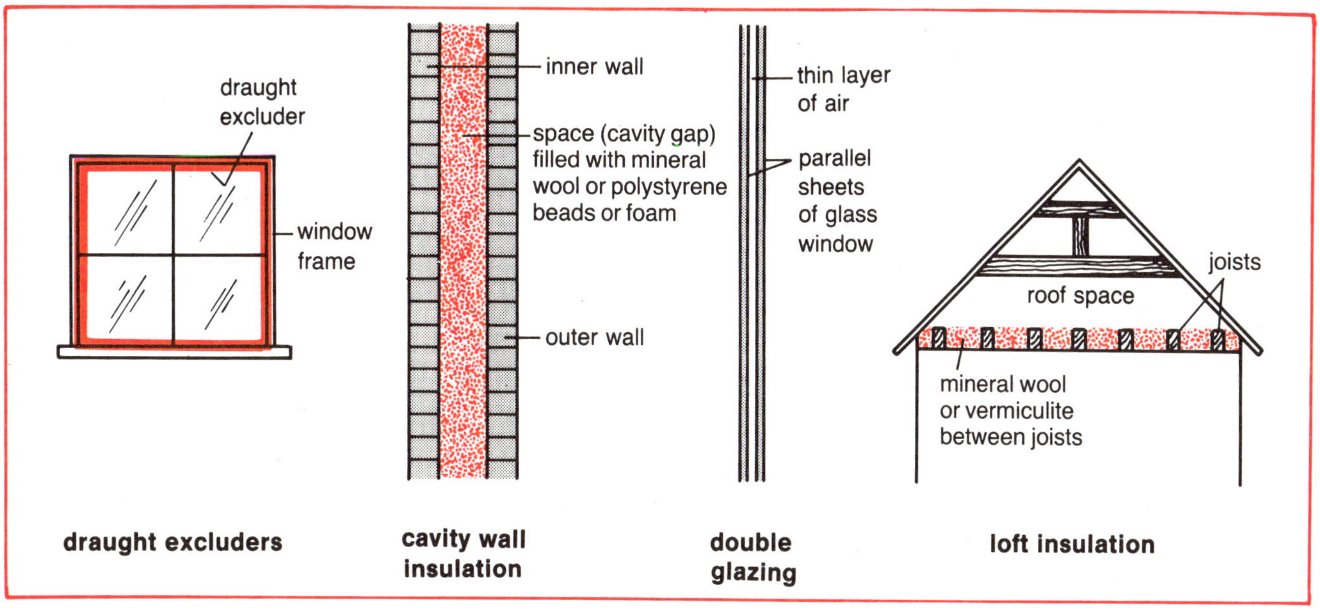

Fig. 24.19 Ways in which we prevent heat loss from our homes

Quick test 24

Questions 1 to 3

A small electric motor is used to lift a load. A meter is used to measure the amount of energy supplied to the motor. The motor is switched on for 10 seconds and the meter shows that 1000 joules of energy have been supplied. During this time the motor does 600 joules of work lifting the load.

1 How fast is energy being supplied to the motor? (2 marks)
2 Work out the power output of the motor. (1 mark)
3 How many joules of energy does the motor waste each second? (1 mark)

(*NEA* (modified), 1988)

Questions 4 to 7

The diagram below shows how energy from fuel is used in power stations.

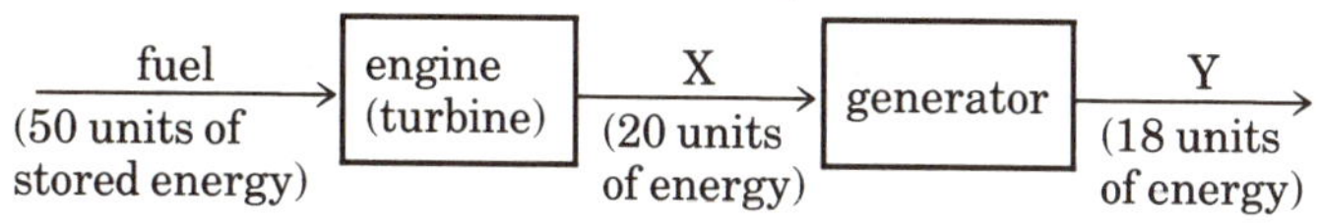

4 Name the forms of energy labelled X and Y in the diagram. (2 marks)
5 How many units of energy are 'lost' from the engine? (1 mark)
6 What has happened to this 'lost' energy? (2 marks)
7 An engineer showing you around the power station tells you that the generator is more efficient than the engine. What does he mean by this statement? (1 mark)

(*NEA*, 1988)

Questions 8 to 12

The graph below shows how the boiling point of water changes with atmospheric pressure.
Use the graph to help you answer the following questions.

8 What is the boiling point of water when the pressure is 76 cm of mercury? (1 mark)
9 What is the boiling point of water when the pressure is 103 cm of mercury? (1 mark)

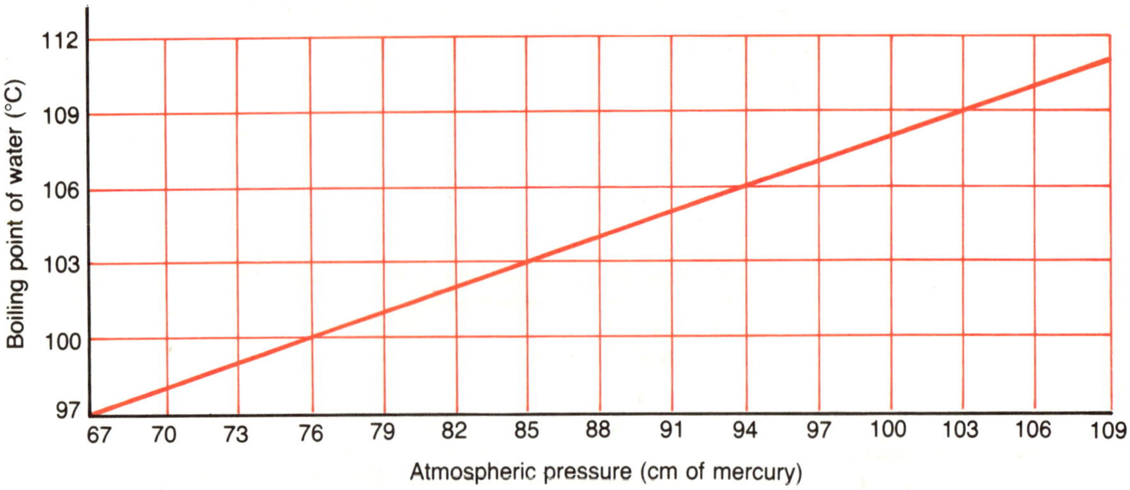

10 Use the information in the graph to explain why food is cooked more quickly in a pressure cooker like the one shown. (3 marks)

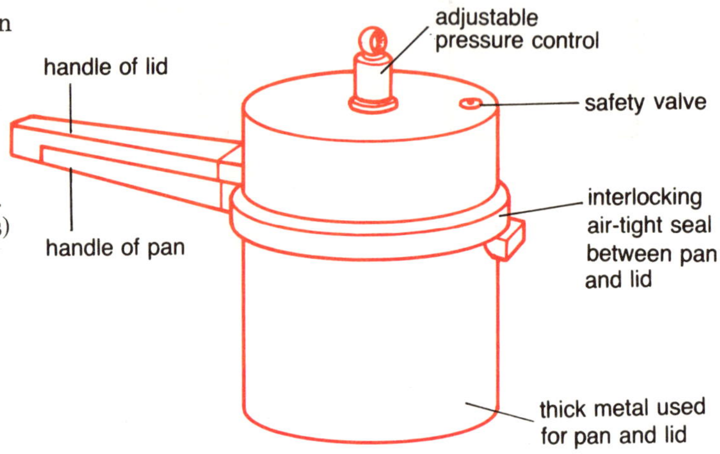

11 Explain the purpose of the safety valve. (2 marks)
12 Explain why thick metal is used for the pan and lid. (1 mark)
(*NISEC*, 1988)

Questions 13 to 14

A girl uses a force of 80 N to push a lawnmower 20 metres across a garden in 5 seconds.

13 How much work does the girl do?
14 How much power does she develop?

Questions 15 to 20

The figure shows a thermostat from an electric iron. End A of the bimetallic strip moves to the right as it cools. Screw B is for adjusting the setting of the thermostat.

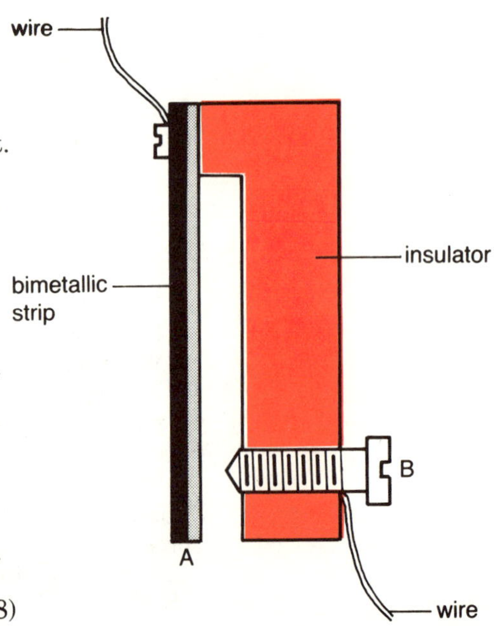

15 What is the purpose of a thermostat like the one shown above? (2 marks)
16 Name a suitable material to be used as the insulator. (1 mark)
17 Explain in detail how the thermostat works. (4 marks)
18 What is the effect on the thermostat of moving screw B slightly to the left (screwing it in)? (2 marks)
19 Explain the effect on running costs of moving screw B to the left. (2 marks)
20 Explain why this thermostat would be unsuitable for use in a refrigerator. (1 mark)
(*LEAG*, 1988)

25 ENERGY AND WAVES

25.1 Introduction

Figure 25.1

Waves play an important part in our lives. They affect our leisure activities, our work and our home life. For example:
– waves on the sea help us to enjoy swimming, surfing and sailing;
– radiowaves enable us to transmit information and messages from one place to another;
– microwaves provide energy for cooking;
– X-rays and gamma rays have important medical uses.
These examples illustrate two important properties of waves:

- **Waves carry energy.**
- **Waves carry information.**

At the present time, various experiments are being carried out to see if the energy of water waves can be converted into useful energy. One experiment involves floating rafts which move up and down with the waves. The movement of the rafts is made to drive a generator and produce electricity.

The most important applications involving waves carrying information are radar, radio and television broadcasts and, of course, the light and sound that carry messages to our eyes and ears.

25.2 Describing waves

Have you ever tried to rescue a ball or a boat from a still pond by making waves? This method is never very successful. The waves move across the surface of the pond, but the water only moves up and down. This means that articles floating on the pond do not move across it with the waves. They only bob up and down.

As the water moves up and down, the wave carries energy from one place to another without the water being carried along. This illustrates another important characteristic of waves:

- **Waves carry energy from one point to another without transferring matter.**

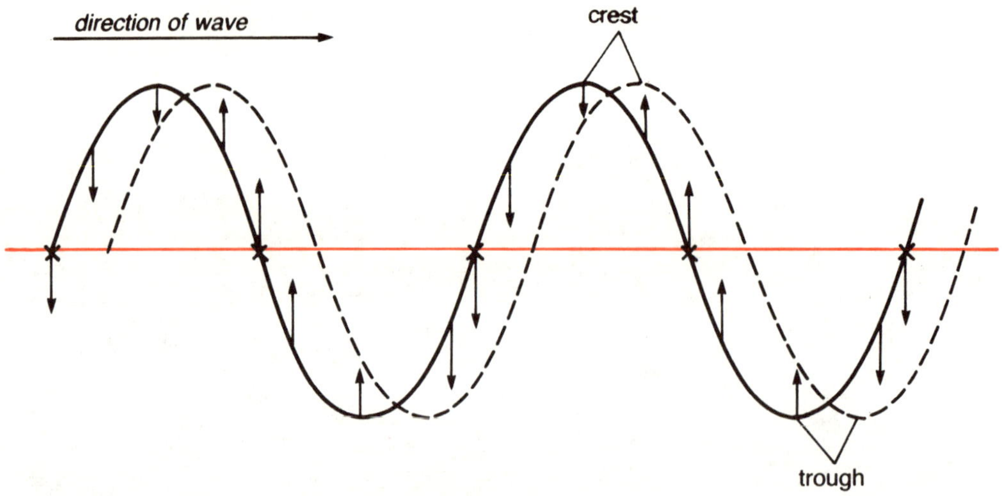

Fig. 25.2 The movement of water producing a wave

Figure 25.2 shows the general shape of water waves. At the points marked by a cross, the water is passing through the *average undisturbed position*. Arrows on the wave show how the water is moving at various points. The dashed curve shows the position of the water and the wave a moment later. The peaks in the waves are called **crests** and the dips in the waves are called **troughs**.

If possible, try the following experiment. Fill a tank or a bath with water to a depth of about 5 cm. Now make waves by dipping a horizontal ruler in and out of the water at intervals of about half a second.

Wavelength

Try to estimate *the distance between one crest and the next*. This distance is called the **wavelength** (see Fig. 25.3). The wavelength is represented by the symbol λ (a Greek letter, pronounced *lamda*).

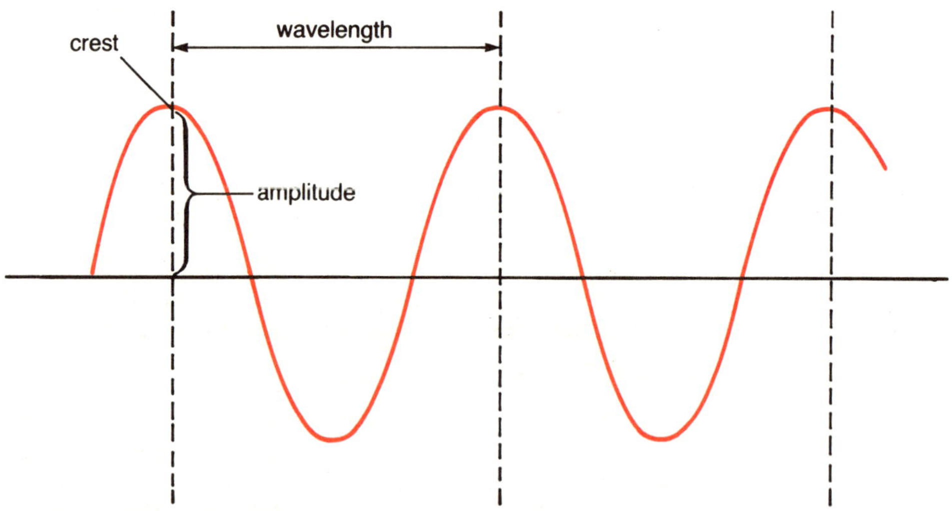

Fig. 25.3 Measuring a wave

Amplitude

Try to estimate *the height of a crest from the undisturbed position* of the water. This is called the **amplitude** of the wave. Think of the amplitude as the height of a hump (crest) in the wave from the undisturbed position. NB: It is *not* the vertical distance from the top of a crest to the bottom of a trough. As the amount of energy carried by a wave increases, its amplitude also increases. We all know that big waves carry more energy and therefore can do more damage than small waves!

Frequency

Carry on dipping the ruler in and out of the water at half-second intervals. Try to estimate the number of wavecrests passing a point just in front of the ruler in ten seconds.

Suppose you count thirty crests in ten seconds. This means that three waves pass the point each second. We say that the **frequency** of the waves is 3 waves per second or 3 hertz. Frequency is *the number of crests which pass a point in one second.* The symbol for frequency is f. The unit of frequency is the **hertz (Hz)**, in the same way that the unit of force is the newton. One hertz is a frequency of one wave per second.

Velocity

The **velocity** (speed) of a wave is *the distance travelled by the wave in one second.* Suppose that three waves pass a particular point in one second (i.e. frequency, $f = 3$ Hz). Suppose also that the wavelength, λ, is 4 cm. This wave is illustrated in Fig. 25.4. Each crest moves forward by three whole waves every second. So over one second the crest at X will have moved to Y.

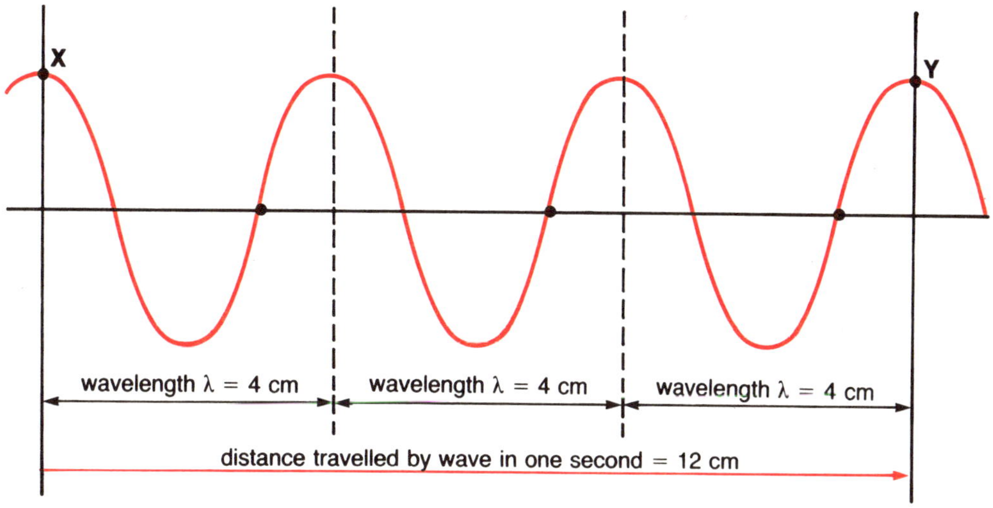

Figure 25.4

Distance moved by a crest in one second = 12 cm,

therefore *velocity of wave* = 12 cm per second.

Notice that the velocity of a wave can be obtained from the following equation:

Velocity = wavelength × frequency

$$v = \lambda \times f$$

This is called the **wave equation**.

Example

A radio station transmits waves with a frequency of 300 kHz and a wavelength of 1000 metres.

$\lambda = 1000$ m $\quad f = 300$ kHz $= 300\,000$ Hz

Therefore, the speed of these radio waves = wavelength × frequency

v = 1000 m × 300 000 per second

= 300 000 000 m/s

= 300 000 km/s

WHEN WAVES HIT MATERIALS

When waves hit materials three things can happen:

1 **The waves can be reflected.**
When waves are reflected from a flat surface, *the angle of incidence* (i) *is equal to the angle of reflection* (r) (see Fig. 25.5 overleaf and section 26.2).

2 **The energy in the waves can be absorbed.**
This causes the material to get warmer. This is what happens in a microwave oven – the microwaves' energy is absorbed by the food which is heated and cooked.

3 **The waves can pass through the material.**
As waves pass into a different material, their *speed changes*. This can change the direction of the wave. The *change in direction* is called **refraction** (see Fig. 25.6 and section 26.3). Note in Fig. 25.6 that the frequency of the waves is the same in shallow and in deep water, but the wavelength is shorter in the shallow water.

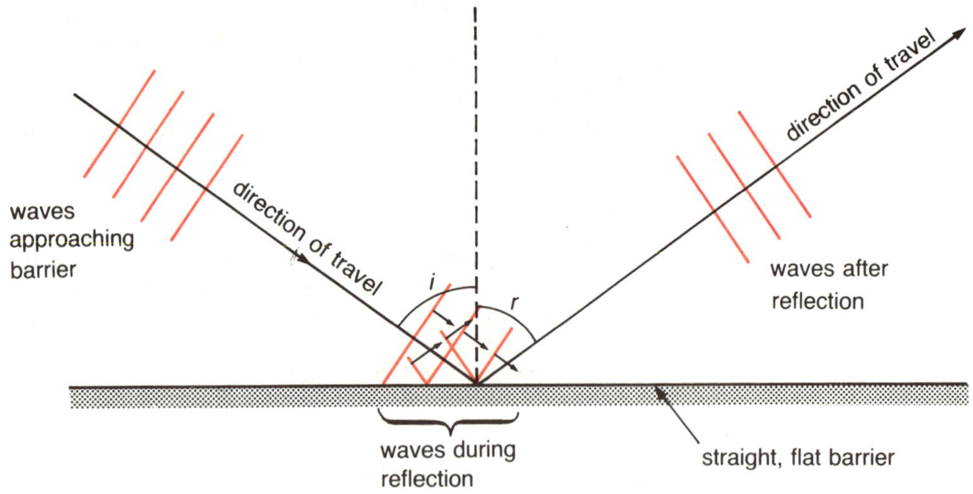

Fig. 25.5 Water waves being **reflected** off a straight, flat barrier

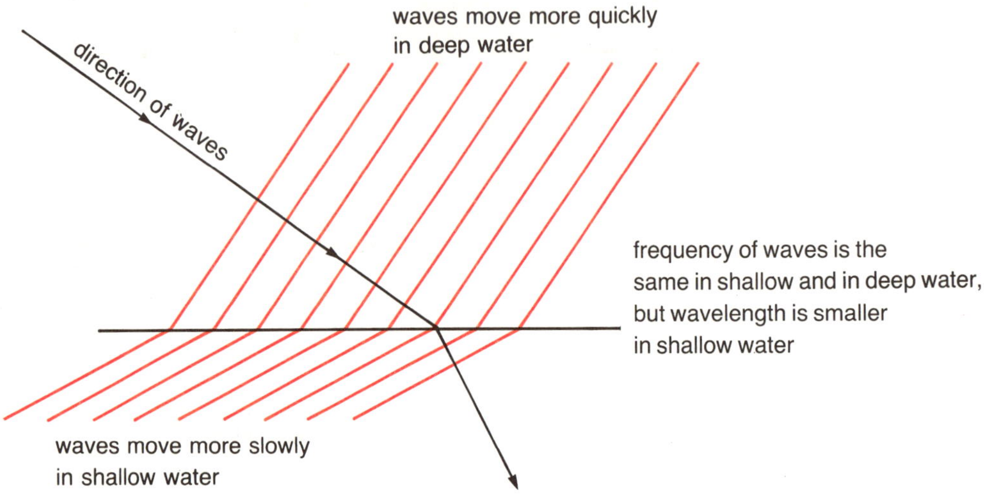

Fig. 25.6 Water waves being **refracted** as they move into shallower water

Under some circumstances, all three of these phenomena can happen at the same time. Part of a wave can be reflected, part absorbed and part of the wave pass through the material.

25.3 Transverse and longitudinal waves

One of the best ways to study waves is to watch ripples on the surface of water. When a stone hits the surface of a pond, kinetic energy in the stone is transferred to kinetic energy in the water. The water *vibrates up and down* and a *wave moves across* the pond. Waves like this, where the *vibrations are at right angles to the direction of the wave* are called **transverse waves** (see Fig. 25.7).

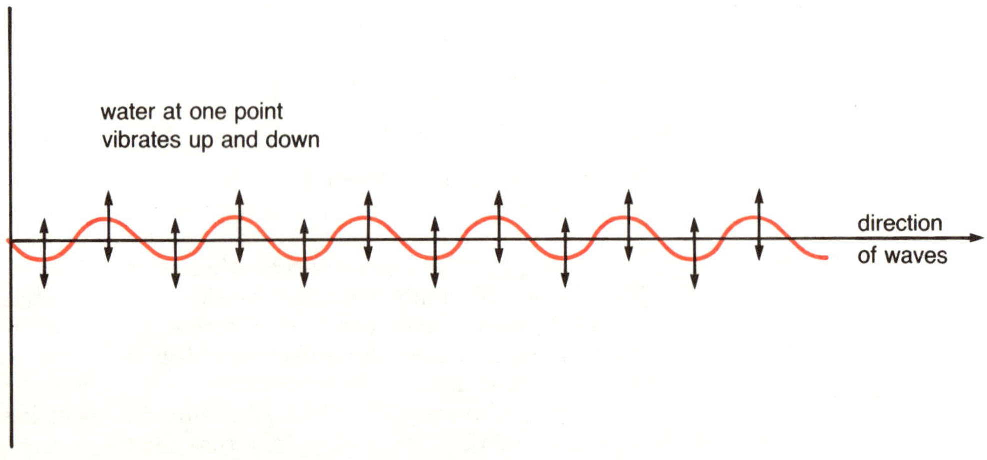

Fig. 25.7 Water waves are **transverse** waves

Light waves, microwaves and radio waves are other examples of transverse waves. Light waves, microwaves and radio waves are produced when electrons in materials vibrate and release energy. As the electrons vibrate, they set up vibrating *electric and magnetic fields*. These vibrating electric and magnetic fields travel through space as waves – light waves, microwaves, radio waves, etc. Because of their electric and magnetic character, these waves are described as **electromagnetic waves** (see section 25.5). In electromagnetic waves, the magnetic and electric fields vibrate at right angles to each other and to the direction in which the wave is travelling (see Fig. 25.8).

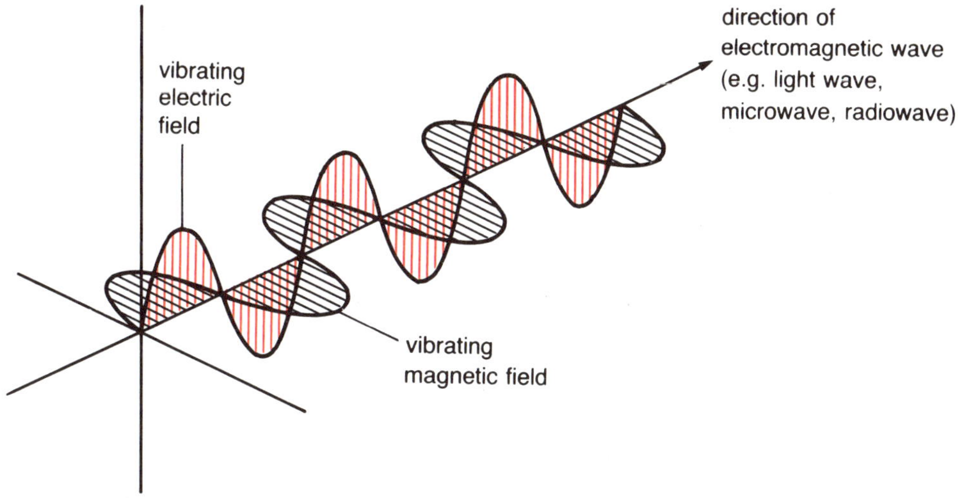

Fig. 25.8 In an electromagnetic wave, the energy is carried by vibrating electric and magnetic fields. These vibrate at right angles to each other and to the direction of the wave

Waves can also be studied using a stretched spring or 'slinky' (see Fig. 25.9). One end of the 'slinky' is fixed. Then a wave is produced by holding the free end and moving your hand quickly to the side and back. The *wave* travels *along* the slinky coil, but the *turns of the slinky coil* move from *side to side*. If you tie a piece of string to the 'slinky' and make some more waves, the string moves from side to side exactly as your hand did to start the wave. These are examples of **transverse waves** – *the turns in the slinky move at right angles to the direction of the waves.*

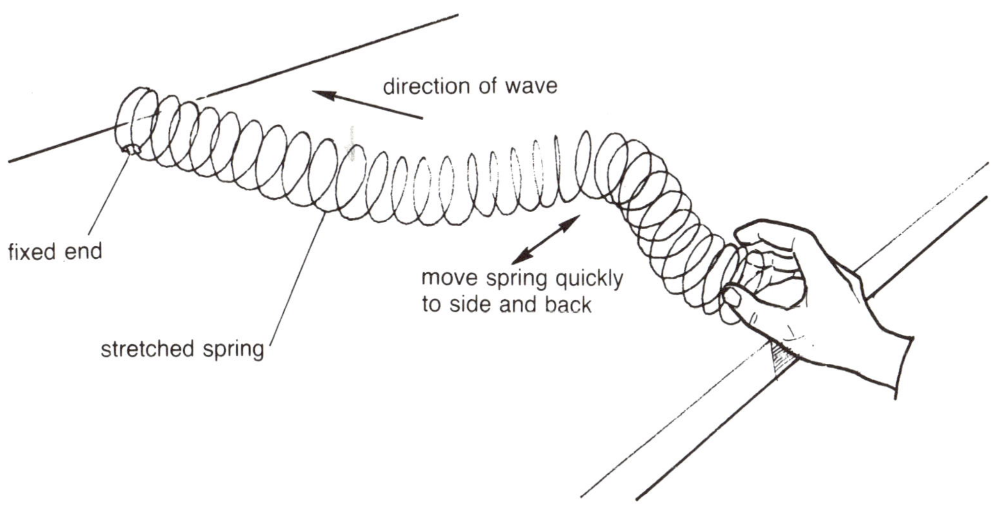

Fig. 25.9 Producing transverse waves in a 'slinky' coil

You can make a different kind of wave in the slinky by moving your hand forwards and then sharply backwards (see Fig. 25.10 overleaf). This movement *compresses* and then *expands* the slinky coil.

This time a wave of closer coils moves along the spring. Tie a piece of string to the 'slinky' coil and make some more waves. The string moves forwards and backwards as each wave passes. This is similar to the way your hand moved to make the wave. The waves are made up of **compressions** and **expansions** which move along the slinky. In the compressions, the turns of the spring are closer than normal. In the expansions, the turns on the spring are further apart than normal. In this case, the turns in the slinky move forwards and backwards in the *same direction* as the wave, *not at right angles* to it.

Waves like this are called **longitudinal waves**. In longitudinal waves, the 'bits'

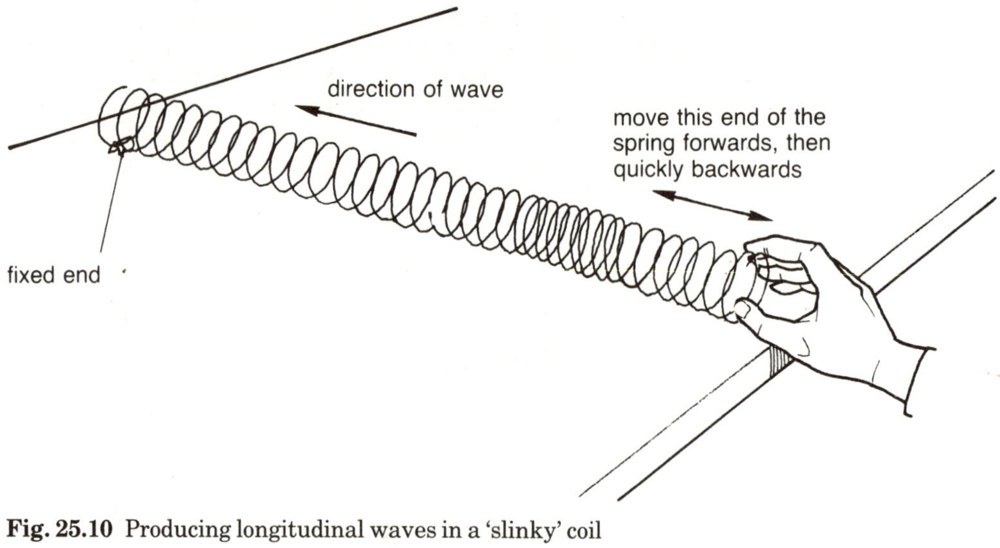

Fig. 25.10 Producing longitudinal waves in a 'slinky' coil

(e.g. the turns of the 'slinky') or the particles in the transmitting material vibrate in the same direction as the wave. Sound waves (discussed in sections 25.6 to 25.10) are probably the most important longitudinal waves.

COMMON WAVE PROPERTIES

There are many different kinds of waves. These waves have different properties and different uses, but they have three important properties in common.

- **All wave motions obey the wave equation,**

$$v = \lambda \times f$$

- **All wave motions transfer energy from one place to another**
- **Wave motions do *not* transfer matter.**

When a wave moves along a spring, across a pond or through the air, kinetic energy is transferred through the material, but the spring, the water and the air finish up where they started.

25.4 Earthquakes – seismic waves

Every year, there are about 800 000 earthquakes around the world. Most of these earthquakes are too small to notice but a few of them are disastrous. When earthquakes happen they produce shock waves (seismic waves). There are **three different kinds of seismic waves** (Fig. 25.11).

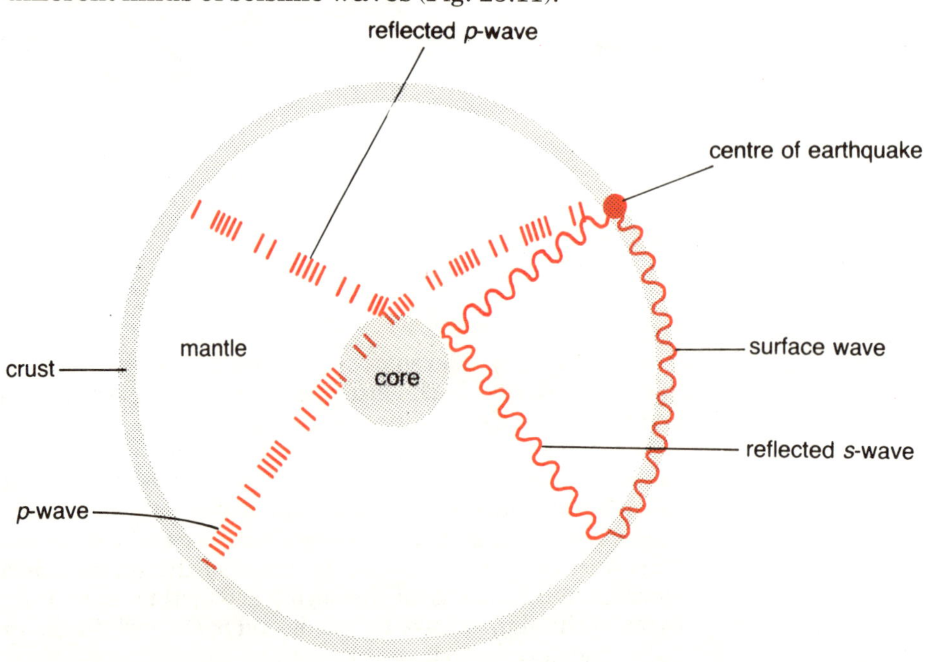

Fig. 25.11 The paths of different seismic waves after an earthquake

1 **Surface waves** roll around the surface of the earth like waves on the ocean. Surface waves are *transverse* waves. The surface waves do most damage to buildings.

2 **Compressional waves** or **p-waves** go through the earth. p-waves are *longitudinal* waves. They travel through the mantle and the core.

3 **Shear waves** or **s-waves** also go through the earth. s-waves are *transverse* waves. They travel through the mantle, but are reflected when they hit the core.

Seismic waves can be detected using a **seismometer**. A large mass is suspended from a beam. Even a slight earth tremor will cause some relative movement between the suspended mass and the earth. This relative movement can be charted by a pen recorder. Figure 25.12 shows how the seismic waves from an earthquake were recorded by scismometers at two different recording stations.

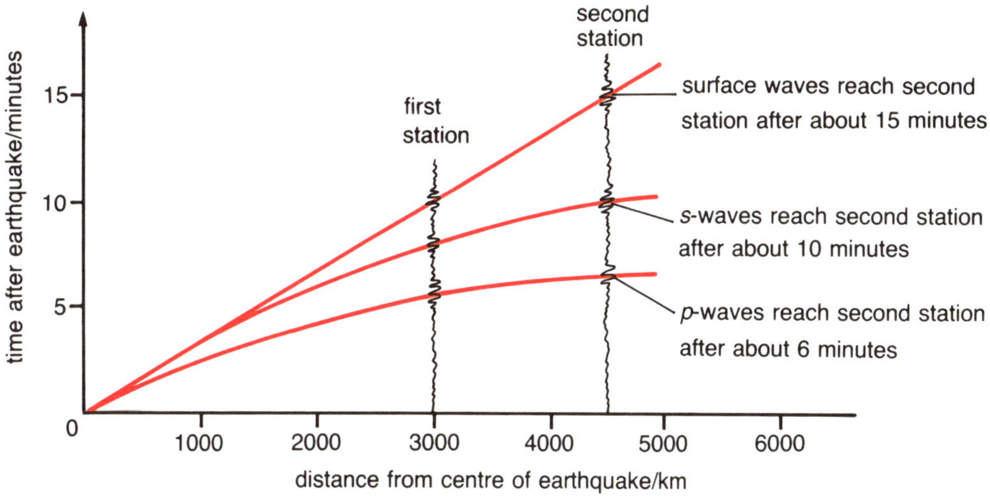

Fig. 25.12 The record of seismic waves by seismometers at two different stations after an earthquake

Notice that the surface waves, s-waves and p-waves travel at different speeds. The scientific study of earthquakes can help to predict when and where an earthquake will occur. In areas where earthquakes are likely to occur, buildings must be designed and built to reduce the extend of damage during a quake.

25.5 Electromagnetic waves

Light waves, radio waves, microwaves, ultraviolet rays and X-rays are all members of a large family of electromagnetic waves. These electromagnetic waves make up a continuous range of waves with different wavelengths and frequencies. The range of waves is called the **electromagnetic spectrum**. The range of wavelengths in the spectrum varies from 10^{-12} metres for gamma rays to ten kilometres (10 000 m) for the longest radio waves.

In spite of this variation in wavelengths, all electromagnetic waves have the following properties:

- They are produced when atoms or electrons lose energy.
- They are transverse waves.
- They transfer energy as vibrating electric and magnetic fields.
- They can travel through a vacuum.
- They all travel at a speed of 3×10^8 m/s in a vacuum. Their speed in air is virtually the same as this.

The properties and uses of the different waves in the electromagnetic spectrum are summarized in Table 25.1 (overleaf).

If you have had an X-ray picture taken, you may have wondered why it was alright for you to be exposed to the radiation, while the radiographer went behind a shield or left the room while the picture was being taken. The short exposure to radiation will not harm you, but radiographers take many X-ray pictures every day so they need to be shielded from the radiation.

	Gamma rays	X-rays	UV rays	Visible light	Infrared rays	Microwaves	Radio waves UHF VHF | short medium long
Wavelength/m	10^{-12}	10^{-8}	4×10^{-7}	7.5×10^{-7}	10^{-4}	1.0	10 | 10^4
	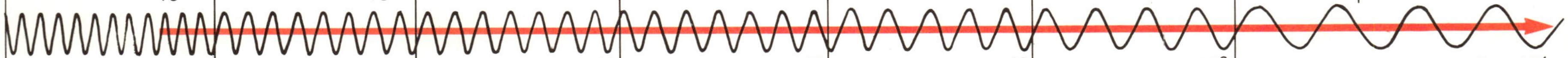						
Frequency/Hz	3×10^{20}	3×10^{16}	7.5×10^{14}	4×10^{14}	3×10^{12}	3×10^{8}	3×10^{4}
Properties	• shortest wavelength of all e/m waves • most penetrating of all e/m waves • can destroy cells and cause mutations	• penetration of matter depends on relative atomic mass of atoms • absorbed by bones and teeth, but pass through flesh • dangerous in high doses	• emitted by the sun and other white hot objects • pass through the air, but **not** through solids • increase formation of vitamin D and melanin (the brown skin pigment that gives a suntan)	• light of different wavelengths appears as different colours to our eyes • violet light has the shortest wavelength; red light has the longest wavelength	• can be detected by special photographic film and heat-sensitive devices • emitted by all warm and hot surfaces – the hotter the surface, the more penetrating the radiation	• absorbed by some materials, e.g. water • reflected by metals • pass through glass, china, paper, cardboard and plastic	• radio waves are e/m waves – they are different from sound waves • radiowaves with $\lambda > 10$ m are transmitted around the Earth by reflection from ionosphere (layers of ionized gas 100 to 400 m above the Earth) • radiowaves with $\lambda < 10$ m pass through the ionosphere – used for communications with satellites
Uses	• treatment of cancer tumours • sterilization of medical instruments and food	• examination of broken bones and of teeth • detecting diseased areas in the body	• sterilization of materials • UV lamps and sun beds	• electric light bulbs	• infrared detectors can be used to track and observe any warm objects e.g. rockets, nocturnal animals, people (e.g. burglars)	• cooking in microwave ovens: water molecules in the food absorb the microwaves, become hot and cook	• carrying signals for radar, telephones, television and radio
	 	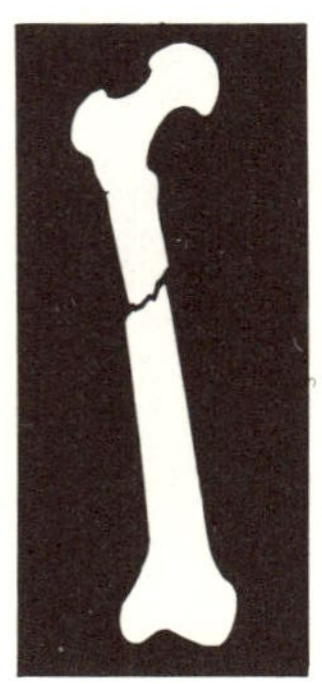				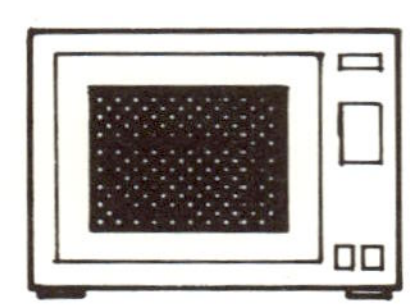	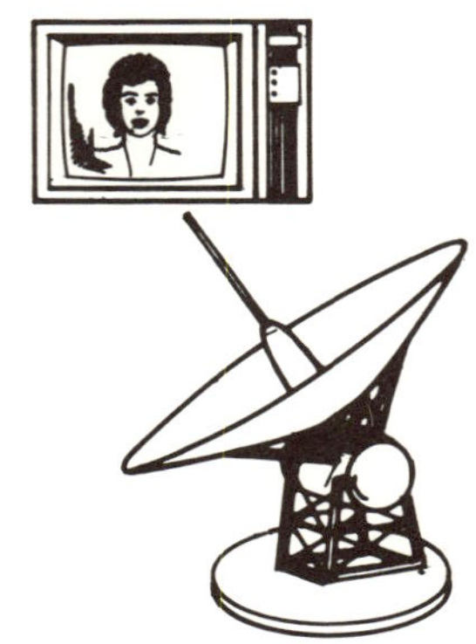

Table 25.1 The properties and uses of different waves in the electromagnetic spectrum

25.6 Sound waves

Sound plays an important part in our lives. It enables us to talk to each other, to enjoy music and to communicate using radios and telephones. Sounds are produced when you speak, when you beat a drum, when you pluck a guitar or blow into a recorder.

All sounds are produced by something vibrating.

The vibrating material might be the vocal chords in your throat, a drumskin, a guitar string or even the air inside a recorder.

Figure 25.13 shows how sound waves are produced by a guitar. As the string on the guitar vibrates, it causes the air to move backwards and forwards in the direction of the sound. As the guitar string moves to the right, it *compresses* the air on the right hand side of it. When the string moves to the left, the air on the right expands (is *decompressed*). As the string vibrates, it pushes out a series of **compressions** (C) and **decompressions** (D), one after the other. In a compression, the air pressure is higher than atmospheric pressure. In a decompression, the pressure is lower than atmospheric pressure. The decompressions are sometimes called **rarefactions**.

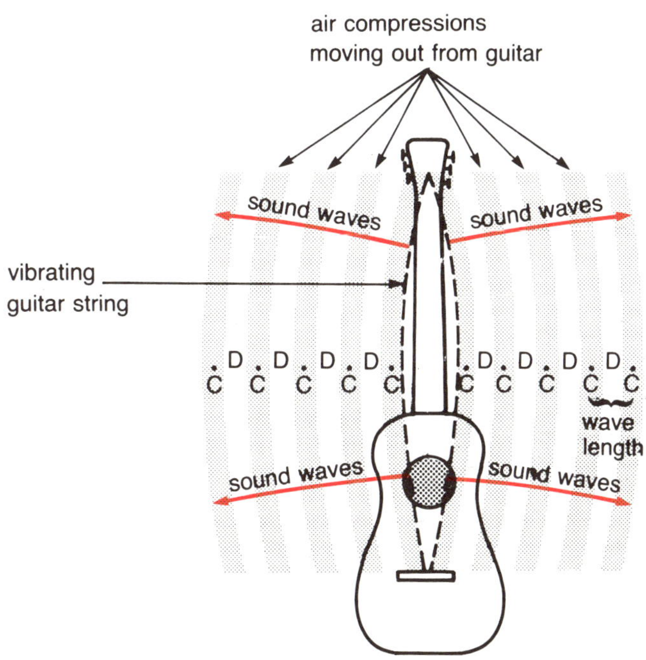

Fig. 25.13 Sound waves from a guitar

The compressions and decompressions move through the air in the same way as compressions and decompressions moved through the slinky coil (Fig. 25.10). When the compressions and decompressions reach your ears, they cause your ear drums to vibrate (refer back to section 8.3). The movements of your ear drum are then transmitted to nerves. These nerves send electrical impulses to your brain and you 'hear' the sound.

Notice that the air itself does *not* move from the guitar string to your ear. Each bit of air is repeatedly compressed and then decompressed. It is the repeated compressions and decompressions which make up the sound waves (see Fig. 25.14).

As the sound waves travel outwards, air molecules are pushed together in a compression and then move apart in a decompression. The molecules in the air are therefore vibrating to and fro in the *same* direction as the wave. Therefore,

sound waves are longitudinal waves.

In this respect, sound waves differ from water waves and electromagnetic waves which are transverse waves.

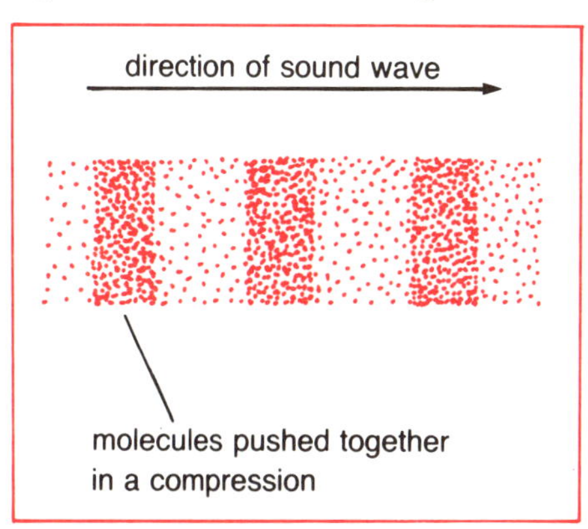

Fig. 25.14 Compression and decompression of air molecules by a sound wave

25.7 Measuring sounds

The distance between one compression and the next gives the **wavelength** of a sound wave. The number of compressions per second is the **frequency**.

As for all waves, the wave equation holds, i.e.

$$\text{speed of sound} = \text{wavelength} \times \text{frequency}$$
$$v = \lambda \times f$$

Using a microphone connected to a **cathode-ray oscilloscope**, it is possible to 'see' the wave nature of sounds. The sounds reaching the microphone make its cone vibrate. These vibrations are turned into electrical vibrations by the microphone and they appear as a wave pattern (waveform) on the screen of the cathode-ray oscilloscope.

The quality of sounds

Figure 25.15 shows the waveforms on a cathode-ray oscilloscope when the note A is produced from a tuning fork, a piano and a violin.

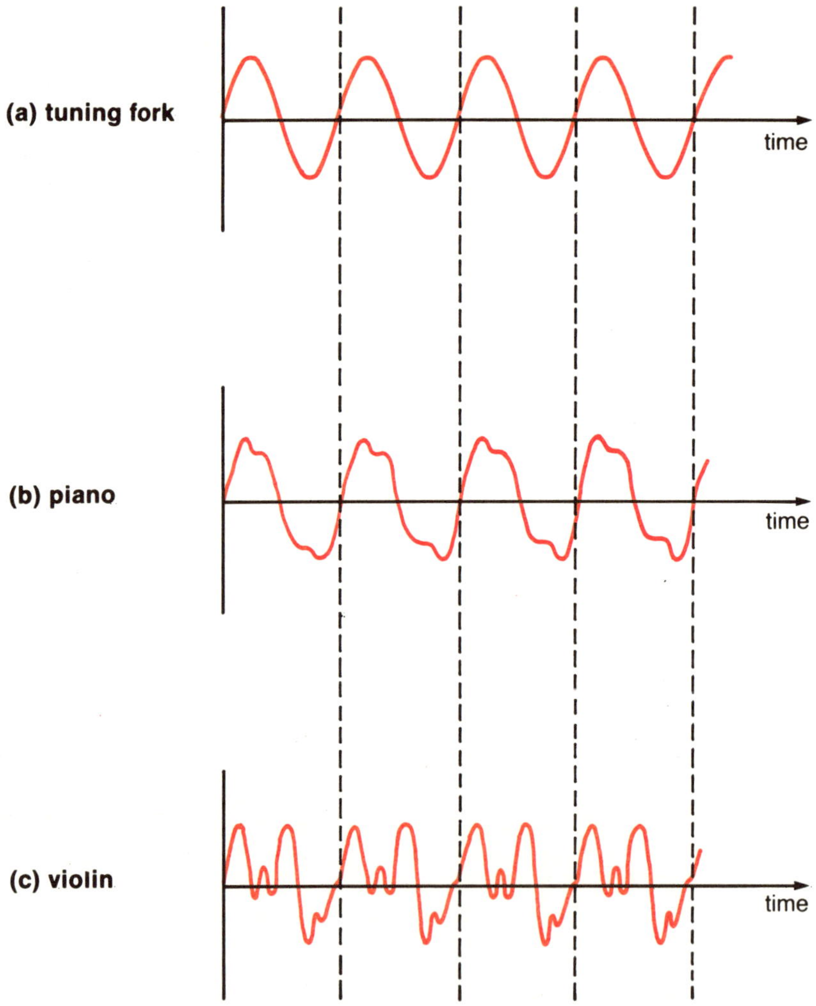

Fig. 25.15 Waveforms on a cathode-ray oscilloscope when note A is obtained from **(a)** a tuning fork, **(b)** a piano and **(c)** a violin

Notice two things from Fig. 25.15:

1 Waveforms with the same frequency have roughly the same shape.

2 Only the tuning fork produces a pure note with a smooth waveform. The piano and the violin have 'squiggles' on their waveforms. This is because other notes with different frequencies and wavelengths are mixed in with note A.

The **quality** of a note depends on the extent to which other notes are mixed in with it. Thus, note A on the tuning fork is purer in quality than note A on the piano. In turn, note A on the piano is purer in quality than note A on the violin. Different instruments produce different mixtures of notes. This gives each instrument its own special sound. This is why note A on a piano sounds quite different from note A on a violin or note A on a guitar.

LOUDNESS

Figure 25.16 shows the waveforms of the same note produced quietly then loudly. Notice that the two sounds have the *same wavelength*, but **the louder sound has a greater amplitude**. This is what we might have expected because the louder sound transmits more energy.

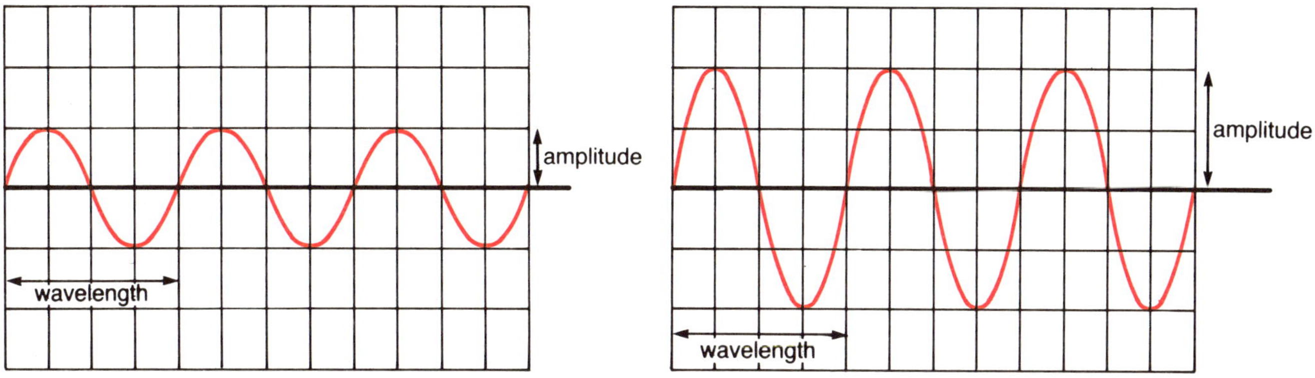

(a) quiet sound from a tuning fork

(b) loud sound from same tuning fork

Fig. 25.16 Waveforms on a cathode-ray oscilloscope when the same note is produced from a tuning fork **(a)** quietly and **(b)** loudly.

Loud sounds cause a greater pressure change on our ear drums than softer sounds. During normal conversation, your ear drum will experience a pressure change of about one newton per square metre (1 N/m^2 or 1 **pascal**). This is tiny in comparison with atmospheric pressure (100 000 pascals). Loud noises can cause pressure waves with an amplitude of 100 pascals or more. These sounds are painful and can damage your hearing. Nowadays there are laws which limit the noise level from industrial machinery and aeroplanes.

PITCH

We use the word 'pitch' to describe how a note or a noise sounds. Bass notes are low in pitch, treble notes are higher in pitch. Some men have very low-pitched voices, whereas young children usually have high-pitched voices.

The pitch of a note depends on its frequency.
High-pitched notes have a greater frequency than low-pitched notes.

Figure 25.17 shows the wave patterns on a cathode-ray oscilloscope from tuning forks of different pitch. (Note that the amplitude of the two waveforms is the same, so these notes are being produced at the same volume.)

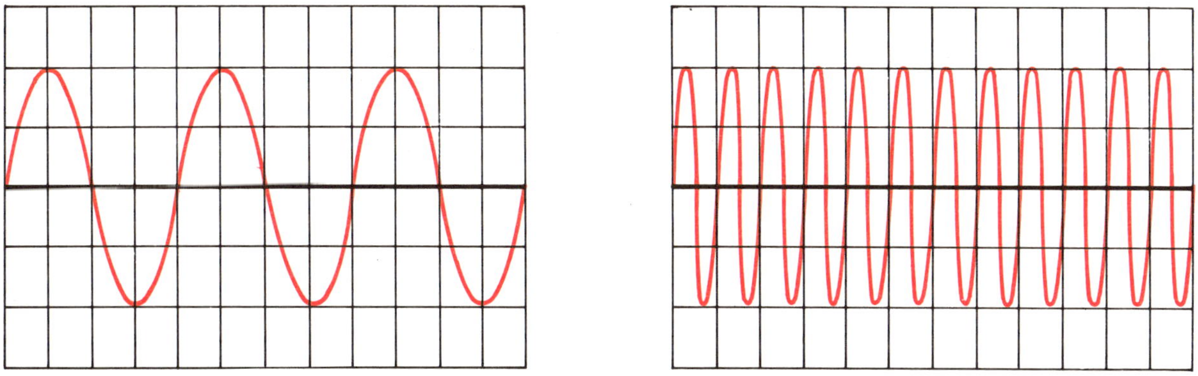

(a) low-pitched tuning fork with low frequency

(b) high-pitched tuning fork with high frequency

Fig. 25.17 Wave patterns on a cathode-ray oscilloscope of notes produced from tuning forks of different pitch

25.8 Hearing sounds

If you sit still and listen, you will hear sounds from all directions. The sounds may travel to you through glass windows, through wooden doors, even through brick walls. This shows that sound waves can travel through all materials. However, unlike electromagnetic waves,

sound waves cannot travel through a vacuum.

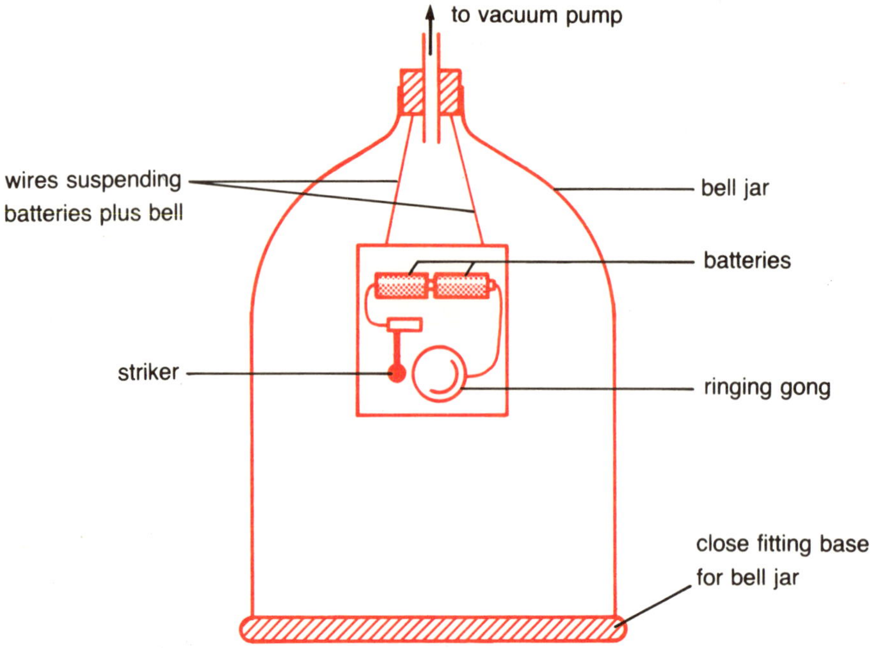

Fig. 25.18 An experiment to investigate whether sound can travel in a vacuum

The experiment shown in Fig. 25.18 can be used to show that sound cannot travel through a vacuum. As the air is pumped out of the bell jar the sound of the bell gets softer. Eventually you can no longer hear the bell at all, even though the striker continues to hit the gong.

Sound waves are transmitted by particles vibrating and knocking into one another. In a vacuum, there are no particles, so sound cannot be transmitted.

The speed of sound depends on the material it travels through. In solids and liquids the particles are packed more tightly than in gases. This allows sound to travel faster through liquids and solids than through gases.

When sound waves hit a material, three things can happen:

- **the sound waves can be reflected** off the material. The reflected noise is called an **echo** (see sections 25.9 and 25.10).
- **the sound waves can be transmitted** through the material.
- **the sound waves can be absorbed** by the material.

Hard, compact materials such as glass, brick and wood reflect about 99 per cent of the sound energy that hits them.

Loose, soft materials, such as carpets, curtains, foam and polystyrene, reflect 50 per cent or less of the sound energy that hits them. The rest is absorbed. Because of this, these materials are useful in soundproofing.

25.9 Echoes – the speed of sound in air

Have you noticed echoes when you have been near cliffs, near large buildings or in mountainous areas? Using echoes, you can easily measure the speed of sound in air.

Stand 50 to 100 metres from a large building and clap your hands. Listen for the echo. Now try to clap your hands so that each clap coincides with the echo from the previous clap. When you do this, the sound travels to the wall and back in the time between two claps. Whilst you are clapping, get a friend to time ten of your claps.

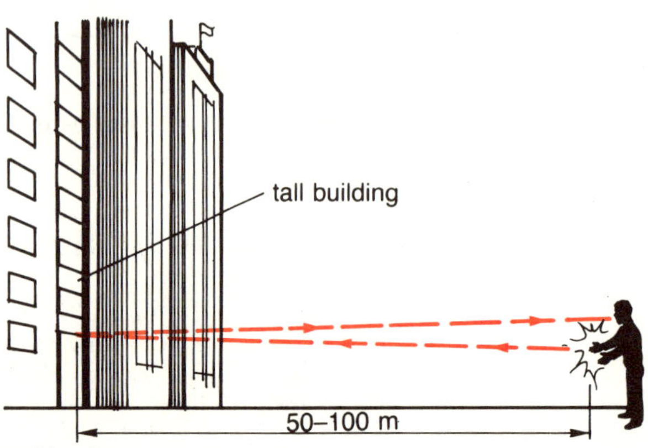

Fig. 25.19 Measuring the speed of sound in air

Suppose you stood 80 metres from a large building and you clapped ten times in five seconds:

distance travelled by sound $= 2 \times 80\text{ m} = 160\text{ m}$

Time between claps $= \frac{5\text{ s}}{10} = 0.5\text{ s}$

From this information we can say that sound travels 160 m in 0.5 seconds,

therefore *speed of sound in air* $= \frac{\text{distance}}{\text{time}} = \frac{160\text{ m}}{0.5\text{ s}} = \underline{320\text{ m/s}}$

25.10 Echoes and ultrasonics

Echoes have some important uses. They have been used to search for oil and to estimate the thickness of the polar ice cap. In these investigations, explosives are detonated at ground level sending waves through the earth. These sound waves are partly reflected when they meet a boundary between different materials such as rock and oil or ice and soil. By timing the echo and knowing the speed of sound through the earth, scientists can estimate the depth of an oil well or the thickness of ice.

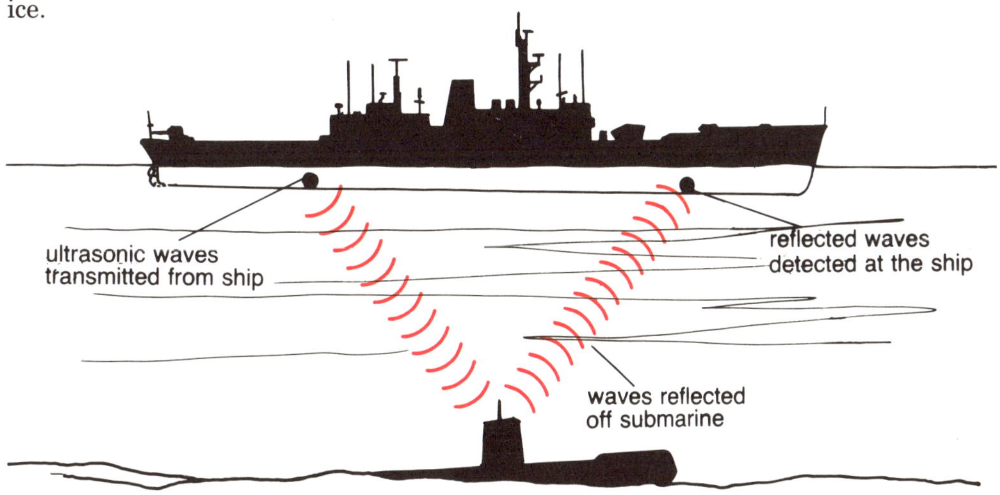

Fig. 25.20 Ultrasonics being used to detect a submarine

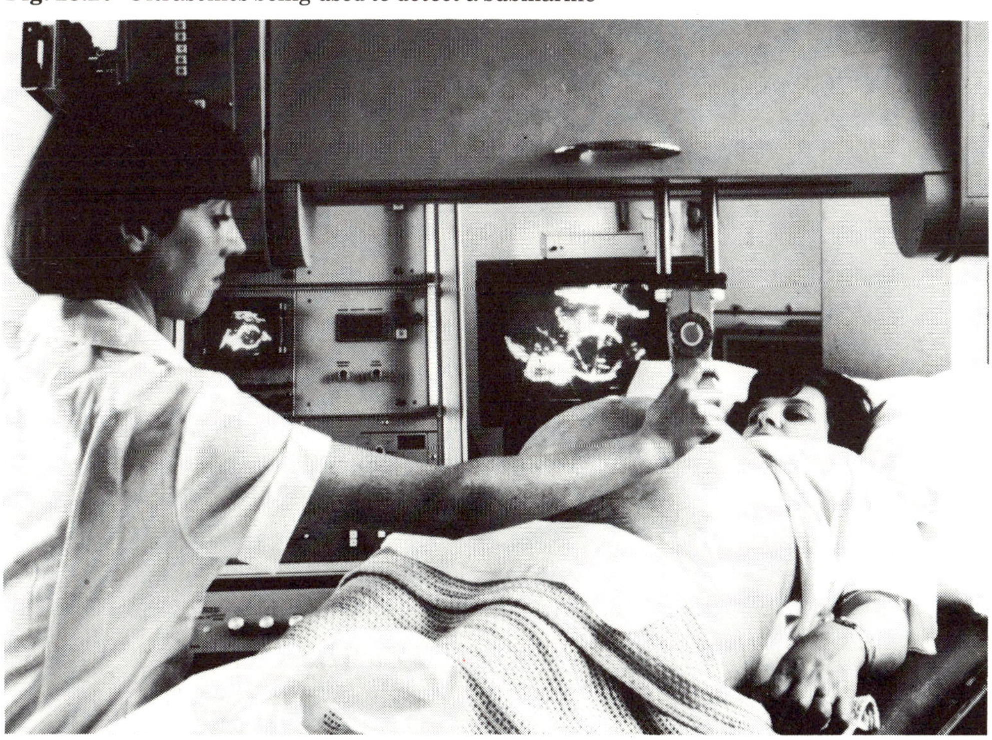

Fig. 25.21 A pregnant woman undergoing an ultrasonic examination. The technician is holding the probe (which produces the ultrasonic waves) to the women's swollen abdomen. An image of the foetus appears on the screen. This can be interpreted as an X-ray picture is interpreted. Ultrasonic examinations are used to monitor growth and/or diagnose many possible abnormalities in the foetus.

Bats also use echoes to detect objects. The sound waves that bats produce have a frequency of more than 20 000 Hz. The frequency of these waves is so high that we cannot hear them. We use the term **ultrasonic waves** (ultrasonics) to describe sound waves like these with very high frequencies that cannot be detected (heard) by the human ear.

Ultrasonics are used to measure the depth of the sea, to detect shoals of fish and to hunt for submarines (see Fig. 25.20). Ultrasonics also have important medical uses. They are used to 'look at' unborn babies (Fig. 25.21) and to scan for tumours in the body. Unlike X-rays, ultrasonic waves are perfectly safe.

Quick test 25

Questions 1 to 5

Questions 1 to 5 concern five types of radiation labelled A, B, C, D and E.

A light B radio waves C microwaves D sound waves E X-rays

Which of these radiations

1 would harm our bodies if it were not absorbed by the atmosphere?
2 has a frequency between those of infrared and ultraviolet rays?
3 cannot travel through empty space?
4 is used for cooking?
5 is most important in communication?

Questions 6 to 9

The diagram below shows five sound waves labelled A, B, C, D and E.

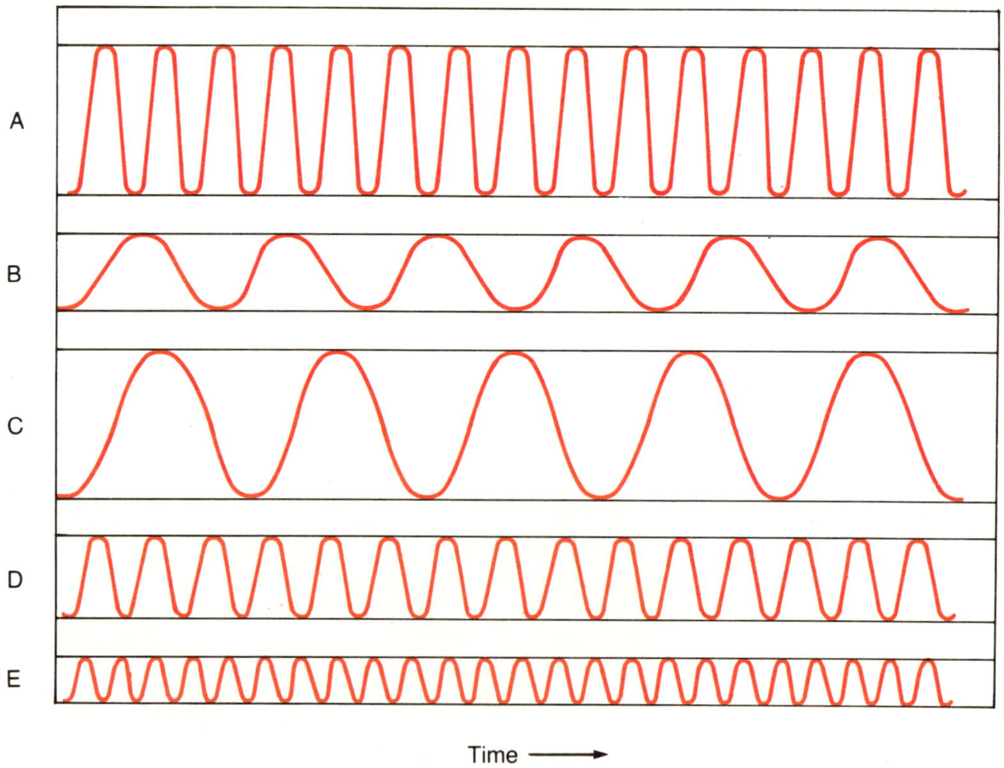

6 Which of the waves has the greatest frequency?
7 Which of the waves has the longest wavelength?
8 Which two waves have the same amplitude?
9 Which two waves have the same pitch?

Questions 10 to 14

The diagram below shows waves on the surface of the sea.

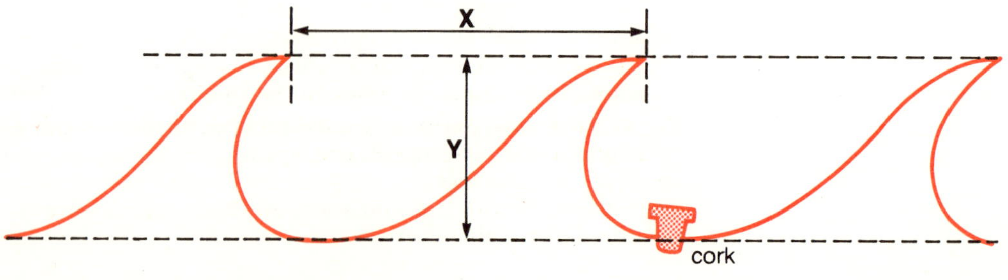

10 What is the distance X called?
11 What is the distance Y?
12 What happens to the cork floating on the surface as waves pass from left to right?
13 How could waves on the sea enable our supplies of fuel to last longer?
14 Suppose the distance between the waves is 10 metres and one wave arrives every 2 seconds. What is the speed of the waves?

Questions 15 – 17

The diagram shows sound waves travelling from a guitar to a person listening.

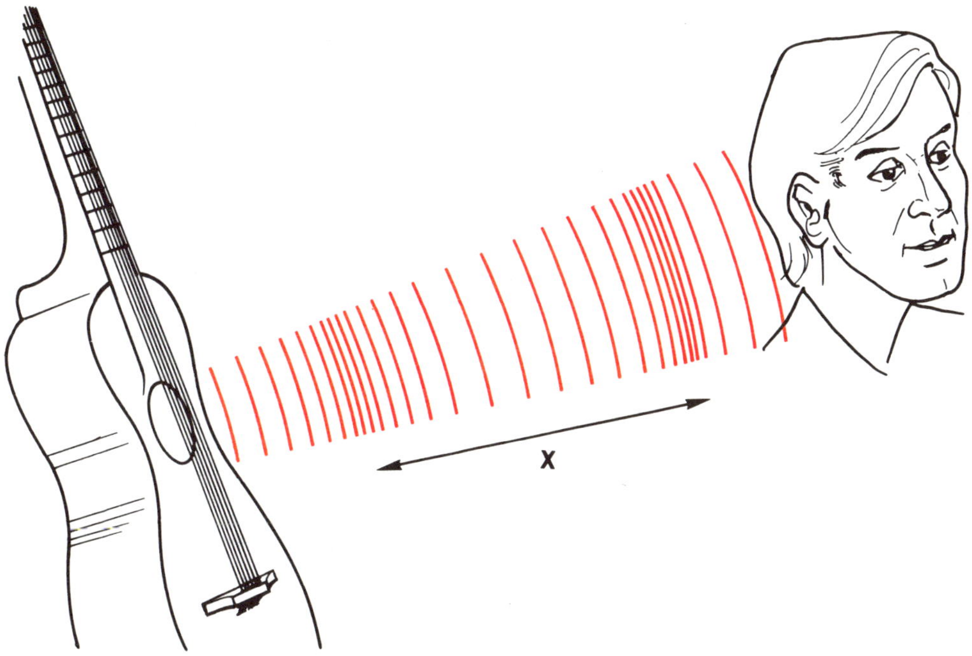

15 By saying what happens to the air molecules in the room, explain how the sound is transmitted from the guitar to the listener. (3 marks)
16 What name is given to the distance marked X? (1 mark)
17 How would you show that the same note repeated on different (musical) instruments does not have the same waveform? (3 marks)
(*MEG*, 1988)

Questions 18 to 21

As part of the planning for a large concert hall, experiments were carried out to determine how much sound energy was absorbed by brick, carpet and tiles at various frequencies. The results are given below.

Material	*Percentage of sound energy absorbed at a certain frequency*		
	125 Hz	500 Hz	2500 Hz
brick	0.05%	0.02%	0.05%
tiles	0.08%	0.5%	0.7%
carpet	0.17%	0.8%	0.9%

18 Which material is the best absorber at a frequency of 125 Hz?
19 Which material is a better absorber at frequencies of 125 Hz and 2500 Hz than at 500 Hz?
20 If 100 joules of sound energy of frequency 500 Hz hit the walls covered with tiles, how much sound energy is reflected?
21 In one particular theatre, the back wall is 33 m from the loudspeakers.
(a) If the speed of sound is 330 m/s, calculate how long it will take the sound from the loudspeakers to reach the back wall.
(b) Give *two* factors that must be considered when thinking about how long the sound will take to die down in the theatre.
(c) Give *one* reason why, when the theatre is full of people, the time for the sound to die down might change. (*WJEC*, 1988)

26 LIGHT AND COLOUR

26.1 Laser beams and light rays

In chapter 25, we learnt that light is a form of energy. It is a form of electromagnetic radiation (refer back to Table 25.1). Scientists believe that glowing (luminous) objects, such as the sun, fires and candles, emit light when their atoms receive large amounts of energy. In an electric lamp, this energy is provided by electricity.

Sometimes all the atoms in a material can be made to emit their excess energy at the same moment. In some cases, a narrow and extremely intense beam of light can be produced. This is the basis of **lasers**. Laser beams are a very concentrated energy source. Lasers can be used for a variety of operations from cutting through metal sheets to performing delicate surgical operations.

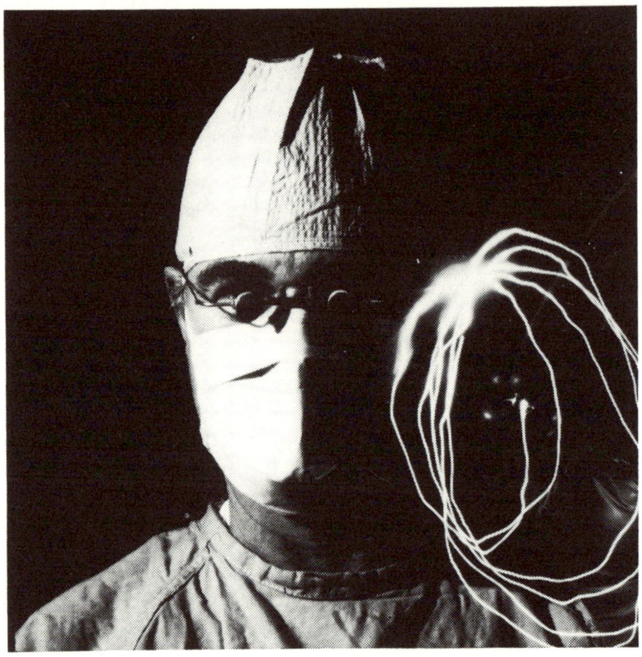

Fig. 26.1 A 'laser surgeon' wearing special operating spectacles which protect his eyes from the intense blue-white laser light

If you have used a torch in the dark you will know that it can be used as a searchlight. The torch can send out a beam of light in one particular direction. Beams of light are also produced by car headlights and when sunlight comes through a break in the clouds (a 'sunbeam'). The sharp edges of the beams from lasers, torches, car headlights and sunlight show that:

light travels in straight lines.

The experiment shown in Fig. 26.2 can also be used to show that light travels in straight lines. In Fig. 26.2, the coloured line shows a **ray**. A ray is a very thin beam of light.

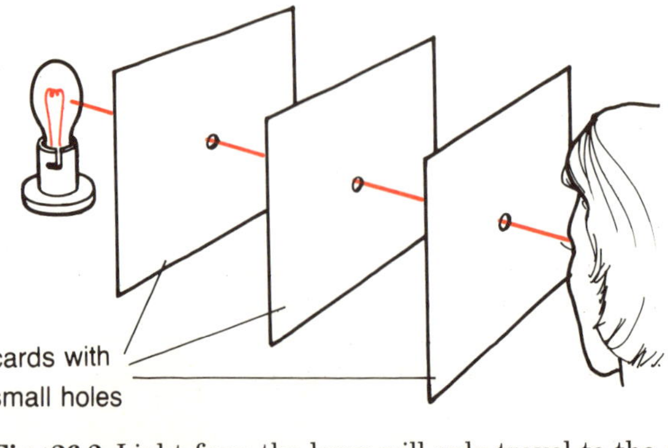

Fig. 26.2 Light from the lamp will only travel to the girl's eye if the holes in the cards are in a straight line

26.2 Reflecting light

When light rays hit a surface, three things can happen:

- **the light rays can be transmitted** (e.g. through glass)
- **the light rays can be absorbed** (e.g. by a black surface)
- **the light rays can be reflected** (e.g. from a mirror).

Most surfaces will reflect some light. Shiny smooth surfaces reflect almost all the light which hits them and they produce clear images. Shiny, smooth surfaces are used for **mirrors**. Most mirrors are made by coating the back of a piece of glass with a thin layer of silver or aluminium.

IMAGES IN MIRRORS

You see objects because they reflect some of the light which falls on them. Rays of light reflected from the objects enter your eyes. Figure 26.3 shows how you see images in mirrors. Rays from the penny travel in straight lines to the mirror where they are reflected. When the rays enter your eye, they *appear* to come from the image behind the mirror.

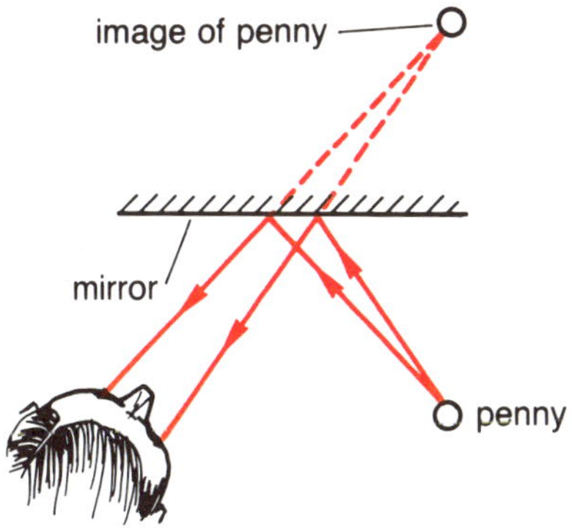

Fig. 26.3 Seeing an image in a mirror. Notice that the image in the mirror is the same size as its object and appears to be as far behind the mirror as the object is in front

This sort of image is called a **virtual image**. Your brain thinks the penny is behind the mirror, but really there is nothing there. Virtual images cannot be projected on a screen or recorded on photographic film. Images that can be projected on a screen or recorded on film (as in a camera) are called **real images**.

When you look at yourself in a mirror, the image you see is different from what your friends see when they look straight at you. If you move your left arm, your image moves its right arm. This effect is called **lateral inversion**. The lettering on ambulances is laterally inverted. The letters on the front of the ambulance are written as '**ƎƆИA⅃UᗺMA**'. Other drivers, looking in their rear-view mirrors, will see '**AMBULANCE**'. To see an effect of lateral inversion, just turn a piece of printed paper over and look at the writing from the reverse side.

REFLECTION BY MIRRORS

Figure 26.4 shows an arrangement to investigate the reflection of light by a mirror. Ray boxes are used to produce thin beams of light.

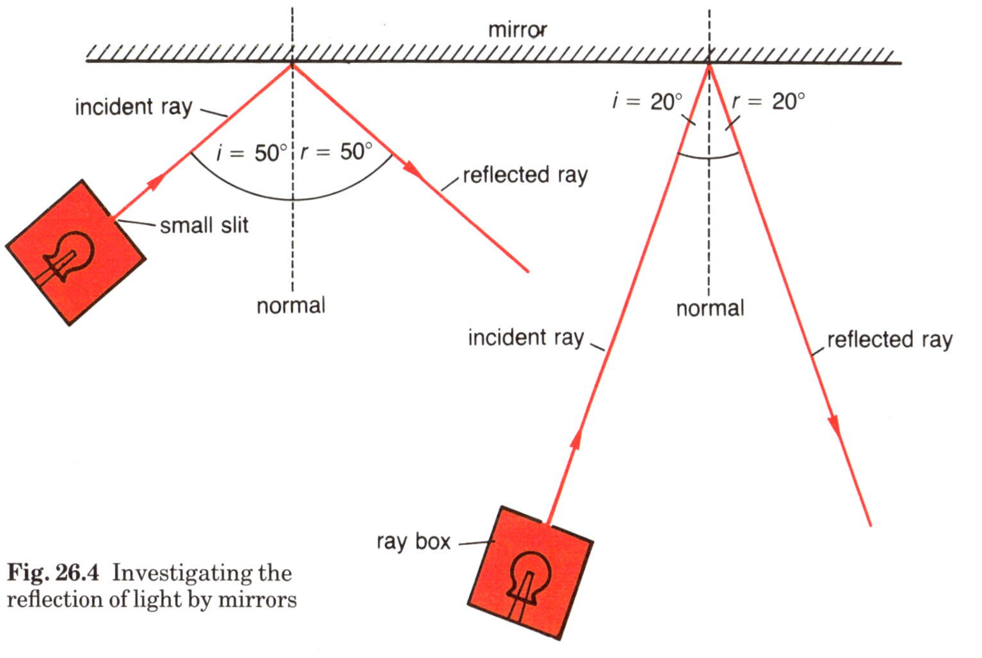

Fig. 26.4 Investigating the reflection of light by mirrors

- Before the ray hits the mirror, it is called an **incident ray**.
- After the ray has been reflected, it is called a **reflected ray**.
- The line at right angles to the mirror where the incident ray hits the mirror is called the **normal**.
- The angle between the incident ray and the normal is called the **angle of incidence, *i***.
- The angle between the reflected ray and the normal is called the **angle of reflection, *r***.

From experiments like the one shown in Fig. 26.4, we know that

the angle of incidence equals the angle of reflection, i.e. $i = r$.

Key points in the reflection of light by flat (plane) mirrors:

- the image is **virtual**
- the image is the **same size** as the object
- the image is **as far behind the mirror as the object is in front**
- the image is **laterally inverted**
- **angle of incidence = angle of reflection**

Using mirrors

Flat (plane) mirrors have many uses, e.g. in bathrooms, in shops, in restaurants and as hand mirrors. Large mirrors are often used in shops and restaurants to make the area seem lighter and more spacious.

Curved mirrors also reflect light rays and produce images. However, their curvature also enables them to concentrate light or spread it out. These properties make curved mirrors very useful – some examples of the uses of curved mirrors are given in Fig. 26.5.

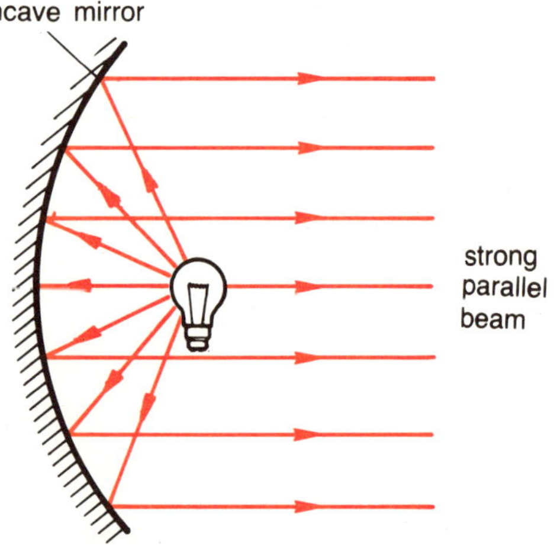

(a) Concave mirrors are used in torches and searchlights to give a strong, parallel beam. They are also used to concentrate the sun's rays, e.g. for solar heating.

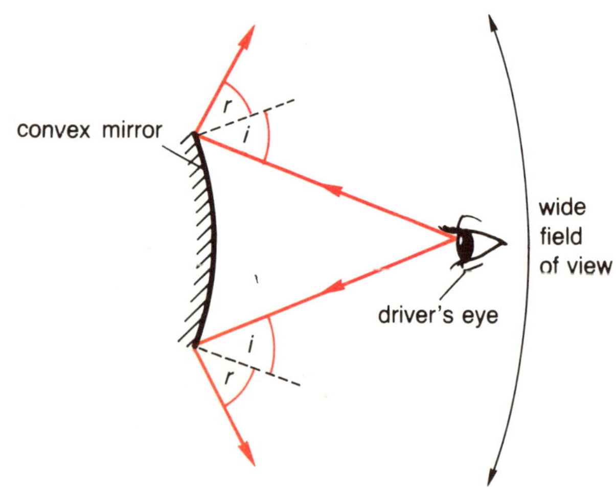

(b) Convex mirrors give a wider field of view than flat (plane) mirrors. Because of this, they are used for driving mirrors.

Fig. 26.5 Uses of curved mirrors

26.3 Refracting light

When a ray of light travels at an angle from air into a clear material such as glass or water, it *changes direction*. This is called **refraction**. Figure 26.6 shows an experiment to study how light rays are refracted (bent) when they travel from air into a glass block.

- The angle between the incident ray and the normal is called the **angle of incidence, *i***.
- The angle between the refracted ray and the normal is called the **angle of refraction, *r***.

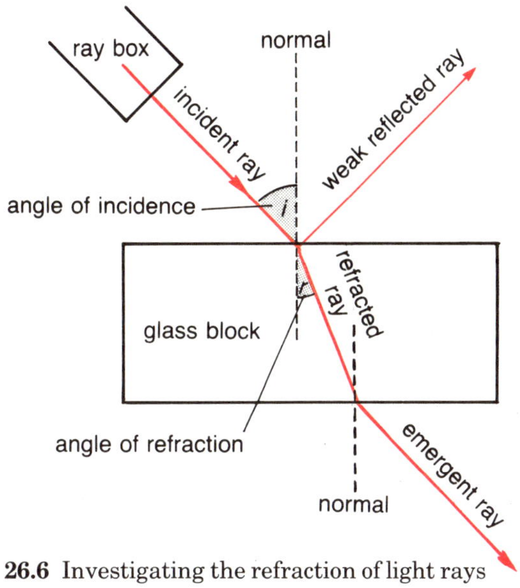

Fig. 26.6 Investigating the refraction of light rays

The results of this and similar experiments show that:

- A ray parallel to the normal goes straight through the glass.
- A ray passing into a denser material (e.g. from air into glass or water) is refracted (bent) towards the normal.
- A ray passing into a less dense material (e.g. from glass or water into air) is bent away from the normal.
- If the block has parallel sides, the ray comes out of the block at the same angle as it went in.

Unexpected effects of refraction

Refraction leads to some unexpected effects. For example, light rays from an object in water are bent away from the normal as they pass from the water into the air. This makes a pool appear shallower than it really is and it makes fish seem nearer the surface than they really are (Fig. 26.7).

Fig. 26.7 The boy fishing thinks that the rays of light come from the image at I, so the fish seems nearer the surface than it really is

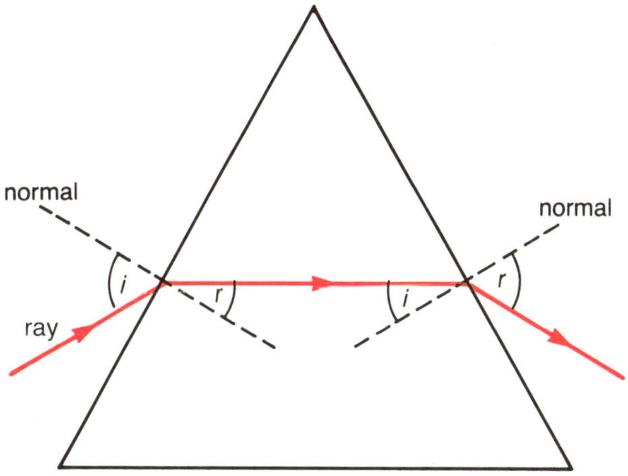

Fig. 26.8 The refraction of a ray of light through a triangular glass prism

The simple results of refraction can also lead to unexpected directions for light rays as they pass through different shapes of glass block. Figure 26.8 shows the direction of a light ray through a triangular glass prism. As the ray enters the glass, it is refracted towards the normal. As the ray leaves the glass, it is bent away from the normal.

26.4 Total internal reflection

When light travels at small angles of incidence from glass or water towards air, the light is refracted as it enters the air (Fig. 26.9**a** overleaf).

However, as the angle of incidence increases, the angle of refraction also increases. When the angle of incidence reaches 42 ° in glass or 49 ° in water, the refracted ray travels along the surface of the denser material (Fig. 26.9**b**). The angle of refraction is now 90 °. When this position is reached, the angle of incidence is called the **critical angle, *c***.

The critical angle for glass/air = 42 °
The critical angle for water/air = 49 °

If the angle of incidence is greater than the critical angle ($i > c$), there is *no refracted ray*. Instead, *all* the light is *reflected* back into the denser material (Fig. 26.9**c**). This is called **total internal reflection**.

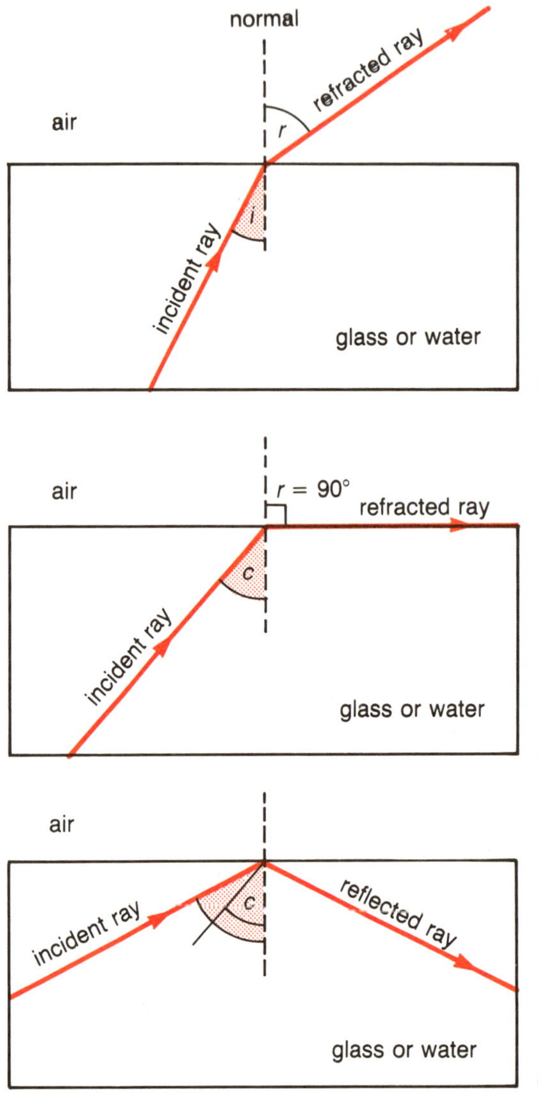

Fig. 26.9 Refraction and total internal reflection of a light ray as it passes from glass or water into air

Uses of total internal reflection

Total internal reflection is put to important use in periscopes, binoculars and cameras. In these instruments, prisms are used to change the direction of light rays (see Fig. 26.10).

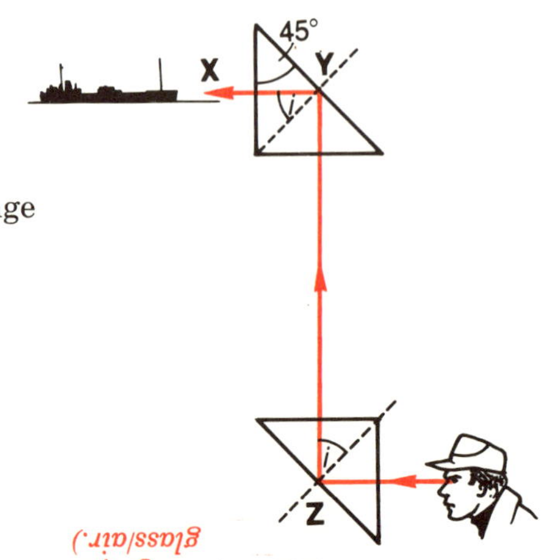

Fig. 26.10 Prisms which allow the total internal reflection of light are used in periscopes. What is the angle of incidence for the ray XY? Why does reflection take place at Y? Why does reflection also take place at Z?

(i = 45° which is greater than 42°, the critical angle for glass/air.)

Total internal reflection also enables glass fibres to carry rays of light. The fibres consist of two parts – an inner part (core) of glass fibre through which the light travels and an outer part of less dense material which protects the inner fibre. This use of glass fibre (optical fibres) is sometimes called **fibre optics**.

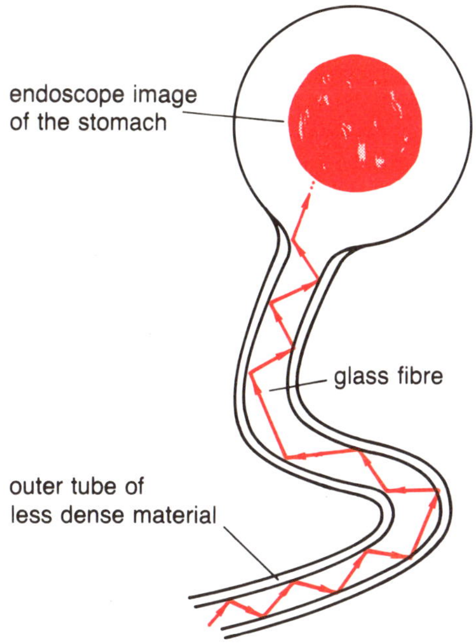

Fig. 26.11 An optical fibre used as an endoscope. Light travels along the inner glass fibre by total internal reflection

Surgeons use glass fibres in a device called an endoscope (Fig. 26.11). This allows them to examine inside a patient's body without cutting them open. For example, it is possible to see right inside the stomach using a special endoscope which passes down the oesophagus. The procedure is called an endoscopy. Optical fibres are also used to carry and direct the laser light in laser surgery.

Electronic messages can also be converted to light impulses and sent along optical fibres. British Telecom are replacing the copper cables in telephone systems with optical fibres.

26.5 Converging and diverging lenses

CONVERGING LENSES

Without converging lenses we would find it hard to survive. There is a converging lens in each of our eyes. These converging lenses help to focus the light coming to our eyes so that we can see things clearly (refer back to section 8.2).

Converging lenses make rays of light come together (converge). They are used in cameras, in binoculars, in telescopes and as magnifying glasses. Converging lenses in these instruments are usually made of glass. They have two curved surfaces. When a light ray enters the glass it is refracted (bent) towards the normal; when the light ray leaves the glass, it is refracted away from the normal (see Fig. 26.12).

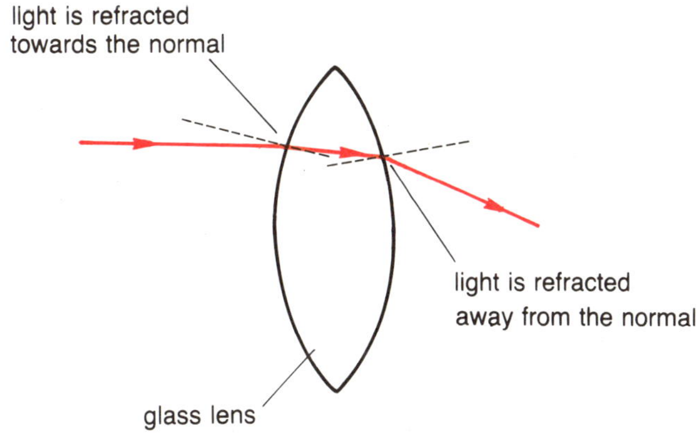

Fig. 26.12 Refraction of a light ray by a converging lens

Figure 26.13 shows what happens when several rays parallel to the **principal axis** pass through the lens. Each ray is refracted by a different amount depending on where it hits the lens. However, all the rays converge to the same point after passing through the lens. This *point at which the rays all meet* is called the **focus** or **principal focus** of the lens. *The distance between the centre of the lens and the focus* is called the **focal length** (see section 26.6).

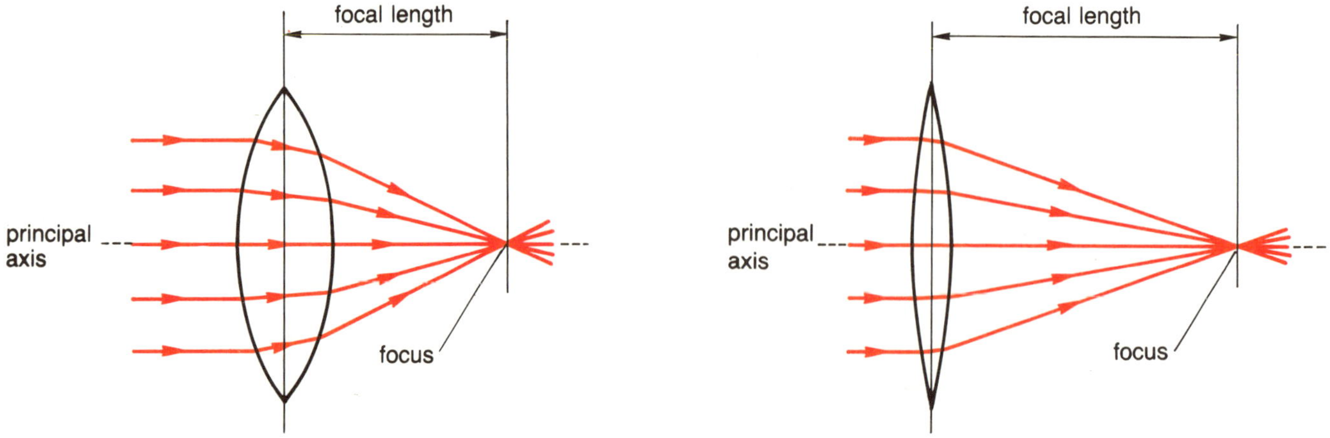

Fig. 26.13 Rays parallel to the principal axis of a converging lens pass through the focus. Notice that the thin lens has a longer focal length than the fat lens. Its surface is less curved than the surface of the fat lens, so it refracts the light less.

Converging lenses are always thicker in the middle than at the edges. They are also called **convex lenses**.

DIVERGING LENSES

Figure 26.14 shows a **diverging lens**. When the parallel rays of light hit a diverging lens, they spread out (diverge). If we trace the rays *backwards* they appear to come from one point. This is the focus of the lens.

Diverging lenses are always thinner in the middle than at the edges. They are sometimes called **concavc lcnses**. Diverging lenses are used in spectacles and contact lenses to correct short-sightedness (refer back to Fig. 8.5, p. 61).

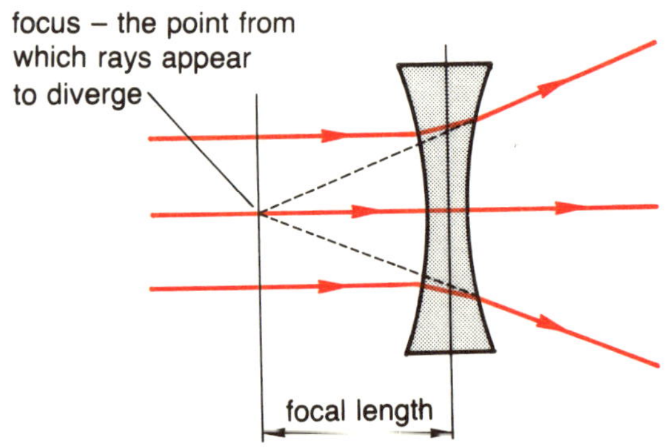

Fig. 26.14 Refraction of parallel rays of light by a diverging lens

26.6 Finding the focal length of a lens

The focal length of a lens tells us how powerful it is. Powerful converging lenses have short focal lengths.

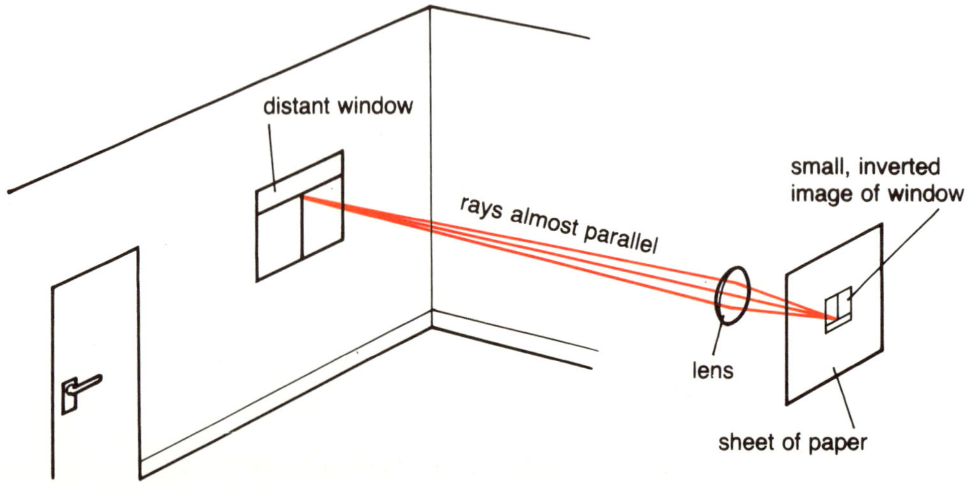

Fig. 26.15 Finding the focal length of a lens. Use the lens to focus light from a distant window on a sheet of paper. (Light rays from any point on the window are almost parallel at the lens.) Measure the distance between the lens and the focused image on the paper. This is the focal length.

You can find the focal length of a lens by using a ray box to produce a few parallel rays. After passing through the lens, the rays will go through the focus as shown in Fig. 26.13.

Figure 26.15 shows an alternative way of finding the focal length.

26.7 Finding images – ray diagrams

If you know: **1** the position of an object
and **2** the focal length of a lens,
you can find the position of an image by constructing a ray diagram.

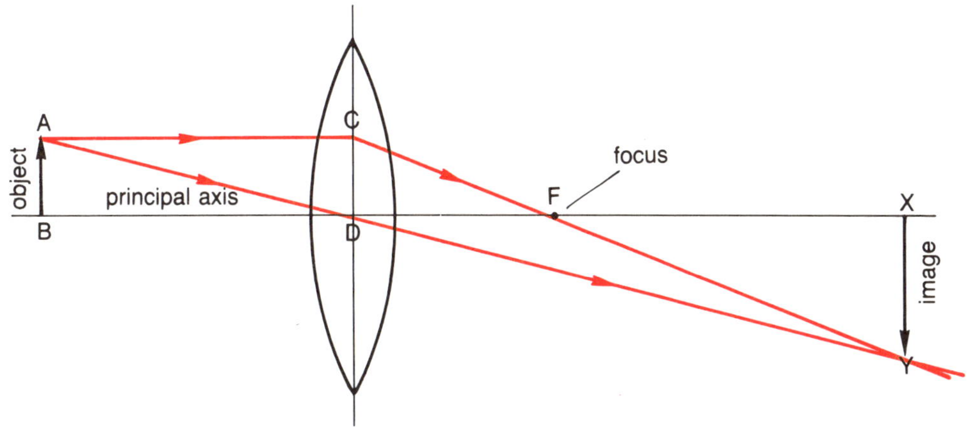

Fig. 26.16 Finding the position of an image by drawing a ray diagram

Figure 26.16 shows the two key rays which help you to find the position of an image:

- Ray AC – parallel to the principal axis, goes through the focus.
- Ray AD – through the centre of the lens, goes straight on.

Both of these rays come from A, the top of the object. An image of A is formed at Y where the two rays meet.

Since it travels along the principal axis, the ray BD passes straight through the lens without being refracted. The image of B (the bottom of the object) will be at X. Notice two things about the image:

1 It is **inverted** relative to the object.
2 It is a **real** image. Light actually passes through it; it could be focused on a screen or photographic film.

Finding the image when the object is *further away* than the focal length

Figure 26.17 shows a **scale drawing** of the image of an object (4 cm tall and 12 cm from the lens) in a converging lens (focal length 3 cm). How far is the image from the lens? How tall is the image?

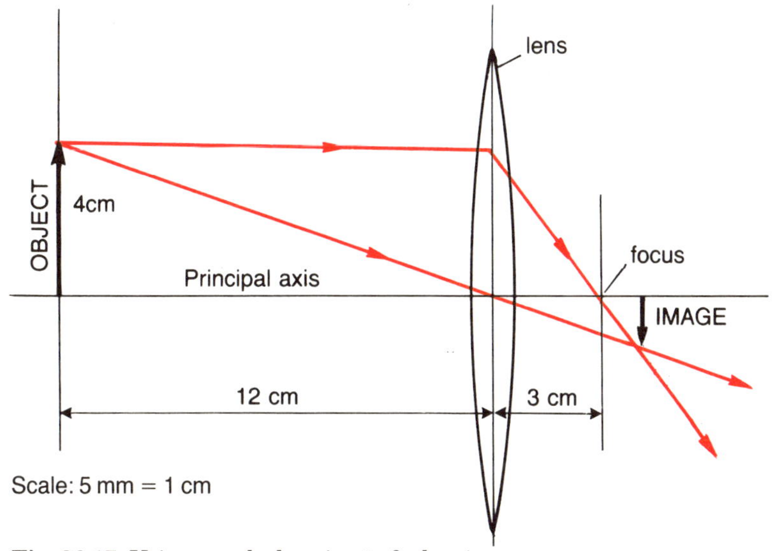

Fig. 26.17 Using a scale drawing to find an image

Lenses similar to the one in Fig. 26.17 are used in cameras. In order to get the clearest photo of the object, the camera film should be placed exactly where the image forms (see section 26.8).

Finding the image when the object is *closer* than the focal length

Figure 26.18 shows a student using a converging lens to look at an insect. Notice that the insect is closer to the lens than the focus. The insect is 3 cm from the lens (focal length 6 cm).

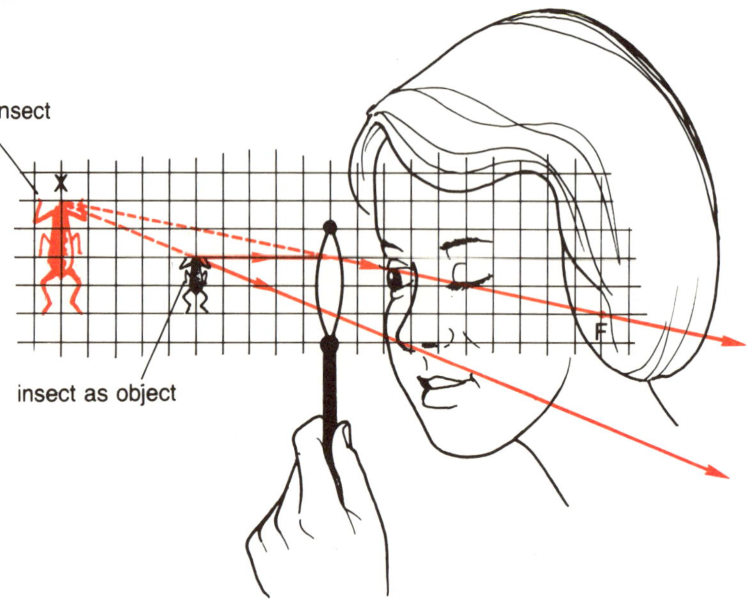

Fig. 26.18 A student using a converging lens as a magnifying lens

As in Fig. 26.17, the two key rays have been drawn. However, this time the rays of light are moving apart after passing through the lens. These rays will never meet, so there is *no real image*. However, to the student it appears that the rays are coming along the dashed line from the image at X. This is a **virtual image**. Rays of light do *not* really pass through a virtual image. If a screen or photographic film was placed on X no image would show there.

So in this case, the image is

1 the **same way up** as the object,
2 **virtual**,
3 **magnified** relative to the object.

Converging lenses with short focal lengths are often used like this as **magnifying glasses**.

26.8 Cameras

Figure 26.19 shows a diagram of a simple camera.

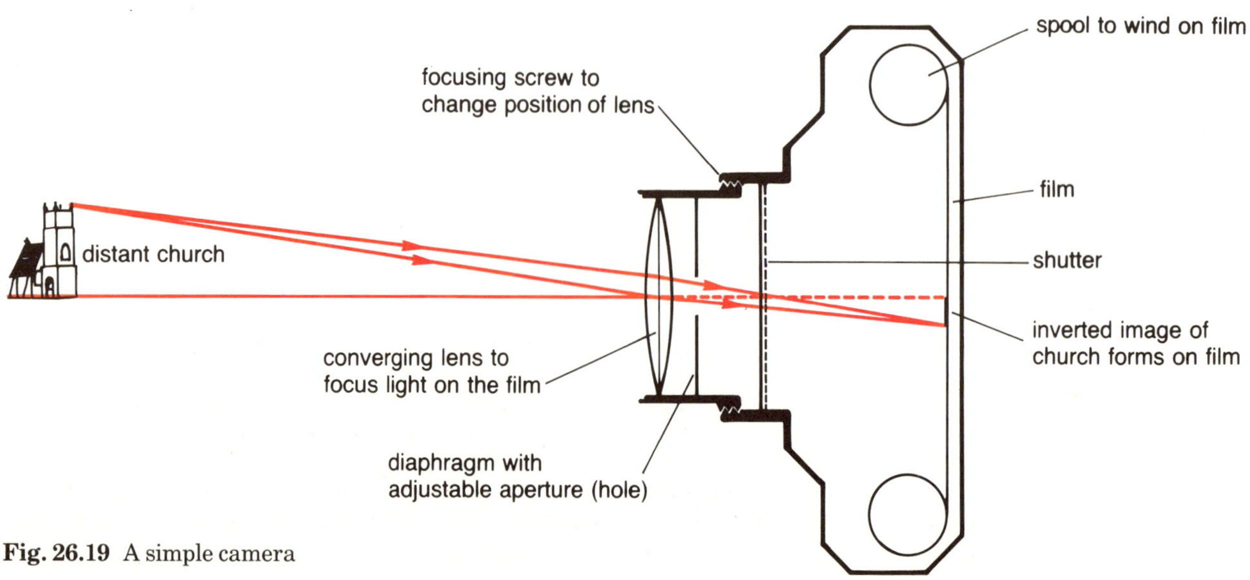

Fig. 26.19 A simple camera

When you take a photo by pressing a button on your camera, the shutter inside the camera opens and closes very quickly. This allows light to fall on the film.

Good simple cameras, like the one shown in Fig. 26.19, have three important adjustments:

1 Focusing
The focusing adjustment moves the lens backwards and forwards so that a clear image is formed on the film. For distant objects, the lens is moved closer to the film. For near objects, the lens is moved away from the film.

2 Shutter speed
The shutter speed controls the amount of light entering the camera. The shutter speed can be adjusted. The shutter might be open for one-thirtieth of a second on a cloudy day, but only one-sixtieth of a second on a sunny day.

3 Aperture size
The aperture size also controls the amount of light falling on the film. The size of the aperture is given as *f*-numbers. For example, a setting of *f*/16 means that the diameter of the aperture is one-sixteenth the focal length of the camera lens.

26.9 Separating colours in light

Light from the sun is a mixture of different colours. These colours can be seen separately in a rainbow. As the sunlight passes through raindrops in the sky, it is separated into different colours. The band of colours is called a **spectrum**.

The various colours in sunlight have different wavelengths and different frequencies. This causes them to be refracted to different degrees when they pass through water in raindrops. This causes the rainbow effect.

We can separate white light into its different colours in the laboratory in two ways:

1 Using a prism

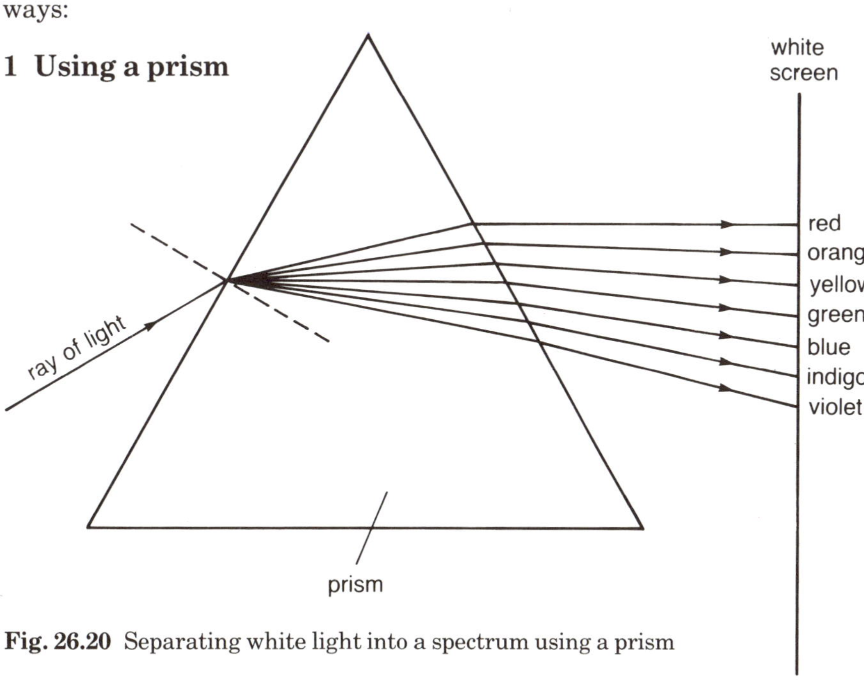

Fig. 26.20 Separating white light into a spectrum using a prism

Figure 26.20 shows how white light from the sun or from a ray box can be separated using a prism. Notice two things in Fig. 26.20.

- The spectrum is usually described as seven different colours – **r**ed, **o**range, **y**ellow, **g**reen, **b**lue, **i**ndigo and **v**iolet. (You can remember these colours (in order) if you notice that their first letters spell a boy's name – **Roy G. Biv**.)
- Violet light is refracted the most and red light is refracted the least.

2 Using filters

If a piece of blue glass is placed between the prism and the screen in Fig. 26.20, the only colours to reach the screen are those in the blue part of the spectrum. The blue glass allows blue light to pass through it. It absorbs the other colours of light.

Coloured materials, such as coloured glass and plastic, which let through some colours of light and absorb other colours are called **filters**. Using filters, we can separate the lights of different colours. Filters are used to produce coloured effects at discos, at theatres and in photography. (For further discussion of filters, see section 26.11).

26.10 Mixing colours of light

When red and blue spotlights overlap, they produce a magenta (purple) colour. Figure 26.21 shows what happens when lights of other colours are mixed.

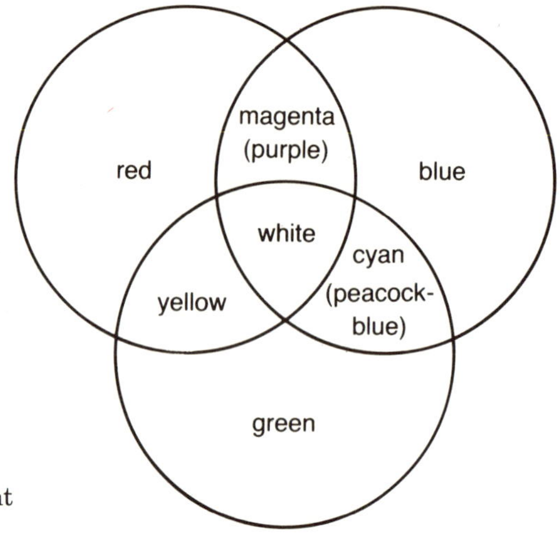

Fig. 26.21 Mixing primary colours of light

Notice, at the centre of Fig. 26.21, that white light is produced from a mixture of equal of amounts of red, blue and green light, i.e. when mixing light

red + blue + green = white

Because of this *red*, *blue* and *green* are called the **primary colours**. Primary colours cannot be made by mixing other colours. Non-primary colours can always be made by mixing primary colours.

Magenta, *yellow* and *cyan* (peacock blue), which are produced by mixing equal amounts of two primary colours, are called **secondary colours**.

Together, the secondary colours contain equal amounts of red, blue and green, so they can be mixed to give white light. Pairs of colours, opposite each other across the white portion in Fig. 26.21, e.g. magenta and green, can also be mixed to give white.

26.11 Absorbing colours of light

The colour produced by a filter depends on the light it transmits (allows to pass through). For example, a red filter looks red because it allows only red light to pass through. It absorbs light of other colours (see Fig. 26.22).

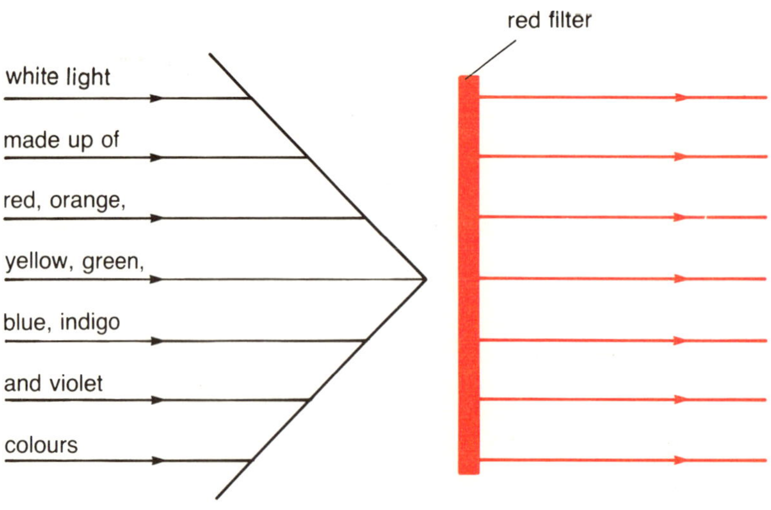

Fig. 26.22 White light passing through a red filter

Most objects are not like filters. They do not allow light to pass through them at all. These **opaque** objects appear coloured because they absorb some colours of light and *reflect* others. For example, a white T-shirt looks white because it reflects all the colour in white light. In red light, it will reflect the red light and appear red. In green light, it will reflect the green light and appear green.

What about a red T-shirt? This looks red in daylight (white light) because it reflects red light, but absorbs all the other colours. Figure 26.23 illustrates this and also shows what happens to the red T-shirt under red and blue spotlights.

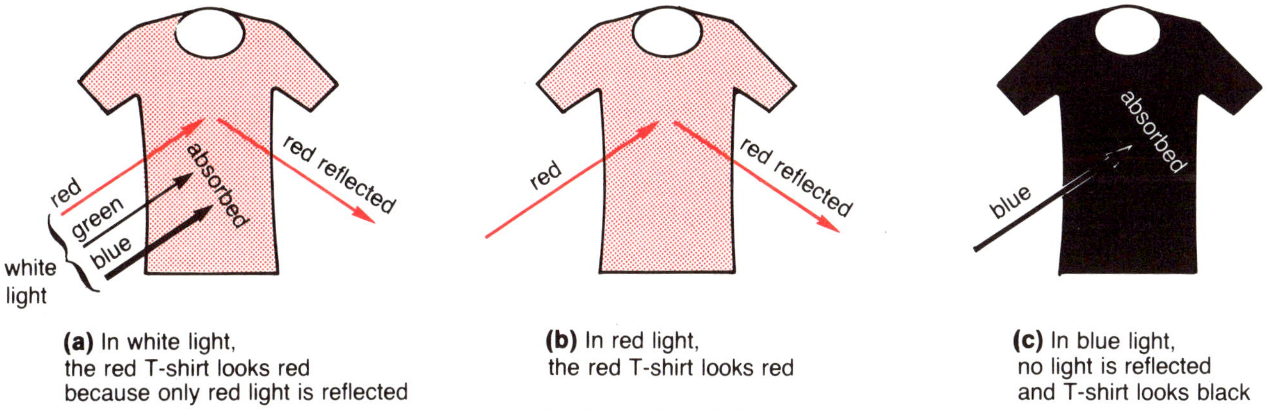

Fig. 26.23 The colour of a red T-shirt in daylight, red light and blue light

Quick test 26

Questions 1 to 3

Questions 1 to 3 concern the five descriptions of images, labelled A to E below.

A the same size as the object
B larger than the object and upside down
C larger than the object and the right way up
D smaller than the object and upside down
E smaller than the object and the right way up

Use the letters A to E to describe the following images.

1 The image of a distant mountain formed by a converging lens in a camera.
2 The image of a stamp using a converging lens as a magnifying glass.
3 The image of your face in a flat mirror.

Questions 4 to 6

The diagram below shows a ray of light travelling in material X, then being reflected or refracted at material Y.

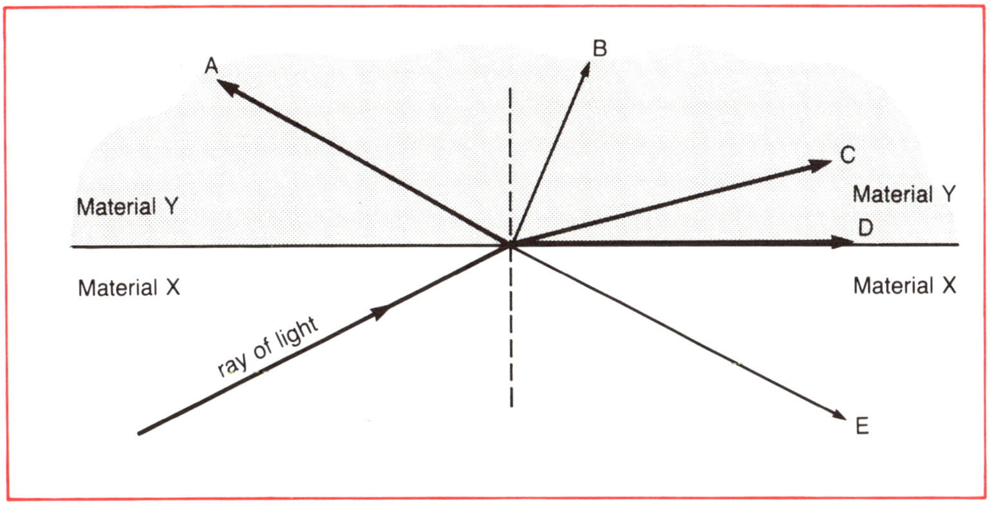

Choose from A to E, the final direction of the ray if

4 X is air and Y is glass.
5 X is glass and Y is air.
6 X is air and Y is a mirror.

Questions 7 to 9

A lamp, a lens and a screen were used to obtain the information below.

Distance from object (lamp) to lens/cm	*Distance from image (of lamp on screen) to lens/cm*	*Height of image/cm*
1000	10.0	0.2
200	10.5	0.5
50	12.0	2.5
20	20.0	7.0

7 What happens to the distance of the image from the lens as the distance from the object to the lens gets smaller?
8 What happens to the height of the image as the distance from the object to the lens gets smaller?
9 What is the focal length of the lens?

Questions 10 to 14

A girl wears a cyan (peacock blue) dress at a disco.
10 What colours of light will the dress absorb?
11 What colours of light will the dress reflect?
12 What colour will the dress appear to be under a red spotlight?
13 What colour will the dress appear to be under a blue spotlight?
14 What colour will the dress appear to be under a green spotlight?

Questions 15 to 17

The diagram shows a screen with a lens in front of it. In front of the lens is a flower.

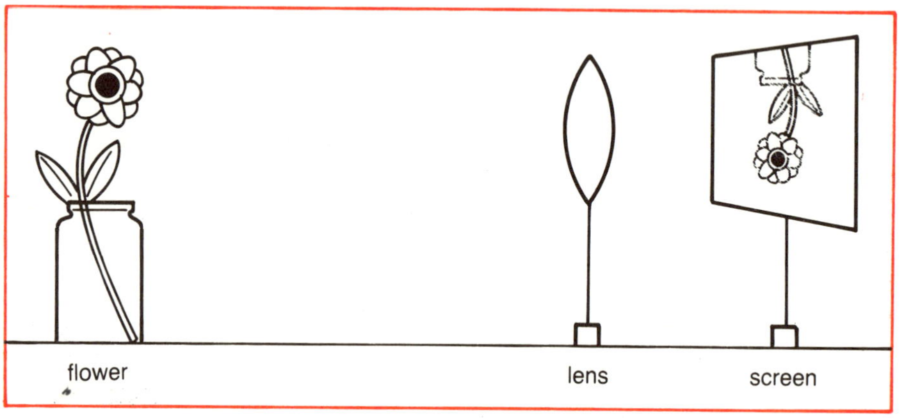

15 The image of the flower on the screen is fuzzy. Suggest *two* ways in which you could make the image sharp. (2 marks)
16 Once the image is sharp, the flower is moved a little way towards the lens. What must you now do with the screen to make the image sharp again? (1 mark)
17 What difference would you see in the image if the lens was replaced by another of the same power, but with only half its diameter? (2 marks)
(*MEG*, 1988)

Questions 18 to 20

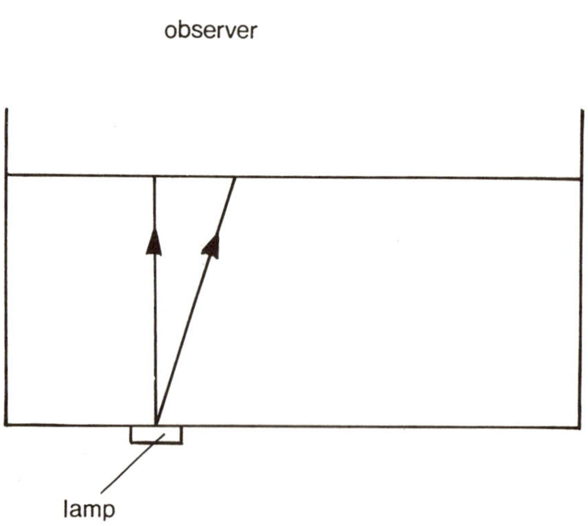

The diagram shows two rays of light from a lamp at the bottom of a tank of water.
18 On the diagram, draw lines to show the direction of the rays leaving the water surface. (2 marks)
19 Draw another line to find where the lamp appears to be to the observer looking directly into the water. Mark the apparent position of the lamp with the letter A. (2 marks)
20 Use measurements from the diagram to explain in what way the apparent depth of the tank differs from its real depth. (3 marks)
(*MEG*, 1988)

27 ELECTRIC CURRENTS AND ELECTRICITY

27.1 Introduction

Most of the time we take electricity for granted. At the flick of a switch or the press of a button, we have electrical appliances which will cook our food, warm our homes, light our rooms and provide us with television pictures. Without electricity our lives would be very different. Most of the electrical devices in our homes use mains electricity. In addition to these, there are other appliances such as torches and radios which use electric currents from cells and batteries.

There are two main reasons why electricity is so useful in our modern society:

- It is a form of energy which is easily and conveniently transferred from one place to another.
- It is readily converted into other forms of energy, e.g. heat and light.

27.2 Electric currents and circuits

Figure 27.1 shows an **electrical circuit**. This type of diagram is sometimes called a **circuit diagram**. Notice the symbols used for the different pieces of equipment. The bulbs are connected to an ammeter, a cell and a switch by connecting wires made of metal.

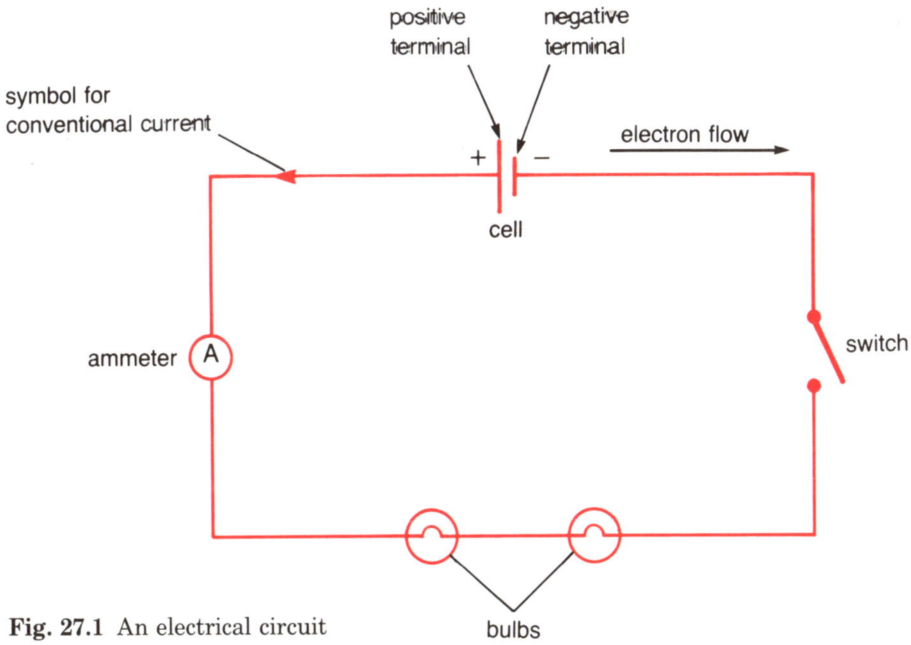

Fig. 27.1 An electrical circuit

When the switch is closed, there is a complete circuit (path) of conductors so an electric current flows. The electric current is measured by the **ammeter**. The electric current is measured in **amperes (A)**.

In metals (e.g. the wires in a circuit), **an electric current is a flow of electrons** (refer back to section 16.2). The electrons flow from the negative terminal of the battery through the circuit to the positive terminal. In solutions and molten ionic compounds, an electric current consists of positive ions flowing to the negative electrode and negative ions flowing to the positive electrode (see section 16.4).

In electrical circuits, scientists have agreed to show the current flowing from positive to negative. This is usually called the **conventional current**. It is shown by *an arrow on the connecting wires* in circuit diagrams. This has been done in Fig. 27.1. We shall use the arrow symbol for the conventional current in circuit diagrams in chapters 27 and 28 which deal with electrical currents, motors and generators.

Be careful though – **electron flow** is from negative to positive. The electron flow in a circuit can be shown by *an arrow at the side of the circuit wires* (as in Fig. 27.1).

SERIES CIRCUITS

In the circuit shown in Fig. 27.1, the bulbs, the cell and the ammeter are said to be **in series**. In a series circuit, there is **only one route** for the current.

Another series circuit is shown in Fig. 27.2. In this circuit there are two bulbs, two ammeters and a battery in series. A **battery** is simply *two or more cells connected together*.

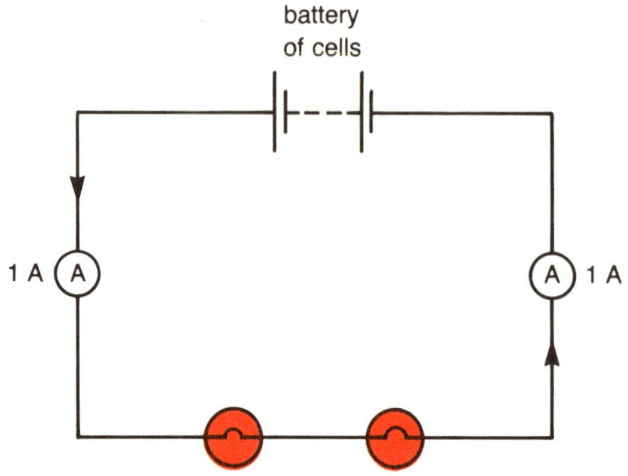

Fig. 27.2 Current in a series circuit

When the circuit in Fig. 27.2 is complete, both ammeters show the same current of one ampere (1 A). You cannot lose current as it goes round a circuit, so the current must be the same at all points in a series circuit.

PARALLEL CIRCUITS

Now look at Fig. 27.3. This time there is a **branch** in the circuit. When the current gets to X, it has a choice of paths. It can either go through bulbs A and B or it can go through bulb C. In this circuit, bulbs A and B are in series with each other, but they are said to be **in parallel** with bulb C.

In parallel circuits, the current does not split equally if one route is easier than the other. In the circuit shown in Fig. 27.3, it is easier for the current to go through bulb C than to go through bulbs A and B. So the current divides, and two amperes goes through bulb C and one ampere goes through bulbs A and B.

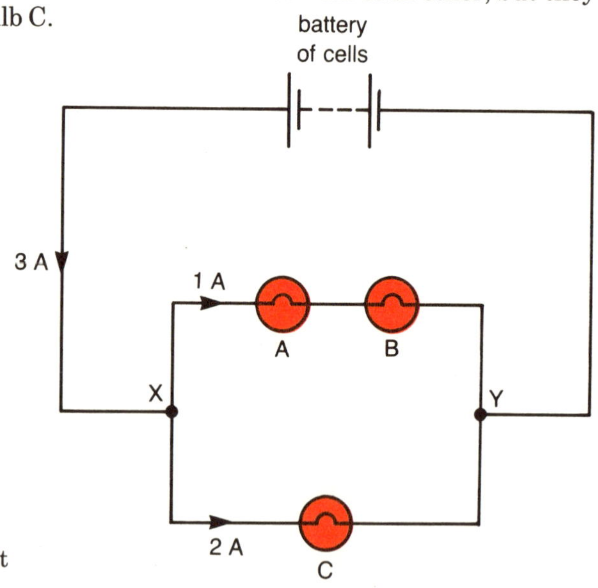

Fig. 27.3 Current in a parallel circuit

A **short circuit** is an example of a parallel circuit. When we cause a short circuit, we provide an alternative, easier path for the current (see Fig. 27.4).

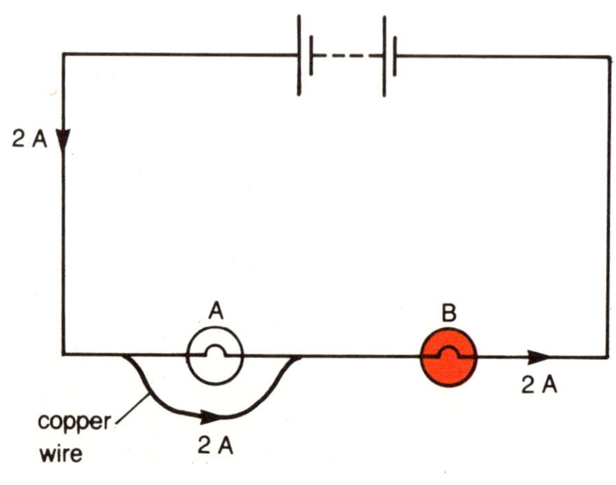

Fig. 27.4 The copper wire short circuits bulb A and provides an easier path for the current. Most current passes through the copper wire. Only a tiny amount of current flows through bulb A so the filament does not glow.

IMPORTANT CURRENT RULES

- In a series circuit, the current is the same at all points.
- In a parallel circuit, more current goes through the easier path.
- In a parallel circuit, the sum of currents approaching a junction equals the sum of currents leaving the junction.

27.3 Measuring current and charge

We could measure the amount of charge flowing in an electric current by counting the number of electrons which pass along. However, electrons have only a tiny charge. Instead our unit of charge is the **coulomb (C)**. One coulomb is the charge on six million million million (6×10^{18}) electrons.

Electric currents are measured in amperes (**amps** for short). When the current is one ampere (1 amp or 1 A), the flow of charge is **one coulomb (1 C) per second**. When the current is two amps, the flow of charge is two coulombs per second (2 C/s).

$$\textbf{Current } (I) = \frac{\textbf{Charge flowing } (Q)}{\textbf{time } (t)}$$

i.e. $I = \dfrac{Q}{t}$ and $Q = I \times t$

Example

During a flash of lightning, 20 coulombs of charge travel from the bottom of a thundercloud to the earth in 0.01 seconds. What is the size of the current?

$$\text{Current } I = \frac{Q}{t} = \frac{20\text{ C}}{0.01\text{ s}} = 2000\text{ C/s} = 2000\text{ A}$$

27.4 Voltage and potential difference

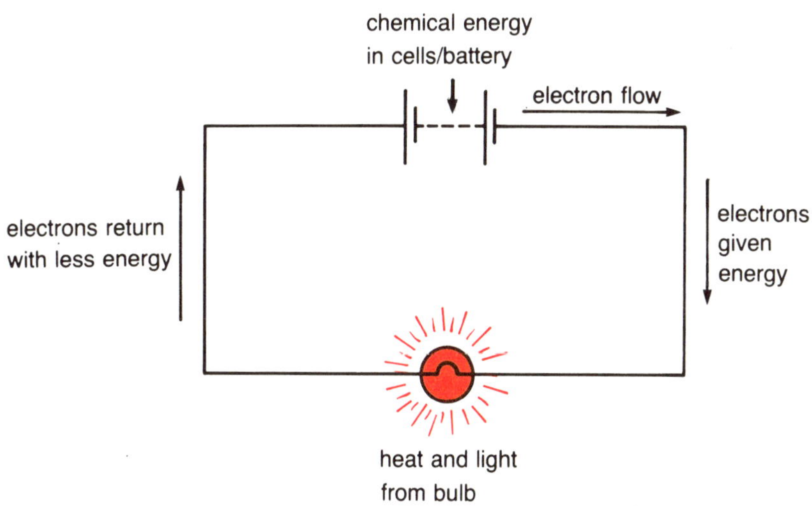

Fig. 27.5 Energy changes in an electrical circuit

In an electrical circuit, the cell or the battery provides the electrons with energy. It turns chemical energy (from the substance inside it) into electrical energy in the moving electrons. The electrons move through the circuit from the negative terminal to the positive terminal. When the electrons reach a bulb, they lose energy. This 'lost' energy is turned into heat and light (see Fig. 27.5). Finally, the electrons return to the positive terminal of the battery with less energy. Therefore, there is an energy difference between the negative and positive terminals of the battery.

This energy difference is measured by the **potential difference (p.d.)** or the **voltage** of the battery. The greater the voltage of a cell or battery, the more energy it can provide. For example, the voltage of a small cell used in a watch or a calculator is probably no more than two volts (2 V). The cells in a transistor radio or a torch provide between six and twelve volts. The voltage of the electricity supply to our homes is 240 V.

The potential difference (voltage) is measured in **volts (V)** using a **voltmeter**. The voltmeter is connected across (*in parallel* with) the parts of the circuit where we want to measure the voltage.

Figure 27.6 demonstrates an important application of voltage. The two headlamps of a car should be arranged in parallel with the battery, *not* in series.

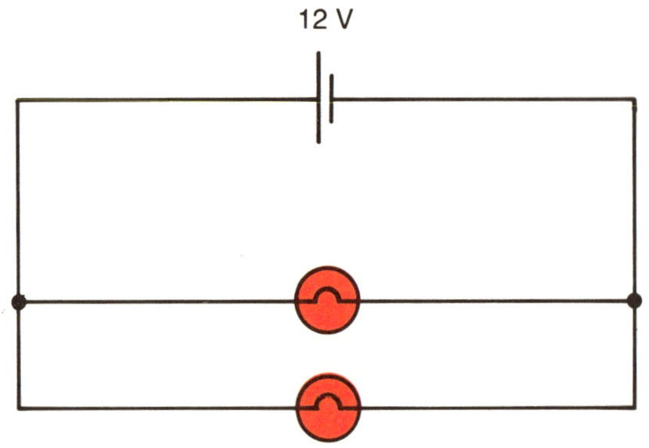

(a) Headlamps in parallel

Each bulb gets a voltage of 12 V from the battery, so the bulbs are very bright

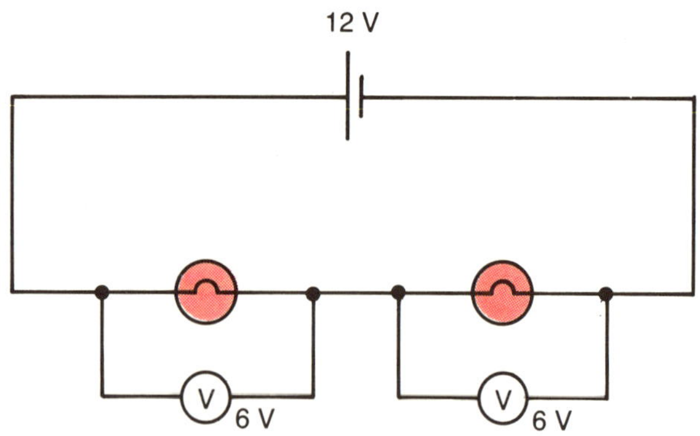

(b) Headlamps in series

Each bulb gets only half the battery voltage (6 V), so the bulbs are dim

Fig. 27.6 The voltages across bulbs in parallel and in series

IMPORTANT VOLTAGE RULES

- Bulbs or appliances in parallel get the same voltage.
- Bulbs or appliances in series share the total voltage.
- Adding the voltages across the bulbs/appliances in a circuit gives the battery voltage.

27.5 Voltage and energy

A battery with a voltage of one volt (1 V) gives one joule (1 J) of energy to each coulomb of charge which passes round the circuit.

one volt = one joule per coulomb

A voltage of 2 V would give 2 joules per coulomb and so on. In other words,

$$\text{Voltage } (V) = \text{Energy per unit charge} = \frac{\text{Energy supplied } (E)}{\text{Charge flowing } (Q)}$$

$$\text{i.e. } V = \frac{E}{Q} \qquad \text{and} \qquad E = V \times Q$$

We know from section 27.3 that

charge flowing = current × time

i.e. $Q = I \times t$

So, substituting for Q in the equation $E = V \times Q$, we get

E	=	V	×	I	×	t
energy	=	**voltage**	×	**current**	×	**time**
(joules)		(volts)		(amps)		(seconds)

Example

A 6 V torch battery delivers a current of 0.5 A for one hour. How much electrical energy does it provide?

E	=	V	×	I	×	t
(joules)		(volts)		(amps)		(seconds)

therefore, Energy = $6 \times 0.5 \times (60 \times 60) = 10\,800$ J

27.6 Resistance and resistors

As the electrons in an electric current move around a circuit, they bump into the atoms in the wires through which they pass. Atoms of different elements impede

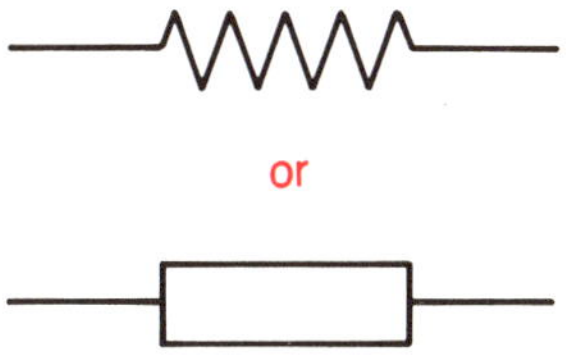

Fig. 27.7 Symbols for resistors

(hold up) the electrons to different extents. For example, electrons pass easily through copper wire, but much less easily through tungsten or nichrome wires. We say that copper has a lower **resistance** than nichrome or tungsten. This is why copper is used for the connecting wires and cables in electrical circuits.

When an electric current passes through thin nichrome or tungsten wire, the electrons cannot flow easily. They collide with atoms in the wire. This causes the atoms to vibrate more quickly. This causes the wire to warm up. If the resistance of the wire is high and the circuit is large, the wire may get red hot. Conductors like this which provide a high resistance are called **resistors**. The symbols used for resistors in circuit diagrams are shown in Fig. 27.7.

IMPORTANT RESISTORS

Figures 27.8 and 27.9 show two important uses of resistors – as filaments in light bulbs and as heating elements in electrical appliances.

Filaments in bulbs (Fig. 27.8) are made of thin tungsten wire. When a current flows through tungsten wire it becomes white hot at about 2500°C. Fortunately tungsten does not melt until 3380°C.

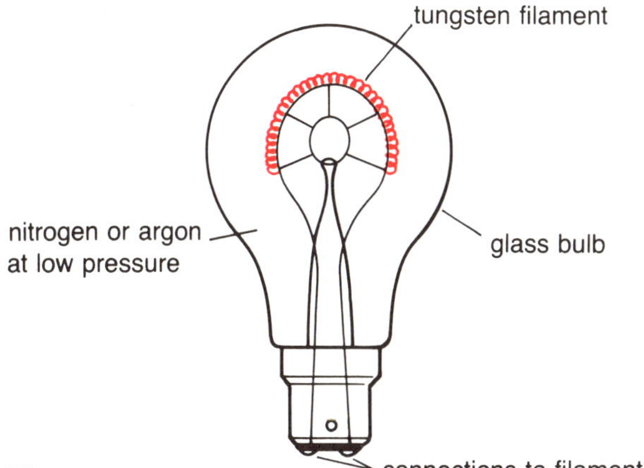

Figure 27.8

Heating elements in hair dryers (Fig. 27.9), irons, electric fires, electric kettles and hot plates are made from nichrome or other nickel alloys. These alloys stay red hot without melting or reacting with air.

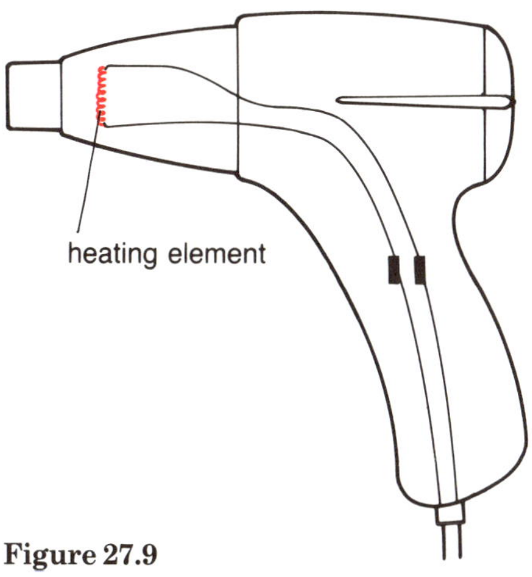

Figure 27.9

Sometimes, it is necessary to vary the resistance in a circuit or in an electrical appliance. **Variable resistors** can be used to vary the brightness of bulbs and the volume of brightness of radios and televisions. The circuit symbols for variable resistors are shown in Fig. 27.10.

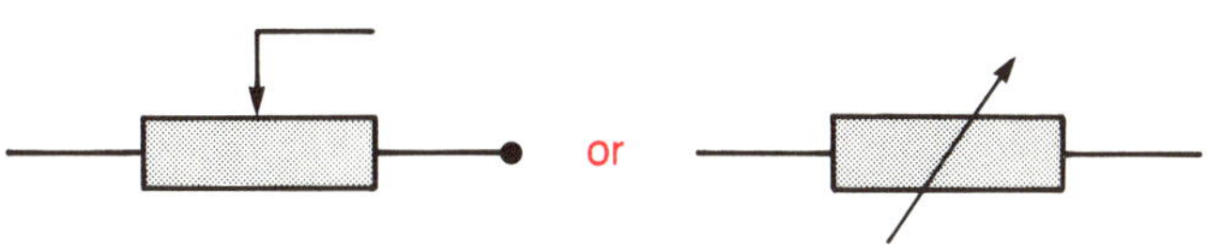

Figure 27.10 Symbols for variable resistors

27.7 Measuring resistance – Ohm's law

During the 1820s, the German scientist, Georg Ohm, investigated the resistance of various metal conductors. The unit which we use for resistance is called the **ohm** in honour of Georg Ohm. The symbol for the ohm is Ω, e.g. five ohms is written 5 Ω.

Ohm used a circuit like the one shown in Fig. 27.11 (overleaf). He measured the voltage across a resistor at different levels of current.

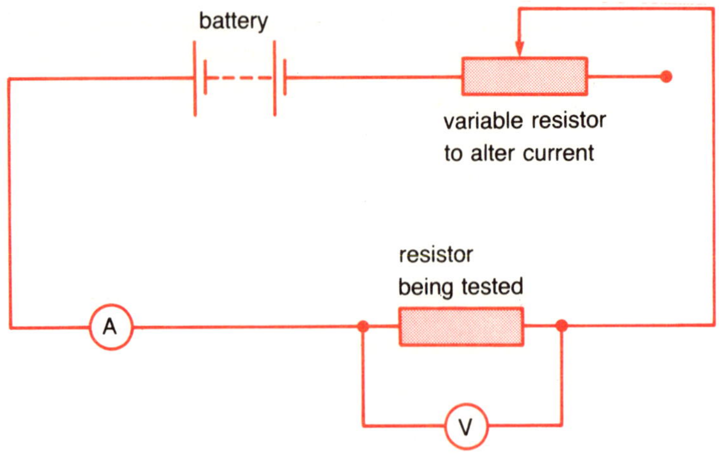

Fig. 27.11 The circuit used to investigate Ohm's Law

Ohm used his results to plot a graph of current (I) against voltage (V) (Fig. 27.12). The results gave a straight line through the origin (O).

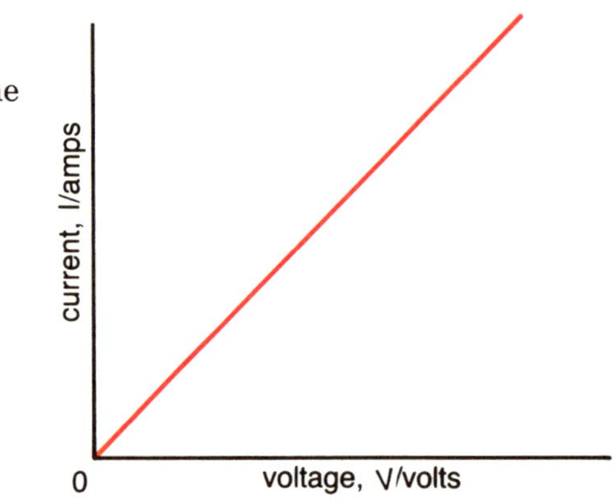

Fig. 27.12 A graph of current (I) versus voltage (V)

This led to **Ohm's law**:

The current in some conductors is proportional to the voltage, provided the temperature stays constant.

This can be written in symbols as

$$I \propto V$$

Because I is proportional to V, we can say that

$$\frac{V}{I} = a\ constant$$

Ohm's results show that doubling the voltage doubles the current. Treble the voltage will give treble the current, and so on. The larger the resistance, the greater the voltage needed to push each ampere of current through it. This led to the definition of one ohm:

A resistor has a resistance of one ohm (1 Ω), if a voltage of one volt (1 V) will drive a current of one ampere (1 A) through it.

If a voltage of two volts (2 V) is needed to drive a current of one amp (1 A) through a resistor, its resistance is two ohms (2 Ω). If 3 V are needed to drive a current of 1 A through a resistor, its resistance is 3 Ω. Notice that the **resistance of a resistor** is the **voltage per unit of current**, i.e.

$$\text{Resistance (ohms)} = \frac{\text{Voltage (volts)}}{\text{Current (amps)}}$$

$$R = \frac{V}{I}$$

Example

A torch has a 6 V battery and a bulb with a resistance of 12 Ω. What is the current when the torch is working?

You are given voltage (V) = 6 V and resistance (R) = 12 Ω.

The formula $R = \frac{V}{I}$ can be rearranged to $I = \frac{V}{R}$

So, current (I) $= \frac{V}{R} = \frac{6}{12} = 0.5$ A

Conductors which obey Ohm's law are called **ohmic conductors**. Metals and alloys are ohmic conductors. **Semi-conductors**, such as silicon and germanium, do *not* obey Ohm's law. The differences between ohmic and non-ohmic conductors are summarized in Table 27.1.

Table 27.1 Comparing ohmic and non-ohmic conductors

Ohmic conductors	**Non-ohmic conductors**
Obey Ohm's law	Do not obey Ohm's law
Metals and alloys	Semi-conductors
Resistance *increases* slowly with temperature Number of electrons carrying the current stays constant as temperature rises. Atoms vibrate faster at higher temperatures and impede electrons more	Resistance *decreases* with temperature Electrons are held strongly by atoms. At higher temperatures, more electrons can escape from their atoms so the current is larger
At very low temperatures, atoms hardly vibrate at all. Resistance is very low and some metals become **superconductors**	Some non-ohmic conductors have resistances which decrease rapidly with temperature. These are called **thermistors**

27.8 Electricity in the home

Electricity is transmitted from power stations to our homes and factories by the National Grid system. The current is carried from power stations to sub-stations by thick cables supported by pylons. Thick cables have a lower resistance than thin cables, so there is a smaller proportion of the electrical energy lost as heat.

Current from the National Grid

The current supplied to our homes by the National Grid is **alternating current (a.c.)**. In an alternating current, electrons flow forwards, then backwards. In the mains supply, the electrons change direction 50 times per second. In comparison, the current from a battery is **direct current (d.c.)**. In a direct current, the electrons flow in the same direction all the time.

There are two important reasons why power stations provide alternating current:

- It is easier to generate than d.c.
- Its voltage can be changed more easily (see section 28.11).

Alternating currents and transmission by the National Grid are discussed further in sections 28.10 and 28.11.

Resistors provide a resistance to an alternating current in the same way as they resist a direct current. So, a.c. supply can be used for heating and lighting in our homes. However, unlike direct current from a cell, alternating current does *not* cause electrolysis (refer back to section 16.4). As the current goes first one way then the other way, each electrode is alternately positive then negative. This happens 50 times per second which is too fast for any reactions at the electrodes.

The mains supply to our homes

There are **two cables** from the mains supply to your home. One cable is **live**, the other is **neutral**. The live wire is the dangerous wire. It is alternately positive and then negative with a potential difference (voltage) of 240 V relative to the neutral wire. The voltage of the neutral wire stays close to zero.

Figure 27.13 (overleaf) shows a general plan of the wiring in a house. The supply from the mains cable passes through a main fuse and then through the electricity meter to a **fuse box**. The fuse box acts as a distribution point for the electricity supply to the house. In the fuse box, there are several fuses. Each fuse leads to a different circuit servicing different areas in the house.

Most houses have two or three **ring main circuits** for the three-pin wall sockets. Each ring main will have about ten sockets. Notice (in Fig. 27.13) that all the sockets are connected to the ring main circuit in parallel, so each one receives the full mains voltage. The long loop or 'ring' of cable which joins the sockets contains three wires – *the live wire*, *the neutral wire* and *an earth wire*. (Hence, it is called a three-core cable.) The ring main is protected by a 30 A fuse in the fuse box. This will melt ('blow') if the total current to the sockets is 30 A or greater.

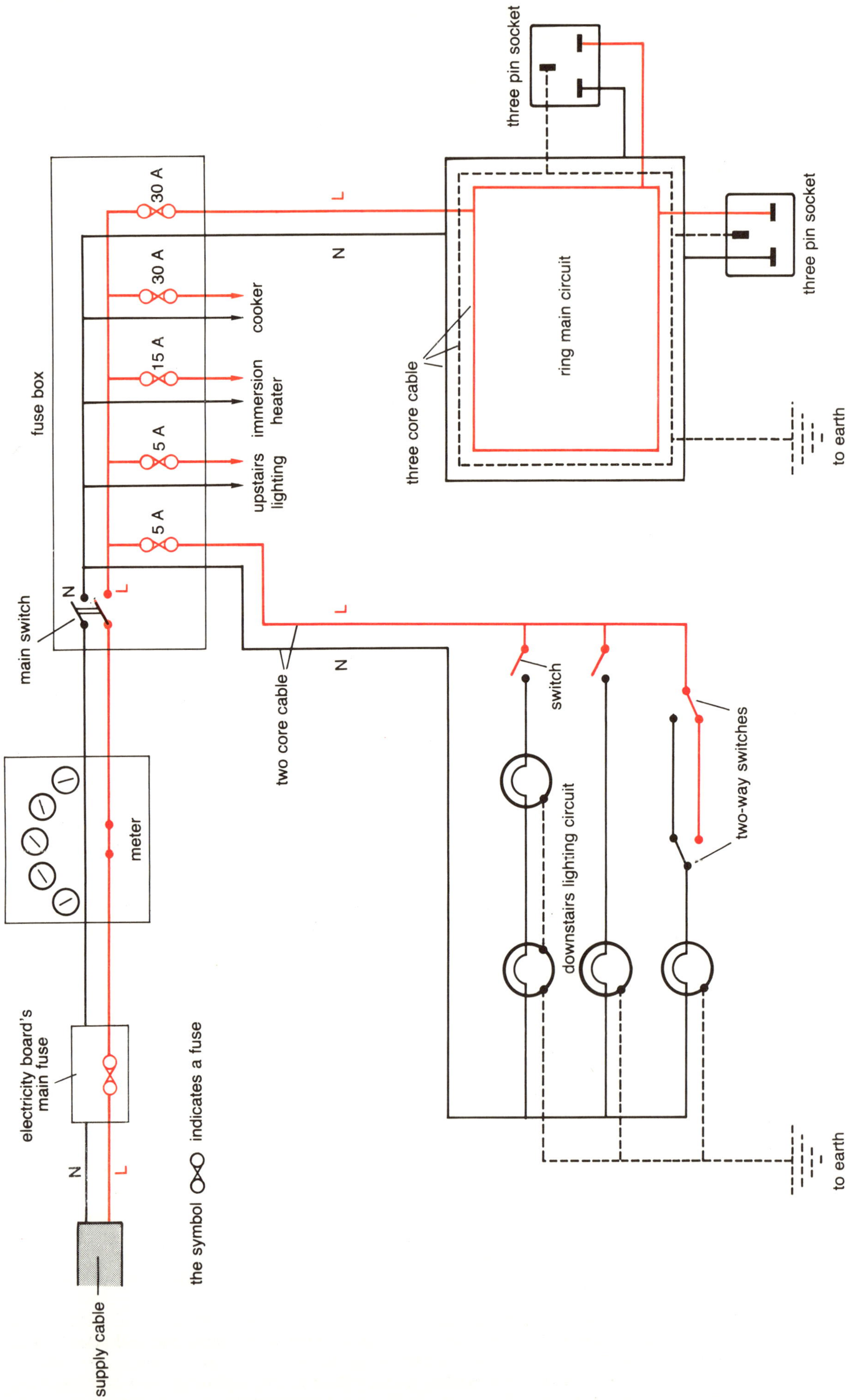

Fig. 27.13 A general plan of the wiring in a house

In addition to the ring main circuits, there are usually two or three lighting circuits and separate circuits for appliances such as cookers and immersion (hot water) heaters which each use large currents.

27.9 Safety in electrical circuits

Faults in electrical circuits can cause fires and very painful, even fatal, electric shocks. There are two main safety components in electrical circuits – fuses and earth wires.

FUSES

A fuse is simply a thin wire which melts if the current passing through it is too large. When a fault occurs, the fuse melts. This breaks the circuit and the current ceases.

The main purposes of a fuse are:

- to prevent fires – fires might easily occur if over-large currents caused part of the wiring to become red hot;
- to prevent damage to electrical appliances.

Fuses are always placed in the live wire (see Fig. 27.14). This will mean that if a fault occurs and the fuse 'blows', the live wire will be disconnected. Switches are also placed in the live wire. If switches were placed in the neutral wire, you could get a shock from an electrical appliance even when it was switched off.

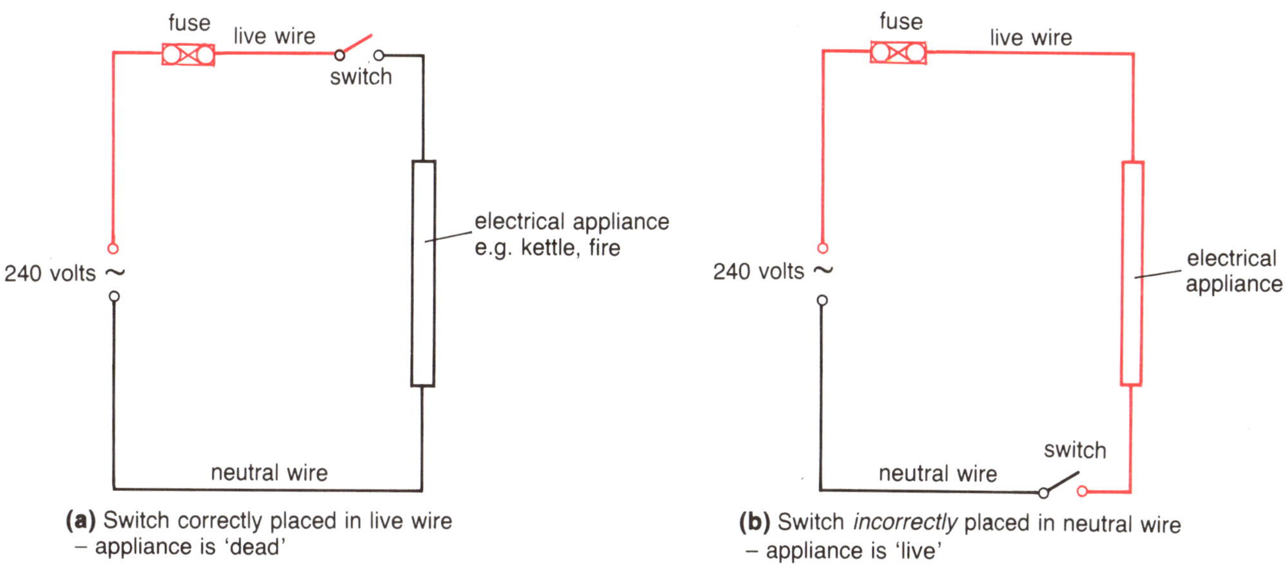

Fig. 27.14 Fuses and switches must always be placed in the live wire

EARTH WIRES

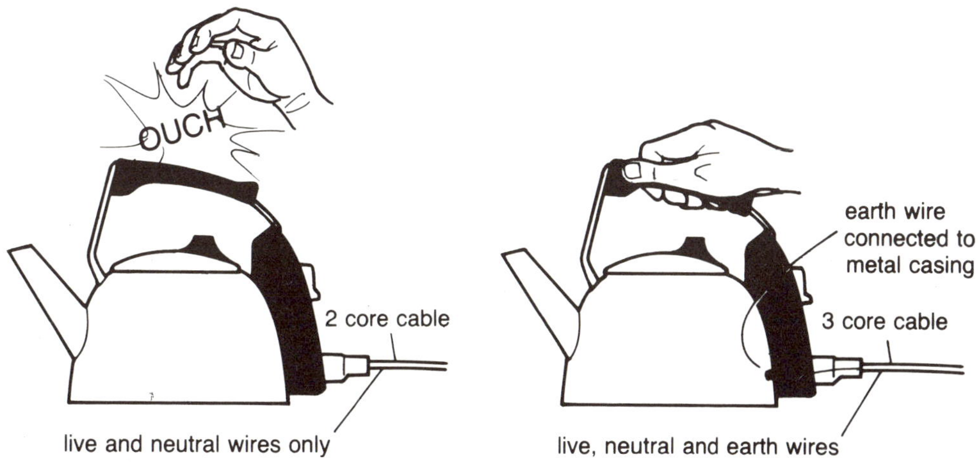

Fig. 27.15 Earth wires are important on electrical appliances with outer metal parts

(a) No earth to kettle
If a fault develops and the live wire touches the metal casing, then anyone touching the metal parts will get a shock

(b) Earth wire connected to metal on kettle
If the live wire touches the metal casing now, any current will flow away along the earth wire

Nowadays, many electrical appliances have outer parts made of plastic. Plastic does not conduct electricity, so these appliances do not usually need an earth wire.

THREE-PIN PLUGS

Three-pin plugs are carefully designed with safety in mind. Figure 27.16 shows a socket on the ring main circuit and a correctly wired three-pin plug.

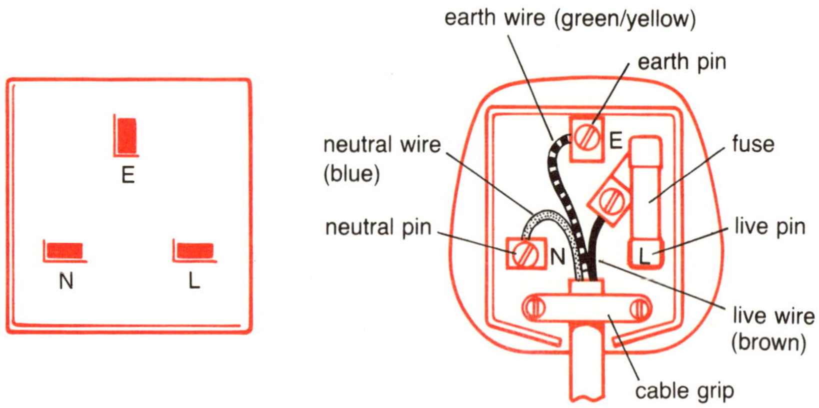

A socket on a ring main circuit **A correctly wired three-pin plug**

Fig. 27.16 Correct wiring for a three-pin plug

Notice the following points:

- The plug carries a fuse in the live circuit.
- The plug has an earth pin.
- The three wires in the cable must be connected to the correct pins in the plug:
  – the brown wire goes to the live pin, L;
  – the blue wire goes to the neutral pin, N;
  – the green/yellow wire goes to the earth pin, E.
- The plug must have a fuse of the appropriate value:
  – appliances such as table lamps, radios and televisions take small currents (well below 3 amps). They should have plugs fitted with 3 A fuses.
  – kettles, irons and electric fires usually take currents of more than 3 amps, so they should have plugs with 5 or 13 A fuses.

27.10 Power ratings

Most electrical appliances carry a **power rating** and an **operating voltage**. For example, an electric kettle may be labelled '2000 W, 240 V'. This means that its power rating is 2000 watts and its operating voltage is 240 volts.

In section 27.5, we found that the electrical energy supplied by a current I, in time t, at a voltage of V, is given by the formula

$$\underset{\text{(joules)}}{E} = \underset{\text{(volts)}}{V} \times \underset{\text{(amps)}}{I} \times \underset{\text{(seconds)}}{t}$$

In section 24.4, power (wattage) was defined as follows:

$$\underset{\text{(watts)}}{\text{Power}} = \frac{\text{Energy output (joules)}}{\text{Time taken (seconds)}}$$

$$\text{i.e. } P = \frac{E}{t}$$

Substituting for E, we get

$$P = \frac{V \times I \times \cancel{t}}{\cancel{t}} = V \times I$$

i.e. $\underset{\text{(watts)}}{\textbf{Power}} = \underset{\text{(volts)}}{\textbf{Voltage}} \times \underset{\text{(amps)}}{\textbf{Current}}$

Using the last equation we can find the current taken by the electric kettle with a power rating of 2000 watts.

power = voltage × current

So, in this case,

2000 watts = 240 volts × I amps

therefore, $I = \frac{2000}{240} = 8.3$ A

The current in the heating element of the kettle will be 8.3 A. A 3 amp fuse would not be adequate. The kettle requires a 10 or 13 A fuse.

Table 27.2 shows the power ratings of some electrical appliances. The power of an appliance tells us its rate of working in watts or joules per second. For example, the television in table 27.2 uses 60 joules of energy per second.

Table 27.2 Power ratings of some common electrical appliances

Appliance	*Power rating/W*
light bulb	100
television	60
electric iron	750
kettle	2000
electric fire	2500

27.11 Electricity bills

Electricity boards charge for the amount of electricity (energy) which you use. The amount of electricity which you use is recorded on a meter. The meter measures energy in units called **kilowatt hours (kWh)**. If you use a one kilowatt (1 kW) electric fire for one hour, you will use one kilowatt hour (1 kWh) of energy (i.e. 1 unit on the meter). The cost of electricity is about 6 pence per unit (i.e. 6 p per kWh).

Electrical energy is measured by the Electricity Companies in kilowatt hours rather than joules, because one joule is a very small amount:

1 kWh = 1 kW for 1 hour

= 1000 W for 3600 seconds

Energy = Power × time

so 1 kWh = 1000 × 3600 = 3 600 000 joules

Example

How much does it cost to use a 2500 W electric fire for four hours if electricity costs 6 p per unit?

Power rating: 2500 W = 2.5 kW

Energy used = power × time

= 2.5 kW × 4 hours

= 10 kWh

1 kWh (1 unit) costs 6 p, therefore total cost will be 60 p (10 × 6 p).

Quick test 27

Questions 1 to 3

The diagram below shows a circuit which has two resistors in series with a 10 volt supply.

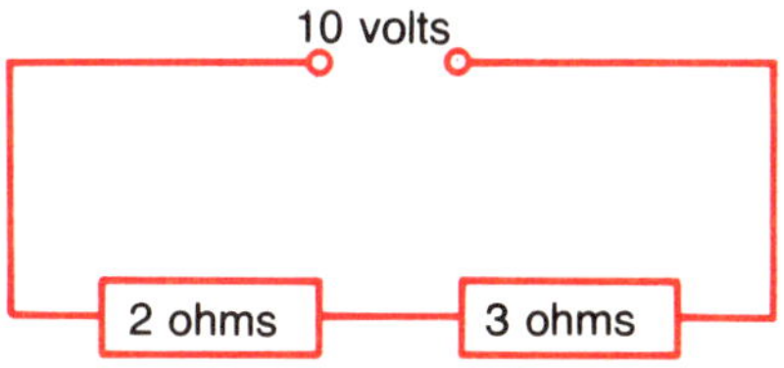

1 What is the total resistance of the two resistors?
2 What is the current flowing in the circuit?
3 What is the voltage across the 2 ohms resistor?

Questions 4 to 6

Many cars have a heated rear window. This is made of wires which are attached to the glass and which get hot when an electric current passes through them. The car's battery provides the electrical energy. Here is the electrical circuit.

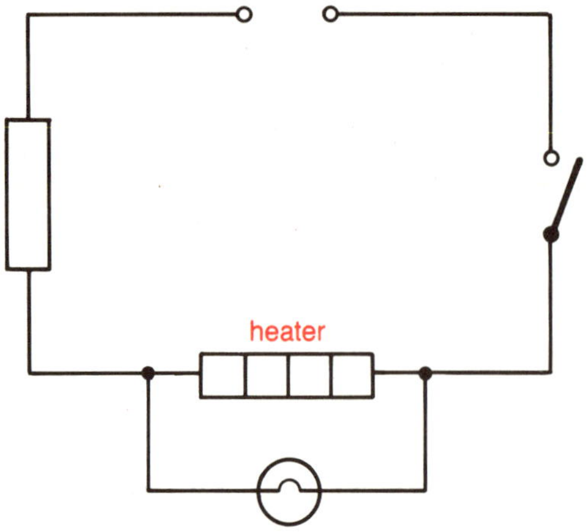

4 On the circuit, label these parts:
switch, bulb (filament lamp), fuse, 12 V supply. (2 marks)

5 What happens if too much current flows in the circuit? (2 marks)

6 On a cold, damp morning the driver cannot see through the rear window because of water droplets (condensation). She turns on the window heater. After a few minutes, the window begins to clear.
Describe in detail, what happens to the water molecules as they gain energy from the heater. (4 marks)

(*NEA*, 1988)

Questions 7 to 10

An electric kettle carries a label as shown here. it brings a kettle full of water to the boil in three minutes.

3 pints/1.7 litres
3 kW
230/240 volts

7 How long can the kettle be used on just one unit of electricity?

8 If the mains voltage is 240 V, what current will flow through the kettle after it is switched on?

9 What difference would there be in the current if the mains voltage was only 120 V?

10 What else would you need to know to find the cost of boiling a kettle full of water?

Questions 11 to 15

The drawing shows a fuse wire card. At points X, Y and Z, the wording has been removed.

At point X several words are missing.

At point Y a number is missing.

At point Z one word is missing.

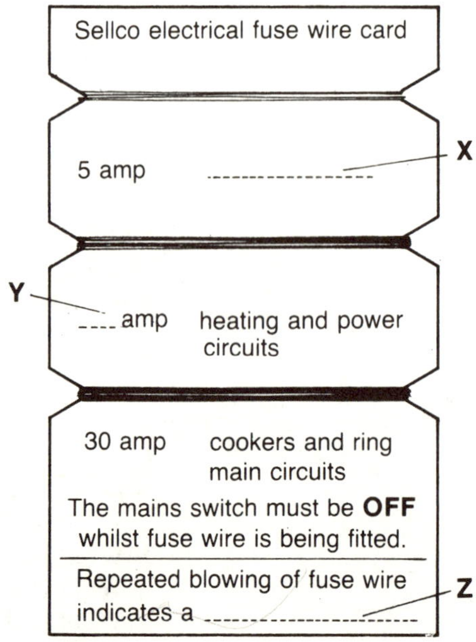

11 Suggest what should be written at **(a)** X, **(b)** Y, **(c)** Z. (3 marks)

12 What is the *physical difference* between 5 amp and 30 amp fuse wires? (1 mark)

13 Why do you think that fuse wire is always made of a metal or alloy? (1 mark)

14 **(a)** What could happen if the mains switch were not off when fuse wire is fitted? (1 mark)

(b) What actually happens to fuse wire when a fuse blows? (1 mark)

(c) How would you deal with a fire caused by an electrical fault? (1 mark)

15 How do you know that the lamps in your classroom are wired in parallel and not in series? (1 mark)

(*WJEC*, 1988)

Questions 16 to 19

The figure shows part of a household wiring circuit.

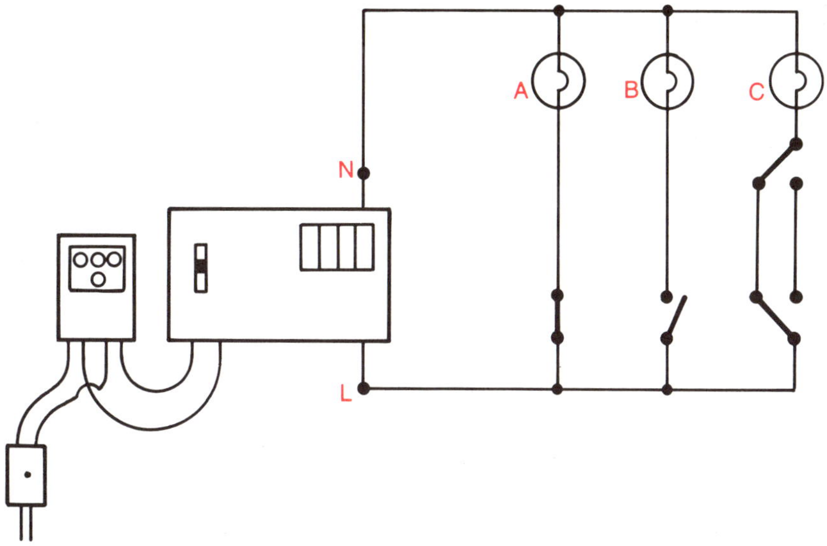

16 **(a)** Mark 'C' on the figure to label the consumer unit (fuse box). (1 mark)

(b) Mark 'M' on the figure to label the meter. (1 mark)

17 Which bulbs are on? (2 marks)

18 Which bulb is connected with two-way switches? (1 mark)

19 What would happen if a wire was added to connect L and N? (1 mark)

(*LEAG*, 1988)

Questions 20 to 21

20 The figure shows the inside of a 13 A mains plug.

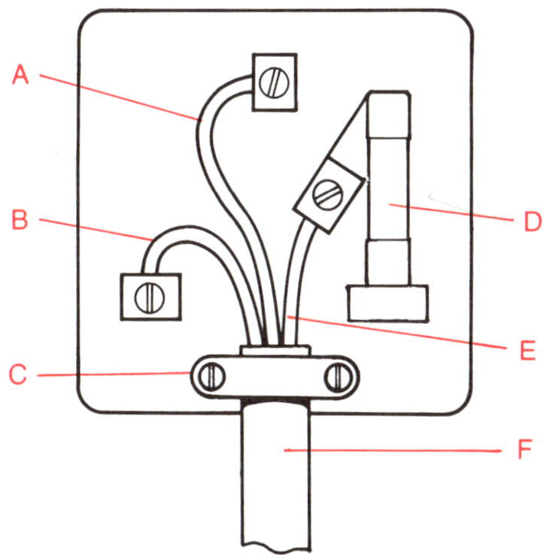

Name the parts labelled A to F. (6 marks)

21 Each year many people are killed in accidents at home involving electricity. Give *four* sensible safety rules for people using electrical appliances. (4 marks)

(*LEAG*, 1988)

28 MOTORS AND GENERATORS

28.1 Magnets and magnetic poles

A few metals including iron, are **magnetic**. They are attracted by magnets. Figure 28.1 shows what happens when a magnet is dipped into a pile of iron filings. The filings cling around the ends of the magnets. These ends of the magnet are called **poles**. The magnetic forces seem to come from these poles.
The magnet will also attract steel pins and nichrome wire, but nothing happens with brass tacks or plastic buttons. The only common materials which magnets attract are *iron, cobalt, nickel and their alloys* such as steel, nichrome and Alnico.

Fig. 28.1 Iron filings are attracted by a magnet

28.2 North and south poles

Figure 28.2 shows what happens when a bar magnet is suspended from a fine thread. When the magnet comes to rest, one end always points north. This end of the magnet is called the **north-seeking pole** or **north pole** for short. The other end of the magnet is called the **south-seeking pole** or **south pole**. Because they behave in this way, magnets are used as compasses.

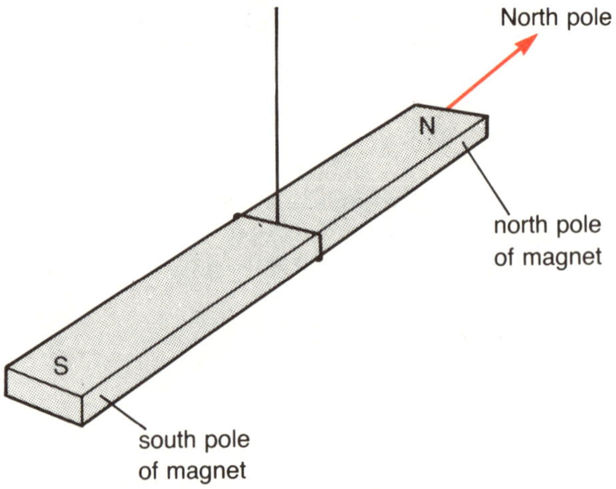

Figure 28.2

Every magnet has a north pole and a south pole. When the poles of two magnets are brought together:

- **Like poles (two N-poles or two S-poles) repel each other.**
- **Unlike poles (a N-pole and a S-pole) attract.**

Compare this with positive and negative charges (refer back to chapter 16).

28.3 Permanent and temporary magnets

When pieces of iron or steel are placed near a magnet, they become magnets themselves. The bar magnet **induces** an opposite pole in the iron or steel nearest itself. This **induced pole** is then attracted to the magnet (Fig. 28.3).

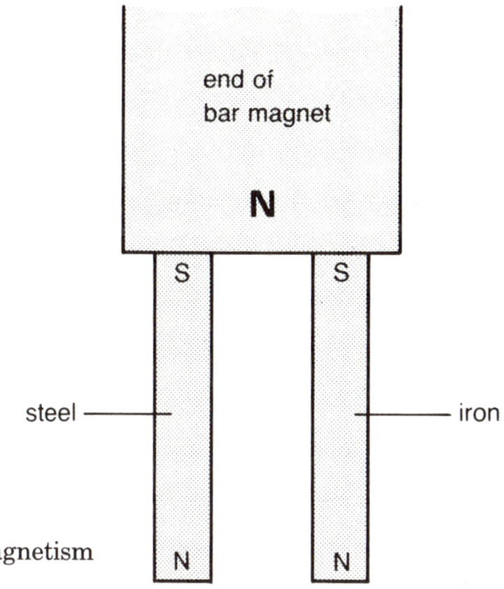

Fig. 28.3 Induced magnetism

Experiments show that:

- Iron is easy to magnetize, but it loses its magnetism when the bar magnet is removed. Iron is said to form **temporary magnets**.
  Because of this property, iron is used in electromagnets, where the magnetism is 'switched' on and off very easily. Iron is often described as *soft iron* when it is used in electromagnets. This is because it is so easy to magnetize and demagnetize.
- Steel retains its magnetism much better than iron. If the bar magnet in Fig. 28.3 is removed the steel will remain magnetized. Steel is used to make **permanent magnets**.

28.4 Magnetic fields

Strong magnets can attract other magnetic materials:

- from a distance away;
- through non-magnetic materials, such as paper and wood;
- through a vacuum.

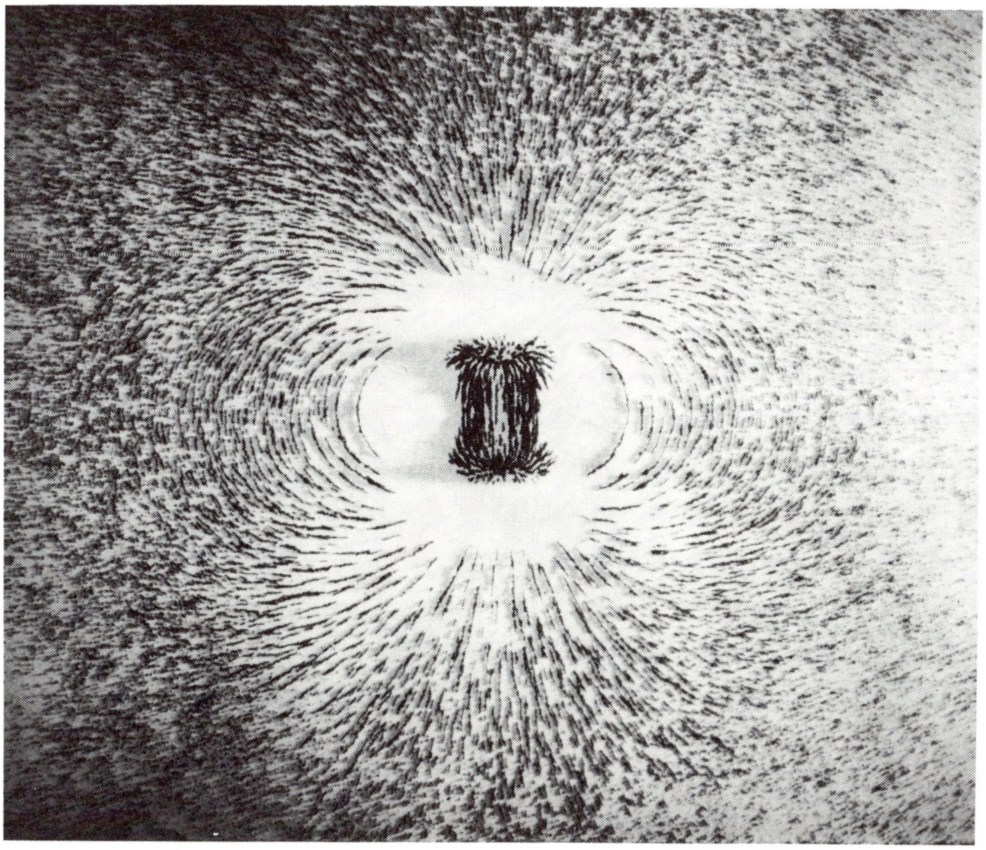

Fig. 28.4 Investigating the magnetic field around a bar magnet using iron filings

The region around a magnet, where its magnetic force acts, is called a **magnetic field**.

INVESTIGATING MAGNETIC FIELDS

Using iron filings

Sprinkle iron filings onto a sheet of paper on top of the magnet. Tap the paper gently. The iron filings are quickly magnetized and line up in the direction of the magnetic field (see Fig. 28.4, p. 303).

Using a plotting compass

This is a more accurate method of defining the magnetic field around a magnet. A plotting compass is a small compass with a magnetic needle. Using the plotting compass it is possible to draw a series of lines running from the north pole to the south pole (see Fig. 28.5). These lines are called **lines of magnetic force**.

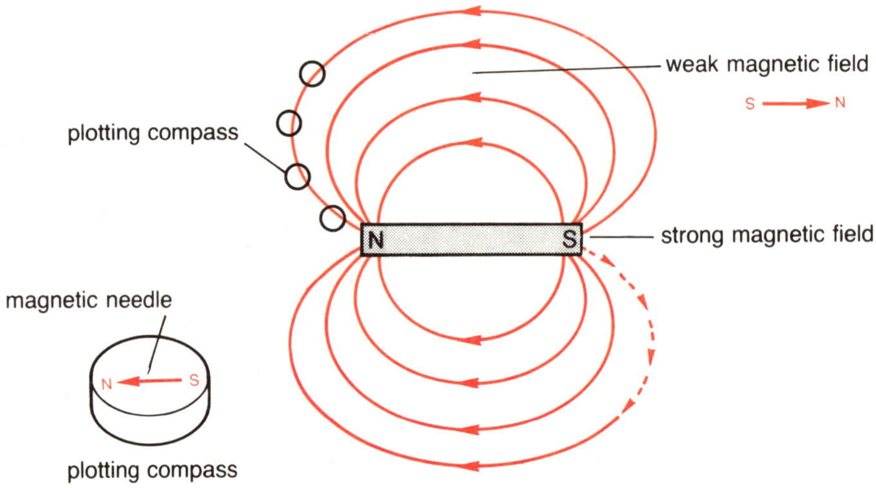

Fig. 28.5 Investigating the magnetic field around a bar magnet using a plotting compass

Notice that the **lines of force**:

- always point away from a N-pole and towards a S-pole.
- never cross.
- are close together where the field is strong and further apart where the field is weak.

28.5 The Earth's magnetic field

The Earth has its own magnetic field. It behaves as if there is a huge bar magnet along its north-south axis (see Fig. 28.6).

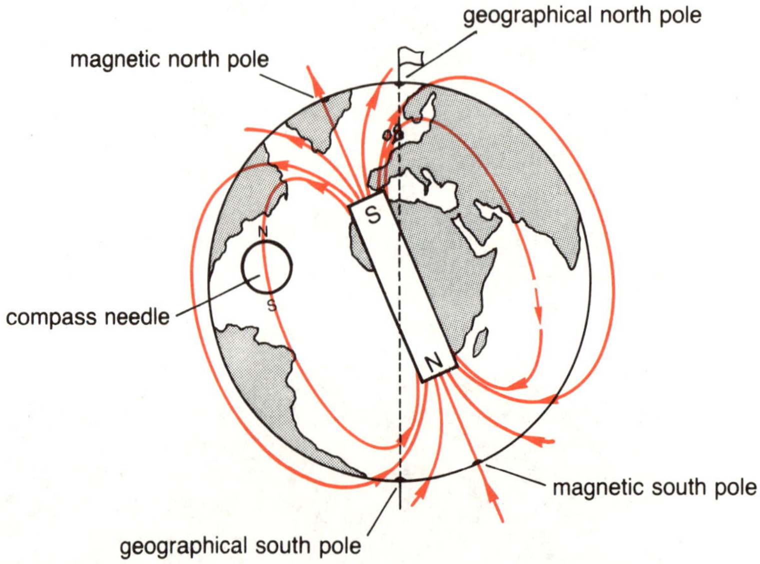

Fig. 28.6 The Earth's magnetic field

Notice two important points shown in Fig. 28.6:

- The Earth's magnetic north pole is not at the same point as the geographical north pole.
- The Earth's magnetic north pole *attracts* the north poles of magnets. Therefore, the Earth's magnetic north is really a *south-seeking pole*.

28.6 The magnetic effects of electric currents

Magnetism can be turned on and off at the flick of a switch. This is possible because

every electric current produces a magnetic field.

The magnetism produced by electricity is called **electromagnetism**.

The magnetic field around a straight wire

The magnetic field around a straight wire can be investigated using the apparatus shown in Fig. 28.7.

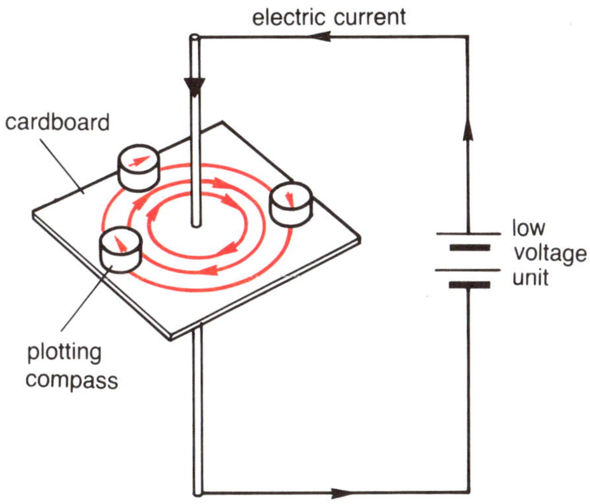

Fig. 28.7 Investigating the field around a straight wire carrying a current

If the current in the circuit is reversed, the compass will point in the opposite direction. If the direction of the current is known, the direction of the field can be predicted by the **right-hand grip rule**:

> *Imagine gripping the wire with your right hand so that your thumb points in the direction of the current. Your fingers will then be pointing around the wire in the direction of the magnetic field.*

The magnetic field around a solenoid

A solenoid is a long coil of wire. Figure 28.8 (overleaf) shows what happens when an electric current is passed through a solenoid. The solenoid acts like a magnet. The lower part of the diagram shows a good way to work out whether the end of a solenoid is a north pole or a south pole. Remember that the arrows on the wires show the direction of the current (conventional current), *not* the direction of electron flow. The arrows come out of the letters N and S in the same direction as the current in the wire.

The strength of the magnetic field around a solenoid can be increased by:

- using a larger current:
- having more coils in the solenoid;
- having a soft iron-core through the solenoid.

The solenoid in Fig. 28.8 will act as an electromagnet. When the current is switched on, the solenoid acts like a magnet. When the current is switched off, the magnetism disappears. Electromagnets like this, based on solenoids, are used in electric bells, telephones, loudspeakers, relays and electric motors.

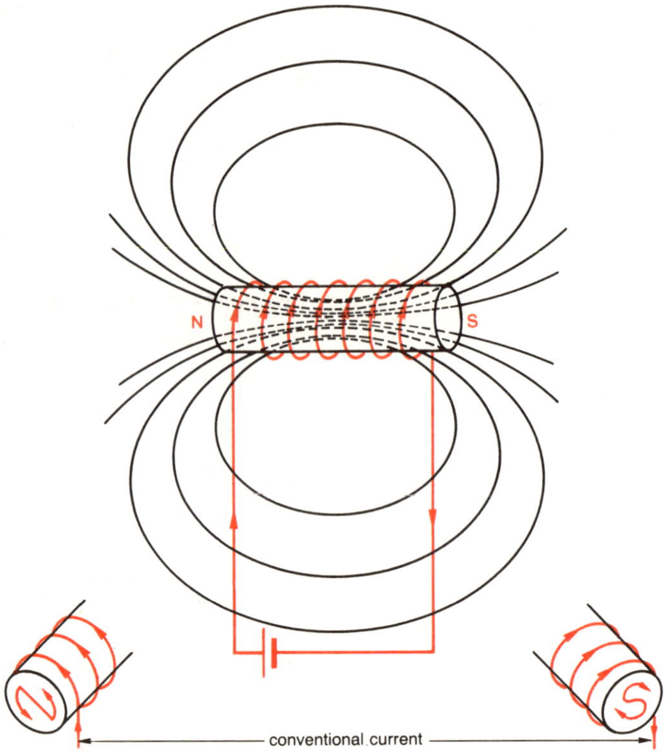

Fig. 28.8 The magnetic field around a solenoid

28.7 Uses of electromagnets

Electromagnetic relays

Relays are used to operate various appliances including automatic doors, burglar alarms and car ignition systems. An electromagnetic relay is a switch controlled by an electromagnet. It works like a relay race. In a relay race, a baton is passed from one runner to the next. In an electromagnetic relay, signals are passed from one circuit to the next by electric currents.

Figure 28.9 shows the electromagnetic relay in a car ignition system. The starter motor requires a very large current (about 100 A). This would normally require a heavy-duty switch. Such a switch might easily produce sparks which would be dangerous to the user. These problems are overcome by using a relay system.

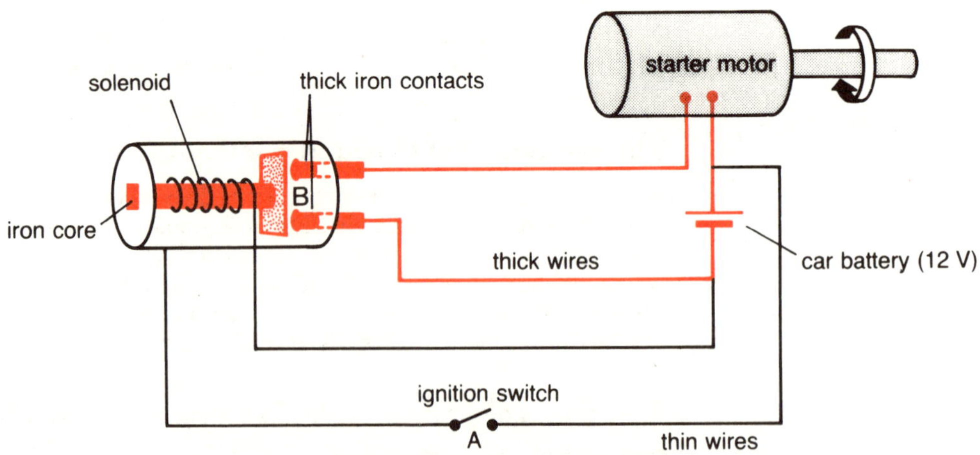

Fig. 28.9 A car ignition system – the relay circuit is shown in red

The relay circuit in Fig. 28.9, (in red) includes an iron core inside a solenoid. When the ignition is switched on at A a small current flows in the solenoid. The iron core is magnetized and attracted towards the thick iron contacts at B. Contact is made at B and a current flows to the starter motor.

Moving coil loudspeakers

Figure 28.10 shows a loudspeaker of the type used in a radio or a television. Notice the solenoid (coil) between the poles of the magnet. Electrical signals from the radio cause the current in the solenoid to change. As this current changes, the force on the solenoid (coil) from the permanent magnet changes and the coil moves. These changes happen very rapidly, making the paper cone vibrate in and out so rapidly that it produces audible sounds.

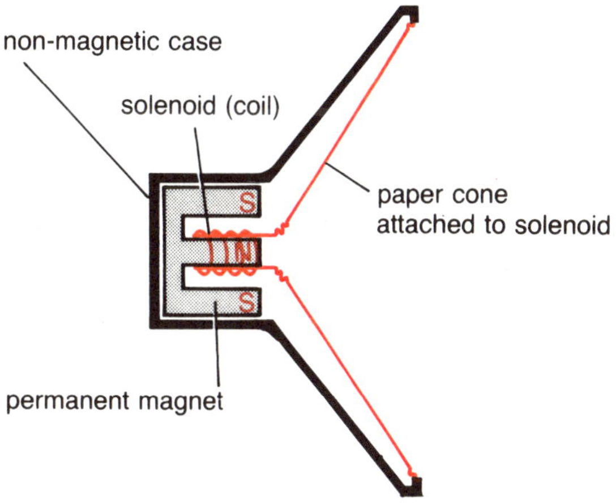

Fig. 28.10 A moving-coil loudspeaker

28.8 Electric motors

An electric motor uses electricity and magnetism to produce movement. This is called the **motor effect**. It can be demonstrated using the apparatus shown in Fig. 28.11.

- The magnet provides magnetism.
- The current provides electricity.
- When the switch is closed, the wire jumps up.
- If the current is reversed *or* the field is reversed, the wire moves downwards.
- If both the current *and* the field are reversed, the wire jumps up again.

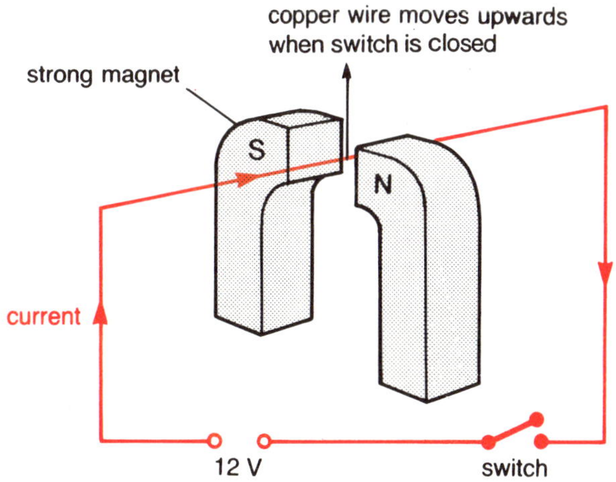

Fig. 28.11 Demonstrating the motor effect

Notice two important points from these results:

- The wire always moves at right angles to the direction of the field and the direction of the current.
- The direction of the wire's movement depends on the direction of the field and the direction of the current.

You can predict the direction in which the wire will move using the **left-hand motor rule**:

Hold the first finger, second finger and thumb of your left hand at right angles to each other (Fig. 28.12). If you place your hand so that the ***f****irst finger points in the direction of the* ***f****ield from N to S and the se****c****ond finger points in the direction of the* ***c****urrent; your thu****mb*** *will point in the direction in which the wire will* ***m****ove.*

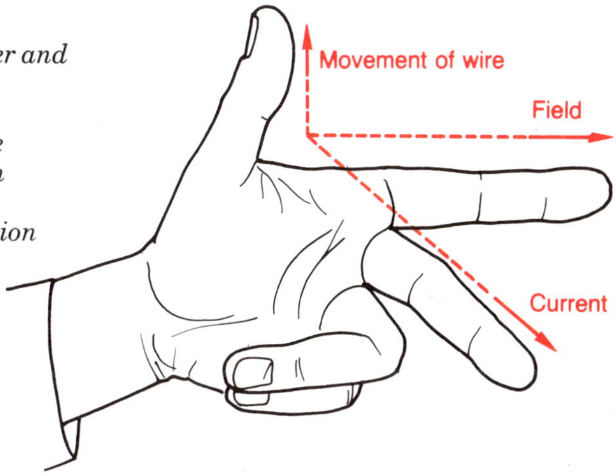

Fig. 28.12 Using the left-hand motor rule

The motor effect is put to use in electric motors:

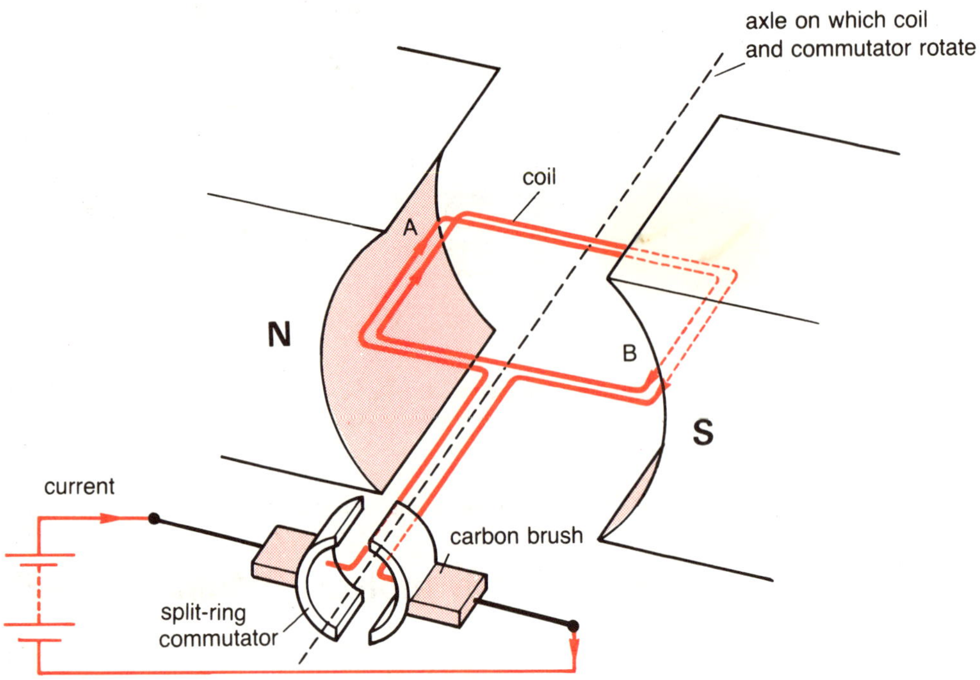

Fig. 28.13 A simple direct current (d.c.) motor

A simple d.c. motor has a coil which can rotate between the poles of a magnet. The ends of the coil are connected to the two halves of a split metal ring called a **commutator**. The commutator rotates with the coil. Two carbon contacts (carbon brushes) press lightly on the commutator.

Applying the left-hand rule to Fig. 28.13:
side A of the coil will try to move down,
and side B of the coil will try to move up.
So the forces acting on the coil will rotate it anticlockwise until it is vertical.

When the coil is vertical, the gaps in the commutator are opposite the brushes. So there is no current in the coil. This causes the coil to slow down, but as it overshoots the vertical position, the contacts at the commutator change over. Side B of the coil is now on the left where side A was before. In this position side B is forced downwards and side A is forced upwards. So, the coil continues to rotate anticlockwise.

In commercial motors:

- *electromagnets* are used rather than permanent magnets because permanent magnets slowly lose their magnetism.
- the coils have *dozens, or even hundreds, of turns* to increase the turning force.
- the coils are wound on a *soft iron core* to increase the strength of the magnetic field.

28.9 Electromagnetic induction

In an electric motor, an electric current passes through a coil in a magnetic field. This causes the coil to move.

i.e. electricity + magnetism ⟶ movement

The motor converts electrical energy into kinetic energy. The process can also be reversed – if a coil is moved in a magnetic field, an electric current is produced.

i.e. movement + magnetism ⟶ electricity

In this case, kinetic energy is converted to electrical energy.

Electric currents produced by this method are called *induced* currents and the effect is called **electromagnetic induction**. This effect is used in dynamos for bicycle lights, alternators in cars and generators in power stations. All these machines use movement and magnetism to generate electricity.

Fig. 28.14 All air passengers must walk through an archway like the one in the photograph. The archway is part of a security check. Metal objects cause changes in an electromagnetic field when they pass below the arch. A circuit detects the changes and warns the security guards.

INVESTIGATING ELECTROMAGNETIC INDUCTION

Figure 28.15 (overleaf) shows an experiment to investigate electromagnetic induction.

- There is no current when the wire is stationary.
- **To produce a current, the wire must move *across* the lines of magnetic force** between the poles of the magnet. Therefore, a current flows when the wire is moved up (direction 5) or down (direction 6). There is no current when the wire is moved in directions 1, 2, 3 and 4 – in these directions, the wire is moving *along* the line of force, not across them.
- The current only flows while the wire is moving.
- Reversing the movement reverses the current.
- An induced current also flows if the wire is stationary and the magnet is moved up and down.
- The induced current is larger when
  – the wire is moved faster;
  – a stronger magnet is used;
  – more turns of wire are used.

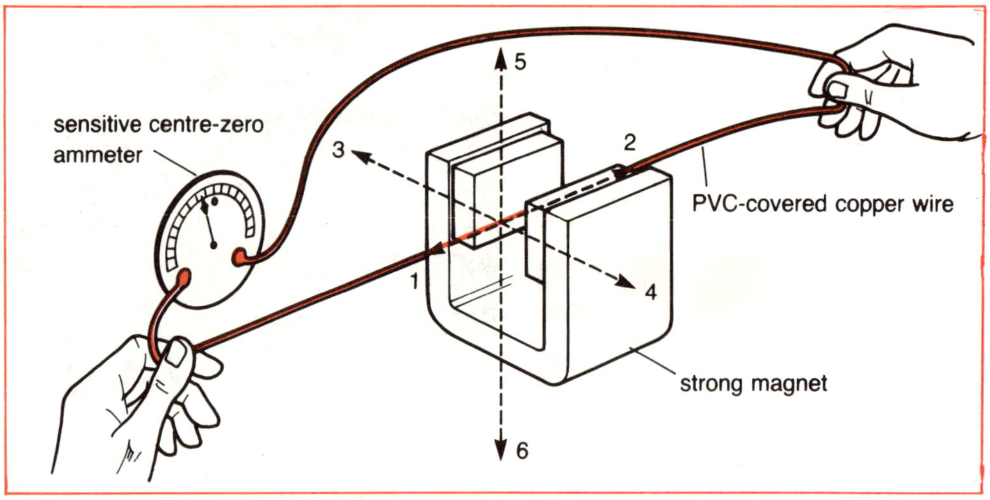

Fig. 28.15 Investigating electromagnetic induction

These results are summarized by **Faraday's law of electromagnetic induction**:

The size of the induced current is proportional to the rate at which the wire/coil moves across the magnetic lines of force.

28.10 The a.c. generator (alternator)

Figure 28.16 shows a simple alternating current (a.c.) generator. The rings on the axle are fixed to the coil and rotate with it. As the axle rotates, the coil moves through a magnetic field and an induced current is generated.

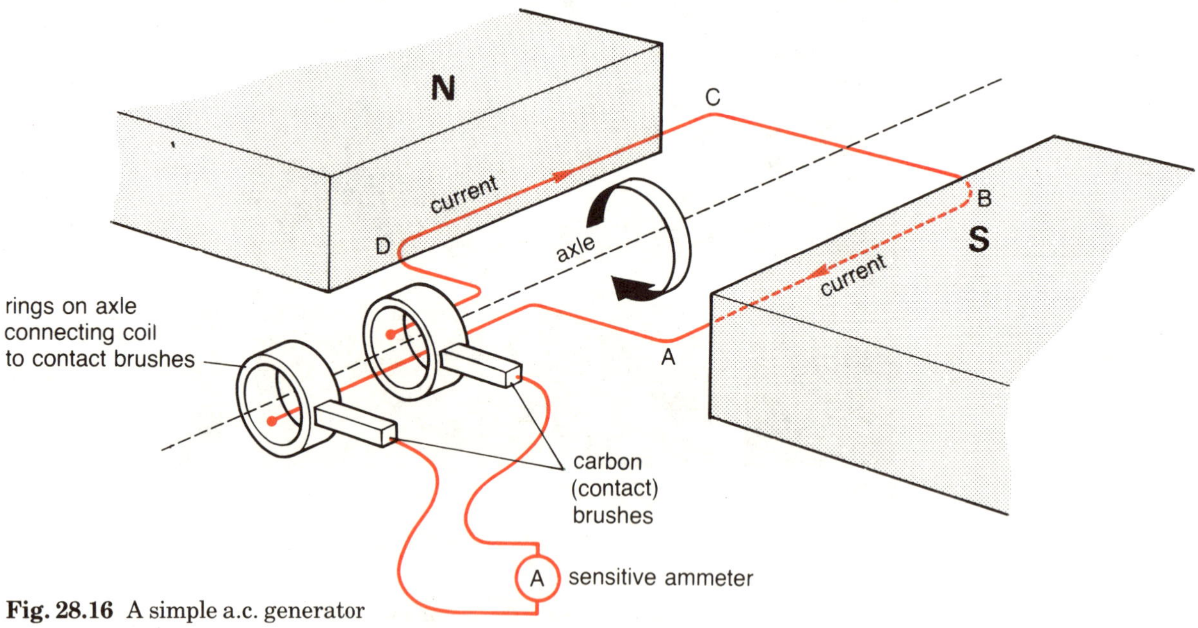

Fig. 28.16 A simple a.c. generator

Figure 28.17 shows how the induced current varies during one turn of the coil:

Position (i) coil horizontal
– cutting lines of force at fastest rate, therefore current is at a maximum. As coil moves towards the vertical position, current falls.

Position (ii) coil vertical
– no lines of force being crossed, therefore current is zero. As coil moves towards the horizontal position, current increases but in *opposite* direction.

Position (iii) coil horizontal
– current in opposite direction reaches a maximum. As coil moves towards the vertical again, current falls.

Position (iv) coil vertical
– current zero again

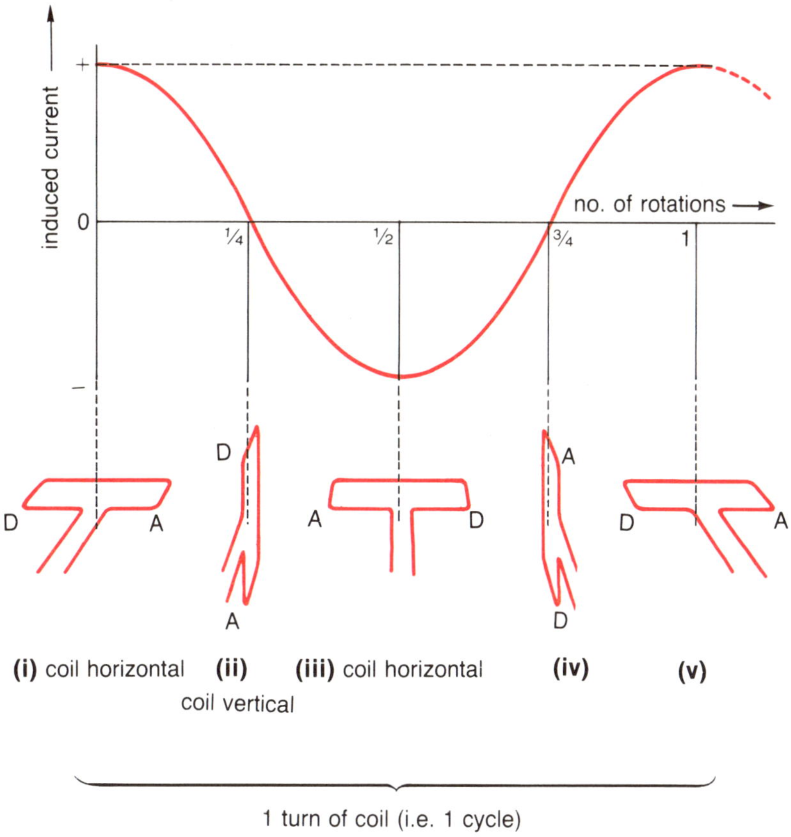

Fig. 28.17 Variation in the induced current during one turn of the coil

Notice, from Fig. 28.17, that the current flowing from the generator is an alternating current. This is why an a.c. generator is sometimes called an **alternator**.

Power stations have huge a.c. generators. These have a rotating magnet rather than a rotating coil. The advantage of this is that rings and contact brushes are not needed. This cuts out the wear and tear from sparks and friction.

This arrangement is also used in car alternators. The engine causes an electromagnet to rotate inside several stationary coils. The alternating current is then changed into direct current so that it can recharge the car's battery.

The alternator (a.c. generator) is easily modified to give direct current. This can be done by using *split* rings (commutators). The commutators and contact brushes are arranged in the same way as in a d.c. motor (Fig. 28.13) so that the current always flows in the same direction (see Fig. 28.18). Generators which produce direct current are sometimes called **dynamos**.

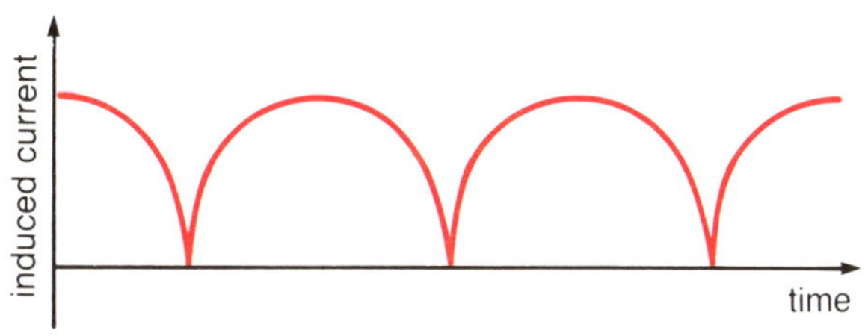

Fig. 28.18 The current from a d.c. generator (dynamo)

28.11 Transformers

In section 28.9, we saw that an induced current is generated in a coil as long as it is cutting *across* the lines of force from a magnet.

An induced current can also be obtained in a (secondary) coil if the magnet is replaced by a coil (**primary coil**) carrying an alternating current. As the alternating current in the primary coil changes direction, the magnetic field continually increases and decreases. The lines of force cutting across the secondary coil continually change and this produces a continuous alternating voltage in the secondary coil.

This is the principle behind **transformers** (see Fig. 28.19 overleaf).

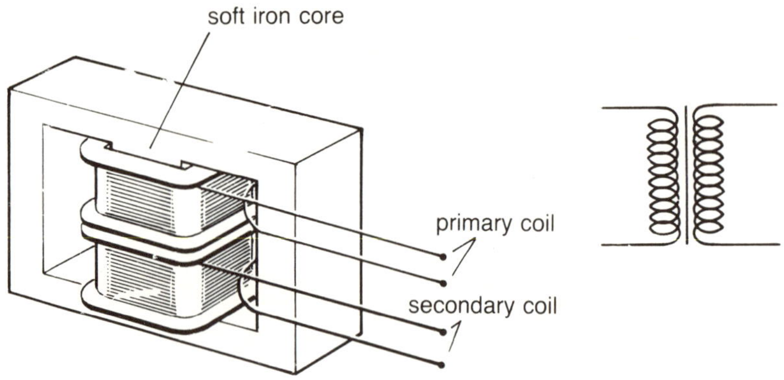

A transformer in which the coils are wound side by side (in some transformers, one coil is wound over the other)

a circuit symbol for a transformer

Fig. 28.19 Transformers

- A transformer is made by putting two coils of wire (a primary coil and a secondary coil) on a soft iron core.
- The primary coil is connected to an alternating current and an alternating voltage is induced in the secondary coil.
- The induced voltage in the secondary coil depends on the number of turns in the two coils. This makes transformers useful because they allow us to change the voltage of a supply.

The voltage, *V*, induced in a coil is proportional to the number of turns, *n*, i.e. $V \propto n$.

This means that:

$$\frac{\text{Voltage across secondary coil } (V_s)}{\text{Voltage across primary coil } (V_p)} = \frac{\text{Number of turns on secondary } (n_s)}{\text{Number of turns on primary } (n_p)}$$

Example

A transformer is being used to reduce the mains supply from 240 V to 12 V for use with a model railway. There are 500 turns on the primary coil in the transformer. How many turns are there on the secondary coil?

$$\frac{V_s}{V_p} = \frac{n_s}{n_p}, \text{ so } \frac{12}{240} = \frac{n_s}{500}$$

therefore, $n_s = 500 \times \frac{12}{240} = \underline{25 \text{ turns}}$

In this example, the transformer is a **step-down transformer**. Step-down transformers give a *decrease in voltage*. They have fewer turns on the secondary coil than on the primary coil. **Step-up transformers** give an increase in voltage. They have more turns on the secondary coil than on the primary coil.

28.12 Transmitting electricity

Transformers are important in the transmission of electricity from power stations via the National Grid. Large power stations generate electricity at 25 000 volts. This is 'stepped up' to 275 000 or 400 000 volts using a transformer before being transmitted through the Grid.

Most transformers can transfer electrical power very efficiently from the primary circuit to the secondary circuit. If the transformer is 100 per cent efficient:

power input from primary = power output from secondary

therefore $V_p \times I_p = V_s \times I_s$

From this equation, it is clear that if the voltage is stepped up from 25 000 to 400 000 volts for the Grid system, then the current must be stepped down proportionally. This is a big advantage. A small current has a much smaller heating effect in the cables. Less energy is therefore lost as heat. The lower current can also use thinner cables with pylons further apart. However, the transmission at higher voltages requires greater insulation.

The Grid voltage is reduced by step-down transformers at sub-stations before it is used in homes and factories. Some industrial plants take electrical energy from the

Grid system at 33 000 or 11 000 V. Transformers reduce this further to 240 V for use in our homes.

From time to time, people complain about the way in which electricity pylons and overhead cables spoil the environment. There is a lot of support for this view, particularly when pylons pass through beautiful countryside. However, laying cables underground would be more expensive and this would increase the cost of our electricity.

Quick test 28

Questions 1 to 6

The diagram below shows a compass placed near one end of a coil in position 1. When a current is passed through the coil, the compass needle points in the direction shown.

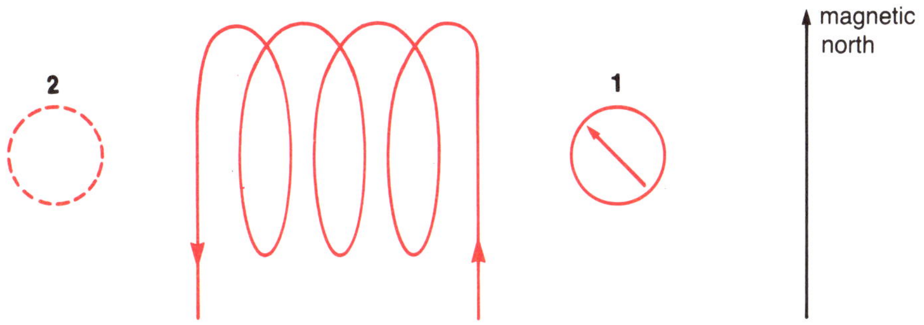

Will the compass needle point
- A closer to magnetic north,
- B further from magnetic north,
- C exactly as in position 1,
- D the same angle to magnetic north, but on the opposite side to that in position 1,
- E directly to magnetic north,

if the
1 current through the coil is decreased?
2 current flows in the opposite direction?
3 compass is moved to position 2?
4 coil has more turns?
5 coil is turned through 90°?
6 compass is moved to position 2 and the current is reversed?

Questions 7 to 9

Questions 7 to 9 concern the following pieces of equipment:
- A commutator
- B diode
- C relay
- D fuse
- E transformer

Which piece of equipment
7 is an essential part of a motor which uses direct current (d.c.)?
8 allows current to flow in one direction only?
9 is essential in the operation of a small 2-volt motor from the mains supply?

Questions 10 to 15

The apparatus shown in the diagram overleaf was used to study the magnetic field produced when an electric current flows through a solenoid. The magnet was placed on the forcemeter and the forcemeter was set to zero. For each current used, readings were taken with and without the iron core present. The results are shown in the table below.

Current/amps	*Forcemeter reading /N*	
	without iron core	*with iron core*
0.2	4	6
0.4	8	11
0.8	15	20
1.0	20	25

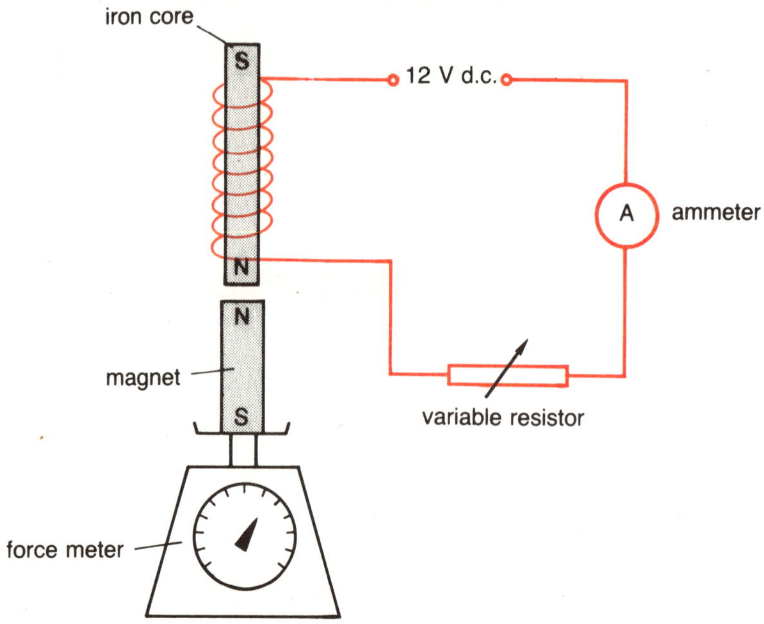

10 Why does the forcemeter not register zero when the apparatus is set up?
11 Why is the forcemeter set to zero?
12 Why is a variable resistor included in the circuit?
13 Explain why the forcemeter shows a reading when there is a current in the solenoid.
14 How does the force from the magnetic field depend on the size of the current?
15 How does the iron core affect the force from the magnetic field?
16 The following article recently appeared in a local newspaper.

> **Overhead versus underground**
> Protestors at yesterday's meeting voted against the proposal that electricity pylons should be built to carry power to remote farms on the island. They wanted the power cables to be buried underground. Some local residents, however, were not in favour of underground cables as some trees would have to be destroyed, and it takes longer to repair underground cables than overhead cables. The Central Electricity Generating Board pointed out that overhead cables capable of carrying 400 kV through the National Grid cost £506 000 per km, whereas underground cable costs £6 509 000 per km.

(a) From this article and your own knowledge, suggest **two** disadvantages of overhead cables and **two** disadvantages of underground cables. (4 marks)
(b) Most domestic appliances in Britain are rated at 220 – 240 V. Why is it necessary to carry electricity through the National Grid at 400 kV (400 000 V)? (2 marks)

(*MEG*, 1988)

Questions 17 to 21

A piece of steel is made into a magnet. It is hung up as shown.

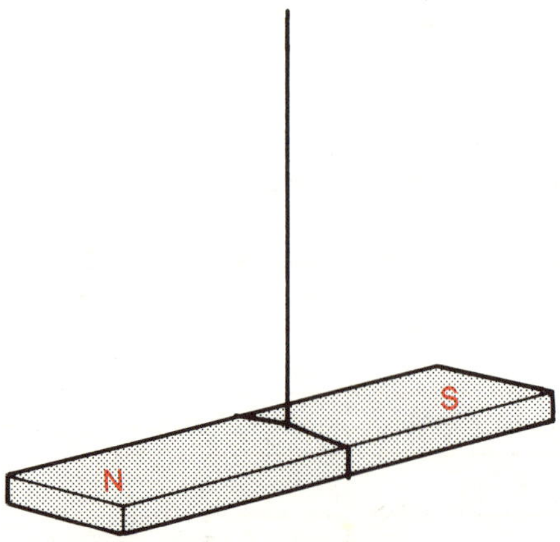

17 When it stops moving another N-pole is brought up to the N-pole of the magnet. What will happen? (1 mark)
18 There is a space around a magnet where it can affect iron filings or another magnet. What is this space called? (1 mark)

Suppose you made a model of the earth to show how a compass works. Here is a picture.

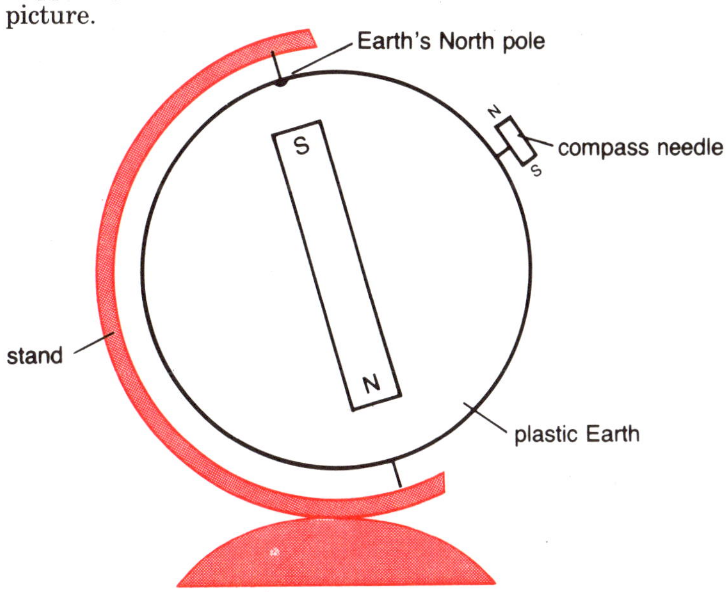

19 Why is the south pole of the magnet at the Earth's North pole? (1 mark)

20 The compass is placed on the surface of the model. It is in the field around the magnet. Explain why the needle will point towards the Earth's North pole. (3 marks)

21 Suggest a suitable material to use to make the stand. (1 mark)

(*NEA* (part question), 1988)

LONGER EXAM QUESTIONS

Most of the questions used in the 'Quick tests' at the end of each chapter were relatively short, objective questions requiring short answers. They were also confined to the topics considered in that particular chapter. In general, they were taken from the general level papers rather than the extension level papers of GCSE science examinations.

The extension level papers are usually designed for those students who are likely to achieve grades A or B. If you are aiming for a grade C or better in your GCSE exams, you will need to gain at least 60 per cent of the possible marks on those parts of the 'Quick tests' which are included in the syllabus for which you are studying. If you are aiming for a grade A you will need to score at least 80 per cent of the possible marks in the relevant parts of the 'Quick tests'.

Almost all the questions in this section are longer, structured questions. They require extended prose (three or four sentences) for the answers to some parts. Some of these questions test ideas taken from several chapters of this book. Most of them are taken from the extension level papers of actual GCSE examinations.

To obtain a grade B at GCSE you should aim to score at least 60 per cent of the possible marks on the relevant questions from extension level papers.

N.B.: Even if you are not aiming for a high grade, remember that the general level papers and the extension papers will both include various types of questions. They will both probably include some structured questions and they *must* both include questions which require extended prose. In addition, both types of paper must devote at least 15 per cent of marks to the applications and issues related to science.

Therefore it is important to attempt the longer exam questions in this section, as well as the 'Quick tests', whatever GCSE grade you are hoping to gain.

The marks allocated to different parts of the questions appear in brackets after the question. Answers are provided on pages 339–50.

Question 1

Front view of a three-pin power socket fixed to a wall

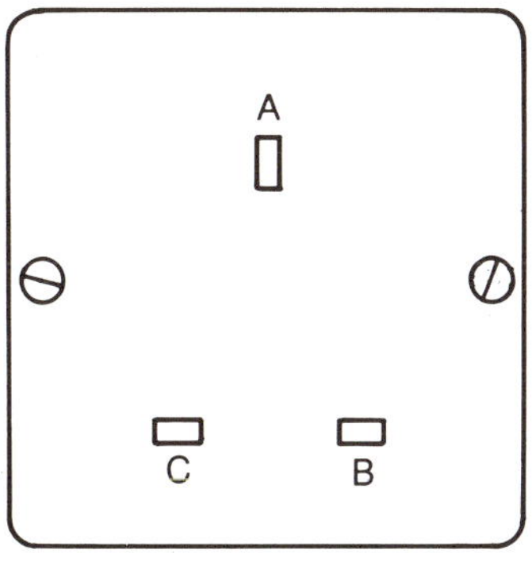

(a)(i) What is the name given to the wire that leads to the opening A? **(1)**

(ii) Why is it even more dangerous when a young child accidentally pushes a metal object into opening B rather than opening C? **(1)**

(iii) Explain why there should be **no** power sockets in a bathroom. **(3)**

(b) Explain why the plastic sleeve makes the new plug safer to use. **(2)**

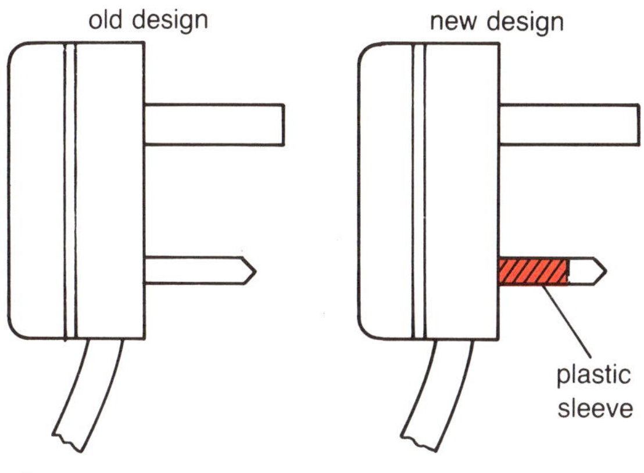

(c) Study the diagram below and answer the questions which follow.

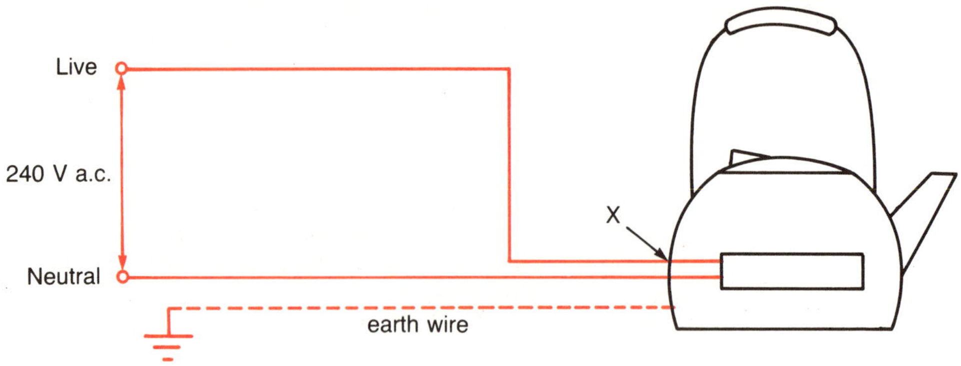

(i) What does 'a.c.' mean? **(1)**

The kettle in the diagram is 'live' because the insulation round the cable has broken and the live wire is in contact with the kettle at X.

(ii) In which part of the circuit (live, neutral or earth) should the fuse be placed? **(1)**

Give a reason for your answer. **(1)**

(iii) The earth wire should stop any user of this kettle getting an electric shock. To what part of the kettle should the earth wire be joined? **(1)**

(iv) What can you say about the resistance of any earth wire? **(3)**

(d) When working properly the kettle is rated at 2.4 kilowatts (kW).

(i) What does 'kW' mean? **(1)**

(ii) What current will flow if the kettle is connected to the mains supply? Show your working. **(4)**

(iii) Calculate the resistance of the wire in the element. Show your working. **(4)**

(e) Use either the word *high* or *low* in order to complete the table below.

Wire	*Melting point*	*Resistance*
Heating wire		
Fuse wire		
Circuit wire		

(6)

(*SEG Integrated Science – Applications, Paper 3, 1988*)

Question 2

(a) Motor car bodies are now designed to crumple in collisions. Give two reasons for this. **(2)**

(b)(i) Front seat passengers must wear seat belts. Why is this also important for back seat passengers? **(2)**

(ii) What has been the effect of the wearing of seat belts on the number of people having kidney transplants? **(1)**

Give a reason for your answer. **(2)**

(c) Write about four different road safety problems that have to be overcome by a vehicle designer who specializes in the building of mini-buses.

(Up to four marks may be awarded for clear expression of your ideas). **(12)**

(d) In a vehicle testing station, a remotely controlled car was driven head-on into a wall.

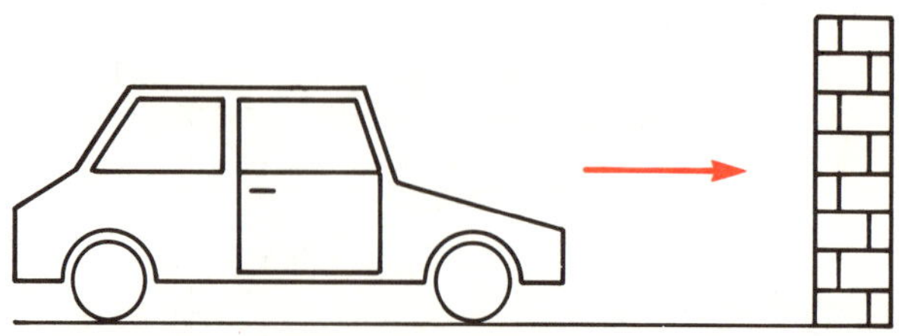

Mass of car = 500 kilogram (kg)
Speed of car = 10 metres per second (m/s)

(i) Calculate the kinetic energy of the car before the crash. Show your working. **(4)**

(ii) What happened to the kinetic energy of the car during the crash? **(2)**

(*SEG Integrated Science – Applications, Paper 3, 1988*)

Question 3

The diagram below shows a container in which fruit flies are allowed to grow and reproduce.

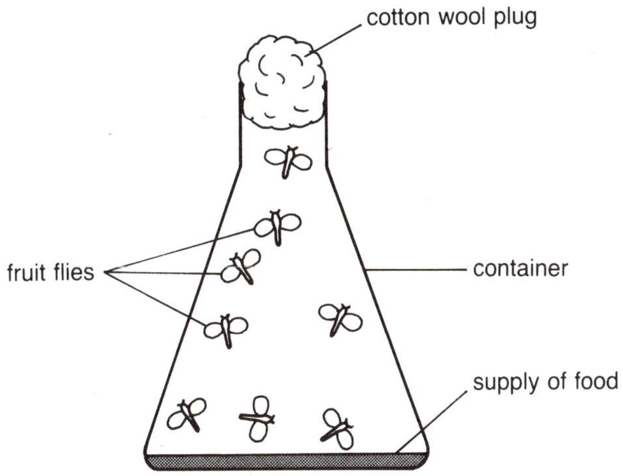

(a)(i) Why does the container have a plug? **(1)**

(ii) Why is cotton wool used as the plug? **(1)**

(b) At the start of an experiment, a container was set up as shown and 30 fruit flies were placed in it. The graph below shows the number of flies counted each week for about 40 weeks.

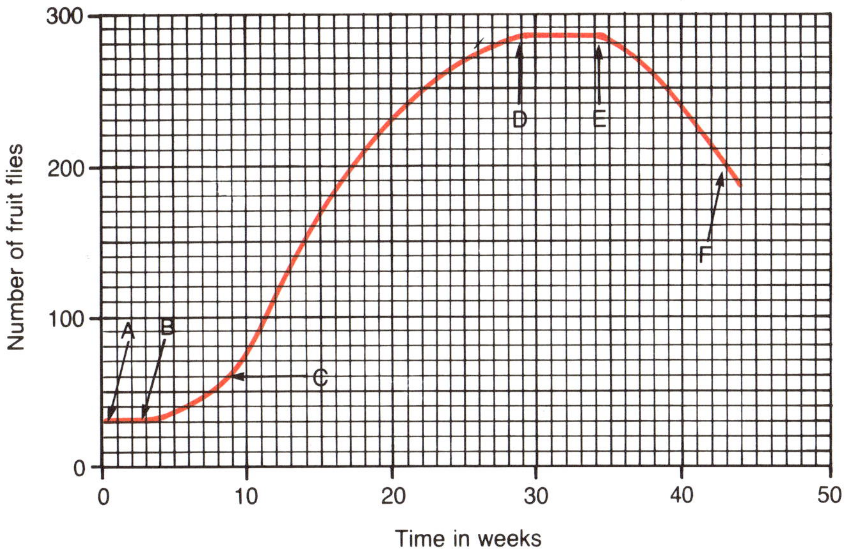

Fill in the table below to describe how the population changed between points A to F on the graph.

	What is happening?	*Reason*	
From A to B			**(2)**
From B to C			**(2)**
From C to D			**(2)**
From D to E			**(2)**
From E to F			**(2)**

(c) In the 19th century, experts used the type of information obtained from the fruit fly experiment to predict that the human population would reach a maximum and then stop increasing.
Explain two reasons why the human population has not yet reached its maximum. **(4)**

(*SEG Integrated Science–Principles, Paper 6, 1988*)

Question 4

Study the table below which gives some characteristics of some groups of animals and answer the questions which follow.

Group of animal	*Example*	*Reproduction*	*Characteristic features*
Bony fish	Stickleback	External fertilization Eggs with soft shell laid in water	Scales Have gills Cold blooded
Amphibians	Frog	External fertilization Eggs with soft shell laid in water	Moist skin, no scales Have lungs Cold blooded
Reptiles	Lizard	Internal fertilization Eggs with shells laid	Horny skin Have lungs Cold blooded
Birds	Pigeon	Internal fertilization Eggs with shells laid	Feathers Have lungs Warm blooded
Mammals	Mouse	Internal fertilization Live birth	Hair Have lungs Warm blooded

(a) Give one characteristic of amphibians which is fish-like, and one feature which is reptile-like.

(i) fish-like: .... **(1)**

(ii) reptile-like:... **(1)**

(b) Give two ways in which a reptile is better adapted to life on land than an amphibian. **(2)**

(c) Animals which have hair or feathers also have one other feature in common. What is this feature and what link does this have with the body covering? **(2)**

(d) Name one further feature, not listed in the table, common to all these groups. **(1)**

(*SEG Integrated Science–Principles, Paper 6, 1988*)

Question 5

Study the following table of substances and their properties.

Substance (in powder form)	*Magnetic properties*	*Solubility in water*	*Solubility in petrol*
Wax	None	Insoluble	Soluble
Aluminium	None	Insoluble	Insoluble
Silicon	None	Insoluble	Insoluble
Cobalt	Magnetic	Insoluble	Insoluble

Using the information, briefly describe one experiment in each case to separate mixtures of:

(a) silicon and cobalt, **(2)**

(b) wax and aluminium. **(2)**

(*SEG Integrated Science–Principles, Paper 6, 1988*)

Question 6

Some students were asked to design and perform an experiment to find out how much heat was needed to warm up some water.

(a) Two students decided to use small electric heaters. They drew the diagram shown at the top of the next page, then set up their experiment with apparatus that was known to work. When they closed the switch, the water did not heat up although the voltmeter gave a reading.

(i) What fault is there in their diagram? **(1)**

(ii) Explain why the water did not heat up. **(2)**

(iii) What would the voltmeter read? Give a reason. **(2)**

(b) State how you would change the circuit so that the water would heat up. **(2)**

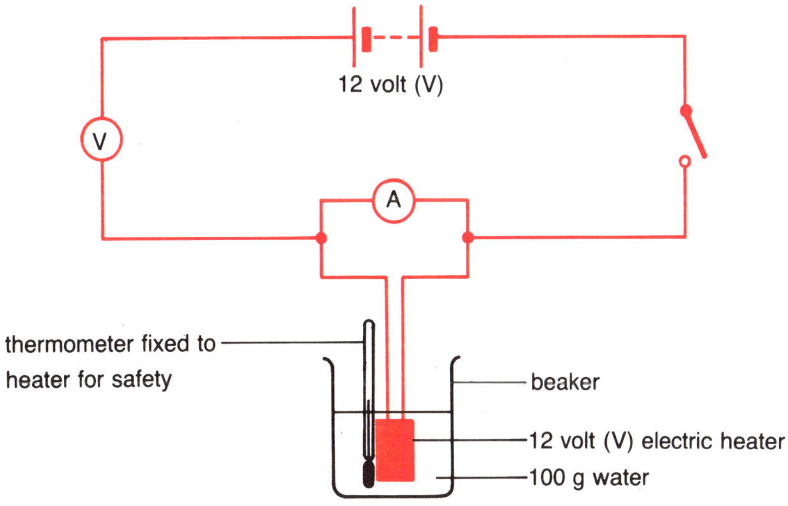

(c) The following readings were taken from the improved experiment.

Ammeter reading	Final temperature
Voltmeter reading	Time taken
Temperature at start	Mass of water used

(i) How would you calculate the energy supplied by the heater? **(2)**

(ii) If the temperature rise of the water showed that less energy than that calculated in **(c)(i)** actually went in to heating the water, where has the 'extra' energy gone? **(1)**

(iii) Suggest two possible safety measures the pupils should have used. **(2)**

(*SEG Integrated Science – Principles, Paper 6, 1988*)

Question 7

(a) Two experiments were set up to measure the rate of take-up of materials by the roots of plants.

In one experiment a growing plant was placed with its roots in a solution and kept at constant temperature. This solution contained a radioactive substance. At fifteen minute intervals the solution was tested for radioactivity.

After one hour, oxygen was bubbled through the solution for several minutes. The results are shown in the graph below.

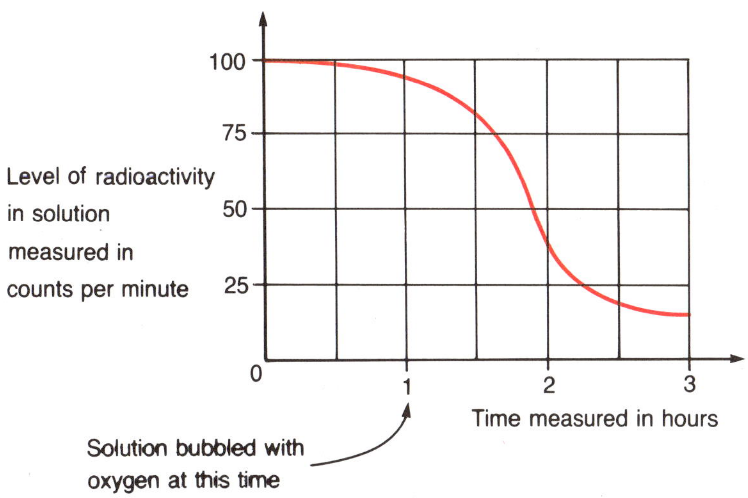

(i) What effect did bubbling the solution with oxygen have on the level of radioactivity in the solution during the next hour? **(2)**

(ii) Explain your answer as fully as possible. **(3)**

(b) In a second experiment, the take-up of the elements potassium and nitrogen by the roots of a plant was investigated. The experiment was repeated using solutions at different temperatures. The results of this experiment are shown in the graph overleaf.

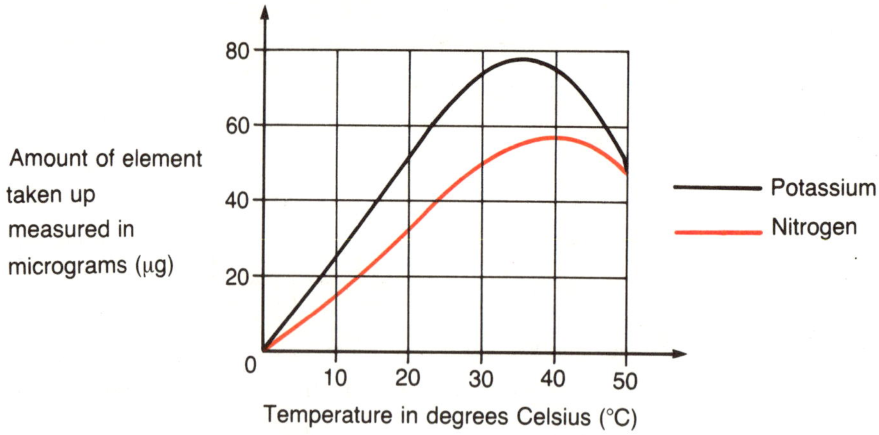

(i) Describe what happens to the take-up of potassium as the temperature is increased. **(3)**

(ii) Describe what happens to the take-up of nitrogen as the temperature is increased. **(3)**

(iii) How does the take-up of potassium compare with that of nitrogen? **(3)**

(*SEG Integrated Science–Principles, Paper 6, 1988*)

Question 8

The energy changes over a period of one hour in a typical coal-fired boiler/turbine unit in a power station are shown in the diagram below.
(The energy unit is the megajoule; 1 MJ=10^6 J)

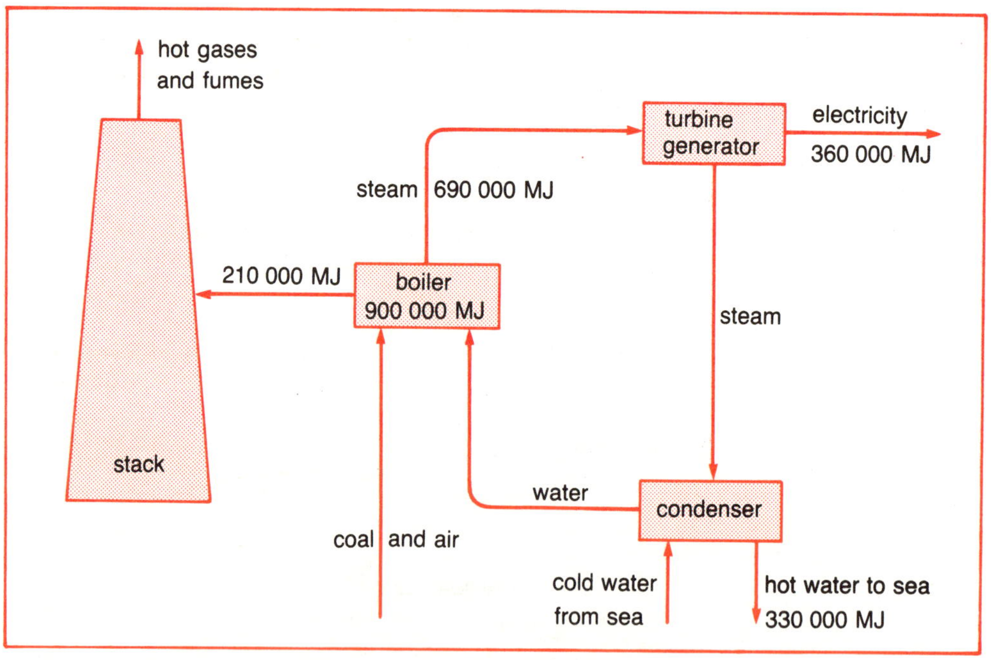

(a) What kind of energy does coal possess? **(1)**

(b) How much energy is converted into a useable form in one hour? **(1)**

(c) How much energy is wasted in one hour? **(1)**

(d) Calculate the percentage efficiency. Show clearly how you got your answer. **(2)**

(e) If the energy obtained by burning one tonne (10^3 kg) of coal is 24 000 MJ and the cost of the coal is £50 per tonne, work out the amount of coal which is used in producing *waste* heat in one hour. Use the result to work out the amount of money wasted each hour. **(3)**

(f) What is the rate of production of electrical energy in megawatts?
(1MW = 10^6 watts = 1 MJ/s) **(2)**

(g) The condenser uses 10 000 tonnes of sea-water in an hour. The temperature of the water entering the condenser is 10°C. What is the temperature of the water leaving the condenser?
(Specific heat capacity of water = 4.2 MJ/tonne °C) **(3)**

(h) Calculate the power a pump would need to develop in order to transfer the sea-water to the condenser if the condenser is 18 m above sea-level. Show clearly how you got your answer.
(gravitational constant g = 10 m/s/s; gravitational force = 10 N/kg) **(5)**

(i) Suggest one way of using the warm water produced in the condenser instead of returning it to the sea. **(1)**

(j) What do you think could be the consequence of pumping warm water from the condenser back into the sea? **(1)**

(k) Name one gas, not present in pure air, which might be present in the gases emitted from the stack, and explain its origin. **(2)**

(l) Suggest *two* reasons why the existing power station is being converted from oil-power to coal-power. **(2)**

(*NISEC Science, Paper 3, 1988*)

Question 9

(a) The extraction of iron is carried out in a blast furnace. A diagram of this plant is shown below.

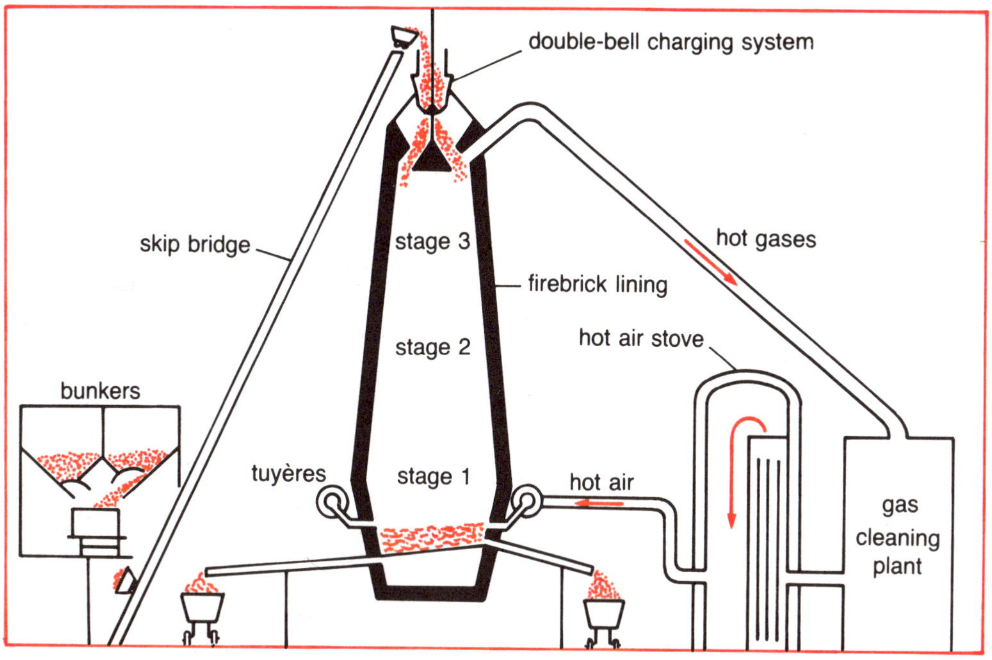

(i) Show on the diagram, by labelling,
A where the raw material enters,
B where the iron is removed. **(2)**

(ii) Besides air, what *three* raw materials are used in the blast furnace? **(3)**

(iii) What word is used chemically to describe the conversion of iron oxide to iron metal? **(1)**

(iv) Write a word equation and a symbol equation for the reaction of carbon monoxide with iron(III) oxide, Fe_2O_3. **(4)**

(v) Describe how iron is produced in the blast furnace. You should mention the chemical changes, the temperatures used, removal of impurities and recovery of the iron. **(5)**

(vi) The diagram below shows the processes involved in a modern integrated iron and steel plant.

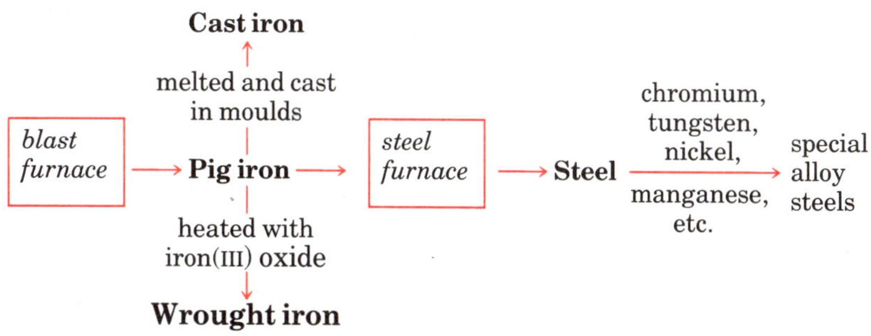

Suggest *two* industries in Northern Ireland which might be large users of steel. **(2)**

(vii) Despite the obvious demand for steel by industry and commerce, no manufacturing plant for iron or steel has ever been set up in Northern Ireland. Suggest three reasons why this is so. **(3)**

(viii) Suppose you were asked to choose a site in Northern Ireland to build an iron and steel manufacturing plant. Describe *three* factors you would consider when choosing the best site. **(3)**

(ix) A commercial grade ore contains 30 per cent by mass iron(III) oxide. Calculate the maximum mass of iron which could be obtained from 1000 tonnes of this ore. (Fe = 56, O = 16) **(4)**

(b) Look at the picture below. This is a photograph of manganese nodules lying on the floor of the Antarctic Ocean. Read the following passage.

Manganese nodules were first discovered in the late 19th century, and are now known to lie at the bottom of most deep oceans as well as in coastal waters and some fresh water lakes. Typical manganese nodules are dull-black, ovoid bodies, roughly fist-sized. The nodules consist of a mixture of fine-grained iron(III) oxide and manganese(IV) oxide. A typical nodule contains about 20 per cent metallic manganese (Mn), 20 per cent iron (Fe) and 1 to 3 per cent nickel-copper-cobalt by mass. It is, however, the presence of trace elements, especially those which are in short supply from land sources (e.g. nickel and copper), which is responsible for much of the interest shown in manganese nodules in recent years. At the present time it is thought to be marginally economic to harvest nodules from the sea floor for the trace elements they contain, and several companies are currently engaged in pilot mining schemes to test the practibility of this idea. Technical and other problems may mean that it remains cheaper to exploit land-based sources of these metals, although it will not be long before mining of deep sea nodules becomes economically viable.

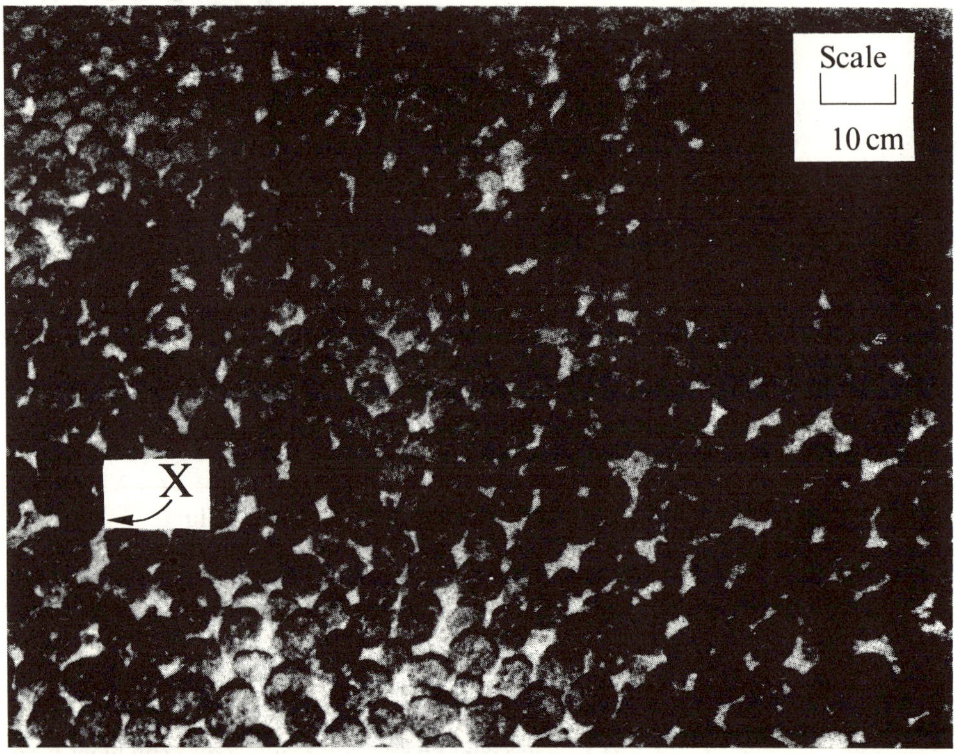

(i) Use the scale given on the photograph to work out the diameter of the nodule marked X. **(2)**

(ii) Give the chemical formula for manganese(IV) oxide. **(1)**

(iii) What is meant by 'trace elements'? **(2)**

(iv) Name *two* trace elements in manganese nodules. **(2)**

(v) Suggest how a trace element discharged from industry into the sea may be harmful to humans. **(3)**

(vi) What is meant by the phrase 'marginally economic'? **(1)**

(vii) Name one industry which might be interested in manganese nodules. Give a reason for your choice. **(2)**

(*NISEC Science, Paper 3, 1988*)

Question 10

(a)(i) Use the information in the table below to construct a key which could be used to classify a vertebrate animal into one of the five groups listed.

Animal group	*Identifying feature*
Fish	fins
Amphibian	soft damp skin
Reptile	hard scaly body
Bird	feathers
Mammal	fur/hair

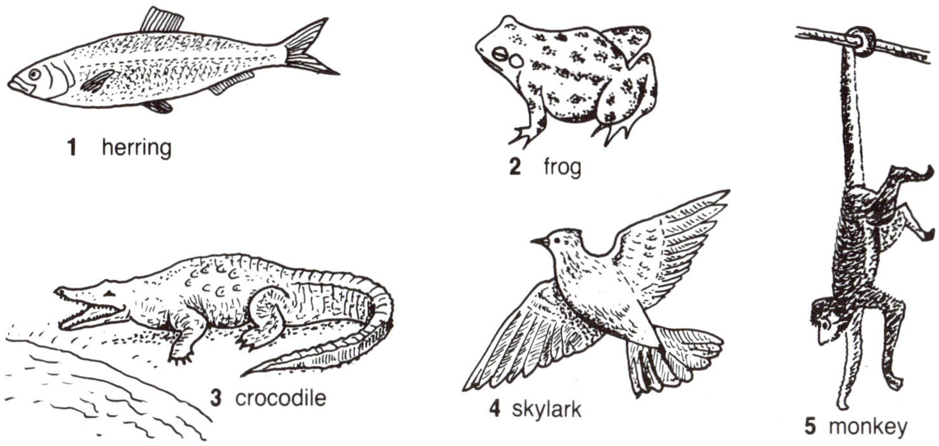

(ii) Use the key to classify the animals labelled 1 to 5 above. **(13)**

(b) Some people have the ability to roll their tongue. Others have not. This characteristic is inherited.

(i) Complete the diagram below by inserting the correct symbols in the circles to show whether the children of two parents who can roll their tongues will themselves be able to.

R is the allele for the ability to roll the tongue.
r is the allele for the inability to roll the tongue.

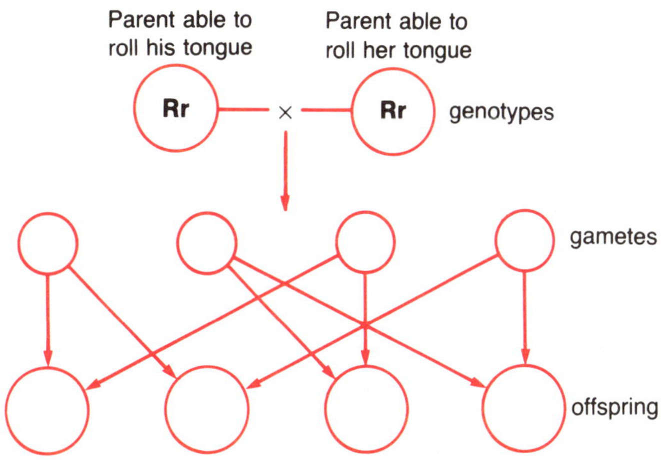

(2)

(ii) What proportion of rollers to non-rollers is produced in the offspring? **(2)**

(c)(i) Some human characteristics are sex-linked. What is meant by the term 'sex-linked'? **(2)**

(ii) One sex-linked characteristic is premature baldness. Using the notation below, show which pairing could produce a prematurely bald daughter.

XY normal male	XX normal female
^{B}XY prematurely bald male	^{B}XX carrier female

Key: X and Y are normal sex chromosomes
^{B}X carries the gene for premature baldness. **(3)**

(iii) Explain briefly why a female with chromosomes ^{B}XX would *not* be prematurely bald. **(1)**

(d) Mr and Mrs Kelly have four children, James aged 12, Peter aged 7 and Patricia and Ann aged 5. Mr Kelly suffers from colour blindness which is a sex-linked characteristic.

(i) Explain *fully* how Mr and Mrs Kelly can have one son and one daughter who are colour blind when their other two children are not. **(8)**
What conclusion can you draw about the genotype of Mrs Kelly? **(1)**

(ii) Tongue rolling is a harmless inheritance. Give one example of a disease caused by the inheritance of a harmful gene. **(1)**

(iii) Explain briefly the implications of being able to work out the possibility of one's children inheriting a harmful gene. **(2)**

(e) An experiment was carried out to investigate the relationship between water intake and urine production in humans. During the 12 hours before measurements were made, the person was not allowed to drink but was allowed to eat.

The quantities of water drunk and urine released were measured and are shown on the graph overleaf.

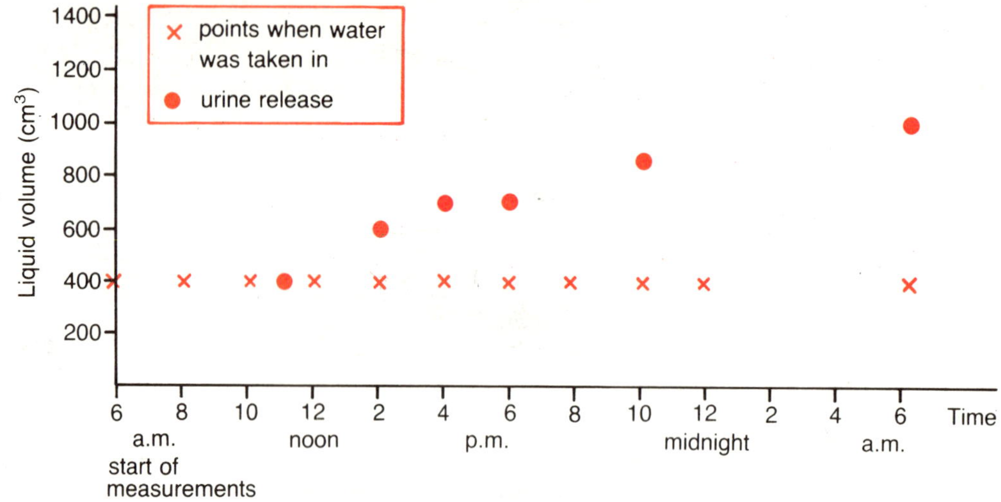

(i) How much water was released between 2 p.m. and 7 p.m.? **(1)**

(ii) Which feature of the experimental method could be responsible for the delay of five hours before urine was first released? **(2)**

(iii) Which one feature of the investigation prevents you making an accurate statement about the relationship between water intake and urine release in humans? **(2)**

(*NISEC Science, Paper 3, 1988*)

Question 11

Your firm is trying to decide which of three insulating materials will be the best one to use to make a sleeping bag for a mountaineer.

(a) You have to do tests with the three sets of equipment shown below so that the insulating materials can be compared.

In *each* of the three tests, carefully explain exactly what you would measure.

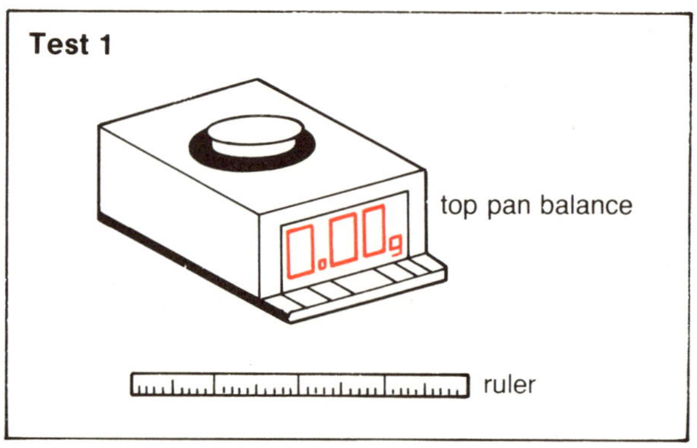

I would note ____________________

____

____________________ **(3)**

I would note ____________________

____

____________________ **(3)**

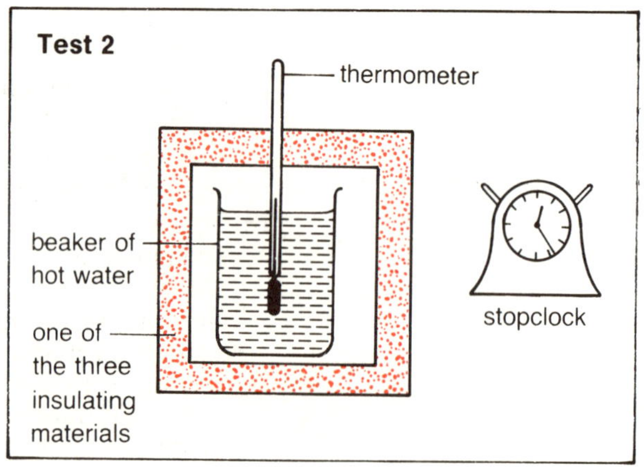

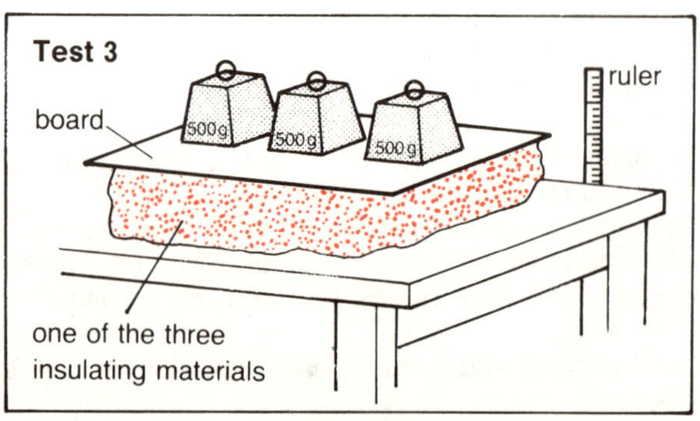

I would note ____________________

____

____________________ **(3)**

(b) Next you have to find out how safe these insulating materials would be in a fire.
Explain what you would do, what you would be looking for, and any safety precautions that you would need to take when carrying out your tests. **(6)**

(*NEA Science (Modular), Module test – Materials, 1988*)

Question 12

You carry out the experiment below to find out whether some foods contain more stored energy than others.

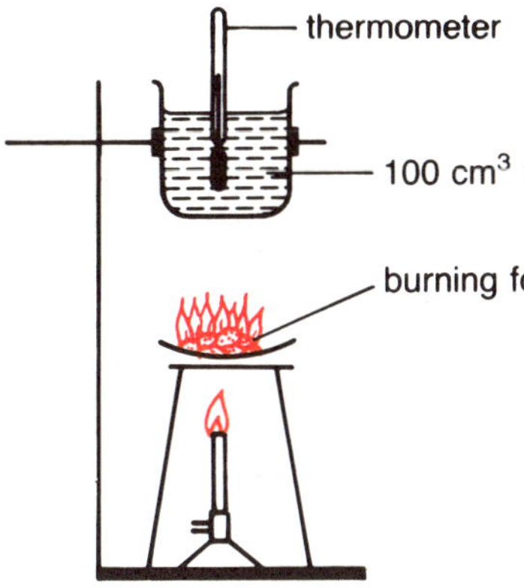

Each food is set alight by heating it with a Bunsen burner. The heat given out as it burns is used to heat up the water in the beaker.

(a) What measurements would you need to make to find out which food contains most energy? **(2)**
(b) State *two* problems you might have in getting the experiment to work. **(2)**

Your teacher does the experiment with the much better apparatus shown below.

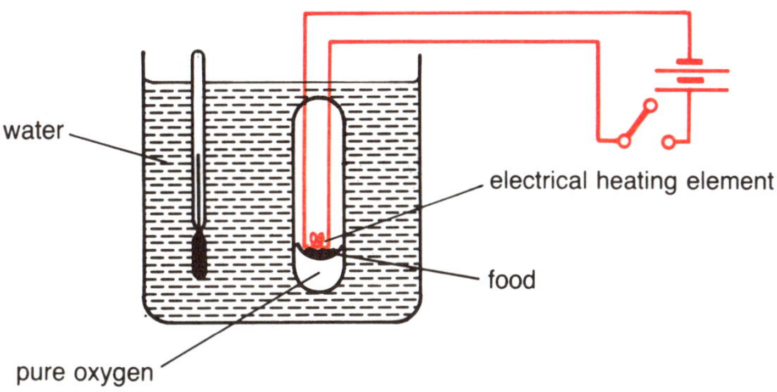

(c) How is the food set alight in this experiment? **(1)**
(d) State *two* ways in which your teacher's apparatus is better than the apparatus in your experiment. **(2)**
(e) When 2 g of *three* different foods are used, the following temperature rises are obtained:

Food A: 4°C
Food B: 10°C
Food C: 3°C

Which food is made up mainly of fat?

(*NEA Science (Modular), Module test – Humans as organisms, 1988*)

Question 13

Dippers are small birds which live in and about upland streams. They feed on aquatic insects such as caddis fly larvae, which in turn feed on smaller insects. This food chain begins with food producers such as water weeds. Dippers are sometimes eaten by peregrine falcons which also eat a variety of other birds including skylarks and pigeons. Skylarks and pigeons often feed on farmland. Trout living in the streams also feed on caddis fly larvae.

(a) Use this information to complete a food web on the outline below. **(4)**

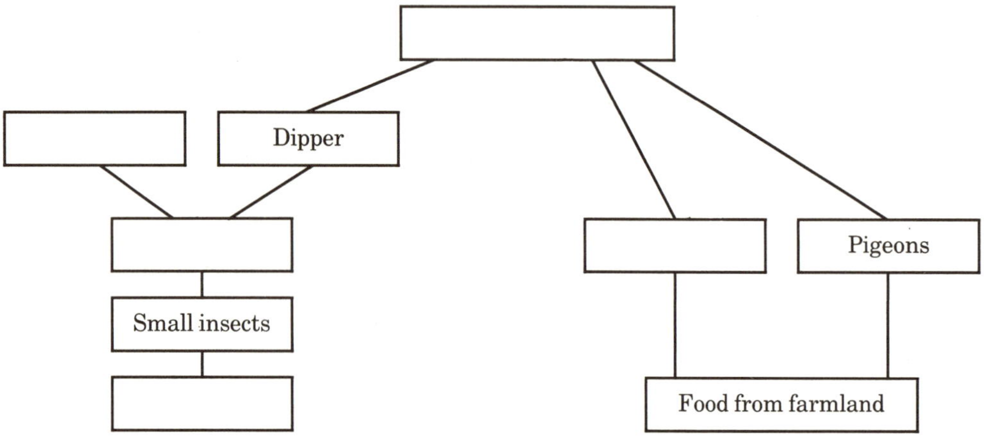

(b) Name a competitor of the dipper. **(1)**

(c) What would be the effect on the number of peregrines if the number of dippers falls? Explain your answer. **(2)**

(d) Consider the following facts.

- ⋆ Anglers fish the streams for trout.
- ⋆ If the numbers of trout fall, local angling clubs re-stock the streams.
- ⋆ Acid rain, caused by burning fuel in local towns, can reduce the numbers of caddis fly larvae.
- ⋆ Before they were put under strict control, certain insecticides caused peregrines to lay eggs with very thin shells which were often crushed by the sitting bird.

Use the above facts to explain how the activities of human beings can affect the numbers of dippers. **(8)**

(NEA Science (Modular), Module test – The environment, 1988)

Question 14

A remote cottage is lit using the electricity produced by a small wind generator.

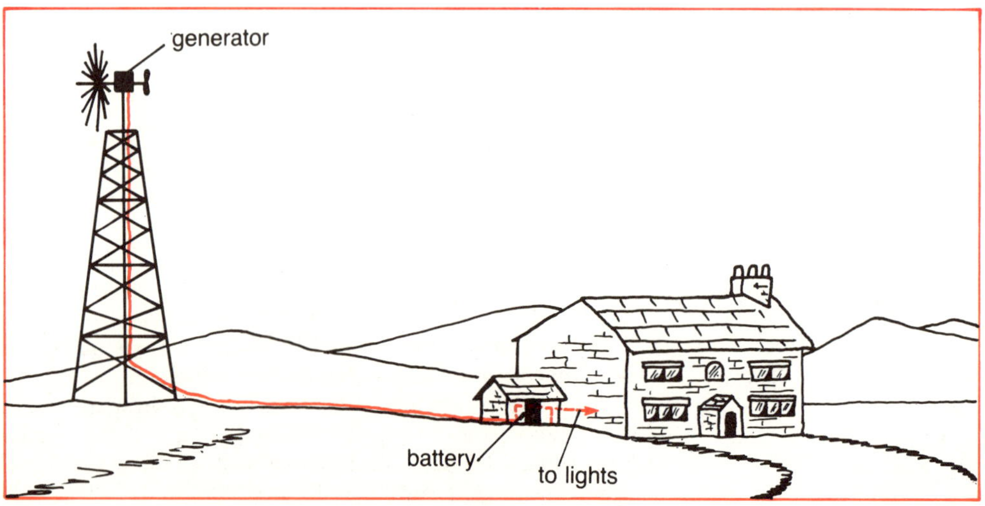

The diagram shows how the system is set up. The re-chargeable lead/acid battery is expensive and the generator will light up the lamps without it. Why do you think the lead/acid battery is used? Give *four* reasons. **(4)**

(*NEA Science (Modular), Module test – Energy, 1989*)

Question 15

The purpose of an electricity sub-station is to reduce the voltage at which electrical energy is transmitted down to the 240 volts which we use in our homes.

(a) What name do we give to the device which makes up this sub-station? Draw a simple labelled *diagram* to show how such a device works. **(5)**

(b) If one hundred homes, all connected to one such device, arrange to draw a current of 20 amperes each, what is the minimum current which must flow into the sub-station from the grid?
(Assume that the transmission voltage is 10 000 volts.) **(4)**

(c) When a table lamp is switched on, it gives what seems to be a steady light. But the voltage applied to the bulb is changing many times each second from 240 V to 0 V. Explain in as much detail as you can how you would find out whether the brightness of the bulb changes over a short period of time. What results would you expect? **(8)**

(*MEG Combined Science, Paper 4, 1988*)

Question 16

(a)(i) Explain what is meant by one mole of substance. **(2)**

(ii) In terms of moles, say what information you can obtain from the equation

$$CH_4 + 2Cl_2 \rightarrow CH_2Cl_2 + 2HCl \qquad \textbf{(3)}$$

(b) The oceans contain, altogether, about 4×10^{17} moles of sodium chloride. If all the sodium was extracted, what *volume* of metal would be produced? Do the calculation in these stages:

(i) Find the mass of sodium. **(3)**

(ii) Estimate the density of sodium from what you know about it.
Density is about ____________________ . **(2)**

(iii) So the volume of sodium would be ____________________ . **(3)**

(c) Sodium chloride is essential to life, but chlorine is dangerous. From your knowledge of the *properties* of chlorine, suggest two ways in which chlorine would cause harm to anyone who inhaled it. **(4)**

(*MEG Combined Science, Paper 4, 1988*)

Question 17

(a) Starch molecules consist of long chains of smaller glucose molecules.

(i) Suggest *two* ways by which starch molecules can be broken down. **(2)**

(ii) What is the name of this process? **(1)**

(iii) Name another product of this reaction. **(1)**

(b) In industrial brewing processes, yeast is added to glucose solution and left to ferment at 25°C.

(i) What does the yeast do to the glucose molecules? **(1)**

(ii) What are the products of fermentation? **(3)**

(iii) What will be the effect of raising the temperature to 35°C? **(1)**

(iv) Explain why boiling the yeast/glucose mixture stops the reaction. **(2)**

(c) Describe how animals obtain and use glucose. **(4)**

(*MEG Science (Syllabus A), Paper 3, 1988*)

Question 18

(a) There are *two* types of reproduction, asexual and sexual.

(i) Distinguish between asexual and sexual reproduction. **(2)**

(ii) Describe some of the ways in which commercial advantage has been taken of the asexual reproduction process. **(3)**

(iii) What are the advantages of sexual reproduction? **(2)**

(b) A plant with red flowers is allowed to self-pollinate. The seeds from this cross were planted and 151 plants grew to produce flowers. Of these plants, 112 had red flowers and 39 had white flowers. Using the symbols **R** for the dominant red gene and **r** for the recessive white gene, draw a diagram showing the cross and state the genotypes of the following:

(i) The red-flowered parent generation.

(ii) The white-flowered offspring.

(iii) The red-flowered offspring. **(5)**

(c) Draw a labelled diagram to show the life cycle of a typical plant. **(3)**

(*MEG Science (Syllabus A), Paper 3, 1988*)

Question 19

The table below refers to the radius of some common atoms and their ions.

Element	*Radius of atom*	*Radius of ion*
Lithium	1.3	0.7
Sodium	1.5	1.0
Calcium	1.4	1.0
Tin	1.4	0.9
Oxygen	0.7	1.3
Sulphur	1.0	1.8
Bromine	1.1	2.0
Iodine	1.3	x

(a) What pattern do you observe about the relative sizes of an atom and its ion when comparing metals and non-metals? **(2)**
(b) Predict the size of the radius of the iodine ion, x. **(1)**
(c) Name **two** elements from the above list which form negative ions. **(2)**

Look at a copy of the Periodic Table (page 212) and identify the position of sodium and lithium.

(d) What is the size of the charge on these ions? **(1)**
(e) Sodium chloride has the following properties:
high melting point
solid
dissolves in water to become an electrolyte
(i) State the type of bonding which holds together the sodium and chloride ions. **(1)**
(ii) Describe, with the help of diagrams, how the bonding between sodium and chloride ions differs from the bonding between two chlorine atoms. **(3)**

(*MEG Science (Syllabus B), Paper 7, 1988*)

Question 20

Read the following account of an experiment, then answer the questions below:

'Some impure sodium chloride was crushed in a pestle and mortar. The powder was mixed with water and stirred with a glass rod. The mixture was poured through a filter paper leaving some black specks. A colourless liquid was collected in an evaporating basin which on heating, until dryness, gave a white powder.'

(a) From this account give one example of each of the following terms:
(i) solute **(iii)** solution
(ii) solvent **(iv)** filtrate **(3)**
(b) State why the mixture was filtered. **(1)**
(c) Give the name of the white powder remaining in the basin. **(1)**
(d) Name the process by which the water was driven off by heat. **(1)**
(e) The following table shows the colours produced when an indicator is added to various solutions:

Solution	*Colour*
Hydrochloric acid	red
Vinegar	orange
Water	pale green
Limewater	dark green
Sodium hydroxide	blue

Name the colour which would be produced by each of the following:
(i) sodium chloride solution
(ii) saliva
(iii) rainwater **(3)**

(*WJEC Science, Paper 2, 1988*)

Question 21

(a) The graph shows the change in volume of the lungs of a person during a period of moderate exercise.

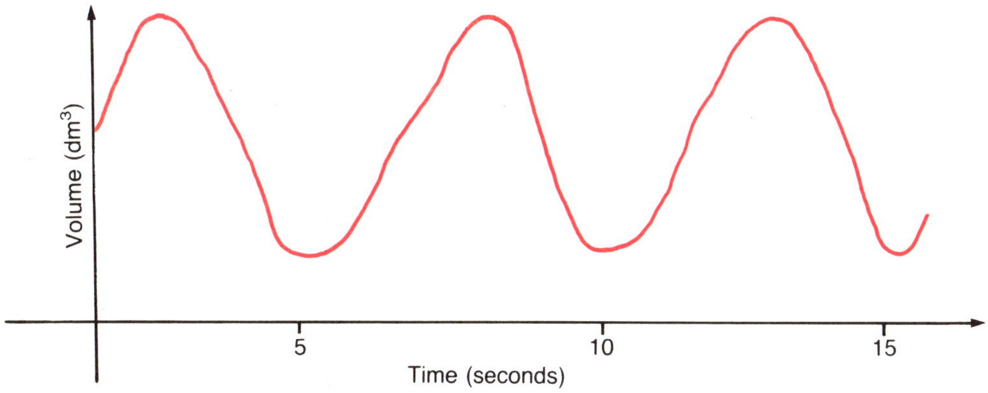

(i) Explain the graph. **(2)**

(b) On axes like those below, draw labelled graphs to show the change in volume of the lungs if the person involved

(i) had just gone to sleep,
(ii) had just received an adrenalin injection,
(iii) were a very heavy smoker.

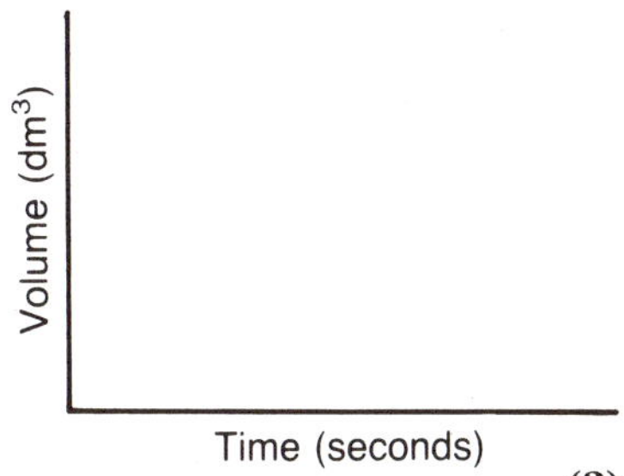

(3)

(c) Explain how you would prove that a sample of exhaled air contains carbon dioxide. **(1)**

(*WJEC Science, Paper 2, 1988*)

Question 22

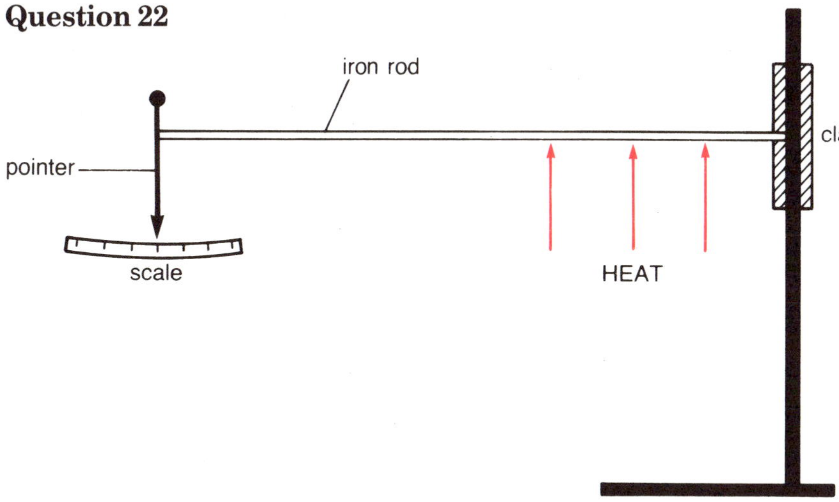

The arrangement shown above was set up. The iron rod was heated as shown.

(a) Name the process by which heat is transferred through the iron rod. **(1)**

(b)(i) Describe what happened to the pointer during the experiment. **(1)**

(ii) Give *one* reason for your answer to **(i)**. **(1)**

(iii) Give *two* everyday examples in which the behaviour of iron as illustrated by the experiment has to be allowed for. **(2)**

(*WJEC Science, Paper 2, 1988*)

Question 23

Explain briefly how the following impurities in water are dealt with at either the sewage or water works:

(a) Solid matter floating on the surface **(1)**
(b) Dissolved gases **(1)**
(c) Bacteria **(1)**

(*WJEC Science, Paper 2, 1988*)

Question 24

The sulphur concentration of lichens (algae and fungi living together) was measured at various points in a town. The map below shows the points A to F where measurements were taken.

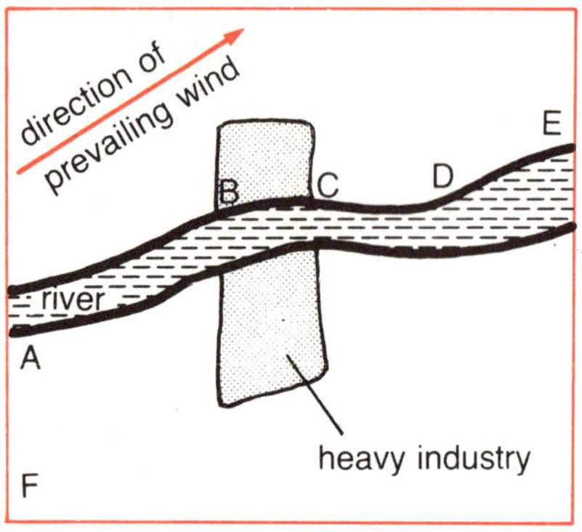

The results were as follows:

Point	*Sulphur concentration*
A	0.02
B	3.30
C	2.40
D	1.70
E	1.20
F	0.01

(a)(i) By studying the map and the table of results, state the connection between the sulphur concentration in the lichens and the distance from the town. **(1)**

(ii) Explain the difference in sulphur concentration between points A and C. **(2)**

(b) Since 1954 the numbers of species of flowering plants living within a radius of 1 km of the town was monitored, together with the output of sulphur dioxide.

Year	*Millions of tonnes of sulphur dioxide*	*Species of flowering plants in a radius of 1 km from the town*
1954	5.5	542
1965	6.4	328
1970	5.8	322
1975	5.4	320
1980	5.6	317

State how the sulphur dioxide appears to be affecting the flowering plants. **(2)**

(*WJEC Science, Paper 2, 1988*)

Question 25

(a) A radioactive source S gives radiations A, B and C whose paths are shown in the cloud chamber pictures below and at the top of the next page.

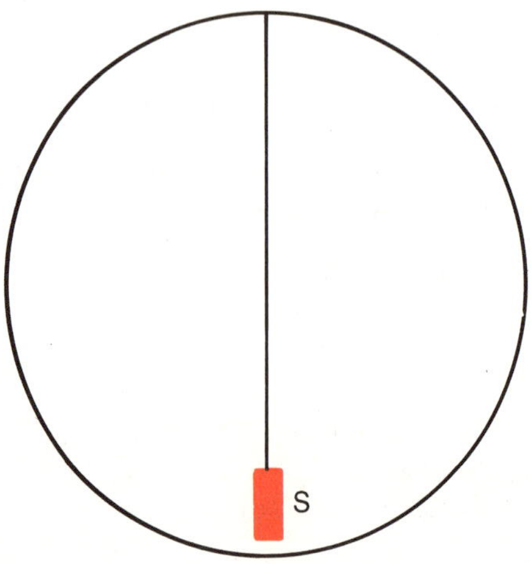

In Fig. 1, the radiations all stay in a straight line.

Figure 1

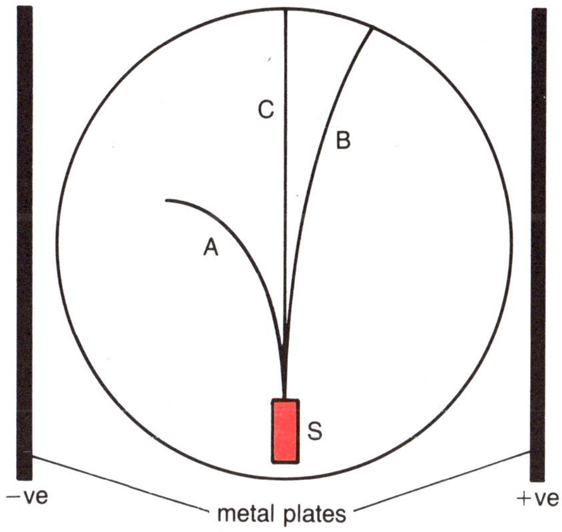

In Fig. 2, two metal plates are placed on either side of the chamber such that an electric field is set up.

Figure 2

(i) Explain why the paths of A and B are curved in opposite directions in Fig. 2. **(1)**

(ii) Give one reason why the path of B is curved less than that of A in Fig. 2. **(1)**

(iii) Explain why C travels along a straight line path in both figures. **(1)**

(iv) Give the names of the radiations A, B and C. **(3)**

(b) A radioactive source was surrounded by three screens as shown in Fig. 3.

The source emits alpha, beta and gamma radiation. It was found that all three radiations passed through the paper screen.

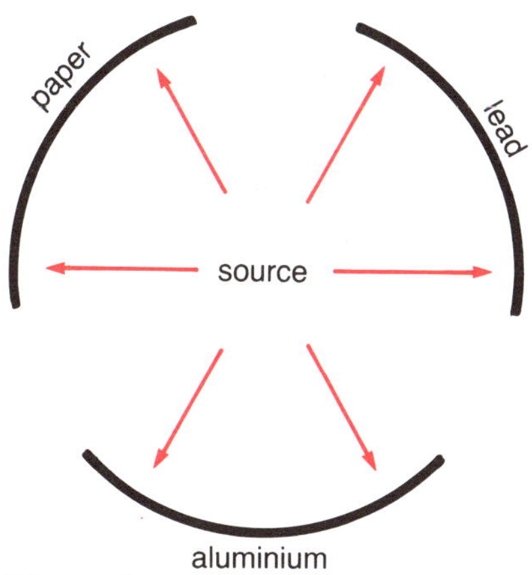

Figure 3

(i) Which two radiations would be likely to pass through the aluminium screen? **(2)**

(ii) Which radiation would be likely to pass through the lead screen? **(1)**

(c) A radioactive material has a mass of 24 g and a half-life of 6 days. What mass of the original sample was still radioactive after:
(i) 6 days (ii) 18 days? **(2)**

(d) Give an account of *two* ways in which radioactive substances have been put to good use by mankind. **(6)**

(*LEAG Science (Syllabus N), Paper 3, 1988*)

Question 26

(a) Mary and Betty are trying to find out which of them is fitter. They decide to run up a long flight of stairs. The stairs have a vertical height of 10 metres. They take their pulse rates at rest (before exercise) and at intervals after their exercise. Their results are shown in Table 1.

Table 1

	Pulse rate per minute					
	Before exercise	*Immediately after exercise*	*30 sec. after exercise*	*60 sec. after exercise*	*90 sec. after exercise*	*120 sec. after exercise*
Mary	60	135	105	85	70	60
Betty	75	155	135	120	105	90

(i) Which girl is fitter? Give *two* reasons for your answer. **(2)**

(ii) What is the relationship between pulse rate and heart beat? **(2)**

(iii) Mary and Betty both sweat after their exercise. Explain how sweating helps to cool them. **(3)**

(iv) Why will the muscles in the girls' legs begin to feel tired as they run? **(2)**

(v) Mary weighs 500 N. How much power will she develop if she runs up the stairs in 8 seconds? Show your working. **(4)**

(b) Three cubes are shown below.

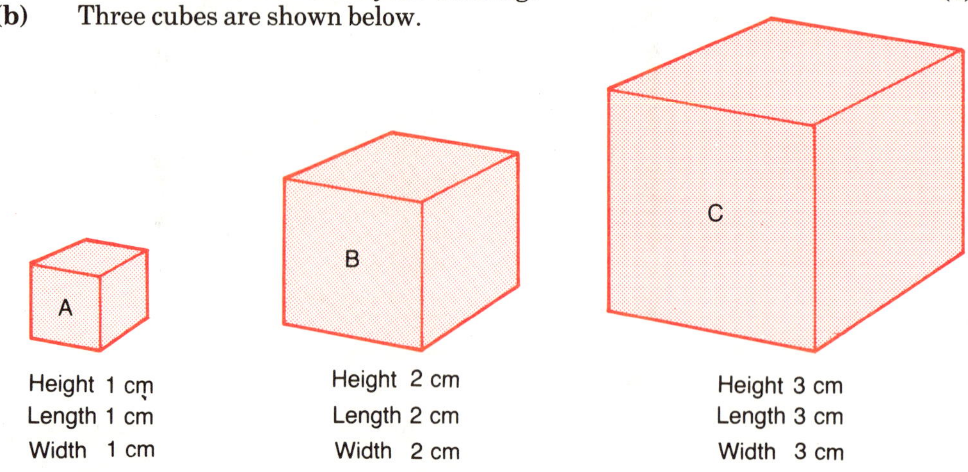

(i) What is the surface area of cube A? **(2)**

(ii) What is the volume of cube B? **(2)**

(iii) Which cube has the largest surface area to volume ratio and what is that ratio? **(3)**

(iv) Name *one* internal part of the body which has a very large surface area compared to its volume. **(1)**

(v) Name *one* substance which diffuses through this area. **(1)**

(vi) There are many species of penguins. One of the smallest is the Blue Penguin and one of the largest is the Emperor Penguin. One of these penguins lives in New Zealand (which has a similar climate to Great Britain) and one of them lives in Antarctica (which is very cold).
Suggest which penguin lives in New Zealand and explain your answer. **(1)**
Why would this penguin not survive in Antarctica? **(2)**

(LEAG Science (Syllabus M), Paper 3, 1988)

Question 27

(a) Greenhouse trials were carried out to find out the effect of temperature on the yield of a particular tomato species. The trials were carried out during the normal growing season of the tomatoes. Three identical greenhouses were used, at 20°C, 25°C and 30°C, respectively. The mass of the tomatoes growing on the 50 plants in each greenhouse was estimated weekly.
The results are shown in Fig. 1.

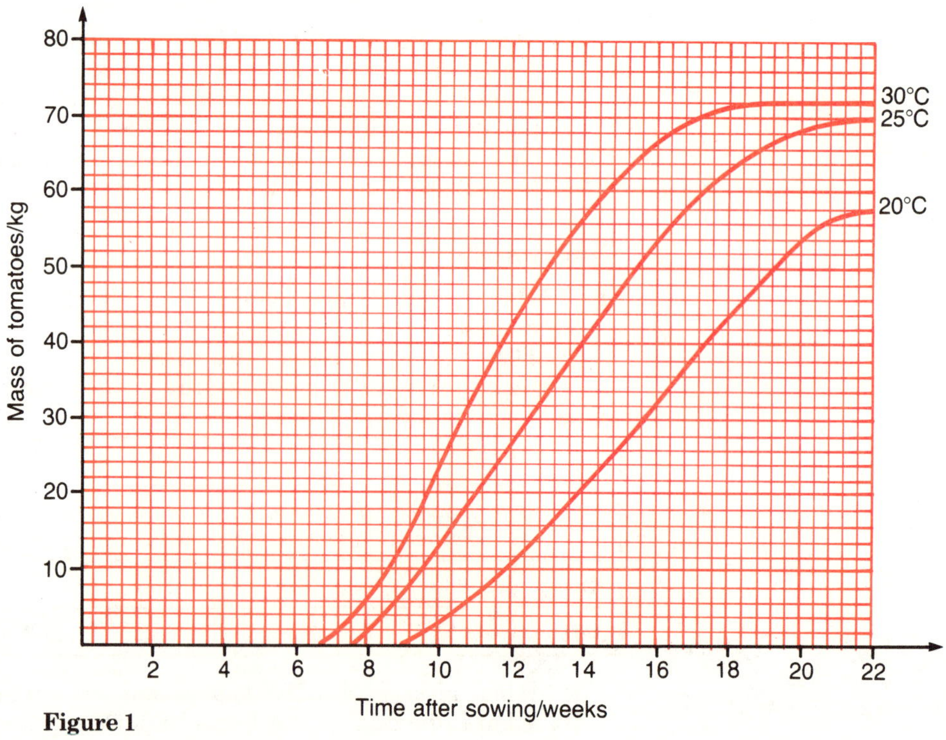

Figure 1

(i) State *two* environmental factors which must be controlled in the greenhouses to make a fair comparison of results. **(2)**
(ii) In the greenhouse maintained at 25°C, what is the average weekly increase in yield between week 12 and week 16? **(1)**
(iii) What was the total mass of tomatoes in all three greenhouses at the end of week 14? **(1)**
(iv) During which week is the difference in mass of tomatoes growing at 20°C and 30°C greatest? **(1)**
(v) What is likely to happen to the tomatoes if they are not picked by the end of week 22? **(1)**
(vi) At which temperature would you grow tomatoes? **(1)**
Explain your choice. **(2)**

(b) The rates at which two different soils drain were investigated using the equipment shown in Fig. 2.

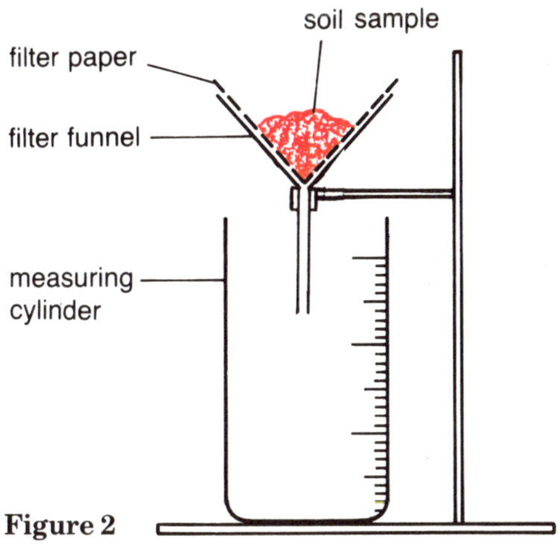

Figure 2

100 cm^3 of water is poured into the filter funnel. The amount collected in the measuring cylinder after 30 seconds was noted. The results are shown in the table below.

	Soil sample A	Soil sample B
amount of water collected after 30 seconds	95.0 cm^3	34.4 cm^3

(i) How much water has been retained by sample B? **(1)**
(ii) Compare the structure of the two soils by using the results of the investigation and suggest how the structures of the soils might be improved. **(4)**
(iii) Explain why most land plants die in waterlogged soils. **(2)**
(iv) Explain the roles of nitrogen, phosphorus and potassium in plant metabolism. **(3)**
(v) What is meant by 'biological control'? **(1)**

(*LEAG Science (Syllabus M), Paper 3, 1988*)

Question 28

(a) Mr Jones buys some green filter sunglasses.
(i) Figure 1 shows the window area of a house. How will the colours shown appear to Mr Jones when he wears the sunglasses? **(3)**

Figure 1

(ii) Would these green sunglasses be suitable for Mr Jones when driving a car? Explain your answer. **(2)**

(b) Figure 2 shows part of the electromagnetic spectrum.

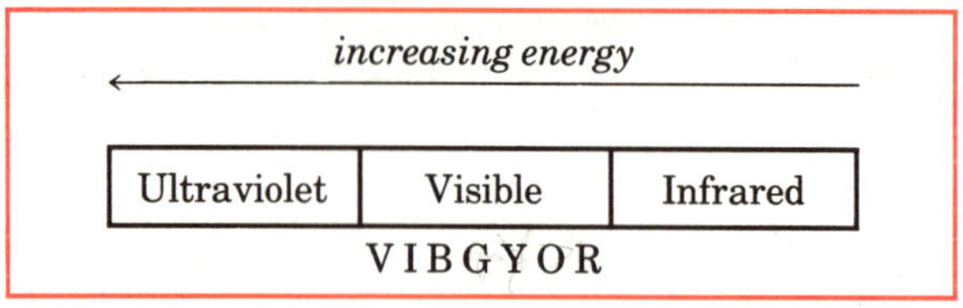

Figure 2

Tungsten is used for the filament in light bulbs. When the filament gets hot it becomes first red (at 1000°C) and then orange (at 1500°C).

(i) Explain why the black filament changes colour as its temperature increases. **(2)**

(ii) Suggest what colour the filament might be at 2000°C and explain your answer. **(2)**

(c) Figure 3 shows a wave travelling down a long spring. The lines show the spirals of the spring.

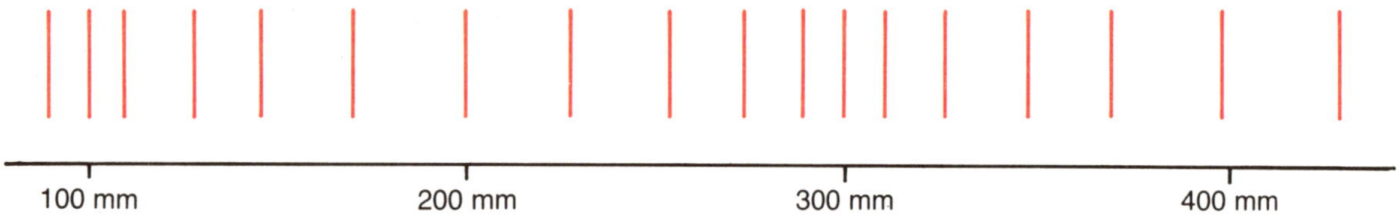

Figure 3

(i) Mark a position of compression with the letter C. **(1)**

(ii) Mark a position of decompression (rarefaction) with the letter D. **(1)**

(iii) What is the wavelength of the wave? **(2)**

(d) Figure 4 shows the continuous waves on water.

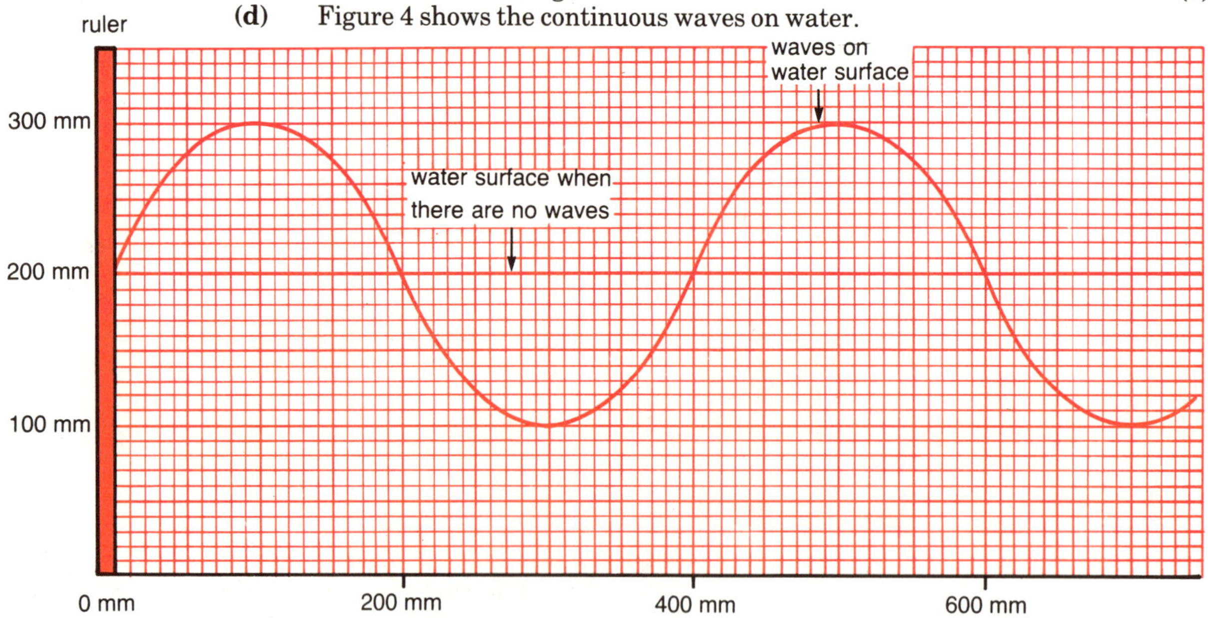

Figure 4

(i) What is the amplitude of the wave? **(1)**

(ii) What is the wavelength of the wave? **(1)**

(iii) If six waves pass a given point every two seconds, calculate the speed of the water waves. **(3)**

(LEAG Science (Syllabus N), Paper 4, 1988)

Question 29

Ammonia (NH_3) is a very useful chemical in the large-scale manufacture of fertilizers. The HABER process is the industrial method by which nitrogen is fixed artificially, using an iron catalyst.

Nitrogen + Hydrogen → Ammonia + Heat

The mixture produced consists of ammonia together with unreacted nitrogen and hydrogen. The percentage of ammonia in this mixture varies with temperature and pressure as shown in the table below.

Temperature/ °C	*Percentage of NH_3 in the mixture at pressure of:*			
	1 atmosphere	100 atmospheres	200 atmospheres	1000 atmospheres
200	15.3	80.6	85.8	98.3
300	2.2	52.1	62.8	92.6
400	0.44	25.1	36.3	79.8
500	0.15	10.4	17.6	57.5
600	0.05	4.5	8.3	31.4
700	0.02	2.1	4.1	12.9
800	0.01	1.2	2.2	–
900	0.007	0.7	1.3	–
1000	0.004	0.4	0.9	–

(a) Describe two patterns shown in this table. **(4)**

(b)(i) From the table, state conditions that produce the largest percentage of ammonia. **(2)**

(ii) Suggest a reason why these conditions are not normally used in the industrial process. **(1)**

(c)(i) What is the effect of the iron catalyst on the reaction? **(1)**

(ii) Explain this effect in terms of the activation energy. You may use the diagram below.

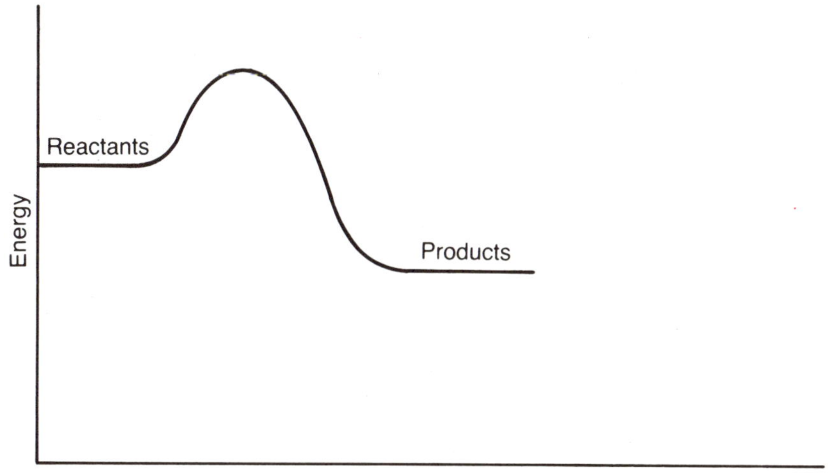

(d) This table shows the boiling points of the three chemicals in the mixture produced.

Using the information given in the table, describe how ammonia can be separated from the mixture.

Gas	*Boiling point/°C*
Ammonia	−33.5
Nitrogen	−195.8
Hydrogen	−253.0

(e) Nitrogen and hydrogen gases are then recycled. Explain why this is done. **(2)**

(LEAG Science (Syllabus N), Paper 4, 1988)

Question 30

A car of mass 1000 kg starts off from rest at traffic lights and accelerates away uniformly, as shown in the graph (overleaf).

(a)(i) What is meant by 'accelerates'? **(1)**

(ii) Calculate the acceleration of the car and state the units. **(3)**

(b) The kinetic energy of a moving body can be found from the pattern

$$\text{Energy} = \tfrac{1}{2}\,\text{mass} \times (\text{velocity})^2$$

Find the kinetic energy of the car at 10 seconds after the start, stating the units. **(3)**

(c) The input energy is produced by petrol burning in the engine. Car engines waste some of this input energy, because not all of it can be converted to kinetic energy.

(i) What is the other main form of energy produced? **(1)**

(ii) What use can be made of this energy? **(1)**

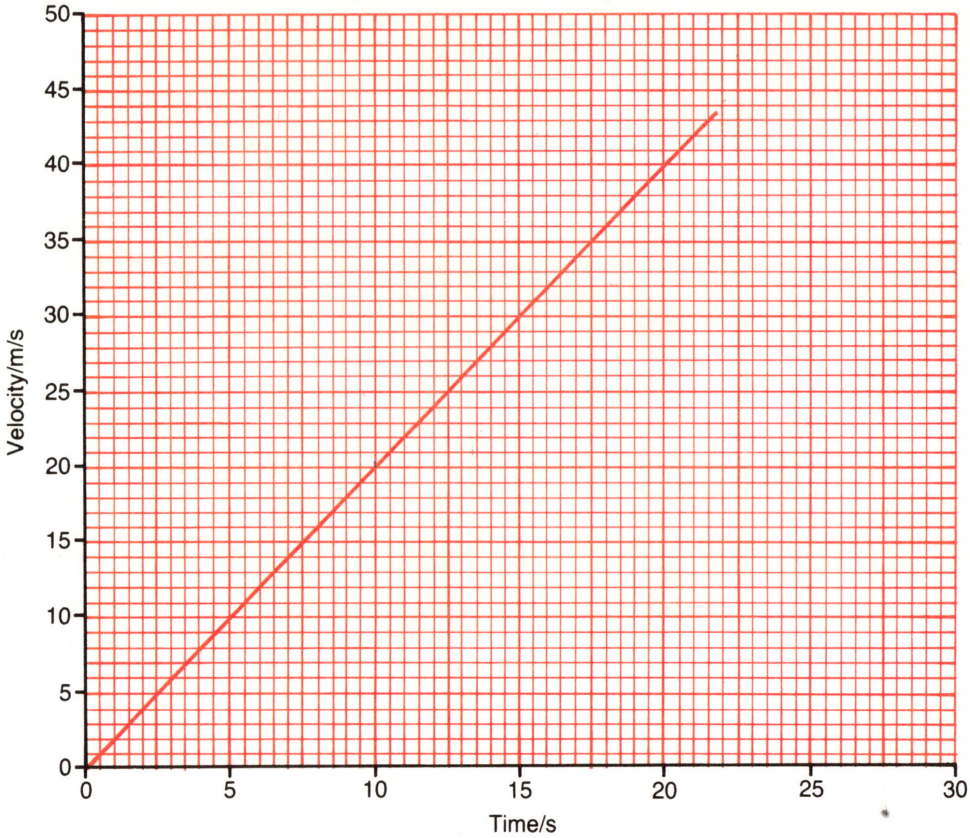

(iii) The car has an input energy of 400 kJ at 10 seconds after the start.
The *efficiency* of the engine is found from the pattern:

$$\text{efficiency} = \frac{\text{kinetic energy}}{\text{input energy}} \times 100$$

Calculate the efficiency of the engine after 10 seconds. **(3)**

(d) 20 seconds after the start, the driver of the car puts on the brakes and comes to a stop in 5 seconds.

$$\text{force} = \text{mass} \times \text{acceleration}$$

Calculate the braking force, stating the units. **(3)**

(LEAG Science (Syllabus N), Paper 2, 1988)

ANSWERS TO LONGER QUESTIONS

Q1(a)(i) earth **(1)**
(ii) B is connected to the live wire **(1)**
(C is connected to the neutral wire)
(iii) water may get on the socket **(1)**
water will conduct electricity **(1)**
therefore, there is a danger of electric shocks **(1)**
(b) If pin is partly removed from socket, **(1)**
plastic sleeve insulates the live pin and prevents it being touched **(1)**
(c)(i) alternating current **(1)**
(ii) live **(1)**
Reason: to cut off the current before it reaches the kettle **(1)**
(iii) outer metal **(1)**
(iv) It should be very **(1)** small **(1)**
so that current will flow away easily **(1)**
(d)(i) kilowatts **(1)**
(ii) $W = V \times I$ **(1)**
$2400 = 240 \times I$ **(1)**
so $I = 10$ amps **(2)**
(iii) $R = \frac{V}{I}$ **(1)**
$R = \frac{240}{10}$ **(1)**
$= 24$ ohms **(2)**
(e)

High	High
Low	High
High	Low

(6)

Q2(a) less damage to whoever/whatever they hit **(1)**
Slows down rate of deceleration **(1)**
absorbs some of the impact **(1)**
(any two)
(b)(i) In a collision, unbelted back seat passengers are also thrown forwards. **(1)**
This can cause injury. **(1)**
(ii) *Effect:* fewer transplants **(1)**
Reason: fewer fatal accidents **(1)**
therefore fewer kidneys available **(1)**
(c) Four marks for clear expression.
Road holding
Movement of seats on collision
Low centre of gravity
Rear vision for driver
Rigid chassis
Prevention of engine moving backwards on collision
Effect of collision on all passengers
Broken glass from windows on collision
} Any 4 sensible concerns related to road safety, 2 marks each **($4 \times 2 = 8$)**
(d)(i) $K.E. = \frac{1}{2} mv^2$ **(1)**
$= \frac{1}{2} \times 500 \times 10^2$ **(1)**
$= 25\,000$ **(1)** J **(1)** *or* 25 **(1)** kJ **(1)**
(ii) Converted to:
Heat due to friction on collision **(1)**
Sound on collision **(1)**
Mechanical deformation (strain energy) **(1)**
(any two)

Q3(a)(i) to keep flies in **(1)**
(ii) to allow exchange of gases **(1)**
(b) A–B stable phase/constant number of flies **(1)**
Reason: no young have yet appeared **(1)**

B–C gradual increase **(1)**
Reason: beginning of reproduction **(1)**
C–D rapid increase **(1)**
Reason: rapid reproduction **(1)**
D–E stable again **(1)**
Reason: births = deaths **(1)**
beginning of food shortage **(1)**
overcrowding **(1)**
limiting factors **(1)**
} (any one)
E–F decrease **(1)**
Reason: lack of food **(1)**
build up of toxic waste **(1)**
} (any one)

(c) Any two suitable reasons, e.g.:
improvements in food production
better agricultural methods are still being adopted
improving medical care
space is still available
} **(2 × 2 = 4)**

Q4(a)(i) external fertilization/soft eggs, laid in water (any one) **(1)**
(ii) have lungs/cold blooded (any one) **(1)**
(b) No need to lay eggs in water
Eggs have shells for protection
Horny skin stops it drying out
(any two)
(c) *Feature:* Warm blooded **(1)**
Link: Hair/feathers act as an insulator **(1)**
(d) They are vertebrates (i.e. they have backbones)/body skeleton **(1)**

Q5(a) Use a magnet **(1)** to attract cobalt **(1)**
(b) Add mixture to petrol **(1)** to dissolve wax **(1)**

Q6(a)(i) Voltmeter and ammeter in wrong places **(1)**
(ii) Current goes through ammeter not heater
or ammeter has too low a resistance **(2)**
(iii) 12 V **(1)**
Reason: Voltage reading is that of supply **(1)**
(b) Swap the meters round **(2)**, *or*
connect ammeter in series with heater **(1)**
and voltmeter in parallel with heater **(1)**
(c)(i) Energy = Current × Voltage × Time **(2)**, *or*
Current in amps × Voltage in volts × Time in seconds **(2)**
(ii) to the surroundings **(1)**
(iii) check circuit before switching on **(1)**
make sure all connections are good **(1)**
do not allow connections to heater to get wet **(1)**
(any two)

Q7(a)(i) Level of radioactivity drops **(1)**
slowly at first, then quickly **(1)**
(ii) Plant absorbs radioactivity **(1)**
Oxygen helps absorption **(1)**
Process probably involved in respiration **(1)**
(b)(i) increases up to 35°C **(1)**
levels off **(1)** and drops above 35°C **(1)**
(ii) Increases up to about 40°C **(1)**
levels off **(1)** and drops above 40°C **(1)**
(iii) Increases more rapidly **(1)**
and drops more rapidly **(1)**
peaks at lower temperature **(1)**

Q8(a) chemical energy **(1)**
(b) (useable form is electricity) 360 000 MJ **(1)**
(c) 540 000 MJ (900 000–360 000) **(1)**
(d) $\% \text{ efficiency} = \dfrac{\text{useful energy output}}{\text{energy input}} \times 100$ **(1)**

$= \dfrac{360\,000}{900\,000} \times 100$ **(1)**

$= 40$ per cent

(e) 24 000 MJ are obtained from 1 tonne of coal

$\therefore$ 540 000 MJ are obtained from $\frac{540\ 000}{24\ 000}$ tonnes **(1)**

$= 22.5$ tonnes

Mass of coal producing waste heat = 22.5 tonnes **(1)**

$\therefore$ money wasted $= 22.5 \times £50$

$= £1125$ **(1)**

(f) Rate of production of electrical energy = 360 000 MJ per hour

$= \frac{360\ 000 \text{ MJ}}{60 \times 60 \text{ s}}$ **(1)**

$= 100$ MJ/s

$= 100(\frac{1}{2})$ MW **($\frac{1}{2}$)**

(g) Heat lost to sea water in one hour = 330 000 MJ

4.2 MJ raises the temperature of 1 tonne of water by 1°C

$\therefore$ 330 000 MJ raises the temperature of 1 tonne of water by $\frac{330\ 000}{4.2}$ °C **(1)**

$\therefore$ 330 000 MJ raises the temperature of 10 000 tonnes of water by

$\frac{330\ 000}{4.2 \times 10\ 000}$ °C **(1)**

$= 7.9$°C

$\therefore$ Temperature of water leaving condenser $\simeq$ 18°C **(1)**

(h) Work = force × distance **(1)**

Work done by pump in one hour = force (weight of water) × distance (height lifted)

$= (10\ 000\ 000 \times 10) \times 18$ J **(2)**

Power $= \frac{\text{work done}}{\text{time taken}}$ **(1)**

$= \frac{10\ 000\ 000 \times 10 \times 18}{60 \times 60}$

$= 500\ 000$ J/s (500 000 W) **(1)**

$= 0.5$ MW (or 500 kW)

(i) Use it to heat the offices and factory areas at the station

Use it to heat homes near the station

(any one) **(1)**

(j) Temperature of sea-water will rise. This might damage organisms in the water/cause ecological changes. **(1)**

(k) Sulphur dioxide **(1)**

from sulphur present in the coal **(1)**

(l) Coal is cheaper than oil

Coal is more plentiful than oil

Coal reserves will last longer than oil

(any two) **(2)**

Q9(a)(i) A at top of furnace below charging system and at tuyères where hot air enters **(1)**

B – along channel from bottom of furnace to trolley on left **(1)**

(ii) iron ore **(1)**, coke **(1)**, limestone **(1)**

(iii) reduction **(1)**

(iv) iron(III) oxide + carbon monoxide → iron + carbon dioxide **(1)**

$Fe_2O_3 + 3CO \rightarrow 2Fe + 3CO_2$ **(3)**

(v) Coke burns in the hot air forming carbon monoxide **(1)**

This reaction is exothermic. The heat produced raises the temperature from 1500 to 2000°C **(1)**

The carbon monoxide reduces the iron ore to iron **(1)**

Molten iron sinks to the bottom of the furnace and is tapped off from time to time **(1)**

Limestone decomposes in the furnace to lime (calcium oxide) **(1)**

The lime reacts with impurities in the iron ore forming slag **(1)**

Molten slag floats on the molten iron and is tapped off periodically **(1)**

(Maximum **5**)

(vi) building industry

shipbuilding industry

motor car industry

(any two) **(2)**

(vii) Cost of plant is too large
Cost of producing iron/steel will be higher than buying it elsewhere
Demand for iron/steel is not sufficiently large
Cost of raw materials is high
Raw materials are not readily available
(any three) **(3)**

(viii) Adequate space for building
Good transport facilities
Least effect on environment
Adequate workforce
Workforce with suitable skills
(any three) **(3)**

(ix) Formula mass of iron(III) oxide, $Fe_2O_3 = 56 + 56 + 16 + 16 + 16 = 160$ **(1)**
i.e. 160 g Fe_2O_3 contains 112 g iron **(1)**
1000 tonnes of ore contain 300 tonnes Fe_2O_3 **(1)**
so 300 tonnes of $Fe_2O_3 \rightarrow \frac{112}{160} \times 300$ tonnes iron
$= 210$ tonnes iron **(1)**

(b)(i) 6 **(1)** cm **(1)**
(ii) MnO_2 **(1)**
(iii) elements required by plants **(1)** in very small amounts **(1)**
(iv) nickel **(1)**, copper **(1)**
(v) Trace elements in the sea may get into fish **(1)**
If humans eat fish, then trace elements will get into humans **(1)**
Some trace elements are harmful to humans **(1)**
(vi) only just profitable **(1)**
(vii) Electrical industry
Reason: copper for wires and cables
(**1** for sensible industry, **1** for reason)

Q10(a)(i)

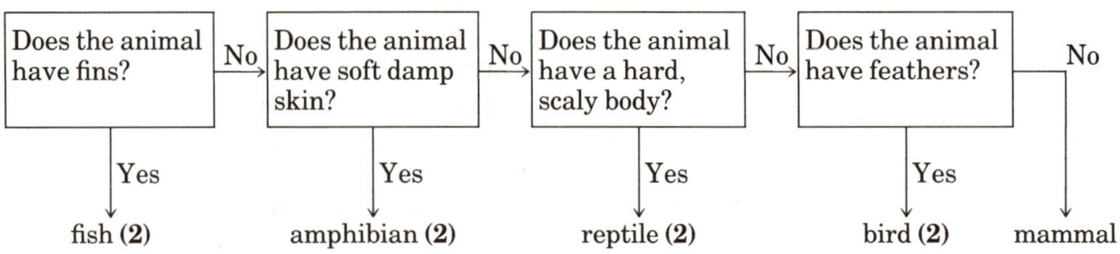

(**2** for each stage × 4 = **8**)
(ii) Herring – fish **(1)**, frog – amphibian **(1)**, crocodile – reptile **(1)**, skylark – bird **(1)**, monkey – mammal **(1)**

(b)(i)

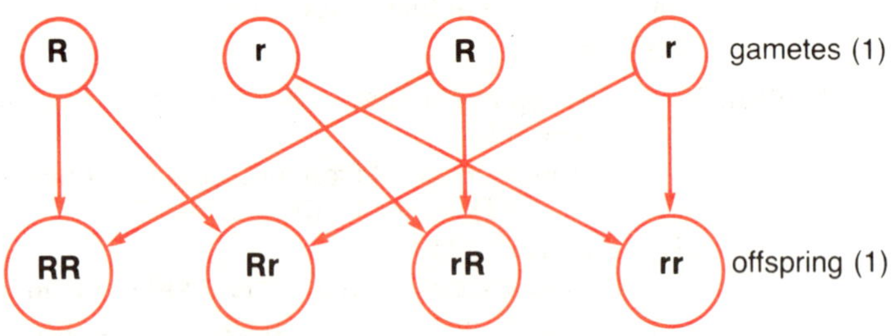

(ii) 3:1 **(2)**
(c)(i) The characteristic is carried by a gene **(1)** on the sex chromosomes **(1)**
(ii)

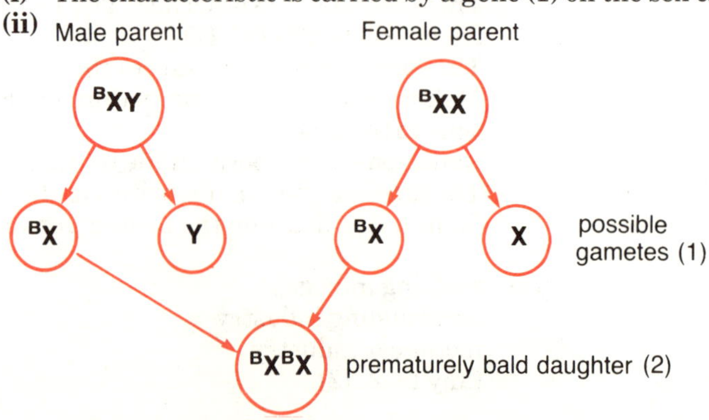

(iii) A female with chromosomes ^{B}XX has:
one chromosome which is normal (X) **(1)**
and one chromosome with the gene for premature baldness (^{B}X) **(1)**
The normal chromosome ensures she is *not* prematurely bald **(1)**

(d)(i) One girl is colour blind, therefore the gene for colour blindness must be on an X chromosome (say ^{C}X) **(1)**
Mr Kelly's sex chromosomes are ^{C}XY **(1)**
The affected son's sex chromosomes are ^{C}XY **(2)**
The unaffected son's sex chromosomes are XY **(1)**
The affected daughter's sex chromosomes are $^{C}X^{C}X$ **(2)**
The unaffected daughter's sex chromosomes are ^{C}XX **(1)**
Mrs Kelly's genotype must be ^{C}XX **(1)**

(ii) cystic fibrosis, haemophilia, etc. (any one) **(1)**

(iii) It is sometimes possible to work out the mathematical probability that a child will inherit a harmful gene and therefore suffer in some way **(1)**
If the probability is high, some couples may decide not to have children of their own **(1)**

(e)(i) $600 + 700 + 700 = 2000\ cm^3$ **(1)**

(ii) The person was not allowed to drink **(1)** during the 12 hours before measurements started. **(1)**

(iii) Food was eaten in the 12 hours before measurements started **(1)**
This food would probably contain water **(1)**

Q11(a) *Test 1: I would note* the weight **(1)** of similar **(1)** shapes and sizes **(1)** of the three materials

Test 2: I would note the temperature **(1)** initially,
then take temperature every 2 minutes or so **(1)**
Calculate rate at which the temperature falls **(1)** for each material

Test 3: I would note the position of the board without the masses **(1)**,
the position of the board after adding the masses **(1)**
Calculate the squashing per unit mass **(1)**
Compare the amount of squashing for the different materials **(1)**
(any three)

(b) Try to melt it/burn it **(1)**
See how easily it melts/burns **(1)**
See how quickly it burns **(1)**
See if there are any flames/fumes **(1)**
See how easily the burning material can be extinguished **(1)**
(any three)

Precautions
Wear safety spectacles/gloves **(1)**
Work in a fume cupboard (or outside) **(1)**
Use small pieces of the material **(1)**
Work on a ceramic tile **(1)**
Have a fire extinguisher available **(1)**
(any three)

Q12(a) The mass(weight) of food taken **(1)**
The temperature rise of the water **(1)**

(b) Difficulty in getting food to burn **(1)**
Difficulty in burning the food completely/smoke from food **(1)**
Loss of heat from burning food goes into the air **(1)**
Water is heated when setting food alight **(1)**
(any two)

(c) By the electrical heating element **(1)**

(d) Almost all heat from food goes into water **(1)**
Food burns more completely in pure oxygen (less smoke) **(1)**
Energy (heat) to start food burning can be calculated **(1)**
(any two)

(e) Food B **(1)**

Q13

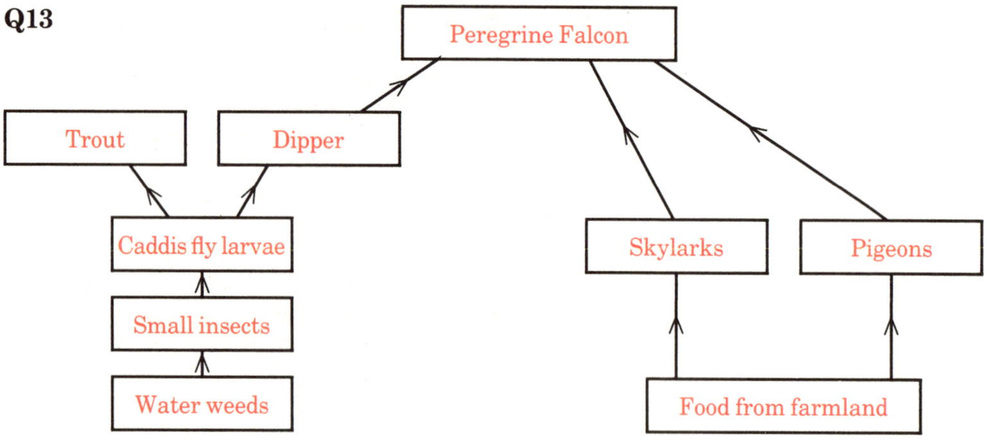

(5 or 4 correct **4**,
3 correct **3**,
2 correct **2**,
1 correct **1**)

(b) trout **(1)**
(c) Little effect if plenty of other food **(1)**
Change in diet/eat more skylarks/pigeons **(1)**
If food is scarce, peregrine population will fall **(1)**
(any two)
(d) *Fishing for trout*
removes competition for food
causes dipper population to increase
Re-stocking with trout
increases competition for food
causes dipper population to decrease
Burning fuel
decreases supply of food
causes dipper population to decrease
Using insecticide
reduces predators
increases dipper population
Controlling insecticide
increases predators
decreases dipper population
(1 mark for each activity up to a maximum of 4)
(1 mark for each explanation/effect up to a maximum of 4)

Q14 The battery can store the energy from the wind generator. **(1)**
The battery will provide a constant voltage. **(1)**
The generator will produce no electricity when the wind does not blow. **(1)**
The house can be lit from the battery if the generator breaks down. **(1)**
The energy stored in a battery is easily converted back to electricity. **(1)**
(any four)

Q15(a) step-down transformer **(1)**

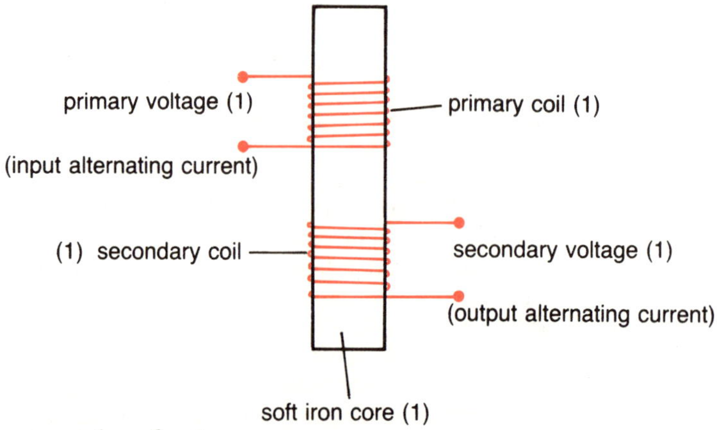

(any four)

(b) Total current taken from sub-station = 100 ×20 A
= 2000 A **(1)**
Assuming the transformer is 100 per cent efficient,

Power input = Power output **(1)**

$I_p \times V_p = I_s \times V_s$ **(1)**

$I_p \times 10\,000 = 2000 \times 240$

so $I_p = \dfrac{2000}{10\,000} \times 240 = 48$ A **(1)**

Minimum current flowing into sub-station = 48 A.

(c) Connect up the table lamp **(1)** to the mains supply. **(1)**
Arrange a photocell (light meter) **(1)** to measure the brightness of the bulb. **(1)**
Read current in photocell (light meter) **(1)** every 15 seconds. **(1)**
The current in the photocell/light meter will stay constant **(1)**
showing that the brightness of the bulb stays constant **(1)**
(A simple light meter could comprise a LDR (light-dependent resistor) **(1)** in series with an ammeter **(1)** and a cell **(1)**)
(any eight)

Q16(a)(i) One mole is the quantity of a substance **(1)** which contains 6×10^{23} particles (atoms/molecules) **(1)** of that substance, i.e. 1 mole of water contains 6×10^{23} molecules of water.

(ii) 1 mole methane (CH_4) (½) reacts with 2 moles (½) of chlorine molecules (Cl_2) (½) to give 1 mole of CH_2Cl_2 (½) and 2 moles (½) of hydrogen chloride molecules (HCl) (½).

(b)(i) Formula of sodium chloride is NaCl, therefore
1 mole NaCl contains 1 mole Na **(1)**
Mass of 1 mole of Na = 23 g **(1)**
so mass of sodium in the oceans = $4 \times 10^{17} \times 23$ g
= 92×10^{17} g **(1)**

(ii) Density of sodium is about 0.9 **(1)** g/cm^3 **(1)**
(Sodium floats on water, therefore its density is less than 1 g/cm^3.)

(iii) Density = $\dfrac{\text{mass}}{\text{volume}}$ **(1)**

So volume = $\dfrac{\text{mass}}{\text{density}}$:

volume of sodium = $\dfrac{92 \times 10^{17}\ \text{g}}{0.9\ \text{g/cm}^3}$ **(1)** $\simeq 100 \times 10^{17}$ cm^3
$\simeq 10^{19}$ cm^3 **(1)**

(c) *Properties:*
Chlorine is a very reactive non-metal **(1)**
It reacts with water to form a very acidic solution **(1)**
containing hydrochloric acid **(1)**
Harmful effects:
Chlorine will attack sensitive lung tissue **(1)**
Inhalation of chlorine would also prevent oxygen uptake in the lungs **(1)**
Chlorine will attack sensitive tissue in the eyes/nose/mouth **(1)**
(any four)

Q17(a)(i) To carbon dioxide + water **(1)**
or to ethanol + water **(1)**
(ii) respiration **(1)**
(iii) energy **(1)**

(b)(i) it breaks them down/decomposes them **(1)**
(ii) ethanol **(1)**, carbon dioxide **(1)**, energy **(1)**
(iii) fermentation will take place at a faster rate **(1)**
(iv) Boiling changes the structure of enzymes in the yeast **(1)**
The enzymes can no longer catalyse fermentation **(1)**,
so the reaction stops.

(c) Animals must eat plants to obtain glucose **(1)**
They obtain glucose by breakdown of starch in the plants **(1)**
Animals use glucose in two ways:
– to produce energy by respiration to CO_2 and H_2O **(1)**
– to store energy by forming glycogen **(1)**

Q18(a)(i) Sexual reproduction involves the union/mating of a male and a female. It involves meiosis.
Asexual reproduction involves only one parent. It involves mitosis. **(2)**

(ii) Cuttings are taken from adult plants to produce new plants (e.g. geraniums)
Grafting of new shoot onto an old root system (e.g. roses)
Runners and stolons are used to grow new plants (e.g. strawberries, spider plants)
Tubers are used for foods (e.g. potatoes) or new plants (e.g. dahlias)
Bulbs are used for food (e.g. onions) or new plants (e.g. daffodils, tulips)
(**1** for each technique, **½** for an example of each technique, to a maximum of **3**)

(iii) Sexual reproduction involves fertilization (**½**)/meiosis (**½**)
Neither of these occur in mitosis (**½**)
Both fertilization and meiosis result in *new genetic combinations* in offspring (**½**)
This allows evolution, natural selection and adaptation to occur (i.e. animals and plants better adapted for survival) **(1)**
It also prevents disadvantages (e.g. harmful diseases) being automatically passed to offspring **(1)**
(maximum **2**)

(b) 151 plants → 112 red, 39 white

approx. ratio 3 : 1 **(1)**
RR or Rr : **rr**

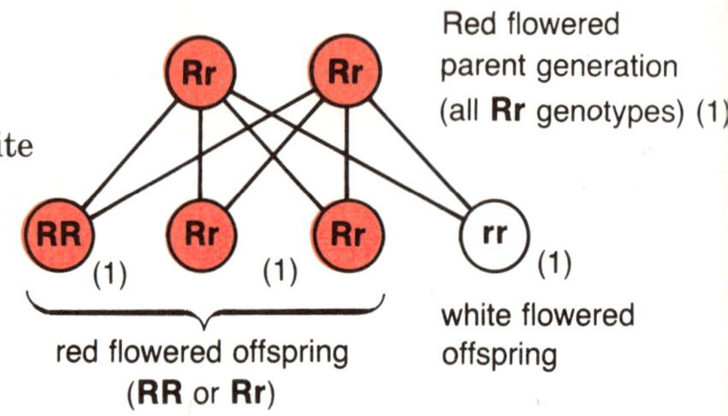

(c) seeds (**½**) —germinate (**½**)→ plant (**½**) —growth (**½**)→ flowers (**½**) —fertilization (**½**)→ seeds (back to seeds)

Q19(a) *In metals*: atom is larger than ion **(1)**
In non-metals: atom is smaller than ion **(1)**

(b) 2.4 (± 0.1) **(1)**

(c) oxygen, sulphur, bromine, iodine (any two)

(d) +1 **(1)**

(e)(i) ionic bonding (or electrovalent bonding) **(1)**

(ii) In sodium chloride (NaCl) there are positive Na^+ ions (**½**) and negative Cl^- ions (**½**). The bonding between these ions involves *electrostatic attraction of* Na^+ *for* Cl^-. (**½**)

The bonding between two Cl atoms involves the attraction (**½**) of the positive nuclei of each Cl atom (**½**) for shared electrons (**½**).

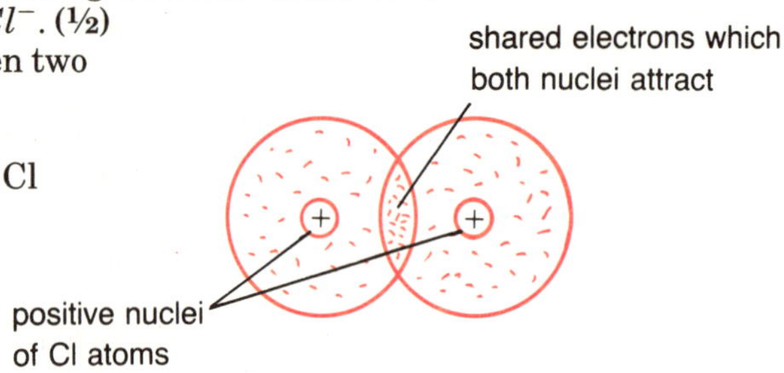

Q20(a)(i) impure sodium chloride (or white powder) (**½**)

(ii) water (**½**)

(iii) the mixture or colourless liquid **(1)**

(iv) colourless liquid **(1)**

(b) to remove insoluble impurities/black specks **(1)**

(c) sodium chloride **(1)**

(d) evaporation **(1)**

(e)(i) pale green

(ii) between dark green and pale green (green) **(1)**

(iii) between orange and pale green (yellow) **(1)**

Q21(a) When air is inhaled, volume increases **(1)**
When air is exhaled, volume decreases **(1)**

(b)

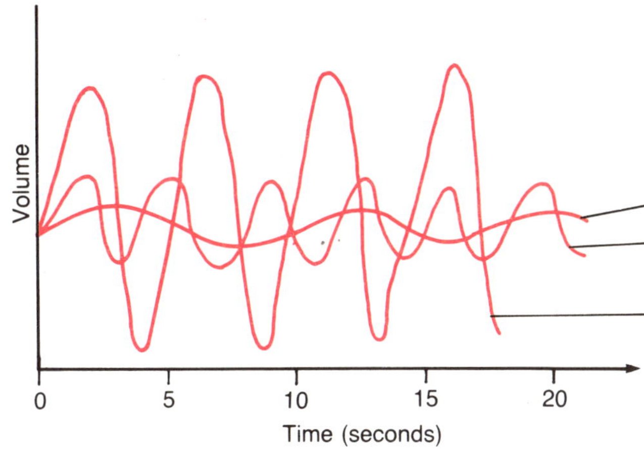

(c) Exhale through a straw, into lime water **(½)**
Lime water turns milky **(½)**

Q22(a) conduction **(1)**
(b)(i) Pointer will move to left **(1)**
(ii) Iron rod expands on heating **(1)**
(iii) railway lines **(1)**
steel bridges **(1)**
overhead cables **(1)**
(any two)

Q23(a) filtration **(1)**
(b) heating or displaced by aeration **(1)**
(c) chlorination **(1)**

Q24(a)(i) Concentration of lichens falls as distance from town increases **(1)**
(ii) The heavy industry produces sulphur dioxide (SO_2) **(½)**
The lichens pick up sulphur from the SO_2 **(½)**
The prevailing winds drive gases from the heavy industry towards C and away from A **(½)**
So sulphur concentration is higher at C than A **(½)**
(b) Initially (1954–65), a large number of species were affected and a large loss in flowering species resulted **(1)**
Since 1965 (1965–80), fewer species have been lost **(1)**
This suggests that the plants remaining are tolerant to the SO_2 levels **(1)**
(any two)

Q25(a)(i) A and B are oppositely charged **(1)**
(ii) B has a smaller charge **(1)**
B is travelling faster **(1)**
(iii) C is uncharged **(1)**
(iv) A alpha (α) **(1)**
B beta (β) **(1)**
C gamma (γ) **(1)**
(b)(i) β and γ **(2)**
(ii) γ **(1)**
(c)(i) (1 half-life) 12 g **(1)**
(ii) (3 half-lives) 3 g **(1)**
(d) Mention of two uses **(2)**
Examples of uses **(2)**
Coherent, clear answer plus safety aspects **(2)**

Q26(a)(i) Mary is fitter
She has a lower pulse rate before and after exercise **(1)**
After exercise, her pulse rate returns to normal sooner than Betty's **(1)**
(ii) Pulse rate = heart beat **(1)**
Each pulse is a surge of blood caused by the heart pumping blood around the body **(1)**
(iii) Sweating allows liquid to escape from pores **(1)**
This liquid evaporates into the air **(1)**
Evaporation takes heat from the body **(1)**

(iv) They deplete their supplies of oxygen and nutrients (e.g. glucose) **(1)** which muscles need for energy **(1)**

(v) Work done = weight × height lifted **(1)**

$= 500\text{ N} \times 10\text{ m}$

$= 5000\text{ J}$ **(1)**

$$\text{Power} = \frac{\text{work done}}{\text{time taken}}\ \textbf{(1)} = \frac{5000}{8} = 625\text{ J/s}\ \textbf{(1)}$$

$= 625\text{ W}$

(b)(i) area of one face = 1 cm^2 **(1)**
therefore surface area of cube A = 6 cm^2 **(1)**

(ii) volume of cube B = $2 \times 2 \times 2$ **(1)** = 8 cm^3 **(1)**

(iii) cube A has largest $\frac{\text{surface area}}{\text{volume}}$ **(1)**

surface area cube A = $1 \times 1 \times 6 = 6\text{ cm}^2$ (½)
volume cube A = $1 \times 1 \times 1 = 1\text{ cm}^3$ (½)
$\frac{\text{surface area}}{\text{volume}}$ cube A = 6 cm^{-1} **(1)**

(iv) lungs (or kidney) **(1)**

(v) oxygen or CO_2 through the lungs; urine/water through the kidneys **(1)**

(vi) Blue Penguin – because it is one of the smallest penguins **(1)**
(or because the climate in New Zealand is mild)
Its surface area to volume ratio is much larger than the Emperor Penguin's **(1)**
This means it will lose heat faster than the Emperor Penguin and could not survive in very cold climates **(1)**

Q27(a)(i) temperature, humidity, soil, watering, light, CO_2/O_2 concentrations (any two) **(2)**

(ii) Increase from week 12 to week 16 = 54 − 27 = 27 kg

Average weekly increase = $\frac{27}{4}$ = 6.75 kg **(1)**

(iii) 21 + 40 + 57 = 118(± 1) kg **(1)**

(iv) week 14 **(1)**

(v) They will become over-ripe **(1)**

(vi) 20°C **(1)**
Reasons: Heating costs will be low **(1)**
Increase in temperature does not have a great effect on final yield **(1)**
(or another temperature, with a sensible explanation for your choice)

(b)(i) 65.6 cm^3 **(1)**

(ii) Soil A allows water to drain through easily – light soil (e.g. sandy soil) **(1)**
Soil B retains water – heavier soil (e.g. peat or clay) **(1)**
Soil A might be improved by adding peat to improve water retention **(1)**
Soil B might be improved by adding sand to allow water to drain through **(1)**

(iii) aeration of soil is prevented **(1)**
roots start to rot **(1)**
in icy conditions, water uptake is prevented **(1)**
(any two)

(iv) N needed for synthesis of proteins/chlorophyll **(1)**
P needed for synthesis of nucleic acids **(1)**
K takes part in the synthesis of carbohydrates and proteins **(1)**

(v) a natural control mechanism **(1)**
as opposed to a man-made (mechanical or chemical) method

Q28(a)(i) Curtain will look black **(1)**
Flowers will look black **(1)**
Leaves will look green **(1)**

(ii) No. The only colour which the sunglasses transmit is green.
So green and white articles will look green, but all other colours will look black. **(2)**

(b)(i) As its temperature increases, it emits light (radiation) with increasing energy **(1)**. i.e. red at 1000°C, orange at 1500°C **(1)**

(ii) Yellow at 2000°C **(1)**
At 2000°C, radiation emitted will have greater energy than at 1500°C **(1)**

(c)(i) C where lines are closest **(1)**

(ii) D where lines are furthest apart **(1)**

(iii) 200 mm **(2)**

(d)(i) 100 mm **(1)**
(ii) 400 mm **(1)**
(iii) frequency = 3 per second = 3 Hz **(1)**
speed = wavelength × frequency **(1)**
= 400 mm × 3 Hz
= 1200 mm/s **(1)**

Q29(a) As the temperature increases, the percentage of NH_3 decreases at each pressure **(2)**
As the pressure increases, the percentage of NH_3 increases at each temperature **(2)**
(b)(i) low temperature (200°C) **(1)**
high pressure (1000 atm) **(1)**
(ii) At low temperatures, the reaction rate is too slow **(1)**
or At high pressure (1000 atm) the reaction vessels and equipment would be too costly because they have to be made to withstand such high pressures **(1)**
(c)(i) It speeds up the reaction **(1)**
(ii) The catalyst introduces a new reaction path **(1)**
This new path has a lower activation energy **(1)**
This makes the reaction easier and faster **(1)**
(d) The mixture is cooled to below −33.5°C **(1)**
but well above −195.8°C (i.e. about −50°C)
The ammonia condenses to a liquid **(1)**
but nitrogen and hydrogen remain gaseous **(1)**
This allows the ammonia to be separated from the mixture
(e) to avoid waste of materials and energy **(1)**
to increase the yield of ammonia **(1)**

Q30(a)(i) increases its speed **(1)**
(ii) $\text{acceleration} = \dfrac{\text{increase in speed}}{\text{time taken}}$ **(1)**
$= \dfrac{40\ \text{m/s}}{20\ \text{s}}$
= 2**(1)** m/s/s **(1)** (*or* 2 ms^{-2} *or* 2 m/s^2)
(b) K.E. = $\frac{1}{2}mv^2$
= ½ × 1000 × $(20)^2$ **(1)**
= ½ × 1000 × 400
= 200 000 **(1)** J **(1)**
(c)(i) heat (thermal energy) **(1)**
(ii) heating the inside of the car **(1)**
(iii) kinetic energy at 10 s = 200 000 J = 200 kJ
efficiency = $\dfrac{200\ \textbf{(1)}}{400\ \textbf{(1)}} \times 100$
= 50% **(1)**
(d) $\text{Acceleration (deceleration)} = \dfrac{\text{change in speed}}{\text{time taken}}$
$= \dfrac{40\ \text{m/s}}{2\ \text{s}}$ **(1)**
= 20 m/s/s **(1)** (*or* 20 ms^{-2} *or* 20 m/s^2)
Braking force = mass × acceleration
= 1000 × 20
= 20 000 N **(1)**

ANSWERS TO QUICK TESTS

Quick test 1

1 *auratus*
2 *Carassius*
3 Fish
4 Animals with backbones
5 Animals
6 A and D
7 C and E
8 cell wall
9 cell membrane
10 nucleus
11 vacuole
12 cytoplasm
13 chloroplast
14 C
15 A
16 D
17 B
18 C
19 B
20 D
21 E
22 A
23 response to stimuli
24 movement
25 requirement for energy

Quick test 2

1 A
2 C
3 D
4 C
5 E
6 C
7 D
8 B
9 A
10 E
11 C
12 W
13 Y
14 Z
15 Cells in layer C are arranged regularly – the arrangement of cells in layer D is haphazard.
Cells in layer C have more chloroplasts than those in layer D.
Cells in layer C are elongated – those in layer D are rounded.
(any two differences)
16 The cells do not contain chloroplasts (i.e. no green chlorophyll)
17 B
18 B and D
19 Increased CO_2 concentration increases the rate of photosynthesis.
20 Water the plants more, increase the light intensity, raise the temperature
21 glucose and oxygen
22 light energy to chemical energy
23 To remove chlorophyll from the leaf
24 The leaf is stained dark blue

Quick test 3

1 protein
2 added sugar, added salt
3 fibre
4 salt
5 fibre and added sugar
6 25 g
7 water
8 500 kJ
9 water
10 roast beef
11 cheese
12 roast beef
13 carrots
14 carbohydrate
15 protein
16 fat
17 170 kJ
18 6000 kJ
19 it increases
20 it decreases
21 amino acids
22 glucose
23 glucose and fructose
24 glycerol and fatty acids

Quick test 4

1 D
2 D
3 B
4 enamel
5 dentine
6 gum
7 pulp
8 cement
9 nerve and blood vessels
10 mouth and duodenum
11 stomach and duodenum
12 duodenum
13 ileum
14 kills germs and helps to break down proteins
15 mouth and stomach
16 pepsin, trypsin and peptidases
17 roughage
18 it increases the surface area for action by enzymes
19 iodine
20 dark blue/black
21 concentration of amylase, concentration of starch, time of experiment
22 maltose
23 acidity

24 6.9
25 3 minutes
26 20/21 minutes
27 Every sweet can produce dental attack for 20–21 minutes. Not eating sweets between meals keeps the period of attack to a minimum.
28 bacteria
29 more than 7 (alkaline)
30 to neutralize acidity in the mouth
31 fluoride

Quick test 5

1 D
2 B
3 A
4 C and E
5 A and B
6 C
7 D
8 B
9 red blood cells
10 white blood cells
11 plasma
12 Japan
13 N. Ireland
14 Finland, England and Wales
15 C
16 Paula
17 Paula has a lower heart rate.
Paula's heart rate returns to normal more quickly.
18 any four of: exercise, stress, disease, smoking, anger, excitement
19 a blood clot forming in a coronary blood vessel
20 lack of iron in the diet
21 any two of: arteries carry blood away from the heart, veins carry blood to the heart;
arteries have thicker walls than veins;
arteries are not as close to the surface of the body as veins;
blood is at a greater pressure in arteries than in veins.
22 blood group test
23

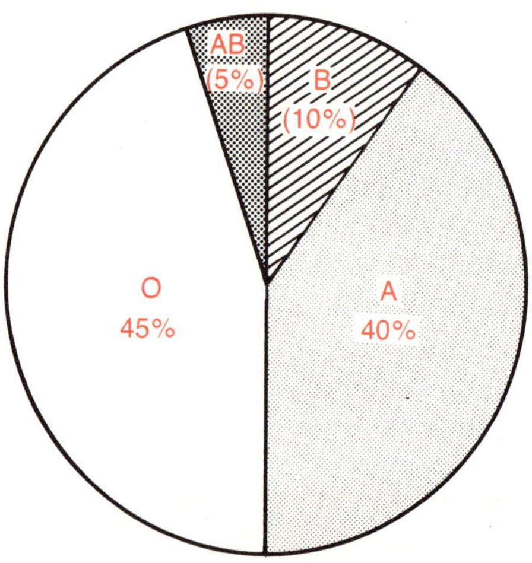

Quick test 6

1 trachea or windpipe
2 bronchus
3 bronchiole
4 alveolus
5 to keep the windpipe open at all times
6 35 000 cm^3
7 25 000 cm^3
8 $\frac{1}{5}$
9 $\frac{1}{5} \times 25\,000 = 5\,000\ cm^3$
10 oxygen
11 carbon dioxide
12 cellular respiration
('respiration' would be accepted)
13 barley (malt)
14 ethanol (alcohol) and carbon dioxide
15 Fermentation will take place more quickly.
16 Boiling kills the yeast.
17 two
18 six
19 to make sure no water came from the incoming air
20 to give a larger surface area to absorb water
21 to prevent water coming directly from the soil in the plant pot
22 to prevent photosynthesis which would use up water
23 mass of tube B before and after the experiment
24 put another calcium chloride tube in the system (before the pump) and check its weight before and after the experiment
25 acidic
26 Coolmist
27 Longsmoke and Tardust
28 $20 \times 0.8 = 16$ mg
29 Plain cigarettes:
burn at lower temperature;
have a darker residue;
contain more nicotine.
(any two)
30 lung cancer, emphysema, bronchitis

Quick test 7

1 C
2 A
3 E
4 B
5 D
6 A and B
7 darker
8 most
9 bone
10 tendon
11 joins muscle to bone
12 humerus (upper arm bone)
13 biceps
14 C gets shorter and fatter (contracts)
15 D gets longer (extends) and thinner
16 A
17 C
18 brain
19 heart and lungs
20 spinal cord
21 C
22 E
23 D
24 two of: allow movement, support the body, make blood cells
25 two of: close packing of cells, cellulose strands, wood

26 Water is frozen and cannot flow up the stem. Cells are no longer stiffened by turgor, so the stems droop.

Quick test 8

1 B
2 C
3 D
4 F
5 B
6 E
7 A
8 F
9 eye
10 ear
11 tongue (strictly speaking tongue and nose)
12 nose
13 F
14 E
15 D
16 B
17 F D E A C B
18 epidermis
19 dermis
20 fat
21 pore
22 sensory cell
23 sweat gland
24 the growing tip
25 test 3
26 to provide a control (comparison)
27 any three of:
the starting size of cutting,
the number of leaves on cutting,
the type of soil used,
the amount of soil used,
the watering of the soil,
the plant pots used (same size and shape),
the position of the pots during the experiment (same temperature, lighting, etc., throughout the experiment).
28 any three of:
more accurate timer should be used;
flicking of switch should start the timer;
pressing of button should stop the timer;
Julie should not be able to see Mary flick the switch;
experiment should be repeated several times and the results averaged.

Quick test 9

1 B
2 E
3 D
4 A
5 15 years
6 10 years
7 12 years
8 18 years
9 urethra
10 penis
11 sperm duct
12 bladder
13 testis
14 to protect the foetus from bumps and jolts
15 to transfer food and oxygen from the mother's blood to the foetus
and waste products from the foetus's blood to the mother's blood
16 to carry the foetus's blood to and from the placenta
17 C
18 D
19 B
20 support the petals
21 attract insects/animals
22 male reproductive organs which produce pollen
23 A→D→E→C→B
24 two of:
maintains similar plants;
maintains healthy plants;
reproduction is more rapid.

Quick test 10

1 D
2 A
3 A
4 C
5 D
6 B
7 female (mother)
8 X
9 X or Y
10 The predator thinks that fly is a bee because of similar characteristics **(1)**,
learns that bee stings **(1)**,
so avoids bee and fly **(1)**.
11 change in a gene
12 Mutation in ancestor produced characteristics of bee **(1)**.
Both bee and fly continued to reproduce **(1)**.
13 Bacteria become immune to antibiotics.
14 grey
15 Grey male has genotype **GG (1)**,
so all babies must have one dominant **G** gene **(1)**.
16 Some grey babies will have the genotype **Gg (1)**.
If two **Gg** parents mate;

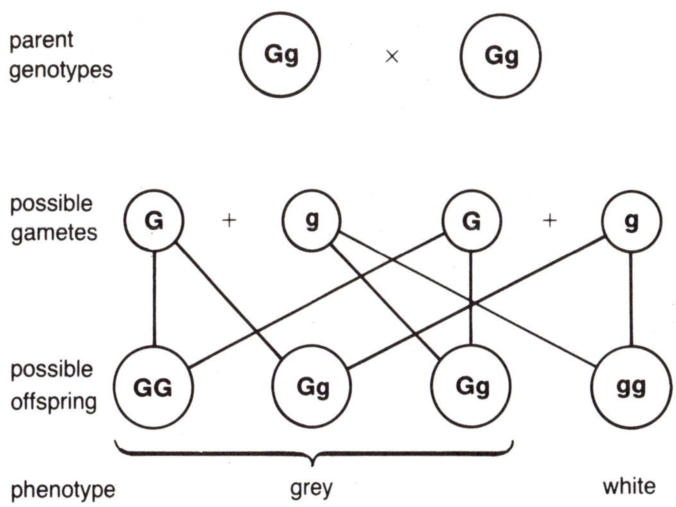

So, two **Gg** parents can mate to produce **gg** babies which will be white **(1)**.
17 Mate two white rabbits **(1)**: they will both have the genotype **gg** and all their babies will have the genotype **gg** and be white **(1)**.

18 Very large ears are needed
– for cooling in hot desert **(2)**;
– to hear prey at night **(2)**.
19 Population B lives in open grassland, therefore they need larger ears
– to hear prey in poor light of early morning or late evening **(2)**;
– to hear predators in open grassland areas **(2)**.
20 thick coat

Quick test 11

1 E
2 C
3 B
4 grass
5 sunlight
6 carnivores
7 the numbers decrease
8 food web
9 foxes
10 grasses and shrubs
11 grasses and shrubs
12 sunlight
13 There would be more grass for sheep
Foxes would be more likely to take sheep
14 Nutrients are taken from soil by hedge
Water is taken from soil by hedge
The hedge provides shade (so the wheat receives less sunlight)
15 any two of:
competition from wheat in the field
the plants prefer shady conditions
wild plants are killed by chemicals used on the wheat
16 any one of:
it destroys habitats
it destroys animals and plants
it makes the countryside less attractive
it removes wind breaks
it increases soil erosion
17 the sun
18 carbohydrates
19 sugar/glucose/starch/cellulose (i.e. any one carbohydrate)
20 chlorophyll
21 photosynthesis
22 decomposers
23 amount leaving = amount entering
24 sunlight
25 It is the first organism in the food chain
or it produces energy (foods) for other organisms in the food chain
26 (a) 100 kJ (b) 10 kJ (c) 1 kJ
27 any two of:
heat during respiration
to maintain chemical processes in organisms
in faeces
in urine.
28 Energy is lost at each stage of the food chain.
Vegetable food is the first link in the chain, therefore less energy has been lost.

Quick test 12

1 A
2 C
3 C
4 B
5 D
6 D
7 B
8 C
9 A
10 E
11 Mass rises steadily from Jan. to Aug.
Mass falls sharply to zero in Aug.
12 Increased temperature and sunlight causes wheat to grow from Jan. to Aug.
Mass falls sharply when wheat is harvested in Aug.
13 any two of:
migration, breeding, increasing food supply.
14 Wheat is food for mice, therefore population of mice fluctuates with wheat (food) supply.
15 Any factor (other than food supply) that could give rise to fluctuations in the numbers of field mice, e.g. migration, death, litters, being prey to carnivorous birds.
16 use of pesticides and other chemicals toxic to bees
17 reduced use of pesticides
18 any one of:
reduced pollination of flowers
interference with food webs
reduced honey production
19 discontinue use of pesticides and other substances toxic to bees
20 30 tonnes in each 100 tonnes of scrap
21 Only $\frac{1}{3}$ of what could be recycled, actually is recycled.
22 to conserve our resources of aluminium

Quick test 13

1 D
2 2
3 C
4 B and D
5 B
6 C
7 A
8 E
9 D
10 C
11 E
12 A
13 D
14 B
15 B
16 C
17 A
18 B
19 food and oxygen
20 carbon dioxide and water

Quick test 14

1 A
2 B
3 A
4 C
5 D
6 D

7 A
8 C
9 B
10 E
11 D
12 C
13 C
14 A
15 E
16 A, B and D
17 B and D
18 C
19 A
20 E
21 D
22 D
23 C
24 A
25 B
26 D
27 C

Quick test 15

1 B
2 A
3 D
4 C
5 B
6 C
7 D
8 E
9 C
10 B
11 D
12 A
13 5
14 7
15 $C + O_2 \rightarrow CO_2$
16 $CH_4 + 2O_2 \rightarrow CO_2 + 2H_2O$
17 $CuO + H_2SO_4 \rightarrow CuSO_4 + H_2O$
18 $N_2 + 3H_2 \rightarrow 2NH_3$
19 480 g
20 8 g
21 mole ratio C:H $= \frac{75}{12} : \frac{25}{1}$
$= 6.25 : 25$
$= 1 : 4$
Therefore formula is CH_4.
22 mole ratio Cr:N $= \frac{0.26}{52} : \frac{0.07}{14}$
$= 0.005 : 0.005$
$= 1 : 1$
Therefore formula is CrN.

Quick test 16

1 negative
2 The negatively charged ions are attracted to the oppositely charged electrode.
3 ammeter
4 ampere (amp)
5 voltage (potential difference)
6 R
7 to adjust the current
8 silver
9 C
10 A
11 carbon
12 **(a)** covalent
(b) ionic
13 Ionic bonds are very strong, so the melting point of salt is very high.
14 ions
15 Sulphur does not conduct
or alcohol does not conduct
16 Any two of:
The liquid would spill easily
The liquid is acidic
Zinc reacts with dilute acid even when the cell is not being used
17 By electrolysis **(1)** of molten **(1)** aluminium oxide **(1)**
18 *Cathode* (−) **(1)** Al^{3+} **(1)** + $3e^-$ **(1)** $\rightarrow$ Al
19 C
20 D
21 A
22 E
23 B
24 C

Quick test 17

1 A
2 D
3 B
4 E
5 C
6 2
7 1
8 it rises from 7
9 Ca, Mg, Fe, Cu
10 hot water tanks/pipes/radiators/saucepans
11 they react violently with water
12 they react with oxygen and/or water
13 **(a)** not at all
(b) a little
(c) a little
(d) a lot
14 two of: oiling, painting, plastic coating, tin plating, chromium plating, galvanizing
15 one of: haematite, magnetite, siderite
16 coke, limestone, air
17 carbon monoxide
18 Dissolve them in water; melt them
19 it can be used to obtain the metal
20 coke will not reduce all ores to the metal
21 silver/gold/platinum
22 it is very unreactive
23 D
24 C
25 E
26 water
27 oxidation/redox

Quick test 18

1 C
2 D
3 B
4 E
5 A
6 B

7 D
8 E
9 C
10(a)(i) zinc and sulphuric acid **(1)**
(ii) sodium hydroxide and hydrochloric acid **(1)**
(iii) copper(II) sulphate and sodium carbonate **(1)**
(b) *Either* zinc sulphate using acid and excess metal as in Fig. 18.9
or sodium chloride using indicator method as in Fig. 18.9
or copper carbonate using precipitation as in Fig. 18.9
11(a) 1 m^2 polythene sheet **(1)**
(b) clean beaker **(1)**
(c) test tube **(1)**
(d) teat pipette **(1)**
12 So as not to affect the acidity (pH) of the rain water collected.
13(a) carbon dioxide **(1)**
(b) pH rises **(1)**
14 H^+
15(a)

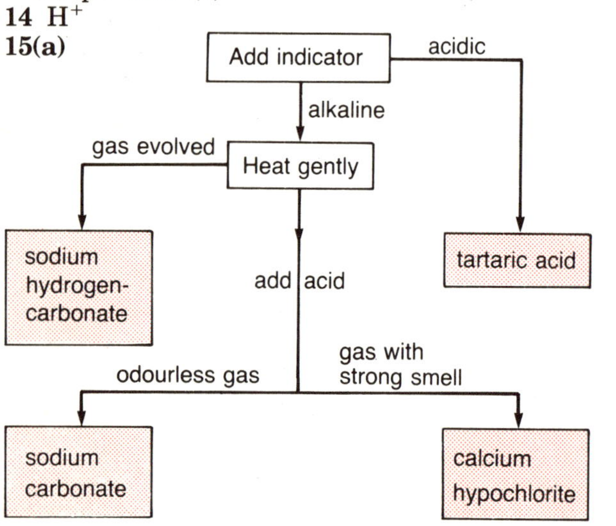

(b)(i) 44 **(1)** (ii) 106
(c) 106 g $Na_2CO_3 \rightarrow$ 44 g CO_2

$$\therefore 1\text{ g } Na_2CO_3 \rightarrow \frac{44}{106}\text{ g } CO_2$$

$$\therefore 212\text{ g } Na_2CO_3 \rightarrow \frac{44}{106} \times 212\text{ g } CO_2$$

$$= 88\text{ g } CO_2$$

Quick test 19

1 B
2 E
3 D
4 A
5 E
6 C
7 A, B and D
8 They cannot convert nitrogen gas to nitrogen compounds which they need to grow and metabolize.
9 Nitrogen compounds are produced by lightning, by decay of dead animals and plants, or by nitrogen-fixing bacteria on leguminous plants.
10 If crops are harvested and not left to decay on the land, the other natural sources of nitrogen cannot replenish the nitrogen compounds in the soil.
11 Hydrogen from steam and natural gas. Nitrogen from the air.
12 to increase the reaction rate
13 ammonia + nitric acid $\rightarrow$ ammonium nitrate
14 35% (see calculation, Table 19.4)
15 The percentage of ammonia increases
– as the pressure increases;
– as the temperature decreases.
16 Low temperature; high pressure
17 N nitrogen; P phosphorus; K potassium
18 They convert nitrogen in the air into nitrogen compounds for plants
19 Some of the nitrates are
– washed out of the soil;
– decomposed by bacteria to nitrogen;
– used by bacteria in the soil.
(any two)
20 In deep soil, in waterlogged soil, in hard, compacted soil, etc.
(any two suggestions which prevent air getting into the soil)

Quick test 20

1 methane
2 It produces no SO_2, which is poisonous and causes acid rain
It produces no CO, which is poisonous
It produces no ash
(any two)
3 tides, waves
4 'sea' power is
– renewable, unlike nuclear power and coal.
– free; nuclear materials and coal are expensive. As nuclear and coal fuel costs increase, they will become more costly to run.
– does not cause smoke/ash pollution.
– has no radiation hazards.
(any three)
5(a) fractional distillation
(b) *larger* molecules have *higher* boiling points and
smaller molecules have *lower* boiling points (or vice versa)
6(a) cracking
(b) high temperatures
or high temperatures and a catalyst
7 oxygen
8 by reduction/removal of oxygen to form water as they respire
9 nitrogen
10 ammonia
11 (a)

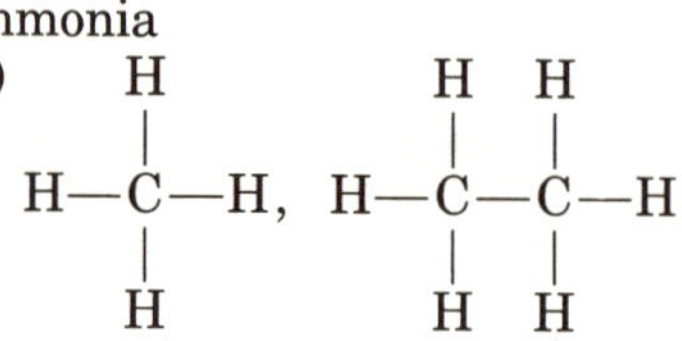

(b)

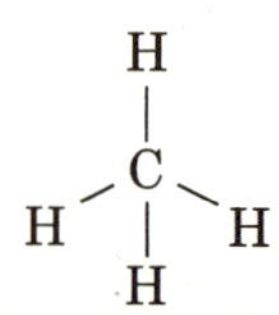

12 The series of compounds have similar properties. There is a gradual change in property from one member in the series to the next.

13 Mass of water = 200 g = 0.2 kg
Temperature rise = 57 − 21 = 36°C
4200 J heats 1 kg by 1°C
so 4200 × 0.2 × 36 heats 0.2 kg by 36°C
i.e. 30 240 J was given out when the butane burnt

14 Mass of butane burnt = 0.6 g
0.6 g butane gives 30 240 J

$\therefore$ 1 g butane gives $\frac{30\,240}{0.6}$ J

$\therefore$ 1 kg butane gives $\frac{30\,240}{0.6} \times 1000$ J
$= 50\,400\,000$ J $= 50\,400$ kJ

15 1 kg butane produces approximately 50 000 kJ
So, 2 kg butane produces 100 000 kJ
Cost of 2 kg butane = £1.00

16 carbon dioxide and water

17 Ensure no heat from burning butane is lost to air.
Calculate heat from burning butane given to metal can.
Ensure butane burns completely.
(any two)

Quick test 21

1 D
2 A
3 E
4 C
5 fluoride
6 chlorine
7 chlorine + iodine
8 14
9 7
10 8
11 3
12(a) they get larger
(b) they increase
(c) they get darker

13 one atom of hydrogen combines with one atom of the halogen

14 ◯ (diameter > that for I)
m.p. between 204 and 244°C; *colour* black; HAt

15(a) 127
(b) 131
(c) $\frac{127 + 127 + 127 + 127 + 131}{5} = 127.8$

or $\left(\frac{80}{100} \times 127\right) + \left(\frac{20}{100} \times 131\right) = 127.8$

16 *m.p.* between 10 and 30°C
b.p. between 450 and 600°C
reaction with water very fast
(m.p. and b.p. are best predicted by drawing graphs of m.p. against RAM and b.p. against RAM)

17 *b.p.* between 100 and 140°C
(from graph of b.p. against RAM
state liquid
reaction with iron fairly fast

18 *Effect of increasing RAM on*

	alkali metals	halogens
m.p.	decrease	increase
b.p.	decrease	increase
reaction	faster	slower

Quick test 22

1 A
2 B and C
3 B and D
4 E
5 D
6 C
7 D
8 A
9 E
10 B

11(a) α particles are positive, therefore they are attracted to upper plate which is negative.
β particles are negative, therefore they are attracted to lower plate which is positive.
(b) both α and β particles will be stopped by the aluminium

12(a) γ-rays can damage cells and body tissues. They are stopped by lead.
(b) It does not remain active (emitting γ-rays) for long enough to cause damage in the person being investigated
(c) Gamma rays sterilize the syringes *after* packaging.
The syringes can become recontaminated during packing after steam sterilization.

13(a) background radiation
(b) radiation from the sun, radioactive isotopes in rocks
(c) a Geiger-Muller tube

14 protons and neutrons
15 27
16 55

17 *decay*: random and spontaneous break-up of radioactive atoms
half-life: the time it takes for half of a sample of radioactive isotope to decay

18 because the half-life of Cs–137 is much longer than that of Co–60

19 In position A, γ-rays escape through the channel.
In position B, any gamma rays emitted would hit the surrounding lead and be absorbed.

20 Keep exposure time as short as possible
Work behind lead or concrete shields
Use remote handling equipment from as far away as possible.

Quick test 23

1 Newton
2 metre
3 kilogram
4 metres per second per second (m/s^2)
5 newton metre or joule (see section 24.1)
6 4 km/h
7 3 km/h NE
8 10 km
9 15 km
10 $\frac{25}{\frac{3}{4}} = 33\frac{1}{3}$ km/h
11 J
12 B, F, K
13 H
14 D, L
15 200 m

16 15 s
17 at the end of the race
18 $\frac{200\text{ m}}{25\text{ s}} = 8\text{ m/s}$
19 the runner
20 90 kg
21 135 N
22 10 m/s (acceleration due to gravity)
23 100 m/s
24 50 m/s
25 500 m
26 force, velocity
27 $\frac{144 \times 1000}{60 \times 60} = 40\text{ m/s}$
28 180 m
29 B
30 B
31 C
32 C
33 D
34 D
35 A
36 C

Quick test 24

1 $\frac{1000}{10} = 100$ J/s (i.e. 100 W)
2 $\frac{600}{10} = 60$ J/s or 60 W
3 40 J
4 X kinetic energy; Y electrical energy (electricity)
5 30
6 The energy is lost as heat to the surroundings from burning the fuel and as friction between parts of the machines.
7 It wastes a smaller fraction (%) of the energy put into it.
8 100°C
9 109°C
10 The adjustable pressure control allows the pressure inside the cooker to rise. This causes the water in the cooker to boil at a higher temperature. This causes a faster reaction, so the food cooks more quickly.
11 It allows gas to escape from the cooker if the pressure gets too high.
12 So that it withstands the high pressure inside the cooker.
13 80 N × 20 m = 1600 J
14 power $= \frac{\text{work done}}{\text{time taken}} = \frac{1600\text{ J}}{5\text{ s}} = 320$ J/s (320 W)
15 To adjust (control) the temperature of the iron
16 plastic
17 When the iron is cool, end A touches the end of the screw. When the iron is switched on, a current flows. The heating element in the iron and the bimetallic strip get hot. This causes the bimetallic strip to bend away from the screw. At a particular temperature, contact with the screw is broken and the current stops.
18 End A will touch the screw at a slightly higher temperature.
19 More electricity is used, therefore running costs will be higher.
20 In this thermostat, the current cuts out when the temperature gets too high. In a refrigerator, the current must continue when the temperature increases so that the pump continues working; the current must stop when the temperature gets too *low* (to prevent food freezing).

Quick test 25

1 E
2 A
3 D
4 C
5 B
6 E
7 C
8 A and C
9 A and D
10 wavelength
11 2 × amplitude
12 it moves up and down
13 waves on the sea could be used to drive small turbines and generate electricity. This would reduce our use of fossil fuels.
14 $\lambda = 10$ m, $f = \frac{1}{2}$ Hz
speed $= \lambda \times f = 10 \times \frac{1}{2}$
$= 5$ m/s
15 As the strings vibrate, the air molecules near the strings are moved backwards and forwards **(1)**. This causes alternating compressions and decompressions of air to be pushed out from the guitar **(1)**.
When the compressions and decompressions reach our ears, they cause our ear drums to vibrate **(1)**.
16 wavelength
17 Connect a microphone **(1)** to a cathode-ray oscilloscope (CRO) **(1)**.
Play the same note on different instruments and observe their different wave forms on the CRO **(1)**.
18 carpet
19 brick
20 99.5 joules
21(a) 330 metres in 1 second, so 33 metres in 0.1 (1/10) second
(b) two of:
the shape of the theatre
the size of the theatre
the number of people present
the materials used for seating, walls, furnishings
(c) people will absorb the sound

Quick test 26

1 D
2 C
3 A
4 B
5 E
6 E
7 it gets larger
8 it gets larger

9 10 cm
10 red, orange, yellow, indigo, violet
11 green and blue
12 black
13 blue
14 green
15 two of:
move the flower a little
move the lens a little
move the screen a little
16 move the screen a little *away* from the lens
17 The image will be less bright
The image will be the same size but less of it will appear on the screen
18 and 19

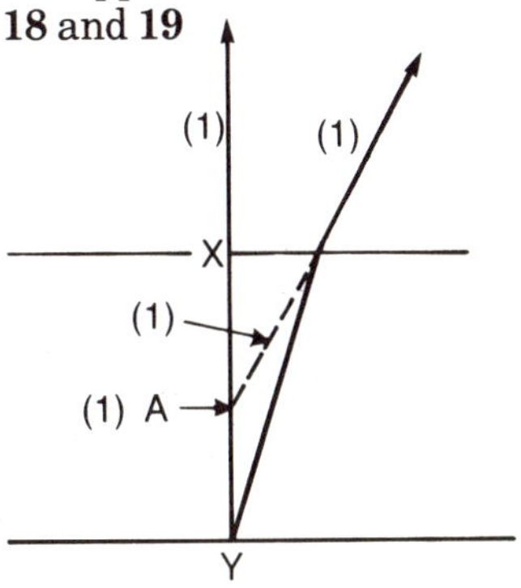

20 Apparent depth is XA; real depth is XY.
Apparent depth is less than its real depth.

Quick test 27

1 5 ohms
2 $I = \frac{V}{R} = \frac{10}{5} = 2\text{ A}$
3 $V = I \times R = 2\text{ A} \times 2\Omega = 4$ volts
4 (½ for each correct label)
5 The fuse wire melts **(1)**
The current ceases **(1)**
6 The water molecules move around each other faster. **(1)**
Eventually some water molecules near the surface of the water droplets have enough energy **(1)** to escape from the droplet **(1)** into the air. **(1)**
The molecules have evaporated. **(1)**
In time, all the water molecules have enough energy to evaporate. **(1)**
(any four)
7 1 unit = 1 kWh
The kettle has a power of 3 kWh
energy = power × time
1 = 3 kW × time (hours, h)
so time used = $\frac{1}{3}$ h = 20 minutes
8 Power = $V \times I$
$3000 = 240 \times I$
so current = $\frac{3000}{240} = 12.5\text{ A}$
9 The current would be twice as large.
10 the cost per unit of electricity
11(a) lighting circuits **(1)**
(b) 15 **(1)**
(c) fault **(1)**
12 5 amp fuse wire is thinner
13 it must conduct electricity
14(a) You could get an electric shock
(b) the wire melts
(c) Switch off the supply at the mains, then use sand, foam or CO_2 to cut off the supply of air.
15 They can be switched on and off one at a time. If they were in series, they would *all* go on and off together.
16(a) C on 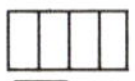
(b) M on 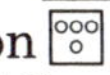
17 A and C
18 C
19 None of the bulbs would light.
20 A earth wire; B neutral wire; C cord grip; D fuse; E live wire; F cord
21 Always switch off at the mains before investigating circuit faults.
Repair appliances/wiring as soon as faults occur.
Disconnect appliances before doing repairs.
Choose the right fuse for each appliance.
Ensure that appliances with outer metal parts are earthed.
Make sure the wires from an electrical appliance are connected to the correct terminals in the plug.
(any four)

Quick test 28

1 A
2 D
3 D
4 B
5 E
6 C
7 A
8 B
9 E
10 Because of the weight of the magnet
11 So that the forcemeter registers only the force from the magnetic field
12 To vary the current through the coil
13 The current in the solenoid creates a magnetic field with a N pole at the lower end of the solenoid.
This repels the magnet and pushes on the forcemeter.
14 current ∝ force from magnetic field
15 The iron core increases the force from the magnetic field.
16(a) *Disadvantages of overhead cables:*
– unsightly pylons and cables
– installation damages environment
– may interfere with radio/TV reception
– danger from electrocution
(any two)
Disadvantages of underground cables:
– trees in the cable path are destroyed
– take longer to repair
– more expensive to lay
(any two)
(b) A higher voltage means that a small current can be used. **(1)**
This has a smaller heating effect in the wire so less energy is lost. **(1)**
17 The N-pole of the suspended magnet will be repelled (the suspended magnet will swing away from the second magnet).

18 a magnetic field
19 The Earth's 'North pole' is really a magnetic south pole because it attracts the N-pole of magnets.
20 The N-pole of the compass is repelled by the N-pole of the magnet and attracted by the S-pole of the magnet. **(1)**
The S-pole of the compass is repelled by the S-pole of the magnet and attracted by the N-pole of the magnet. **(1)**
If the needle is pivoted freely it will therefore swing so that it points towards the Earth's N-pole. **(1)**
21 plastic or wood (or other non-magnetic material)

INDEX

INDEX